A NATION FOR ALL

ENVISIONING CUBA

Louis A. Pérez Jr., editor

ALEJANDRO DE LA FUENTE

A Nation for All

Race, Inequality, and Politics in Twentieth-Century Cuba

THE UNIVERSITY OF NORTII CAROLINA PRESS   Chapel Hill & London

© 2001

The University of North Carolina Press

All rights reserved

Manufactured in the United States of America

Set in Monotype Garamond and Meta types

by Keystone Typesetting, Inc.

The paper in this book meets the guidelines for

permanence and durability of the Committee on

Production Guidelines for Book Longevity of the

Council on Library Resources.

Library of Congress Cataloging-in-Publication Data

Fuente, Alejandro de la, 1963–

A nation for all : race, inequality, and politics in Twentieth-

Century Cuba / Alejandro de la Fuente.

    p. cm.—(Envisioning Cuba)

Includes bibliographical references and index.

ISBN 0-8078-2608-1 (cloth: alk. paper)

ISBN 0-8078-4922-7 (pbk.: alk. paper)

1. Cuba—Race relations. 2. Equality—Cuba—History—

20th century. 3. Cuba—Politics and government—20th

century. 4. Race discrimination—Cuba—History—20th

century. I. Title. II. Series.

F1789.A1 F84 2001

305.8'0097291—dc21   00-046693

05   04   03   02   01   ·   5   4   3   2   1

Parts of this book have been reprinted in revised form

with permission from the following works: "Myths of

Racial Democracy: Cuba, 1900–1912," *Latin American

Research Review* 34, no. 3 (Fall 1999): 39–73; "Recreating

Racism: Race and Discrimination in Cuba's Special

Period," in *Georgetown University Cuba Briefing Paper Series*,

no. 18 (1998); "Two Dangers, One Solution: Immigra-

tion, Race, and Labor in Cuba, 1900–1930," *International

Labor and Working-Class History* 51 (Spring 1997): 30–49;

and "Race and Inequality in Cuba, 1899–1981," *Journal of

Contemporary History* 30, no. 1 (1995): 131–67.

To Patri and Isa

To my parents, who taught me to love Cuba

and its people

To Wilfredo "Willy" Capote,

wherever he is

CONTENTS

FIGURES AND TABLES

ACKNOWLEDGMENTS

I began thinking about the intricacies of Cuba's modern race relations in the early 1990s, in the peace of my Havana personal library, surrounded by precious books and by the warmth of my extended family. I finished it in Tampa, Florida, nearly ten years later. Gone is the library; also gone is the easy access to my family. But during all these years something remained: the love and support of my wife, Patricia. Academics frequently thank their spouses last in book introductions. I thank mine first and foremost. More recently, I thank her for helping me resist the advances of our three-year-old daughter, Isabel. Isa always had plans for me, admittedly better than my revising this manuscript.

It was my privilege to conduct much of this research at the University of Pittsburgh, where I had the opportunity to work with a remarkable group of scholars—Seymour Drescher, Peggy Lovell, and Carmelo Mesa-Lago among them. George Reid Andrews and Harold Sims have read and commented on countless versions of this manuscript, and I have learned in the process what academic excellence and collaboration are all about. I give special thanks to them both for their generosity and support. I am also grateful to Susan Fernandez, my colleague and friend at the University of South Florida (USF), for carefully reading the entire manuscript and for her suggestions and criticisms in questions of form and substance.

Rebecca Scott's pioneering work on race, politics, and mobilization in Cuba has been, together with her dedication and enthusiasm, a source of inspiration. Our mutual interests have led to several collaborative efforts that have involved the participation of other scholars, such as Ada Ferrer, Orlando García Martínez, and Michael Zeuske. I must acknowledge that in this process I have always received more from them than I was able to give in exchange.

Other colleagues who read and critiqued different sections of the manuscript include the noted Colombian anthropologist Jaime Arocha, Jorge de Carvalho, Carmen Diana Deere, Laurence Glasco, Olabiyi Jay, Helen Safa, Ward Stavig, and Kevin Yelvington. In Cuba, I benefited from the comments and questions raised by Jorge Ibarra, a leading student of Cuban nationalism, culture, and society. Tomás Fernandez Robaina, a long-term collaborator and friend, shared with me his extensive knowledge of Afro-Cuban history and sources. It is fair to say that his support was crucial to my finishing this project. Walterio Carbonell clarified questions and provided background information that is seldom found in written sources. The late Conrado Bequer shared his personal experiences as labor organizer and political activist during the second republic. Historian Carmen Almodovar helped me collect information during the early stages of the research. So did my parents, José de la Fuente and Sara García. Lourdes Serrano and Juan A. Alvarado Ramos, from the Centro de Antropología de Cuba, discussed their work with me, and we have collaborated in several common projects. I owe a very special note of thanks to people at two organizations in the island: to Orlando García Martínez, president of the Cienfuegos branch of the Unión de Escritores y Artistas de Cuba, and to the staff at the Centro Juan Marinello in Havana, especially Rafael Hernandez and center director Pablo Pacheco, for the opportunity to present my work before a Cuban audience. I also thank the efficient and dedicated staff of the Archivo Histórico Provincial de Cienfuegos, who always go out of their way to facilitate my work there.

In its final stages, the manuscript benefited from the comments and suggestions of Louis A. Pérez and Thomas Holt, who read the book for the University of North Carolina Press. In addition to thanking her for her patience and resourcefulness, I am grateful to Elaine Maisner, editor of the book, for her choice of readers, whose criticisms made this book infinitely better. Thanks to Elaine, what typically is a stressful process has been in fact a pleasant experience.

My research was generously funded by a Peace Scholar Award from the United States Institute of Peace, by the Institute for the Study of World Politics, and by the Harry F. Guggenheim Foundation. I did some preliminary writing while holding a Rockefeller Visiting Scholarship at the University of Florida. Additional research for the book was made possible by a Grant for Research and Writing from the John D. and Catherine T. MacArthur Foundation and a postdoctoral grant from the United States Institute of Peace. A Faculty Development Grant and a Presidential Young Faculty Award at USF provided funds for traveling and field research. The History Department at USF generously gave me free time to finish the writing. I thank my colleagues at USF for a collegial and pleasant work environment.

Finally, I must acknowledge the support of those who were always with us during these sometimes difficult years: my parents and parents-in-law, Noel Gonzalez and Yolanda Maicas, who were never distant even though we could not see them; Maria and Luigi Tatichi, who literally gave us refuge when we needed it most; Lola Maicas, Luis Miguel García Mora, Humberto and Berta Gonzalez, Harry and Odalys Valdez, Gena Wodnicki, and Elena and Carmelo Mesa-Lago, who did everything possible to make us feel at home when it seemed that we had lost our own home forever. To them, I would rather say it in Spanish: *muchas gracias*.

ABBREVIATIONS

CANF
: Cuban American National Foundation

CFN
: Conjunto Folklórico Nacional (National Folkloric Ensemble)

CNOC
: Confederación Nacional Obrera de Cuba
(National Workers Confederation of Cuba)

CTC
: Confederación de Trabajadores de Cuba, later Central de
Trabajadores de Cuba (Confederation of Cuban Workers)

FDMC
: Federación Democrática de Mujeres Cubanas
(Democratic Federation of Cuban Women)

ICAIC
: Instituto Cubano de Arte e Industria Cinematográficos
(Cuban Institute for the Art and Industry of the Cinema)

KKKK
: Ku Klux Klan Kubano (Cuban Ku Klux Klan)

MOPI
: Movimiento de Opinión Progresista Integral
(Movement of Integral Progressive Opinion)

M-26-7
: Movimiento 26 de Julio (26th of July Movement)

OLAS
: Organization of Latin American Solidarity

ONRE
: Organización Nacional de Rehabilitación Económica
(National Organization of Economic Rehabilitation)

PC
: Partido Conservador (Conservative Party)

PCC
: Partido Comunista de Cuba (Cuban Communist Party)

PIC
: Partido Independiente de Color (Independent Party of Color)

PL
: Partido Liberal (Liberal Party)

PP
   Partido Popular (Popular Party)
PRCA
   Partido Revolucionario Cubano Auténtico
   (Cuban Revolutionary Party, Authentic)
PSP
   Partido Socialista Popular (Popular Socialist Party)
SNOIA
   Sindicato Nacional de Obreros de la Industria Azucarera
   (National Workers Union of the Sugar Industry)
TNC
   Teatro Nacional de Cuba (Cuban National Theater)
UNITA
   Union for the Total Independence of Angola

More than thirty years had passed when, in the summer of 1993, a white, upper-class Cuban-American woman from Miami returned to the island for a visit. She was greeted there by her former maid, now retired, a black woman who was the mother of two children: an engineer and a medical doctor. It was an emotional encounter, full of common memories and mutual happiness. But when the unavoidable issue of a post-Communist Cuba came up during the conversation, the black ex-maid asked: "Will my children be maids again?"[1]

Will her children be maids again? A reflection of the anxieties typical of the early 1990s conjuncture, when Cuban society entered its worst crisis since the revolutionary triumph of 1959, this question also reflects Afro-Cubans' long-standing anxieties over political changes more generally. Together with other disadvantaged social groups, Afro-Cubans have been traditionally dependent on state actions for economic and social opportunities. Government policies can either create avenues for blacks' and mulattoes' inclusion in the nation or preclude their participation in areas of the country's economic, social, and political life. Whereas some of the elements of the 1990s crisis were without precedent, the apprehension with which Afro-Cubans perceived the possibility of impending political changes was certainly not.[2]

These anxieties were based not only on the impact that government changes can have on the daily lives of ordinary citizens but also on the knowledge that political transitions in Cuba's modern history have often resulted in racially defined social tensions, even violence. Given the centrality of race in the construction and representation of the Cuban nation, this is hardly surprising. It is during periods of crisis and transformation, when competing visions of the nation and its people openly clash for legitimacy and consolidation, that the place of Afro-Cubans in society has been more vividly contested. Some social actors have seen these periods as opportunities to minimize blacks' access to the polity and to the most desirable sectors of the economy. Others, including many Afro-Cubans, have seen them as possibilities to advance José Martí's dream of a racially egalitarian republic, a nation with all and for all.

Although Martí's vision remained an unfulfilled project in the early 1990s, the Cuban revolutionary government had taken significant steps toward turning his dream into a reality. The poor had enjoyed substantial social mobility since the early 1960s, as exemplified by the former maid's own children, who had become professionals.

Yet some authors would probably contend that this is not a typical example. The literature on the impact of the Cuban revolution on race relations is characterized by the existence of radically divergent, irreconcilable points of view, ranging from the belief that the revolution inherited and solved the racial problem, to the argument that it has actually reinforced racism and that Fidel Castro himself is a racist. "The Cuban revolution [has] eliminated in less than three years an evil that lasted more than three centuries"[3] is a typical statement at one end of the spectrum; the claim that "Fidel Castro is a calculating racist" or that "the revolution, in its own way . . . is also, perhaps due to the very nature of communism, fundamentally racist" exemplifies the other end.[4]

Although some of these authors have created serious and provocative pieces, the best scholarship on race in contemporary Cuba has been produced by scholars who have adopted a more balanced, intermediate position. Not surprisingly, their contributions are better substantiated, more carefully researched, and less aggressive in tone.[5] They have argued that Cuba is neither the racial paradise depicted by Cuban authorities, official scholars, and sympathetic observers nor the racist hell portrayed by some of the detractors of the revolutionary government. Cuba has undoubtedly made progress toward equality, these authors claim, but it has not solved the "race problem." Beyond this point of consensus, however, they strongly disagree about the revolution's impact on race relations and fluctuate between a clear support for the government and its policies to an open, although moderate, criticism on the subject.

But as Lourdes Casal argued years ago, one of the issues being contested is the nature of Cuba's prerevolutionary society, how racist and racially unequal it was.[6] Although, to my knowledge, no serious scholar has claimed that the republican society was free from discrimination,[7] some authors do stress that the trend toward a more racially equal society predates the 1959 revolution; that opportunities for social mobility existed, including access to elite jobs; that the 1940 constitution proscribed discrimination; that institutional racism was unknown; and that there existed a long-term trend toward "racial integration" in the country.[8] Arguments of this form tend to minimize the impact of the socialist revolution on race relations. On the other hand, Casal and other scholars have asserted precisely the opposite: that pre-1959 Cuba was a deeply racist society, in which blacks were systematically kept at the bottom of the social hierarchy.[9]

This discussion is informed not only by the contending ideological positions of the authors but also by the lack of systematic research on the subject. As Marifeli Pérez-Stable argues, the nature of Cuban prerevolutionary society is "a rather neglected theme in the literature" and "uncharted terrain for sociological analysis."[10] This is especially true for studies on race, despite the peculiarities of Cuba's historical experience. The island received African slaves into the 1860s and was the last Spanish colony to abolish slavery (1886), an event that was itself related to the struggle for independence and the formation of a cross-racial nationalist coalition. Furthermore, it was in Cuba that blacks first organized a racially defined national political party in 1912. And last, but certainly not least, the country provides a unique example to study the impact of socialism on race relations in the Americas.

This lack of scholarship corresponds with a dominant, long-term interpretation of Cuban nationalism that posits the divisiveness and dangers involved in the discussion of a subject that might threaten national unity and Cuba's racial fraternity. Indeed, according to this vision it is not only dangerous and antipatriotic to inquire about race—as a white intellectual put it in 1929, "The black problem exists only when it is talked about, and that is to play with fire"[11]—but unnecessary as well, for race has no role among true Cubans.

Nonissues are not for study. When they are, they are frequently relegated to the convenience of the past or to areas of minimal political conflict. During the republican period, most studies on race sought to glorify the lives, the political and military trajectories, of prominent black leaders, especially those who had participated in the struggles for independence. By emphasizing blacks' contribution to the cause of Cuban independence, these writings also had, of course, a direct political purpose. Not coincidentally, most of these contributions were written by black authors.[12] With very few exceptions, studies dealing with Afro-Cubans during the postindependence period were more critiques of their subordination in Cuban society than scholarly studies.[13]

It was only in the area of "culture" that Afro-Cubans' contribution to national life was acknowledged, researched, and publicized in mainstream intellectual circles as part of national folklore. Studies about the African ingredients—"roots" was the term coined—of Cuban music, dance, food, and language proliferated after the 1920s as part of a broader effort to redefine the very meaning of Cubanness. In the process, symbolized above all by the Afrocubanista literary movement, Cuba was reconstructed as a mulatto or mestizo nation.[14]

The 1959 revolution did not fundamentally alter these intellectual trends and does not appear to be, in this respect, the "great divide" that it is usually assumed to be.[15] On the one hand, cultural authorities selectively acknowledged, sponsored, and publicized the African roots of popular culture as key ingredients of Cubanness and national folklore. On the other hand, building upon long-term dominant interpretations of Cuban nationalism, the revolutionary government imposed its own brand of official silence on race. Beginning in the 1960s, the new authorities claimed that racial discrimination had been eliminated from the island. "Discrimination," Fidel Castro asserted in 1966, "disappeared when class privileges disappeared, and it has not cost the Revolution much effort to resolve that problem."[16] Race was treated as a divisive issue, its open discussion as a threat to national unity. The government had "solved" the racial problem: to speak about it was to address a nonissue.[17]

Although this is not the place to discuss the merits of Cuba's official position, it should be emphasized that this ideological environment greatly discouraged scholarly research on the role of race and the place of individuals of African descent in Cuban society. The initial revisionist attempts of Walterio Carbonell in *Crítica, cómo surgió la cultura nacional* (1961) and Juan René Betancourt in *El negro: Ciudadano del futuro* (written before the revolution, but published in 1959) were both, despite their significant differences, unsympathetically received and met with official resistance.[18] Instead, domestic historians focused their attention on the study of slavery and the plantation economy (a crucial element in understanding Cuba's underdevelopment), the United States' political control and economic penetration of the island, the wars for independence, and the labor movement. Valuable studies were also conducted on *maronage* and other forms of black resistance, and biographies of some prominent Afro-Cubans were published.[19] Although racism and racial discrimination could have been integrated into the narrative of the "precedents" of the revolution, race was seldom addressed by domestic historians and was frequently treated as a mere by-product of class contradictions.[20] Tomás Fernández Robaina's revisionist *El negro en Cuba* is the most notable exception to this trend, for in it the author emphasizes not only the discriminatory nature of republican society but also blacks' permanent struggle to oppose it and to achieve full and effective equality.[21]

But recent scholarship has started to open up this important area in Cuban historiography. Rebecca Scott's pioneering studies on the transition from slavery to free labor have been complemented by Ada Ferrer's research about black participation in the wars for independence and the discourse of race in the construction of national identities.[22] Rafael Fermoselle, Thomas Orum, and, especially, Aline Helg have provided a much more comprehensive view of racial politics in the early postindependence period and have underlined as well the negative influence exercised by the U.S. occupation governments in the island, a subject to which Louis A. Pérez Jr. and other scholars had already devoted their attention.[23] Valuable studies have also appeared concerning the evolution of racial ideologies in Cuba and their interaction with national culture.[24] Within the island, historians and anthropologists are showing a renewed interest in race—and in areas previously closed to scholarly inquiry. Anthropologists, for instance, are conducting research on contemporary issues that were taboo until recently, including the persistence of prejudice and racist stereotypes in Cuban society.[25] Quite obviously, the concerns of the former maid quoted at the beginning of this introduction are not hers alone.

This book, in turn, seeks to incorporate the study of "race" and of racial inequality into the general question of national formation and the evolution of Cuban society during the postcolonial period. It is understood that an approach like this has certain limitations. By concentrating on national trends, this study does little justice to the complexities and infinite variations of local conditions. Local situations are always richer than any national abstraction. And although numerous local events are mentioned in the book, they are used to illustrate certain general statements—not the other way around. Following the same logic, the book analyzes the impact that government policies, economic conditions, and different forms of social action have had on discourses of race and on patterns of racial inequality in the island. Thus the book emphasizes the social end of what Thomas Holt calls the continuum "between behavioral explanations sited at the individual level of human experience and those at the level of society and social forces."[26] Of particular interest are the connections that mediate between these actors: how different social groups influenced the formation of state policies and how the state shaped in turn the composition, goals, and strategies of those groups. Different notions of race and *cubanidad* competed for acceptance and legitimacy through this interaction.

Concretely, this book seeks to answer three basic questions. First, how racially unequal has Cuban society been during the twentieth century in areas such as access to education, the labor market, and power resources? We know that race has played a fundamental role in Cuban society since the colonial period, but to what degree has race constrained individual life chances in Cuba, both under the republic (1902–58) and under the revolution (1959 to the present)? What impact did the revolution's class-based program have on Afro-Cubans' situation? This work, however, attempts to establish not only how racial inequality changed but also, to a certain extent, why it did. Thus, the second and more challenging question is what factors explain the relative position of blacks and whites in the areas mentioned above, a question that is in turn related to the third one: what roles have racial ideologies played in defining the terms of racial coexistence within the Cuban nation? Dominant racial ideologies are not mere reflections of structural conditions but integral parts of social realities. They define what is politically possible. Thus, the book seeks to determine the social and political opportunities and limitations that contending notions of Cubanness and national identity have created for blacks and whites in Cuba's postcolonial history.

THEORETICAL PERSPECTIVES

The existing literature does not provide a coherent explanation for the often ambiguous roles that perceptions of race have played in Cuban society, economy, and politics. Scholars still differ widely on what happened during the twentieth century; some authors underline the racist character of Cuban prerevolutionary society, whereas others emphasize blacks' progress under the republic. Nowhere are these divergent theses more sharply defined than in their interpretation of the so-called race war of 1912. Thus, whereas Helg claims "the slaughter of 1912 dealt a long-lasting blow to Afro-Cubans," Jorge and Isabel Castellanos interpret the same events in a quite different way: "[T]he disaster of 1912 briefly deterred, but did not stop, the movement toward equality and for the spiritual and material advancement of the Cuban population 'of color.' "[27] I will refer to these alternative theses as "the dominance of racism" and "the possibility of integration."

These positions provide at least a point of departure for discussion. To the questions posed above, the advocates of the racism thesis respond that republican Cuba was racially unequal. They explain this condition in terms of the racist character of Cuban society and the effects of a "myth of racial equality" that, while claiming that all Cubans were equal, served in fact to keep blacks at the bottom of the social ladder. This scholarship provides important insights, such as a possible interpretation of the character and purpose of Cuban nationalist ideology, the centrality of race in the construction of the nation, and ample evidence of Afro-Cubans' relentless struggle to achieve full economic, social, and political equality. That these authors have broken the long-standing silence on race in Cuban scholarship is itself a significant achievement.[28]

The arguments of the integration thesis are less developed. Its proponents recognize the existence of inequality and racism in pre-1959 Cuba, but they stress the continuing progress of blacks in several key areas (education, employment) and the integrationist nature of Cuban nationalist ideology. Important contributions of this literature include the perceptions that the nationalist ideology might have contributed to the integration of blacks and whites into a shared notion of Cubanness and that objective, measurable inequality did in fact decline in certain areas and periods under the republic.[29]

Their contributions notwithstanding, none of these positions takes us very far in explaining the changing meanings of race in postcolonial Cuban society. The integration thesis detects black progress but offers only vague explanations about why it happened—and why it did not in some periods. Its proponents imply that Cuban nationalism allowed for all racial groups to participate in society, but they fall short of explaining how this ideology was translated into concrete opportunities for blacks' advancement, why racial inequality persisted under the republic, or why blacks were openly excluded from certain occupations and social spaces.

The racism thesis, in turn, asserts that Cuban nationalism served to maintain blacks in a subordinate position, but it fails to explain why blacks improved their position relative to whites in several important areas, including positions of leadership in politics and the government bureaucracy. Its characterization of racism as something inherent to Cuban society provides little insight about the economic, social, and political conditions in which it operated, its changing nature, and its potential decline—a possibility that might not even be considered. To borrow the expression from a student of race in the United States, these authors assume that Cuban society operated on a racially biased automatic pilot.[30] Furthermore, by emphasizing race—in what typically becomes a "white versus black" approach—proponents of the racism thesis tend to downplay the importance of other social identities. It does not suffice to claim that race was an important "social construction" in Cuba—it was and still is. It is necessary to explore its importance in comparison to other forms of social organization and identity.

The critique of the so-called Cuban myth of racial equality by the proponents of the racism thesis follows trends similar to the literature about race in Latin America. Starting in Brazil, where the UNESCO-sponsored studies conducted in the 1950s demonstrated that the country was not the racial paradise it was expected to be, the trend in recent scholarship has been to stress that these ideologies are elite creations that serve to demobilize blacks—thus contributing to maintaining the status quo—while blaming them for their lack of success in societies that are supposed to provide equal opportunities for all. "Like their peers in several Latin American countries," Helg contends, "Cuba's white elites cleverly resorted to a myth of the existence of racial equality in the nation so as to justify the current social order. . . . The ultimate function of Latin American myths of racial equality was . . . to place the blame for blacks' continuing lower social position entirely on blacks themselves." Furthermore, "Cuba's myth of racial equality, by denying the existence of discrimination on the basis of race, undermined the formation of a black collective consciousness."[31]

Criticism has also been directed against the incongruence between an ideology that rests on the alleged fraternity and equality of all racial groups, on the one hand, and the persistence of gross inequalities associated with race, on the other. Michael G. Hanchard explains: "Within the economy of racial democracy . . . blacks and mulattoes are being excluded from employment and educational opportunities reserved for whites, and relegated largely to positions of inferior economic and social status. Thus, the myths of racial exceptionalism and democracy proclaim the existence of racial egalitarianism . . . while producing racially discriminatory belief systems and practices at the same time." The advocates of racial democracy frequently emphasize the mild character of race relations in Latin America, particularly in comparison to the United States, but the reality, anthropologist John Burdick claims, "is not quite so pretty."[32] The conviction that these "myths" were designed to hide the harsh realities of fundamentally racist societies has grown along with each piece of scholarship documenting the persistence of racial inequality, particularly in Brazil.[33]

But just as social realities are not "so pretty," the Latin American paradigms of racially mixed, integrated nations are not so ugly. The rhetorical exaltation of racial inclusiveness as the very essence of nationhood has made racially defined exclusion considerably more difficult, creating in the process significant opportunities for appropriation and manipulation of dominant racial ideologies by those below while limiting the political options of the elites. By portraying the ideologies of racial democracy as forces that operate in a unidirectional sense of subordination and demobilization, the critics have downplayed the capacity of blacks and other groups to use these myths to their advantage. This explains why some of these critics have significant difficulties accommodating in their narratives whatever presence blacks have enjoyed in leadership positions in Latin America, a presence that is frequently explained in terms of the cooptation of a few select leaders.[34]

A logical and virtually unavoidable corollary of the racism thesis is that blacks should mobilize separately and that racially based political mobilization is the legitimate—perhaps even only—way to fight racism effectively. This might be true in societies that have been racially segregated, in which racial identities are constantly enforced from above, leading to forms of mobilization that are racially defined. The existence of a rigid and legally defined racial order relegates all members of the oppressed racial group to a subordinate social position, regardless of education, income, or other socially relevant variables. But Latin American societies are characterized precisely by the lack of these state-sanctioned racial orders—"not a trivial distinction," as George Reid Andrews argues.[35]

Ideologies of racial democracy have made mobilization along racial lines difficult, but they have also opened opportunities for other forms of social action.[36] Analyzing these myths as demobilizing forces tends to imply that racial mobilization is the only legitimate way to struggle for racial equality. This is an assumption born out of the very North Atlantic ideologies that the critics ultimately attack (that is, the essentialness of race), and it is based on the peculiar historical experience of racial segregation in the United States.

The study of Latin America through a North Atlantic theoretical "lens" is understandable, however. Studies about race in the United States are significantly more developed than those about race in Latin America, and available theories of racial stratification are based on studies dealing with the emergence and consolidation of these racial orders. As William J. Wilson explains, these theories can be grouped into two main categories.[37] One group emphasizes the role of the elites in creating a racial order that works to their advantage because it divides the working class, guarantees the existence of a pool of cheap reserve labor, and depresses wages. Drawing from neoclassical economic analysis, the other group contends that racial divisions restrict the free movement of labor in an open market, which is against business's true interests. The elimination of free workers' competition for jobs benefits higher-paid labor, not capitalists or the elite. Thus, the emergence of a racial order is linked by these theorists to the interests of the racially privileged sector of the working class. It is because of their level of organization and power that workers in the privileged sector are able to impose on capitalists the additional cost of a segmented labor market.[38] Other authors, such as political scientist Stanley Greenberg, apply a combination of both theories.[39]

Despite their differences, these authors agree on at least two crucial points: the methodological importance of social classes (capitalists, working class) for the study of race and the centrality of politics. Social classes might have a vested interest in the creation and consolidation of a racial order, but forms of racial domination will be institutionalized only if those groups have the power resources to access, influence, and eventually monopolize the state. This is a political question—it takes political power to define and enforce the socio-legal status of a racial other as inferior.

THE CUBAN CASE

A study that seeks to explain Cuban race relations must likewise place state policies at center stage and explore the economic, social, and ideological constraints under which social classes and racial groups interacted. That is the focus of this book. Yet as any scholar of colonial or dependent states is aware, in a colonial situation government policies are frequently a better reflection of imperial goals than of local pressures. Cuba is no exception to this trend. Although my analysis concentrates on the influence that domestic factors—that is, social and interest groups, political parties, unions—exercised on different administrations and on government responses to them, in Cuba some of the most influential "domestic" factors were, in fact, foreign. Especially during the first republic (1902–33), not only did U.S. investors control key economic activities such as sugar production, but they represented a formidable political force as well.

Given the extent of U.S. investors' hegemony over Cuban affairs, the capacity of this group to determine government policies was greater than that of any other elite. In addition to their economic power, they had the ability to access and influence official circles in the United States, where policy decisions were ultimately made. As previous scholars have noted, U.S. hegemony not only limited Cuban independence but also assured the survival of the very social order that the *independentistas* (anticolonial forces) sought to transform.[40] Foreign capital and Washington demanded order and stability; building a nation that was truly for all required decisive state action and drastic social transformations. In the context of Cuba's imperial subordination, a modicum of independence could be maintained only at the expense of social justice. As Pérez-Stable contends, "Containing the *clases populares* was the *sine qua non* of mediated sovereignty."[41] For instance, the possibility of yet another U.S. military intervention in 1912 contributed to unleashing the wave of repression against the Partido Independiente de Color and to presenting their activities as a threat to the very survival of the republic.

U.S. interference in domestic politics diminished under the second republic (1933–58), but North American interests and concerns continued to shape internal affairs in important ways. The extension of cold war politics to the island in the late 1940s, for instance, led to the displacement of the

Communists, who had made racial equality one of their most important political goals, from the leadership of the labor movement. Even during the postrevolutionary period, when the Cuban government succeeded in shattering the bases of U.S. influence, the autonomy of the state remained limited by external factors. In order to claim a leading role in the struggle against imperialism and racism in the context of the cold war, for instance, Cuba had to deem its own race problem solved. The country's reinsertion into the international economy in the 1990s, in turn, exposed again the vulnerability of the Cuban state to foreign influences and the impact that these influences can have on Cuban society.

Most of these effects have been neither intended nor predictable. U.S. hegemony frequently provoked the very ills it sought to prevent: chronic instability and disorder. Given the relationship between national independence and social justice, the struggles to build a nation for all could be easily couched in the language of nationalism and sovereignty, using symbols with which Cubans across class and racial lines could identify. These struggles were potentially revolutionary, for they implied the elimination of U.S. control and their allies in the island. Yet the possibility of U.S. intervention could also legitimize repression, as in 1912, or be used by government authorities to diffuse the threat of popular mobilization. Likewise, public demonstrations against racism in the United States questioned the values of North American democracy and boosted national pride, but they were also used to remind Afro-Cubans that they lived already in a racial paradise. Scientific ideas of race led to the creation of national counterdiscourses such as Afrocubanismo in the 1920s and 1930s, yet these discourses reproduced the notion that race was central to the representation of the nation.

Polar explanations such as those discussed above are barely adequate to explain the complexities of Cuba's racial politics and to account for the contradictory and often unexpected effects of the nationalist ideology of racial fraternity, formed largely in response to those foreign influences. Neither unqualified racial integration nor linear exclusion characterizes the history of Cuba as an independent nation. Theories about the institutionalization of racial orders provide important analytical insights, but they study precisely what Cuba lacked: a social order based on rigid, codified distinctions of race. I share their emphasis on state policies and social actors, but with the qualifications imposed by Cuba's dependent status in the international arena. Ambiguity is what best defines the evolution of race relations in twentieth-century Cuba.

The very creation of the republic is a superb example of these ambiguities.

Early republican Cuba is in fact a textbook example of what Greenberg calls the period of "intensification" of a racial order.[42] Commercial agriculture was in full expansion, and farmers formulated, with some success, several proposals to expand the role of the state in the labor market and to guarantee a steady supply of cheap and politically disempowered labor. Racial divisions permeated the nascent labor movement; white workers in at least some sectors would have benefited from a system that kept blacks out of competition. Adding to these conditions was the U.S. hegemonic control over the island, which came accompanied by scientific racism, an open disdain for darker, lower-class Cubans, and support for the traditional colonial elite. The creation of a racial order was a possibility indeed.

But other forces worked in the opposite direction. The republic was born after several decades of cross-racial mobilization and nationalist myth-making. Individuals of African descent had played a very prominent role in the ranks and leadership of the liberation army, and their prestige and visibility could not be easily erased after the war. During the struggle against Spain, the Cuban people had invented "revolutionary traditions" that proclaimed all Cubans to be equal. The nationalist ideology envisioned a new republic that would be not only politically independent but egalitarian and inclusive as well—a republic "with all and for all," as José Martí had called it. The existence of "races" was seen as a social reality, but within an encompassing notion of Cubanness that was supposed to subsume, and eventually erase, racial identities. These competing notions of nationhood coexisted in an environment of political uncertainty. At stake was nothing less than how different the "new Cuba" would truly be.

The first great battle between these competing notions of nationhood was fought over the question of citizenship and the definition of suffrage. The notion of universal male suffrage prevailed in the Constitutional Convention of 1901 and became a central tenet of Cuban politics, despite the objections of some members of the traditional elite and the fierce opposition and maneuvering of the U.S. occupation government. This, in turn, suggests that the ideal of racial equality operated in ways more complex than just as a tool to maintain blacks in a subordinate position.

Universal male suffrage made Cuba unique among countries with a substantial population of African descent in the early twentieth-century Americas. At the time universal suffrage was being introduced in Cuba, electoral rights were being significantly reduced in Brazil, the U.S. South, and Venezuela. In Brazil, the electoral reform of 1881 and the Constitution of 1891, which created the oligarchic first republic (1889–1930), provided electoral rights only to literate men, effectively barring most Afro-Brazilians (and most Euro-Brazilians as well) from the country's political life. In the U.S. South, the failure of Reconstruction gave way to the emergence of segregation, the creation of a disenfranchised class of black laborers, and effective control by the white southern ruling elite. Access to the ballot became, as George M. Fredrickson notes, a "main objective in the battle against white domination." In Venezuela, universal suffrage was established in the Constitution of 1893, but only to be restricted in 1901.[43]

If Cuban "revolutionary traditions" had precluded Afro-Cubans' exclusion from the polity, universal suffrage guaranteed the salience of race in national politics and opened opportunities for blacks' advancement under the republic. As a contemporary newspaper put it, "[I]n a country of universal suffrage it is not possible to disregard popular feelings."[44] No political party could afford to utterly ignore the circumstances and preferences of more than one-third of the electorate. The most conservative political sector fully understood this reality: hence their repeated efforts to restrict the franchise by introducing voting requirements similar to those used in the U.S. South. When these efforts failed, they resorted to manipulation and corruption of the whole electoral process. As elsewhere, the ballot was an important resource for Afro-Cubans, but its actual effectiveness depended, of course, on intra- and interparty competition. Thus, the control of the political machinery by the Conservatives during the 1910s undermined not only elections but also Afro-Cubans' chances to be represented in government. The proportion of blacks in Congress declined after 1912, the year of the Conservatives' political victory and of the much-debated revolt of, and racist repression against, the Partido Independiente de Color (PIC, Independent Party of Color).

Although the activities of the PIC have received ample attention from scholars, its creation was only one of the forms of mobilization and political participation practiced by Afro-Cubans in the early republic. Efforts to organize blacks separately failed not only because of repression but also due to the mainstream parties' successful campaign to attract Afro-Cuban voters and the pervasiveness of a nationalist ideology that called for all Cubans to be equal. The racist repression against the PIC in 1912 became politically viable precisely because a racially defined political party was not compatible with the dominant discourse of a racially inclusive Cubanness. Based on this interpretation of Cubanness, the organization of the party was easily construed as a "racist" act—the Independientes could be accused of having placed race above national identity.

This environment proscribed as un-Cuban any attempt at racially based mobilization, but it also made the construction of a legally defined racial order a political impossibility. The ideal of a racially integrated and harmonious nation did not reflect social realities accurately, but the legitimacy of the idea itself was so strong as to impose its acceptance on all quarters of Cuban society, even the most reluctant ones. And although it limited Afro-Cubans' choices for political action, the integrationist ideal also opened up opportunities for their participation in republican society—opportunities that they made good use of.

The inviability of Afro-Cuban autonomous political mobilization was also a function of these opportunities, which led to social mobility and to a growing fragmentation of what was referred to in the late 1800s and early 1900s as "clase de color" (the colored class). Afro-Cuban intellectuals themselves stressed that by the 1920s there was little resembling a *class* of "colored" people. Since the first years of the republic, a growing number of Afro-Cubans took advantage of a desegregated public school system, expanded their education, and moved into the world of white-collar employment and the professions. The emphasis that elites placed on formal schooling as a prerequisite to social advancement and to holding public office served initially to justify the exclusion of Afro-Cubans from white-collar jobs,[45] but these very requirements were turned into a socially acceptable route for mobility. Thus, like their African American contemporaries, Afro-Cubans came to regard education as sacred. In contrast to the United States, however, in Cuba blacks benefited from a public school system to which access—the evidence suggests—was not racially based.[46]

The result was the formation of a sizable group of black and mulatto professionals who, given the precariousness of their recently acquired status, sought to distance themselves, socially and culturally, from the masses of black manual workers. Social and cultural distances were emphasized precisely because many Afro-Cuban professionals were dangerously close to working-class blacks through family and community links. These Afro-Cuban professionals also saw themselves as the leaders and the voice of the whole "colored race." They were both, to a degree. Black and mulatto intellectuals did address issues that concerned all Afro-Cubans regardless of socioeconomic status, but most of their efforts revolved around the barriers that the highly educated and "civilized" blacks faced in Cuban society. What we frequently perceive as black discourse is, in fact, black middle-class discourse. And because racial barriers hardened along with the desirability and prestige ascribed to professional jobs—the higher and better-paid an occupation, the whiter—the black middle class became the most visible target of racial discrimination. In response, Afro-Cuban professionals created their own exclusive societies and fought against exclusion from the closed social spaces of the white bourgeoisie.

In turn, race was only one of many factors affecting the lives of the black and mulatto manual workers. The process of proletarianization of the black rural population was fairly advanced by the late 1920s, and according to official statistics, by the 1940s race had a limited impact among manual workers' incomes and employment opportunities in the largest sectors of the economy, including agriculture, manufacturing, and personal services.

Inequality in the occupational structure declined until the Great Depression, despite the deliberate efforts of employers and the state to flood the labor market with immigrant workers. In this respect the Cuban experience was hardly unique. As elsewhere in the Americas, employers in Cuba's first republic implemented immigration, hiring, and promotion practices that contributed to the construction of what Gay Seidman calls "racialized labor markets, racialized labor processes, and racialized interpretations of class and social status."[47] In contrast to the United States and South Africa, however, in Cuba and other Latin American countries workers insisted for the most part on the need to create alternative, cross-racial class identities.

But even if white workers in Cuba had sought to enforce a monopoly over the best sectors of the market—and, given the dominant ideology of racial fraternity, there is no evidence that they ever did—they lacked the political power to do so. When they got access to power, it was as part of a Communist-led, militant, cross-racial labor movement that by the late 1930s had emerged as a major actor in the Cuban political scene. Under Communist leadership, the labor movement extracted significant concessions from employers and the state, giving salience in the process to class identities in Cuban society.

Contributing to the salience of class, in addition to the politics of state patronage, was the ideology of *mestizaje* produced by the nationalist intellectuals who formed the Afrocubanista cultural movement in the late 1920s and 1930s. A reformulation of the nationalist myth of racial equality, Afrocubanismo had taken Martí's notion of Cubanness one step further, inventing a synthesis that proudly proclaimed miscegenation to be the very essence of the nation—a mulatto "Cuban race." As did many of their colleagues in Latin America, however, these intellectuals reacted to North Atlantic ideas of race by exalting miscegenation without abandoning the notion that race was central to the representation and future of the nation. The new ideology signaled the bankruptcy of the elite's dreams of a Caucasian paradise in the tropics—Cuba was definitely not white—but was only one step short of claiming that there was no racial problem in the island, merely an economic one. Racial inequality was thus increasingly perceived as a by-product of class inequities.

This ideology of *mestizaje* was not a mere ideological representation devoid of real content. As in Brazil or Venezuela, this ideology represented an ideal that individuals and institutions could not blatantly ignore without risking social condemnation and eventual legal action. Flagrant violations of the ideal could be presented as antinational acts, thus eliciting repulse across race and class lines. That is why instances of discrimination against African American public figures generated unusual publicity and condemnation across Latin America. These racist acts were frequently presented as a *national* shame, for they exposed the inconsistencies of Latin American racial fraternities, so central to nationalist pride. Thus when three hotels in Caracas refused accommodation to African American singer Robert Todd Duncan in 1945, authorities reacted by passing legislation that outlawed discrimination in all public services. In Brazil, the widely publicized refusal of a hotel to host African American dancer Katherine Dunham resulted in the approval of the Afonso Farinos Law of 1951, which declared illegal all forms of discrimination in jobs and public spaces. In Cuba, a similar incident involving African American House of Representatives member Arthur Mitchell resulted in a public outcry in 1937.[48]

Together with other factors, instances of discrimination such as that perpetrated against Representative Mitchell contributed to maintaining race at the core of the political struggles in Cuba's second republic (1933–58), the salience of class notwithstanding. With the collapse of the authoritarian regime of Gerardo Machado (1925–33), conditions were ripe, again, to create a "new" Cuba—perhaps even the true republic for all envisioned by Martí. But, as in 1898, there were contending notions of what "new" meant and what blacks' place should be in the sociopolitical order under construction. Emergent political actors such as the Communist Party and the labor movement envisioned a radical, racially egalitarian republic. Others saw an opportunity to reverse whatever gains Afro-Cubans had made under the first republic, and they invented the notion that blacks had been the main supporters and beneficiaries of the fallen regime—and that thus they deserved to be excluded from the new order. Racial tensions escalated to the point of rupture, leading to different forms of racially defined violence and mobilization. Through the 1930s, race remained an explosive political issue, and

Cuba oscillated between the hope of racial fraternity and the threat of racial confrontation.

In another similarity with conditions at the turn of the century, these competing notions of Cubanness clashed over the formation of the new political order in the Constitutional Convention of 1939. Suffrage was no longer at stake; suffrage had been truly universal since 1934, when women obtained the right to vote. Rather, discussions centered on the state's role in combating racial discrimination and other forms of social injustice. The Communists envisioned an activist state that would actively pursue racial equality and condemn racist behavior, but others remained committed to a vague notion of racial fraternity in which government intervention was neither necessary nor convenient. As with many other issues discussed in the convention, the result was a compromise. The Constitution included a general antidiscriminatory principle, but it deferred the specifics of government action in this area to future legislation. Following Jorge Domínguez, this books thus argues that the struggle for racial equality became linked to the fortunes of the radical labor movement and to the "performance" of the political system.[49] Groups not represented by organized labor, such as the unemployed and domestic servants, did not benefit from the new political system—and blacks were overrepresented in these groups. Likewise, labor's bargaining capacity was dependent on its autonomy, severely curtailed after the expulsion of the Communists from the leadership of the labor federation in 1947. On the one hand, the weakening of the labor movement and the ban of the Communist Party in 1952 meant that the cause of racial equality had lost its most formidable and militant political allies. On the other hand, the political system did not deliver. An antidiscriminatory law complementary to the Constitution was never approved, so the true republic with all and for all would have to be made through other means.

When change came through revolution in 1959, Fidel Castro insisted that this time "it was for real."[50] Real enough it was, but what the revolution would mean for blacks remained open to different interpretations. Some signs were ominous. Race barely figured in the political agenda of the 26th of July Movement (M-26-7), despite the fact that some of their programmatic documents read like a catalog of all the economic, social, and political ills of the republic. The leadership of the movement itself was predominantly white. As in 1933, rumors circulated presenting blacks as the main beneficiaries and supporters of the fallen dictator—in this case, Fulgencio Batista (1952–58), himself a mestizo, according to the white elite. Again, these rumors sought to legitimize the exclusion of blacks from the new order. At the same time, however, the unprecedented commitment of the revolutionary government to benefit the humblest sectors of Cuban society would benefit blacks, for they comprised a significant portion of the *clases populares*. Recognizing that race could be turned into a formidable ideological weapon against the United States and into a source of domestic and international political support, Fidel Castro publicly attacked racial discrimination in jobs and public spaces, linking racism to a past that was about to be transformed and to social groups that were about to be destroyed. Reinforcing previous ideological trends, racial inequality was presented as a by-product of "class privileges." Once these privileges were eliminated, the revolutionary government could triumphantly proclaim the elimination of racial discrimination from the island.

Analyzing the impact of socialism on race relations in Cuba defies any simple formulation. First, the revolutionary government dismantled the old structures of segregation and discrimination (private clubs, recreation facilities, and schools). The socialization of the previously segregated spaces was not achieved without resistance, and eventually black clubs and societies were dismantled as well. It could not be otherwise: the very existence of these clubs defied the revolution's vision of a color-blind society and symbolized the survival of the past. Not only were Afro-Cuban organizations eliminated, however; some Afro-Cuban religious ceremonies were temporarily banned, and race itself was erased from public discourse. By the early 1960s authorities referred to racial discrimination in the past tense, so any attempt to incorporate race into the political agenda was deemed to be counterrevolutionary—a divisionist act. Race surfaced only in the relatively safe area of culture, or as a political issue in the international arena.

Meanwhile, the class-based program of redistribution of wealth and social services had a significant impact on objective indicators of inequality, including life expectancy, education, and jobs. Contrary to what is frequently believed, by the mid-1980s blacks and mulattoes were well represented in managerial positions. This may have been the end point of a process of social ascent, or it may have been the result of the Communist Party's effort to promote blacks to positions of leadership. As an African American scholar who visited the island in 1993 proclaimed with optimism, Cuba, "while not a racial Utopia, is as close to a racial democracy as we have on this earth."[51]

But it takes more than structural change to build a racial democracy. It requires a transformation of what one of my collaborators in the island referred to as "people's heads." Indeed, heads have been remarkably resilient to change. Although the government's educational and cultural programs were explicitly antiracist, the official silence on race allowed the survival and reproduction of racial ideologies that found a fertile breeding ground in the remaining private spaces. As Holt contends, it is at the level of "everyday-ness," through daily "acts of name calling and petty exclusions," that race is reproduced and constantly made.[52] Indeed, the Cuban case strongly suggests that this reproduction occurs even in the midst of an institutional environment committed to racial integration and equality. Recent anthropological research suggests that the acute housing shortage, in turn, facilitated the transmission of racial prejudice in multigenerational households.[53] Through their ancestors, Cuba's youth remained tied to a past that refused to simply vanish.

The link between revolution and racial justice is itself problematic. It implies that racial equality depends on a particular set of structural conditions and on the state's capacity to deliver them. As in the second republic, racial justice is thus linked to government "performance." But the capacity to "perform" is what the government lacked in the 1990s due to the crisis officially labeled as the "special period." The slow but growing privatization of the economy has eroded the very bases that undergirded racial and other forms of partial social equality in the past. This erosion has opened new spaces for racist ideologies to operate more freely—racist ideas are not confined to people's heads anymore.

As in the 1930s, the combination of these racist ideologies with an environment of scarce economic resources stimulates openly discriminatory practices and leads to growing racial tensions. That is why some analysts claim that race is "at the heart" of Cuba's crisis.[54] Adding to these tensions is the possibility that in a not-too-distant future the largely white Cuban-American community might regain some influence in Cuba's economic, social, and political affairs. After all, it is not by chance that in the anecdote that opened this introduction, the black ex-maid's question was posed to a white visitor from Miami. Not only is Cuban Miami overwhelmingly white; it is also part of one of the most racially tense cities in the Americas—a reality that Cuban authorities have not failed to recognize and publicize.

The existence of a largely white exile community adds another racial dimension to the current crisis, but the relationship between "race" and "crisis" is certainly not new in Cuban modern history. As in the past, there are social sectors whose leaders will attempt to minimize blacks' participation in the new Cuba. Whether those forces will succeed is something that this book does not attempt to predict. The ex-maid's question, thus, remains unanswered.

PART I THE FIRST REPUBLIC
1902-1933

Race and the Contending Notions of Cubanidad

The term "Cuban" refers to the Cuban people (not Negroes).
—U.S. Senate, Reports of the Immigration Commission,
   Dictionary of Races or Peoples (1911)

Cubans are known to be . . . whites born in Cuba, descendants mainly of
Spaniards.
—Rafael Montalvo, "Discurso" (1884)

A Cuban is more than mulatto, black, or white.
—José Martí, "My Race" (1893)

Cuba and Cubanness were represented in vastly different ways in 1899, when the defeated Spain had to relinquish sovereignty over its Caribbean colony. Despite their differences, all these definitions had a common element: the shared belief that "race" was at the very core of the nation. Race was, and remained, central to the process of national construction. The competing visions that by the end of the nineteenth century clashed over the creation of the republic and of the new Cuba disagreed not only on questions of property relations or institutional arrangements but also—indeed, primarily—on how racially inclusive and egalitarian postcolonial Cuba should be.

Each of these visions was supported and linked to different social and political actors whose place in the new order was yet undefined in 1898. On the one hand, there was the Liberation Army, nominally victorious and with an enormous prestige among the populace. In a long process involving three separate wars and thirty years of struggle, Cubans of all colors and social origins had created a formidable cross-racial coalition and forged a nationalist revolutionary ideology that claimed all Cubans were equal members of the nation, regardless of race or social status. This coalition had gone to war in 1895 to bring about social change and political independence. They envisioned a new Cuba that would be independent, socially egalitarian, and racially inclusive—a republic "with all and for all," as Martí had called it. Although social and racial tensions plagued the Liberation Army and the nationalist discourse was open to contending and even contradictory interpretations, racial inclusion remained the main thrust of Cuba Libre (Free Cuba): the existence of "blacks" and "whites" was recognized, but they would equally participate in the nation under construction.[1]

On the other hand, the Liberation Army was not in power. Some functions of government, such as tax collection, policing, and justice administration, were performed initially by units of the army, but all these functions came gradually under the control of the U.S. invading forces when the government of military occupation was organized. By 1899 it was the U.S. Army who ruled the island. And although they had entered the war with the avowed purpose of encouraging Cuba's independence, American authorities entertained serious doubts about Cubans' capacity for self-rule and proper government, particularly due to the racial composition of Cuba's population. General Leonard Wood and other American officers did not hide their disdain for dark, lower-class Cubans, and they openly supported what they referred to as "the better class."[2] Wood's own vision of Cubanness was unequivocally explicit in a 1901 letter to Senator Orville H. Platt, after whom the famous amendment limiting Cuban independence was named: "[W]e do not want to get *the real Cuban people*, I mean the producers and merchants, against us."[3]

Planters, merchants, and other members of the former elite had suffered during the war, but they had not been annihilated. American officials did not want a confrontation with them, as Wood stated in his letter to Platt, but more important, under the occupation government the properties and privileges of the former elite were fully respected. U.S. authorities hoped that these "real" Cubans would play a prominent, even leading, role in the creation of the republic, and they gave them support and favor in the appointments to public office. A group that might have been displaced by the victory of the revolutionary coalition was, as a result of intervention, guaranteed continued access to power. Independence had not been achieved. Social change under these circumstances seemed highly unlikely. Supported by American authorities, some members of the "better classes" even questioned whether Cubans of African descent were real and full members of the nation. During the revolution they had sided with Spain precisely because of the racial composition of the Liberation Army and the fear that Afro-Cubans might create a black republic in the island. Some of the members of this traditional elite had staunchly defended the Spanish character of Cuban civilization and could easily connect and sympathize with North American racial ideologies.

Clashing for primacy, these competing ideologies and interests envisioned radically different ways to constitute the nation. Each had its own claims to legitimacy and sources of support. The nationalist paradigm of a racially inclusive nation appealed to large sectors of the population and rested solidly on the prestige and patriotic merits of Cuba's dearest heroes—particularly Martí and the mulatto general Antonio Maceo—and of the Liberation Army. Racially exclusionary notions of nationhood did not have the same popular appeal, but they took their legitimacy from the superiority of North Atlantic science and found political support in the occupation government and the propertied classes.

To complicate things further, some sectors within the white leadership of the Liberation Army were also interested in minimizing blacks' participation in the new Cuba, especially during a period of scarce economic resources and opportunities for employment. Members of the civil and military branches of the Liberation Army formed a powerful political class, led the dominant Liberal and Conservative Parties, and competed ferociously for public office. Despite differences in political denominations, the leadership of these parties shared views of race and nation that were virtually identical. They did not dispute the legitimacy of the nationalist principle of racial democracy, but they treated racial equality as an achievement of the war for independence, not as a goal requiring further social and political action—a conquest rather than a program. The result was an interpretation of Cuban nationalism that denied or minimized the existence of a "race problem," avoided or condemned its public discussion as an affront to the nation, and contributed to maintaining the status quo. This conservative interpretation of the nationalist ideology, linked to the dominant political parties and elite political actors, lingered on through the republic. Despite their formal commitment to a racially fraternal Cubanness, the proponents of this view fully endorsed the notion that whiteness was a precondition for stability and progress and lent support to racially defined immigration programs. In this aspect, the new political elite coincided with, and shared the fears of, the traditional elite and the American occupation forces.

That it was possible to support whitening while pledging allegiance to the ideology of racial fraternity exemplifies the complexities and contradictions of this ideology. Beyond its apparent coherence, the *mambí* revolutionary ideology was in fact open to contending interpretations. Different social groups could refer to the same foundational discourse to explain the relationship between race and nation in radically different ways. Rather than a finished product, the nationalist ideology itself was permanently contested and redefined. In contrast to the elite, conservative version of Cuban racial democracy, a popular interpretation of the same ideology referred to Martí's egalitarian republic as a goal in the unfinished process of nation-building, opposed any attempts to silence the issue, and called for different forms of social action. This radical interpretation was defended initially by only a handful of Afro-Cuban voices. After the 1920s, it was endorsed also by the radical labor movement and the Communist Party.

Thus, clashes occurred not only between Cuban racial democracy, on the one hand, and the racially exclusionary ideologies of the U.S. occupation forces and the traditional white elite, on the other. Clashes also took place within the nationalist ideology. This chapter discusses these formulations of race and nation, their differences and similarities. In order to facilitate the analysis, the first section traces the formation of the nationalist ideology of racial democracy and discusses its ambiguities and contradictions, which enabled various social groups to advance vastly different interpretations of the same ideology. I have grouped these interpretations into two main categories: a conservative, elite version of race and Cubanness and a radical, popular view. A second section discusses the availability of ideas that, in opposition to the ideal of racial fraternity, legitimized Afro-Cubans' exclusion from the nation and the creation of a legally defined racial order. A final section explores the discourse of whitening, in which elite interpretations of racial democracy and the scientific racism manufactured in the North Atlantic countries most visibly coincided.

RACIAL DEMOCRACY

The formation of a nationalist ideology advocating racial inclusiveness was a long and contested process that developed in Cuba from concrete political needs. While the white elites were troubled by the visible racial diversity of the island's population, it was clear that they could not achieve political independence from Spain without the formation of a multiracial alliance, with all its unforeseeable consequences. Cautiously, the white leadership of the first war for independence—the 1868–78 Ten Years War—moved from an opportunistic defense of slavery to the advocacy of abolition. The first constitution of Cuba Libre (1869) had stipulated that all the inhabitants of the republic were free and equal, but it was not until 1871, when the last ordinance approved by the revolutionary authorities concerning freedmen was annulled, that abolition and equality became dominant themes in the nationalist rhetoric. Moreover, the experience of war and the presence and leadership of blacks within the army reinforced the image that independent Cuba would have to be egalitarian and inclusive.[4]

It was to attract blacks to the pro-independence camp that an ideology advocating racial fraternity was further elaborated and systematized. Leading these efforts was nationalist intellectual and activist José Martí, whose militant campaign for a "cordial" republic "with all and for all" became gospel in Cuban nationalist ideology. Martí and other nationalist leaders understood well that unity was a precondition to launch a successful new war for independence. Unity, however, would not be achieved if race continued to separate Cubans. Spanish authorities had effectively used the fear of race war to discourage white Cubans from joining armed attempts against the colonial order, emphasizing in the process that racial diversity and nation were two incompatible entities.[5]

The challenge, then, was to create a new notion of Cubanness that conciliated racial diversity with white fears. This Martí achieved by claiming that Cuban racial fraternity had been forged during the Ten Years War, a revolution that had given freedom and honor to the slaves and in which blacks and whites had fought and died together to form a new Cuba. "Dying for Cuba on the battlefield, the souls of both Negroes and white men have risen together. In the daily life of defense, loyalty, brotherhood, and shrewdness, there has always been a Negro standing beside every white man."[6]

Unity and brotherhood were emphasized because they were politically crucial, but Martí himself recognized that racial unity was more a goal than an accomplished reality. Indeed, such emphasis would have been unnecessary in an environment of true racial fraternity. "Always to dwell on the divisions or differences between the races, *in people who are sufficiently divided already*, is to raise barriers to the attainment of both national and individual well-being, for these two goals are reached by bringing together as closely as possible the various components that form the nation. . . . A man is more than white, black, or mulatto. A Cuban is more than mulatto, black, or white." Consequently, Martí condemned any attempt to classify or separate people according to "races" as a "sin against humanity" and a violence against "Nature."[7] In "Our America" (1891), he even challenged the legitimacy of the concept itself: "There can be no racial animosity, because there are no races. The theorists and feeble thinkers string together and warm over the bookshelf races which the well-disposed observer and the fair-minded traveler vainly seek in the justice of Nature where man's universal identity springs forth."[8]

To counter Spanish propaganda, this discourse stressed that race and nation were compatible also because blacks would never attempt to gain control of the republic. Blacks would not rise against their white brothers who had fought to end slavery in the island. "Made by slaveowners, the revolution declared slaves free," Martí asserted. Thanks to the revolution, "the Negro race" had "returned to humanity" and had been "rescued" from the ignominy of its previous existence. Martí suggested that rather than being seen as a racial threat, blacks should be seen as grateful recipients of white generosity—constructing in the process what Ferrer has termed the image of the "subservient insurgent." Afro-Cuban heroism and contributions to independence were not ignored, but emphasis was placed on blacks' "virtues," "generosity," "prudence," and love for "sensible" freedom. Afro-Cubans aspired to freedom, work, and justice, but they did so as Cubans, not as members of a racial group, insisted Martí.[9]

This foundational discourse recognized the existence of different races but included them within an encompassing notion of Cubanness that was supposed to supersede racial identities. If to be Cuban was "more than" being white, black, or mulatto, then there was no need even to refer to these particular groups, whose very existence competed with the formation of an inclusive, raceless Cubanness. To insist on someone's blackness or whiteness could then be easily construed as a "racist" and un-Cuban act. As Martí put it, "[T]he Negro who proclaims his racial character . . . authorizes and brings forth the white racist. . . . Two racists would be equally guilty, the white racist and the Negro." In these circumstances, silencing the whole issue of race was a desirable strategy and an act of patriotism. Martí himself had written in 1892: "It should be enough. This constant allusion to a man's color should cease."[10]

Reflecting the multiple tensions and contradictions it was supposed to solve, the nationalist ideology was open to different interpretations. The only element that remained nearly uncontested was the primacy of the *mambí* ideology itself.[11] The first and most important point of contention was whether Martí's republic with all and for all had been achieved during the wars for independence, or whether it remained a desirable but unfulfilled goal. The political implications of these divergent interpretations were, of course, vastly different. The former, voiced by elite political actors, opposed any grievance associated with race as a threat to the nation's racial harmony. The latter, sustained by Afro-Cuban intellectuals and, after the 1920s, by the radical labor movement and the Communist Party, called for social change and was at least potentially revolutionary.

Not surprisingly, elite interpretations were frequently couched in a deliberately vague language that tended to further obscure the issue of race. As early as 1905 the dominant Partido Moderado, for instance, did not include any allusion to race in its program because it considered that "the current generation has realized the ideals for which the Cuban people suffered."[12] That these "ideals" included racial fraternity was taken for granted. Other elite political actors did not disagree with this view. They emphasized that the Cuban people were and should always be "one, without any divisions," and they claimed to be the true heirs of the "heroic generations that had sacrificed themselves to obtain a vigorous nationality, united, fraternal, without privileges or castes, and protective of the juridical principles of equality."[13] In no other country in the world, they claimed, was the "man of color" as "appreciated or equal" to whites as he was in Cuba.[14]

Equality itself was vaguely defined in formal terms and tied to questions of merit, virtue, patriotism, and education. But even in the absence of equality, blacks should be grateful for the abolition of slavery and recognize the great sacrifices that whites, particularly wealthy whites, had made to "liberate them." In this interpretation, Cuban racial fraternity did not necessarily rest on equality, however defined, but on blacks' indebtedness to whites. This way the republic could be unequal and "for all" at the same time. As a contemporary newspaper put it, "There is no country in which the white has done as much for the black. For blacks to be free . . . many prominent whites struggled and died. . . . Blacks by themselves never would have become free."[15] The political elites argued that even during times of slavery race relations had been "softer" and more "harmonic" in Cuba than in other countries. Slavery itself had been abolished due to the "titanic" efforts, dedication, and generosity of a group of worthy white Cubans who had raised their voices in the Spanish parliament to impose manumission on the colonial government or by those, equally worthy, who had sacrificed their own well being, fortune, and family to fight for their freedom (see figure 1.1). "In this respect, I think that what white Cubans have done has no parallel," Enrique José Varona, a prominent intellectual and leader of the Conservative Party, declared.[16] White patriot Manuel Sanguily, secretary of state and member of the opposing Liberal Party, agreed: "We pauperized and ruined ourselves on their account. . . . [W]e suffered as much as they did, indeed more than they did, and bravely fought for our own liberty and for [their] manumission." The conservative La Discusión would then ask rhetorically: "Don't those who . . . elevated and dignified [the black race] deserve, at least, some gratitude?"[17]

This version of Cuban racial democracy had at least two important implications. First, it assumed that no racial problem existed in Cuba. Second, to the degree that racial inequalities persisted, they were to be explained by

FIGURE 1.1. *White Generosity. The discourse of white generosity and black gratefulness is represented in this cartoon, which portrays Carlos Manuel de Céspedes, initiator of the Ten Years War, granting freedom to one of his slaves. From* La Discusión, *October 10, 1905. (Biblioteca Nacional "José Martí")*

the injustices of slavery and the colonial past, which had rendered blacks unprepared for republican life. If someone was to be blamed for black inferiority, it was blacks themselves, who had not been able (or had not had the time) to take advantage of the opportunities created by the egalitarian republic.[18] "Coming out of slavery a few years ago, redeemed from the social and political yoke in a period shorter than the life of a man, [the "colored" race] has not been able to give to civilization more than a handful of talents. . . . Slavery . . . [and] the colonial system left in the agitated soul of the man of color, the pernicious trace of all its ills," a Liberal politician declared in 1916.[19] These "ills" were numerous, including an "inferiority complex," lack of education and work habits, and a "bad moral status." The solution, thus, rested with blacks themselves. As white intellectual Jorge Mañach wrote, "[The solution] can't be other than a constant effort at improvement. . . . [The black] must become increasingly attractive [to whites]."[20]

Blacks' social subordination was this way presented as a black problem—not a social one. White participation in their subordination was reduced to a "cultural" issue, a problem of innate "ethnic instincts" and "aesthetic" perceptions, a "psychological mechanism" that time itself would correct through "indirect" and "gradual" means, never through open confrontation. Those seeking to confront the issue of racial discrimination were portrayed as instigators of racial violence who desecrated Martí's memory and undermined the significance of the struggle for independence in which Cuba's racial fraternity had been forged. "The black problem exists only when it is talked about, and that is to play with fire."[21]

The ambiguities of the Cuban national discourse regarding race and the convenience of avoiding this issue were echoed by an imprecise racial terminology and by the fluidity of racial ascriptions. Martí himself had stated that to classify people according to races was a "sin against humanity." Racial classifications challenged the very idea of a raceless Cuba and undermined the silence advocated by this interpretation of Cuban nationalism. As an Afro-Cuban intellectual stated, it was better "to avoid classifications."[22]

Classifications did not disappear, although in the early twentieth century blackness got frequently diluted into general categories such as "race of color" and "class of color," which had the virtue of avoiding the use of specific racial labels—*negro, moreno, pardo*, and *mulato*. "I am white, but before that . . . I am a Cuban who loves *la patria* [the motherland], who desires the best for *la patria*, and . . . does not speak of *negros*, but of the Cuban Race of Color," a reader of *La Prensa* commented.[23] These constructions tended to underline the common experience of subordination and discrimination suffered by all Afro-Cubans, but they did not enjoy universal acceptance among nonwhites, and specific racial labels survived. "The mulatto does not agree to be mixed with the black," a reader of Ramón Vasconcelos's column asserted in 1915.[24] Especially in Oriente, where the "colored" population was larger and the process of miscegenation had been traditionally more common, the color line between *negros* and mulattoes was stronger. As was usual outside Havana, they attended separate social clubs and mutual-aid societies.[25]

A clearer example of how blackness got diffused in the racial terminology is that of the label *mestizo*, which appears in the censuses and other statistical sources since at least 1899. The label was used by scientists in the late nineteenth century to denote the extensiveness of miscegenation in the island, but it was opposed on the ground that it designated so many racial mixtures as to become scientifically meaningless.[26] In his studies, criminal anthropologist Israel Castellanos frequently despaired over the lack of precision of this term and complained that mestizos were being classified only on account of their skin color, which ignored relevant variables such as hair type, prognathism, and other cranial and facial features that he claimed defined human races.[27]

It was precisely the ambiguity of the term, however, that made it attractive. In opposition to other racial labels such as *negro* or *mulato*, deemed to be more precise in Cuban racial imagery, the denomination *mestizo* had the virtue of detaching a significant portion of the Cuban population from blackness. "I use the term *mestizo* with the delicacy of a white woman who does not want to hurt . . . the mulattoes who honor her with their friendship," a feminist leader declared in the early 1930s.[28] By the 1950s, the label *sepia* was also occasionally used, in what seemed to be an effort to further avoid referring to someone as *negro*. Felipe Elosegui popularized this term in his column "1000 noticias en sepia" (1,000 News in Sepia), published by *El Tiempo*. Furthermore, by this time a final move was made toward erasing Cuba's racial diversity. Since in the Cuban racial democracy there was no reason to classify people according to the color of their skin, race labels started disappearing from official statistics.[29]

What neither the elite interpretation of the national discourse nor the deliberate obscurity of racial labels could hide was that for a significant sector of the Cuban population life chances remained tied to African ancestry. For this reason, elite expectations about black gratefulness were never fulfilled. If this was playing with fire, then blacks and other popular actors were nothing short of arsonists. Using the same foundational discourse, their interpretations challenged, point by point, every assertion of the elite vision of Cuban racial democracy. To the arguments that racial fraternity had been achieved during the independence struggle and that the Cuban republic had been created with all and for all, they countered that it was precisely for those reasons that blacks deserved full and equal participation in the economic, social, and political life of the country. It was exactly because of their extensive participation in the struggle, to which they had contributed more than their proportional share, that they had gained the right to full citizenship. To the argument that blacks were indebted to whites for their freedom, they offered, amid protests of racial fraternity, a counterargument: the abolition of slavery was not an example of generosity by Cuban masters or Spanish colonial authorities but a "conquest" by black insurgents in the 1868 war. As Lino D'Ou asserted, "restituir no es ceder" (to give back is not to cede).[30]

This popular nationalism portrayed Martí's cordial republic with all and for all as a goal, an unfulfilled program in the yet-to-be-completed process of national formation.[31] For them, *la patria* was not just a territory free from foreign domination that preserved the same injustices that Cubans had fought against. "*La patria* must be the agreement resulting from the legitimate satisfaction of all, produced by justice and equity," Rafael Serra, black intellectual and collaborator of Martí, wrote in 1901.[32] Afro-Cuban intellectuals ridiculed the dominant discourse of a Cuba with all and for all as a "cantilena" used by politicians to attract votes in election times and stressed that the republic had in fact betrayed Martí's vision of a racially fraternal nation. The republic had been made by all, but it provided for the well-being of only a few.[33] "We speak and work practically so that the ideal of the Apostle of our freedoms, José Martí, who dreamed and wanted a cordial Republic 'with all and for all,' may be a reality and not a myth," a black woman asserted in 1929. In opposition to the elite version of racial democracy, this popular interpretation stressed the need to build Martí's "true" republic.[34]

This discourse asserted as well that blacks' entitlement to unqualified membership in the nation and to all the benefits of the republic was not a white concession but a conquest of Afro-Cuban insurgents, whose participation in the wars of independence had made *la patria* possible. The question of black participation itself became hotly contested, turning numbers and proportions into political weapons.[35] "When the war ended, the talk started about whether the blacks had fought or not. I know that ninety-five percent of the blacks fought in the war. Then the Americans began to say that it was only seventy-five percent. Well, no one criticized those statements," black veteran Esteban Montejo recounted.[36] In fact, such statements did not go uncontested, and black participation in Cuba Libre was frequently emphasized in this radical interpretation of Cubanness. The very creation of the Partido Independiente de Color in 1908 was explained in terms of the rights blacks had acquired because of their participation in the war, which PIC leaders set at 85 percent.[37]

Whereas the elite interpretation tended to deny the existence of a race problem and blamed Afro-Cubans for their continuing subordination in society, this popular nationalism stressed precisely the opposite: there was a race problem in the island that needed to be addressed and that could not be reduced to blacks' alleged lack of preparation for republican life. As a result, attempts to silence the race issue were never successful. Black intellectuals and activists repeatedly stressed that the only way to achieve real racial fraternity was to acknowledge the existence of a race problem and to discuss it openly. "Poor us if we continue with this sepulchral silence!" black veteran Ricardo Batrell exclaimed in 1907. "Lies, hypocrisy, and dissimulation will only bring greater ills. . . . It must be screamed, it must be denounced: . . . the evil discrimination because of skin color is still practiced," another black intellectual stated in 1952.[38] The attempt to deracialize Cuba through silence failed due to a combination of factors. In addition to Afro-Cuban activists and to their remarkable literary and journalistic production,[39] silence was never viable because the Cuban political system, based on male universal suffrage, forced dominant political parties to pay at least lip service to Afro-Cubans' demands, particularly during elections.[40]

Rather than seeing it as a "black problem," the radical interpretation of Cubanness claimed that Afro-Cubans' economic and social subordination could not be explained by their alleged deficiencies. The solution was not to turn every Afro-Cuban into a famous mathematician, as mulatto poet Nicolás Guillén put it. This was a social problem that required social transformations. "The white, that is the problem," Guillén wrote. Another radical Afro-Cuban intellectual, Angel Pinto, elaborated on the subject: "[The black] has been told that he is a 'great patriot' and he has believed it, that 'Cuba is a republic with all and for all' and he has believed it, that 'all Cubans are equal before the law' and he has believed it. . . . Cuba is divided in classes, but at the same time its people are divided in groups according to the color of their skin. . . . The republic in itself is an abstract thing. . . . It is governed by one of the social classes . . . from which blacks are excluded. This class . . . [is composed] precisely of the most obstinate racists." This radical vision was not shared by all black middle-class intellectuals, however. Many openly endorsed the elite notion that the Afro-Cuban masses should "earn" their place in society through education and progress.[41]

That the *mambí* ideology of Cubanness was open to divergent interpretations should not obscure the fact that some of its central claims were barely equivocal and enjoyed significant acceptance. Even in the midst of this controversy some consensus existed. A republic with all and for all was at least a desirable goal, so a proposal that sought to overtly and systematically exclude blacks was almost unambiguously un-Cuban. The political elites might have dreamed about a *patria* in which blacks were symbolically or literally absent, but the elites' own allegiance to the notion of an inclusive Cubanness limited their political choices and provided Afro-Cubans with legitimate tools to fight for inclusion in a nation that virtually no one denied was also theirs. Besides, the vision of a truly egalitarian and racially fraternal nation was sustained not only by blacks. It was also championed by white radical intellectuals and, particularly after the 1920s, by the radical labor movement. Contending interpretations crossed both color and class lines. The black middle-class intelligentsia, for instance, frequently denied that the republic was really inclusive, but they shared the elite notion that the masses of black manual workers should de-Africanize themselves and join the bandwagon of white progress. White veterans who entered politics were reluctant to debate questions of race, but they frequently opposed measures that resulted in the blatant exclusion of blacks. The republic with all and for all was a misrepresentation of reality, but as with any other dominant ideology it affected reality itself, creating in the process unexpected limitations as well as opportunities for social and political action.

A superb example of how this discourse operated in practice is provided by Jesús Masdeu in his novel *La raza triste* (The sad race), written in the 1910s.[42] Although the explicit purpose of the novel is to denounce the persistence of racism under the republic, several of Masdeu's white characters defend the need to treat blacks and whites as equals and frame this need in the language of the nationalist ideology. Thus, when the all-white "notables" of Bayamo gather in a local club to fund the education of two children, a proposal quickly emerges: "One of them white and the other of color." "The Negroes are to carry water," replies a veteran of the Ten Years War, a former slave owner. "I believe that there are blacks who are suited for something else," argues a young lawyer and millionaire who was also a colonel of the Liberation Army. "Besides," adds another participant, "that whole thing of blacks and whites is over in Cuba. Today, those who have been born in this country are citizens of Cuban democracy. . . . The republic is with all and for all. . . . If we, who are the designated ones, do not open our arms to the blacks, who helped us achieve independence . . . we will place ourselves at the same level as the bad patriots." Good patriots, Masdeu implies, are not supposed to be racially conscious, much less discriminatory.

How inclusive Cubanness would be was not just a question of ideological and discursive symbols, regardless of how powerful they might have been. Adding to the strength of the nationalist ideology was the presence of blacks in the leadership and ranks of the Liberation Army. Individually and collectively, Afro-Cubans had emerged from the war with a public presence and prestige they did not enjoy before the struggle began. Two out of six of the regional armies were under the command of black generals when the war ended.[43] Planter Edwin Atkins noted that blacks had become "very outspoken" and that they went into the public plaza, "which was never allowed before." Immediately after the war the insurgents controlled numerous country towns, "collecting taxes and managing affairs quite independent of other authority," and not infrequently "under negro officers." Havana, according to black veteran Esteban Montejo, was "a carnival" where blacks "had fun anyway they could."[44]

The confidence and determination that Afro-Cuban soldiers had acquired during the war are well exemplified in an anecdote concerning their interaction with American soldiers. This case, recalled by Montejo, took place in Cienfuegos in 1899, when a number of *mambises* (members of the Liberation Army) attacked some American soldiers because of their disrespectful manner toward Cuban women. Montejo, who boldly stated that he "could not stand" the Americans, declared that they addressed Cuban women by saying "Fuky, Fuky, Margarita" and that he had never felt as angry at any time in the war as when he saw them in Cienfuegos. The fact that these *mambises*, among whom there were several blacks, violently enforced what they believed was proper order suggests not only that they considered Cienfuegos to be their own territory but also that they believed they had the right to regulate life in it.[45]

Afro-Cubans' collective visibility and assertiveness was matched by the prominence of black military leaders whose names were intimately linked to the independence cause. Some of the highest-ranking black officers, such as Antonio and José Maceo, Flor Crombet, and Guillermo (Guillermón) Moncada, had perished, and they were elevated to the status of national heroes. Black generals Jesús Rabí, Agustín Cebreco, Quintín Bandera, Juan Eligio Ducasse, Prudencio Martínez, Pedro Díaz, and others had survived, and their contribution to Cuba Libre could hardly be disputed. These generals were living symbols of the Afro-Cuban participation in the war for independence, and they represented a potential source of leadership to resist the efforts of those who wanted to minimize blacks' role in the making of the nation.

The social significance of these black veterans was guaranteed through endless banquets in their honor, the eagerness of the emergent political parties to attract them, and the creation of social and political clubs named for them. Their social and political activities received generous press coverage. In 1900, for instance, a "cordial banquet" was given in Santiago de Cuba in honor of General Rabí, with the participation of "all" the civil, religious, and judiciary authorities, plus representatives of several corporations, newspapers, and the "most valuable citizens" of the city.[46]

Quintín Bandera is another example of black heroes' visibility and prestige. In 1899, he organized and presided over the Partido Nacional Cubano de Oriente (Cuban National Party of Oriente), later called the Liga Nacional Cubana (Cuban National League). In 1900 Bandera toured the island, visiting numerous towns in the provinces of Havana, Matanzas, and Oriente. The "hero," as *Diario de la Marina* referred to him, was everywhere received by local authorities and "notables." In Arroyo Naranjo (Havana), for instance,

Bandera and his companions were given a royal welcome by the mayor of the municipality, visited the local headquarters of the Rural Guard, where the chief gave a banquet in their honor, and were hosted by a local prominent landowner. Similar banquets and festivities were organized in other towns by local committees of the Partido Nacional Cubano, labor clubs, and even Spanish organizations such as the Casino Español of Colón. Meanwhile, a recreational club with his name was being created in Havana.[47]

That Afro-Cubans' contribution to Cuban independence could not be hidden became obvious in patriotic acts such as the very inauguration of the republic on May 20, 1902. That day a group of soldiers from the former Liberation Army, described by the press as a "Cuban force, most of it with a brown face," marched through the streets of Havana under black general Pedro Díaz, chief of the Sixth Army and a personal friend of Antonio Maceo's. Black generals were also prominent in other public acts of patriotic significance, such as those commemorating the beginning of the Ten Years War.[48] Pensions and positions for the families of dead black liberators were provided by municipalities, the Cuban Congress, and even by U.S. authorities, while public funeral ceremonies were held with the attendance of prominent white politicians.[49] Rabí's illness and death, for instance, was closely followed by the national press, with front-page coverage. The funeral procession of black patriot Rafael Serra y Montalvo, a collaborator of Martí's, was headed by none other than Alfredo Zayas, the white vice president of the republic in 1909; that of Martín Morúa Delgado a year later was headed by the president himself.[50] Even if the top white government officials participated in these public acts only in order to lure the black vote, by doing so they were also giving public recognition to Afro-Cubans' central role in the formation of the Cuban nation.

Leadership and visibility were also provided by a number of black patriots who did not have such prominent military credentials but had also contributed to the cause of independence. Juan Gualberto Gómez was, of course, the most conspicuous of these Afro-Cuban leaders. The son of slaves and a close collaborator of Martí's, Gómez had become the most notable Afro-Cuban leader in the island by the 1890s, when he presided over the Directorio Central de Sociedades de la Raza de Color (Central Directorate of Societies of the Colored Race) and began publishing the newspaper *La Igualdad*. The importance of the Directorio in supporting independence and in opposing discrimination against Afro-Cubans is widely acknowledged. The organization encompassed about 100 societies throughout the island by 1893, and it waged a successful campaign for the recognition of

Afro-Cubans' civil rights and legal equality.[51] The Directorio also provided a place in which Afro-Cuban activists acquired organizational and political skills that would later allow them to play an active public role in the republic.

Manuel Delgado's life clearly exemplifies this trajectory. In 1892 the society La Luz, a black club from Yaguajay, appointed him delegate before the Directorio. Delgado later joined the Liberation Army, becoming a *comandante*. After independence, he served as lieutenant of the rural guard, member of the provincial council in Las Villas, and representative in the national Congress. Under President Machado, Delgado became a member of the cabinet, first as secretary of agriculture, then as secretary of the interior.[52]

Another black public figure who had been involved with the Directorio and the newspaper *La Igualdad* before taking part in the war, in which he earned the rank of colonel fighting as a member of José Maceo's staff, was journalist and writer Lino D'Ou. D'Ou organized several black societies in Santiago de Cuba and Guantánamo and became a Conservative Party representative from the province of Oriente in 1908. U.S. authorities described him as someone who hated whites, "particularly Americans." D'Ou remained a prominent political and intellectual figure until his death in 1939.[53] Also linked to the Directorio were Laudelino García, Juan Travieso, and Ramón Canals. García finished the war as a captain of the Liberation Army and was later a member of the provincial council of Las Villas, where he owned a pawnshop. Travieso became a representative and was later referred to as the "patriarch" of his native town, Bejucal, near Havana. Canals was a shop owner who, although he went into exile during the war, served on Havana's town council in 1908–10 and 1912–16.[54]

Even dead, black heroes of independence provided visibility and prestige to Afro-Cubans. Besides Martí, Antonio Maceo was the most revered, quoted, and contested symbol of Cuban racial fraternity. Maceo's death in battle was commemorated every year with massive processions to his grave that invariably included the most prominent politicians and representatives of the black clubs and societies. Congress celebrated special sessions in his memory, and parks were built, monuments erected, and streets named in honor of the mulatto general. As part of his efforts to attract Afro-Cuban support, President Gerardo Machado declared the date of Maceo's death a national holiday in 1930.[55]

Contestation over Maceo's memory and legacy reached a point in which his own "race" became the subject of controversy. When the general's remains were exhumed in September 1899, it was stated that his skull presented an "interesting anomaly . . . frequent in the indigenous race, particularly of

South America, which is known as the 'bone of the Inca.' " A subsequent anthropological study concluded that, although a mulatto, Maceo was closer to the white racial type than to the black.[56] Portraits and drawings portrayed him and other prominent Afro-Cuban patriots as "almost white."[57] Attempts were made also to downplay Maceo's talent as a military chief or to minimize or deny altogether the racist obstacles that he had encountered during his years of service to the cause of Cuba Libre.[58]

Despite efforts to deprive Afro-Cubans of their most cherished icon, Maceo continued to be used in the struggle for racial equality through the end of the republic. The politicians' manipulation of the general's legacy was frequently scorned in the black press—and later in that of the Communists and the radical labor movement.[59] Whereas elite politicians used black heroes to stress the fraternity of the Cuban nation or to lecture ordinary blacks about their alleged deficiencies, black intellectuals used Maceo to denounce their subordination in Cuban society. In a "conversation" with the bronze statue of the general inaugurated in Havana in 1916, an Afro-Cuban activist explained to the hero: "Yes, General, the Constitution says that . . . all Cubans are equal before the law, but . . . in the republic that . . . was created with your effort, all Cubans are not treated as equals."[60] Popular interpretations of Maceo did not stop at denunciations of racism, however. They also called for social action to build *la patria*, egalitarian and inclusive, dreamed of by Martí and the Afro-Cuban general. As another black activist stated, "[I]t is upon us, the Cuban youth, to finish peacefully what was not accomplished militarily because of Maceo's death."[61] An American observer thus stressed the need to rescue the patriot's memory from the masses, "so that the exaltations to the highest peaks of glories of the mulatto champion of independence . . . shall not be, as it has been, a source of worry [for] the authorities."[62]

The visibility and prestige of Afro-Cuban heroes and veterans were indicative of an unavoidable reality. Even those who "didn't care much for the blacks," as Montejo claimed in reference to Americans, had to acknowledge blacks' existence and to confront the delicate issue of their participation in the emergent political order. As a contemporary observer stated, "The existence of the blacks must be reckoned with in every phase of the reconstruction of the island."[63] This task of reconstruction, however, fell under the control of the American occupation forces.

RACIAL ORDER

At the same time that Martí was creating the notion of a racially inclusive and fraternal Cubanness, American scientists were busy proving blacks' innate inferiority. Numerous anthropometric studies had concluded that blacks were naturally inferior and thus unfit to participate in civilized societies and condemned to eventual disappearance in the inevitable process of competition with the superior white race. At the peak of their glory, social Darwinists had taken these conclusions one step further, arguing that the struggle for the "survival of the fittest" explained not only blacks' subordination but also the ascent of certain nations and races in a world that seemed to have no place for backward peoples.[64]

The American occupation forces brought this ideology—and the segregationist practices it justified—with them to the island.[65] They encountered in Cuba a population that, according to their own racial ideology, was made up largely of "Negroes" in need of guidance and supervision. Doubts might have existed about Cubans' capacity for improvement and eventual self-rule; none existed about their collective inferiority. As Kathy Duke argues, the U.S. military operated on the firm belief of Anglo-Saxons' cultural and racial superiority over the Cuban people, whom they considered a "race of ignorant savages." Even "well-meaning" Americans, a contemporary observer admitted, arrived on the island feeling like missionaries "among savages of various degrees of gentleness."[66]

Cubans' inferiority was, of course, racial. "We are dealing with a race," Governor Leonard Wood wrote to President William McKinley, "that has steadily been going down for a hundred years and into which we have got to infuse new life, new principles and new methods of doing things."[67] It could not be otherwise, he explained, because after being the "Spanish criminal dumping-ground" for centuries, the island just had too much "mixed blood" to enter successfully the concert of civilized nations. "There is today a decided negro strain in many of the whites of Cuba," a professor at Oxford University wrote. Blackness was so pervasive in Cuba, another observer concurred, that the majority of the population was nonwhite. "Based on our standards, it is doubtful whether five percent of the population can show clean white strain."[68]

Such a high level of miscegenation was seen as Cuba's greatest ill, a legacy that the island could not escape. Miscegenation, American scientists had concluded after substantial research into the subject, resulted in mongrelization. "The anthropometry of the Mulatto is decidedly against him," Tulane University professor William Smith argued. Mongrelization, in turn, violated nature's harmony and led to "racial decadence."[69] According to the influential geneticist Charles Davenport, mulattoes combined "ambition and push" with "intellectual inadequacy," making them "unhappy hybrids" prone to

disrupt a harmonic social order.[70] The consequences for Cuba were ominous, an American journalist explained: "Cuba is politically impossible, socially impossible, economically impossible, because morally rotten.... These
Cubans are ... the whittling of a race.... They can't rise out of themselves.
The fault is racial. Cuba ... yields a hard, indocile mixed blood that riots in
depravity."[71]

Even those who did not share such negative views about the island's
population agreed that Cubans were lazy, childish, inconsistent, and afflicted
by an acute "feeling of inferiority." The Cuban teachers who visited Harvard
in 1901 to be trained in American values were described as "grown up
children ... who could not understand the significance of what they saw."[72]
This vision, based on the notion of Anglo-Saxon racial superiority, outlasted
the American occupation. As late as 1946 a similar portrait, still informed by
the same racial premises, emanated from the U.S. legation in Havana: "Many
of them [Cuban politicians] possess the superficial charm of clever children,
spoiled by nature and geography, but under the surface they combine the
worst characteristics of the unfortunate admixture and interpenetration of
Spanish and Negro cultures—laziness, cruelty, inconstancy, irresponsibility
and inbred dishonesty."[73]

Americans thus felt the need to lecture Cubans about their many deficiencies and to supervise the establishment of self-government in the island,
a possibility that was itself in question. "What you Cubans need," presidential
envoy William Taft admonished in the opening ceremony of the academic
year at the University of Havana in 1906, "is to feel the urge to make money,
establish great enterprises, and promote the prosperity of this beautiful island."[74] In addition to instilling these basic Anglo-Saxon values, North Americans could also teach Cubans how to deal more effectively with the so-called
"Negro" problem. "In some respects we have done better with the negro
than has any other people," a U.S. journalist asserted in a local newspaper in
1899. "We have made him work when free; have instilled an ambition to own
his own house and land and live like a white man."[75] Blacks, several U.S.
journalists stressed, had to submit to white control if they were going to be of
any use in the future republic. The very example of the Spanish-American
War had shown that it was only under "white influence" that blacks acted
according to civilized norms. The behavior of black regiments under "Negro
officers" during the war was conclusive: it was characterized by "uncontrolled
savagery." This was the lesson Cubans should learn: "When blacks get ex-
cited, they resemble a fierce hound which has killed already and feels the
furious desire to exterminate whatever comes into his path."[76]

Afro-Cubans were portrayed as the lowest of the low, the most savage among the uncivilized. No matter how much progress blacks had made, "African nature" was still "strong" in them. That this "nature" turned Afro-Cubans into little more than beasts who loved disturbance, "with its attendant opportunities to loot," was not even questioned. "In the mind of the African the right to eat is unconditioned. It does not depend upon work. This makes him a thief," a colonel in the U.S. Army explained. Blacks were naturally criminal, thus a constant "source of possible trouble" for the authorities and the established order. Indeed, American observer Charles Pepper contended that any discussion concerning crime was superfluous when it came to "the African race." Afro-Cubans' only advantage was their resistance to harsh climatic and labor conditions—another clear indication of their inferiority and savagery. They were lazy, inefficient, and irresponsible workers whose limited abilities and inferior intellect were "congenial" only with cane cutting. "His grave defect is lack of serious purpose. . . . No race can show less for what it does."[77]

North American beliefs of Afro-Cubans' innate and inescapable inferiority were based on an extensive body of scientific research that found its way into the island, permeating local intellectual circles and racial ideologies. Although Cuban physicians and health practitioners, like many of their Latin American colleagues, were influenced by French and Spanish scientific ideas, the U.S. occupation and influence in Cuban affairs facilitated the transmission of the North American "science" of race.[78] The works of U.S. eugenicists were frequently referred to and analyzed in Cuban publications, and the contending theories of heredity that were being discussed in the academic centers of Europe and the United States were well known in the island. In a 1918 lecture on the laws of heredity and applied biology, University of Havana professor Arístides Mestre reviewed the theories of Lamarck, Darwin, De Vries, Galton, Mendel, and Weismann and their contributions to what he termed "the central problem" of biology: heredity. A member of the American Genetic Association and a subscriber to its *Journal of Heredity*, Mestre was au courant of the major findings and publications of every major North American eugenicist, including William Bateson, Charles Davenport, and Thomas Morgan.[79] He participated in the creation of the League of Mental Hygiene of Cuba in 1929, modeled after a similar institution created by his friend Clifford Beers in New York.[80]

Also replicating U.S. scientific practices, Cuban intellectuals studied and debated the convenience of sterilizing incorrigible criminals, "degenerates," and the mentally handicapped. A Cuban delegate to the Congress of the

National Prison Association held in Richmond in 1908 reported that the attendees supported the sterilization program as the only viable solution to growing criminality. U.S. studies also showed, Cuban scientists observed, that this method did not result in any physical harm or loss of sexual capacity to the individual, whose "mental strength" actually increased after the procedure. By 1910, Dr. Francisco Fernández, later secretary of sanitation and founding member of the Cuban League of Mental Hygiene, was advocating the introduction of sterilization in the island as a way to "preserve the race." A law was even introduced in Congress to that effect.[81]

Fernández was also the chairman of the first Pan American Conference on Eugenics and Homiculture held in Havana in 1927, attended by Davenport himself.[82] The gathering unequivocally demonstrated the degree to which Cuban intellectuals had been influenced by North American ideas of race. "It is fortunate," the secretary of state declared in his inaugural speech, "that our Hemisphere is, in great majority, populated by two superior races. They are the ones that have given to contemporary civilization its formidable impetus; the Latin, born and developed in . . . the shore countries of the European Mediterranean, and the Saxon." Similar concepts were voiced by Dr. Domingo Ramos, secretary of the conference and a follower of Davenport, whom he had met in New York during the Second International Congress of Eugenics in 1921. Ramos stated that although "all the races"— Native Americans, blacks, and whites—had contributed to the Americas, the continent itself was "the greatest historic proof of the power and spirit of progress of the white race." Environmental factors might better an individual, but it was "absolutely erroneous" to consider all men as equals, for it was necessary, Ramos concluded, to "integrate first the inheritance factor."[83]

The influence of these ideas was guaranteed not only by the respectability and avowed neutrality of leading scientists and the economic, political, and cultural presence of the United States in Cuba's life. These racial ideologies also found a sympathetic ear among planters, merchants, and other Cuban elites, who were convinced already of the racial inferiority of peoples of African descent. Concerning the traditional white Cuban elite, U.S. officers, journalists, and scientists were preaching to the converted. It was precisely because of their apprehension about Afro-Cubans and the possibility that they might play a significant role in Cuba's future political order that some members of the colonial elite had fully endorsed the colonial notion of the black peril and opposed independence. "No more blacks, Chinese, or Hindus," they had demanded since before the war. For Cuba to become a "truly civilized" country, Rafael Montalvo explained in a 1888 conference, it was imperative to nurture the superiority of the "Caucasian elements that constitute today the majority of the inhabitants of Cuba." Montalvo added that Cuba's most important problem was its multiracial population, so every "good Cuban" should ensure that "the descendants of Aryans keep forever the material and political superiority that they currently enjoy, in such a way that . . . the control of public affairs never escapes their expert hands."[84]

This group also shared with the U.S. occupation forces their misgivings about Cubans' capacity to establish a successful independent republic, free of North American tutelage. In a well-known ethnographic and sociological analysis of the island's history, politician and writer Francisco Figueras argued that the deleterious effects of Cuba's racial composition could be opposed only through the adoption of Anglo-Saxon mores. His skepticism was shared by other public figures, who claimed that Cubans' inclination to misgovernment was to be explained by "atavism or the law of inheritance of the race."[85] Spanish culture and colonialism not only had rendered Cubans incapable of self-government but also had encouraged the appearance in the population of the "inferior types masterfully described by Herbert Spencer, characterized by wittiness, frivolity, and propensity to jokes."[86]

Blacks led the list of these inferior types, against which a North American protectorate or the outright annexation of the island were the only defenses. "We seek annexation because it is convenient. . . . Cuba [is] one of the most heterogeneous countries in the world, in which races and nationalities are infinitely mixed."[87] Annexation, however, was not possible. Opposition to it was massive in the island, while within the United States numerous voices questioned the convenience of acquiring an island "inhabited by a mongrel race" and "unused to self-government." Protectorate status was both viable and necessary, for it would reassure those concerned with the racial question that the "black peril" was under control.[88]

The importance and magnitude of this peril became obvious in April 1900, when the results of the 1899 census were released. An editorial in the conservative *Diario de la Marina* summarized the apprehension of the white elite: "To be honest, we did not expect the black race to constitute one-third of the Cuban native population; we thought it would be lower. . . . It can be stated without any doubt that the black population has grown in the last thirty years in a proportion similar to whites, even though it has not received . . . a constant immigration. Taking this into consideration, the danger can be seen . . . for the white race if the immigration flow is interrupted. . . . [T]he need is to promote it in greater scale . . . so the said danger is definitely eliminated." The editorialist warned, however, that the benefits of the immigration program would be felt only in a remote future; in the meantime, plans concerning the situation of the country would have to deal with the fact that one-third of its population belonged to the "Ethiopian race."[89]

Possible solutions to this "danger" ranged from overt repression and confrontation to different forms of coexistence and eventual racial integration— from subordination and exclusion to equality and inclusion. On one point there was near consensus among white intellectuals and employers in the early republic, however: whitening Cuba was a desirable goal, indeed a precondition for civilization and progress. As elsewhere in the Americas, planters, merchants, and many intellectuals in Cuba did not question the notion that Africanness equaled savagery and symbolized backwardness. Even those who subscribed to the ideal of a racially fraternal nation agreed that Cuba should be predominantly white and culturally European. To achieve this the country needed to attract as many desirable white immigrants as possible and to de-Africanize its own black population. Whitening was cultural as well as racial.

WHITENING

A transformation of the racial makeup of the Cuban population was linked only in part to selective immigration. It was hoped that blacks' lower rates of natural growth would eventually cause the race to disappear. Some Cuban intellectuals shared with social Darwinists an "obsession" with "health and population trends" to monitor these expectations.[90] That the 1899 census showed that the proportion of blacks had not diminished was of course disheartening to such hopes, particularly because the expectation was that the war had decimated the black population.[91] The evidence notwithstanding, the authors of the census report concluded that the decrease of blacks relative to whites since the mid–nineteenth century was conclusive evidence of their racial inferiority, "another illustration of the inability of an inferior race to hold its own in competition with a superior one."[92] Demographic studies in North America had purportedly demonstrated already that if biology and heredity were allowed to operate unhindered by government intervention, the black race would progressively degenerate into total extinction.[93] In Cuba, the same belief was widely shared, although frequently explained in less deterministic terms. Using population statistics, the head of statistics of the secretary of sanitation, Jorge Le-Roy y Cassá, remarked in 1915 that black female mortality was higher than white female mortality, a fact that Cambridge professor Walter Heape had established previously. Based on these data, the press claimed that the "colored" race was, slowly but uninterruptedly, disappearing from the national territory.[94] In his racist tract, Gustavo Mustelier described this process as "optimistic," adding that blacks were declining due to lower natural growth and immigration, the high incidence of prostitution among Afro-Cuban females, and the large number of males in prison.[95]

This process, however, was too slow for its supporters and needed to be accelerated through the immigration of racially desirable people. Although the whole immigration question was in fact a planter-engineered attempt to increase the supply of labor and flood the labor market with cheap workers, it operated under the racist assumption that only white laborers, particularly Spaniards, were congenial with Cuban civilization.[96] "The Spaniard," a newspaper from Cárdenas explained in 1900, "will always be the best ally in our efforts to sustain the Cuban personality. Race, language, religion, and customs form very strong bonds."[97] The first immigration project presented to Governor Wood with the support of the Planters Association stated unequivocally that whites were "the only convenient" immigrants and claimed that on this particular topic the country's opinion was "unanimous." These immigrants, the proposal added, should come from southern Spain or the Canary Islands; those populations had already demonstrated the capacity to endure the "rigor" of the tropical climate. Indeed, to make these proposals acceptable it was necessary to challenge the widespread notion that the white race degenerated in a tropical environment.[98]

Cuban migration policies explicitly sanctioned the racial and cultural advantages attributed to whites and favored colonization programs—that is, the immigration of white families—over the importation of seasonal contract labor. Contract laborers—the so-called *braceros*—were an ideal solution to the sugar companies, which employed them only during the harvest, but these workers did not settle in the country and made no contribution to the improvement of the population stock. Thus, out of the $1 million appropriated by the immigration law of 1906 to subsidize immigration, 80 percent was to be used to pay the moving costs of families from Europe and the Canary Islands, and the balance to subsidize the introduction of *braceros* from Norway, Sweden, Denmark, and northern Italy.[99] Several years later the Cuban government appointed a special delegate of immigration and colonization with residence in Europe whose main duty was to publicize the advantages of Cuba as a migratory destination.[100] The Cuban government also agreed to subsidize the importation of 5,000 to 6,000 workers from the Panama Canal, but only of "the right class of men . . . Portuguese or Spanish or other white labor."[101]

It was only reluctantly, and under steady pressure from the powerful sugar companies, that Cuban governments agreed to open the door to the seasonal migration of black workers. In 1904, President Estrada Palma refused to grant the United Fruit Company permission to introduce Jamaican laborers for their plantations in Oriente, claiming that he considered the importation of these workers a "serious problem." Likewise, an authorization granted to the Ponupo Manganese Company, an American mining company established in Oriente since 1895, to import 2,000 laborers was later canceled on the ground that it had not specified that the workers "were to be white." In its second attempt, the company was given permission by President José Miguel Gómez to import 500 laborers, but the decree clarified that they could be brought only from Spain.[102]

In the 1910s, however, the Cuban government began authorizing the importation of Antillean workers and lifted the legal barriers that prevented their massive introduction. Several hundred thousand Antilleans entered the island and contributed to the spectacular expansion of sugar during and after World War I. Although these workers were supposed to be returned to their points of origin after the harvest season, many stayed. The dominant discourse decried their presence as a lethal blow to the whitening ideal and a step toward the "Africanization" of Cuba. Opponents used sanitary, economic, cultural, and political arguments against the importation of Antilleans. Although explicit racial arguments were not the most frequently voiced, the deeply racist character of this campaign was barely hidden. The whole notion of "undesirability" applied to the Antilleans was racially defined.

Most frequently portrayed as a public-health danger to the country, Antillean immigration was compared to an invasion of deadly germs. Whereas other immigrants were allowed in the country "with only the usual precautions," Antilleans were subjected to special sanitary measures, including quarantines and blood tests to detect infectious diseases.[103] Malaria and typhoid fever were the diseases that most concerned medical authorities. Occasional outbreaks of smallpox were also linked to the introduction of workers from "infected countries," but since it was believed that this disease "seldom attacked white people" it was not given priority attention. In 1920, 97 percent of the cases of smallpox registered in the island occurred in the provinces of Camagüey and Oriente, where the large majority of West Indians were employed. By 1919, 75 percent of the deaths caused by malaria also occurred in these eastern provinces.[104]

This regionalization of morbidity and mortality was quickly used to prove with hard, scientific data the undesirability of the Antillean immigrants. Hygienists, physicians, and politicians expeditiously concluded that West Indian laborers were to be blamed for the surge of epidemics in the island. President Alfredo Zayas described them as "devoid of even the most elementary notions of hygiene" and portrayed the island as a besieged territory "surrounded by intense focuses of epidemics and quarantinable diseases." Antilleans were presented as members of a race with "hereditary pathological defects or propensities" and a "cerebral organization" inadequate to civilization. National medical congresses demanded a rigid prohibition on all "undesirable immigrations," and so did the office of the secretary of sanitation.[105]

Regardless of the scientific tone of these speculations, Cuban public officials and medical authorities were misreading the very data they used to demonstrate the biological and medical undesirability of the West Indian immigrants. It is true that some of these diseases were common in Haiti and other Caribbean territories, just as malaria and other contagious diseases were more prevalent in the eastern provinces, where most Antilleans worked and lived. But at least two important facts were conveniently overlooked. First, the number of cases of malaria had always been higher in the provinces of Camagüey and Oriente in proportion to the total population. In other words, the rates of morbidity of this disease were higher in the eastern part of the island well before Antilleans began entering in large numbers in the mid-1910s. Second, the trend toward an increasing concentration of the disease in this area of the country also antedated the massive immigration of Antilleans. The share of Camagüey and Oriente in the total number of deaths caused by malaria had increased steadily from 1900 to 1915: 32 percent in 1900, 42 percent in 1905, 68 percent in 1910, and 89 percent in 1915.[106] It is noteworthy that years later, in 1940–44, when Antillean immigration had been effectively closed for almost a decade, malaria was still a disease of eastern Cuba, where 84 percent of the registered cases occurred.[107]

If sanitary and political authorities misread the data and propagated the image of Antillean immigrants as epidemic vectors, it was because they needed a scientific, objective justification for their prejudices. As a science supposedly detached from any ideological influence, medicine provided the evidence and the arguments needed to elaborate a deracialized notion of undesirability. West Indian laborers were opposed in the name of a clean, healthy social body. The sanitary arguments, however, barely concealed what seemed to be the actual reason for rejecting these immigrants: their race. The U.S. consul in Santiago de Cuba commented on this subject in a confidential letter in 1916: "[N]either the health authorities here nor in Havana nor elsewhere entertain any serious apprehension with regard to the introduction of malaria, filaria or miasmatic germs of whatever character. . . . This idea is but a voluntary deception which has been given general publicity . . . for the express purpose of preventing if possible, or at least curtailing the constantly increasing influx of these neighboring islanders. . . . There are practically no objections to them at all, physically, but chiefly on account of their color. They are most all as black as coal and the authorities here view with alarm this constant augmentation of the already high percentage of Negroes in this vicinity."[108]

Indeed, according to press reports, many white Cubans feared that with the increase of Antillean immigrants blacks would become predominant in the island and would attempt to "dominate whites." The old "black peril" was revived. A widely read article published by *Gráfico* in 1916 claimed that the population of the island should be increased with "ethnic elements similar to the more numerous group of inhabitants, which is that of the white race," and reminded readers what racist ideologue José Antonio Saco had claimed in the nineteenth century: that Cuba's "future and prosperity" depended on the increase of the white population. The progressive blackening of Cuba was identified with its "slow decadence, its certain intellectual ruin," and was blamed on foreign sugar barons who sought to turn the country into a huge dark plantation: "When the prosperity of an industry depends on the indispensable employment and introduction of laborers of an inferior race, such an industry is not a healthy one." What was at stake, white Cubans warned, was nothing less than the "racial and cultural future" of the country. "This is the great racial tragedy of Cuba: its growing Africanization."[109]

The Antilleans' undesirability was based also on their alleged propensity to commit crimes and the supposed primitiveness of their religious beliefs, two attributes linked by the dominant racial ideologies to blackness. Concerning crime rates, the statistical evidence was again conspicuously misread. In the 1,303 cases of homicide officially reported between 1908 and 1918, only 8 (that is, less than 1 percent) had been committed by male foreign blacks. The "desirable" white immigrants (mostly Spaniards), in turn, were responsible for 16 percent of the reported cases. The situation was not very different among female offenders. Spanish convicts represented 9 percent of the total number of women sentenced to jail between 1903 and 1928, a proportion well above their population share. When the secretary of the interior recommended the expulsion of all Antillean convicts in 1928, they represented only 2 percent of the prison population.[110]

Antillean religion was considered an even greater threat, for the Cuban government had made significant efforts to eradicate Santería and other Afro-Cuban religious and cultural manifestations from the island. It was argued that contacts between the Antilleans' savage religious rites and Afro-Cubans' own atavistic *brujería* could only produce aggravated forms of criminality and fetishism, thus obstructing the cultural program that sought to de-Africanize the black native population.[111]

Repression of African-based cultural practices was not new, but the U.S. occupation government had given the process renewed impetus and legitimacy. Shortly after the occupation, processions and public demonstrations by Afro-Cuban religious societies were prohibited. North Americans viewed Afro-Cuban religions as a "mass of foolishness" in which Catholicism and "African demon-worship" had become "grotesquely mixed." Black public dances, considered to be obscene and leading to sexual indulgence and degradation, were also forbidden.[112]

An essentially identical vision permeated the institutional response of the Cuban government and intellectual circles to Afro-Cuban cultural practices, particularly to religion. The very denomination of these beliefs as *brujería* (witchcraft) evoked images of ancestral, primitive rites mixed with human sacrifices and even acts of cannibalism. In the eyes of the elites and those of the black middle class, *brujería* symbolized Africanness, the very antithesis of progress and modernity. The press constantly reported cases in which practitioners—the *brujos*—allegedly kidnapped, killed, and eventually ate children, typically blonde girls, whose blood and organs were supposedly used to perform curative religious ceremonies.[113] Although frequently these cases rested on weak and contradictory evidence, popular rumors and the press blamed *brujería* for almost any unexplained death. In a typical case in 1906, the "mysterious" illness and death of a young white female in Candelaria, Pinar del Río, was quickly attributed to *brujería*. Supposedly, the lover of the deceased's boyfriend had contacted some *brujos* who might have induced the victim to take "harmful substances," provoking her death. Even though, in a final disclaimer, the journalist asserted that he was only repeating what he had heard, the story clearly served to reinforce stereotypes about the bloody nature of *brujería*. A 1910 article entitled "The Crimes of *Brujería*" referred in fact to the homicide of a woman by gunshots. Reports about the incident, the journalist acknowledged, were contradictory and vague, "but they tell me that *brujería* . . . is the principal cause of this horrendous event." In 1907, a brujo was detained and his home searched following the death of a child, even though a physician had certified that the death was actually caused by meningitis. The autopsy confirmed the diagnosis, but the event was still publicized as "*Brujería* in Havana."[114]

These racial and cultural stereotypes facilitated and encouraged the repression of any Afro-Cuban cultural practice. Santería and other Afro-Cuban religious beliefs were all referred to as *brujería*. Simple possession of ritual objects or performance of harmless religious ceremonies were persecuted.[115] Afro-Cuban carnival dances and processions were prohibited, and a special law proposed to repress the "practice of *brujería* and quack medicine." In a 1922 resolution, the secretary of the interior banned all Afro-Cuban religious ceremonies and dances on the grounds that they were offensive, that they were opposed to culture and civilization, and that "experience showed" that they frequently "led to robberies, kidnappings, or killings of children of the white race."[116] Indeed, if the alleged victim was a black child, then the crime was not conceptualized as *brujería*.[117] This contributed to further racialize *brujería*, although abundant evidence demonstrated that these popular beliefs had in fact a vast multiracial following.

The racist character of these de-Africanization efforts, which included opposition to the black immigrants from the Antilles, exemplifies the degree to which whitening was accepted as an intrinsic part of Cubanness. Only a few Afro-Cuban voices, joined since the 1920s by the radical labor movement and later the Communists, protested against the campaign waged against these darker immigrants and exposed its racist character. To the argument that West Indians were primitive and responsible for the Africanization of the country, black intellectuals responded that Cuba was not white and that what the supporters of such an argument truly sought was to whiten the island through the elimination of its black population. Moreover, they labeled as hypocritical any discourse that opposed West Indians in the name of native workers while encouraging, at the same time, the massive entry of white workers from Spain.

Black intellectual Rafael Serra led these efforts, arguing as early as 1901 that the dominant immigration discourse was an attempt to "destroy" blacks. The 1906 immigration law was opposed from the pages of *El Nuevo Criollo* and by black representative Antonio Poveda Ferrer, who argued that more than enough immigrants were coming to the island from Spain every year. In their notable "Manifesto" to the people of the "colored" race (1907), Batrell and Nenínger reminded their audience that politicians from all parties supported the law, which sought to encourage the immigration of families, but only from countries where there were no blacks. They then accused white politicians of trying to reduce the Afro-Cuban population.[118]

Black intellectuals also claimed that Caribbean immigrants were not to blame for depriving natives of jobs and higher salaries. It was Spaniards who flooded the cities and presented a ruinous competition to nationals. They also contested the notion that these white immigrants were intellectually or in any other way superior to West Indians. As Lino D'Ou stated, neither Ramón y Cajal, Pablo Iglesias, Blasco Ibáñez, nor Pío Baroja had come to Cuba as immigrants.[119]

Afro-Cubans also opposed the notion that a massive entry of black immigrants represented a danger to the future of the republic. Although they usually agreed that it was not beneficial to encourage the introduction of West Indians, they resented the racist explanations given by the mainstream press.[120] Haitians and Jamaicans should be opposed for "sociological or other reasons," not for being black. Whereas the dominant media stressed the white character of Cuban civilization, the Afro-Cuban journal *Labor Nueva* responded that the island could proclaim anything except being a "land of white people." Consequently, they opposed the importation of *braceros* from any source and argued that if permanent colonists were needed, then their race and national origin should not be important.[121]

Both the immigration debate and the efforts to whiten the island, racially and culturally, reflected the different ways in which Cuba and Cubanness were envisioned.[122] Black immigration was opposed because of the belief, shared by authorities and most members of the economic and cultural elites, that the island "had already more than sufficient Negroes," or, as President Machado put it, that "Cuba's negro population was already quite as large as was desirable."[123] As a white intellectual told Afro-Cuban journalist Gustavo Urrutia, "Cuba will be white, or it won't be."[124] That these ideas could coexist with the rhetoric of the republic with all and for all is a clear sign that racism could safely operate even under the Cuban ideology of racial democracy. Immigration laws in the 1920s and 1930s maintained the preference accorded to Spaniards while excluding Antilleans and other "races prejudicial to good eugenics."[125] Even in the midst of the wave of anti-immigrant feeling that followed the 1933 revolution, authorities insisted that Spanish immigrants were superior because they were "brothers of race, language, religion, and ideas."[126]

Contending racial ideologies during the early republic thus created a range of often contradictory possibilities for social organization and political action. Under Cuba's racial democracy, blackness was frequently denigrated as atavistic and savage, yet this ideology also called for all Cubans to be equal members of an ideal republic with all and for all. The same public figures who disparaged black immigrants courted Afro-Cuban support and repeatedly called for racial fraternity. Adding to this complex environment were North American ideas of race, which openly endorsed a consolidation of the color line and blacks' exclusion from the nation. More to the point, these ideas enjoyed some institutional support: they were shared by sectors of the local traditional elite and favored by the military occupation government. The American troops themselves introduced segregationist practices in the army and public services. When the occupation government departed in 1902, it left behind the Platt Amendment, which guaranteed the United States continuing influence in Cuban affairs. Also left behind were a growing number of investors who were in a privileged position to implement their racist ideas through discriminatory practices in the labor market and social activities.

The construction of a legally defined racial order would have required, however, Afro-Cubans' exclusion from the polity. The experience in the U.S. South demonstrated that a politically disempowered black population was a precondition to their systematic subordination and exclusion—a reality that U.S. authorities and local elites understood well. Whether that was possible in a republic that was supposed to be racially fraternal and inclusive was, of course, an altogether different question. Open to question also was the possibility of erasing the prestige, visibility, and popularity of the Afro-Cuban veterans. Despite its contradictions, the ideology of racial democracy represented at least an obstacle, a wall against the crudest forms of racism coming from within and without. The ideal republic envisioned by Martí bore little resemblance to social realities and the political design of the elites, but the vision was popular enough to be a contender in the struggle for the definition of the political order. Both the U.S. authorities and local elites learned this lesson firsthand when they tried to mold Cuba's citizenship and political order according to their own visions in the constitutional debates that inaugurated the republic.

It is impossible to speak about the black problem in Cuba without mentioning politics.
—David Grillo, *El problema del negro cubano* (1953)

The definition of the political order was the first and most important step in the creation of an independent Cuban republic. The nature and character of the political system would indeed delineate how "new" the emergent republic was in comparison to the colonial past. An inclusionary polity was unavoidable if the republic was to claim that it was "with all and for all." Thus it was in the political arena that the strength of the nationalist ideology of racial equality was tested and that different visions of Cubanness and citizenship competed for legal sanction and recognition.

The military occupation government fully understood the importance of this process and exerted considerable pressure to assure that the republic would not be with all, much less for all. U.S. authorities and their local allies considered citizenship, particularly voting rights, a privilege to be accessed through education and income—a monopoly of the "better classes," the producers and merchants that according to Governor Wood constituted "real" Cubans. Although this notion made no explicit allusion to race, it obviously excluded the overwhelming majority of Afro-Cubans. Had the North American vision become the law of the land, Cuba could have moved toward the creation of a rigid, legally defined racial order.

But it did not. Despite the strong objections of American authorities, who feared that an inclusive franchise would turn Cuba into a second Haiti, the Constitutional Convention of 1901 sanctioned universal male suffrage. Invoking the revolutionary "traditions" of the Cuban "people," the nearly all-white assembly granted electoral rights to all males, regardless of race, literacy, or income. The appeal and legitimacy of the nationalist ideal of racial fraternity were strong enough to prevent Afro-Cubans' exclusion from the polity.

As Carnoy states, "[P]olitics is shaped by normative rules—how things *should* be, not how they are."[1] Voting rights represented a crucial avenue for participation, but they did not guarantee blacks equal access to public office and the government. Among other things, the effectiveness of suffrage depended on political competition and on the integrity of the electoral process.

What universal male suffrage did guarantee was the salience of race in Cuban politics. From the first presidential campaign onward, elections were fought over who was the true representative of Martí's racial fraternity. In the process, the dominant political parties were forced to incorporate blacks into their webs of patronage and clientelism, opening opportunities for Afro-Cubans to participate in mainstream politics. Some parties even reserved a number of positions for black candidates—a type of affirmative-action program. Political rhetoric—and, to a degree, practice—contributed to legitimize the ideal of a racially inclusive republic. If Cuba's revolutionary traditions had prevented the disenfranchisement of blacks, universal male suffrage in turn prevented Afro-Cubans' exclusion from republican politics.

An inclusive franchise resulted in unusually high levels of political participation. Several decades of mobilization and nation-making had prepared Cubans, black and white, to exercise voting rights. Whereas only 30 percent of adult males voted in the U.S. South in 1910, 71 percent voted in the 1908 presidential elections in Cuba. Voters represented less than 2 percent of the total population in Brazil in 1906 compared to 21 percent in Cuba.[2] In this context, and given that whites were indeed divided between the Liberals and Conservatives, the dominant parties had little choice but to appeal to broad sectors of the population, Afro-Cubans included. No party could dare to utterly affront one-third of the electorate without risking electoral defeat.

Despite these levels of cross-racial political participation, Cuban historiography has devoted limited attention to black participation in mainstream politics during the republic. With few but notable exceptions, previous historians have focused almost exclusively on blacks' autonomous mobilization during the 1900–1912 period, when Afro-Cubans created the PIC.[3] The post-1912 period has been virtually neglected in the existing literature. Although little agreement exists among the few authors who have written about the subject,[4] these authors tend to coincide on one important point: 1912 marked the end of black mobilization in the island.[5]

The repression of the PIC signaled, however, the end of only one form of Afro-Cuban mobilization and participation in politics—and even this is open to question. The effects of the 1912 events were multiple and unexpected. White racism did consolidate, but as in the early years of the republic, other forces worked in the opposite direction. Unlike the aftermath of Reconstruction in the U.S. South, 1912 did not result in a disenfranchisement of Afro-Cubans. Office seekers still needed the black vote to win elections, and this need created opportunities for black participation. Besides, black leaders understood that government action, or lack of it, could either accelerate, retard, or even halt altogether the creation of Martí's republic with all and for all—and thus their struggle to maintain control over Afro-Cuban voters and to gain equal participation in politics. In a political system characterized by its "pluralization," in which authority and influence came from a variety of sources, those who managed to organize were in position to exact concessions of various kinds from the state.[6]

Yet Afro-Cuban politicians operated within significant constraints: efforts to give institutional form to their electoral support could be construed as un-Cuban and "racist." The ultimate center of power in Cuban politics was external—located in Washington, D.C.—and clearly unsympathetic to any black ascendance in national politics. Despite these obstacles, blacks and mulattoes managed to exercise a modicum of power and to maintain and assert their presence within the state and the government bureaucracy. In the process, two important precedents were set: electoral politics in the island would be by definition cross-racial, and the struggle for racial equality would be increasingly linked to national politics and government action. The second republic turned both precedents into full trends. That is why Afro-Cuban politician and author David Grillo asserted that it was impossible "to speak about the black problem in Cuba without mentioning politics."[7] One could argue, in turn, that it is equally difficult to understand republican politics without reference to the "black problem."

DEFINING CITIZENSHIP: THE SUFFRAGE CONTROVERSY

Discussions about political rights began immediately after the occupation government took possession of the island. The census itself had been conducted as a first step in the creation of the new political order. The enumeration was deemed crucial not only to determine the number of potential voters but also to ascertain their racial composition. As *La Lucha* explained in 1899, "In Washington they believe that in order to devise a political constitution and an election law for Cuba, it is unavoidable to have a precise knowledge of the ethnic elements that form its population."[8]

Given their perceptions about Cubans in general and their disdain for the "illiterate mass of people" in particular, American authorities decided to restrict political rights even before the census returns were known. In a January 1900 meeting with "the most important people in Cuban politics," Governor Wood defended the need to deprive illiterates of political rights. Cubans themselves were divided over the issue; members of the traditional elite sided with the military governor, whereas veterans such as Bartolomé Masó, general and former president of Cuba Libre, contended that anything short of universal (male) suffrage was not acceptable to the revolutionaries. There was a "firm" consensus, however, that members of the Liberation Army should enjoy electoral rights without qualification, a concession that Wood considered an unavoidable evil.[9]

With the support of the occupation government, the restrictive vision initially prevailed. The first municipal elections (1900) and those for the Constitutional Convention of 1901 took place under the electoral law approved by U.S. authorities in March 1900. Succinctly, it stipulated that persons could vote only if they were male, twenty-one years of age or older, natives or Spaniards who had not explicitly declared their allegiance to the Crown of Spain, and residents in the municipalities for at least thirty days. In addition to these general requisites, voters had to be literate, had to own property worth $250 (American gold), or had to have served in the Liberation Army prior to July 18, 1898.[10] Following the precedent set in the southern states, where blacks had been effectively disenfranchised, these restrictions were designed to appear racially neutral. But what officials did not proclaim publicly they recognized in private. The law, Wood admitted, had the virtue of excluding "the sons and daughters of Africans imported into the island as slaves" from the political process, which would in turn prevent a "second edition of Haiti or Santo Domingo in the future."[11]

This exclusion was hardly compatible with what the nationalist press labeled as "democratic principles" and "traditions" of the Cuban people. Opposition to a restrictive suffrage came from *ayuntamientos* (town councils) across the island, from the Centro de Veteranos, and from some of the emergent political parties.[12] The occupation government reacted by creating a commission to study the question, but its members soon learned that it was not in their power to change the principles established by the Americans. Understanding this, Martín Morúa Delgado, the only Afro-Cuban appointed to the commission, resigned.[13] It was then up to the almost all-white constitutional convention to restore the principle of universal male suffrage, despite the clear opposition of American authorities.[14] But whereas a broad statement of equality—"all Cubans will be equal before the law"—was unanimously approved without any discussion, on the suffrage issue there was division among Cubans themselves.[15]

What must be noted, however, is that all the competing proposals that circulated on the floor adhered to the principle of universal male suffrage, and they disagreed only in aspects of secondary importance. General José B. Aleman, the author of one of the proposals, articulated the dominant revolutionary position, arguing that suffrage was an "acquired right," a popular "conquest" that could not be ignored by an elected body that was supposed to represent the Cuban people. No delegate dared to oppose openly the principle of universal male suffrage itself. Rather, opponents focused on whether it was convenient or appropriate to include such a provision in the constitutional text. One of the most eloquent opponents of the principle, for instance, felt compelled to assure the convention—and the public—that he "did not fear universal suffrage," nor was he "concerned with the exercise of such right by the Cuban people."

"If no one here opposes universal suffrage, then what is the issue?" white veteran Manuel Sanguily demanded. He argued that, even if unmentioned, the real debate was whether illiterates should be allowed to vote. Those against universal male suffrage, he claimed, feared that this would open the doors of the government to "the masses" and with it to "ignorance." But Sanguily argued that with the exception of a few "illustrious" individuals, neither the middle class nor the remaining aristocracy was worthier than the Cuban "people," and he supported General Aleman's argument that the right to universal male suffrage had been previously recognized by revolutionary authorities and even the Spanish colonial government. To restrict male electoral rights, Sanguily concluded, was to introduce a "repugnant privilege." In the end, the convention approved with only three votes in opposition the inclusion of universal male suffrage in the constitutional text.

The adoption of universal male suffrage had several important consequences that did not go unnoticed to contemporaries. Compared to the first electoral law, the number of potential voters increased only some 12 percent, but the proportion of blacks within the voting population, once the literacy requirement was dismissed, almost doubled: it rose from 20 percent to 36 percent. Afro-Cubans represented 32 percent of the voting population by 1907.[16] Blacks, the mainstream press warned, would play a prominent role in politics, for they were "too many" to be ignored by candidates. No matter what their personal feelings and prejudices, political figures were forced by universal male suffrage to pay at least lip service to the ideal of an inclusive republic. As the author of an antiblack tract published in 1912 stated, certain "undeniable truths" could be said only by those who did not ask for votes. In other words, Cuban politicians could not afford to be openly racist.[17]

Furthermore, office seekers needed Afro-Cuban electoral support in order to win. In election periods, candidates of all parties protested their commitment to Cuba's racial fraternity and made vague promises to include Afro-Cubans in their government. As D'Ou stated during the presidential elections of 1916, "[I]t is our turn to be flattered and to receive tributes; it is the electoral period." Another Afro-Cuban writer speculated that if a Russian or Swede decided to run for town councillor in Cuba, he would surely claim to represent the interests of "the colored race."[18]

Afro-Cubans' mockery of the electoral process notwithstanding, they recognized that electoral politics created opportunities for them. During elections, "precisely in this hour of political wheedling," as black journalist Pedro Portuondo Calás called it, blacks could challenge publicly the performance of any politician or party.[19] Electoral competition also opened opportunities for Afro-Cuban professionals and public figures to advance socially and politically, which in turn allowed the entrance of some of their clients and supporters into the administration, the rural guard, and the army (see Chapter 3). Even detractors and critics of the Cuban political system had to admit that competition for the Afro-Cuban vote had forced the dominant parties to make concessions to their black constituents and to include black leaders among their candidates.[20] As a U.S. military officer later wrote, "[T]he blacks see in the Republican form of government an opportunity to advance and are taking advantage of it."[21]

It was precisely because of the opportunities opened by universal suffrage that several attempts were made to restrict electoral rights. The debate about contending notions of citizenship reemerged immediately after the Constitutional Convention of 1901, with several conservative political leaders advocating a restriction of voting rights. Instead of depriving illiterates of their right to vote, they proposed moving away from the one man, one vote principle and awarding multiple votes based on literacy and property—the so-called plural vote.[22] This system pledged formal allegiance to the notion of an inclusive citizenship while minimizing in practice the electoral power of those referred to in the convention as the Cuban "people."

White intellectual Enrique José Varona, later president of the Partido Conservador (PC, Conservative Party), opposed universal male suffrage on the ground that a society recently emerged from a "plantation colony" could not be transformed overnight into a real democracy. In a 1905 debate sponsored by Havana's most prominent cultural circle, the Ateneo, Varona asked whether the Cuban people, "composed of perfectly heterogeneous elements," could suddenly exercise their electoral rights to provide the republic with an appropriate government. In his view, suffrage was not a "right" but a "responsibility" that should be exercised only by those who had the necessary "moral and intellectual conditions." Rafael Montoro defended a similar position before the Comisión Consultiva, which drafted a new electoral law during the second U.S. government of intervention (1906–9). Montoro argued that the plural vote was a "means to compensate for the inconveniences of universal suffrage" and mentioned that in the U.S. South, especially in those states that were closer to Cuba in terms of "social structure" and "historical conditions," suffrage had been effectively limited in several ways. In his view, male citizens with higher education, property holders, and those who lived in legal marital unions should be entitled to more than one vote.[23]

But the idea did not prosper. In his response to Varona in the Ateneo's debate, Alfredo Zayas, a leader of the Partido Liberal (PL, Liberal Party), underlined the links between the nationalist ideology and the notion of popular participation in the political life of the country. Zayas argued that the revolution had to transform everything, especially politics, and that suffrage was a "right," not a "function" as Varona presented it. Acknowledging that several decades of cross-racial, popular mobilization could not be easily reversed, he stated: "[I]n our fatherland it is not possible, without grave and serious consequences, to restrict suffrage." The revolution had not been made exclusively by those who held noble titles or real estate but also had been made by an "enormous mass" who did not have assets and did not know how to read and write. Suffrage, Zayas concluded, was "the right of every citizen."[24]

This position was endorsed by black intellectuals as well. Although none of those who opposed universal male suffrage explicitly referred to race, race was indeed a major factor in their fears. Varona's claim that unqualified citizenship was not viable in Cuba given its "heterogeneous elements" and Montoro's reference to the U.S. South were both clear allusions to race. From the pages of *El Nuevo Criollo*, edited by black intellectual Rafael Serra, Varona was attacked for seeking to establish "feudalism" and "an aristocratic republic" in Cuba.[25] In the Comisión Consultiva, Juan Gualberto Gómez replied to Montoro's arguments that, unlike in the U.S. South, in Cuba blacks and whites had fought together for abolition and independence. In the context of these debates over the meanings of citizenship, efforts to restrict electoral rights continued, but universal male suffrage remained a central tenet of the political system. Afro-Cubans would play some role in republican politics.

ELECTORAL POLITICS, 1900–1908

The dominant parties followed several strategies to gain blacks' political support. Both Liberals and Conservatives courted blacks, included Afro-Cuban leaders in party nominations for public office, and rhetorically exalted the validity of the Cuban myth of racial fraternity. Depending on the level of competition, candidates attacked each other for not giving proper attention to Afro-Cuban issues. As one newspaper stated, despite the agreement that "there should be no distinction in politics between the two races," presidential campaigns were in fact based on "a special appeal to the colored people."[26]

Indeed, all the presidential campaigns during the first decade of the republic (1901, 1905, and 1908) were largely fought over what candidate was the true representative of an inclusive Cubanness. During the first campaign, candidate Masó underlined the need to attract, with "consideration and respect," the "class of color," which he labeled a "family of heroes," an "essential factor of our social existence" that should exercise the "participation it deserves in our political personality." He declared opposition to any privilege that contradicted the combined legacy of Martí and Antonio Maceo and called for all Cubans to unite in times of peace as well as war. After he arrived in Havana in late October, the first place he visited was the black society Centro de Cocineros, where his own campaign committee was established.[27] Also supporting Masó were some of the most prominent black public figures of the period, such as Juan Gualberto Gómez and veterans Quintín Bandera, Silverio Sánchez Figueras, and Generoso Campos Marquetti. As members of the Masó Campaign Committee, Gómez and Sánchez Figueras spoke at numerous demonstrations, visited black societies, and explicitly called for Afro Cubans to vote for their candidate in the spirit of the republic that Martí had envisioned.[28] Moreover, they reminded black voters that the opposing candidate, Tomás Estrada Palma, had lived in the United States for a long period of time and that under his government blacks would be treated "as the American Negro is."[29] Several newspapers thus anticipated that "the entire colored vote" would go to Masó.[30]

What should be emphasized, however, is that Estrada Palma and his followers reacted to this campaign by stressing their support for the same nationalist discourse that was being used to attack them. Rather than challenging the terms of the debate, they countered that their candidate did not distinguish between blacks and whites, that all Cubans belonged to the "same family," and that Estrada Palma would be the one to build the "cordial republic with all." Indeed, they contended that Estrada Palma, not Masó, was the legitimate heir of Martí.[31]

This political debate was reproduced in subsequent elections, always within the parameters defined by a racially inclusive notion of nationhood. In the campaign of 1905, the Liberal Party accused Estrada Palma and his Partido Moderado of being antiblack. In electoral meetings throughout the island, Juan Gualberto Gómez remarked that the incumbent candidate "despised" blacks, while a number of Afro-Cuban Liberals published a letter asserting that the president did "not even want blacks to clean his shoes."[32] To further lure the black vote, the Liberals even campaigned using Afro-Cuban rhythms and dances and attended social and funeral functions of the Congos Libres, a cultural and mutual-aid association of former slaves of Congo origin and their descendants.[33] In 1908 the Liberals again accused the Conservative Party, heir of Estrada Palma's Moderados, of attempting to introduce "caste divisions" in Cuban society through their opposition to universal male suffrage. Black voters were reminded that vice presidential candidate Rafael Montoro, a former leading member of the pro-colonial Partido Liberal Autonomista, had refused to work for the benefit of Afro-Cubans while he was a representative in the Spanish parliament in the 1880s. Black Liberals also claimed that Montoro had publicly congratulated Spanish military governor Valeriano Weyler in 1897 for the death of Afro-Cuban general Antonio Maceo.[34] As usual, both the Moderados and the Conservatives claimed that they truly represented the ideal of a racially integrated republic while accusing the Liberals of fostering racial hate among the population. "Those who try to exploit the colored race . . . should know that they are, above all, Cubans; that blacks and whites, together, created . . . this republic," was the argument they voiced to oppose Liberal propaganda.[35] In 1908 they repeated that the Conservative Party recognized "no races, no colors, no hierarchies" and denied the charge that they were trying to introduce "odious privileges" in republican politics through suffrage limitations.[36] In the opening ceremony of the presidential campaign at the National Theater, with six black generals in attendance, Montoro was asked to embrace Afro-Cuban general Jesús Rabí in public. The hug, hailed by the conservative press as the consummation of Martí's dream of a republic with all and for all, was also intended to show that black veterans of the highest military rank were siding with the Conservative Party.[37]

While at a rhetorical level this fierce political competition for the black vote reinforced the notion of a racially inclusive nationhood, at a practical level it opened concrete opportunities for Afro-Cuban participation in national politics. The Estrada Palma administration showed that, unless the incumbent had complete control over the electoral machinery, public displays of racism could be publicized by the opposition and incur a heavy political cost. A well-known 1905 incident illustrates this point. Senator Martín Morúa Delgado and Representatives Antonio Poveda Ferrer and Generoso Campos Marquetti were invited to attend an official reception at the presidential palace, but without their wives and families. Both representatives refused to participate and denounced in a public letter what they considered to be an "insult" against their race.[38] Rafael Serra, a political supporter of Estrada Palma, criticized the exclusion but said that it was not the president's fault; no candidate would have invited Afro-Cubans' families to the palace. To prove that Estrada Palma was not himself a racist, Serra pointed out that the president had invited black generals Rabí and Cebreco to his own house. Serra realized the political importance of the incident: he asked contending Liberals not to use it for electoral purposes.[39]

But the opposition did not comply with Serra's request. Rather, the incident was invoked in numerous meetings during the Liberal campaign across the island. A local black leader from Perico (Matanzas) claimed that the president had violated the Constitution, introducing illegal "preferences" among Cubans. An Afro-Cuban orator from Colón remarked that if the president had dared to humiliate the families of black congressmen, he would not hesitate to do the same with less prominent blacks. "We have nothing to thank don Tomás or his government for," he stated, "because he has done nothing for us."[40]

Political competition for the black vote also opened opportunities for black candidates to exercise pressure within the parties. When the Partido Moderado dropped Juan Felipe Risquet, a mulatto representative from Matanzas, from its ticket in the congressional elections of 1905, the Liberals immediately attacked. In a public manifesto addressed to Afro-Cuban voters, they characterized as "wicked" the "act of robbing the colored element of the meager representation" they had in the national government, and they used the occasion to offer their support to run black candidates for the government of "the Republic dreamed by Martí: with all and for all." (For a graphic representation of the Liberal propaganda, see figure 2.1.) Black Moderados, in turn, took advantage of this environment to pressure their own party. In a telegram sent to the head of the party in Matanzas, the black voters from Cárdenas asserted "the need to have adequate representation in the parliament, as a full demonstration that the party does not disregard them, refuting in practice the constant assertions" made by the Liberals. They also threatened to launch Risquet's candidacy as an independent. The Conservative Party learned the lesson: it took Risquet back to Congress in 1908.[41] Meanwhile, in Oriente, blacks were also asking for proportional representation in the positions and nominations of the party. In a similar incident, when Liberal Juan Gualberto Gómez withdrew from the senatorial race in 1908, the Conservative Party expediently offered him a senatorship, which he refused.[42]

FIGURE 2.1. *"The Liberal Program." This cartoon portrays the candidates of the Partido Liberal, José Miguel Gómez and Alfredo Zayas, endorsing Martí's project of a nation "with all and for all." From* La Lucha, *November 23, 1906. (Library of Congress)*

As a result of this competition for the black vote, the participation of Afro-Cubans in the national government tended to increase during the first decade of the republic, although in a proportion well below their percentage in the voting population. In 1905, only 4 out of 63 representatives to the House were black,[43] but at least 14 blacks and mulattoes were elected to Congress in 1908. Thus the proportion of black congressmen (including those in the Senate and House of Representatives) was somewhere between 13 and 15 percent of the total. Blacks were still quite underrepresented in the legislative body, but this proportion more than doubled the 6 percent they had obtained after the partial elections of 1904. Both parties were equally responsible for the presence of blacks in the new Congress. Among eleven well-identified representatives, six were Liberals and five Conservatives.[44] The highest proportion of blacks had been elected in Matanzas and Oriente, the two provinces with a large percentage of Afro-Cubans in the total population. Out of ten representatives elected in Matanzas, at least three were black: Ramiro Cuesta Rendón and Silverio Sánchez Figueras from the Liberal Party and Juan Felipe Risquet from the Conservative. In Oriente, 7 out of 18 representatives elected were black, including such well-known Afro-Cuban politicians as Lino D'Ou, Rafael Serra, Francisco Audivert, and General Agustín Cebreco from the Conservative Party and Alberto Castellanos, José Pagliery, and Manuel Lores Llorens from the Liberal. The number of Afro-Cuban candidates in each party was even larger, but not all were elected. For instance, among the Liberals, neither General Miguel Lores from Pinar del Rio nor Venancio Milián or Juan Travieso from Havana made it to Congress. According to D'Ou, 46 percent of provincial councillors, 9 percent of municipal mayors, and 40 percent of all town councillors in the island were also black.[45]

In order to guarantee Afro-Cuban representation in Congress, political parties on occasion even reserved a number of positions for the black candidates in their slate. In Oriente, the provincial assembly of the Conservative Party discussed only 14 of the 18 possible nominations in 1908: the remaining four had been previously set aside for black and mulatto candidates. Although this system guaranteed a minimum of Afro-Cuban participation among the candidates—a sort of affirmative-action program—it did not necessarily work to the advantage of black candidates, nor was it based on the principle of raceless equality advocated by all parties. Afro-Cuban candidates were forced to compete among themselves for these limited positions, so their total number among the elected officials would never exceed certain margins previously defined by the party's leadership. D'Ou was right when he complained that this practice was not congruent with the ideals of "justice" and "cordiality" on which the Cuban republic was allegedly based.[46]

The growing Afro-Cuban presence in Congress by 1908 also reflected the prominent participation of blacks in the Liberal revolt of August 1906, which overthrew the Estrada Palma government and provoked a second American intervention. A contemporary observer estimated that 80 percent of the rebels were blacks. American officials concurred that the movement enjoyed widespread support among the "poorest" and the "uneducated" classes.[47] In the heat of the 1905 electoral campaign against the Moderados, the Liberal Party had promised to build the republic with all and for all, had virulently criticized Estrada Palma and the Partido Moderado for not giving blacks what they deserved, and had even appropriated Afro-Cuban dances and rhythms for political purposes. Blacks' expectations of participation and rewards in a new liberal and populist republic had consequently grown. Blacks were also well represented among the losers. Indeed, the Partido Moderado had enjoyed the support of most Afro-Cuban veterans of the highest military ranks.[48] During the revolt, both rebel and government troops were commanded by black officers. Colonel José Galvez headed the loyal troops that defended Guanajay against the Liberal forces led by another Afro-Cuban veteran, Generoso Campos Marquetti.[49]

Since participation and rewards would be measured primarily in terms of the number of bureaucratic positions and public jobs distributed among the different factions, this environment was certain to increase competition for resources. "Here politics is reduced only to the question of public jobs," *La Discusión* asserted in 1906. And public jobs were not in great supply, given the large number of potential seekers. As a U.S. officer commented from Santiago, "There cannot be enough patronage places created to satisfy the majority of those expecting positions. . . . There will be so many expecting to get something for their political support that some must be disappointed."[50] Blacks were certainly in the forefront of those expecting to get something. It was largely they who had ended Moderado rule, through their support for the Liberal revolt. Writing in late 1906, an American resident in Cuba noticed that after the revolt blacks were demanding "greater consideration" and that this might lead to "sharper" racial divisions in the island.[51] His words were prophetic: in the following years, racial tensions increased to the point of rupture.

BLACK AUTONOMOUS MOBILIZATION: THE PIC

The organization of a racially defined political group was a sensible strategy in a system in which those in control of voting blocs could exact significant concessions from the state. If successful, a black political party could become a key broker in Cuban elections. Even if the party was unable to win by itself, its support would be indispensable to the success of either Liberals or Conservatives in national elections.

What was sensible politically, however, was unacceptable ideologically. The nationalist ideology of racial fraternity made it difficult to exclude Afro-Cubans' from the polity, but it also made it possible to delegitimize any attempt at racially defined political mobilization. While it was possible to justify the need for a black organization on the grounds that Martí's republic remained in fact unrealized, the dominant interpretation of Cubanness would proscribe such an attempt as un-Cuban and an act of "racism." According to this interpretation, the organizers and members of a racially exclusive party would be placing race above national identity—being black would be more important than being Cuban and not the other way around, as Martí had wanted.

Creating an Afro-Cuban party was a strategy to gain access to public office. Although the black share in Congress and the government increased during the early years of the republic, blacks remained underrepresented in the structures of power. Besides, previous experience showed that, when organized, blacks were able to obtain at least token concessions from the state. In the late nineteenth century, the Directorio Central de Sociedades had managed to impose on Spain a recognition of Afro-Cuban civil rights. In 1902, the Comité de Acción de Veteranos y Sociedades de la Raza de Color had lobbied President Estrada Palma and Havana's provincial governor with some success to increase blacks' representation in the police, the rural guard, and other public jobs.[52]

The experience of the committee showed the opportunities that Afro-Cuban mobilization could create, on the one hand, and its limitations and difficulties, on the other. Under the leadership of Generoso Campos Marquetti and with the support of Juan Gualberto Gómez, the committee included black veterans as well as delegates of the Afro-Cuban clubs and societies of Havana, of which at least eleven were represented.[53] They met with the president, introduced a motion in Congress to nullify the racist measures approved by the U.S. occupation government, and obtained an allocation of eighty positions for blacks in Havana's police and twelve in the mail service.[54] But as soon as the committee organized, it was accused of instigating a racial war in the island. Not even the support of Juan Gualberto Gómez, a radical integrationist, protected the committee from such rumors. Campos Marquetti denounced such charges in a public letter, claiming that it was not until the American intervention ended that blacks had even tried to redeem "part of their violated rights," so they could not be accused of endangering the republic that they had helped create.[55]

The committee's activities provided other enduring lessons as well. First, disputes over the distribution of patronage could easily disrupt these organizational efforts. Just one month after its creation, a commission of the committee complained that some of the positions allocated in the police were being filled with candidates not recommended by them—a clear move to undermine the authority and effectiveness of the organization. By November 1902 a dissident faction had appeared and the Comité de Acción was virtually dead.[56] Furthermore, the main leaders of this and similar organizations were frequently incorporated by the dominant parties. Campos Marquetti was elected to Congress by the Liberals in 1904. Most of the leadership of the Directorio de la Raza de Color created in Havana in 1907 ended up in Congress as well. This included Rafael Serra and Lino D'Ou, both of whom were elected to Congress on the Conservative ticket in 1908. Tiburcio Aguirre, the subsecretary of the Directorio, was organizing public acts to honor the Conservative presidential candidate the same year. The secretary of the organization, Miguel A. Céspedes, became a congressional representative in 1912, and he was later president of the exclusive Club Atenas.

This Directorio was only one of the various efforts undertaken by Afro-Cuban leaders to assert their place in Cuban politics after the Liberal revolt. In the summer of 1907, numerous meetings took place throughout the island. In San Juan y Martínez (Pinar del Río), the Protest Committee demanded fair participation for blacks in the distribution of public jobs.[57] In Camagüey, the Directorio de la Raza de Color issued a manifesto calling for blacks to organize in a "common convention" for the moral, economic, and political improvement of the "colored" race. It opposed the formation of an independent political party. Rather, what this Directorio proposed was the creation of an organization that could exercise effective pressure on the political parties, forcing them to give proportional representation to Afro-Cubans in all public positions. It asked its followers to deny support to those parties that did not fulfill such aspirations.[58]

This initiative was followed by the creation of the Havana directorate in a meeting attended by more than 200 people in the society Arpa de Oro. Some of the participants, such as Campos Marquetti, argued against creating an autonomous black organization, claiming that many of the goals mentioned in the Camagüey manifesto already had been fulfilled. Lino D'Ou, in turn, asked Campos Marquetti to reconsider his position and stressed that legal equality alone had not prevented the exclusion of Afro-Cubans from important sectors of national life. Despite Campos Marquetti's opposition, a provisional directorate was created, with Juan Bravo as president and Miguel A. Céspedes as secretary.[59]

The discussion in Havana's Directorio illustrates that Afro-Cubans did not share a common view concerning political activism. On the one hand, a number of Afro-Cubans felt the need to create some sort of organization that would enhance their capacity to pressure the existing political parties. These leaders sought to maximize the return for their participation in the political process, just as white public figures did. Although they did not propose to establish an autonomous black political movement and fully subscribed to the integrationism of the nationalist ideology, they did stress the need to realize in practice "the rights that citizenship gives us." This position was, in fact, just one step short of the creation of an all-black political party.[60]

On the other hand, Afro-Cuban leaders such as Campos Marquetti, Juan

Gualberto Gómez, and Morúa Delgado defended the need to work within the existing political parties and opposed any attempt at separate racial mobilization. Not infrequently, political allegiances were stronger than feelings of racial solidarity. Just a few days after its release, the Camagüey manifesto was contested by a large group of black Liberals from the same province, who agreed that blacks had the legitimate right to fully participate in the country's public affairs but argued that such a right "had never been contested or denied by the Liberal Party, with which most colored men in Cuba [were] affiliated." What the Directorio would do, they claimed, was to debilitate the Liberal Party and disturb the harmonious coexistence of the two racial groups.[61]

A third position called for Afro-Cuban autonomous political mobilization as the only way for blacks to get their share as citizens of a republic that they had fought so hard to create. A manifesto published by a group of veterans in Lajas unequivocally endorsed this position. It asserted that blacks would not be deceived any more by politicians, whose electoral promises were always disregarded later. It proposed to form "a great independent party, so when the moment of the elections come we select our local and national candidates, for we are tired of promises and offers."[62]

A black independent political party was finally organized under the leadership of Evaristo Estenoz in Havana on August 7, 1908. The new group, called Agrupación Independiente de Color (later Partido Independiente de Color), was formed after the defeat of numerous black candidates in provincial and municipal elections (August 1). In their programmatic documents, the Independientes made clear that they had organized to obtain full participation "in all the governments of the Cuban Republic, so that we are well governed."[63] Among other goals that were not racially specific—an eight-hour workday, free immigration for all races, distribution of land among veterans—they demanded black representation in the diplomatic service, the army, and the different branches of the government. Although the PIC's program did not advocate racial separatism, pledged allegiance to the ideal of a racially integrated Cuban nation, and contained goals of broad popular appeal, its very name suggested that the organization was only for people "of color," who were organizing "independently," that is, separate from whites.

The PIC joined together mainly former members of the Liberal Party, particularly from the faction led by José Miguel Gómez (the so-called Liberales Históricos). Estenoz's links to this group were not severed until just a few months before the creation of the PIC. As late as August 1907 Gómez and Estenoz were attending Liberal rallies together. In a public demonstration in Trillo Park, Havana, Gómez reportedly applauded what an American newspaper called "barbarous remarks of General Estenoz and other heroes of the colored race."[64] Not surprisingly, the Conservative press treated the creation of the "colored" party as a simple disagreement "within the Liberal family."[65]

That this was more than just a disagreement became obvious in the national elections of 1908, in which the PIC participated with a complete list of candidates for Congress in the provinces of Havana and Las Villas. Their performance, however, can only be described as catastrophic. In Havana, the Independiente candidate with the largest number of votes was Agapito Rodríguez, who got only 116. Conversely, each Liberal candidate received more than 47,000 votes, and no Conservative aspirant got fewer than 23,000. Estenoz, the leader of the PIC, attracted only 95 votes, the sixth among the candidates of his own party.[66]

For Estenoz this was the last failure in what had been a varied but largely unsuccessful career that included being a labor leader, a militant in various mainstream political parties, a rebel in at least two uprisings, and even a would-be entrepreneur. After the war for independence, which he finished with the rank of captain, he joined the Partido Unión Democrática, which grouped a number of veterans and ex-Autonomists.[67] Estenoz was a master mason and, as president of the masons' guild, organized a strike for the eight-hour workday in 1899. The strike failed, and he was detained with other labor leaders.[68]

In 1902 Estenoz joined the Committee of Afro-Cuban Veterans, which lobbied for access to public jobs. Two years later, he tried to establish an exclusive fashion store in Havana, apparently without success, although his wife was a well-known milliner.[69] By this time, he had entered the Liberal Party, and he complained that blacks were kept in lower roles within the party and never considered for important positions, either political or administrative. In a public document circulated in late 1905, he also asserted that he was not interested in any nomination, nor would he accept one. "I aspire to be among those who become wealthy through their personal work," he declared.[70] A few months later he joined a brief uprising against the Moderados on December 1, election day, returning home a few days later. The following year he joined the August revolt that ended the government of Estrada Palma and provoked the second American intervention in the island. Afterward, Estenoz led a commission that represented the grievances and aspirations of the black participants. Apparently, he also attempted but failed to be nominated on the Liberal ticket in 1908 for the governorship of Matanzas.[71]

Although the party had organized only shortly before the elections, this alone does not explain its electoral failure. The PIC's platform mainly addressed the needs of urban veterans and black Liberals who had not been included in the distribution of offices and patronage. Its capacity to attract support was seriously undermined by the opportunities for social ascent that mainstream political parties could offer, as well as by the other parties' active efforts to lure Afro-Cubans to their ranks. Furthermore, the 1908 presidential elections had brought a relatively large number of blacks to positions of power and prestige within the state under the auspices of the major parties, challenging the notion that Afro-Cubans were not well represented in Cuban political life.

It is not by chance that legal action against the Independientes was not brought until 1910, a year of partial congressional elections. In fact, the whole chronology of the PIC is marked by political events. The party was created prior to the national elections of 1908; it was banned just prior to the congressional elections of 1910; and it revolted and was destroyed just a few months before the presidential elections of 1912. The PIC alone did not represent a serious challenge to the Liberals, but in alliance with the Conservative Party, it was indeed a major threat to Liberal control of the black electorate. Indications of such an alliance were widespread. The Conservative press had been supportive of Estenoz's activities since the end of the Liberal revolt in 1906. Some of the leaders of the PIC, such as Gregorio Surín and Pedro Ivonnet, had been active in the Conservative ranks.[72] The president of the Veterans Council in La Maya (Oriente province) in 1903, General Ivonnet, as he was referred to, had been on good terms with Estrada Palma, who appointed him veterinarian in the rural guard.[73] A prominent member of the Partido Conservador, Freyre de Andrade, undertook the defense of Estenoz and other Independientes when they were detained in 1910.[74] According to the American ambassador, Conservatives had done "everything in their power to assist the negroes. Their interest in them has increased conspicuously during the progress of the electoral period." He also stressed that the bail of several Independiente leaders had been paid by "prominent white members of the Conservative party."[75] To make things even worse for President Gómez and his followers, the Zayista Liberal faction had also maintained a cautious and at times friendly attitude toward Estenoz, in a clear move to attract his followers to their ranks.[76] As a contemporary cartoon showed, the "race fire" had been fed by the contending political forces, their electoral promises, and their flattery of "racist passions."

At this point, Morúa Delgado, the leading Afro-Cuban figure among the

FIGURE 2.2. *Martín Morúa Delgado with his wife, Elvira Granados de Morúa, and their daughters, Vestalina and Aravella. From* El Fígaro*, September 12, 1909. (Author's collection)*

followers of President Gómez, introduced a bill in the Senate establishing that any group composed of individuals of a single race or color would not be considered a political party. Morúa argued that he was opposed to "any" racially exclusive political group, for Cubans should not get used to the idea of being separated according to their race. Furthermore, he claimed that a black political organization would automatically generate its opposite, an all-white organization, and that this was precisely "the conflict" that the bill attempted to prevent. He also warned that if unchecked these trends could end up "drowning us all" and stressed that all parties had in fact tried to attract the largest possible number of black voters.[77]

Although the PIC was banned by this bill, the Liberals also tried to maintain their image as the legitimate representatives of the "colored" race in the island. In March 1910, just before the detention of Estenoz and other leaders of the PIC, President Gómez toured the island. In Cienfuegos, one of the cities in which the Independientes had established a branch in 1908, the president visited the "colored" Sociedad Minerva, while Morúa Delgado and Vice President Zayas toasted the unity of all Cubans in a banquet offered by the local customs house. In Santiago de Cuba, representatives of the Afro-Cuban societies met with Gómez; a day later he and his companions were greeted at the Luz de Oriente society. And in Pinar del Río, Gómez actually met in private with the local representatives of the PIC, while Zayas visited black clubs in Artemisa and called, in conjunction with several black orators, for an end to racial divisions. Also, in a political gesture addressed to "the element that he represents," Morúa Delgado—whose term in the Senate was about to expire—was named secretary of agriculture, the first black member of a Cuban cabinet.[78]

These overtures were not successful. In May 1912, the PIC revolted in protest against the Morúa law and was ruthlessly repressed. Racist repression became politically possible due to a combination of factors. First, the Independientes' revolt was easily construed as an attempt to break the fragile boundaries of Cuban racial democracy and therefore as a threat to the very existence of the republic. As a press editorial explained, "[T]hose who follow Estenoz are evil because they prefer to be blacks rather than Cubans."[79] The PIC and its leaders were labeled "racist"—that is, a group that placed "race" above national identity. The fact that the Independientes constantly asked for the recognition of the U.S. government helped to reinforce the image that they were not good patriots.[80] Furthermore, between 1910 and 1912 the antiwhite rhetoric of the PIC's leaders, as reported by the mainstream press, increased dramatically. The press probably exaggerated the Independientes' declarations, but the party's own official documents show that they had become more vocal and outspoken. In a letter to a local judge, a member of the PIC in Oriente warned that the abuses against the organization would have to end, either by peaceful means or by force.[81]

By 1912 it was also obvious that, despite his efforts to reincorporate Estenoz and his followers into the party system, Gómez would not have the

Independientes' support in the forthcoming elections. As late as February 1912, the president was still offering to repeal the Morúa law if the Independientes dropped the word "colored" from their party name, a request they rejected. It was only at this point that Gómez openly threatened "to put every possible obstacle" in the party's way.[82]

Yet the initial government reaction was slow and ambivalent. A U.S. representative in Havana reported that although the government had sufficient forces in Oriente to crush the rebellion, not a single confrontation of importance had occurred. He speculated that either the movement had some official sanction, or the government was trying to negotiate some sort of agreement with the rebels. "I cannot see any reason why the Cuban government cannot quell this revolt if energetic and immediate measures are adopted to suppress it," he asserted. At the same time, sugar mill owner Manuel Rionda described the event as "a regular Cuban 'rumba' creating considerable noise, but little or no actual harm."[83]

This "rumba" quickly degenerated into what was widely perceived as a race war. The mainstream press greatly exaggerated and distorted the Independientes' actions, fueling the fears of whites and helping to consolidate their sense of racial solidarity and legitimizing the slaughter of innocent blacks.[84] Pressures from within and without the island mounted for the Liberal government to take decisive action against the Independientes, who had caused some property damage and disrupted production in southern Oriente. Property owners complained that they were unable to control the labor force and demanded armed protection from the government. The Conservative presidential candidate, Mario García Menocal, offered to crush the revolt with three thousand volunteers under his personal command, embarrassing the Liberal administration in the process.[85] Foreign investors protested their defenselessness to U.S. representatives—"We have been practically at the tender mercy of the negro bands," the vice president of the Cuba Railroad Company reported—and lobbied the State Department to provoke intervention.[86]

The U.S. government reacted by dispatching troops to the Guantánamo base with the alleged purpose of protecting American citizens in the region. A large naval force was assembled at Key West, Florida, and additional ships sent to Nipe Bay and Havana. The U.S. government warned Cuban authorities that if they failed to "protect the lives or property of American citizens," the United States would "land forces to accord necessary protection." That the official American note specified that this was "not intervention" did not make things easier on Gómez, who strongly opposed these measures on the grounds that they placed his government in a "humiliating" position, "causing it discredit within and without the country." Thus, Gómez asserted that his government had largely succeeded in crushing the revolt and that rebel activity still persisted only in Oriente. For a president who, as a U.S. journalist wrote, had made "political capital out of his patriotic, anti-American attitude," intervention would have been disastrous, especially in an electoral year.[87]

As a result, President Gómez faced what proved to be an impossible situation. Anything short of open confrontation with the Independientes would be interpreted as a sign of weakness and further erode the credibility of a government that was notorious for its corruption and inefficiency. Gómez did as much as he could to reassure U.S. authorities that he had the situation under control and that another intervention was not necessary. He even told the U.S. ambassador in Havana that he "had the Negroes completely terrorized." Indeed, racist terror was increasingly perceived as the only viable solution to the crisis. As a railroad manager stated, "[N]othing short of a reign of terror will end the revolt in Oriente."[88]

Terror ensued, and at two different levels. First, Gómez sent General José de Jesús "Chucho" Monteagudo, a long-standing and reliable collaborator, to Oriente to crush the rebellion. Monteagudo's work was facilitated by the suspension of constitutional guarantees in the province, granted by the Congress at the beginning of June. This, a contemporary observer noted, would allow the army "a chance to kill Negroes without the courts mixing in the matter, and many, good and bad, will be killed." Indeed, just a few days later, reports that "many innocent and defenseless Negroes" were being "butchered" began to circulate. By mid-June there was consensus that the government forces were killing all prisoners without distinction and "cutting off heads, pretty much without discrimination, of all Negroes found outside the town limits." Monteagudo himself acknowledged that the operations had degenerated into "butchery."[89]

Racist terror also spread through the formation of white civilian militia units throughout the island. The press campaign depicting the Independientes as a horde of savages who had started a race war generated panic in the white population, which began arming itself against a potential attack by blacks. The government itself encouraged the formation of volunteer units to offset its own inability to provide effective protection to all properties and urban centers. As evidence of his commitment to crush the revolt, Gómez himself wrote to U.S. president Taft that he had "awakened the public spirit" and distributed more than nine thousand rifles for the defense of farms and villages.[90]

Whites were thus given the power to control and patrol urban centers as well as the most important productive enclaves in the rural areas, such as mines and sugar mills. For the first time since the inauguration of the republic, social control was explicitly defined in racial terms. It was also unhindered by government intervention or by the mediation of office seekers concerned with electoral results. Once the restraining walls represented by an inclusive Cubanness were successfully presented as broken, white racism was allowed to operate almost freely. Racist repression was not only politically possible but also presented as an act of patriotism. In this respect, Morúa's admonition about a white response to a black party proved to be correct. Flooded with sensationalist press reports, ordinary Cubans were likely to accept the notion that "blacks" had started a "racist" movement to destroy national independence. The widespread vision, then, was that Afro-Cubans themselves had broken the fragile boundaries of Cuban racial democracy.

Repression set the tone of the government's response to the revolt, but some efforts were also made to restore the myth of Cuban racial fraternity and to restrain indiscriminate repression. The government realized that it had become politically necessary to crush the revolt at any cost, but not even in the midst of the racist hysteria that swept the country was the importance of the Afro-Cuban vote totally forgotten. In fact, as late as May 1912 it was anticipated that the government would not use severe force against the rebels "for fear of alienating sympathy" among Afro-Cuban followers. In some cities local authorities supported the participation of blacks in the police and the regular army, despite the opposition of white citizens.[91] Blacks also were well represented in the army that chased the Independientes in Oriente, according to Monteagudo, and at least one of the officers in command, Arsenio Ortiz, was perceived as nonwhite.[92] President Gómez warned that he would not tolerate abuses against peaceful blacks, and similar statements were made by mayors and public officials in several cities, although with little practical results. The secretary of justice instructed all local justices to "guarantee the rights of the peaceful elements of color" and to oppose "unjustified persecutions" against Afro-Cubans.[93] Occasionally, the press also criticized whites' attempt to use the revolt as an excuse to deprive blacks of "rights granted to [them] in Cuban democracy." The amnesty of the Independientes in mid-June was also an effort to restore racial peace for political purposes.[94] By this time the revolt had been crushed. Both Estenoz and Ivonnet were caught and killed in the following weeks.

Although the brutal defeat of the Independientes was a function of white repression, it was facilitated by the PIC's limited appeal among blacks. As

Orum argues, the party "was only marginally accepted by Cuba's Negro community."[95] The testimony of Lázaro Benedí Rodríguez, an Afro-Cuban resident of the shanty town of Las Yaguas interviewed by Oscar Lewis in 1969, confirms this assessment. Recalling 1912, he asserted: "I fought hard against the movement of the Independientes de Color. Why? Because I understood that, according to the Constitution, which stated that all Cubans were equal before the law, we blacks should never come to organize a political party represented by one race only."[96]

Opposition to the PIC had started at the very time of its creation. Public manifestos condemning the creation of a black political party had been published by Afro-Cuban Liberals from Regla, Havana, Sancti Spíritus, San Juan de las Yeras, and Manzanillo as early as 1908.[97] Similar public statements were made later by black Liberals from Cárdenas, Güines, and other places. Those of Güines argued that in the local town council "half of the employees [were] men of [their] race," clear proof of the "good faith" of the Liberal Party. Moreover, all these documents stressed the fact that blacks were, above all, Cubans: "[W]e belong to a race that is called Cuban," a manifesto from Cárdenas asserted.[98]

The PIC's activities were also opposed by the most prestigious Afro-Cuban veterans,[99] "colored" societies,[100] and black politicians. In 1910 the black members of the legislature criticized the PIC and what they described as its "racist campaign." In 1912 they issued a public manifesto, also signed by Juan Gualberto Gómez, who was not a member of Congress, asserting that there was no racial problem in Cuba and that the rebels were disgruntled former members of the mainstream political parties who had failed to gain preeminence in national politics. They insisted that the Independientes represented a tiny fraction of the Afro-Cuban population and that their revolt should not create a "race problem" in the country, for most blacks did not support the movement. At the same time, they also called for whites to endorse the doctrine of racial fraternity and to avoid provocations against the "colored" race.[101]

Racist provocations, however, were common during the wave of repression that followed the Independientes' revolt. After 1912, even the possibility of Cuba's racial fraternity was open to question. Never before had Martí's integrationist creed been challenged so openly. Since the PIC was a racially defined political party, the widespread perception was that "blacks" had revolted and that it was only a matter of time before they did it again. Racist whites seized 1912 as a golden opportunity to exclude Afro-Cubans, once and for all, from national life. In the following years, black cultural symbols were frequently repressed and persecuted. Efforts were made to introduce or consolidate segregationist practices in several public spaces. The immigration of West Indian workers was used to revitalize a national discourse that unabashedly proclaimed whiteness to be the essence of Cubanness. In 1928 a chapter of the Ku Klux Klan was created in the island. The events of 1912 seemed to open, again, the possibility of constructing the racial order that elements of the Cuban elite and their American patrons had envisioned for the island since the days of the military occupation government.

Afro-Cubans' electoral power, however, was not destroyed. Blacks still represented more than one-third of potential voters. Moreover, the Morúa law, which the Independientes had opposed so vigorously, remained on the books. It prohibited the creation of another black party, but it also prevented whites from organizing their own racially defined, exclusionary political party. The law promoted the ideal that national public life had to be racially integrated and condemned racially based mobilization as inherently "racist."

THE AFTERMATH OF 1912

The effects of 1912 on Cuba's society were varied, in many ways unexpected, and difficult to assess. Racial tensions remained high in the following year. A bolder, more aggressive, and undisguised white racism led to several incidents of confrontation and violence that were defined as racial. Despite their varied nature, all these incidents had a common origin: whites' attempts to impose their own notions of the "proper place" for blacks and Afro-Cubans' resistance to these attempts. Several black authors referred to deepening racial divisions as a central trait of Cuban society after 1912.[102]

Nowhere were these tensions more obvious than in the conflicts over access to and use of public spaces. Blacks' unrestricted access to parks, streets, and other spaces represented a visible indicator of their "place" in society and a daily test of the validity and veracity of Cuba's racial fraternity. That is why, during the PIC revolt, efforts had been made to "drive the blacks off the streets." Violent incidents provoked by white opposition to Afro-Cubans' presence in parks, certain streets, and bars took place in Havana and other cities. The city park of Sagua la Grande (Las Villas) was reportedly converted into a "battlefield" of whites and blacks, with several people wounded.[103]

Writing shortly after these events, novelist Jesús Masdeu captured the new environment. When the mulatto protagonist of one of his novels holds a white woman by the arm in Bayamo's park, it provokes whites' anger. In a public assembly, whites shout, "We do not want more Negroes," "back to Africa," and "out of Cuba," and they agree, by acclamation, "to prohibit blacks from walking through the park."[104] Either public spaces were being resegregated or old segregationist practices were receiving renewed support. In fact, it is difficult to assess whether these practices had totally disappeared in the early years of the republic. During the first American occupation, open racial segregation frequently met with resistance, but some sort of accommodation of American segregationist practices seems to have prevailed in the following years. According to a press report, an American-owned café was ordered closed by Havana's provincial governor in 1899 because the proprietor refused to serve drinks to Afro-Cuban general Juan Eligio Ducasse. By 1910, however, the refusal of American hotels "to entertain Negroes" met with acceptance rather than confrontation. President Gómez and the mainstream press called on "all patriotic colored Cubans not to persist in enforcing their rights," claiming that their "intrusion" would only increase "the animosity of Americans" and halt tourism revenues.[105]

The available evidence suggests that in the wake of 1912 local white elites attempted to at least formalize—as in Masdeu's novel—what could previously have been an unspoken custom. In the mid-1910s, racial violence erupted twice in the cities of Camagüey and Cienfuegos when blacks dared to walk in park sections traditionally occupied by white families. Both cases resulted in several people being wounded and the eviction of blacks from those areas, on the grounds that local "traditions" were being violated.[106] Similar traditions were invoked when racial clashes occurred twice in Santa Clara's Parque Vidal in 1925. As on previous occasions, the mainstream press blamed blacks for the explosion of violence. "Colored men living in civilized societies," *La Discusión* stated, "should never lose sight of their social position, submitting without resentment to conventions sanctioned by society."[107]

These events show that Afro-Cubans did not easily submit to these racist conventions. Defining sections of the central parks as off-limits to blacks was as much an act of white control over spaces as it was an act of white control over the symbols of the state. The "centrality" of these squares was not merely a question of physical layout: they were civic spaces surrounded by the most important institutional buildings in the locality. The designation of whites-only sections within the parks was an act of resistance against Afro-Cubans' inroads into the polity and a sharp reminder that true racial integration remained elusive. These parks reflected and reproduced the uneasy coexistence of forces for racial exclusion and inclusion found in society at large.[108]

The reaction of local black leaders in Santa Clara to the violence in Parque Vidal demonstrates that some of these segregationist practices were so embedded—they were referred to as "traditions"—that they could not be transformed without racial confrontation. After the initiative of Afro-Cuban Isaac Pérez, president of the city council, representatives of the "colored" societies Bella Unión and Gran Maceo met with members of the black local elite, including businessmen and professionals, to define their position. What they proposed was "to maintain at any cost [racial] fraternity . . . keeping at the same time the existing tradition in Parque Vidal."[109] Order was to be maintained by condoning a racist tradition—a decision hailed by white local authorities as an act of "patriotism."

This tradition bore little resemblance to the "revolutionary traditions" invoked earlier to create an inclusive polity, but the ideal of a racially egalitarian republic was not totally dead. The blacks who had entered the park's white areas were walking symbols of it. The legitimacy of the ideal was also demonstrated by the cross-racial movement of protest against the local agreement. Protests came from black residents in Santa Clara, black officials and public figures elsewhere, Afro-Cuban students at the National University, Club Atenas, and even some white organizations. In a public letter to the governor of Las Villas, black representative Marcelino Garriga referred to the agreement as "disgusting" and to its participants as "cowards." Black university students called it "degrading," while Club Atenas labeled the tradition "humiliating."[110] Some white veterans joined the campaign and, using the language of racial fraternity, called for "absolute equality, without limits, for all Cubans." The emerging radical student movement also condemned the events. White Communist leader Julio Antonio Mella called for blacks to take justice into their own hands and asserted that racial fraternity was not possible without equality. "Justice," he said, "is to be conquered; otherwise slavery is deserved."[111]

The national government reacted to these events and to the wave of protests against the "cordial" settlement engineered by the local authorities in two different ways. First, in order to prevent additional violence, the government dispatched a military supervisor to the city. One month after the events, the Parque Vidal was still occupied by the army, and tensions between blacks and whites were reportedly high. Second, the reply of the secretary of the interior to local authorities in Santa Clara was unequivocal: the settlement could not be enforced, for the Constitution clearly stated that all Cubans were equal before the law. Anyone, regardless of race, could make use of "public" spaces.[112] Under pressure, the Cuban state had little choice but to publicly endorse the validity of the national myth of racial democracy, fully sanctioned by the Constitution.

But as the previous example shows, the Constitution in itself did not guarantee blacks' equal participation in national life. Mobilization and political pressure did. Afro-Cubans understood that political influence was crucial for their becoming effective members of the nation, but any real or imaginary attempt at organizing quickly resulted in charges that blacks were preparing to avenge the killings of 1912 and initiate a new racial war. These rumors of black conspiracies sought to minimize the benefits that blacks might get from their participation in politics and to keep the momentum for racial repression alive. In fact, these alleged conspiracies were invariably reported during electoral periods.

The first of these rumors circulated in 1913, after the Liberals' electoral defeat. In Cienfuegos, the Partido Liberal was supposedly cooperating with former leaders of the PIC and "inciting the Negroes" to revolt. In Santiago, it was said that Mauricio Monier, a self-titled "Brigadier General of the Revindicating Army," had sent a telegram to U.S. authorities announcing that a new black revolt was about to start. At the same time, another rumor asserted that black Liberal representative Hermenegildo Ponvert was leading a band of thirty armed men toward the town of Ariza, Las Villas, where a new partial election involving his own appointment was going to take place. It was later revealed that Ponvert had left Santa Clara only to go to Havana.[113]

Allegations of a new black conspiracy emerged again in 1915, prior to the general elections of 1916, when the political club Amigos del Pueblo organized in Oriente under the leadership of former members of the PIC. According to press reports, in a meeting of the club held in the house of Eugenio Lacoste, different speakers asserted that a new revolt was under way and that blacks were now better prepared than in 1912.[114] Rumors of Afro-Cubans preparing an armed movement were also reported in Las Villas, Guantánamo, Jatibonico, and even Havana, where the conspiracy was linked to the political aspirations of Juan Gualberto Gómez. In the Havana suburb of Regla, a black man barely escaped lynching after allegedly stating in public that "this time, whites would be the ones to die."[115]

The creation of the Amigos del Pueblo in 1915 seems to have been a political move to thank President Menocal for the amnesty and final release of the Independientes that same year. Menocal was named honorary president of the organization, and one of the leaders of the club, Isidoro Santos Carrero, publicly declared that "other than General Menocal" they had no political "commitment" to any candidate.[116] By presenting themselves as "neither Liberals, nor Conservatives," Lacoste and the Amigos were trying to guarantee their participation in the process of nominations and distribution of patronage in Oriente through the endorsement of selected candidates. In other words, they hoped to use their real or alleged control of the Afro-Cuban vote to bargain with contending candidates. Lacoste himself received a monthly payment as an "electoral agent," thanks to his influence over black voters in the region of Guantánamo. Thus the appraisal of mulatto journalist Vasconcelos was: "This is all . . . politics, a business of well-known personalities who exploit the blacks as an electoral factor." Vasconcelos treated "racism"—that is, race propaganda—as a "political hook," a "recruitment center" that guaranteed a candidate some share of the black vote.[117]

Rumors about a new "Negro revolution or insurrection" circulated again in 1919, prior to the general elections of 1920. Such concerns were voiced by property owners in Oriente, fearful that with the withdrawal of U.S. troops from the region, the new elections would degenerate into violence. Only in Havana were those rumors linked to the possible creation of a black political group—a new party purportedly called El Buen Camino, which according to police sources had been organized in the heavily black neighborhood of El Cerro. No further evidence indicates that this party was ever created.[118]

These conspiracies were invented precisely because Afro-Cubans remained an important factor in republican politics. Since the violence of 1912 did not disenfranchise blacks, their vote could not be ignored. The revolt had barely ended when Liberals and Conservatives began maneuvering again to attract black voters to their ranks. Even some of the most conspicuous protagonists of the repression adopted a conciliatory tone toward blacks. For instance, as early as July 1912, General Monteagudo declared that he had no doubts about the loyalty and patriotism of black soldiers, who, he asserted, represented 40 percent of the army. At the same time, the elitist Club San Carlos of Santiago canceled a dance to honor Monteagudo and his staff because the previous night they had participated in a social function organized by Luz de Oriente, one of the main "colored" societies in the city.[119]

Some isolated white voices protested the repression and advocated the repeal of the Morúa law, frequently seen as the immediate cause for the Independientes' revolt. The president of the National Council of Veterans declared in late June 1912 that what the government troops were actually doing in Oriente was "hunting" people who, although mistaken in their actions, were still Cubans. Another white veteran declared that the situation was dangerous because whites were out of control, not blacks, most of whom were in hiding for fear of repression. Juan Gualberto Gómez denounced publicly the "unnecessary and excessive cruelty" with which the Independientes' revolt had been repressed, while white Conservative representative Bartolomé Sagaró from Oriente condemned, before Congress, what he called the "bloody actions" of the army and blamed political parties for their "censurable silence" during the repression.[120]

Silence, however, did not last long. Seeking to disassociate themselves from the repression and to reconstruct their image as supporters and friends of the "colored race," both Liberals and Conservatives supported a sweeping amnesty of the former members of the PIC. President Gómez himself recommended as early as September 1912 the amnesty of nearly a thousand blacks who were in prison because of the revolt. The eagerness of both parties to acquit the Independientes was, as an American diplomatic source stated, "a move to conciliate the negro vote."[121]

The black vote also was courted by using the 1912 events as a subject of political propaganda. Just as the opposition attacked Estrada Palma for excluding Afro-Cuban politicians from official ceremonies in 1905, the racist repression was used as a political tool against Gómez. In the electoral campaign of 1912, a few months after the PIC revolt, the Conservatives presented their candidate as the only one who could "restore the motherland of all and for all," a thinly veiled allusion to the racial strife that had taken place under Liberal rule.[122] More explicit charges were also made. In fact, José Miguel Gómez was blamed for the "bloody racial war [that] exasperated blacks and whites . . . and endangered national independence." The opposition press represented the PL as a vulture devouring the Cuban soul, the killer of the republic. This image referred to their notoriously corrupt handling of the national treasury, on the one hand, and their incapacity to prevent racial troubles and American intervention in Cuban affairs, on the other.[123]

Denunciations of the 1912 repression were even blunter in the election campaigns of 1916 and 1920 (see figures 2.3–2.6). Political competition increased in 1920 because the PL divided again over the presidential aspirations of its main leaders: Zayas and Gómez. When the latter obtained the official nomination of the party, Zayas, with the customary support of Juan Gualberto Gómez, created the Partido Popular (PP, Popular Party) and allied with the Conservatives, his old adversaries, giving birth to the National League. As the vice president of the first Liberal administration, Zayas needed to distance himself from the 1912 repression as much as possible. To achieve this, full responsibility for the events had to be placed on President Gómez's shoulders.

The Zayista press thus presented Gómez as the Afro-Cubans' greatest enemy—the "butcher" and the "assassin of a noble race."[124] He was quoted as ordering General Chucho Monteagudo to "sweep away all the blacks

Tiburón en Oriente

LA SOMBRA DE ESTENOZ

ESTENOZ.—No solicites del negro
su voto, José Miguel,
que aún se estremece pensando
en lo que hiciste con él.

Y pues contar con su apoyo
en ti fuera una locura,
piensa que todavía está
caliente mi sepultura.

FIGURE 2.3. *"Tiburón in Oriente." This cartoon portrays Estenoz coming out of his grave to indict José Miguel Gómez. "Estenoz's Specter. Estenoz: 'Don't ask for the black vote, José Miguel. They still tremble at the memory of what you did to them. You would be crazy to think you can count on their support; my grave is still warm.'" From* La Política Cómica, *October 10, 1916. (Biblioteca Nacional "José Martí")*

without compassion" in 1912. In Santiago, leaflets with photographs of Estenoz's body with a caption stating, "Why blacks cannot be Miguelistas," were distributed in public rallies. In Las Villas, a broadsheet containing a caricature of Gómez in a cemetery, surrounded by the graves of the Independientes, circulated widely.[125] Symptomatically, on November 1, election day, the Zayista *La Opinión* ran on its front page the following two headlines: "Colored Race, Remember the Great Slaughter of May" and "The Eternal Demagogue, the One Who Machine-Gunned the Colored Race in Oriente, Will Today Get the Punishment He Deserves for His Crimes."

Manifestos calling on the "colored" race to oppose the Liberal candidate were published by black voters in Matanzas, Guantánamo, Santa Clara, and other cities. In Guantánamo, the Afro-Cuban Club Moncada closed its doors when Gómez toured the city. Similar actions were undertaken, according to

El macheteo de los negros

EL PICO DE TURQUINO

Aún recuerda con horror,
estremecida la gente,
el macheteo destructor
de los negros en Oriente.

Y fue tal la mortandad
dispuesta por Bacuino,
que con cráneos puede hacerse
otro pico de Turquino.

FIGURE 2.4. *"The Killing of Blacks." This cartoon compares the tallest elevation in Cuba, the Turquino peak in Sierra Maestra, Oriente, to a mountain of skulls of the Afro-Cuban victims of 1912. On top, President Gómez is represented as a vulture. "The Turquino Peak. People still remember with horror the* macheteo *of blacks in Oriente. Under Bacuino's [Gómez's] command mortality was so high, that it is possible to build with skulls another Turquino peak." From* La Política Cómica, *October 15, 1916. (Biblioteca Nacional "José Martí")*

the Zayista press, by "colored" societies in Camagüey, Santa Clara, and Sagua la Grande.[126] In Havana, a group of Afro-Cubans organized the so-called Vanguardia Popular Nacional with the purpose of grouping together all the opponents of Gómez, irrespective of their political affiliation. Although this organization was referred to as a "Popular Directory of the Colored Race," its leaders disclaimed any racial label and stated that they opposed Gómez because his presidency would be harmful to the nation as a whole. Still, all the main leaders of the Vanguard were black: ex-Independiente Pantaleón Julián Valdés, public notary Oscar Edreira, Francisco Barada, and Jacinto Poey, a delegate to the municipal convention of the Partido Popular in Havana.[127]

RECUERDO DE UNA "CACERIA" 1912

MATANDO "TOTIS"

Este ilustre cazador
que veis aquí retratado,
su escopeta ha disparado
a la raza de color.
Y tal estrago causó
en la oriental sitiería,
que más de seis mil tumbó
con su mortal puntería.

1916

FIGURE 2.5. "'Hunting' Souvenir 1912." This cartoon depicts President Gómez as a hunter holding the heads of Estenoz and Ivonet. The knife sheath reads, "Kill blacks." "Killing 'Totis' [black birds, a pejorative term used to designate blacks]. This illustrious hunter, who is portrayed here, has used his rifle against the race of color. He caused so much destruction in Oriente's countryside, that he killed more than six thousand with his deadly aim." From La Política Cómica, October 15, 1916. (Biblioteca Nacional "José Martí")

The use of 1912 for electoral propaganda allowed a new interpretation of these events to emerge. In the heat of the campaigns, the new vision briefly found a privileged space in the mainstream press and in national political discourse. In 1912, the PIC and its leaders were presented as a threat to the nation and to Cuba's racial harmony. By 1920, the emphasis had shifted to their repression by the government. Rather than being seen as the savior of the republic, Gómez was charged with killing mercilessly thousands of Afro-Cubans. In the process, the former "patriot" became a "butcher," the de-

DESDE EL CACAHUAL

LA VOZ DE MACEO

FIGURE 2.6. *"From Cacahual: Maceo's Voice."* *The specter of Estenoz, who is compared in this cartoon with Afro-Cuban national hero Antonio Maceo, guides black voters to the ballot box in the 1916 elections. Their ballots read, "Vote for Menocal." On the wall hangs a picture of Ivonet. From* La Política Cómica, *November 19, 1916. (Biblioteca Nacional "José Martí")*

fense of national integrity, a "slaughter." The alleged heroism and efficiency of Gómez's generals, initially hailed almost unanimously by politicians and the press, had been transformed into acts of "assassination" and undue "cruelty."

Through this reconstruction of the events of 1912, even the meaning of "racism" was subverted. Whereas the Independientes' attempt to form a racially separate organization was labeled at the time as "racist," eight years later the use of such a label for the PIC was being openly challenged. A black contributor to *La Opinión* put it unequivocally: those who called the Independientes "racists" were trying to cover up their own "assassinations" and "cowardice." Rather, Gómez was the "racist" because of his alleged desire to whiten Cuba through the annihilation of the "colored" race. "Yes, Tiburón

[Shark, a nickname used to refer to Gómez] Is a Racist," read the headline of one of the articles published during the 1920 campaign. Another article referred to 1912 as the "ill-named racist war." At the same time, the image of some of the Independiente leaders, the former "racists," was being reassessed. When Gómez visited Oriente in August 1920, the opposition press asked whether he thought that the "assassinated" General Pedro Ivonnet was no longer mourned in the province. Whereas in 1912 Ivonnet was characterized as an African savage trying to establish a black republic, in 1920 he was remembered as a "brave soldier for independence."[128]

The embattled Liberals responded to these accusations with some of their own. They claimed that the Conservatives were in fact the ones who had demanded "the extermination of blacks," extending repression to innocent black citizens. They accused Freyre de Andrade—who had undertaken the defense of the PIC leaders in 1910—of instigating the "racist war" and reminded Afro-Cuban voters that Menocal had volunteered to "asphyxiate in blood" the PIC revolt. Meanwhile, candidate Gómez vowed to "bring about peace and patriotic forgetfulness of past events, which must not be repeated."[129]

It is difficult to determine the importance of this campaign and of the memory of 1912 in the electoral defeats of the Liberals in 1912, 1916, and 1920. Years later, an American observer stressed that Gómez never again won reelection because of the "loss" of the black vote after the repression of the PIC. There is some merit to this assertion, although the fact that his opponents found it necessary to constantly use the race issue to discredit him suggests that Gómez continued to have a large Afro-Cuban following.[130]

The Liberals lost the province with the largest Afro-Cuban population, Oriente, to the opposition, an indication that they might have paid a political price for the repression. In the general elections of 1912 the Partido Conservador carried the province, reversing the Liberal majority in 1908.[131] In 1920 the Liberals lost in every municipality in the province in which Afro-Cubans represented more than 50 percent of the population, with the sole exception of Palma Soriano. Zayas and his Partido Popular, described in a contemporary report as "especially strong with the uneducated negro element in Oriente," took one-fifth of the total vote in the municipalities with a black majority. When the Liberals contested the accuracy of the official electoral returns before American authorities, the province of Oriente was excluded.[132]

Although this was the kind of contested environment in which Afro-Cubans could exercise pressure on political parties to increase their representation in public office, armed violence and the open manipulation of elections both tended to undermine the effectiveness of blacks' most important weapon: suffrage. The triumph of the Conservatives in 1912 was not auspicious: the leadership of the party had consistently voiced doubts about the capacity of lower-class Cubans to exercise political rights in a responsible way. In 1920, a black delegate to the Conservative national convention protested the party's reluctance to nominate blacks and introduced a formal motion to that effect.[133] Incentives to incorporate Afro-Cubans had been particularly low in 1916, when Menocal sought to win reelection through fraud with the backing of the army. At the same time, the Liberals' attempt to reconstruct its image as a "responsible" political force that would protect the interests of the "better class" also conspired against the ascent of blacks to positions of power. As a contemporary newspaper stated, Liberalism was trying to "aristocratize" itself and had lost its original strength, which lay in the "humble" classes.[134]

Still, nothing close to a sweeping whitening of Congress or government took place. In 1912, some new Afro-Cuban politicians entered Congress for the first time. They included journalists Primitivo Ramírez Ross, a Conservative from Matanzas, and Saturnino Escoto Carrión, a Zayista Liberal from Havana; lawyer Miguel A. Céspedes; and Luis Valdés Carrero, a Conservative from Havana. Other well-known Afro-Cuban politicians were either reelected or their term had not expired. This was the case for Campos Marquetti, Manuel Delgado, Hermenegildo Ponvert, and General Agustín Cebreco, who was beginning his third term in Congress. Two years later, Juan Gualberto Gómez finally became a member of the House of Representatives. By the mid-1910s, about ten members of Congress were individuals categorized as black or mulatto. Their proportion had declined since 1908, but it was still higher than in 1905.

The Afro-Cuban representation in Congress, however, declined further after 1916, when only a handful of black candidates were elected. In Havana, Juan Gualberto Gómez became a member of the Senate on the Liberal ticket, but both Céspedes and Valdés Carrero failed to secure reelection to the House. The other black candidate from the province, Juan Bell, also was defeated. The situation was no different in Matanzas. Journalist and writer Ramírez Ross, one of the editors of *Labor Nueva*, was nominated but did not get the votes needed to stay in the House. He was the Conservative candidate with the fourth largest vote in the province, but only the first three (all white) entered Congress. Also unsuccessful were lawyer Ramiro Cuesta, a follower of José Miguel Gómez, and Juan Verdugo. Among the four black candidates to the provincial council, only one, Aquilino Lombard Thondique, a Liberal, was elected. Two years later, in the partial elections of 1918, he became a member of the House of Representatives. Equally unsuccessful were Dr. José Maria Beltrán from Pinar del Río and Dr. Emilio Céspedes from Camagüey, as well as Hermenegildo Ponvert and General Manuel Delgado from Las Villas.[135]

Thus, by 1916 Congress was a considerably whiter institution. This situation did not change much in 1920, when several well-known Afro-Cuban public figures—such as Campos Marquetti, Félix Ayón, and General Delgado—were again nominated but did not gain the votes to win. In Oriente, several black Liberal politicians protested that they had been excluded from the party's nomination process. Blas Masó published a letter demanding proportional representation of Afro-Cubans in electoral posts, while nomination seeker Américo Portuondo created a "Popular Directory" within the party "to defend the interests of the Liberals of color." It was again the manipulation of the nomination process within the party that explained the relative lack of success of Afro-Cuban aspirants. A commentator from Santiago explained that blacks did not have the financial resources to "buy" delegates to the municipal assemblies, so they did not receive the necessary support at the provincial or national level. The political parties' traditional attention to the racial composition of their candidates had clearly given way to the corruption and commercialism of the nomination process and the elections.[136]

Yet both Liberals and Conservatives tried to accommodate at least the most prominent Afro-Cubans within the public administration or to place them in town and provincial councils. At least five of the nominees for the Havana town council in 1916 were black. The Liberals placed Idelfonso Morúa Contreras and Prisciliano Piedra in the provincial councils of Havana and Matanzas in 1920. Those who failed in the elections or even in the nomination process were frequently offered positions in the public administration. Miguel Angel Céspedes received an appointment as public notary after failing to be reelected in 1916. José Galvez, who was not nominated by the Conservatives despite his friendship with Menocal, was given a position as department head in the Ministry of Public Works. In Oriente, unsuccessful nomination seeker Jonás Galán was named municipal physician in Alto Songo.[137] American historian Charles Chapman noted in 1926 that "political jobs for negroes" had been granted "rather lavishly" after 1912, "though not those involving any high degree of responsibility, beyond the duty of adding up their pay and collecting it and of delivering a number of votes to a party chief." Even some prominent ex-members of the PIC were reincorporated into the political machinery. Pantaleón Julián Valdés, who had been arrested with other Independientes in 1910 and 1912, was elected to the Havana Board of Education with the support of the Partido Liberal. Rufino Pérez Landa became a member of the Havana Provincial Council and was later nominated to Congress by the Conservatives.[138]

The corruption of the electoral process was only one of the numerous symptoms indicating the bankruptcy of republican institutions. During the Zayas administration, corruption and graft reached unprecedented levels. The sugar industry recovered from its 1920 collapse, but at the price of falling under the nearly total control of American financial interests. National banks had virtually disappeared. In politics, the unveiled interference of U.S. ambassador Enoch H. Crowder in government affairs was a national humiliation. The political establishment had become increasingly discredited, together with the generation of veterans that had controlled the republic since its creation. According to Fernando Ortiz, 20 percent of the candidates for public office in the elections of 1924 had a criminal record.[139]

In this environment, the candidacy of General Gerardo Machado represented a hope of restoring the credibility of republican institutions. The Liberal candidate campaigned on a populist agenda that promised to expand education, improve public health, create a labor code, and clean up the administration. Machado also promised to support the economic, social, and political betterment of the "colored" race, as well as blacks' aspirations to ascend to government positions that had been previously closed to them.[140] The republic's credibility could not be restored without rebuilding the ideal of Cuban racial fraternity.

"RECONQUERING THE NEGRO ELECTOR": MACHADO, 1925–1933

To a larger degree than most of his predecessors, Machado lived up to his electoral promises. Several blacks attained power and visibility in his administration. General Manuel Delgado occupied the top position in three important secretariats—agriculture, interior, and communications. Manuel Capestany, a lawyer from Las Villas, was named subsecretary of justice. Journalist Ramón Vasconcelos and Dr. Raúl Navarrete were appointed to the foreign service—up to that time a branch of government completely closed to Afro-Cubans, as the Independientes had made clear in 1908. Other Afro-Cubans received prominent positions in the public administration, such as Benjamín Muñoz Ginarte, named chief of section in the Secretariat of Agriculture and secretary of the Cuban delegation to the Panamerican

Conference of Agriculture and Animal Industry, which took place in Washington, D.C., in 1929.[141]

Machado frequently hailed Cuban racial fraternity in his speeches, signed a law turning December 7, the date of Maceo's death, into a national holiday, and gave Cuba's highest decoration, the Carlos Manuel de Céspedes Order, to Juan Gualberto Gómez.[142] In 1928, his government opposed the creation of a chapter of the Ku Klux Klan in Camagüey and ordered its dissolution.[143] At the same time, the number of Afro-Cubans in the legislature increased. Liberals Felix Ayón (Havana), Lombard and Prisciliano Piedra (Matanzas), Manuel Capestany (Las Villas), and Américo Portuondo (Oriente) won election to the House. Carmelo Urquiaga and Eladio González were elected on the Popular ticket; Marcelino Garriga, on the Conservative. Unsuccessful candidates included Campos Marquetti, Vasconcelos, and Justo Salas for the Liberals; Escoto Carrión for the Populares; and Pío Arturo Frías, Francisco Audivert, and Jonás Galán for the Conservatives.[144] Blacks remained heavily underrepresented in power structures, but they had regained political visibility in the national government, leading a U.S. political analyst to assert that the "process of reconquering the negro elector . . . was not attained until Machado's regime"[145] (see figure 2.7).

The image of Machado as a pro-black president was greatly enhanced by a massive public homage rendered to him by the Afro-Cuban societies in 1928. Presented as a demonstration of thankfulness by the whole "colored race" for the appointment of several Afro-Cubans to government positions, the act was in fact organized by the very beneficiaries of those policies: black politicians and the black middle class. The idea to offer a public dinner to Machado had been originally proposed by Américo Portuondo and Manuel Capestany, two Liberal congressmen who were also members of Club Atenas. The organizing committee for the event was headed by Aquilino Lombard, also a representative and the president of Atenas, while Miguel A. Céspedes, vice president of the club, was scheduled to speak during the ceremony. The whole organization of the event was in fact conducted at Atenas, where invitations and requests for participation were handled.[146]

By any account, the homage was a great success. On September 5, 1928, the representatives of 186 Afro-Cuban societies from throughout the island met at the National Theater to render their tribute to the president, who attended with all his cabinet, several provincial governors, and the chief of the army. Sharing the presidential table were Lombard and Delgado, together with the vice president, the mayor of Havana, the president of the House, and other government officials. A classic opera performed by black

EN EL CIRCULO POLITICO

Los Senadores por la Habana

FIGURE 2.7. *"In the Political Club: Havana Senators." This cartoon depicts cross-racial electoral politics during the Machado era. From* La Política Cómica, *November 2, 1930. (Biblioteca Nacional "José Martí")*

musicians, with Afro-Cuban star vocalist Zoila Galvez as a soloist, was designed to show Afro-Cubans' success in the "conquest of civilization," as Céspedes stated in his speech. Claiming that the republic "could be cordial, with all and for all," he asked the president to "completely erase" any difference that might "subsist" between blacks and whites in Cuba. "We now aspire," Céspedes declared, "that our equality before the law and politics, the administration and the government, be not just a legal formula."[147]

At the same time that the Afro-Cuban societies were honoring Machado, however, opposition to his government was mounting. In order to extend his rule without resorting to reelection (which he had promised in his campaign not to seek), Machado engineered a constitutional change that established a longer presidential term. This he did with the support of the traditional Conservative opposition in Congress. On the grounds that his national reform program should not be opposed, he promoted the alliance of all parties in what was called *cooperativismo*, thus allowing for the consolidation of his increasingly authoritarian regime. But Machado's success was the failure of the republic. *Cooperativismo* was the most visible indicator of the traditional parties' incapacity to modernize the political structure of the country and give any concrete meaning to republican democracy. The birth of *cooperativismo* corresponded with the death of one of the foundational principles of the republic: universal male suffrage and its most immediate consequence, competitive politics. As Pérez-Stable has noted, "[T]he new arrangement signaled a rupture in the pattern of Cuban politics."[148]

This rupture occurred at different levels. In contrast with previous moments of turmoil, opposition was now mounting from all quarters of Cuban society, threatening to turn a political quarrel among contending groups into a full social crisis. New actors were emerging in the national political scenario: university students demanded autonomy and organized the Directorate of University Students. Urban professionals and white-collar workers grouped in ABC, a society based on clandestine cells that responded to Machado's repression with its own violence. As living conditions deteriorated due to the sugar crisis of the mid-1920s and the Great Depression, the working class, organized under the Confederación Nacional Obrera de Cuba (CNOC, National Workers Confederation of Cuba), became more radical and militant. The nascent Cuban Communist Party (PCC) was gaining in strength, organization, and appeal. And within the traditional political class, a dissenting faction opposed *cooperativismo* and created the Unión Nacionalista in 1928.

Attempting to conduct politics as usual, the Unión Nacionalista used racial arguments against Machado and his followers. It strongly attacked the notion that Afro-Cubans had in any way benefited from his administration and criticized Havana's mayor, Miguel M. Gómez Arias (son of José Miguel Gómez), on the grounds that in 1912 he, together with his father, had sought the "extermination" of all blacks. The party's official newspaper devoted a permanent section to Afro-Cubans, under the title "Problems of the Element of Color." One of those columns summarized its criticism of Machado: "Collectively, the Cuban colored race has no motive for special gratitude toward the current president. With a laughable participation in the public administration, with the offices in private companies closed to the cultured element, with workers of both sexes almost eliminated from industry in the big cities, what has the current government done to protect the colored race . . . and to alleviate their situation of misery?"[149]

Politics as usual would not solve the republican crisis, however. The appeals of the Unión Nacionalista to the whole "colored race" overlooked the fact that by the late 1920s blacks were increasingly divided by socioeconomic status. While Afro-Cuban intellectuals, professionals, and government employees gathered in the exclusive club Atenas to honor the president for opening some opportunities for Afro-Cubans in the government bureaucracy, most black workers were struggling to survive in a declining economy that would soon fall into depression. Black workers faced a situation of misery, as the opposition charged, but misery was in fact widespread and affected workers of all colors.

The depression, in turn, threatened to reverse the gains Afro-Cubans had made in the occupational structure. Although race continued to play a significant role in the labor market, during the first republic blacks and mulattoes made significant progress in entering jobs and economic sectors that were previously closed to them. This "progress" was partly a function of how low their status had been at the turn of the century, but it reflected also the opportunities that blacks enjoyed in a republic that claimed to be racially fraternal and politically inclusive. Such opportunities—and the social polarization they generated—help to explain, in turn, the limited success of Afro-Cuban autonomous mobilization. The experience of blacks and mulattoes remained heavily affected by race and discrimination, but the character and nature of racial barriers differed greatly depending on the social status of the individual. For black manual workers, race was only one of several factors determining their subordinate position in society.

PART II INEQUALITY
1900-1950s

Blacks are denied even the most elementary of all citizen rights, which is that of work.
—Pascual M. Vegueri, *El negro en Cuba* (1955)

While it was primarily in the political arena that the nationalist paradigm of a racially egalitarian and inclusive Cubanness was tested, for most Afro-Cubans the meaning of such a paradigm was far more concrete. The republic would be truly for all only if it provided blacks with equal opportunities for employment and advancement in Cuba's expanding economy.

Political rights per se did not guarantee economic power, but they were in fact related. A racially inclusive political practice implicitly proscribed the most extreme forms of racial segregation and reduced the barriers that might have otherwise existed for blacks to obtain jobs, particularly in the growing public sector. At the same time, the limited intervention of the state in the economy during the first republic allowed significant racial discrimination to operate unhindered in the labor market. As in the case of Santa Clara's Parque Vidal mentioned in Chapter 2, the Cuban government occasionally reacted against segregation and exclusion, but only under significant pressure and in places defined as public. Private spaces, from factories to social clubs, remained beyond the regulations of a state committed to minimal interference in the economy and society. When the state did intervene, it was to consolidate and expand racial and ethnic divisions in the labor market. This was clearly exemplified by government immigration policies, inspired by the sugar interests' drive to secure abundant, cheap, and politically disempowered labor for the fast-growing export economy.[1]

Immigration was designed to lower salaries not only by increasing the labor supply but also—perhaps primarily—by creating a multiethnic and multinational labor force divided by linguistic, cultural, and national barriers.[2] Immigrant presence in the labor market was so prominent that it tended to obscure racial differences among native workers. Indeed, in the early years of the twentieth century, "race" was frequently understood as a line that separated Cuban and foreign workers rather than native workers of different skin colors.[3]

IMMIGRATION

As mentioned in Chapter 1, the migration policies of the Cuban state were informed by a central belief: the proportion of blacks in the total population was too high for Cuba to become a "modern" nation. The census of 1899 made this social reality painfully clear. But the census unveiled an equally unpleasant fact: for the first time since the nineteenth century, the island's total population had declined. Whereas members of the cultural and non-sugar elites complained that there were too many blacks, the sugar planters cried that there were too few workers.

Plantation owners and other employers bemoaned the disruption of the labor market and the "scarcity" of labor. Sugar interests voiced their concern that, should the situation persist, the crops of 1900 and 1901 would be seriously compromised, not the least because workers were "conscious of the advantages of their position" and determined to obtain higher salaries. Operating in a market with a limited labor supply, employers were unable to impose their own conditions and were forced to bargain with labor. Employers referred to the "demoralized" condition of workers and to their "exaggerated pretensions" concerning payment and, in the best slavery tradition, suggested that the establishment of forced labor was the only viable solution.[4]

White immigrants were thus seen as the solution to two separate but intimately linked "dangers": those of blacks and labor. As Military Governor Wood stated, "The solution of both the *social* and *economic* problems in the Island of Cuba depends principally on endowing it with a population of 8 or 10 millions of white inhabitants." Such endowment could only be achieved, as Wood himself recognized, by encouraging white immigration.[5]

Solutions for these two "dangers" were only partially compatible, however. Although a steady flow of permanent white immigrants increased the supply of labor and was therefore sympathetically viewed by the sugar interests and other employers, these employers were not eager to pay for the resettlement costs of the potential immigrants. Nor was there any guarantee that they would remain available to be employed whenever needed. Especially in the sugar sector, in which labor demands were highly seasonal, the promotion of stable settlers was not, in purely economic terms, the most desirable solution. Companies would have to provide their workers with plots of land, thereby diminishing their own land reserves, and would be forced to supply housing and some sanitary services to the workers' families. And still there was little guarantee that, during harvest times, workers would abandon their personal plots to work the central, especially for the salaries companies were willing to pay. It was cheaper to dispose of an unlimited supply of workers during the *zafra* (sugar harvest), whose maintenance during the remainder of the year was not the company's responsibility.

Thus two alternative migration policies quickly emerged as possibilities. Bearing the black "danger" in mind, the Cuban state openly favored a "colonization" solution that advocated the immigration of stable European families, which would "improve"—that is, whiten—the composition of the native population. The sugar companies, in turn, favored the migration of seasonal workers and saw in the West Indies a great source of cheap labor.

Government-sponsored colonization efforts were disappointing. Although close to 800,000 entries from Spain were reported by Cuban government sources between 1902 and 1931, this was not the family-based migration that Cuban authorities had encouraged. Rather, this was basically a movement of single young males who came to the island for several months to work during the sugar harvest. Rates were usually higher than four men per woman, and more than 80 percent of all the migrants were between 14 and 45 years old.[6] In 1911, the secretary of agriculture recognized the failure of the colonization initiative and complained that "while large numbers of Spanish men came to Cuba for the winter . . . each year [during the *zafra*], it was very difficult to induce Spanish families to immigrate." He then suggested that to guarantee sugar production the introduction of contract labor—so-called *braceros*—would have to be allowed.[7]

The free introduction of Antillean *braceros* is what sugar investors had been demanding since the days of the American occupation government (1899–1902), through organizations such as the Círculo de Hacendados (Planters Circle), Liga Agraria (Agrarian League), and Fomento de la Inmigración (Promotion of Immigration). The sugar interests exercised enormous pressure on the Cuban state to liberalize and encourage the introduction of foreign workers and to repeal all the legal obstacles, based on U.S. immigration laws, that prevented the importation of contract labor. By the mid-1910s, the expansion of sugar production had created a need for a labor force that neither the colonization attempts undertaken by the Cuban government nor the annual migration of seasonal workers from Spain and the Canary Islands could meet. The Cuban population had increased more than 30 percent during the first decade of the republic, but sugar production had multiplied sixfold during the same period, from some 300,000 tons in 1900 to more than 1,800,000 tons in 1910. Moreover, the expansion had taken place mainly in the eastern provinces, where population densities were the lowest. Between 1901 and 1913 the proportion of sugar produced in Camagüey and

Oriente had doubled, from 15 to 30 percent. In terms of laborers this meant that if the 1902 *zafra* had used 4,500 cane cutters, for 1913 at least 21,000 would be needed.[8]

Under pressure from the sugar companies, the importation of *braceros* was allowed. A presidential decree authorized the United Fruit Company to introduce 1,000 West Indians in 1913. Four years later, when Cuba formally entered World War I and sugar production was deemed a question of national security, the traffic in Antillean labor was fully legalized. According to Cuban fiscal sources, between 1917 and 1931 some 300,000 Haitians, Jamaicans, and other workers from the Caribbean region entered the island to work on sugar plantations. Although the companies were supposed to repatriate workers after the end of the harvest, many stayed. The Cuban government had sacrificed whitening to sugar production because, as a popular saying put it, "sin azúcar no hay país" (without sugar there is no country). In turn, the sugar barons claimed that without West Indians there was no sugar.

This immigration was to be allowed only for as long as the war lasted, but the sugar companies mobilized their vast political resources whenever their supply of cheap black laborers was jeopardized by foreign authorities, the Cuban government, or both. Two incidents exemplify the capacity of the sugar interests to guarantee, despite the objections of vast sectors of the Cuban population and the reluctance of the state, the importation of Haitian laborers. In the first case, which took place in late 1918, the Haitian government halted emigration to Cuba, alleging that sanitary conditions in the island were bad. Cuban authorities acknowledged that there was an epidemic of influenza but asserted that it was "very mild." Meanwhile, the sugar companies and U.S. representatives in Havana asked for the intervention of the U.S. State Department, claiming that the prohibition would "seriously affect" the *zafra* and that there was an "urgent need" for cane cutters. Their efforts bore fruit. The State Department quickly instructed its legation in Port-au-Prince to "discuss this matter immediately with the Haitian government," which lifted the prohibition in January 15, 1919, when the sugar harvest was about to start in Cuba.[9]

A second prohibition occurred in 1928, in the midst of a declining economy and growing opposition to the immigration of Antilleans. According to the Haitian minister in Havana, President Louis Borno had decreed a suspension of emigration to Cuba in response to the "very offensive" campaign waged in the press against Haitians and to a circular of the Cuban immigration service that referred to them as "inferiour [*sic*] races."[10]

Showing its traditional reluctance to allow the immigration of black workers, the reaction of the Cuban State Department was timid and slow. The undersecretary of state informed the U.S. Embassy in Havana that the department was "satisfied" with the prohibition, as "Cuba felt that it already had more than sufficient Negroes and did not desire Haitian immigrants." President Machado had frequently reiterated his opposition to this "undesirable" immigration, so he was actually pleased that this result had been achieved through an action taken by Haitian authorities.[11]

The president enjoyed the support of the nonsugar interests represented by the recently created National Economic Defense Commission, but the sugar companies were not pleased.[12] As soon as the prohibition was announced, a representative of the powerful Mill Owners Association conferred with the secretary of agriculture, stressing that such a measure would be ruinous to the industry not only because Cuban labor in sufficient abundance could not be obtained but also because native "cane cutter[s] would not accept the wage offered to the Haitian laborer." Although the government was little inclined to take any action to reverse this policy, it did withdraw the offensive circular referred to by the Haitian minister in Havana. In turn, the sugar companies mounted their own diplomatic offensive and reached a separate agreement with the government of Haiti. The United Fruit Company, for instance, succeeded in getting authorization from President Borno to import 9,600 Haitian laborers for its plantations in Oriente. Bypassing Cuban immigration authorities altogether, these immigrants would enter the country through the United Fruit Company's own port of Antilla, not through Santiago, as was customary.[13]

Although the sugar companies kept pressuring the Cuban government for authorization to import *braceros*, the collapse of the sugar economy due to the Great Depression and the rise of unemployment effectively halted immigration by the early 1930s. Between 1929 and 1933 sugar prices declined 60 percent, production collapsed, and the harvest period was reduced from 150 days to 70. Whereas in 1928 14,353 Haitians had come to the island to work in the sugar harvest, by 1930 their number had declined to 5,126. This was the last year in which a contingent of Antillean field laborers entered Cuba legally.

Not only were more immigrants no longer needed, but those who lived in Cuba had suddenly become redundant. Given the enormous weight of the sugar sector, its collapse also meant a collapse of the economy at large. Amid rising unemployment and social turmoil, the immigrants became a visible target for the nationalists' desire to alleviate the situation of native workers. In 1934 it was estimated that of 514,000 field workers, no more than 280,000 could be employed during the *zafra*.[14] That is, even during the brief harvest period, 45 percent of the agricultural labor force was considered surplus. Since a significant proportion of the economically active population was foreign, the expulsion or repatriation of foreigners was increasingly defended as the only patriotic solution to the labor crisis.

Antilleans became the preferred targets of such a campaign. Although the process of "repatriation" began as early as 1931, it was the brief populist government of Ramón Grau San Martín (1933–34), born out of the so-called revolution of 1933, that adopted the most stringent measures against immigrants and effectively provided for their repatriation. A presidential decree of October 18, 1933, ordered the "forceful repatriation of all foreigners residing in the republic, who are out of employment, and deprived of all kinds of resources." The order referred to all immigrants regardless of color or nationality, but it was applied almost exclusively to Antilleans, especially Haitians.[15] Jamaicans were protected by British consular authorities, who had occasionally complained to Cuban officials about the way the Crown's subjects were treated in the island.[16]

If Antilleans were affected the most by the October 18 order, Spanish immigrants were the main target of decree 2583, the Provisional Law of Nationalization of Labor, approved by President Grau on November 8, 1933. This law established that 50 percent of all occupations had to be performed by native workers, who were also to be given preference in hiring. Additionally, foreigners were to be discharged before natives. This way, the labor market was enlarged for native workers through a political act, a "truly nationalist" policy that tended to divide the labor movement along ethnic lines and to enlist labor's badly needed political support. This strident nationalism notwithstanding, Grau also stated that Spanish immigration would be preferred again in better times, for Spaniards were "brothers of race, language, religion, and ideas." For ordinary Spanish workers, this brotherhood meant little: regardless of what the president said, the "Fifty Percent Law" took jobs away from them, and many were forced to emigrate or to become naturalized Cubans in order to survive.[17]

The effects of these labor and immigration policies became evident in 1943, when a new census was conducted. Compared to 1931, there were 100,069 fewer Spanish-born people living in the country, a 40 percent decline. Although this figure also includes mortalities, it is beyond doubt that several tens of thousands of Spanish immigrants had left the island during the 1930s. Furthermore, the 1943 census figure included several thousand Spaniards who had entered Cuba in the early 1940s as war refugees, so the real emigration was actually greater. The Antillean decrease was even sharper. The 102,307 blacks born outside Cuba in 1931 had been reduced to 40,091 in 1943, a decline of more than 60 percent. Scant evidence suggests that some of the deported workers had been able to return prior to 1943 with help from the sugar concerns and local corrupt authorities, so again the real volume of repatriations might have been larger. It is likely that this illegal immigration continued into the 1940s, for in 1953 the number of Haitians and Jamaicans living in the island had not declined compared to 1943. An alternative, of course, is to speculate that Antilleans were massively under-registered in 1943. The Haitian minister in Havana guessed, in fact, that about 80,000 Haitians lived in Cuba in the early 1940s.[18]

The "Cubanization" of the labor market also affected the makeup of the population in terms of citizenship. In 1931, 14 percent of all whites living in the island had been born in Cuba but were considered foreign citizens. These were mainly the Cuban offspring of Spanish immigrants, who kept the citizenship of their parents. By 1943 their proportion had declined to a negligible 0.1 percent. Since access to jobs was increasingly difficult for foreign citizens, many of these Cuban-born "Spaniards" had become Cuban citizens during the decade. Furthermore, the 1940 constitution endorsed the principle of *ius solis* and considered as Cuban any person born in the island. By 1943 the proportion of foreigners in the total population was the lowest since the beginning of the republic, only to decline even further thereafter. Cuba would never open its doors again and could be considered, as an analyst stated in 1955, "sealed off to any important amount of immigration." Rather, after the 1940s whenever the doors were opened it was to let Cubans emigrate, mainly to the United States.[19]

THE "FIRST VICTIMS" OF *LATIFUNDIA*

Foreign sugar interests not only succeeded in opening the country's doors to the immigration of contract labor but also controlled a growing share of productive lands and other resources. They owned 15–20 percent of the national territory by the mid-1920s.[20]

U.S. investors were the main beneficiaries of this process. Between 1899 and 1905 some 13,000 U.S. corporations and individual investors acquired about 60 percent of all rural properties in Cuba. This process was particularly intense in the province of Oriente, where the total number of farms declined 50 percent, from 21,550 to 10,854. In some municipalities, such as San Luis and Alto Songo, the process of land concentration was even more acute, with the number of independent farms declining 70–90 percent.[21]

TABLE 3.1. Percentage Distribution, Land Ownership, by Race, 1899–1931

Category	Number of Farms		Total Farmland	
	1899	1931	1899	1931
Whites	75.3	88.4	84.0	91.5
Owners	24.0	37.1	33.3	45.6
Renters	51.3	51.4	50.7	45.9
Blacks	24.7	11.6	16.0	8.5
Owners	5.3	5.1	3.7	4.4
Renters	19.4	6.5	12.3	4.1

Sources: U.S. War Department, *Report 1899*, 555; Cuba, *Censo 1931*, table 37.
Note: Black includes mulattoes.

This trend affected all Cubans, but it was particularly harmful to Afro-Cubans. Especially in Oriente, there was a good chance that each acre acquired by foreign investors and devoted to sugar production represented an acre lost to Afro-Cubans' subsistence and independent farming. In 1899, blacks controlled 25 percent of the total number of farms in the island as owners or renters, but in Oriente they controlled a much higher proportion: 43 percent. Afro-Cubans controlled 48 percent of the land devoted to rice production in the province, 59 percent of coffee, 61 percent of cocoa, and 61 percent of malanga. "The Cuban negro has a marked trait in the instinct of land ownership," an American observer remarked in 1899. Some of the southeastern municipalities in which the process of land dispossession was more intense were also those with the island's highest proportion of Afro-Cubans. Sugar expansion took place in the northern area of Oriente as well, but population densities were significantly lower there.[22]

The long-term effects of this process can be summarized in just a few words: the proletarianization of the Afro-Cuban peasantry, particularly in the east. Between 1899 and 1931 blacks' control over land decreased 50 percent both in terms of the number of farms and the total farmland (table 3.1). By 1931 Afro-Cubans represented approximately 28 percent of the total population but controlled only 8.5 percent of the farmland in the country. No wonder Ramiro Guerra stated in 1929 that blacks had been "the first victims" of sugar *latifundia*. The proportion of black ownership, however, had remained stagnant: those who suffered the most had been the so-called renters, who in many cases had lived and farmed public and other lands of dubious ownership. In 1946, when sociologist Lowry Nelson conducted his rural survey of Cuba, he estimated that 51 percent of the "Negro" rural workers were wage workers, compared to 22 percent of whites. Nationally, according to the National Agriculture Census (1946), wage workers represented 57 percent of the rural labor force. In the sugar-producing region of Camagüey, they represented a staggering 77 percent.[23]

Even for wage workers, employment opportunities were restricted in the countryside. It was estimated that blacks represented about 50 percent of the labor force on the sugar plantations by 1899, but employers frequently asserted that they were almost useless for any productive activity except cane cutting. "Only in the cutting of cane can the Cuban, and especially the Cuban negro, be said to excel. This work he understands and finds congenial." Another observer concurred: "Admittedly the black does not do well at fruit-raising, and the intricacy of tobacco cultivation is too great for him to become a successful veguero, or tobacco farmer. In the cane fields he is at his best as a laborer."[24]

Given their prejudices against blacks, employers hired Afro-Cubans mainly as cane cutters, but they restricted their access to the industrial sector. The number of black cane cutters was especially high in the provinces of Matanzas and Las Villas, where the proportion of native workers in the harvest was much higher than in the east. After the 1910s, when the modern sugar *centrales* of Camagüey and Oriente managed to flood the labor market with a massive importation of cheap labor from the Antilles, employment opportunities for native workers decreased. Seasonal migrant laborers from Spain were also employed during the sugar harvest in Las Villas and Matanzas, but their proportion in the total labor force seems to have been lower.[25] Nevertheless, foreign whites steadily increased their representation in the agriculture and mining sectors (see table 3.3 below), and growing numbers of them were employed in these activities. In 1899, 27 percent of foreign whites (most of them Spaniards) with a gainful occupation were employed in agriculture and mining, and the proportion had increased to 37 percent by 1931. In this sense, the world of sugar agriculture was (as it had been since colonial times) a multiracial and multiethnic world in which native whites and Afro-Cubans, Spaniards, West Indians, Chinese, and others worked together. Luis Felipe Rodríguez re-creates this multiracial world of cane in his story "La Guardarraya," written in the 1930s, in which the labor force is composed of Haitians, Jamaicans, Spaniards, Puerto Ricans, Dominicans, and Cubans.[26] After the 1930s, with the drive toward the nationalization of labor, Afro-Cubans' participation in cane cutting increased, especially in the western part of the island, where the harvest was "almost entirely done by natives." In 1938 about 60 percent of the labor force devoted to cane cutting in the province of Matanzas was composed of native blacks and mulattoes.[27]

The industrial and administrative sides of sugar production were much whiter, in part because foreigners were better represented in these better-paid positions. In 1925, 62 percent of the members of the board of directors of sugar mills in the island were foreigners. This proportion decreased among lower white-collar employees, but still 37 percent of them were non-Cubans. About the same period, all of the thirty managers and "upper employees" of the Morón, Senado, and Adelaida sugar mills in the province of Camagüey were white. As the CNOC denounced in 1934, thousands of Afro-Cubans worked as cane cutters, but their proportions declined significantly in more skilled and better-paid occupations. The higher the salary, the lower the presence of blacks, the CNOC concluded.[28]

The facts are scarce, but it seems safe to state that a large proportion of the labor force employed in the manufacturing side of sugar was white and that Afro-Cubans' opportunities to enter these positions were limited at best. A sugar factory superintendent commented in 1901: "We employ only Spaniards. They equal in industry and endurance American workingmen. . . . I have had more than twenty years experience in Cuba as a factory and plantation manager, and have seldom found native Cubans efficient in occupations requiring physical endurance or personal skill."[29] In central Soledad, blacks seem to have been regularly excluded from work at the mill.[30] A 1934 consular report also describes the ethnic and racial divisions introduced by employers in sugar-related jobs in Camagüey: "The cane cutters have been Haitians and other black West Indians. . . . The haulers, weighers and foremen are usually Cubans, and the mill employees, railroad section hands, etc., are mostly Spaniards."[31] According to census data, "foreign whites" were overrepresented in sugar-manufacturing-related occupations. Of the "mechanics," 20 percent were foreign in 1907, 22 percent in 1919. Afro-Cubans, conversely, were significantly underrepresented.

Racial barriers to accessing the most skilled occupations in the industry persisted through the end of the republic. According to Conrado Becquer, a union leader who became general secretary of the National Federation of Sugar Workers, as late as the 1940s and 1950s blacks were excluded from the most skilled positions within the industry, regardless of their experience or ability. "I recall the case of a mulatto," he stated, "who was in charge of grinding and knew the mill from top to bottom. He was not appointed machine operator until after the triumph of the revolution—the Americans did not accept having blacks in positions of command. Things like this happened in the whole industry." Furthermore, U.S.-owned mills maintained racially segregated facilities (barber shops, housing), in the style of the U.S. South.[32]

Foreign labor was even more important in the mining sector. According to the 1907 census, 94 percent of all miners were white foreigners. Although this proportion had declined substantially by 1919 (to 54 percent), it was still well above their proportion in the working-age population (15 percent). The Spanish American Iron Company had used immigrant labor since the late nineteenth century, and it imported 400 laborers from Spain to work in its mines in 1900. In fact, the company maintained a labor agent in Spain. If the nationality of the workers treated in the company's hospital is accepted as a fair indicator of their national composition, then the presence of Spanish miners was overwhelming: 82 percent of the 4,811 workers registered in the hospital (1901–3) were Spaniards, 15 percent were Puerto Ricans, and less than 2 percent were Cubans. Industrial analyst Victor Clark confirmed that, in Oriente, the mining companies imported "much of their labor from Spain." The employers' preferences for immigrant workers were also evident in the Matahambre copper mines in Pinar del Río: "Work underground is performed by Spaniards. Cooking, laundering, etc., are done by Chinese nationals. Cubans . . . cannot be depended on to work steadily."[33]

By the mid-1920s job opportunities and land availability in the countryside were becoming increasingly limited. The process of sugar expansion had reached its limit, and no new mills were built after 1925, when Cuba's sugar production surpassed five million tons for the first time. The foreign-owned sugar *latifundia* had consolidated in the eastern provinces of the island, to the detriment of native small landholders. Sugar prices tended to decline throughout the 1920s, so the mills increasingly turned to cheap imported labor in an effort to reduce costs, further reducing employment opportunities for native workers. "[I]f there are few native Negroes among the peasantry," Afro-Cuban Communist activist Pérez Medina denounced in the early 1930s, "it is because they have been obliged to take refuge in the cities on account of the competition in cheap labour and resistance to poor living conditions." Furthermore, in an attempt to check the decline of prices, a policy of restricted harvests was implemented, and the number of mills in operation actually decreased during the late 1920s. Out of 176 *centrales* producing sugar in 1926, only 135 were in operation in 1933.[34]

Not only were fewer employment opportunities being generated by the sugar industry, but existing jobs were available for a decreasing period of time. During the 1920s the length of the sugar harvest shortened, with the consequent growth of the so-called dead season. According to figures from the United Fruit Company, between 1920 and 1924 the *zafra* was reduced from 249 to 151 days and by 1928 had declined even further to 125 days. Consequently, the dead season, during which a large proportion of the cane cutters became unemployed, doubled. By 1928 sugar workers were out of work for about two-thirds of the year. Planters themselves asserted that in bad years only 20 percent of the regular work of industrial repair and field preparation was done before the harvest. An official of the American Central Hormiguero in Las Villas declared that the mill employed 600 field workers during the crop season and only 50 during the dead season. In the manufacturing sector, including the mill, railroad, shops, and other services, about two-thirds of the labor force became unemployed once the *zafra* was over. Central Soledad employed 350 men in these departments during the harvest but retained only 120 for the rest of the year. "Only those employees of an official or semi-official character remained." In all, well-informed sources estimated that about 90 percent of the labor force became idle during the dead season.[35]

Afro-Cubans' choices in the countryside were limited, to say the least. The aggressive land policies of U.S. investors, combined with the insolvency of national owners, tended to proletarianize natives. Afro-Cubans' prominent presence in subsistence agriculture in the eastern part of the island meant that they were the main victims of land dispossession in Oriente, where this process was particularly intense. But for blacks to lose their land was only the beginning. At the same time, the massive importation of laborers from Spain and, after the 1910s, the West Indies severely limited employment opportunities in the rural areas. The new landless proletarians had to compete with the Antilleans, considered by many employers as "ideal" workers for cane cutting, and with the Europeans for better-paid and more skilled occupations.[36] Afro-Cubans then had little choice but to seek better opportunities elsewhere.

URBANIZATION

The destination was the city. In 1899, urbanization rates for whites and blacks were almost equal in Cuba. Forty years later, 44 percent of Afro-Cubans lived in urban centers with a population of at least five thousand, compared to 37 percent of whites, for a black/white ratio of urban residence of 1.18 (see table 3.2).[37]

The process of urbanization occurred in phases. Between 1899 and 1907

TABLE 3.2. Ratio of Percentage of Black and White Residents in Urban Centers (5,000 or More), by Province, 1899–1943

Province	1899	1907	1919	1931	1943
Cuba	1.02	1.04	1.04	1.09	1.18
P. Río	1.34	1.50	1.45	1.40	1.21
Havana	1.19	1.19	1.21	1.23	1.23
Matanzas	0.78	0.85	1.19	1.36	1.43
Las Villas	1.36	1.42	1.73	1.89	1.74
Camagüey	1.68	1.61	1.33	0.87	1.11
Oriente	1.32	1.18	1.13	1.18	1.38

Sources: U.S. War Department, *Report 1899*, 194–99; Cuba, *Censo 1907*, 314–19; Cuba, *Censo 1919*; Cuba, *Censo 1931*, table 6; Cuba, *Informe Censo 1943*.
Note: Black includes mulattoes.

the percentage of urban residents actually declined from 47 to 44 percent. Although this decrease was basically a white phenomenon (the proportion of Afro-Cubans living in urban centers increased slightly), it is evident that the Cuban countryside attracted a large number of settlers in the immediate postwar period. The initial recovery of sugar and agriculture produced this trend. In the eastern provinces of Camagüey and Oriente, the black/white ratios of urban residence declined, although it is important to note that after 1907 this result was greatly influenced by the massive introduction of Antilleans to the region. Conversely, in the old sugar-producing areas of Matanzas and Las Villas, where the Antillean presence was negligible, a growing proportion of blacks moved to the urban centers compared to whites. In 1899 Havana was already a preferred destination for Afro-Cubans. Of the province's blacks, 67 percent lived in the city and its surroundings (Marianao, Guanabacoa), compared to 56 percent of whites. When Esteban Montejo visited the city around 1898, he expressed surprise at finding such a large black population in Havana—"Wherever you looked there was a black," he asserted.[38]

It was in the 1920s, however, that both the urbanization process in general and the race differential in urbanization rates in particular accelerated. Between 1919 and 1931 the percentage of residents in urban centers of five thousand or more jumped from 30 to 37 percent. Whites' proportion increased 6 percent (from 30 to 36 percent), while that of Afro-Cubans increased 8 percent (from 31 to 39 percent). A contemporary observer theorized that these figures were a clear indication of what he called an interesting trend: "that of the colored population to concentrate where economic opportunity is less abundant and more primitive. This concentration in the cities is really an indication of their relative poverty and dependence upon manual and casual labor."[39] Urbanization was indeed an indication of Afro-Cuban "poverty," but it can hardly be argued that employment opportunities were "more primitive" in the urban centers.

On the contrary, the acceleration of urbanization and Afro-Cubans' increasing migration to the cities was explained not only by land dispossession but also by the city's power of attraction. As in the United States, urban migration opened opportunities for better employment and the possibility to access social services—notably education—that were not available in the countryside.[40] Stimulated by the sugar export boom, manufacturing, trade, transportation, and the public sector experienced a significant expansion in the 1910s and 1920s. Between 1907 and 1919 the manufacturing sector generated 62,923 new jobs, all of them located in urban centers. This represented a 51 percent increase, compared to a 28 percent increase of the working-age population in the island. Light manufacturing, such as cement, paper, shoes, soap, perfume, liquors, and clothing, developed around Havana and other cities. Although expanding at a slower rate than the population, the trade and transportation sectors grew 25 percent in the 1920s, while manufacturing increased 14 percent, due largely to protectionist tariffs introduced by the Cuban government during the decade (the Tariff Reform of 1927). In the mid-1920s it was estimated that about seventy new industries had been established in the island. The public sector, however, grew at record rates. Between 1899 and 1931 it increased 8.5 times, generating 44,315 new positions (including jobs within the army and the police). During the same period, the only sector that grew at a faster rate was that of professional services, also related to the urban world.[41]

The Great Depression stimulated further movement to the cities. The elimination of the importation of Antillean laborers and their gradual expulsion from the country opened up new opportunities for native workers, but in the early 1930s the zafras became even shorter. The harvest of 1933 lasted only fifty days. Meanwhile, news of movements of unemployed farm laborers to the urban centers were reported with alarm. "[U]nconfirmed reports have appeared in the press to the effect that bands of hungry countrymen are marching toward the cities in search of food and employment," stated a U.S. official in Havana. "Working people have been discharged from the mills and the fields and are making their way into the towns," commented Ambassador Guggenheim.[42]

But during the Depression the situation in the urban centers was no better than in the countryside. The collapse of sugar exports was felt in all other areas of the economy. National per capita income declined about 60 percent between 1920 and 1933.[43] Manufacturing and other urban activities had expanded during the decade, but population had grown faster. In an effort to secure a stable labor supply and to soften the social tensions generated by this situation, an increasing number of mills allowed part of their labor force to produce subsistence staples during the long dead season. The measure had been urged by the secretary of agriculture as a way to cope with "the usual seasonal fear . . . that these unemployed harvest hands may invade the cities." To forestall migration, the government also appropriated a small sum to distribute seeds among rural workers.[44]

The movement to the cities continued during the 1930s, though at a slower pace than in the previous decade. The trend toward an increasing racial differentiation in the rates of urbanization also continued. Between 1931 and 1943 the proportion of whites living in urban centers increased from 36 to 37 percent, but that of Afro-Cubans grew 5 percent: from 39 percent in 1931 to 44 percent in 1943. Consequently, the ratio of blacks to whites living in urban centers had expanded significantly by 1943 (table 3.2). Due to the shorter *zafras*, unemployment and "surplus" labor became structural features of the Cuban economy, especially during the long dead seasons. Conversely, opportunities in the cities were brighter: the manufacturing sector recovered slowly but steadily after 1934 and generated about sixty thousand new jobs during the decade. Significant growth was experienced also by commerce, transportation, professional services, and the public sector.[45]

World War II created a new cycle of prosperity. Import substitution and industrial diversification were encouraged, with a growing interventionism of the Cuban state in the economy and other areas of national life. Under protectionist tariffs, manufacturing expanded, and more than 100,000 new jobs were created in this sector during the 1940s and early 1950s. A 1945 law of "industrial promotion" authorized the free importation of machinery, and the Bank of Agricultural and Industrial Development was created in 1950 to stimulate investments in sectors other than sugar. Economist Jorge Pérez-López estimates that manufacturing output doubled between 1940 and 1950, and it had increased an additional 40 percent by 1957. Most of this industrial capacity was installed in Havana, where one-fifth of the total population lived by 1953. Other sectors, such as professional and personal services, commerce, and transportation, also expanded at a faster rate than the working-age population. In addition, new jobs were created by the booming tourist sector, which more than doubled in terms of visitors between 1946 and 1954. Finally, the growth of the public sector was again the largest in relative terms: by 1953 about 9 percent of the Cuban working population held government jobs.[46]

Migration to the urban centers created acute housing problems, especially in the case of Havana. Since the early republican period, the inadequacy of workers' housing and the existence of the so-called *solares*, *ciudadelas*, and *casas de vecindad* (tenement houses—usually old colonial mansions inhabited by numerous low-income families) were subjects frequently addressed in public discourse and political propaganda. In 1904 it was estimated that 2,839 *casas de vecindad* existed in Havana and that about one-third of the city's population, including "people of all classes, conditions, ages and races," inhabited them.[47]

The housing situation deteriorated in the late 1920s and early 1930s, when the sugar collapse drove large numbers of peasants into the cities. Added to the old *solares* and *ciudadelas*, dispersed throughout the city, were slums on the outskirts of the capital. These poverty-stricken neighborhoods grew significantly during the post-Depression period. In 1951 there were twenty-one such neighborhoods in Havana, with a population that varied between 40,000 and 50,000. An estimated 200,000 additional people lived in the *solares* and *casas de vecindad*, so about one-third of the city's population lived in conditions of extreme poverty.[48]

Both the slums and the urban *solares* were frequently inhabited by individuals of all colors, but blacks and mulattoes seem to have been greatly over-represented in this population. Although the concentration of Afro-Cubans in the slums can be explained in part by their higher rates of urbanization, the identification of *solares* as black spaces was a construct aimed at excluding the poorest from the city's geography and society, a cultural validation of social hierarchies. In the mainstream press, the slums were linked to marginality, crime, and promiscuity—attributes frequently used to characterize blackness. Regardless of skin pigmentation, residents of slums and *solares* were socially identified with blackness. In his magnificent short story "La luna de los ñáñigos" (1932), Lino Novás Calvo describes the transformation of Garrida, a white maid who lives in a *solar*, into a black woman. Garrida not only becomes "all but black inside" while living in the shantytown but also accomplishes the ultimate miracle of dancing among "Negroes" without being noticed. "Only the devil," an old Afro-Cuban resident of the *solar* remarks later, "could have painted her black during the dance." Sharing the *solar's* social and cultural spaces had turned Garrida into a black woman. In 1948, David W. Ames, an American scholar who conducted field research in Cuba, defined "solares" as "the term . . . which is now used in Havana to denote Negro tenement houses." Ames studied a *solar* located in the periphery of the residential district of Vedado and found that 69 percent of the residents were what he labeled "Negro."[49] Other sources refer to an even larger Afro-Cuban percentage. Juan Chailloux, who surveyed fifty *solares* in Havana in the mid-1940s, found that a staggering 95.7 percent of the tenants were black or mulatto and that frequently the *solares* were all-black. His results coincided with the 97.5 percent estimate made by the National Convention of Cuban Societies of the Colored Race in 1936.[50] It is apparent why Afro-Cuban intellectuals had devoted systematic attention to the housing problem since the early years of the republic.[51]

In the final analysis, the solution to the slums and to the movement of the population to the cities lay in the countryside, where a highly concentrated rural structure had prevented the formation of a stable peasantry. As Afro-Cuban journalist Benjamín Muñoz stated in 1929, the only real alternative to accelerated urbanization was land: "Land! Cheap land for Cuban farmers!"[52] Land never became available, so it was in the cities that a growing proportion of Afro-Cubans had to work and live.

BETWEEN TWO EVILS

Inadequate housing was far from being the only problem faced by Afro-Cubans in the cities. Although employment opportunities were more diverse and in many cases more lucrative in the urban centers, getting access to them was not an easy task. Afro-Cubans had to compete for available positions not only with white Cubans but also with a large contingent of European (mostly Spanish) immigrants, many of whom, to the dismay of the sugar planters, stayed in Havana and other major cities. Afro-Cubans were, in Muñoz's words, "between two great evils: foreigners in the cities and foreigners in the countryside."[53]

The white immigrants were indeed well represented in the urban occupational structure, both because of their concentration in productive ages and because of the large proportion of men among them. Between 1899 and 1919, the rates of economic activity of this segment of the population were about double those of the general population. In the 1907−19 period they made up 15 percent of the working-age population but controlled 21 percent of the available jobs, and their share was even higher in the urban occupations.

Table 3.3 summarizes the evolution of the participation of each group

TABLE 3-3. Index of Participation, Economic Sectors and Occupations, by Race and Nativity, 1899–1943

Category	1899			1907			1919			1931			1943		
	NW	FW	B	NW	FW	B	NW	FW	B	NW	FW	B	NW	FW	B
Agriculture, fishery, mining	105	76	101	104	93	96	100	97	102	103	75	110	103	101	92
Trade and transportation	70	389	29	80	314	32	83	268	45	84	208	62	103	234	68
Merchants	74	393	22	73	350	28	73	319	37	78	241	53	84	450	82
Railroad and tramway	91	324	22	58	380	39	121	104	57	90	170	75	97	0	125
Telephone, telegraph	135	207	1	159	78	4	151	50	27	141	100	23	127	36	34
Manufacturing	81	115	124	75	118	137	71	131	140	75	115	138	83	110	147
Carpenters	68	142	133	65	144	142	65	137	149	63	101	169	67	121	188
Masons	34	100	205	39	147	187	45	134	188	50	105	191	59	125	212
Mechanics	127	137	42	111	133	64	92	145	92	92	104	122	—	—	—
Shoemakers	55	121	163	55	121	170	53	102	191	58	129	160	67	127	187
Tailors	35	185	168	33	155	194	36	156	196	—	—	—	48	204	228
Cigar factories	102	84	104	99	51	125	94	46	140	94	60	136	85	27	155
Professional service	129	186	19	129	144	26	131	97	40	128	100	48	110	186	58
Lawyers	166	89	1	161	79	1	160	52	8	165	14	32	123	35	48
Bookkeepers	120	263	2	110	253	8	—	—	—	—	—	—	116	103	55
Dentists	148	99	25	137	100	34	148	59	28	159	38	28	119	36	58
Nurses	53	395	54	93	260	36	99	171	64	125	131	33	122	192	21
Pharmacists	157	66	7	163	38	19	128	62	28	—	—	—	—	—	—
Civil engineers	97	308	20	105	275	6	119	196	12	130	139	18	117	309	17
Teachers	142	156	11	144	94	24	133	95	39	140	60	49	106	99	82
Physicians	154	130	2	160	80	2	146	87	17	164	23	27	125	50	38
Personal service	63	119	151	53	125	173	69	149	135	85	145	101	66	155	187
Government	115	178	45	115	121	63	132	43	67	138	25	76	114	13	77
Officials, employees	132	194	11	112	224	18	150	37	37	138	29	74	114	21	76
Army, police	113	176	48	115	118	64	121	48	88	138	19	80	114	0	78
No occupation	120	40	93	118	38	98	115	51	96	104	94	96	94	113	115

Sources: U.S. War Department, *Report 1899*, 438–39, 462–63; Cuba, *Censo 1907*, 514–15, 545–46; Cuba, *Censo 1919*, 632–33, 666–67; Cuba, *Censo 1931*, tables 16, 21, 24; Cuba, *Censo 1943*, 1042, 1056, 1112.
Note: NW: native whites; FW: foreign whites; B: blacks (includes natives and foreigners). Index: percentage in each category divided by the percentage of the group in the working population (1899, 1907, and 1919: 15 years and over; 1931 and 1943: 14 years and over).

(native whites, foreign whites, and blacks) in the occupational structure for the 1899–1943 period. As mentioned above, white immigrant workers were underrepresented in agriculture, but their participation in the sector increased steadily from 1899 to 1919. Blacks' index, conversely, declined initially (between 1899 and 1907) but increased thereafter due to the growing West Indian population. In the 1930s, when the traffic in Antilleans ceased and a large number of them were expelled from the island, blacks' participation in agriculture declined again.

Not only were commerce and transportation foreign-owned sectors of economic activity, but access to them was rather limited for Cuban workers, especially for Afro-Cubans. Indeed, Spaniards' indices of representation in this group were the highest in the whole occupational structure. Of all merchants, 54 percent were foreigners (mostly Spaniards) in 1899. This proportion had declined by 1931 (to 43 percent), but it was still well above their share of the working population. Spaniards controlled, for instance, 59 percent of the wholesale trade in the province of Las Villas in the late 1930s and some 60 percent of all mercantile establishments in the city of Matanzas.[54] Conversely, Afro-Cubans were vastly underrepresented in this privileged sector of the labor market, although their proportional participation more than doubled between 1899 and 1931. Indeed, the first issue addressed by Gustavo Urrutia in his column *Ideales de una raza* was the "participation of blacks in commerce."[55] By 1943 their index of participation was moving closer to the ideal and was virtually identical to that of native whites, whose share in this activity had slowly increased throughout the republican period.[56]

Conditions for Afro-Cuban women were worse than for men or white women. In 1919, women of all colors represented a meager 2 percent of the labor force employed in "trade and transportation," and Afro-Cuban women occupied only 11 percent of those jobs. The result is that fewer than four hundred black women found employment in stores and other commercial establishments throughout the island. This "painful reality," as Urrutia called it, had not improved by 1931. The proportion of women employed in the commercial sector had not changed, and Afro-Cubans' share was virtually the same: 12 percent. The Communist-oriented Federación Democrática de Mujeres Cubanas (FDMC, Democratic Federation of Cuban Women) consistently denounced the exclusion of black women from trade-related occupations, noting that although retail trade generated thousands of jobs, blacks in general, and black women in particular, were never hired. The most fashionable department stores rarely employed black women, and when they did, it was in positions in which these women had little or no contact with the public. It was not until 1951 that mulatto women were hired for the first time to work in some of Havana's upscale stores, such as El Encanto, Fin de Siglo, and La Filosofía.[57]

The way these women got access to the Havana department stores is in itself an excellent example of the barriers they faced in this sector of the economy. They were hired only after Carlos Prío, the president of the republic, personally intervened on their behalf. Under pressure from the Frente Cívico Cubano, a black middle-class organization that sought to increase Afro-Cuban representation in better-paid occupations, President Prío approved a decree condemning racial discrimination, also devised as a response to the Communists' repeated attempts to pass an antidiscrimination law in Congress. The president and his minister of labor met in private with representatives of Havana's commercial houses, encouraging them to hire a number of "black" women in their stores.[58]

In the end, four women began working in El Encanto on December 1, 1951, and three more were hired by Fin de Siglo and La Filosofía. Four additional women were supposed to join them some time during the month, when extra employees were needed for the Christmas season. All the women hired were light-skinned ("mulatas," in Cuban racial terminology) and had been recommended by public figures or institutions, including journalists, famous baseball players, and the president himself. They all had high school degrees—one from a U.S. high school, another from a secretarial academy—and three were attending the university, where they studied pharmacy, pedagogy, and medicine. And still these highly educated women considered it a privilege and a triumph to be offered positions as store clerks. The event was praised by the mainstream press as a clear sign of Cuba's racial fraternity, and Labor Minister Buttari went so far as to say that there was no racial discrimination in Cuba. White politician and journalist Sergio Carbó commented: "The secret of this success consists in having chosen girls who are refined, cultured, and gentle . . . which demonstrates that there is not, in reality, racial prejudice. What there is, and there will always be, is prejudice of education." A month later, however, the Communist daily *Hoy* was among the few to note that after the Christmas season all of these women were removed from their positions.[59]

Trade was not the only area in which blacks found limited employment opportunities. Afro-Cubans were also poorly represented in transportation and communication. Transportation, which included urban tramways and the extensive railroad network that covered the island, shared with commerce a major trait: a massive foreign presence. Arredondo estimated that more than 80 percent of the railways were controlled by foreign capital and that immigrant workers were vastly overrepresented in their labor force, especially during the first decade of the republic (see table 3.3). Blacks found it hard to enter some better-paid fields, such as that of locomotive engineers, whose union exercised a tight control over the system of promotion. In fact, the first black engineer secured this job in 1901 thanks to a conflict between the company and the engineers' union.[60] "Those familiar with the labor movement in Cuba know that a member of the colored race cannot be a conductor in the railways," Communist leader César Vilar asserted in 1940. Access to white-collar positions within the sector was even more difficult: all office work was performed by white workers. Nicolás Guillén, the great mulatto poet and writer, recounted that in the 1920s he had tried to obtain a "modest position" in the offices of the railroad in Camagüey with no success: "[T]hat company has many black employees, but only in the mechanical shops."[61]

In the cities, the U.S.-owned tramway companies controlled 98 percent of the market in terms of the number of passengers carried, and they generated 97 percent of the jobs in the sector. That they discriminated against native workers is clearly suggested by the fact that by the mid-1920s only 44 percent of their total labor force was native, compared to 89 percent in the small Cuban-owned companies. This underrepresentation occurred not only in the higher echelons of the company, in which only 32 percent of the employees were Cubans, but also at the lower end: native workers represented a meager 34 percent of the craftsmen and laborers employed by Havana Electric and other American companies.[62]

Afro-Cubans steadily increased their representation in transportation-related jobs in the 1899–1931 period (table 3.3), but some specific occupations were closed to them altogether. It was not until 1947, for instance, that the first black tramway conductor was seen in the streets of Havana. The promotion of Marino Peña, a black worker for Havana Electric, to such a position was made possible by the combined efforts of the Communist union and the related Tramway Committee against Discrimination, which sought to promote blacks to more lucrative jobs within the company. The symbolic importance of breaking whites' traditional monopoly in this and other jobs was not trivial: an anonymous communication received by the U.S. Embassy in Havana predicted that incidents of this kind would cause nothing less than a Communist-inspired racial war in the country. The Communist labor movement indeed hailed the measure, not only because it represented a concrete step against racial discrimination but also because it had been imposed on an "imperialist" company that was well known for its discriminatory conduct.[63]

Black organizations also cheered the accomplishment, but they said that a single case was merely an exception and that similar steps should be taken in other public utility companies, such as the Cuban Telephone Company, which often discriminated against Afro-Cubans.[64] Their criticism was valid. Blacks' participation in the telephone industry was minimal throughout the whole republican period and was still very low in 1943, despite the fact that foreign workers were also underrepresented (table 3.3). In 1943, phone companies hired Afro-Cubans in a proportion that was two-thirds below their share in the working population. Although in absolute numbers this sector was not a significant source of employment (it usually employed fewer than 2,000 people), women represented about 40 percent of the industry's labor force, so educated black women were the main victims of these discriminatory practices. A simple glance at *Unidad*, the official organ of the Federation of Telephone Workers of Cuba, shows that the situation had not changed by the late 1940s and early 1950s: the sector was still overwhelmingly white.[65]

Competition for employment opportunities occurred also in more massive and less attractive sectors of the urban labor market. As table 3.3 shows, between 1899 and 1919 white immigrant workers increased their participation in manufacturing activities and personal services, which were traditional Afro-Cuban sectors. Referring to blacks' participation in manufacturing, Pepper commented in 1899 that they made up 20–25 percent of the cigarmakers and worked "at the same bench with whites" with equal pay, and that similar conditions prevailed in the shoe shops, tanneries, and building trades.[66] Despite competition from immigrants, Afro-Cubans' indices of participation in the manufacturing sector increased almost without interruption until the 1940s. Behind this trend was the proletarianization of both the black peasantry and urban artisans who could not compete with the massive importation of cheap manufactured products, especially from the United States.[67] At the same time, the expansion of manufacturing allowed increasing numbers of immigrants as well as Afro-Cubans to find employment in the factories. Native whites were the only group whose index of participation declined in the 1899–1919 period.

Manufacturing provided opportunities for employment, but access to better-paid positions was again restricted. If indicators other than participation in the broad manufacturing sector are used, the patterns of racial inequality begin to appear. Blacks represented, for instance, a sizable and growing proportion of the labor force employed in the tobacco industry, but they were disadvantaged in at least two respects. First, their presence was much more prominent in cigar than in cigarette factories, in which salaries were, on average, 30 percent higher. Second, even within the cigar industry Afro-Cubans were concentrated in the worst-paid and least-attractive positions. In the mid-1920s they formed 30 percent of the labor force employed in cigar factories, in which the average yearly salary was 714 pesos, but only 4 percent in cigarette factories, in which the average salary was 935 pesos. Not surprisingly, the distribution of Spanish immigrant workers was exactly the opposite: they made up only 10 percent of the workers in the former industry and 19 percent in the latter. Within cigar production Afro-Cubans made up one-third of the worst-paid cigar-makers but were heavily underrepresented among salesmen, clerks, drivers, and other employees. Conversely, foreigners occupied 52 percent of these better-paid positions. According to Vilar, this situation had not changed significantly by 1940, although at that point the Spanish workers had become naturalized and were considered Cubans for all legal and practical purposes. The tobacco industry, then, replicated the pattern found in the sugar industry: blacks were employed in the sector, but they were kept within the less attractive, worst-paid positions.[68]

This was also true in other areas of production in which a foreign presence was prominent. Immigrant workers represented an already high 30 percent of the labor force employed in the alcohol distilleries, but their share of the better-paid positions was much higher. Fifty percent of the technicians, 40 percent of the factories' directors, 39 percent of the managers, 43 percent of the chemists, and 42 percent of office workers were foreign. Conversely, their proportion in activities such as packing (23 percent) or the unskilled labor force (25 percent) was much lower. Even in the province of Oriente, where immigrants represented only 11 percent of the total labor force in the distilleries, 60 percent of the technicians, 50 percent of the chemists, 42 percent of the directors, and 27 percent of the managers were foreign.[69] No wonder Afro-Cubans identified Spaniards as one of the leading causes of their displacement from attractive jobs. A young Afro-Cuban who went to Havana to study in 1916 commented that it was extremely difficult to find a job in any trade because the shops were full of white workers, "most of them from other lands." He continued, "Formerly, mason and cigar-maker were synonyms for Cuban. Not today; most construction in Havana is done by Catalan masons, and . . . large numbers of Spaniards work in the tobacco factories." The Afro-Cuban journal *Labor Nueva* was categorical: Spanish immigration was harmful not only to Afro-Cubans but also to all native workers.[70]

Things were no better at the lowest end of the labor market, the "personal services" sector, in which many Afro-Cuban women found employment. Immigrant workers' index of participation in these activities increased steadily during the 1899–1943 period, especially during the second decade of the century (1907–19), when the annual immigration of Spaniards reached its highest point. "How much have many Cuban women who were formerly domestic servants suffered . . . since Spanish women began . . . to dedicate themselves to those tasks?" a black journalist demanded in 1916. White immigrants made up 18 percent of all female servants in 1919, but they represented only 8 percent of the female working-age population (15 years and over), so their index of participation was 226, higher than black women's 186. And the last figure includes an unspecified number of West Indian female immigrants, for censuses grouped native and foreign-born blacks in a single category. American families, in particular, preferred Jamaican and other English-speaking servants. Advertisements in the local American press often made explicit that Jamaican houseworkers, and not others, would be hired. In other cases it was Afro-Cuban women who were explicitly excluded.[71]

Spanish female immigrants entered other sectors and activities in which Afro-Cuban women had traditionally found employment opportunities, such as manufacturing. In 1899 black women represented 55 percent of the female labor force employed in manufacturing. Thirty years later their proportion, although still above their share in the working-age population, had declined to 40 percent. Native whites' relative participation had remained basically stagnant (rising from 42 to 44 percent): those who had increased their share in manufacturing were the "white foreign" females, whose percentage had jumped from 3 percent in 1899 to 16 percent in 1931.[72] The immigrants' growing participation in the labor market, combined with the economic stagnation of the late 1920s and early 1930s, had a tremendous impact on black women's overall activity rate, which in 1931 (6.5 percent) was just a fraction of what it had been in 1899 (23 percent). Doubtless, many more than 6 percent of black women worked in 1931, but they increasingly did so in occupations that escaped the statistical efforts of the Cuban state. It is easy to imagine how the census would consider "without gainful occupation" someone such as "La Larga" (literally, the Long One), a black female character in Jesús Masdeu's La raza triste. In the novel, La Larga is formally unemployed but actually distributes her time between two different activities: laundering and prostitution. The household receives additional resources through her two (also formally unemployed) daughters: one has been "rented" to babysit a white boy; the other is a prostitute.[73]

The immigrant workers' presence alone does not explain Afro-Cubans'

TABLE 3.4. Index of Dissimilarity in Occupations, by Race and Nativity, 1899–1943

Category	1899	1907	1919	1931	1943
Native whites/foreign whites	31.1	27.4	22.8	25.5	16.9
Blacks/foreign whites	35.4	34.8	24.8	23.5	18.3
Blacks/native whites	20.2	25.2	17.6	9.8	17.5

Sources: U.S. War Department, *Report 1899*, 438–39, 462–63; Cuba, *Censo 1907*, 514–15, 545–46; Cuba, *Censo 1919*, 632–33, 666–67; Cuba, *Censo 1931*, tables 16, 21, 24; Cuba, *Censo 1943*, 1042, 1056, 1112.

---

concentration in the less attractive sectors and activities of the Cuban economy. In addition to their lack of formal schooling, Afro-Cubans had restricted opportunities because employers applied racialized notions of efficiency and suitability that provided white immigrant workers with advantages in hiring and promotions. The whole discussion about how "beneficial" this immigration was for Cuba is thus useless. Spaniards and other immigrants contributed and benefited from the country's economic expansion during the pre-Depression export era, but Afro-Cubans and native workers in general had little to gain from their presence. As usual, what was beneficial for some might not have benefited others. Afro-Cubans were not among the former.[74]

The impact of this massive introduction of white workers should not be underestimated. In fact, the indices of dissimilarity in the distribution of blacks and native and foreign whites in the occupational structure were *always* lower among black and white native workers than between natives (of any color) and foreign workers.[75] In other words, differences between native and foreign workers were consistently greater than between white and black Cubans (table 3.4). The only exception occurred in 1943, largely because many workers who were formerly Spanish had become naturalized Cubans by the 1940s, transposing to the "natives" column part of the dissimilarity previously accounted for in the "foreign whites" category. Among natives, in fact, the index had decreased significantly after 1907, and it was less than ten in 1931.

These differences were largely the result of a conscious policy that sought to divide workers according to their nationality. Differences in employment were in fact so large that in the early decades of the century "race" was occasionally construed as a line separating native and foreign workers. Planter Edwin Atkins, for instance, grouped the Cienfuegos dockworkers into two different categories: Spanish, on the one hand, and "Negroes and Cubans," on the other.[76] Likewise, when a labor analyst reported in 1902 that tobacco workers were divided into two unions, one for Spaniards and one for Cubans, he referred to this division as "an element of *race antagonism* among the cigar operatives."[77]

Employers manipulated these divisions to their advantage. Foreigners were used to break workers' resistance. Ethnically diverse workforces were hired, and at times isolated, to minimize their capacity to organize. The convenience of this tactic was made plain by a superintendent of the Jatibonico sugar mill: "Owing to the trouble last year with the centrifugal force, we have decided to contract this work with Chinese, and at the same time to house them in the *batey* separate from all other labor. Chinese . . . should put an end to strikes in this department . . . which have been taking place for the last three years." A manager of the Francisco sugar mill reported in 1917 that although native workers had used the Liberal revolt to "leave the cane fields," grinding had not stopped thanks to the Antilleans: "Our salvation in the matter of cane supply has been the Haitians and Jamaicans. They are all scared."[78]

Foreign workers were also used as strikebreakers, particularly in those sectors related to the all-important sugar industry: waterfront activities, railroad transportation, and, of course, sugar production itself. In the case of harbor strikes, American and British ship lines imported their own laborers, sometimes disguised as crew members, or turned tasks over to Antilleans or newly arrived unemployed immigrants.[79] If qualified workers were not available to replace strikers, they were imported. In 1916, the Cuba Railroad Company responded to a strike that paralyzed all traffic in the crucial sugar region east of Camagüey with a request to its New York office: "Engineers joining the strike. Please get one of the organizations in the United States which make it a business to break strikes to send thirty engineers with their firemen."[80]

These divisionist tactics further encouraged hostility among workers of different origins, which occasionally erupted into open violence. In 1916, the Cuban and Haitian cane cutters of the Cuba Company's Jatibonico sugar mill clashed over salaries due to the latter's acceptance of wages 20 percent below those demanded by natives. "[T]he Cubans attempted by force to prevent the Haitians from cutting," reported a manager at the mill. A similar conflict was "narrowly averted" in 1922 in a mill of the Atlantic Fruit Company. Two years later, a full riot left one Haitian dead in the town of Sagua de Tánamo (Oriente), when Spanish and Haitian workers battled over limited employment opportunities and salaries. Troubles between Cubans and Spaniards also developed among the Havana dockworkers in 1917, whereas the native stevedores at Antilla went on strike in 1921 under the leadership of black local leader Antonio Fernández with the motto "Cuba for the Cubans."[81]

Divisions between Cuban and Spanish workers permeated the labor movement through the 1920s. The well-known 1902 "apprentices' strike" is a case in point. Called by the Liga General de Trabajadores Cubanos, native workers demanded equal access to the tobacco trades "without distinctions of race" and condemned "the odious privileges in the distribution of jobs" that gave preference to Spaniards. The league itself was created in 1899 to give Cuban workers "the same advantages and guarantees" that foreigners enjoyed in the island.[82] In 1909, socialist activist Carlos Baliño withdrew from the Partido Socialista de Cuba, led by Spanish socialists, because of its disregard for native workers' rightful struggle for employment opportunities. "There are guilds," Baliño denounced, "where work is so monopolized by Spanish workers that few white Cubans work in the trade, and *not one black*."[83] Divisions were also evident in a 1911 strike of the workers employed in the construction of Havana's sewer system, of whom about 75 percent were foreign. The Partido Socialista de Cuba, which organized and led the strike, resented the lack of support among Cuban laborers, claiming that it was opposed to any privilege favoring Spaniards and that one of its main leaders had even refused to deal with contractors who did not admit the employment of black masons.[84] But some unions, such as the Association of Naval Machinists of Cuba, which was affiliated with the reformist Federación Cubana del Trabajo, remained segregated along ethnic and national lines as late as 1931.[85]

Divisions were also reinforced by Cuban workers' attempts to regulate the access of foreigners to employment—a strategy that sought to counteract the employers' discriminatory practices through government intervention in the labor market. Protective legislation for natives was sought by a labor group from Cienfuegos as early as 1900 and by the Círculo de Trabajadores from Santiago in 1905. After the end of the second American occupation, the Obreros de la Patria, Asociación de Cubanos Nativos, requested that President Gómez pass a law reserving 75 percent of all jobs for natives, as well as a general prohibition on immigration. The issue was endorsed by the Labor Congress of 1914, which demanded a similar proportion of apprenticeship positions and public contract jobs for Cubans.[86] Not surprisingly, Afro-Cubans were well represented among those advocating these measures: it was they who fared the worst in the competition for employment with foreign workers.[87]

The most important legal battle to pass a bill protecting native workers took place in 1925, when black representative Aquilino Lombard introduced a proposal reserving 50 percent of all positions, with the exception of agriculture, for Cubans.[88] Popular mobilization in support of this measure proved to be crucial for its approval by the House. The representatives worked under heavy pressure from a multitude of native workers who invaded the House galleries and surrounded the building every day. The president of the House was forced to address the public on several occasions, reassuring them that the project would be approved and that all representatives had the workers' well-being in mind. Cheered by those in attendance as the "defender of Cuban workers," Lombard seized the moment and got the bill approved.[89]

But opposition mounted as well. Local chambers of commerce from throughout the island implemented a well-orchestrated campaign, arguing that the law would render unemployable "valuable elements" who had created Cuban families (that is, the Spanish immigrants); that qualified personnel for retail trade could not be improvised (another reference to the Spaniards); and that the bill would hinder all "desirable" immigration to Cuba (Spaniards). Also opposed was the National Association of Economic Corporations.[90] The U.S. Chamber of Commerce called for a special session to discuss the bill, concluding that it was "detrimental to American interests and in some respects confiscatory." And last, but certainly not least, the U.S. government instructed its embassy in Havana to "strongly impress" upon Cuban authorities its hope that such legislation would not be enacted.[91]

As usual, Cuban authorities retreated rather than cope with these pressures. Machado declared his support "in principle" for a bill benefiting native workers, but he expeditiously assured American authorities that U.S. interests would not be affected and that he would veto the bill unless it was modified. Likewise, a senatorial committee turned down the proposal on constitutional grounds while pledging "absolute identification with the principle of nationalism and the protection of Cubans."[92]

In the final analysis, the discussion about the implications of the Lombard bill was as much about race as it was about labor. Not only was the bill's proponent a black congressman, but initial support in the House was provided by Afro-Cuban representatives Marcelino Garriga, Carmelo Urquiaga, and Américo Portuondo. Moreover, the whole argument about the impact of the law on immigration was a racial one. "The sugar industry and farmers are exempted from the provisions of the bill. So our doors will continue to be open to the undesirable Jamaican and Haitian immigration, but on the other hand we close them to the desirable immigration from Spain," commented

Heraldo de Cuba. An editorial in *La Lucha* was even more explicit: "Let us think of the deplorable gangs of Jamaicans and Haitians who by becoming Cubans . . . would cause regretful damage to our race." Even those who supported the bill used racial arguments in favor of its implementation. "It is silly to assert that this measure would be harmful to the Spaniards in Cuba," *El Día* stated, "and highly protective for the Cuban Negro or colored elements, because at least 90 percent of the Spaniards in Cuba are able to take our citizenship. . . . This is precisely . . . what pleases us most."[93]

As mentioned above, a law protecting native workers was not approved until 1933. A bill providing Cuban workers with privileged access to the labor market blatantly contradicted the migration policies that the Cuban state had implemented and the economic interests that had successfully promoted them. It made little sense to flood the market with cheap immigrant workers only to restrict their access to employment. Under a regime of legal protection for natives, immigrants lost their raison d'être: to depress labor costs either by increasing the supply of workers or by fragmenting the labor movement. But even if the Cuban government was willing to provide protection for native workers, the sugar interests could always turn to Washington, D.C.—the ultimate arbiter in Cuban politics—for support. In fact, they frequently did. The failure to have such a law approved until 1933 was also an indicator of organized labor's incapacity to exercise effective political pressure.

Although employers and the state succeeded in fragmenting the labor movement along ethnic and national lines, their ultimate goal—the creation of an acquiescent and submissive labor force—was never achieved. The construction of race as a line separating workers of different nationalities tended to obscure racial differences among native workers and to facilitate their cooperation. "Negroes and Cubans," as Atkins described them, frequently joined the same unions and shared their leadership. Besides, neither Spaniards nor West Indians were the submissive workers that employers expected them to be. In the late 1920s immigration was being halted not only because of deteriorating economic conditions but also because foreign workers were seen as a constant source of labor troubles. Indeed, government deportation policies emphasized that labor conflicts were an imported evil and tended to reinforce the line between native and foreign workers. Even more frightening for the elites was the tendency of these workers to collaborate with natives of all colors in unions and strikes.[94] The immigrants had a privileged access to employment, but since they lacked the political resources needed to monopolize these positions, their situation remained in fact precarious. They were singled out for repression and could be replaced at any time. Under these conditions, the anarchists' doctrine that workers had no nationality served to bridge the gap that otherwise separated workers of different national backgrounds. As a Spanish leader from the bakery trades wrote in 1919, "The real fatherland is the perfect union of all workers, without distinctions of race and nationalities." Workers, an anarchist newspaper claimed in 1909, "could not be foreign in any place."[95] After the 1920s, the radical labor movement turned workers' equality into one of its programmatic principles and elaborated an alternative notion of workers nationalism: "Cuba must be for the Cubans. This does not mean hatred for the *foreigner*; it means hatred for *foreign capital*."[96] By the time the immigrants' presence in the labor force declined in the 1930s, native workers had developed a long tradition of cross-racial cooperation.

These traditions notwithstanding, the halt of immigration and the changing composition of the labor force contributed to heighten competition among native workers after the 1930s. Whereas in the early republic "race" had often referred to workers' national and ethnic origins, after the Great Depression perceptions of race served exclusively to differentiate Cubans of European and African descent and to separate blacks from whites. Blacks and mulattoes had always encountered greater obstacles in getting jobs than whites, but "racial" barriers in the first republic's labor market contributed to place Cubans of all colors in a disadvantageous position relative to the Spanish immigrants. Post-Depression barriers, while still racial, applied primarily to Afro-Cubans.

Furthermore, although immigration tended to obscure race differences among natives, it heightened competition among Cubans in those sectors that foreign workers found it more difficult to enter: the growing public sector and professional services. In those sectors, which had represented a mere 2 percent of total employment in 1899 but expanded to about 10 percent in 1931, Afro-Cubans would have to compete with white Cubans for employment opportunities.

THE CUBANS' "ONLY INDUSTRY"

Natives had been left with relatively few avenues of economic and social ascent. Sugar-producing land, industries, banks, public utilities, domestic and foreign trade, and the transportation system were all controlled by foreign investors. Easier for natives to access was the public sector, which generated several thousand (after 1907, tens of thousands of) white- and blue-collar jobs at the national, provincial, and municipal levels. Politics, public employment, and access to the nation's budget opened up opportunities for mobility among Cubans of modest origins with few other chances to move up the social ladder. "What is the national budget if not the only big business open to Cubans in general?" a journalist asked in 1929. Quite often gained through corruption and graft, a public post of the right kind could mean the transition from poverty to wealth. "The salaries in public office as a rule are small, but the opportunities for 'extras' are many."[97] At the very least, public jobs provided some temporary financial security. That is why Miguel de Carrión wrote in 1921 that politics was the Cubans' "only industry," and administrative fraud the natives' only path to fortune. As a black writer explained, if the majority had neither land nor capital, they had to look elsewhere for advancement.[98]

Access to public employment depended on political connections. Victorious political parties and candidates distributed jobs and appointments through a complex system of patronage that started in the neighborhood and ended up in the presidential palace. Although no specific study has analyzed the operation of the system, the endless denunciations of favoritism and partisanship in the distribution of appointments permit at least a broad characterization of this process. These complaints were voiced even under the U.S. occupation government, when as early as 1899 the appointed secretaries were accused of filling their departments with friends, cousins, brothers, and other relatives. As soon as he assumed the presidency (May 1902), Estrada Palma had to face an endless stream of visitors seeking to enter the government payroll or to recommend relatives or friends for public positions. The president proved to be a quick learner: his 1905 reelection was largely guaranteed through the appointment of political followers to the expanding public sector, a practice that led to the Liberal revolt of August 1906.[99]

Succeeding administrations entrenched the system further by expanding the budget and creating an increasing number of imaginary bureaucratic jobs (the so-called *botellas*). Political contacts and recommendations were indispensable to get any job in public administration. Afro-Cuban intellectual and politician Rafael Serra asserted that teachers, physicians, and other white-collar workers of all colors needed "powerful influences" to be appointed to public schools, hospitals, and the bureaucracy.[100] This was true also for more menial and less skilled jobs. A young manual worker from Cienfuegos commented that he had obtained a blue-collar job in Havana only after securing a "high recommendation" from a public figure. Likewise, the political director of the Atarés neighborhood committee of the Partido Liberal requested four positions in the city council for his followers in the barrio: one for a copyist and the others for a doorkeeper and street cleaners. After the 1930s, influence was needed even to work as a stevedore, and bureaucrats in the Ministry of Labor sold or distributed these positions according to their interests.[101]

Getting a job in the public sector was difficult, but losing it was much easier. A presidential change resulted in a complete reshuffling of the labor force, despite legislative attempts to hinder this practice. To reward their followers and to honor political commitments, winning factions had to discharge previous employees. The Auténticos' triumph in 1933, for instance, resulted in the dismissal of all the employees of Havana's city council, who were quickly replaced with political followers. In the central government, the "entire personnel" of the Department of Public Works was discharged in 1936 when a new administration took over. As had happened under Estrada Palma in 1905, thousands of employees not affiliated with the party in power were fired prior to elections and replaced with followers and sympathizers. The system had become, as the Havana press stated in the mid-1940s, a "perpetual disgrace" to Cuba.[102] Political parties were perceived as "cliques . . . headed by a leader who holds his followers largely by promises of patronage in the event of success." As *Atenas*, the monthly of the famous black club, wrote, the parties were nothing less than "mutual-aid societies for employment and insurance against poverty."[103]

Under heavy political pressure, the public sector expanded at an astonishing rate. In fact, this was the fastest growing source of employment in Cuba during the 1899–1953 period. In 1899 only 1 percent of the working population was employed in government (civil and military) activities, but the proportion had multiplied ninefold by 1953. Civil jobs accounted for about 62 percent of this increase. The number of public employees (including the army and the police) doubled in the 1920s, from 26,000 in 1919, to 47,000 in 1925, to 51,000 by the end of the decade. And these figures included only "permanent" workers.[104] On top of this, the Cuban government paid large sums for a number of *botellas*. The secretary of the treasury estimated in 1921 that about 15 million pesos were paid annually for such jobs, an amount that represented more than 40 percent of what the state paid to "real" employees. In other words, *botellas* were equivalent to the annual average salary of 19,000 additional employees.[105]

Afro-Cubans did gradually access the public sector, but they remained underrepresented throughout the whole republican period, and their participation clearly stagnated after 1931. Their endless protests denouncing the lack of equal opportunities to enter the state bureaucracy and the army were therefore well grounded, especially because they had envisioned a republic in which blacks would occupy "all public spheres."[106] The reality, however, hardly matched Martí's dream of a free Cuba for all. In 1901, an Afro-Cuban society denounced the fact that out of 7,000 public appointments during the American occupation, fewer than 100 had been given to black Cubans. White veterans blamed the U.S. occupation government, but blacks were still left out of the distribution of patronage after the republic was formally established in 1902. They complained that only seven or eight out of fifty mailmen in Havana were black, and not even one customs inspector was black; that the secretary of state employed two blacks, and the secretary of the interior just one. Blacks were also absent from Havana's local government, and their presence among police officers was minimal.[107]

Given their prominent participation in the August 1906 revolt against Estrada Palma, blacks expected a growing participation in the distribution of patronage once the Liberals became the dominant political force. Amid growing competition for public office between contending factions within the Partido Liberal, however, Afro-Cubans' expectations for a proportional share of public jobs were as difficult to realize as ever. As Charles Magoon recognized, competition for employment in the public sector and the lack of opportunities for advancement in other areas of the Cuban economy were fostering racial tensions in the island.[108]

Blacks' participation in the public sector did increase during the first decade of the republic, however, and this trend was not interrupted by the 1912 racist massacre against the Partido Independiente de Color. Rather, during the 1910s and 1920s a growing number of Afro-Cubans obtained civil and military posts, and by 1931 their index of representation in the sector was approaching the ideal (table 3.3). In part, this had been possible through the displacement of Spaniards, whose participation in the public sector declined some 80 percent between 1899 and 1931. The 1911 veterans' campaign to expel the so-called *guerrilleros* (Cubans who bore arms for the Spanish cause) from public office and to "Cubanize" the sector was in fact an attempt to open new employment opportunities at the expense of Spaniards. Even if this process was mainly, as Arredondo claimed, a white affair, blacks did benefit from the expansion of the public sector.[109]

The area in which the public sector was hardly exceptional was the distribution of jobs among the racial groups. The pattern was similar to the private sector: as a trend, Afro-Cubans were kept within the lower echelons of the public administration, and some specific activities and branches of the Cuban government were closed, or nearly closed, to them. Afro-Cubans became well represented among mailmen, street cleaners, other manual jobs, and the lower bureaucracy, but their numbers declined in the justice system, the higher bureaucracy, and the diplomatic service. Blacks protested, for instance, when after the fall of Machado they were not given a proportional number of positions in the court system.[110]

Likewise, they frequently demanded representation in the diplomatic service. Indeed, this was one of the first issues mentioned in the program of the PIC, which underlined "the urgent need to appoint citizens of the colored race, so that the republic will be represented as it is." Afro-Cubans were conscious that to represent the nation before foreign governments had a tremendous symbolic value: a way to acknowledge that they were Cubans in the fullest sense of the term and that the country was not exclusively white. As the white local boss of the PL tries to explain to Miguel Valdés, the mulatto protagonist of Masdeu's *La raza triste*, "certain people" cannot be included in the "genuine" representation of Cuba before the world.[111] Machado appointed a few Afro-Cubans to the diplomatic service, but this branch of government remained overwhelmingly white.

The military was no exception to this pattern. Blacks increased their representation in the army and the police, but ascending to officers' rank was difficult at best. As previous historians have noted, when the U.S. occupation government organized the army and the rural guard, it established a number of prerequisites that tended to reduce the participation of blacks.[112] To enlist, candidates were required "to furnish at [their] own expense [their] horse and equipment and uniform." They had to be literate, to be "of good character and standing in their community," and to provide two letters of recommendation from well-known citizens, "preferably property owners." According to a press release reproduced by *Diario de la Marina*—although not confirmed by other sources—the appointed chief of the rural guard, Major General Alejandro Rodríguez, had ordered the "progressive expulsion" of Afro-Cubans from the corps. Although the rural guard was reorganized later under republican rule, Batrell and Nenínger asserted in their manifesto that blacks had been excluded again.[113]

Blacks' presence in the artillery corps was even more controversial. Military Governor Leonard Wood attempted, in fact, to create an all-white artillery corps in the island, and it was only under pressure from the veterans of the Liberation Army that blacks were given the opportunity to enlist. In the name of the Council of Veterans, General Alemán and Colonel Estrampes, both of whom were white, asked Wood "not to exclude men of color from the artillery." The officers reminded Wood that blacks and whites had fought together for the freedom of Cuba, many times under the command of "colored chiefs," and that Afro-Cubans' exclusion was contrary to "justice" and the "democratic and revolutionary traditions" of the Liberation Army. In other words, white veterans made clear that there was a blatant contradiction between the integrationism of Cuban nationalist discourse and the segregationist policies of the U.S. occupation government. Wood's solution was typical, however. He replied that he had never intended to hurt "the feelings of the Cuban people" and promised that the artillery corps would be composed of equal numbers of blacks and whites "without distinctions or privileges." What he did not say was that they would be grouped into two racially segregated companies. To add injury to insult, a few months later he ordered the enlargement of the corps, but only with members of the "white race," so in the end there were two white companies and one black.[114]

Thus, whereas the strength of the nationalist ideology of racial fraternity prevented the formation of an all-white artillery corps, the power of North American racism succeeded in introducing segregation into the army. To create an army in which blacks and whites were equally represented and enjoyed roughly similar opportunities for promotion—as in the Liberation Army, which had forged the "revolutionary traditions" invoked by the white veterans in their interview with Wood—republican governments would have to reverse the policies of the military occupation government. This is what the Comité de Acción sought in 1902 when it obtained 80 positions for Afro-Cubans in Havana's police force.

Given the level of electoral competition and the dominant parties' formal commitment to the ideal of a racially inclusive republic, the creation of a white army was a political impossibility. There is no doubt that blacks did enter the military. In fact, by 1919 their representation in the sector almost equaled their share in the working population of the island (table 3.3). The army and the rural guard expanded significantly in the 1910s, creating ample opportunities for enlistment. By 1906 the total armed forces comprised about 6,000 members, but this figure jumped to some 13,000 by 1919. Meanwhile, the proportion of the budget allocated to military expenses rose from 11 percent in 1907 to 23 percent in 1919.[115] The literacy and other requirements that tended to exclude the poorest sectors of Cuban society from entering the army and the navy were maintained in subsequent modifications of the military laws, but they were frequently ignored in practice.[116]

What was truly difficult for blacks was to ascend within either the army, the rural guard, or the police. In the early 1900s, black intellectuals and public figures claimed that there were no black officers in the artillery and that the black company never participated in acts honoring foreign representatives.

In the police, blacks were seldom named "first class" guards and some black officers had been removed from their posts. There were just two black officers in Havana's police: a lieutenant and a captain. In the rural guard, with the exception of two or three lieutenants, all the officers were white. Máximo Gómez, the head of the Liberation Army, exhorted Wood to appoint General Pedro Díaz as chief of the rural guard in 1900, but the Afro-Cuban general was denied the position. Instead, it was rumored that Díaz would be offered a position as police inspector in Pinar del Río.[117]

The military replicated the pattern found in other sectors of the Cuban labor market, in which racial competition increased in the higher echelons. These positions were political appointments that conferred prestige, power, and higher salaries. A major earned three times the salary of a first sergeant and five times as much as an enlisted man. Many officers had graduated from American military schools, including West Point, in which blacks were not allowed. The highest officers, without exception, were white. In 1922 the chief of staff, the adjutant general, the quartermaster general, and all the district commanders were white. Some particular officers deliberately took steps to drive blacks out of the army, and blacks' access to some elite corps was restricted. When in 1918 the Cuban army decided to train forty men for an aviation squadron, they were all described as white. It was not until 1942 that the first license was granted to a black pilot in Cuba, and even then he was unable to fly military planes because of "certain legal obstacles."[118]

As in the civilian branch of government, access to leadership positions was difficult but not impossible for Afro-Cubans. Some Afro-Cuban officers from the Liberation Army, such as General José González Planas, enjoyed positions of command after the war. González Planas became the first chief of the fourth district of the rural guard in the province of Las Villas before his death in 1901. Afro-Cubans' access to positions of command seems to have been significantly easier in the rural towns than in Havana and other major cities. To mention but one example, in 1907 nine of the eighteen members of the police squadron of Camajuaní were black, including the chief of the municipality, Serafín Rodríguez.[119]

A few officers, such as Arsenio Ortiz, veteran Bernardo Sandó, and Ramón Cabrales, acquired national visibility and prestige. Ortiz, described as "colored" and "nearly black," rebelled against Estrada Palma in 1903 and 1906 and then entered the army as a lieutenant. Ortiz had a distinguished record in the repression against the Independientes' revolt in 1912, an indication that even then the color line was not consistently enforced. In 1917 he remained loyal to the Conservative government against the Liberal revolt and was promoted to major. Three years later he was named military supervisor in Holguin during the elections, becoming known for his intimidation of Liberal voters, a reputation shared by Major Sandó, also a military supervisor in the province. In the late 1920s Ortiz became a commander, the military supervisor of Santiago de Cuba, and one of Machado's most hated officers. The opposition called him "the jackal" and considered him "the most ferocious of all the assassins of the period." In 1931 he was replaced as military supervisor by Cabrales, described by U.S. officers as "quite colored." Both Ortiz and Sandó were supposed to have "a large Negro following."[120]

The number of black officers in the army increased after the overthrow of Machado and the "sergeants' revolt" of September 4, 1933, led by Fulgencio Batista. Opportunities for the rebellious lower officers were guaranteed through the dismissal of a large number of high officers. As early as September 16, 1933, an executive order dismissed a total of 518 officers, including 7 colonels, 16 lieutenant colonels, 41 majors, and 125 captains. As many as 70 percent of the officials higher than second lieutenants were replaced.[121] In Matanzas, out of the seventeen officers stationed at the city in December 1933, only three were former officers. The U.S. consul in the city commented that some of them could "hardly read and write" and added that eight of them were "negroes." The new chief of the rural guard in the province was also black. Batista, himself of dubious whiteness, had several black soldiers in his personal escort, providing Afro-Cubans with a growing visibility within the army. U.S. military intelligence sources asserted that after the September 4 revolt the proportion of blacks in the army had increased. They estimated that 30 percent of the soldiers were "pure blacks," 35 percent mulattoes, and 35 percent whites, including "many so-called whites who have a small admixture of negro blood." Among the officers, it was estimated that 20 percent were "negroes."[122] These proportions were even higher in Oriente: 40–75 percent of the soldiers were blacks and mulattoes, as were 40 percent of the officers. Furthermore, in the newly created women's reserve, "mulattoes predominated."[123]

Increasing numbers of Afro-Cubans became officers in the new army, but not without resistance. In the post-Depression years, the army represented one of the few avenues for social ascent. "The army is the supreme power in Cuba today," claimed the U.S. consul in Santiago de Cuba. Military chiefs controlled not only their own resources but also the local distribution of patronage. "The army's tentacles have grown until they reach out to the control of the insignificant municipal jobs, such as the appointment of street sweepers and other jobs." Only "close relations and friends" of the officers and soldiers could obtain such jobs. The cohesiveness of the army itself was guaranteed through the distribution of patronage among the officers and soldiers in the way of housing, food, recreational facilities, and opportunities for graft.[124]

When competition for promotions intensified, tensions became progressively racialized. White soldiers were reportedly "hostile" to the "influx of negro officers," and cases of open racial violence developed in several garrisons throughout the island. Matanzas witnessed street fights between whites and blacks and a white soldiers' plot to remove "all negro soldiers and officers" from the army. In the Cabañas garrison, a riot occurred after a white soldier refused to obey a black officer. Manifestos calling for racial violence among the soldiers multiplied, and rumors of black conspiracies against the white race spread. Meanwhile, the "better classes" made it repeatedly clear that they had little in common with the darker leadership of the new army. In an effort to attract the "upper stratum" to the army's social events, "negro officers" or their families were excluded. The mulatto chief of the Nuevitas Naval District, for instance, felt compelled to attend dances and other events without his wife, described as a "full blooded Negress."[125]

White resistance achieved at least two concrete results. The leadership of the army remained white—although Batista's "race" was always a contested issue—and Afro-Cubans' representation in the armed forces and the police actually declined slightly during the 1930s (table 3.3). Black journalist Manuel Cuéllar Vizcaíno was right when he stated that under Batista the army had "whitened" and that black officers were in many cases barred from social events in the army's clubs. He also noted that blacks remained underrepresented in the navy and that they were not admitted to the School of Officers in Mariel. Indeed, the "race question" had been traditionally described as "more acute" in the navy than the army.[126]

Some blacks, such as Generals Hernández Nardo and Gregorio Querejeta, reached positions of command at the national level, but the control of the army and the police remained in white hands. The highest thirty officers of the National Police were white in 1945, the same year in which the Afro-Cuban club Unión Fraternal felt compelled to pay homage to the chief of police for having promoted a descendant of Maceo from sergeant to second lieutenant. In 1938, in the army, all the commanders of regiments and military districts were white.[127] Querejeta would eventually become chief of a regiment, inspector general of the army, and chief of Fort Cabaña in 1946, only to be retired two years later. A captain by the time of the sergeants' revolt, he was promoted to comandante but transferred immediately to the department of the quartermaster general, where he had no direct command of troops. Although he performed the duties of the actual quartermaster general, Batista never appointed him to that position, "presumably because [he] was unwilling to have a negro officer among his three auxiliary colonels." Querejeta's retirement from the army in 1948 was interpreted as the result of a policy "aimed at eliminating negroes from positions of high command in the Cuban army."[128]

Blacks' difficulties in ascending within the military and the bureaucracy, and even in getting some skilled manual jobs, conformed to a general pattern: the higher the position on the socioeconomic ladder, the harder it was for blacks to be hired. By the early 1930s blacks had made remarkable progress in all sectors of the Cuban economy in terms of participation, with one partial but notable exception: that of professional services. In Cuba, as in other places in Latin America, racial inequality had gradually moved up from the most massive sectors of the economy to the most desirable ones. But even in those massive sectors some occupations remained closed, or nearly so, to blacks, including highly skilled industrial jobs or positions that involved direct contact with the public—from store clerk to tramway conductor. The organized labor movement managed to break some of the barriers, but its struggle demonstrates that the barriers were real indeed. Race, however, was a far greater obstacle to blacks trying to access the professions. Income differences were virtually negligible among manual workers, but they increased significantly among professionals. Also, it was in this sector that blacks' indices of representation were the lowest.

The Cuban black has, before him, an unsolved problem that can be
considered the most important of all problems: education.
—Rafael Serra, *El Nuevo Criollo* (1905)

The same unbalance that exists among whites' social classes exists . . . among
the colored.
—Ramón Vasconcelos, *La Prensa* (1915)

When a black man succeeds in any activity, he suffers even more humiliation
and racial discrimination.
—Juan R. Betancourt, *Doctrina Negra* (1954)

Access to the professions and white-collar employment depended on
several factors. Education, understood as formal schooling, was of course
crucial. The republican state was committed to a notion of modernity in
which academic merits and formal training were key. On this aspect, both the
former members of the Liberation Army and the U.S. occupation government tended to agree. Widespread illiteracy was not compatible with the
building of a modern nation. The nature, character, and goals of educational
programs and institutions, however, remained contested. Moreover, whereas
some white intellectuals, politicians, and employers perceived Afro-Cubans'
lack of education as a manifestation of the "black problem," blacks themselves explained it as the result of slavery and colonialism.

The meritocracy on which Cuban republican society allegedly rested
worked in complex and contradictory ways. On the one hand, merits and
preparation were invoked to minimize the participation of Afro-Cubans and
poor whites in the administration or in white-collar, private-sector employment. As General Wood stated as early as January 1899, "[T]he better appointments required men of education," very few of whom where black.[1] On
the other hand, merits and education served to map a "route" for social
ascent and mobility that could be followed by those at the bottom of the
social ladder. Furthermore, literacy and at least some elementary education
were considered indispensable to "fulfill the duties of citizenship and universal suffrage" for which Cubans had fought so hard.[2] Afro-Cubans thus
treated schooling as virtually sacred and actively campaigned to improve

their education. They also demanded that the government create enough schools. If education was construed as a requisite to be an effective member of the republic with all and for all, the Cuban state that claimed to represent this ideal had to provide opportunities for schooling.[3] Indeed, the improvement of education always figured in party platforms, and some candidates, such as Machado, made it a centerpiece of their electoral campaigns.[4]

Attaining education was not sufficient to allow Afro-Cubans to access the liberal professions and white-collar employment, however. Social and political contacts were also needed. Jobs in the public sector were distributed through networks of patronage controlled by the main political parties and public figures. A black mathematician explained in 1929 that he could not find a job because he was not involved in politics.[5] Similar positions in the private sector, in turn, were informally distributed through social and family links that were out of reach for most Afro-Cubans. The segregated social clubs of the white bourgeoisie provided most of those contacts and potential clients.

Despite these and other obstacles, a growing number of Afro-Cubans attended school, became literate, expanded their education, and eventually entered the professions. Translating educational gains into vocational mobility proved to be more difficult. As late as the 1940s blacks remained heavily underrepresented in professional occupations, and in these activities income differences by race were the largest. In response to the segregationist practices of the white social clubs, highly educated blacks created their own exclusive societies and used them as a platform to exercise political pressure to expand their representation in the public administration. Speaking in the name of the whole "race of color," they also denounced the most overt forms of racial discrimination. But whereas race and discrimination linked these Afro-Cubans to the masses of black manual workers, the need to consolidate their recently acquired middle-class status led black professionals to emphasize the social distance that separated them from the "low" elements that they claimed to represent. Education and "culture" were the cornerstones of this discourse. Manipulating the same social conventions that initially served to minimize Afro-Cuban participation in government, educated blacks demanded equal access to and representation in white-collar employment.

EDUCATION

Writing in 1899, an American author reported that Afro-Cubans wanted "education for their children."[6] Indeed, Rafael Serra considered lack of education the most important of all problems affecting blacks and saw schooling as the only way to achieve true racial equality. Only through education, Serra explained, would blacks be able to "move out of the status of inferiority in which they are forced to live under the Cuban republic." In the eyes of Serra and other Afro-Cuban intellectuals, education was not only a route to individual mobility but also a social and political strategy for Afro-Cubans to participate, equally and effectively, in the republic that they had helped create. "Modern democracy," Serra also wrote, "is progress, . . . improvement of the individual's intelligence to its highest degree." Afro-Cuban veteran Ricardo Batrell Oviedo, who was eighteen years old and illiterate when the war ended, fully understood the need for education. After the war, he retreated from public activities for six months to learn how to read and write, which in his own words was indispensable to obtain a "suitable position" in free Cuba.[7] Education was thus perceived as a step in Afro-Cubans' struggle for equality—in a sense, a sequel to their participation in the Liberation Army.

As did their African American contemporaries, whose educational progress Afro-Cubans followed closely, blacks in the island came to regard education as a sacred right and duty. "Let us turn teaching into the true religion," *El Nuevo Criollo* advised in 1905.[8] Afro-Cuban societies frequently included learning and instruction among their most important goals. Since its creation in 1887, for instance, the Directorio Central de Sociedades de la Raza de Color sought "the creation of elementary schools for children of both sexes, or their admission into those established for children of both races."[9] A few societies maintained their own schools and academies, including night schools for adults. Unión Fraternal had a well-known academy with a library in Havana, and since its creation in 1890 the organization had made "the diffusion of instruction" its main goal. Club Benéfico (Havana) maintained an elementary school, while Nueva Aurora in Colón (Matanzas) and Club Unión Fraternal (Nueva Paz, Havana) had libraries and provided classes for members and their families. In 1905 a group of mutual-aid associations agreed to create a new institution to promote postelementary education among blacks.[10]

The number of separate black schools did not proliferate, however. A desegregated public school system made them, for the most part, unnecessary. Although for different purposes, the need to create schools and expand education was recognized by nationalists and the U.S. occupation government alike. The former saw schooling as a way to overcome Spain's legacy of colonialism and slavery; the latter, as an instrument to socialize Cubans with Anglo-Saxon values, which American authorities deemed indispensable to achieve progress and stability.[11]

The result was the expansion of educational opportunities. The number of students attending public elementary schools had increased sevenfold between 1895 and 1900. The number of schools multiplied from just a few hundred in the late nineteenth century to 3,660 in 1929. Despite this impressive growth, the public school system never fulfilled the needs of all the population, particularly after the 1910s. The postwar baby boom generated an increasing demand that the government seemed unable to match. According to census data, the rates of school attendance were lower in 1919 than in 1907. The percentage of registered students in the school-age population had been close to 50 percent during the first decade of the century, but it fell to 39 percent in 1920, when the country was hit by the collapse of sugar prices.[12] Education became a hotly contested political issue, with nationalist intellectuals crying that Cubanness and illiteracy were incompatible. "In Cuba," Fernando Ortiz declared, "to preserve culture is to preserve liberty."[13] The campaign had a favorable effect. Under President Machado, whose populist agenda included building schools as one of its leitmotivs, rates of enrollment recovered. By 1926 they had reached an estimated all-time high of 63–71 percent, according to different sources.[14]

The available evidence strongly suggests that public elementary schools were open to all, regardless of race. Since the years of the American occupation, public school advertisements made explicit that they would receive students "without national or racial distinctions."[15] That Afro-Cubans took advantage of these opportunities is beyond any doubt. In fact, their rates of schooling through the 1920s were slightly higher than those of whites. According to census data, in 1907 and 1919 the black/white ratios of school attendance were 1.04 and 1.03, respectively. Their representation declined after this date, but it was still congruent with their share in the total population (see table 4.2 below).

Afro-Cubans' drive to obtain education, plus the opportunities created by a school system to which access was not racially defined, had a strong impact on literacy rates. In 1899 only 30 percent of blacks 10–19 years old were literate, compared to 40 percent of whites, for a black/white ratio of 0.75 (table 4.1).[16] Thirty years later the rate of black literacy had more than doubled compared to 1899, and it was slightly higher than 70 percent. More to the point, the 1899 racial gap had almost disappeared by 1931. The race differential in literacy was less than 3 percent, a three-fourths decline since the time of the American occupation.

The Great Depression interrupted this educational improvement. By 1942 the registration rate had declined to 31 percent, the lowest in the whole

TABLE 4.1. Literacy Rate of Population 10–19 Years Old, by Race, 1899–1953

Year	Total	Whites	Blacks	Ratio Blacks/Whites
1899	36.6	39.7	30.0	0.75
1907	68.7	69.5	66.9	0.96
1919	61.3	63.0	56.6	0.90
1931	73.6	74.3	71.5	0.96
1943	73.0	74.3	69.2	0.93
1953	70.8	—	—	—

Sources: U.S. War Department, *Report 1899*, 361–62; Cuba, *Censo 1907*, 465–66; Cuba, *Censo 1919*, 568–70; *Memorias 1931*, 233; Cuba, *Censo 1943*, 926; Cuba, Oficina Nacional, *Censo 1953*, 119–24.

---

republican period. The proportion of enrolled children increased during the 1940s, but it was still at about 50 percent during the early 1950s. Literacy figures confirm these trends (table 4.1). After 1931 the literate proportion of children 10–19 years old tended to stagnate and was in fact lower in 1953. This was true especially for blacks, whose literacy rate declined 2 percent between 1931 and 1943, while that of whites remained the same. For blacks 15–19 years old, the literacy rate declined 4 percent, compared to a 1 percent decline among native whites. People in this age group should have attended school in the early 1930s, when the public school system deteriorated due to the economic crisis and to political chaos. A decline in public education affected mostly the poorest social groups, in which blacks were overrepresented. As the National Convention of the Cuban Societies of the Race of Color asserted in 1936, the relative number of blacks attending schools had suffered a considerable decline. Furthermore, Afro-Cuban societies were also affected by the crisis, and some had to cancel operations, including instructional efforts.[17]

Sociologist Lowry Nelson commented that Cuba's failure to make any gains in literacy during the 1930s was "a somewhat startling revelation." Improved education was one of the ideals of the 1933 revolution, and the 1940 constitution established universal compulsory education, proclaimed the need to expand schooling for adults, and prescribed that the budget of the Ministry of Education should not be less than the ordinary expenditures of any other ministry. The fact that the literacy rate had declined even further by 1953 certifies that these ideals were not being realized in practice. A large proportion of the Ministry of Education's budget went to *botelleros*, of whom there were about 9,000 in 1946. The mission of the International Bank for Reconstruction and Development, the so-called Truslow mission, visited Cuba in 1950 and described the "general trend in the school system" as one of "retrogression."[18]

But while "retrogression" characterized the educational public sector, the number of private schools increased. About 13 percent of the total number of elementary schools in the 1900–1930 period were private, but this proportion decreased during the 1930s due to the parents' inability to pay tuition during the crisis. In 1936 only 6 percent of all elementary schools were private. Between 1940 and 1945, however, the number of pupils in private primary education doubled, from 31,000 to 72,000, and it almost doubled again by the late 1950s. Of all elementary school students, 10 percent went to private schools in 1945 and 16 percent in 1958. The Truslow mission commented: "A general lack of confidence in the public schools is reflected in a disproportionate increase of private school enrollment, with a tendency to intensify social class divisions."[19]

Private schooling was even more prominent in secondary education. In the 1920s there were only six public high schools in the island, compared to forty private schools, which controlled about 75 percent of the total enrollment. Of all secondary schools, 86 percent were private in 1936. Although the number of public high schools expanded later, in 1942 the minister of education asserted that private schools represented the majority. Indeed, in 1958, 60 percent of all secondary schools operating in the country were private.[20]

In contrast to public schools, private institutions were virtually segregated. Data to evaluate the racial composition of students in private schools are considerably scarcer than for government institutions, but they provide a consistent picture: black students were heavily underrepresented in these schools, and their proportion declined steadily from the 1900s to the 1920s (table 4.2). Afro-Cuban teachers seldom found employment in these institutions, another important contrast with the public schools, in which their share of total teaching jobs increased gradually through the 1920s. Afro-Cuban teachers' underrepresentation in private schools was closely related to two fundamental features: in addition to their elitist character, most of these schools were religious and foreign-controlled. In the 1920s, 38 percent of the teachers in private schools were foreign and had a religious affiliation. A 1933 report estimated that 70 percent of teachers in private schools were foreign.

TABLE 4.2. Public and Private Education, Indicators of Inequality, 1901–1934

Year	Schools	Children/ Classroom	Students/ Teacher	Percentage Black Students	Percentage Black Teachers
Public Education					
1901–2	—	—	61	35.6	3.4
1908–9	2,139	92	49	33.7	7.3
1910–14	2,271	109	59	31.5	9.8
1915–19	3,450	91	59	27.8	13.1
1920–24	3,415	108	60	26.4	15.8
1925–29	3,660	93	48	24.9	16.3
1930–34	—	—	—	24.2	—
Private Education					
1909	316	22	—	14.7	—
1910	305	—	—	15.2	—
1911	443	—	—	12.2	—
1916	340	24	—	8.8	—
1920	297	—	—	—	3.0
1921	416	27	24	8.0	2.8
1923	551	24	19	7.9	3.2
1924	596	21	19	8.1	5.1
1925	606	21	19	7.9	3.4
1926	484	—	21	7.3	—
1929	563	23	19	6.9	3.6

Sources: "Report of the Secretary of Public Instruction" and "Annual Report of the Commissioner of Public Schools," in Cuba, Military Governor, *Civil Report 1901*, 9:84–85, 169–85; "Report of Matthew E. Hanna," in Cuba, Military Governor, *Civil Report 1902*, 1:49–75; "El censo escolar," *La Lucha* (June 8, 1902); Magoon, *Report of the Provisional Administration*, 304; Cuba, Presidencia, *Memoria de la administración del Presidente*; "Estadística escolar," *Revista de Instrucción Pública* 1, no. 1 (January–February 1918), 3, no. 3 (March–June 1920); "Mensaje [presidencial] al Congreso," *Gaceta Oficial* (November 22, 1918; November 8, 1921; November 25, 1924; November 15, 1928; November 6, 1929; November 4, 1931); Carlton Bailey, Report: education in Cuba, Havana, December 10, 1926, USNA, RG 59/837.42/21; Cuba, Secretaría de Educación, *Estadística general, 1931–1936*.

Some of the best schools in the country, such as Ruston Academy, Candler College (Methodist), La Progresiva (Presbyterian), and Cathedral School (Episcopal), were American and open only to whites. As Pérez contends, "[S]egregated schools became one of the landmark features of Protestant schools during the early decades of the republic."[21] Other religious schools, such as Colegio Champagnat (Marist) and Colegio de Belén (Jesuit) were Spanish and equally discriminatory. In the Colegio de Belén there was not a single Afro-Cuban in a student body of more than four hundred in the mid-1910s. Also all-white were the student and teaching bodies of Colegio Champagnat in the late 1920s. Catholic schools for girls, such as La Domiciliaria and El Sagrado Corazón in Havana, were equally segregated.[22]

The limited evidence available suggests that the racially exclusive character of these institutions was not altered under the second republic. On the contrary, private institutions flourished not only due to the public sector's inability to keep pace with demand but also because they provided middle-class and wealthy white Cubans with the opportunity to segregate their children into a privileged, racially homogeneous world. Buenavista, Candler's prestigious sister school for girls, "was known for its exclusion of Blacks up until the mid-1950s." In the Havana Military Academy, a school created in 1947 that provided elementary and secondary education, there was not a single black in a student body of more than five hundred. A few light-skinned mulattoes were allowed in the school, but their proportion was negligible—below 3 percent. Its twenty-nine professors also were white. This situation was reproduced in La Progresiva, the prestigious school founded by Presbyterians in Cárdenas. According to the testimony of several former students, in the late 1940s and 1950s a few *mulaticos* (light-skinned mulattoes) attended the school, but the student body was overwhelmingly white. In the Instituto Edison, a Havana lay high school with a branch affiliated with Fairleigh Dickinson College (Rutherford, N.J.), only 2 out of 122 graduates could be considered light-skinned mulattoes in 1955. Not a single Afro-Cuban was to be found among its forty-three teachers.[23]

It is therefore hardly surprising that when a growing nationalist campaign demanded the "Cubanization" of private schools and their supervision by the state in 1941, the issue of racial discrimination figured prominently. Foreign influence (American and Spanish), dominant religions (Protestant and Catholic), class elitism, and racial discrimination had become identified with private schools. The campaign to "Cubanize" the sector was loaded with implications. Socially exclusive and racially segregated spaces were defined as antidemocratic and un-Cuban. "The real Cuban school," an Afro-

Cuban intellectual asserted, "is egalitarian and against all discrimination." The campaign to desegregate these schools was justified in the name of a racially inclusive Cubanness and tied to the struggle for independence under the slogan "for the Cuban school in free Cuba." When the Communist Party launched a political campaign to approve a law regulating private education in the island, it did so from the highly visible Club Atenas, the most exclusive of the Afro-Cuban societies. Dr. Miguel Angel Céspedes, president of the club, explained that Atenas supported the Communists' project because it opposed "a school system that excludes the poor and discriminates against the black."[24] The law was never approved by Congress, but the campaign attracted considerable support and did highlight the discriminatory nature of these institutions.[25]

Access to private schools was particularly important because they were major avenues for social ascent. Their infrastructure, curricula, foreign contacts, and socioracial exclusiveness were all symbols of high-quality education. Education, in turn, was a marker of class status. In an effort to evaluate the differences between private and public schools, table 4.2 includes a ratio of students per room and per teacher. The number of students per classroom was four times higher in public schools than in private schools; that of students per teacher two times higher. Public schools were, as the press reported, "crowded."[26] Furthermore, private control over secondary education functioned in practice as a barrier to blacks attempting to enter the university and the liberal professions. Afro-Cubans were conscious that their exclusion from private schools meant more than a random act of racial discrimination: it represented a formidable obstacle to their aspirations for mobility. As the president of Atenas explained, "[T]he Cubans who get an education in private institutions enter public and social life with a feeling of superiority . . . whereas those who attend public schools might feel that they are placed on an inferior level. This results in the predominance of the private institutions . . . which damages the prestige of the public school, which is the one that is truly nationalist and democratic."[27]

Social perceptions about private education paved the way to mobility and reproduced the social and racial inequities that characterized republican society. As Communist leader Juan Marinello asserted in 1940, "[A]ll secondary and technical education of any value is dispensed in schools for white kids and youths."[28] Attendance in public secondary schools of Afro-Cubans and poor whites somehow compensated for their exclusion from the private sector, but their limited number made it more difficult for these students to continue their education beyond the elementary level. Blacks' representation in public secondary education was always below their population share. In the Havana Institute for Secondary Education they represented about 14 percent of the student body in 1906–8. In some professional schools, such as those of commerce, their share was allegedly lower. Even in the normal schools the percentage of black students was well below their proportion in the school-age population. Only 10 percent of the students enrolled during the opening year of the Havana normal school for female teachers (1915) were nonwhite. The proportion of black women in the school increased, but it was still only 17 percent ten years later despite the fact that enrollment opportunities had expanded significantly with the creation of similar institutions in most provinces. In the normal school for male teachers, 18 percent of the graduates during 1918–28 were black or mulatto.[29]

Opportunities were not greater in higher education. Enrollment at the University of Havana increased steadily, but it could accommodate only a limited number of students. Its student body had grown from about 600 in 1904 to 3,000 in 1921, 5,000 in 1930, and 15,000 in the late 1940s and early 1950s.[30] Blacks and mulattoes made up 11 percent of the students and 16 percent of the graduates in 1925–26. Their proportion among the students was similar in the late 1920s, and, if Betancourt's estimates are correct, it was not much higher in the early 1950s (15–20 percent). In the private Universidad Católica Santo Tomás de Villanueva, black representation was of course negligible.[31] Afro-Cubans entered universities since the very beginning of the republic, but in a proportion below their population share.

Patterns of participation and advancement within the educational system mirrored trends found in society at large, particularly in the labor market. Black representation decreased in secondary and higher education and was nonexistent in the most prestigious schools, which were invariably private and segregated. But few obstacles seemed to have existed for Afro-Cubans to enter public schools, either as students or teachers. The cross-racial nature of public educational institutions should not be taken as proof that they were free from racial discrimination, however. Admittedly rare, instances of discrimination were far from absent in public schools. For instance, a French planter from Oriente recalled in 1919 that in his boyhood there were about five hundred students in the Institute of Santiago de Cuba, of whom "over" four hundred were white. By the late 1910s, he asserted, this situation had been "reversed" and a growing number of blacks were entering the institution. "The majority of the coming practicing lawyers of Santiago are Negroes," he said. This "reversal" had not taken place without resistance, however. "The principal of the institute does not want to give degrees to the

Negroes but says that despite the obstacles he puts in their way he is forced to give them degrees, and not to the whites because the latter are degenerate and unambitious." In the equally public normal schools, according to Marinello, there was a "real conspiracy" to keep the number of Afro-Cuban students to a minimum. If admitted, they were barred from activities that implied visibility and the representation of the school in social events, such as music bands. At the university level, blacks complained in 1929 that they were consistently given lower grades than whites.[32]

Likewise, although Afro-Cuban teachers found employment in the public sector, getting a job might have been more difficult than the statistical figures suggest. In the early years of the republic, American efforts to train Cuban teachers resulted in the exclusion of Afro-Cubans. As part of their efforts to court the black vote, the Liberals argued that under Estrada Palma black teachers had been displaced from public school classrooms and that conscious efforts were being made to whiten the profession. Furthermore, as with any other job in government, teaching positions were distributed through networks of patronage to which blacks and mulattoes did not have equal access. Tranquilino Maza Cobián, an Afro-Cuban from Santiago who obtained a teaching license in 1906, recalled later that it had been "a challenge" to be appointed. Another black professor was denied a position in Bayamo's technical school in 1951 because an allegedly less qualified white candidate was the daughter of a local political boss. In a typical example of the accommodational practices that seem to have mediated race relations in republican society, the competition was declared formally void while the white teacher continued to be "temporarily" hired.[33]

Despite these obstacles and the financial constraints imposed by their concentration in the lower strata of society, a growing number of Afro-Cubans succeeded in expanding their education beyond elementary school, acquired professional and college degrees, and taught in public institutions. Urrutia was correct when he claimed that blacks had educated themselves en masse after independence.[34] In addition to the cross-racial nature of public schools, this process was facilitated by the concentration of Afro-Cubans in the cities, where most schools were located. Rural education was in fact quite deficient. In 1931 the literacy rate for the ten largest cities in the country was 91 percent, compared to 64 percent for the remainder of the country. Only 22 percent of the rural population 5–24 years old attended public schools in 1953, compared to 45 percent of the urban population.[35] This overall advancement of Afro-Cuban education was recognized by both blacks and whites. Afro-Cuban intellectuals interpreted it as a demonstration of blacks' intellectual capacity; some whites perceived it as a threat to the social order and to racial hierarchies, and others claimed it exemplified the wonders of Cuban racial fraternity.

There were elements of truth in each of these interpretations. Blacks' educational advancement was primarily a reflection of their own efforts and their capacity to take advantage of public educational opportunities—but opportunities existed. Thus, whereas *Heraldo de Cuba*—a newspaper edited by white Liberal congressman Orestes Ferrara—referred to black progress in education as "comforting" and claimed that white Cubans should pride themselves for not establishing racial barriers in education, *Labor Nueva* contested that Afro-Cubans had advanced "without anybody's help."[36] What the *Heraldo* construed as a white concession, *Labor Nueva* deemed an Afro-Cuban conquest. A conquest it was, for it was through mobilization and political pressure that blacks obtained from the colonial government equal access to educational institutions in the late nineteenth century. Reversing this gain was unthinkable in a republic that claimed to be racially inclusive and that was based on universal male suffrage. White racists understood the implications of this conquest, which they perceived as a threat against the social order and political stability. Two white Cubans stated bluntly in a 1922 private letter, "It is quite true that there is not a single negro who is not studying to be a doctor." Blacks' "tendency to compete with and even excel" over whites, they claimed, would inevitably result in a racial war.[37] A U.S. military official concurred: "[B]lacks are gradually attaining mental superiority over the whites. . . . The relative standing of whites and blacks in the lower and higher educational institutions . . . brings out the fact of negro ascendancy." Personal ambition and mobility were supposed to be positive individual traits, but in the case of blacks they represented a motive of "alarm." By being "ambitious and studious," Afro-Cubans were becoming "racially conscious of their strength and therefore demanding their proportionate share of offices and graft."[38] Indeed, blacks were trying to translate educational gains into occupational mobility. In the process, they entered social spaces and activities that had traditionally been white domains.

AFRO-CUBAN PROFESSIONALS

The number of black professionals was negligible at the beginning of the republic, although several Afro-Cubans had excelled since colonial times in writing, journalism, medicine, dentistry, education, and music.[39] By 1899 there was only one Afro-Cuban lawyer, ten physicians, two bookkeepers, and four clergymen. There were 102 Afro-Cuban teachers. Just a few hundred blacks worked in occupations related to what the census considered "professional services," less than 1 percent of the working population.

Three decades later, a social sector of black professionals was clearly distinguishable. By 1931, the number of black lawyers had increased to 174, including 3 women. There were also 158 black physicians, 5 of them female, 49 dentists, 71 pharmacists, and 1,375 teachers. About 4 percent of the black working population was employed in the "professional services" sector, and this proportion expanded further, reaching an estimated 5.3 percent in 1943. Afro-Cubans were right when they claimed to have "competent professionals in all the disciplines" who constituted "an abundant class of our society."[40]

But the relative "abundance" of Afro-Cuban professionals was the problem. Their growing number represented or was perceived as a threat to whites' ability to control access to lucrative jobs. Two students of race relations in the island captured this process in 1928: "Other factors in the racial division, which is largely economic and cultural, are undoubtedly the rising level of education of the colored and their increasing familiarity with political methods and procedures."[41] Education itself was a marker of status, but it resulted in economic security only in relation to new employment opportunities. Afro-Cubans thus denounced what they perceived as a growing gap between preparation and employment. As Afro-Cuban author Ruiz Suárez said, to perform an unworthy job was not acceptable after "qualifying for the symbols of capacity represented by a degree from institutions of learning."[42]

Frustration grew in relation to educational attainment. "A novel could be written," asserted Alberto Arredondo, about the "extraordinary obstacles" faced by ascending blacks. In fact, such novels were written. Eulogio Valdés, the central character of Hernández Catá's *La piel* (The skin, 1910s), exemplifies the difficulties and obstacles faced by a highly educated Afro-Cuban in overcoming the barriers represented in a racist society by skin color—"la piel." Another Valdés, Miguel of Masdeu's *La raza triste*, also recreates the deep sense of frustration and despair felt by educated blacks in response to their exclusion from better-paid jobs and exclusive (at times, not so exclusive) public spaces. Miguel Valdés's only hope to establish himself as a physician in Bayamo is to be appointed head of the municipal hospital, but such a position had been traditionally occupied by a white doctor. "I think I am a good doctor. But I descend from blacks, I am a mulatto and the medical profession has been not only a whites' privilege, but a privilege of the most illustrious families." Both Hernández Catá and Masdeu chose to let their black protagonists die, conveying the pessimism of the emergent black middle class.[43]

The barriers faced by Miguel Valdés were neither a literary invention nor unique. Like him, some Afro-Cubans rose to middle-class status from very modest social origins. One example is that of Florencio Baró. A native of rural Matanzas, where he worked as a water carrier in the Santa Rita sugar mill, Baró moved first to the city of Matanzas, then to the capital. As an urban resident he performed a great variety of jobs: apprentice to a baker, street merchant, rural guard, policeman, and journalist. He was one of the founding members of the journal *Labor Nueva* (1916) and by 1929 had become the owner and principal of a professional academy of English, bookkeeping, and stenography in Havana. Tranquilino Maza's story was not too different. Born in Santiago de Cuba to a poor family, Maza became a tailor as soon as he finished his elementary education. For several years he combined his work with additional studies, and in 1906 he succeeded in getting a teacher's license. Looking for educational opportunities, Maza moved to Havana, where he attended the university, earning a degree in dental surgery in 1913 and another in medicine in 1916.[44]

Some Afro-Cuban women also obtained college degrees against all odds. María E. Matehu, an immigrant to Havana from Jovellanos, attended medical school with the support of her mother, who came to the city to work as a seamstress. In another case, a student of Havana's normal school for women wrote a public letter in 1929 asking for help to get a summer job to buy uniforms and books for the following academic year. Her father, she explained, did not have "acquaintances" in the city, so he was poor and could not obtain a job recommendation for her. Family support was crucial to educational advancement. Despite these financial obstacles—or perhaps because of them— her father encouraged her to get a professional teaching degree. Consuelo Serra, a teacher in the normal school who completed university degrees in pedagogy and philosophy, recalled that her mother had one goal: to demonstrate that blacks could "triumph in life." Success, in turn, depended on education, which her mother understood not only as schooling.[45]

Given these difficulties, it is not surprising that although the number of Afro-Cubans with professional degrees increased further by 1943, they remained heavily underrepresented in the professions. The proportion of blacks among lawyers, nurses, pharmacists, engineers, and physicians was less than half of what it should have been under conditions of equality (see table 3.3 above). The only profession in which Afro-Cubans were close to

TABLE 4.3. Percentage Distribution, Economic Sectors, Occupations, and Professions, by Income and Race, 1943

| | Low Income | | | High Income | | |
| | Whites | Blacks | Ratio | Whites | Blacks | Ratio |
Category	(1)	(2)	(2/1)	(3)	(4)	(4/3)
Economic sectors (total)	80.2	88.0	1.1	1.8	0.9	0.5
Agriculture, fishery	95.5	97.1	1.0	0.5	2.5	5.0
Mining	55.6	84.4	1.5	2.7	1.1	0.4
Construction	60.7	66.2	1.1	1.9	1.1	0.6
Manufacturing	74.8	82.9	1.1	1.7	1.1	0.6
Transportation, communication	50.0	58.3	1.2	3.3	1.7	0.5
Banking	34.8	61.2	1.8	10.5	11.6	1.1
Domestic service	91.2	96.0	1.0	0.8	0.4	0.5
Recreational service	69.9	82.8	1.2	3.2	0.6	0.2
Professional service	45.2	63.3	1.4	11.1	3.5	0.3
Government	55.5	67.0	1.2	2.3	0.8	0.3
Occupations						
Peasants	96.0	97.6	1.0	0.6	0.6	1.0
Owners, managers	66.2	82.3	1.2	4.3	2.9	0.7
Clerks, vendors	62.0	79.1	1.3	2.6	1.0	0.4
Trained industrial workers	69.9	78.2	1.1	1.7	1.0	0.6
Nontrained industrial workers	85.4	89.5	1.0	0.8	0.6	0.7
Security service	83.4	85.0	1.0	1.5	0.8	0.5
Personal service	86.0	91.2	1.1	1.4	1.1	0.8
Agricultural workers	96.3	97.4	1.0	0.2	0.4	2.0
Professions	35.4	52.1	1.5	8.4	2.5	0.1
Lawyers	20.2	40.2	2.0	23.0	5.7	0.2
Bookkeepers	29.1	50.0	1.7	23.6	18.2	0.8
Dentists	20.2	23.2	1.1	12.0	10.2	0.8
Nurses	46.7	77.8	1.7	2.1	0.0	0.0
Pharmacists	44.3	43.8	1.0	6.1	12.5	2.0
Civil engineers	8.2	18.8	2.3	43.2	0.0	0.0
Teachers	23.1	24.5	1.1	1.4	0.6	0.4
Physicians	10.3	15.2	1.5	27.8	15.2	0.6

Source: Cuba, *Censo 1943*, 1098, 1203–5.
Note: Low income, up to 59 pesos per month; high income, more than 200 pesos per month.

being proportionally represented was teaching, the very bottom of this sector in terms of salary. Professions such as nursing were actually whiter in 1943 than they had been at the beginning of the republic. In no other sector of the labor market was racial inequality so acute. Afro-Cubans learned that the hardest barrier to overcome was the one that opened the gates to the middle class. Betancourt, himself a university graduate, explained a decade later that it was the lack of appropriate networks that hindered blacks' access to these positions. They could not enter the social clubs and associations of the white elite, where many attractive jobs were informally distributed through recommendations and family connections. But overt racial discrimination also played a role, and Betancourt underlined that those in higher positions were discriminated against most.[46]

Strong evidence supports his claim. Although income differentials by race characterized the whole occupational structure in the early 1940s, they were significantly lower in the more massive sectors of the Cuban economy. In agriculture and manufacturing, which covered about 65 percent of all employment, income differentials by race were low (table 4.3). Conversely, inequalities were larger in more selective, better-paid activities (banking, professional services) and occupations, especially among professionals, clerks, and vendors. In general terms it is possible to agree with Betancourt that the higher the occupational category, the greater the differential.[47] Among the worst-paid occupations, those in which more than 80 percent of the total labor force received no more than 59 pesos per month (that is, peasants, agricultural workers, personal services, and unskilled industrial workers), income differences by race were not significant. Race had a more limited impact on the life chances of the poor. It was among professionals that differences were larger. Only 2.5 percent of black and mulatto professionals entered the higher income groups, while white proportions were three and a half times larger (8.4 percent). The opposite was true in the low-income bracket: blacks represented 52 percent of the professionals making no more than 59 pesos a month, compared to 35 percent of whites. And the gap was even wider in some of the most exclusive professions, such as law.

The social situation of black professionals was in fact precarious. Although education and "culture" made this group eligible for middle-class status, their skin color, social origin, and financial situation, as well as white racism, kept them dangerously close to the world of poverty and manual labor that they were trying to escape. As mentioned above, half of all black professionals earned a monthly income similar to that of workers in the most massive sectors of the economy—hardly a middle-class symbol. In response to this situation and in reaction to dominant perceptions and social practices that regarded and treated blacks as a homogeneous social group, upwardly mobile and educated Afro-Cubans stressed the cultural abyss that separated them from the masses of black manual workers.

As in the United States, this discourse was addressed to the government and to white politicians, intellectuals, and employers, those who defined the spaces available for the black middle class to exist and expand. By emphasizing their cultural superiority to lower-class blacks, Afro-Cuban professionals sought to enlarge these spaces, create new opportunities for themselves, and eliminate the barriers that hindered their social advancement. As Urrutia stated, once they achieved "cultural progress," the "cultivated blacks" should be given the opportunity to demonstrate their capacity to contribute to Cuba's "civic life," that is, to perform white-collar jobs in the public sector.[48]

Afro-Cuban intellectuals thus challenged the white notion that all blacks were equal—that is, equally inferior—or belonged to the same "class." Lino D'Ou addressed this topic in 1916: "Our aspiration to progress and happiness is screaming for the establishment of a well-defined social scale. . . . Neither all whites nor all blacks are the same. There is a feasible equality that nobody has the right to deny to us: the equality of the good people, the conscious and responsible ones, those with a decent household, those in the arts and the liberal professions." Ramón Vasconcelos also was definite about this: "The same unbalance that exists among whites' social classes exists, relatively speaking, among the colored ones." Likewise, in response to a white physician who referred to blacks as a "class," Urrutia asserted in 1929: "So the whole black race constitutes a single class? This is the height of improvisation."[49]

As part of their efforts to carve out a well-defined social position in a hostile environment, Afro-Cuban intellectuals frequently referred to "low" blacks in pejorative terms. Urrutia called them the "other" blacks; Vasconcelos, "la negrada," which he defined as the "stupid mass that has taken only superficial things from progress, misunderstands democracy as demagogy, and ridicules the minority that deserves all sorts of considerations." A reader of his columns referred to poorly educated blacks as "the ignorant mob"; Afro-Cuban poet José Manuel Poveda called them the "blind masses."[50]

These "low" blacks were not only ignorant. It was more important to the black middle class that they displayed their lack of education and proper manners in "public." Afro-Cuban professionals feared that public demonstrations of what they deemed "primitive" cultural forms served to reinforce the link between lowness and blackness. They called upon blacks to de-Africanize themselves while condemning Santería and other Afro-Cuban cultural expressions, particularly when they reached the public sphere. As Vasconcelos stated, referring to the Afro-Cuban *comparsas* (processions) during the 1916 carnival: "Go to the wilderness, where you can unleash your rapture and obscenity without offending the sight and refinement of those who want to live in a civilized society, not in an African village. . . . As long as a drum exists, there will be barbarism." Another Afro-Cuban, a reader of *La Prensa*, condemned the *comparsas* as a colonial legacy of "sensual licentiousness in the middle of the street." The implications of these public acts for the black middle class were obvious to Lino D'Ou, who stressed that he did not want "white racism" to believe that all blacks participated in such spectacles—an argument that could be used to justify the exclusion of Afro-Cubans from "high" social circles.[51]

For similar reasons, gender roles, family stability, and "decency" figured prominently among the concerns of these professionals. Indeed, a lack of nuclear families had been long understood as an inherent trait of blackness, another indication of their congenital inferiority. A North American observer summarized this view in 1907: "Morality does not enter into original African religions. From then [slavery] until today, the Cuban negro[es] . . . have propagated and continue to propagate largely without regard to family or marriage. . . . [F]amily is to a large extent made upon passion and broken on whim; it is little regarded."[52] Population statistics seemed to corroborate this impression. Blacks were systematically underrepresented in marriages and overrepresented in illegitimate births. The 1907 census estimated that two-thirds of all illegitimate children were black or mulatto. This percentage had not changed by 1931. With horror, Urrutia reported that in 1928 the proportion of marriages among whites was almost double that of blacks, whereas rates of illegitimacy were three times higher among Afro-Cubans.[53]

Afro-Cuban intellectuals feared that these statistics could be used to confirm white stereotypes about the lack of family life among blacks. "We must establish among ourselves the moral concept of family," D'Ou admonished. "We must elevate our social morale," concurred Urrutia. Improvement was not to be achieved, however, if Afro-Cuban women did not fulfill what was defined as their main social role: their family duties. Writing in 1916, Vasconcelos claimed that women were "the greatest obstacle in the regeneration of blacks." Afro-Cuban females, the journalist explained, were intellectually and morally deficient. Specifically, the "mulatas," whose physical beauty turned them into the easy prey of men's sexual appetites, allegedly preferred prostitution over an honest life of scarcity and hard work. Indeed, Vasconcelos asserted that half of all *mulatas* lived in consensual unions, one-third became prostitutes, and only 10 percent ever married. The challenge, thus, was "to restitute women to the household," for, as Afro-Cuban intellectual Ramiro Neyra explained, when black women "fell," they "dragged with them the honor of all other women and a good part of the respect that males, as men, deserved."[54] Both images, that of black females lacking honor and virtue and that of black males commanding no respect, were equally threatening. The former confirmed racist stereotypes about Afro-Cubans' promiscuity and the sexual availability of black women. The latter threatened the manhood and respectability of black males trying to assert their place in society.

Virtue, marriage, and family were stressed by some Afro-Cuban women as well, and some agreed with Vasconcelos that black women disregarded marriage, entered consensual unions too easily, and lacked culture and morality. But other women attacked Vasconcelos and asked what black men had done for the moral and intellectual improvement of Afro-Cuban women. In a response to his column, a black woman who signed as "Indiana" replied that whereas it was a woman's duty to guide her household, men were supposed to protect and take care of their families, not to have mistresses and to abuse their wives.[55] Some male intellectuals also challenged Vasconcelos's sexist remarks, stressing that it was the lack of opportunities that explained the social behavior of black women.[56]

This middle-class rhetoric of honor, virtue, and privacy was a defensive strategy against dominant conventions that denied the possibility of such attributes among blacks, their income and education notwithstanding. As anywhere else, "spatial inequalities made many activities engaged in by the working-class more visible because, lacking private facilities, their work and leisure were more public."[57] Since some white members of the ruling elite did not recognize a private sphere among blacks, the Afro-Cuban professionals had to construct one, emphasizing in the process the distinction between low and cultured elements, regardless of race. As Urrutia stated, "[W]hen we consider our population according to social classes . . . we see that the educated people of both races share the same ideals, interests, and morality."[58]

Furthermore, the necessity of this discourse was stressed by the realities of everyday social relations, in which instances of racial discrimination figured prominently. Although racism and prejudice permeated all social groups, discrimination against ascending blacks was particularly vicious and visible. They were attempting to enter what the white bourgeoisie perceived as its own social, occupational, and physical spaces. The line of color was considerably more porous and fluid among the poorest in society—a reality that frequently led foreign observers to stress that race did not affect social relations in the island. The line that separated "low" whites from blackness was frequently broken in everyday life through their adoption of "black" cultural symbols such as religion, dance, and music or through interracial sexual relations. Castellanos's descriptions (1914) of the lowest in society exemplify this point. He referred to the underworld as a social sphere in which "promiscuity between blacks and whites" was rampant and in which "blacks' lascivious dances attracted degraded and lustful whites." This intense racial mixing among popular sectors was noticed by foreign visitors as well: "The scum of all races danced together, with an abandonment and vulgarity that I have never seen elsewhere."[59]

Race was a considerably more obvious hindrance in social areas defined as exclusive or elegant. In fact, race affected every important aspect of the lives of highly educated blacks, from housing opportunities to jobs. Although social practices that were openly and indistinguishably racist were not common—they could generate bad publicity and even lead to different forms of mobilization and protest—they did occur. One such case took place in the Soledad sugar mill in 1952, when the American manager denied the only dentist in the *batey* (the mill-related town), a black man, the right to work in the company's medical pavilion. Another case took place in Havana in 1947, when an advertisement published in *Información* announced the rent of three "only for whites" houses. Both incidents generated protests and were presented as blatant violations of Cuba's racial fraternity. In the case of Soledad, the mill workers protested against the administration, asserting that Cuba was "Martí and Maceo's land . . . not that of the KKK and lynching." In the example of the apartments, Club Atenas presented the case to the attorney general, claiming that the advertisement violated the constitutional rights of all black citizens. The National Federation of Societies of the Colored Race also intervened and demanded from the president of the republic a "clear and concise" declaration against racial discrimination. Supporting the efforts of both Atenas and the federation was the Communist Party.[60]

More often, however, discrimination was disguised under socially acceptable practices and was consequently more difficult to perceive and document. White racists devised strategies that, while appearing to be racially neutral, resulted in the actual exclusion of Afro-Cubans. For instance, in the 1950s, when it became illegal to document the race of job candidates, institutions such as the Bank of Agricultural and Industrial Development and the War Economy Council required their employees to have a good "personal appearance," a requisite that only whites could fulfill in practice. Furthermore, they asked prospective employees to comment on their affiliation with social or recreational clubs and used that information to determine the race of the applicants.[61]

The most common strategy was to disguise public spaces as private, for-members-only, clubs. This stratagem was applied in bars, restaurants, cabarets, beaches, and many other recreational facilities that became, as a result, racially segregated. This was particularly the case in luxury places and those that catered to the growing audience of North American tourists. As Urrutia stated, whenever a public place became "fashionable," the first thing the managers did was to exclude blacks. Such places were converted by wealthy whites into their own private preserves. And private spaces were untouchable. Neither the constitutional principle of equality nor the myth of a race-less Cubanness applied there. Quite the contrary: luxury itself became a racial icon in Cuban society, a symbol of whiteness and exclusion. Writing in 1952, Felipe Elosegui asserted that to find evidence of racial discrimination one had only to make a brief tour around the "luxury cabarets" of Havana.[62]

Struggles over social spaces thus centered on whether they were public or private. An incident that occurred during the Second Central American Sport Games (Havana, 1930) exemplifies this point. While President Machado welcomed the visiting athletes "with open arms," the swimming team of Panama and black spectators were denied access to the facilities of the Havana Yacht Club, where a competition was going to take place. What is interesting, however, is that when Club Atenas denounced this affair, it emphasized that the event had been announced in the daily press as one of "public character." The secretary of public works, himself a member of the Havana Yacht Club, agreed: if it was opposed to blacks visiting their quarters, then the club should never have agreed to host a public competition. In his Sunday column, Urrutia stressed as well that the games were public and could be attended by anyone who wished to do so.[63] Most of the press concurred with this view but also described the club's decision as an act of incivility and barbarism—a "moral lynching," according to *Avance*.[64] Only Juan Gualberto Gómez challenged the private-public dichotomy by categorically stressing that, like any institution in which race prejudice was nurtured, the Havana Yacht Club should disappear.[65]

But the dichotomy persisted. Racist owners frequently invoked the law of associations to justify the exclusion of Afro-Cubans from public establishments on the grounds that they were private clubs. In 1951, the son of Felipe Ayón, an Afro-Cuban political boss in the neighborhood of Dragones and a personal friend of then senator Batista, was denied service at a Maxim cabaret, even though, it was denounced, "this cabaret is far from being covered by the law that regulates the functioning of private societies." The same law was invoked by the owners of El Casino Deportivo when they refused entrance to a group of black physicians attending a banquet organized by the National Medical Congress in 1939. When confronted, the casino's restaurant manager argued that, according to the bylaws of the club, they could not provide service to "people of color."[66]

Similar incidents happened elsewhere in the country. In Matanzas, a group of black students participating in a picnic organized by the University of Havana's College of Education were refused service at the Club Monserrate, which despite its denomination was in fact a restaurant. In Santiago de Cuba, the doorman of the bar-restaurant San Pedro del Mar denied entrance to a group of "distinguished personalities from the black population of Santiago" who attempted to patronize the place. And in Guantánamo, the Pan American Club refused service to none other than Antonio Maceo y Font, grandson of Afro-Cuban national hero Antonio Maceo. The person in charge explained that he had orders "not to allow people of color" into the bar.[67]

Those who could not disguise their establishments as private clubs followed different strategies. Hotel managers, for instance, claimed to have no rooms available when black customers sought accommodation. For example, a black female teacher who made a reservation at the Andino Hotel, Havana, in 1940 was denied a room when she presented herself at the desk. More prominent blacks were subject to similar discrimination. In 1929, Cuba's greatest boxing champion, Eligio Sardiñas y Montalvo—better known as Kid Chocolate—was denied lodging in two luxury hotels in Santiago, where he was being entertained by local authorities as a guest of honor. Since hotels were, by definition, establishments open to the public, the owners explained that it was because of the lack of empty rooms that they had not accommodated Kid Chocolate.[68] Something similar happened to African American congressman Arthur Mitchell when he visited Havana in 1937. Mitchell was denied service at Saratoga Hotel, which the owner claimed was "full." The manager of Hotel Sevilla, William Hogan from Tennessee, also refused to accommodate black customers.[69]

Discrimination because of race was prevalent in other areas as well. Often, when a black person tried to rent an apartment in some of the fancy areas of Havana he or she was informed that it had been rented already. Urrutia relates the case of a friend who, after sending his white servant to arrange for an apartment, went in person to sign the papers. Once the owners saw that the tenant was black they attempted to cancel the agreement. According to Urrutia, "decent" black families had great difficulties in getting access to "skyscrapers" and modern apartment buildings. Fancy barbershops also denied service to black customers, arguing that they did not know how to do blacks' hair. Even Havana's dog track, which was operated by a North American firm, claimed to be a private club and designated a separate area for blacks.[70]

These examples are only a sample of what was probably an everyday reality for middle-class blacks. Instances of discrimination are known to researchers only when they were publicly denounced, received press coverage, or generated some sort of institutional response. Indeed, all the cases mentioned above resulted in protests, mobilization, and even legal action. The National Medical Congress canceled its banquet and condemned publicly the discriminatory practices of El Casino Deportivo. The university students who were discriminated against in Matanzas took their case to the courts. The San Pedro del Mar restaurant in Santiago was closed by the town council in response to a wave of protests from several political organizations and Afro-Cuban clubs. The Guantánamo case ended up in the courts as well. And the national government was literally flooded with telegrams and letters demanding action against the management of the Saratoga Hotel for discriminating against Representative Mitchell.

That these racist practices did not go unchallenged does not mean, however, that discrimination was always denounced or protested. In everyday social relations, accommodation, not conflict, was probably the most prevalent solution. As Nicolás Guillén stated in 1929, blacks had slowly withdrawn from luxury cafés, sumptuous official events, and elegant boulevards, so "cultured" blacks, of whom he was himself an excellent example, did not have access to those places anymore. Urrutia concurred. "Just by seeing the luxury of a place," he argued, blacks "abstained from visiting it."[71] When protests did occur, they centered on the "public" character of these recreational establishments—as in the case of the Havana Yacht Club mentioned above. Implicit in these arguments, of course, was that discrimination and exclusion were legal, perhaps unavoidable, in places that were "truly" private. Thus, in a sense, the "clean and decent blacks with money in their pockets," as Urrutia described himself and other Afro-Cuban professionals,[72] had given up the conquest of these spaces. Instead, and in response to discrimination and lack of opportunities for advancement, they created their own private spaces and exclusive societies.

AFRO-CUBAN SOCIETIES

The creation of exclusive black spaces rested on a long tradition of Afro-Cuban organizing. Blacks had come together in religious, cultural, and mutual-aid societies since colonial times, first in *cabildos de nación*, which brought together groups of African slaves of common origin, later in the "societies of the colored race" that proliferated in the island after the abolition of slavery. As previous scholars have noted, these societies played a key role in the survival, adaptation, and transmission of African cultural and social practices while contributing at the same time to the emergence of a new Afro-Cuban identity.[73]

Many of these organizations continued their activities well into the republican period. Although their purposes varied, most included recreational activities, mutual aid, and the celebration of other "social events." Other societies organized along occupational lines, giving workers of the same trade the opportunity to socialize and share their common problems and concerns.[74] Still others were devoted to a very specific purpose, such as the promotion of theater and other cultural activities.

Not infrequently, Afro-Cuban associations registered with the government as mutual-aid societies were in fact centers where African religions and Santería were practiced under disguise. African slaves learned to hide their own gods and rituals behind a facade of Catholic saints and lawful associations. After the 1880s, when the Spanish government ordered the closure of the *cabildos de nación*, this practice of disguising them as mutual-aid societies intensified. In some societies, such as the Sociedad de Socorros Mutuos Nación Congo Real or the Sociedad de Socorros Mutuos Las Cinco Naciones, the change in denomination barely hid the African character of the societies. Since repression of African cultural practices continued under the republic, so did this exercise of masking. The Sociedad Santa Rita de Casia y San Lázaro, for instance, created in 1902, presented itself as a "singing, dancing, and mutual-aid society" but actually brought together, according to its own members, "those who profess the Lucumí religion." The associates claimed, however, that by providing assistance to their members they were also fulfilling Jesus' preaching of universal love. Of similar purpose was the Sociedad de Instrucción y Recreo Nación Congo-Portugués y sus Hijos Santa Teresa de Jesús Meditando, created in Cienfuegos in 1922. Police Inspector Rafael Roche y Monteagudo, who actively participated in the repression of *brujería* during the early republic, complained that the "extinguished brotherhoods of African idols" had found refuge in the new social clubs and were still practicing their "repugnant fetishism."[75]

However, a central trait of most of these societies was their avowed apolitical and areligious character. Associates were forbidden to discuss political or religious matters in the club. The ordinances of Unión Fraternal, one of the main associations in Havana, stated that the society would keep "away from any political tendency" and "from all contact . . . with religious or sociological problems."[76] But as the struggle for independence and the activities of the Directorio Central de Sociedades de la Raza de Color had clearly shown, cultural and mutual-aid societies could play a crucial role in the political mobilization of Afro-Cubans. Independence did not change this. Quite the contrary, in the republic these societies became a locus of electoral propaganda and a preferred target of politicians. The fact that presidential and congressional candidates made Afro-Cuban societies an unavoidable stop on their tours indicates that their electoral importance did not go unnoticed.

This was true even for those associations that, because of their African character, were generally reputed to be criminal. In their quest for votes, politicians did not hesitate to court the support of the ñáñigos, a secret fraternal society of African origin that was frequently presented as a criminal syndicate of African savages. In 1920, for instance, an American source reported that "secret organizations of African origin" had shown signs of revival due to "the unusual license of a bitterly fought election." Thanks to political influence, a ñáñigo leader named Marcos Berrios, alias "Cayuco," previously sentenced to twenty years imprisonment, had just been pardoned. But as Gerardo del Valle recounts in one of his masterful short stories, ñáñigos' support could be crucial for a political office seeker to succeed in a popular neighborhood. In "Para concejal" (For town councillor), he narrates how Mano Abierta (Open Hand), a white boss of the "Palotista Party" in the black neighborhood of Colón, had obtained the nomination for representative through the support of Candela (Fire), the chief of a ñáñigo association in the area. Candela, in return, had been nominated for town councillor, an example of the reciprocal relationships typical of clientele politics in the republic.[77]

Afro-Cuban societies and politics were linked in other ways as well. Several clubs designated well-known public figures as their honorary presidents, including prominent Afro-Cubans such as Juan Gualberto Gómez and Generoso Campos Marquetti. In 1919 the honorary presidents of Club Moncada in Cruces (Las Villas) included Gómez; Liberal politician and journalist Saturnino Escoto; Pablo Herrera, who became president of Club Atenas; and other prominent Afro-Cuban public figures based in Havana.[78] Other societies were named after these leaders, such as the Sociedad de Recreo Juan Gualberto Gómez in Regla and one with a similar name in Quiebra Hacha (Pinar del Río).[79]

These practices were designed to give members access to and some influence over the political establishment and the distribution of patronage. And patronage they received. When members of the Club Hermanos Unidos were accused of *brujería*, their legal defense was undertaken by none other than Representative Campos Marquetti. The Juan Gualberto Gómez Center constantly requested all sorts of favors from him, including public jobs and scholarships for members and their families. Favors were also asked from white public figures. When a prominent member of Unión Fraternal was left off the payroll of the office of the secretary of public works, the club asked the minister to rehire him. Likewise, the Movimiento de Opinión Progresista Integral (MOPI, Movement of Integral Progressive Opinion), requested President Batista to grant a scholarship to Afro-Cuban soprano Olimpia Cabrera in 1952.[80]

Some societies also managed to obtain loans, financial contributions, and other subsidies from the state. In the mid-1910s Unión Fraternal received a yearly subsidy from Havana's city council. Club Atenas obtained public lands and a $50,000 contribution in 1925. After the 1930s, it became customary for Afro-Cuban clubs to be considered for government subsidies drawn from lottery funds. Eighty-six societies asked President Batista for subsidies in 1944. Unión Fraternal and Club Atenas were among the forty-four institutions benefiting from these subsidies in 1943. Both Grau and Batista also gave thousands of pesos to the National Federation of Societies of the Colored Race in the late 1940s and the 1950s.[81] Political figures' refusal to support a black society might lead to public condemnation in the black press, hurting their electoral chances in the future.[82]

The "colored societies" thus represented a major route for Afro-Cubans' social and political ascent. The societies were a means to develop valuable social contacts and networks. As the statutes of *La Unión* from Morón, Camagüey, explicitly stated, "[T]he purpose of this society is to provide the colored race with a center of common fraternity and unbreakable union, where loyalty shines."[83] Through the societies, lawyers, pharmacists, and public accountants found clients; physicians, dentists and midwives found patients; musicians and artists found audiences. Some of the larger associations, such as Unión Fraternal, provided all these services to their associates. Black professionals and aspirants to public office found a niche in which to consolidate their social and professional prominence, and they were quite frequently the leaders of the societies. For instance, the president of the Club Unión Fraternal in Nueva Paz (Havana province), created in 1910, was Sixto Ayón, later a candidate for the provincial council on the Popular Party ticket. The secretary of Divina Caridad in 1902 was Tiburcio Aguirre, an active member of the Moderate and Conservative Parties during the early years of the republic. In the 1920s, the Antilla Sport Club was led by Pedro Portuondo Calás, a renowned Afro-Cuban journalist; Unión Fraternal, by Ramón Hugues, an employee of the office of the secretary of communications.[84] Most of the presidents of Unión Sagüera in Sagua la Grande (Las Villas) had been town councillors at some point. Ricardo Valdés Morales, the founding president of Bella Unión in Martí (Matanzas), was also town councillor. The leadership of El Fénix in Trinidad (Las Villas) included a journalist and the president of the municipal council; that of Unión Club in Lajas (Las Villas), the son of a well-known independence patriot and a lieutenant of the municipal police. The vice president of Club Moncada in Cruces (Las Villas) was Dr. Agustín Iznaga Mora, a lawyer. In Pinar del Río, Atenas Occidental was headed by Rufino Hernández, a notable "industrialist" from the region.[85]

These societies also created opportunities in areas that remained difficult for Afro-Cubans to access. This was the case in sports. The white social clubs sponsored their own amateur teams, to which blacks and mulattoes had no access. In fact, with the partial exception of professional baseball, racial segregation seems to have prevailed in most sports and the amateur leagues by the 1920s and thereafter. The Afro-Cuban clubs and societies participated in national competitions with their own all-black teams, and they were grouped into a different association. Although no formal "Negro league" existed in the island, black sportsmen were not accepted in the Unión Atlética de Amateurs de Cuba, created in the 1920s by some of the most aristocratic social clubs of Havana—the Havana Yacht Club and the Vedado Tennis Club among them—to promote sports. Rather, Afro-Cuban sportsmen were grouped into a loose organization called the Liga Intersocial, comprised of well-known black clubs such as Club Atenas, Magnetic Sport Club, Unión Fraternal, and Antilla Sport Club. In the 1940s, most black athletes belonged to a separate organization called Organización Deportiva Amateur de Cuba. Athletes from the National University participated in the Unión Atlética, but in the athletic games sponsored by the university in 1929, black teams were grouped into a separate, so-called independent group. University teams avoided black players so as not to offend the teams of the white elegant societies.[86]

Given the importance of the Afro-Cuban societies and clubs, it is not surprising that their control was frequently contested. By the 1910s a new generation of Afro-Cuban professionals were pushing to make their way into what they described as the "old" and "traditional" societies. Especially after 1912, when the road for black autonomous political mobilization was effectively closed, they launched a furious campaign against the existing clubs, ridiculing their purposes and composition. These young intellectuals argued that black societies were colonial, atavistic, and out of touch with the needs of "modern" and "civilized" blacks. They labeled them "African *cabildos*" and "dens of iniquity" whose only function was to organize dances. "In Havana there is not a single society with a library, but they all have bars," complained Vasconcelos.[87]

One of the most criticized associations was the Centro de Cocheros. Created in 1880, when coachmen represented a privileged sector of the black urban labor force, it was organized as a mutual-aid society under the patronage of Our Lady of Charity. By the 1910s it was reputed to be "the most prosperous" of all the black societies in Havana, with two hundred male and four hundred female members.[88] Still, young Afro-Cuban intellectuals criticized it on the ground that it was an African *cabildo* that had not evolved since colonial times. "The Centro de Cocheros," Vasconcelos explained, "represents the ancient ideal: mutual aid, veneration of sacred images . . . , soirées on their anniversary . . . , dances during Carnival and domino games the rest of the year." He encouraged them to "de-Africanize" so they could turn their *cabildo* into a "modest, but decent society" that could fulfill the needs of modern men: books, baths, and sports.[89]

In fact, "decency" had always figured prominently in the statutes of the Afro-Cuban societies, and most of them included requisites such as "honesty, good morality, and hard work" for membership. Furthermore, it was not true that all they had done was sponsor dances and recreation or that none of them had a library, as Vasconcelos claimed. On the contrary, as mentioned above, the societies played a key role in the expansion of educational opportunities among Afro-Cubans. The young Afro-Cuban intellectuals' criticism was more a function of their self-identification as "modern," "cultured," and "clean" than of the alleged deficiencies of the societies themselves. It was a conflict born out of their recognition that there was "an enormous discord in the interests and aspirations" of Afro-Cubans due to their "uneven mental and moral level." As Vasconcelos said, "[W]hat is called the colored race is an ethnic conglomerate integrated by superimposed social strata: some belong to the eighteenth century, and others to the current one."

Their elitist view of the lower sectors of the Afro-Cuban population was summarized in a graphic sentence: "Scratch lightly [the skin of] a black, and you will find a Congolese."[90]

For these young Afro-Cuban intellectuals, "decency" was actually a matter of selectivity and representation. To achieve both, these young professionals created their own "new" societies. For instance, in 1908, "a group of youths" who "deplored the hodgepodge" of the Afro-Cuban centers created Jóvenes de L'Printemps, where the "best" of Afro-Cuban society socialized. Similar in kind was the Agrupación de Asaltos Jóvenes del Vals, created in 1916 as a place to hold "intimate parties" and to which only fifty members of "irreproachable morality and behavior" would be admitted.[91] Whereas public dances were considered by the new professionals to be immoral and primitive, social gatherings in private spaces in which all participants where acquaintances of known reputation and morality were deemed to be respectable and civilized. As with many other issues, in this the Afro-Cuban new elites were hardly unique compared to their equals in the United States or Brazil.[92]

Some of the new societies had purely intellectual ends. The Booker T. Washington Society, created in 1915, organized a yearly series of lectures and refused to admit either "corrupt old people" or "electoral traffickers." The society appealed to the educated youth and presented itself as their "greatest moral and intellectual monument." A similar effort was that of the Sociedad de Estudios Científicos y Literarios, created in 1914 to show "the capacity of the youth of the colored race." Organized to eradicate illiteracy and propagate high culture among Afro-Cubans, the society presented itself as "the greatest intellectual movement initiated by Cubans" and published its own journal, *Aurora*.[93]

Given their alleged cultural character, these organizational efforts were well received by many white intellectuals and politicians, who hailed any attempt at "uplifting" the black population as patriotic.[94] But literature and music were not the only subjects addressed by members of these societies. Cuban youth demanded recognition and criticized the "prejudices" of the Cuban government against them. They voiced their right to "social reparation, collective justice, and good government," while clearly stating that a democracy was real only when it represented the "whole" society. As the president of the Sociedad de Estudios stated, "the new generation" demanded "reparation, equality, justice," and "legitimate representation" in all the affairs of the country.[95]

Young professionals went even further. Since none of their societies truly

achieved national prominence and the number of blacks in the upper echelons of the Cuban state tended to decline, they started to proclaim the need
for Afro-Cubans to "unite."[96] Unity would not be achieved easily, however,
precisely for the very reasons that had impelled young Afro-Cuban professionals to create their own clubs. Afro-Cubans were also politically divided
over their allegiance to the mainstream political parties. The only real point
of consensus was that blacks—that is, the black middle class—deserved a
larger share of the public-office pie as a reward for their electoral support and
intellectual progress.

Two alternatives quickly emerged in response to this need for unity. The
first, promoted by the Afro-Cuban sector of the political class and inspired
by the example of the old Directorio Central de Sociedades, proposed to
create a new directorate that would unify all the Afro-Cuban clubs under a
single organization. Not surprisingly, this idea gained momentum in late
1915, just before the nomination process for the general elections of 1916
began. Its main proponents were lawyer Miguel A. Céspedes, whose term in
Congress was about to expire, and Gómez, at that point a senatorial aspirant
and one of the organizers of the old directorate.[97] Moreover, Gómez had
tried to organize, without success, a cross-racial Asociación Fraternal Cubana to restore racial harmony in the island after the slaughter of 1912.[98]

That the new attempted directorate was politically inspired is beyond any
doubt. Its organizing committee was composed exclusively of black politicians. In addition to Céspedes and Gómez, it included Representatives Escoto Carrión, Ramírez Ross, and Ponvert; Havana town councillors Canals
and Madan; and provincial councillors Mamerto González and Pérez Landa.
Also present were a number of aspirants, such as Gálvez, Risquet, D'Ou, and
Venancio Milián.[99] Regardless of party allegiances, they all had something
in common: the need to demonstrate their electoral appeal among Afro-
Cubans in order to secure a nomination. The directorate was supposed to
provide them with both and to show that they were still the unquestioned
leaders of the Afro-Cuban population.

But 1915 was not 1887 (the date when the old directorate was organized),
and the new attempt to unify the Afro-Cuban societies did not prosper.
Several factors contributed to its failure. First, young Afro-Cuban intellectuals who felt excluded from the initiative criticized it as yet another attempt
of the "old" leaders to control the black vote. Poet José Manuel Poveda
bluntly stated that the unification represented a "danger for the youth" and
that the "new superior class" of black professionals did not need an organization representing "the ancient blind masses who wait for the recognition

of their rights." Writer and politician José Enrique Morúa complained that younger Afro-Cubans had been excluded because of their rejection of the "obsolete" societies. Moreover, the leadership of some clubs resisted giving up their control and autonomy. Lastly, some white politicians, most notably Enrique José Varona, opposed the project on the usual ground that it represented a danger to Cuban racial harmony.[100]

The second alternative was to create a large "new" and "modern" society that, through the "scrupulous selection" of its members, would guarantee what members of the Afro-Cuban middle class envisioned as an adequate representation of their race before Cuban authorities and society. The idea was to replicate the powerful Spanish regional centers and to have a club that reflected the middle class's "flowering state of civilization."[101] In opposition to the directorate, which sought to unify Afro-Cubans across class lines, the new selective society was conceived as an elite organization that explicitly recognized the deep gap separating the emerging middle class from what Poveda called the "blind masses" of Afro-Cubans. Even if they claimed to speak in the name of all Afro-Cubans, by creating a separate association on their own they were in fact renouncing the leadership of most Afro-Cubans. Black workers would have to look for representation and leadership elsewhere.[102]

Due to the objective process of social fragmentation experienced by Afro-Cubans, their limited but growing participation in different branches of the economic and political life of the country, and the appeal of the traditional parties, the alternative of the new society triumphed where the directorate had failed. In fact, among the founding members of the new society were almost all the original supporters of the proposed directorate. In 1917, they created what would be the most famous black association in the republic: Club Atenas.

Exclusivity and selection were indeed issues. The club was created to prove the degree of "preparation" achieved by a sector of the black population and to obtain the social and political "consideration" to which they were entitled. "We are an institution," claimed its organizers, "that reflects the degree of culture, spiritual elevation, and intelligence of the elements that we represent, as well as their aspirations toward constant progress." Thus, only the very "best" of Afro-Cuban social circles were allowed to join. The composition of the 68 founding members is telling. The largest single group was that of professionals (32 percent), which included 2 lawyers, 3 engineers, 6 journalists, 1 physician, 2 architects, and 6 professors; 18 members were public employees (26 percent); 7 were students (10 percent); and 13 were merchants, "industrialists," and "property owners" (19 percent). Only 4 of the founding members could be loosely considered blue-collar workers: 1 tailor and 3 cigar-makers.[103] This social composition would characterize the club throughout its long life. Among those requesting to join in 1930, for instance, there were 2 students, 3 lawyers, 2 merchants, 1 professor, and 1 public employee.[104]

Selection and exclusivity were also gender-based. Although women were allowed to participate in the club's activities through the "Ladies' Committee," full membership was restricted to men. Reproducing dominant moral values, the black middle class endorsed the notion that women's first responsibility and social function was to create stable families, and its members angrily criticized what they perceived as Afro-Cuban women's lack of morality and decency. Vasconcelos went so far as to doubt whether it was even possible to find two hundred black women whose "public and private conduct, and level of culture," would allow them to join the new society. As it turned out, among women, those who defined themselves as part of "a minority who reads and studies" fully agreed with the idea that what should typify the "new" black female was her respect and consideration for marriage, family, and household duties.[105] However, black middle-class women also recognized their disadvantageous position in society. Since they had little voice either in Afro-Cuban clubs or in the feminist movement, which tended to overlook the specificity of their situation, their particular needs were not being properly addressed. By the late 1920s, Afro-Cuban women were not only talking about general women's issues such as suffrage rights, but they were exercising pressure to be recognized in both Afro-Cuban and feminist associations.[106] Still, as late as the mid-1940s Club Atenas only granted membership privileges to men.

Many of the founding members of the club played a prominent role in politics. Indeed, most Afro-Cuban politicians at the national level joined the club, including Gálvez, Cuesta, Céspedes, Ramírez Ross, Pantaleón J. Valdés (the club's first president), Policarpo Madrigal (a congressional aspirant from Las Villas in 1916), Pérez Landa, D'Ou, Ponvert, and Idelfonso Morúa Contreras, elected by the Liberals to Havana's provincial council in 1920. Other political figures joined in the 1920s, such as Representatives Lombard, Garriga, Prisciliano Piedra, and Manuel Capestany.

Several of Atenas's presidents between the creation of the club in 1917 and the end of the republic were members of Congress, held important government offices at the national level, or both, including Céspedes, Lombard, Capestany, and Piedra. Céspedes was elected representative in the 1912–16 period and was appointed secretary of justice by Batista in 1952.

Lombard's active public life included many congressional terms—as representative in 1922, 1926, 1932, and 1940 and as senator in 1954. Capestany was appointed subsecretary of justice under Machado and elected representative in 1932 and senator in 1944. Piedra began his long political career as a Liberal provincial councillor in 1922 and spent his adult life in Congress, to which he was elected in 1924, 1930, 1938, 1942, 1946, and 1948. Other club presidents, such as Benjamín Muñoz Ginarte and Pío Arturo Frías, held important government jobs.

With such a prominent membership, the club's ability to access national authorities and influence government policies was all but guaranteed. Like other black associations, Atenas identified itself as a "cultural" club "detached from any political or religious tendency," but it vowed at the same time to struggle for the integration of all Cubans, regardless of race, and for the fulfillment of the principle of equality established by the Constitution. Those vows had clear political implications. Thus, the club used its prestige to denounce and criticize incidents of racial discrimination, such as the expulsion of blacks from Santa Clara's Parque Vidal in 1925 or the exclusion of black spectators and the Panamanian swimming team by the Havana Yacht Club in 1930. In both cases, their campaign received a favorable official reaction.

Club Atenas worked closely with members of Congress and courted their support and friendship in a systematic way, through invitations to public festivities, lunches at the society, and so on. Together with Unión Fraternal, for instance, they supported Senator Alberto Barreras's campaign to build a statue of Quintín Bandera in 1930.[107] Two years earlier, the club had been the main actor in a public homage rendered by the Afro-Cuban societies to President Gerardo Machado (see Chapter 2). These political contacts proved to be exceedingly profitable. In 1925, Congress passed a law granting Club Atenas a parcel of public land and a $50,000 donation to build its new headquarters. Although the measure was opposed by a few white representatives, who were suspicious about the real purposes of the institution, it was strongly defended by black congressmen Lombard, Garriga, and Carmelo Urquiaga, all of whom happened to be members of the club. Indeed, Atenas had its own voice in Congress. As part of his active campaign to court the support of Afro-Cubans, Machado signed the law in June 1925.[108]

Thus, by the end of the 1920s Afro-Cuban elites had developed the institutional means to assert their presence in Cuban society and politics. Black professionals and politicians understood well that government action was indispensable to fight racial discrimination and to break the barriers that impeded their full access to the country's most exclusive social and occupational spaces. They also recognized that state action was likely only if they were able to exercise effective political pressure, which was largely dependent on their ability to mobilize the masses of Afro-Cuban voters and coordinate the efforts of the black societies. To these tasks they turned in the competitive political environment of the second republic.

PART III THE SECOND REPUBLIC
1933–1958

Nation and black cannot be separated in Cuban society.
—Alberto Arredondo, *El negro en Cuba* (1939)

The first definite step of the revolution is to dignify the Cuban race of color.
—Directorio Social Revolucionario Renacimiento (1934)

The black peril is just another pretext to make the revolution fail.
—Gustavo Urrutia, "Armonías" (1934)

The first republic ended amid social warfare, economic depression, and political chaos. Machado's political control unraveled as opposition to his government mounted from within and without. Economic crisis reduced government and national income, limited the president's ability to distribute patronage and conduct politics as usual, paralyzed his public-works plans, and led to growing unemployment and labor unrest. Displaced by hunger and joblessness, rural workers marched to the cities in search of relief or squatted on lands deemed to be private. Machado's decision to extend his term in office through a spurious constitutional change in turn alienated a sector of the political class, which went on to form the Partido Unión Nacionalista (Nationalist Union Party) in 1928. Opposition sprang as well from students and professionals who responded to government repression with their own violence. By 1933 Cuba was immersed in chaos; the United States' traditional support for Machado wavered.[1]

Unlike previous episodes of political violence under the republic, on this occasion opposition was neither led nor defined by the aspirations of a displaced sector of the political class. The year 1933 was not 1906 or 1917, when Liberals and Conservatives had clashed over election results and the spoils of the national budget. Rather, most of the opposition had organized outside the party system, challenging the control of the traditional parties, contesting Cuba's dependency vis-à-vis the United States, and questioning the whole republican order. Despite their substantial differences, many of these Machado opponents shared the belief that it was imperative to build a "new" Cuba. As in the late nineteenth century, conditions existed for the political conflict to become a social revolution.

The reformist impulse had gained momentum since the early 1920s. The sugar collapse and the financial crisis of 1920 exposed the vulnerability of Cuba's dependent economy, liquidated what remained of the domestic banking system, and exposed the incapacity of the political class to provide sustained economic prosperity. As corruption and electoral fraud grew, so did public distrust in republican institutions. Young professionals and representatives of a nascent entrepreneurial bourgeoisie began to demand participation in public affairs. Through organizations such as the Asociación de Buen Gobierno (Association of Good Government, 1922), Junta Cubana de Renovación Nacional (Cuban Junta of National Renovation, 1923), and the Movimiento de Veteranos y Patriotas (Movement of Veterans and Patriots, 1923), they criticized corruption, decried Cuba's subordination to the United States, and called for cultural renovation.[2] Machado's *cooperativismo*—the alliance of Liberals, Conservatives, and Populares in Congress—destroyed even the illusion of political competition and the possibility of legal opposition.

Given the expansion of U.S. cultural and economic penetration of the island, reformism frequently expressed itself in nationalistic language. In the early years of the Zayas administration, the United States meddled in Cuban affairs daily. U.S. penetration was resented by vast sectors of Cuban society: by domestic entrepreneurs seeking government protection of their interests; by workers in foreign-owned enterprises struggling to improve working and living conditions; and by nationalist intellectuals who decried the growing Americanization of Cuban culture.

Since U.S. control was usually rationalized on the ground that racial inferiority rendered Cubans incapable of self-government and civilization, it became imperative to reconceptualize the relationship between race and nation. If Cuba was debased by being black, then blacks had to be vindicated in order to save Cuba. Thus, as in the 1890s, forging a new Cuba implied not only confrontation with a foreign power; to reinvent *cubanidad*, it was necessary, again, to minimize social and racial differences internally so as to challenge the U.S. racist stereotypes that depicted all Cubans as biologically inferior and politically unfit.

THE "CUBAN RACE"

The reinterpretation of Cubanness in the 1920s and 1930s sought to reconcile the perceived social reality of racial plurality with the need to forge a culturally homogeneous, politically stable, and economically prosperous modern nation. As the first republic plunged into economic disarray and political chaos, such needs became ever more pressing—particularly in the face of the growing Americanization of the island and the undisguised interference of the United States in Cuban affairs.

But *cubanidad* could not be reinvented without dealing with race. The inability of the first republic to achieve progress and stability was frequently explained by northern observers as a racial, biologically determined flaw. The combination of U.S. racial categorizations—according to which, one drop of "black blood" made someone "black"—and the belief that blacks were inferior and racially mixed degenerates placed most (if not all) Cubans in a situation of inescapable inferiority and condemned the island to perpetual backwardness. As Fernando Ortiz stated in 1937, "[W]e Cubans, whites, blacks, and mixed, know well how frequently we are all denigrated without distinction and en masse by some foreigners."[3] Even such prominent figures as Presidents José Miguel Gómez and Alfredo Zayas were deemed to be of dubious whiteness by some Americans.[4]

Racial composition, U.S. observers concluded, explained the inviability of the Cuban nation and Cubans' incapacity for self-government. "The majority of the voters in Cuba are of the Negro race (Spanish Americans)," an investor asserted, "who never will be able to govern themselves." A lawyer from Pennsylvania with properties in Isla de Pinos agreed with this characterization: "Both American life and American property . . . are subject to the laws, whims and caprices of an ignorant class of Blacks who are utterly incapable of governing themselves and who would exterminate the Americans if they were not fearful of the United States."[5] Since "black" and "Cuban" were treated as equivalent concepts, all Cubans were targeted by segregationist practices in the United States: "Cubans not admitted," read a billboard on a Tampa beach in 1915; "Neither . . . Negroes and China men, nor Cubans in official institutions," instructed the governor of Virginia circa 1920.[6]

To reconstruct Cubanness thus implied a revalorization of black contributions to the formation of the Cuban nation, for by the late 1920s it was clear that Cuba could not claim to be a white country. Despite government efforts to attract "desirable" European immigrants, blacks and mulattoes remained a sizable proportion of the total population. Whitening had failed. Cuban nationalist intellectuals would have to reconcile modernity with racial diversity, two concepts that North Atlantic racial ideologies had systematically presented as incompatible. As elsewhere in Latin America, nationalist intellectuals solved this ideological conflict through the exaltation of autochthonous cultural elements. But whereas in the early twentieth century Americanization was resisted through the celebration of the "Latin race," by the 1920s an autochthonous culture was increasingly understood as the fusion of the white and black elements that had produced a synthesis deemed to be uniquely Cuban.[7]

In more than one sense, this ideology upheld traditional notions of race and nationhood as much as it challenged them. Through the rhetorical exaltation of cultural and racial miscegenation, the emergent discourse of *cubanidad*, which found in the Afrocubanista cultural movement its most visible expression, challenged dominant conceptions of blacks' inferiority and the negative effects of racial mixing. What U.S. scientists explained as rigid biological processes, Cuban nationalists understood in terms of culture and other historical factors. Where Americans saw race degeneration and mongrelization, the Cubans saw racial improvement. To theories that ranked races according to their alleged capacity and civilization, nationalist intellectuals in Cuba responded that science had conclusively demonstrated that all races were equal.[8]

Yet this notion of *cubanidad* also remained tied to the past. Despite its contestation and creativity, the new nationalist discourse was still framed in the language of "race." Cuban intellectuals denied that some races were naturally inferior and shifted their emphasis from biology and heredity to culture, climate, and history, but they seldom argued about the concept of race itself. Following the latest scientific and anthropological findings, Ortiz had entertained doubts about the meaning and validity of the concept since at least the late 1920s, but it was not until World War II that the notion of race was systematically scrutinized and discussed by the Cuban intelligentsia.[9] Rather, in the early 1930s nationalist intellectuals referred to the new *cubanidad* as a "Cuban race."[10]

Scientists played a prominent role in the formulation of the new ideology. U.S. racist characterizations of Cubans rested on a body of scientific research that had to be challenged for Cuban nationalists to articulate a counterdiscourse in which blackness and miscegenation were not seen as insurmountable obstacles in the road to progress. Despite the strong influence of U.S. science and scholars in the island, some Cuban scientists did not accept northern racial ideologies uncritically. Besides, even in the United States and Great Britain the scientific respectability of racial-biological classifications to predict social developments had begun to decline.[11]

Following what Nancy Stepan calls the "Latin tradition" within eugenics, some Cuban physicians emphasized the role of social factors to explain poverty, mortality, and degeneration.[12] This was the position of Enrique Lluria Despau, a physician born in Matanzas who spent part of his life in France and Spain. In his most noted book, *Evolución superorgánica* (1905),

Lluria argued that social decay, social inequalities, and poverty were caused by mankind's disregard for natural laws and that men degenerated because they did not live in a "propitious environment for their development." Although Lluria's ideas about society were strongly influenced by evolutionism, the environment played a crucial role in his conception. In fact, he dismissed as "arbitrary" the theories of heredity that denied the importance of environmental factors and the transmission of acquired characters.[13]

As one would expect, *Evolución superorgánica* was well received in Cuban intellectual circles. Lluria's ideas created a way out of the determinism typical of racial theories advocating the survival of the fittest. In a review published in the Havana press—entitled "A Great Cuban Book"—the author asserted that Lluria had done all Cubans "an immense favor" by opposing "the erroneous conception that we had about the fittest, telling us that life is not an endless fatal competition in which the strongest wins and reproduces, but a process of progressive improvement." Using the avowedly neutral language of respectable science, Lluria provided Cubans with the possibility of gradual progress at a moment in which the republic seemed destined to disappear under Anglo-Saxon domination. "What a relief, what a spiritual balm!" concluded the reviewer.[14]

Lluria's conceptions about social medicine and the importance of the environment were shared by other physicians, hygienists, and intellectuals in the island.[15] Some, such as Dr. Juan Guiteras, used medicine and science to advance an explicit nationalist agenda. In a 1913 study about mortality in Cuba, Guiteras challenged the notion that the white race degenerated in the tropics and argued that the "tropical climate [was] compatible with the highest forms of human activities." High morbidity and mortality rates in the tropics, Guiteras explained, were not due to racial inferiority or degeneration but were caused by poor social conditions. Taking his arguments one step further, he applied the same principle to analyze mortality rates among whites and blacks in the island. "In my opinion, [differences in mortality rates between blacks and whites] are due to their social position, rather than to ethnic factors. . . . The black race . . . represents the majority of the poor, who generally live in bad conditions of hygiene, and its mortality is, naturally, higher than that of the white, which represents the majority of the wealthy classes."[16]

While using different arguments, Guiteras's conclusions were similar to those of Lluria: improvement was possible; the tropical climate was not a deterrent to progress. Mortality in Cuba might have been high, but this was explained as a function of poverty and social inequality, not racial degradation. Social factors, not congenital inferiority, explained Afro-Cubans' higher mortality rates as well. Guiteras realized that to justify scientifically the viability of the Cuban nation it was necessary to challenge the notion of blacks' biological inferiority. A reevaluation of blacks and blackness was thus indispensable to reimagine the Cuban nation.

Similar arguments were used in the late 1920s in the debate about the etiology and nature of tuberculosis. The rates of morbidity and mortality associated with this disease were much higher among Afro-Cubans than among whites. About 40 percent of all deaths caused by tuberculosis in the 1904–28 period were of blacks and mulattoes. In 1937–38, the Tuberculosis Survey of Cuba found that 42 percent of the infected subjects were Afro-Cubans.[17] With these statistics in hand, racist ideologues concluded that tuberculosis was a disease of the "mixed races"—yet another demonstration of the unfitness of peoples of African descent.[18] Some Cuban physicians countered with the usual argument: this was a social problem that could be solved—a "social disease," in Dr. Gustavo Aldereguía's words. Dr. José A. Taboadela agreed: "To prevent tuberculosis and its diffusion it is necessary to prevent poverty," he explained. Consequently, the solution to tuberculosis should be centered on issues such as higher salaries, better housing for workers, and improved nutrition.[19]

Physicians, hygienists, and scientists elaborated a much-needed rationale to assert that a racially diverse, mixed Cuba was a viable entity, not fatally condemned to perpetual subordination and backwardness. What scientists explained in academic halls and journals, writers and artists popularized in literature, paintings, sculpture, dance, and music. This artistic movement, known as Afrocubanismo, drew heavily on the "black motifs"—as blacks' cultural expressions were referred to in the period—to create a new cultural discourse that was widely perceived as authentically Cuban.

As Vera Kutzinski argues, the evolving notions of *cubanidad* and the exaltation of autochthonous cultural symbols cannot be separated from the antagonistic relationship between the United States and Cuba in the first republic.[20] The defense of a national culture was seen as a means to stop the growing Americanization of the island. The elimination of English from the public school curriculum in 1915 was a step in that direction. In a 1921 article, Ramón Vasconcelos denounced the crisis in Cuban cultural symbols. Only two things, he argued, were left of what once had been a vibrant Cuban culture: the *danzón*—a ballroom dance genre—and the *dril cien* (white suits). Both were on the verge of disappearance under the cultural influence of the United States, which included American music, dance, poetry, and social

Los bailes americanos

LA AGONIA DEL DANZON

FIGURE 5.1. *"American Dances: The Agony of Danzón."* In this cartoon, a nationalist denunciation of North American influences over Cuban culture is represented by the mestizo danzón. *From*
La Política Cómica, *June 18, 1922. (Biblioteca Nacional "José Martí")*

mores. Vasconcelos went on to criticize Cuban composers for their lack of
creativity: "Oh, Miguelito Faílde, oh [Arturo] Valenzuela and [Jorge] An-
ckerman [famous *danzón* authors and players]! They have also degenerated,
they have also become annexationists. . . . Instead of the old rhythm, [the
danzón] adapts to the tastes of Yankeeland and at times it gets dressed as fox-
trot, one-step, and even worse. . . . This infamous betrayal to Cuba we owe to
our composers who are unable to find inspiration in the Cuban environment. . . . This is the definite surrender . . . the 'decubanization' of Cuba."[21]

The *danzón* was a sensible choice to represent the national culture that
Vasconcelos sought to protect from U.S. influence (see figure 5.1). During
the nineteenth century, elements perceived as African influences in the *danzón* had created considerable controversy and opposition to the genre—the
danzón was even banned in some municipalities by colonial authorities. It was
only after the war of independence, when the island became wide open to the

influence of U.S. music and dances, that the *danzón* became accepted as a Cuban musical symbol.[22] Under the threat of foreign penetration and in a moment of political transition and social crisis, a genre that had been initially rejected for its alleged African influence became acceptable to Cuban elites. A similar process would take place in the late 1920s and the 1930s and for similar reasons. Cultural forms that in the early republic were considered to be primitive and savage due to their African influence were gradually incorporated into mainstream national culture.

This process took place in almost every realm of artistic creation, but it was particularly evident in poetry and music. In the late 1920s and the 1930s a literary outburst of *poesía mulata* swept the island. Written by both whites and Afro-Cubans, this poetry used "black motifs"—language, music, dances, and beliefs—to exalt Cubanness and national independence. Writer and Communist activist Juan Marinello described this production as "cubanísima."[23]

Although some of the writers who followed this "black craze" portrayed blackness in highly stereotypical terms, others used cultural expressions of perceived African origins to assert Afro-Cubans' seminal contribution to Cubanness and to Cuban culture, emphasizing in the process the mestizo character of the Cuban nation. Among the former, José Zacarías Tallet's poem *La Rumba* (1928) is perhaps the best example. Fernando Ortiz described it as "white art with black motifs." Tallet's composition portrays *la rumba*—a term that encompasses a variety of Afro-Cuban inspired compositions—as an exotic, lascivious spectacle of sweaty bodies that engage in an overtly sexual game.[24] Nicolás Guillén's collections of poems *Motivos de son* (1930) and *Sóngoro cosongo* (1931) represent the other end of the spectrum. Guillén exalted blackness as a central ingredient of "lo cubano," denounced racial oppression and violence, and represented Cubanness as a cultural and racial synthesis that constructed a mulatto nation. As he wrote in 1931, "Cuba's soul is mestizo, and it is from the soul, not the skin, that we derive our definite color. Someday it will be called 'Cuban color.' "[25]

A similar process took place in other areas of cultural expression. Through what Moore calls a process of stylization, Afro-Cuban popular music was incorporated into mainstream musical culture and elevated to the category of a national cultural symbol. Popular genres that only a decade before had been rejected because of their African influence were adopted by middle-class performers, were conveniently purified to remove them from the slums and streets in which they had been born, and became respectable expressions of Cubanness and Cuban culture. By the 1930s, for instance, commercial rumba was widely perceived as the most genuine example of Cuban music. By 1932 nationalist intellectual Emilio Roig de Leuchsenring proclaimed that Afro-Cuban influences were the most "essential and characteristic" elements of Cuban music.[26]

The so-called black motifs entered painting as well. Some of the most representative members of the *vanguardia* painters—an artistic avant-garde that emerged in Havana in the late 1920s—used Afro-Cuban themes to create what they described as a "new," authentic Cuban art. Eduardo Abela, Carlos Enríquez, Víctor Manuel, and, later, Wilfredo Lam all explored Afro-Cuban popular culture as part of their common efforts to represent Cubanness in the language of art. As was the case in literature, these depictions were sometimes representations of blacks as sensual, rhythmically oriented people (see, for instance, Abela's *El triunfo de la rumba* [The triumph of the rumba, ca. 1928]). But, as Juan Martínez argues, the visual arts also helped create a "new and positive view of Afrocubans and of their previously ignored contribution to Cuban culture."[27] At the same time, some minor figures within the movement, such as Afro-Cuban painter Alberto Peña (known as Peñita) and black sculptors Teodoro Ramos Blanco and Andrés Alvarez Naranjo, used their work to offer a critical view of Afro-Cuban economic and social conditions.

For all its ambiguities and contradictions, this process was nothing short of a cultural and ideological revolution. In contrast to the early republic, in which Cuba's future was frequently identified with the demographic expansion of its white population and the consolidation of its Spanish cultural ancestry, by the late 1920s the Afrocubanista movement was asserting that African influences were at least equally important in defining the character and nature of the Cuban nation. As in the late nineteenth century, a crisis in legitimacy and the need to affirm the singularity of the Cuban experience resulted in a discursive strategy that tended to reconcile internal differences within the shared notion of a racially inclusive nationhood. Inclusiveness remained central to the representation of the nation. But whereas in the 1890s Cubanness was seen as superseding distinctive racial groups, the nationalist discourse of the 1930s celebrated a racial and cultural synthesis—*mestizaje*—as the very essence of what was typically Cuban. The dominant discourse had shifted from Martí's "Cuban is more than white, black, or mulatto" to Guillén's "Cuban color." By the late 1930s and early 1940s, this new vision had become dominant: "Cuba is neither white, nor black, but *mulata, mestiza*," proclaimed white intellectual José A. Ramos in an elite club in 1937; "Without the black, Cuba would not be Cuba," asserted Ortiz in 1943.[28]

Previous authors have argued, correctly, that this incorporation of blackness into national culture was frequently achieved through the commodification and folklorization of Afro-Cuban secular and religious culture. Rumba, for instance, became a national symbol only after it was deprived of some of its most visible African influences and was "reconciled in a musical sense with traditions derived from Europe, the United States, and elsewhere."[29] Likewise, when the *comparsas*—Afro-Cuban carnival processions—were authorized again in 1937 after a twenty-year ban, they were seen primarily by the authorities as an expression of popular folklore that constituted a picturesque attraction for tourists.[30] The description offered by a tourist magazine is telling: "[The *comparsa*] is not a typical Cuban spectacle: it is an outgrowth of the day of slavery. . . . However it has come to be accepted as one of the interesting features of the Carnival season of Havana."[31] In 1937 the *comparsas* were temporarily banned again by authorities because of "inadequate costuming" and because they were not "up to the standard required by present regulations."[32]

Critical studies of Afrocubanismo thus emphasize that black popular culture was accepted mainly on white, middle-class terms or that the movement served to conceal and reproduce Afro-Cubans' subordination in society. These authors interpret the movement as a reconstruction of the elite's hegemony through what Winant calls "the incorporation of oppositional currents in the prevailing system of rule" and "the reinterpretation of oppositional discourse in the prevailing framework of social expression."[33] As Kutzinski explains, "Afro-Cubanism had all the makings of a folkloric spectacle whose political effect was to displace and obfuscate actual social problems and conflicts, especially racial ones." She thus characterizes *poesía mulata* as "the site where men of European and African ancestry rhetorically reconcile their differences and, in the process, give birth to the paternalistic political fiction of a national multiculture in the face of a social system that resisted any real structural pluralism." In her view, the discourse of *mestizaje* actually helped "further entrench" racial hierarchies in Cuban society.[34]

Despite their merits, such characterizations of Afrocubanismo and the nationalist ideology it helped create are problematic. They assume that this ideology served mainly—if not exclusively—to enlarge and consolidate the representational power of the ruling elites without making any significant concessions, or without providing any meaningful opportunities for those who were being represented. But Afro-Cubans were not just passive objects of representation. They were active participants in the contested formulation of an ideological and cultural product that was neither stable nor coherent.

Thus, if on the one hand Tallet's depiction of the rumba is sensual and stereotypical, on the other hand, Guillén's mulatto poems celebrate black street culture, and other authors, such as Regino Pedroso and Marcelino Arozarena, chant to workers and the dispossessed and criticize what the latter called the "bourgeois" comprehension of Afro-Cuban culture.[35]

Similarly, while some of the *vanguardia* painters depicted blacks in terms similar to those of Tallet, others used their art to stress both Afro-Cubans' contribution to the nation and their subordinate social position. Peñita's work, for instance, cannot be reduced to a folkloric portrayal of the black motifs. His subjects are black manual workers who struggle to make a living in an unjust society. Social concerns dominate some of his most important paintings, such as *Workers* (figure 5.2), *Preparing the Road* (in which a black worker builds a road, presumably to the future), or his superb *Mother Dolorosa*, a representation of Cubanness as an old black female who, full of pain, survives in the streets of the city. This is not a ludicrous, sexualized image of the mulatto woman. It is an alternative representation in which the nation is identified with the most humble among the humble: manual workers, the unemployed, and peasants. As Afro-Cuban intellectual Enrique Andreu stated, Peñita painted "ideas." His whole work was perceived as a "lively protest against oppression and social injustices."[36]

One of the most interesting exponents of the new nationalist art was black sculptor Teodoro Ramos Blanco. Ramos frequently emphasized the need to create a genuine national culture in which blackness was not reduced to a merely decorative element in an exotic environment. For Ramos, blackness was "beauty, screams, rebelliousness, and pain." As part of his efforts to celebrate the black ingredients of Cubanness, Ramos's art frequently honored Afro-Cuban heroes such as Juan Gualberto Gómez and Mariana Grajales, mother of Antonio Macco. As a contemporary noted, what was truly unique about Ramos Blanco was that he proudly displayed his blackness as a symbol of dignity and rebelliousness.[37]

Within Afrocubanismo there were disparate, contentious visions of race and of its relationship with national identity. The movement and the discourse of *mestizaje* it helped to consolidate created spaces for some radical authors to express a vision of Cubanness that might otherwise have been difficult to propagate. This vision sought to identify *cubanidad* with the fortune of those who had been marginalized by a republic that was supposed to be with all and for all: manual workers, peasants, unemployed, blacks. It was possible to interpret this discourse as suggesting that the representatives of

FIGURE 5.2. Trabajadores *(Workers), by Alberto Peña (Peñita), oil on canvas, 1934. (Courtesy of Museo Nacional de Cuba)*

power—allied with the United States and consumers of its culture—had not only destroyed the republic but were the antithesis of what was truly Cuban as well.

It is because Afrocubanismo contained these potentially unsettling elements that the acceptance of blackness as a pillar of Cubanness was neither universal nor uncontested. Some white intellectuals opposed the notion that African elements had a significant role in Cuban culture. White composer and musicologist Eduardo Sánchez de Fuentes, for instance, claimed that Cuban music was "almost totally exempt of African influence" and that if there was any, it was obvious only in the rhythm and cadence of some folkloric songs—a question of form, not substance.[38] Other critics reproduced this vision of a white culture, arguing that African elements were less important than European and indigenous influences in the formation of Cuban music. "The 'rumba,'" one of these critics noted, "though not representative of what Cuban music really is, has gripped the public in its exotic rhythm and made Cuba known all over the world just as jazz. . . . The power that both possess finds its origin in the same Negro Race. It is music that holds because it does not need to be understood, it does not rise to the higher levels of true art, but speaks to the senses, to the primitive senses of man."[39]

The political importance of these attempts to minimize the influence of black elements in the formation of a national culture was noted by contemporaries. As black intellectual Salvador García Agüero stated, "the black phobia in music" was just an example of a more general phenomenon: the persistence of racism in Cuban society. "It is not by stabbing the drum and by killing black music," explained García Agüero, "that the artistic level of Cuban society can be elevated, but by lifting the barriers that try to keep the black man in the shadows of an unjust position."[40]

What García Agüero was suggesting was that the acknowledgment of Afro-Cuban cultural expressions as an intrinsic part of Cubanness *could* expose some of the barriers that had kept most blacks in a subordinate social position under the republic. Guillén himself spoke about his "Cuban color" as a future event, a possibility that his mulatto poems sought to realize in practice sooner than later. The formal recognition and valorization of blackness and Afro-Cuban culture could lead to the realization that, for all its *mestizaje*, Cuban society remained racially unequal. A founding member of the movement, poet Ramón Guirao, recognized in 1938 that although literary "incursions" into black themes had not "altered the social destiny of the black man," they had helped create an awareness of the problem. Their literary work, he explained, "made us think . . . about the possibility for blacks to acquire equal opportunities." Guirao at least realized that such equality did not exist.[41]

Afrocubanismo and the ideology of *mestizaje* were thus open—like Martí's ideal republic with and for all—to disparate interpretations. The invention of a "Cuban race" and the representation of the country as a mestizo land in which everyone had some African ancestry worked in contradictory and not always predictable ways. Those notions could be used to downplay the importance of race and to "obfuscate," as Kutzinski says, racial conflicts in Cuban society. In this sense, the new ideology might indeed serve to "entrench" traditional racial hierarchies. In the 1940s, President Ramón Grau

San Martín epitomized this conservative vision of *cubanidad* with his famous political slogan: "La Cubanidad es amor" (Cubanness is love).[42] Furthermore, as noted above, the acceptance and incorporation of black secular and religious culture into mainstream dominant culture was quite ambiguous—and hotly contested. Some Afro-Cuban popular practices—especially Santería—remained denigrated and persecuted as symbols of retrogression and barbarism.[43]

But Afrocubanismo and *mestizaje* could also emphasize that whiteness and European culture did not define Cuba. In fact, blackness and Afro-Cuban practices were typically presented as the most effective deterrent to foreign influences—"antidotes to Wall Street," as novelist Alejo Carpentier called them.[44] After all, Afro-Cubans had been tenaciously vocal about the need to preserve national independence as the only way to avert the introduction of U.S. racist practices in Cuban society. "The black Cuban must hate anything that smells Yankee," Serra wrote in 1901. "For us black Cubans," D'Ou stated thirty years later, "the neighbor to the north . . . is the race that lynches!"[45] Blacks and radical political actors used *mestizaje* to underline that Martí's ideal republic remained a goal that had not been realized in practice and that precisely because of blacks' contribution to the formation of the nation, Afro-Cubans deserved full, equal, and unrestricted participation in its economic, social, and political life. Manifestations of open racism could be presented as un-Cuban, thus lending legitimacy to the struggle against racial discrimination. As Urrutia stated in 1935, white racists were the antithesis of Cuba.[46] Indeed, they were frequently presented as symbols of cultural and ideological subordination to the United States. In the process, racism became identified with the United States' continuing influence in Cuban affairs and with their allies in the island—an association of potentially explosive political consequences, for it implied that racism could be eliminated only through a major transformation of the republican order. Alternatively, this association could also be used to claim that to fight imperialist domination effectively, racism had to be obliterated from the island.[47] In both scenarios, Afrocubanismo and *mestizaje* could highlight racial injustices and subvert established racial hierarchies.

Furthermore, even when used to downplay racial pluralism and conflict, the effects of this national ideology were probably unintended and certainly undesirable to the dominant groups. By concealing racial conflicts, the ideology of *mestizaje* helped expose other forms of social conflict and identity. In the 1930s, a growing number of intellectuals and social activists referred to the increasing importance of "class" as a fundamental identity in Cuban society. An Afro-Cuban Communist activist asserted in 1932, for instance, that "the struggle [was] not one of races, but of classes." Likewise, a white journalist argued, "In Cuba, the racial question is subordinated to the intellectual and economic question." Even Ramón Vasconcelos, who had devoted a good part of his intellectual career to discussing Afro-Cuban issues, claimed in 1937 that "class consciousness" had become stronger than race identity among blacks.[48] These notions tended to reduce the "black problem" to a question of maldistribution of resources, but in the process they facilitated other forms of cross-racial social action that could potentially transform Cuban society. Such transformation seemed possible, even imminent, in the summer of 1933, when a general strike overthrew the debilitated government of Machado and the dictator fled the island.

RACE AND SOCIAL WARFARE

That organized labor dealt the coup de grâce to Machado's government is itself indicative of some of the transformations that Cuban society and politics were experiencing. Although labor mobilization was not new, never before had workers been able to exercise such influence in national affairs. With the fall of Machado, a radical and independent labor movement, led by the Communist-controlled CNOC, emerged as a key player in national and local politics. After 1933 no politician would dare repeat what José Miguel Gómez had stated in 1916: "I do not call on workers, nor do I need them."[49]

Contributing to the rise of the CNOC was the disintegration of the reformist federations that Machado had supported in a failed effort to incorporate the labor movement into the government machinery.[50] The two main organizations—the Federación Cubana del Trabajo and the Unión Federativa Obrera—were so intimately linked to Machado that they were fully discredited by the time the regime fell. Individual unions seeking coordination and support thus flocked to the "red" CNOC, whose importance and strength multiplied accordingly.[51]

The growing importance of the CNOC and of the Partido Comunista de Cuba (PCC, Cuban Communist Party) was explained as well by their ability to organize workers across ethnic and racial lines and by their partial success in mobilizing sugar workers in the previously neglected agricultural sectors, in which large numbers of Antilleans found occupation. While the reformist unions responded to the deterioration of the economy in the late 1920s and early 1930s with demands to stop all immigration and requests to repatriate Antilleans and unemployed foreign workers, the radical wing of organized labor reacted by stressing the need for all workers to unite, regardless of race and national origin.[52] The Communists and their allies understood that to create a truly national labor organization it was indispensable to organize sugar field workers, many of whom were Haitians and Jamaicans.

To forge such an alliance in the midst of an economic depression was a challenge indeed. Not only did the Communists have to transcend the narrow nationalism that tended to blame the immigrants for widespread unemployment and other economic problems, they also needed to challenge the dominant racial discourse that, vis-à-vis foreigners, portrayed all Cubans as equal members of a racially harmonious nation. Likewise, the issue of racial discrimination in the workplace and the unions had to be confronted. The Communists' notion of nationhood and nationalism was articulated in a manifesto of the Anti-Imperialist League: "Cuba must be for the Cubans. This does not mean hatred for the *foreigner*; it means hatred for *foreign capital*."[53] In 1929, the "grievances program" of the CNOC included among its goals the equality of all workers regardless of race and nationality, whereas the political platform of the PCC (1932) devoted a whole section to the issue. The Communists denounced the exploitation and mistreatment of West Indians, the deportation of Spaniards, the discrimination against Chinese, and the persecutions of the so-called Polish—Jews and Eastern Europeans— in the island.[54]

To a degree, the Communists' efforts to create a pan-racial/national movement based on class identities were successful. Spanish workers were drawn together with natives into Communist-organized mass demonstrations and hunger marches. In one incident in Santiago, "an unidentified Cuban negro" waving a red flag mobilized "a group of unemployed Spaniards" until the police intervened, wounding several of them.[55] West Indians were also attracted by the PCC's propaganda, and some of the first Jamaican Marxists were exposed to this ideology while working in Cuba. The longshoremen's union at Nuevitas included Cubans as well as Haitians and Jamaicans, some of whom had become Cuban citizens. The U.S. consul in the area reported in 1931 that "a spirit of unrest was prevalent among them," even though they had been previously apathetic to labor mobilization. Antillean dockworkers also joined natives in a strike at the port of Alto Cedro, Ciego de Avila (Camagüey), according to the testimony of one of the participants.[56]

It was in the sugar sector, however, that the Communists' mobilization efforts proved to be most fruitful in the long run. In 1932 they organized the Sindicato Nacional de Obreros de la Industria Azucarera (SNOIA, National Workers Union of the Sugar Industry), which successfully led some of the most important strikes after the fall of Machado, with the cooperation of native and West Indian workers. As a U.S. observer noted, the Communists successfully mobilized workers in the sugar mills, regardless of national origin. "The Cuban negro came into close contact with the Haitian negro, converted into a slave working for 10 or 12 cents a day. . . . In some cases the Haitian negro seconded the Cuban negro, forming part of red syndicates." In September 1933, a group of Americans traveling by train to the Miranda sugar mill in Oriente were forced to obtain a pass from a Jamaican worker who identified himself as "corporal of the Red Guard." Thus, Communist leader Rubén Martínez Villena asserted rhetorically that "a perfect union between white and black workers" had been achieved during the strikes and that the theories blaming the Antilleans for the situation of sugar workers had been "discredited again with the active participation of these foreign workers in the common struggle."[57]

Although the Communists and the CNOC stressed the need for workers to unite along class lines, regardless of race or national origin, by the early 1930s they also realized that such unity was not possible unless the issue of racial discrimination in the workplace and in labor organizations was confronted. In a 1934 declaration, the CNOC recognized that one of their "fundamental mistakes" had been not taking proper account of "the specific demands of the blacks in their workplace" and ignoring the "black question" in general. A similar pronouncement was made by the radical students grouped in the Ala Izquierda Estudiantil. The CNOC thus called on its affiliated unions to demand a proportional participation of blacks in those occupations in which they were not represented, to secure equal pay for similar work, and to launch a full campaign against all forms of social, political, and cultural discrimination against Afro-Cubans.[58]

These concerns were conspicuously absent, however, from the PCC's agenda before the late 1920s and were not incorporated until after the Sixth World Congress of the Comintern in 1928. The PCC's initial structure included commissions on unions, youth, propaganda, women, and other issues, but not race. By the early 1930s, however, its cells included a "black secretary."[59] Among the first few black militants were Sandalio Junco, expelled from the PCC in 1932 under charges of "Trotskyism"; longshoremen leader Margarito Iglesias; Julián Rivero Bango, a founding member of the party in Matanzas and a leader in the building trades sector; and Antolín Dickinson Abreu, leader of the sugar union SNOIA and editor of its journal. Even so, by 1931 a Communist leader asserted that there were practically "no Negroes in the party."[60]

By this time, however, the Communists were devoting full attention to the "black question." Following the theses and resolutions of the Comintern congress, which advocated championing "the oppressed Negro race for full emancipation" and "the right of Negroes to national self-determination," the Cuban Communist Party followed a double strategy.[61] On the one hand, it launched an intensive campaign for racial equality and against all forms of racial discrimination. It denounced the "economic discrimination" against blacks' access to employment, the "political discrimination" symbolized by the Morúa law that prevented blacks from organizing autonomously, and the "social discrimination" practiced in parks, theaters, and other public spaces.[62]

On the other hand, the party attempted to apply the thesis of black self-determination to Cuban conditions. Following the Comintern's instruction to promote "the revolutionary struggle of race and national liberation from imperialist domination of the Negroes in various parts of the world," the PCC characterized blacks as a "national minority" with a common territory, economy, language, and culture. Oppression of blacks was interpreted as neither a class question nor a racial question. "The black question in Cuba is a national question with a strong class component," the Communists declared in 1934. In its first national conference, the PCC proclaimed that it would support the creation of a black independent state within the island, in the so-called *faja* or *franja negra* in Oriente, where Afro-Cubans made up more than half of the total population.[63] Even the term "faja negra" was borrowed from outside, an almost literal translation of the United States' "black belt."[64]

Cuban Communists also denounced racism in the United States and used race to foster anti-imperialist feelings among Afro-Cubans. In 1931, they waged a campaign denouncing the death sentence imposed on nine blacks in Scottsboro, Alabama, as "an assassination en masse." In a printed circular, the CNOC vigorously condemned "the imperialist assassins of the United States" for the "massacre" they were about to commit and explained it in terms of the "fierce oppression exercised by the Yankee capitalist magnates against blacks." In 1933, when the regional committee of the Liga Juvenil Comunista (Communist Youth League) in Cienfuegos denounced the interference of "the Yankee imperialists" in the island, it appealed specifically to Afro-Cubans: "You will be more oppressed and discriminated against by the military boot of the American bourgeoisie that endeavor to assassinate the young Negroes of Scottsboro. Struggle together with the white native workers for your national liberty."[65]

Although the campaign for self-determination met with opposition among some Afro-Cuban intellectuals, the Comintern's directives had at least one positive effect: they turned the struggle for racial equality into a centerpiece of the PCC's work.[66] Afro-Cuban militants were promoted to positions of leadership and were later elected to various posts in the national government. By 1934 the general secretary of the organization was a mulatto, Blas Roca Calderío, who remained the head of the party for many years. Another Afro-Cuban, Lázaro Peña, headed the CNOC. For all their dogmatic narrowness, the Comintern's directives contained another valuable element: they highlighted the specificity of racial oppression. Thus, the PCC frequently allied with Afro-Cuban clubs in the struggle for racial equality and saw race as a peculiar form of exploitation that deserved specific attention in the context of the workers' general struggle against capitalism.[67]

The party's militant antiracism had several long-term consequences, the most immediate of which was a significant increase in the number of Afro-Cuban followers. By 1934 a Communist leader asserted that one-third of the militants were black; ten years later it was estimated—doubtless with exaggeration—that their proportion had reached a staggering 75 percent.[68] The most important consequence, however, was the association between communism and racial equality itself. After the fall of Machado, these two categories became so intimately mixed that they were at times identified as one and the same. As a U.S. observer noted later, communism in Cuba had "to a large degree taken the form of a racial struggle." The PCC was seen as a "Negro party" and its campaigns for equality attacked as a threat to national unity and stability. Thus, the old specter of a race war was identified with the fear of a Communist-inspired social cataclysm.[69]

Despite their relative success in mobilizing workers and in becoming identified with the struggle for racial equality, the Communists' capacity to lead the revolutionary movement unleashed after the fall of Machado was seriously undermined by at least two factors. One was the party's own mistakes; the other was related to the activities of other political groups that sought to consolidate their own position in this volatile political environment. The PCC framed its condemnation of racial discrimination in the language of nationalism and used the traditional icons of Cuba's nationalist ideology (particularly Martí and Maceo) in its campaigns, but its early support for black self-determination and statements that Afro-Cubans constituted a separate nationality blatantly contradicted the very ideology that the party claimed to represent. Indeed, other progressive groups and radical Afro-Cuban intellectuals condemned this aspect of the Communists' propaganda.[70] Until 1935, when the self-determination thesis was abandoned as a mistake, the PCC called for class-based unity while preaching racially defined separation.

Among those competing to gain the support of workers, particularly

Afro-Cuban workers, were the university students, professionals, and nationalists who supported the government of Ramón Grau San Martín, which came to power in September 1933 as a result of a military revolt led by then sergeant Fulgencio Batista. Opposed by the United States, these groups advocated a type of nationalism that was considerably different from the Communists'. Their vision was summarized in the slogan "Cuba for the Cubans." The new government, which called itself and was widely perceived as "revolutionary," proclaimed that its main goal was "the creation of a new Cuba."[71]

The Grau administration turned to this task during the one hundred days it stayed in power. In his first public act, Grau abrogated the Platt Amendment, the most visible and hated symbol of U.S. control over Cuba. His government also enacted important labor legislation, gave women the right to vote, and dissolved the old political parties associated with Machado. U.S. ambassador Sumner Welles reported with alarm that a "social revolution" was "under way" in the island.[72]

And so it seemed to be. Workers of all colors perceived the establishment of the provisional revolutionary government as an opportunity to advance their claims and to consolidate their position vis-à-vis employers. The traditional structures of power had collapsed. For the first time the national government was rightly perceived as sympathetic to labor. Indeed, foreign investors asserted that one of the factors encouraging labor militancy was the intervention of the newly created Secretariat of Labor, which they claimed was, "if not of soviet tendency, of evident inclination to favor the proletarian classes."[73] By late September, workers had seized thirty-six sugar mills, established community "soviets" in some of them, created red militias, and taken control of local power. In a few cases, management personnel, typically Americans, were held hostage or expelled from the properties. A fearful U.S. consul in Matanzas reported that "a large percent of labor, especially the negro class, believe firmly that it is only a question of a few more days or weeks before all properties, including the sugar mills, will belong to them." By the end of the year, an executive of the Cuban Trading Company summarized: "This is a changed Cuba. In all places, workers are perfectly organized and united, with a marked tendency toward communism. The government, which is weak and can only afford minimal guarantees to capital and respect for property, is on the side of the workers to get their support, so workers feel strong and in control. . . . It is not that they come to ask, it is that we must do what they impose on us."[74]

The previous assessment was correct. Badly needing popular support, the provisional government devoted significant attention to labor issues and granted important benefits to workers. Regulations included the establishment of the eight-hour workday, a minimum wage, paid annual vacations, and accident insurance. Translating his "Cuba for the Cubans" campaign into concrete political acts, Grau also provided for the forced repatriation of foreign agricultural workers—that is, Antilleans—decreed that 50 percent of all employees in any given business had to be born in Cuba, and ordered that only natives could be officers in the syndicates and labor unions.[75] These measures resulted in a tremendous boost of popularity for the provisional regime, particularly among the unemployed, who were legion. Many native workers, including Afro-Cubans, identified more with this nationalist vision—which resulted in the creation of employment opportunities in activities that had been traditionally under the control of immigrants—than with the Communists' abstract campaign for racial self-determination.

But opposition developed as well, and it came from the most radical sectors of the labor movement, controlled by the CNOC and the Communists, who claimed that the reforms were a "fascist" maneuver to divide workers.[76] The struggles surrounding the approval and implementation of the so-called law of nationalization of labor thus exemplify the radically different ways in which a new Cuba was conceived in the volatile political environment of the early 1930s. Fights regarding this law and its application took place at every level of Cuban society, from individual unions and businesses to the national government.

Adhering to the position of the PCC, some scholars have characterized the Fifty Percent Law as a "bourgeois" divisionist tactic.[77] The law, however, was approved in response to popular pressures and was in fact opposed by employers. In October 1933, immediately after the fall of Machado, a "Committee Pro—80 Percent" was created in Havana to lobby for a presidential decree that would limit the participation of immigrant workers in the labor market. A delegation of this committee met with President Grau several weeks later, demanding that 80 percent of all jobs be given to natives and that unemployed foreign workers and "undesirables" be repatriated.[78] The president reacted favorably to these demands, although as an act of deference to the Spanish government—which, in opposition to the United States, had officially recognized the provisional administration—the decree mandated that only 50 percent of all positions be occupied by natives. "Cubans now have a free *patria*," Grau proclaimed triumphantly at a mass rally in which, the U.S. consul in Havana reported, "the large majority [of participants] . . . appeared to have African blood in varying degrees."[79]

This and similar reports probably overstated the level of Afro-Cuban participation in public demonstrations of support for the administration, for U.S. officials were eager to demonstrate that the government's main social base consisted of "laborers of the lowest class, negroes predominating." Blackness was used to convey the image that the island was in a state of virtual anarchy and that the government was unable to provide adequate protection to employers against what they described as "the crowds, largely negroes, of unemployed Cubans, who are in great part armed." As a result, the social conflicts surrounding the nationalization of labor were frequently portrayed as being of a "racial" nature.[80]

These reports were not just manipulations. The island was in a state of anarchy. The government was unable to control popular mobilization. And since Afro-Cubans had suffered the most on account of the preferential treatment given to workers of Spanish origin, they were indeed the main beneficiaries of antiforeign measures. In fact, black participation in the different organizations and committees that promoted the "nationalization" policies seems to have been quite prominent. For instance, the president of an "Association of National Reconquest," which lobbied for the Eighty Percent Law, was black. In their first national convention in 1936, the Afro-Cuban societies and clubs demanded that the Fifty Percent Law be included in the Cuban Constitution and that the proportion of natives in all jobs increase by 10 percent every four years. Writer Alberto Arredondo asserted that blacks welcomed the law as "an indisputable step toward the elimination of prejudice and discrimination." In his view, and that of other observers, it was Afro-Cubans who constituted the backbone of the "Cubanization" process with which the revolution was frequently identified.[81] Furthermore, the organizations that supported the "nationalization" of labor also recognized that opportunities for employment were more limited for black than for white Cubans, adding further visibility to the racial dimension of this campaign. "The race of color," the president of the "Supreme Council Pro–80 Percent" declared, "is ignored by all enterprises to the benefit of foreigners. If it were not for the Fifty Percent Law, in five years the heroic race would become a multitude of indigents, whereas the favored foreign workers . . . would keep sending money to their countries."[82]

But as mentioned above, Afro-Cuban support for these policies was not unanimous. Black leaders associated with the radical CNOC and the Communist Party seconded the criticism of their organizations, which characterized the provisional government as "fascist" and interpreted the nationalization of labor as a divisionist tactic that sought to debilitate the labor movement and to divide workers along racial and ethnic lines. Afro-Cuban workers, the leaders of the CNOC charged, were being used as instruments against the unions.[83]

The opposition of the Communists reflected their conviction that class should supersede other social identities such as race or nationality, but it was also inspired by more practical considerations. Some of the most important unions affiliated with the CNOC were controlled by immigrant workers who would not peacefully surrender their jobs in the midst of an economic depression. These included railway workers, employees in commercial establishments of various kinds, and, of course, sugarcane cutters affiliated with SNOIA, many of whom were Antilleans. In early December 1933, the CNOC-affiliated Federación Obrera de la Habana created a "Central Committee against the Fascist Laws" and called on all its members to strike in protest of the Fifty Percent Law—a position that the national confederation fully endorsed.[84]

Tensions escalated, leading to various forms of violence. The Federación Gastronómica, which included numerous restaurant and café waiters of Spanish origin, refused to fill the positions created by the removal of foreign workers, only to be "raided" later by sympathizers of the Fifty Percent Law.[85] The Sindicato General de Empleados de Cuba (Union of Employees of Cuba) went on strike and paralyzed retail trade in Havana on December 19. A few hours later, however, groups of "soldiers and sailors, followed in many cases by . . . civilians, chiefly Negroes, forced the proprietors to open."[86] Communist demonstrations against the law elicited counterdemonstrations of support and "revolutionary" seizures of establishments that refused to comply with the law. A famous Havana department store, Fin de Siglo, was inspected by a group "to see whether the Fifty Percent Law was being complied with." When the manager declared that both Spaniards and Cubans worked in the store, a member of the group threatened: "[M]any more Cubans will have to be employed. Otherwise we close the store with fire." Heading a procession that a local businessman described as "most alarming," the president of the Supreme Council Pro–80 Percent also threatened to burn down the establishments that did not hire native workers.[87]

As the Communists anticipated, divisions weakened organized labor and popular mobilization, and they did so at a moment in which popular pressures might have used the weakness of the traditional structures of power to launch a full-scale social revolution. The Communists' campaign for unity met with limited success because the nationalization campaign appealed to the immediate needs of thousands of unemployed native workers—and especially Afro-Cubans—who had been systematically relegated to the least-desirable jobs in the labor market. Their defense of foreign workers placed the PCC and the CNOC in the uncomfortable company of their archenemies: the foreign corporations, which, for totally different reasons, also opposed the Fifty Percent Law.[88] In the ferocious competition that developed between the "revolucionarios auténticos" (authentic revolutionaries) of President Grau and the PCC for the control of the labor movement in the following decades, the former frequently emphasized the "party's submission to Moscow" to highlight its disregard for "national" interests.[89]

Race was central to these divisions. Since the nationalization of labor was widely perceived as working to the benefit of Afro-Cubans, the inclusion of racial equality in the Communists' political agenda was forced also by local conditions. As mentioned above, by early 1934, the CNOC and other Communist-affiliated organizations were recognizing publicly that they had not devoted proper attention to this issue. The implementation of the Fifty Percent Law thus fostered competition for Afro-Cuban support and placed the whole question of Afro-Cubans' social position in a new Cuba at the center of the social conflicts that unfolded in post-Machado Cuba.

Also contributing to rising racial tensions was the social origin and racial composition of the participants in the "sergeants' revolt" of September 1933, from which the "revolutionary" government of Grau emerged. The revolt expressed long-standing grievances of junior officers against the predominantly white senior officers and was itself led by someone described by Ambassador Welles as "a mulatto with an admixture of Chinese blood": Fulgencio Batista. The revolt resulted in the removal of a large number of officers and, at least initially, opened unprecedented opportunities for blacks to advance within the army (see Chapter 3). According to U.S. military intelligence sources, after the coup, "negroes" came to represent about one-fifth of the officers, and their proportion was much higher in some garrisons, such as those of Matanzas and Oriente.

The displaced officers, many of whom came from privileged social backgrounds and were linked to the Machado regime, gathered at the Hotel Nacional in protest. The struggle that followed was occasionally interpreted as yet another indicator of the racial conflict that threatened to engulf the republic. Under the leadership of Batista and black officers such as Gregorio Querejeta, the resisting officers were ruthlessly eliminated. Some radio stations even propagated the rumor that a crowd of black women of "the worst class" had insulted and attacked the wives—referred to as "ladies"—and family members of the officers gathered at the hotel.[90]

Furthermore, the "better classes" did not hide their revulsion toward the new darker army and did not accept Batista as one of their own. "They cannot adjust themselves," the U.S. consul in Santiago explained, "to having the old officers of their own social strata removed by those whom they consider inferior." In Cienfuegos, members of the elite referred to Batista as "that mulatto."[91] The most exclusive club of Matanzas, El Liceo, refused to honor "the mulatto sergeant" in a social function planned by local officers. Paraphrasing the views of the local elite, a local source reported: "[T]here are too many Negro officers in the army. . . . [W]hile the Negro officers remain, there is bound to be dissatisfaction. . . . The officers cannot expect to attain admission into civilian society as long as these conditions continue."[92]

The opposition of the upper classes to what they perceived as an assault on traditional white social and economic spaces was not limited to denying ascending blacks entrance into their exclusive clubs and circles. Members of the elite, displaced officials from the Machado regime, and opponents of the nationalist government of Grau San Martín propagated fantastic rumors of black conspiracies and used race to generate chaos and confusion. They feared that a new Cuba would be darker not only at a discursive level, as the Afrocubanista movement proclaimed, but also in terms of the distribution of power and employment, as changes in the racial composition of the army seemed to confirm. Some contemporaries even claimed that, after the revolution, blacks had taken control of Cuba. A caricature published by *El Crisol*, for instance, portrayed blacks taking jobs in the government bureaucracy without being prepared for them. The cartoon's message was unmistakable: it was uneducated Afro-Cubans who gained from Cuba's social and political crisis.[93]

These racist rumors, which were disseminated through the press, radio stations, and flyers, typically appealed to ingrained racial fears and stereotypes to create divisions and confrontation. Drawing on the long-standing stereotype of the black rapist, for instance, a poster called on Afro-Cuban males in Havana to assault white women and force them to bear black children. Its language suggested that it had been made by blacks, but Grau supporters claimed that its real authors were "white reactionaries" who wanted to destroy the revolution. To support their accusations, Grau's followers mentioned the case of Emilio Soto, the chief of police in Santiago under Machado, who had allegedly posted flyers with the caption: "Whites have 24 hours to leave Santiago." Posters advocating racial violence also appeared in the army barracks, calling on blacks to revolt as a way to "redress previous injustices."[94]

Appeals to racial violence and the revival of the old black peril were used to stop a revolutionary movement that threatened to transform Cuba. The radical populism of the provisional administration of Ramón Grau was couched in a language of social and racial equality that appealed to the lower strata of society—thus the charge that Grau had stirred up a black revolt. Political rhetoric presented the revolution as a new episode in the long struggle for independence and social justice—the "new" Cuba would be the republic with and for all that Martí had envisioned. As Urrutia stated, racism had persisted in Cuba precisely because the revolution for independence had been "frustrated" by foreign intervention and the betrayal of national leaders. Racial justice was thus linked to the revolution's success, whereas counterrevolution was portrayed as the work of "traitors, interventionists, and racists."[95]

The link between revolution and racial justice was potentially explosive. It was Afro-Cubans' participation in the war for independence that had prevented their exclusion from republican politics. If blacks' future social standing was somehow based on their revolutionary credentials, then it was necessary for antiblack forces to represent the anti-Machado revolution as a "white" accomplishment in order to minimize Afro-Cubans' gains in the new Cuba.

Thus the myth emerged that "blacks" supported Machado.[96] As conservative politician Enrique José Varona stated, "[T]he black race has been indifferent to the hardships suffered by our unfortunate republic during the struggle against the Machado tyranny."[97] Several facts were selectively recalled in support of this invention: that Afro-Cuban clubs had offered a royal banquet to Machado back in 1928, that several black politicians had been promoted to positions of leadership and visibility within the administration, and that the number of blacks and mulattoes in Congress had increased under Machado. Machado himself was quoted as saying that he would remain in power with the support of blacks and the army, whereas black representative Aquilino Lombard was allegedly ready to mobilize more than twenty thousand Afro-Cubans in defense of the regime. Summarizing this view, a Havana-based journalist explained in a report to the U.S. Embassy: "Naturally, upon the fall of Machado, the persecution against the negro was unquestionable. It was a consequence of the crumbling tyrannical government. In the province of Oriente, where there are large masses of negroes, the struggle was more tenacious and bitter, between the negro who desired to maintain the position he had gained, and the white who came to take it away from him. It is also to be noted that while Arsenio Ortiz was a half-breed (*mestizo*), he found accomplices among his own race to commit one hundred and fifty murders. . . . The opposition did not find any support in the negro masses. . . . On the other hand, the police had among the negro masses its best stool-pigeons and the most resolute defenders of the regime."[98]

This construct ignored the fact that the mainstream political parties, whose leadership was overwhelmingly white, collaborated with Machado through the very end of his regime. It also ignored the fact that the army, charged with committing numerous atrocities, was commanded by white officers. The press singled out the case of Arsenio "The Jackal" Ortiz as the epitome of repression and barbarism, but in a "Gallery of Assassins" published by *Bohemia* in August 20, 1933, only one out of sixteen was nonwhite.

The creation of the legend of black support for Machado was perceived as a necessity for another reason. Race came to the forefront of the social crisis not only because of the campaigns of contending political actors such as the Communists or the nationalists of Grau; Afro-Cubans from different social strata themselves saw the revolution as an opportunity to reverse their traditional subordination, and they mobilized accordingly. Whereas black workers participated for the most part in cross-racial labor unions, the Afro-Cuban intelligentsia tried to organize an autonomous voice.

Leading these efforts were a number of young black intellectuals who criticized the traditional leadership of Afro-Cuban societies for their subservience to Machado. In some regions, such as Santa Clara, "revolutionary committees for the reorganization of the black societies" were created. These committees, whose members defined themselves as "revolutionary youth," charged that the leadership of the Afro-Cuban clubs had in fact contributed to nurturing the belief that Machado enjoyed the support of the black masses, despite the fact that "the youth" had fought against the tyrant. They thus proceeded to "wipe out the leading elements of our institutions . . . who are the continuation of the fallen regime." "To implement this cleaning," the committee from Santa Clara declared, "we took control of our institutions in a revolutionary way (*revolucionariamente*)."[99] Club Atenas was also soundly criticized for its "aristocratic" pretensions and its intimate links with the dictatorship.[100]

The drive to "renovate" did not stop at the reorganization or condemnation of the existing clubs. New societies, identified with the revolution's nationalist program, were established, and efforts were made to coordinate the activities of all clubs and to form a national federation. The Directorio Social Revolucionario "Renacimiento" (Social Revolutionary Directorate "Renaissance") and Club Adelante characterize the type of Afro-Cuban organizations that emerged after the fall of Machado. Created in 1933, Renacimiento described itself as a "revolutionary group" that was not linked to any political machinery whose main goal was to achieve "the respect and consideration that men of color deserve in our country." Both Renacimiento and Adelante were careful to note that they did not promote "racial campaigns," but they claimed to represent the legitimate aspirations of the "most oppressed and criminally exploited of all the groups that form the Cuban population." For the revolution to be real, the new societies stressed, it had to "dignify" the Cuban population of color. At a more concrete level, Renacimiento demanded that all political parties include a proportional representation of black men and women in all appointments.[101]

The situation of Afro-Cuban women was another concern of these societies. Traditionally, the directors of the Afro-Cuban clubs had sought to limit the role of women to charitable work and the organization of "ladies' committees." By late 1933, however, conditions had changed: after years of struggle, women had the right to vote and to be elected to office. Renacimiento thus called on Afro-Cuban clubs to allow women to participate in all of their activities. Adelante condemned gender discrimination and noted that subordination based on sex and subordination based on race were in fact related and quite similar. Furthermore, Afro-Cuban women themselves mobilized. In the fall of 1933, they organized several committees "for the defense of women" and pressured their own institutions for participation and acceptance.[102]

Renacimiento and Adelante shared as well a common vision of the need to unify and coordinate the efforts of individual societies into a national movement. Attempts to create a national federation had failed in 1916 and again in 1928, when the Havana-based Sociedad Benéfica Santa Eugenia organized a provincial congress with little success.[103] But by 1933 the idea had gained momentum. In the hotly contested post-Machado environment, the coordination of the Afro-Cuban societies in some sort of federation represented a clear strategy to consolidate the position of blacks in the new Cuba under construction. Speaking again in the name of "the youth," black intellectuals such as journalist Pedro Portuondo Calás, Ramiro Cuesta, and Pastor de Albear held in the fall of 1933 an "inter-provincial" convention of societies from Havana and Santa Clara that designated a preparatory commission for the national convention. Renacimiento supported these efforts, arguing that blacks' demands would not be met unless they created a "unified social front." Adelante sent a delegate to the meeting and used its journal to appeal for unity.[104]

Because of the country's chaotic political situation, it was not until late 1935 and early 1936 that some of the provincial conventions were held. Unity would not be achieved easily, however. Some of these conventions were criticized for being reduced to merely a process of inscription of delegates without serious discussion of the problems affecting the black population. The representativeness of the resulting federations was also challenged, for, as Adelante pointed out, most Afro-Cubans were not affiliated with any club. Furthermore, some societies interpreted this movement as yet another political move by a group of office seekers and refused to participate.[105]

The program of the 1936 National Convention of Cuban Societies of the Race of Color reflected these tensions. It was broad enough to appeal to different sectors of the population, but it was so general that its implementation would require a major overhaul of republican politics. The program advocated a number of constitutional reforms; the reorganization of the economy, particularly in the countryside; the protection of native workers; a reform of the public school system; and recommendations in the area of public health, including the persecution of "all forms of quack medicine," even though many popular healers were themselves Afro-Cuban. Only two of the convention's agreements referred specifically to race: one requested that the future constitution provide that all jobs in public administration be distributed "taking into account the ethnographic composition of the Cuban population in each province, region, or city"; the other called for concrete penalties against any privilege of "class, sex, or race."[106]

The question of blacks' proportional representation in public administration, which Renacimiento also voiced, was one of the central concerns of an obscure political party formed in Havana in 1933: the Asociación Nacional Revolucionaria y Partido Asteria (National Revolutionary Association and Asteria Party). In contrast to Adelante, Renacimiento, and similar associations, Asteria was registered as a political party that sought "to support the government that resulted from the revolutionary coup of September 4." The group did not define itself in racial terms, but its main leaders were black—its first vice president was Pastor de Albear, one of the organizers of the national convention of Afro-Cuban societies—and the party advocated the proportional division of all jobs and appointments "between the two great ethnic portions that constitute Cuban society." These two elements, by themselves, led to a characterization of the group as a black party. Urrutia referred to it as "a secret society of blacks," organized in response to similar groups among whites.[107] If Asteria did not generate the controversies that had surrounded the Partido Independiente de Color twenty years before, it was because the party never achieved national standing and had a very brief political life. In the 1935 elections, Asteria registered as a municipal party in Havana and supported the candidacy of Antonio Beruff Mendieta for mayor, but it did not get the 3,700 votes needed to survive.[108] Some of its leaders, such as Albear, joined other groups, particularly the recently created Partido Revolucionario Cubano Auténtico (PRCA, Cuban Revolutionary Party, Authentic) of Grau San Martín.

But the example of Asteria also shows that any attempt at black autonomous mobilization was adamantly opposed by many whites and even by some blacks, regardless of how minuscule or unsuccessful the attempt might have been. In December 1933, the association's headquarters were bombed.[109] This, it should be noted, was not an isolated event. In response to Afro-Cubans' growing assertiveness in the post-Machado revolutionary situation, a systematic campaign of racist violence was launched against blacks and their organizations. Together with Asteria, the most important black clubs of Havana fell victim to bombings: Club Atenas, Unión Fraternal, Jóvenes del Vals, and Sol de Occidente. Also attacked were Minerva, Cienfuegos's most important Afro-Cuban society, and Bella Unión in Santa Clara.[110]

This sabotage was probably related to the formation in September 1933 of a new Ku Klux Klan Kubano (KKKK, Cuban Ku Klux Klan). Organized as a secret society based on the U.S. model, members of the KKKK did not disguise their white-supremacist views or their deep hatred for Afro-Cubans. They flatly rejected the notion that Cuba was a mestizo nation and advocated racial segregation in the island. In their first public manifesto, the organization interpreted the 1933 revolution as a black assault on white society and called for the formation of a "great army of racial defense": "Currently the black, with unbelievable insolence . . . has been extending its influence as a malignant plague, demanding rights that he has carried to the extreme, SUCH AS THE POSSESSION OF WHITE WOMEN. Our brothers of Santiago de Cuba have been the first victims of such outrage. The enormous proportion of blacks in that province has incited them to demand entrance to the bathing places of the social centers, being so bold as to threaten the whites. . . . Faced with this difficult problem . . . the white population has been forced to raise its protest, backing it, if necessary, with force, and to this end it is organizing not only for the defense of its rights, but to conserve the moral principles that always have been the base and pride of (white) Cuban society." To emphasize that blacks deserved no special place in the new Cuba, the manifesto elaborated as well on Afro-Cubans' alleged support for Machado, claiming that blacks had "constituted one of the strongest pillars" of the fallen regime.[111]

As the KKKK made clear, the question of Afro-Cubans' "place" in Cuban society occasionally took the form of conflicts over access to social spaces that had traditionally been closed to them, such as the private beaches of Santiago. The best-known incident occurred in Trinidad in January 1934, when a group of white and black strollers clashed over access to the "white section" of the Céspedes Park. In this regard, Trinidad was hardly exceptional: many parks in the provinces of Las Villas and Camagüey had been traditionally segregated. For some Afro-Cubans, however, the revolution meant an opportunity to challenge these and other racist traditions, for, as Urrutia stated, the revolution's very essence was the eradication of all "republican vices."[112] Neither vices nor traditions would surrender peacefully, however. When someone described as "mestizo" entered the white section of the park in Trinidad, he was attacked by a white citizen, and the incident quickly degenerated into a street fight. According to some accounts, the police—who anticipated trouble and had asked the Afro-Cuban societies not to enter the white area of the park—opened fire, wounding several whites. This, in turn, generated an antiblack backlash in which several black-owned businesses were looted and an Afro-Cuban, Justo Proveyer, was lynched.[113]

As in previous occasions during the republic, central parks became the locus of confrontation over access to and control of public space. A U.S. observer noted after the fall of Machado that "the negroes of the street" had developed "an increasingly impertinent and disrespectful attitude."[114] According to the Communists, episodes of racial violence similar to Trinidad's took place in other localities, such as Alquízar, Placetas, and Güines. In Cienfuegos, where racial tensions were reportedly very high, violence was averted on New Year's Eve only after the police placed a machine gun at a visible place in the Martí Park and prohibited blacks from walking through the park.[115]

For Afro-Cubans, such prohibition meant not only that racism was alive and well in the island but also that, all the rhetoric of revolution notwithstanding, in order to prevent disorder local authorities would in fact side with the forces of old Cuba. Especially after January 1934, when the army overthrew the provisional administration of Ramón Grau, the momentum for social revolution began to run its course. Headed by Carlos Mendieta, the leader of Partido Unión Nacionalista, backed by Batista, and blessed by the U.S. Embassy in Havana, the new administration represented in many ways the beginning of a counterrevolutionary reaction. Following the traditional pattern of republican politics, Mendieta appointed some prominent Afro-Cubans to government positions while disregarding Afro-Cubans' specific claims for justice.[116] The government's response to racist violence in Trinidad is a good example. The mayor of the city, Herman Patterson, was removed, but no concrete sanction was imposed on him. Likewise, the military supervisor of Trinidad was transferred to another position but was not punished. To add injury to insult, in October 1934 Patterson was reappointed. It was only after a wave of protests led by the Communist-inspired Committee for the Rights of Blacks and the United Front of Black Societies that Patterson was forced to resign.[117]

But this was only a minor success. The new environment was not favorable to Afro-Cuban mobilization, for after 1934 the Cuban state was clearly opposed to any form of popular mobilization. Social warfare did not recede with governmental change—the deep contradictions that besieged Cuban society had not been solved—but the army was now on the side of repression and order. A presidential decree—Decree-Law 51, "For the defense of the republic"—embodied this political change. It outlawed any organization that threatened the established order for "social, proletarian, racial, or political reasons" and created "national defense courts" to punish such activities in a summary fashion.[118] That the balance of power had changed became evident in March 1935 when the CNOC launched its last revolutionary offensive through a formidable general strike. Although it involved nearly 200,000 workers, the movement was violently suppressed. The unions that seconded the strike were dissolved, their leaders imprisoned, killed, or forced into exile.[119] By mid-1935, the forces advocating a radical vision of a new Cuba had been defeated.

For the Afro-Cuban intellectuals seeking to organize autonomously, this environment could hardly be less auspicious. Their success was largely dependent on the general fate of the nationalist revolution—and by 1935 the revolution was in retreat. Thus, when the Afro-Cuban clubs gathered to celebrate their provincial conventions in the fall of 1935 and early 1936, they were immediately labeled "racist" and were perceived as a threat to political stability and social order. In Las Villas, the celebration of the conventions coincided with the announcement by the government of a vast "racial conspiracy" that allegedly involved the leaders of some of the most important Afro-Cuban clubs in Cienfuegos, such as Minerva and Antonio Maceo. Members of these societies, local police reports contended, belonged to a black revolutionary movement with centers in Havana, Santa Clara, and even the United States—an accusation that the Afro-Cuban clubs from Cienfuegos publicly disavowed.[120] As on previous occasions, these rumors were based on very shallow evidence, but on this occasion they led to the arrest of several prominent black citizens of Cienfuegos and the dismissal of three black members of the local police.[121]

The new environment was also inauspicious because the Mendieta administration included members of the ABC, a secret terrorist anti-Machado organization that had been frequently criticized for its racist leanings. The ABC's main social base included businessmen, merchants, and white-collar employees—"substantial elements," as a contemporary described them, among whom blacks were of course poorly represented. Cuban political commentators also noted that, for a change, the proportion of blacks attending ABC rallies was fairly low.[122] Adding to the perception that this was a racist organization was the fact that one of its main leaders, intellectual Jorge Mañach, had publicly advocated the need for blacks to improve themselves as a precondition to full participation in the national life, a position that several Afro-Cuban intellectuals had angrily criticized. Furthermore, although the party professed not to "make distinctions between Cubans with white hands and Cubans with black hands," its program did not contain a single allusion to blacks or to the so-called race question.[123] This silence, some of its critics noted, was indicative of its disregard for Afro-Cubans and their peculiar social situation. Instead, the ABC's program advocated limiting suffrage according to literacy, a position that was rightly depicted by critics as "aristocratic" and "fascist."[124] Afro-Cuban journalist Vasconcelos characterized the ABC as not a party, but a "phobia." The Communists accused the ABC of instigating racial hatred and violence against blacks—an accusation that novelist Jesús Masdeu endorsed publicly. And a contemporary writer went so far as to claim that ABC members constituted the backbone of the KKKK.[125]

But neither Mendieta and Unión Nacionalista nor the ABC were in the position to dictate the future of Cuba and the fate of the nationalist agenda of 1933. The army was. The U.S. Embassy, which Batista had visited on September 5, the day after the coup, realized that the army was the only institution that could preclude the danger of social revolution and offered to grant recognition and legitimacy to the new military authorities in exchange for their support for a government more amenable to U.S. interests, such as that of Mendieta. Batista, his spurious claim to power and racial background notwithstanding, was identified as the only source of real authority in the island. Many wealthy whites never fully accepted him as one of their own, but by the mid-1930s they also had come to realize that Batista was the lesser of two evils and welcomed his efforts to curb popular mobilization.[126]

Batista's rise to the status of Cuba's strongman had important racial implications, however, for the command of the armed forces and real government power were in the hands of, in Welles's words, a mulatto with some Chinese ancestry. To legitimize Batista it was thus necessary not only to emphasize his military and political abilities but also to modify his racial background. As with Afro-Cuban heroes Antonio Maceo and Jesús Rabí in the early republic, Batista's racial transformation was achieved by discovering some "indigenous" root in his origin—indeed, his close friends later referred to him as "el indio."[127] The need to reconstruct Batista's race was candidly summarized by the U.S. military attaché in Havana: "It has been impossible to definitely determine Batista's antecedents. . . . I am very much inclined now to believe that Batista is either of Chilean-Indian extraction or of Chilean-Mexican extraction, and not as was first believed, half negro and one-quarter Chinese. I consider the importance of this to be that the Chilean-Indian or the Chilean-Mexican is apt to be more courageous, more sagacious and more crafty than the mixed negro-Chinese-Cuban."[128]

Batista turned out to be well supplied with courage, sagacity, and craftiness. Although general elections were celebrated in 1935, following the defeat of the general strike in March, Batista and the army remained the real power in Cuban politics. When, in 1936, the elected president Miguel Mariano Gómez—son of the Liberal *caudillo* José Miguel Gómez—opposed the army's interference in civilian affairs, he was impeached. As Pérez-Stable asserts, "[A]fter 1936, the old political class never again attempted to regain power."[129] His authority consolidated, Batista embarked upon building a social base that was not restricted to the army. To foreign investors he offered order and stability; to traditional and newly formed political actors, the opportunity to peacefully participate in electoral politics; to the popular sectors that he had crushed, political amnesty and social reforms. Himself a product of the "revolution," Batista by 1937 had appropriated the reformist agenda of the early 1930s and presented himself as a radical populist concerned with the fate of workers, peasants, and the dispossessed. His "Plan Trienal" (Three-year plan) included most of the demands of the revolutionary agenda of the early 1930s: workers' protection, land distribution, massive educational efforts in the rural areas, and the expansion of a state-sponsored health care system.[130] Through this ambitious program, Batista sought to snatch the reformist agenda from the Revolucionarios Auténticos of Grau—his most feared political opponent—and to be viewed as the incarnation of the 1933 revolution. This metamorphosis from army colonel into democrat was accompanied by a general amnesty in 1937, the legalization of the Communist Party and the CNOC, and preparations for a constitutional convention and presidential elections in 1940.

Although by the late 1930s the decade had not fulfilled its promise of a new Cuba, the promise itself remained politically compelling. Old Cuba, with its two dominant parties and the Platt Amendment, had perished, although neither Liberals and Conservatives nor U.S. influence in Cuban affairs was gone. Multiple political actors, from the leftist Communist Party to the populist Partido Revolucionario Auténtico and the conservative ABC, fought in a ferociously competitive political environment for popular support and control of organized labor.[131] The growing political importance of the unions, in turn, provided salience to "class" issues in the social and political struggles of the second republic. The social revolution had been defeated, but its ideals remained alive: popular demands and the rhetoric of the new Cuba were incorporated into the programs of all parties, regardless of affiliation. Which vision of the new Cuba would ultimately prevail depended, to a large degree, on the composition and character of the impending constitutional convention. As at the turn of the century, the culminating battle of a revolution that started amid political violence and social unrest would be fought, bitterly but peacefully, in the halls of Congress.

The real revolution, if finally there is one, must take place in the constitutional convention.
—José Armando Plá, letter to Gustavo Urrutia (1934)

Black men do not want democracy, as contained in the Constitution, to be a mere formula but a reality. . . . Until this [antidiscrimination] law is approved, the equality referred to by the Constitution will not be fully guaranteed.
—Evelio Chen, speech at Club Atenas (1951)

The first racist institution in Cuba is the state.
—Aquilino Lombard Thorndike, motion to the Senate (1955)

Discussions about the need to hold a constitutional convention had taken place since the fall of the Machado government. The 1901 constitution had been mocked by the spurious 1928 modifications implemented by Machado to expand his term in office and was "permanently stigmatized," as Louis A. Pérez states, by the Platt Amendment and by the inefficiency and corruption of republican institutions.[1] A new Cuba required a new constitution.

A number of favorable conditions facilitated the constitutional gathering in the late 1930s. Labor mobilization and revolutionary violence receded after 1935 and electoral politics was partially restored, but the army's interference in civilian affairs was resented by various political actors, who demanded a return to constitutional normalcy. Exhausted by years of class warfare and repression, even the most radical groups, such as the Communists and the Revolucionarios Auténticos of Grau San Martín, saw in a new constitution the possibility to reinsert themselves in Cuban politics and salvage some of the popular measures that, under pressure, several governments had approved through the 1930s. Furthermore, only a constitution would give a sense of permanence and security to the profuse social legislation of the decade, all of which had been approved by unstable governments of dubious legitimacy. For the most progressive sectors, the constitutional convention provided the opportunity to legislate the new Cuba that popular mobilization had failed to accomplish. For the forces of old Cuba, the convention represented a chance to limit popular conquests by making them as abstract and meaningless as possible.

The rise and expansion of fascism in Europe further reinforced the perception that democratic institutions had to be consolidated in the island. The polarization that fascism generated between liberal democracy and barbaric totalitarianism was echoed in Cuba, where several groups with pro-fascist sympathies were organized in the late 1930s, including a Nazi Party.[2] Counteracting fascist propaganda and the Nazi danger became the absolute priority of progressive and liberal political actors, including the Communists. The Seventh World Congress of the Comintern (1935) had identified the struggle against fascism as the main goal of the movement and instructed Communist parties to build alliances with other groups, resulting in the so-called popular fronts. As was the case in the United States, the Cuban Communists had in fact applied this strategy before the Comintern congress and continued to do so during the 1930s and beyond.[3] With other groups, members of the Communist Party lobbied for a general amnesty, supported the Spanish republicans, and condemned the Italian invasion of Abyssinia. By the end of the decade the party had developed considerable skills in coalition-building and was ready to participate in electoral politics. As Eric Hobsbawm asserts, fascism created an exceptional historic situation in which unlikely alliances became possible.[4]

Fascism also reinforced the centrality and visibility of race in the legal configuration of a new Cuba, for Nazi Germany contemptuously represented the unabashed horrors of racism and its relationship with labor repression and the obliteration of democratic freedoms. The fight against fascism, the Afro-Cuban intellectuals realized, was also a fight against racism. Thus Urrutia's claim that "it is good and necessary that the black Cuban has shown, shows, and continues to . . . be in favor of democracy . . . and against Nazi-fascism and falangism."[5] Afro-Cuban activists called for "national unity" against Hitler's "arch racism" and warned that, with fascism "at the doors," a democratic constitution was indispensable for Cuba to survive as a nation.[6]

Race was also central to the elaborations of the new constitutional order because, as with many other popular demands, the project of a new, racially egalitarian Cuba remained an unfulfilled promise of the revolution. To the general grievances against the 1901 constitution Afro-Cubans added a specific one: its abstract principle of legal equality frequently had been a dead letter in practice. The constitutional convention was seen as an opportunity—if not *the* opportunity—to legislate effective equal rights for blacks, turn racial discrimination into a punishable crime, and effectively eliminate racism from the island. "[I]t is not enough," the general secretary of the Havana Federation of Societies of the Race of Color, Nilo Zuasnábar, asserted, "to say that 'all Cubans are equal before the law'; it is imperative to regulate explicitly the degree of responsibility incurred by any person or institution . . . that dares to behave otherwise."[7] Some Afro-Cubans, such as journalist José Armando Plá from Camagüey, even equated the convention with the "real" revolution.[8]

Linking racial equality to the fate of the Constitution meant that the struggle against racism would be channeled through state institutions such as the courts, the legislative branch—if additional legislation was required—and the executive branch, in charge of enforcing these measures. Racism and inequality had always been linked to politics, but under the new order the pursuit of racial equality became a responsibility of the state. The credibility and respectability of governments in the second republic would be measured by their capacity to deliver this and other social goods included in the constitutional text. So if on the one hand the convention symbolized the culminating battle of the 1933 revolution, on the other hand it represented the departing point for a new period in the struggles for racial equality.

REDEFINING CITIZENSHIP

The constitutional battle would be bitterly fought. The numerous groups that vied for representation in the convention entertained different visions concerning the organization of the state, the meaning and extent of civil rights, and the government's role in the protection of those rights. The bitterness of this battle, however, was also a function of the fragmentation of the party structure and the sheer number of parties participating in the elections to the constitutional convention. Eleven parties nominated candidates nationally; nine sent delegates to the assembly. Needless to say, for the most part these parties were neither organized along ideological lines nor representative of the interests and aspirations of a single, well-defined social sector. With the partial exceptions of the labor-based Communists and the most conservative groups such as the ABC—whose urban, middle-class base was widely acknowledged—all these parties were both multiclass and cross-racial in their composition.[9]

Ideological lines were further eroded by the fact that most of these groups adopted some of the rhetoric and substance of the revolutionary program as their own. This was true even for the Partido Liberal, in power when Machado's dictatorship was overthrown. Party leaders asserted that the PL of

1939 "was not that of 1933" and claimed that the "program of the Revolution of September 4" (the sergeants' revolt led by Batista in 1933) included "all the democratic aspirations" that the Liberals had always supported. The Communists, in turn, dropped their previous opposition to the "nationalization" of labor (a major conquest of the revolution) and joined all other parties in endorsing the need to curtail immigration to the island.[10] The ABC, the Partido Unión Nacionalista, and the Revolucionarios Auténticos of Grau San Martín all displayed revolutionary credentials based on their opposition to Machado.

However vague, allegiance to the "revolution" and its principles meant that some broadly defined issues commanded enough popular support to be recognized by virtually all political groups, regardless of affiliation. Enlarging the control by nationals of Cuba's economic resources was one of these issues. Another was the need to ratify and systematize the profuse labor legislation generated in the aftermath of the revolution. Competing for the support and control of organized labor, all parties deemed the protection of workers to be one of the centerpieces of the emerging political order.[11] Even the least-progressive groups agreed that the state should play an active role in promoting workers' welfare, for, as a leader of the Partido Unión Nacionalista asserted, "to distribute [wealth] is, sometimes, a conservative way." The shared notion that the state should guarantee employment to every Cuban and mediate conflicts between capital and labor attested to the widespread perception that regulating "class struggle" had become the "main concern" of any government.[12]

A comparable consensus did not exist concerning the questions of racial discrimination and government involvement in this area. All parties nominally condemned discrimination and endorsed the principle that the new Cuba ought to be egalitarian and inclusive, but deep differences set them apart as to whether discrimination existed at all and which laws and institutions, if any, were required to fight against it. That racism was not compatible with Cuban nationalism was not open to question. Even the Nazi Party took exception to this aspect of the Nazi doctrine in its application to the Cuban case, noting that in the island there were not "racial or religious questions to be settled."[13] In turn, the concrete economic, social, and political meanings of such incompatibility were hotly contested.

The first contentious issue was whether racial discrimination was a real problem requiring some sort of government action. Several conservative political parties either denied the existence of discrimination or referred to the problem in the vaguest possible terms. A representative of the Conjunto

Nacional Democrático (National Democratic Union), one of the heirs of the old Conservative Party, declared, for instance, that discrimination had "no relevance in the superior order of the law" because racial differences had been eliminated in Cuba since the times of the wars of independence.[14] The ABC's position was nearly identical to this. The party's program made no reference to race, and its leaders shared the Conjunto Nacional Democrático's opinion that "since the moment in which blacks and whites joined together to fight for the same ideal . . . all differences . . . between the white and the black were abolished forever." Likewise, a spokesman of the Partido Unión Nacionalista doubted the existence of discrimination and declared that any differences that might have existed in republican institutions did not constitute a true "discriminatory reality."[15]

At the other end of the spectrum, the Communists and other radical political groups asserted that racial discrimination was so pervasive as to render the constitutional principle of equality virtually meaningless. Juan Marinello, president of the Partido Unión Revolucionaria—a political group that merged with the Communist Party before the convention elections— declared that racial discrimination was "evident" in employment and educational institutions, particularly in private schools. A leader of the small Socialist Party was equally categoric: since the creation of the republic, the "black race" had suffered "unforgivable humiliations" and had been discriminated against in every area of Cuba's social and political life. The populist Partido Popular Cubano—a minority party organized by Alfredo Zayas and Juan Gualberto Gómez around 1920—concurred that discrimination was widespread, particularly in access to jobs and private education.[16]

A second contentious issue, derived from the first one, referred to the kind of legislative action required to confront discrimination. Those who denied the existence of racism in Cuban society supported the inclusion in the constitutional text of a general principle of equality along lines similar to those of the 1901 constitution.[17] By contrast, those critical of Cuban racial realities advocated explicit antidiscrimination statements, sanctions for racist acts, and even the introduction of a quota system that would guarantee a proportional participation of blacks in all sources of employment, political candidacies, and appointments.[18] "Inequality in social relations does not improve with abstract declarations of equality and fraternity," the general secretary of the Communist Party, Blas Roca, explained, "but through legal precepts that oppose objective inequalities and punish those who create them. . . . Here, to redress inequality, there is no solution but to apply an unequal measure, 'forcing' the employment of a minimal number of blacks in all trades."[19]

The largest political parties, such as the Partido Liberal and the Partido Revolucionario Auténtico, remained somewhere in the middle concerning their perceptions of the so-called black problem. Leaders of these parties acknowledged the existence of discrimination but tended to see it as a consequence of the lack of economic opportunities and, also, of what a Liberal congressman called blacks' "inferiority complex." Their most important difference from the radical groups, however, related to the solution of the problem. The Auténticos saw it mainly within the framework of their own "nationalization" of labor—"as egalitarian as a law can be"—but endorsed the principle that the Constitution should punish racial discrimination. The Liberals remained committed to a general declaration of equality while supporting the approval of a separate law to regulate and punish discrimination. But they came closer to the most conservative groups in their strenuous opposition to racial quotas, claiming that such a solution was worse than the problem and warning that the use of race for political purposes should be avoided, for it tended to generate "black racism, which is as harmful as white racism."[20]

Which position would ultimately prevail in the convention depended, of course, on the success of each party in getting its delegation candidates elected, on the delegates themselves, and on whether significant popular pressure could be built up around this issue. As members of a mass-based party, the Communists understood fully the importance of mobilizing voters around the goal of racial equality as a way to narrow the political options of the conservative opposition. As in their past campaigns, the battle against discrimination became—together with issues such as labor rights and agrarian reform—one of the leitmotivs in the Communists' electoral campaign for the convention. But whereas labor rights and land distribution were supported by many other political parties, the Communists' vigorous antiracist campaign contributed to singling them out as the true champions of Afro-Cuban rights.

Commentators of Cuban politics unanimously concurred that this campaign was being favorably received by Afro-Cubans not affiliated with the party. The Communists' efforts "to arouse class and racial hatred in the minds of the overwhelming Negro population . . . are having a certain effect," reported the U.S. consul in Santiago. "They [the Communists] are having considerable success in increasing their ranks, especially from the unemployed and the negroes," concurred his colleague in Matanzas. In Sancti Spíritus, another U.S. representative asserted, "there is a considerable movement among the negro element towards organization and strengthening their social and economic position."[21] Election results tended to confirm these impressions. The Communists ended up fifth in the elections at the national level, with 9 percent of the vote. In some areas with a large Afro-Cuban population, such as Santiago de Cuba, they attracted the largest number of votes.[22]

The association between the Communists and the cause of racial equality was reinforced further by the racial composition of their delegates. Of a total of seventy-six delegates to the convention, only five were nonwhite; three of them—Blas Roca, Salvador García Agüero, and Esperanza Sánchez Mastrapa—were affiliated with the Partido Unión Revolucionaria Comunista.[23] Half of the Communist delegates were black or mulatto, and a large percentage of Communist candidates were nonwhite.[24] Another member of the delegation, Romárico Cordero from Oriente, was deemed to be either "a negro or possibly mulatto" by U.S. officials, but he was considered to be white by most Cubans, including members of his own party.[25]

By interpreting the Communists' electoral success in racial terms, their enemies also helped legitimize the party's claim that Communists were the true leaders of the struggle for racial equality. Just a few days after the election, Senator Manuel Capestany, a mulatto and leader of the Partido Liberal in Santa Clara, accused the Communist Party of racism—that is, of using racially divisive tactics to attract the black vote.[26] For the Liberals this was a particularly sensitive issue because they had traditionally claimed to represent the bulk of Afro-Cuban voters and promoted blacks and mulattoes to positions of command within their party and the government.[27] In Santiago de Cuba, some sectors of the predominantly white propertied class interpreted the Communists' unexpected success as nothing short of a black assault on the structures of power, a construct that explicitly exposed the intersections of race, class, and political power. As the U.S. consul reported, the election's outcome had caused considerable concern "to the whites, businessmen, and property owners." These groups, he asserted, had begun to mobilize in order to prevent a "negro and communist control of Santiago."[28] In late November, an unsigned letter "typed on very good imported paper" circulated through the mail calling for "war on communism" in the framework of racial antagonism: "More than 90,000 Communists have voted in the elections to the convention! In the next elections we will have COMMUNIST MAYORS AND GOVERNORS, INCLUDING SOME BLACKS. ALL BLACKS ARE

COMMUNISTS! We must prepare to defend our families from being raped by those who have no PATRIA OR FAMILY and pursue the equality of RACE."[29]

Being identified as the party of blacks and workers—two categories that were frequently used interchangeably—was itself a significant achievement for the Communists, who interpreted the election's results as a clear popular mandate to move forward with their antiracist campaign. As a party member from Oriente explained, "On November 15 [election day], citizens expressed their desire to build a strong and harmonious Cuba free of unjust discriminations because of skin color or sex, and to have a constitution that establishes severe punishments against individuals who behave in such a way."[30]

To advance this mandate in the convention, the Communists were forced to make alliances with other groups, for their six votes amounted to only 8 percent of the total. Theoretically, the parties represented in the assembly belonged to two distinct groups. One, the "government" block, supported the presidential candidacy of Fulgencio Batista. This group included the Partido Liberal, the Communists, the Unión Nacionalista, the conservative Conjunto Nacional Democrático, and the Partido Nacional Revolucionario. The "opposition," defined only in terms of its antagonism to Batista, included allies as unlikely as those forming the government block: the Revolucionarios Auténticos, Acción Republicana, and the archconservatives ABC and Partido Demócrata Republicano of García Menocal.[31] Although the opposition elected a majority of delegates, Menocal's party switched sides, giving the government coalition a slight majority in the convention.

This, however, did not mean much. These coalitions were based on sheer political convenience—mainly as a way to secure access to government patronage—and did not reflect any kind of ideological split. Differences among parties and delegates within each block were frequently greater than between parties in the opposing coalitions. In the discussion of a specific issue, support would likely be found among delegates nominally belonging to the opposite group. Being a member of the majority government coalition by no means guaranteed that the Communists' radical views on race and discrimination would easily prevail in the convention.[32]

Nevertheless, the Communist delegates succeeded in promoting an open discussion of racial discrimination and how it affected citizenship rights such as those of equality and equal access to work. In the process, they forced members of other parties to publicly define their positions on these issues, for the sessions were open to the public and received ample, though partisan, coverage in the daily press. Further pressure was placed on the convention by the Afro-Cuban clubs, which had called for the inclusion of antidiscrimination measures in the Constitution and organized public events to advance their views.[33] The most publicized event was a series of conferences sponsored by Club Atenas in early 1939. The club invited representatives of all the major political parties to express their opinions concerning several issues previously defined by the board of directors: economic problems, immigration, work, public education, and racial discrimination. No party refused to participate. Although these conferences were presented as an effort to inform the citizenry, their main purpose was thinly veiled. "The popular masses want to know," the club's president explained in his opening speech, "to what degree is Cuban democracy ready to promote the aspirations of the people . . . especially concerning the evident discrimination in the distribution of work."[34]

Representing these concerns, the Communists tried to define the meanings of citizenship rights and racial equality as concretely as possible in the constitutional text. Race became a controversial matter, particularly in the discussions of two proposed articles: one, which became Article 20 of the Constitution, dealt with the principle of equality; the second, Article 74, dealt with equal access to work.

The definition of equality (Article 20), the U.S. ambassador reported, was "acrimoniously" discussed.[35] Although the drafted article submitted to the convention by a preparatory commission established that "any discrimination because of sex, race, class, or any other motive" was "illegal and punishable," Afro-Cuban delegate Salvador García Agüero argued that a general statement against discrimination would not solve the problem.[36] He thus introduced a new proposal defining discrimination as "any regulation or act that prevents any citizen from gaining access to services and public places, to employment and culture in all its aspects, and to the full use of his civic and political functions." His proposal also prescribed sanctions against discrimination that would be defined by law during the first six months after the approval of the Constitution.[37] This proposal, García Agüero argued, further clarified the statement of the commission by enumerating the areas in which discrimination against Afro-Cubans was more pervasive: public spaces, work, and education, particularly in private religious schools—"here, even God . . . discriminates against blacks," charged the Communist delegate. In short, García Agüero asserted, in spite of the constitutional principle that guaranteed the "absolute equality" of all Cubans, the "citizenship rights" of Afro-Cubans were being violated daily.

Those opposed to his proposal either appealed to the usual argument that Cubans were all brothers living in a fraternal nation or used technical arguments to claim that the general statement of the commission was in fact superior to the Communists' version. Delio Núñez Mesa, a Liberal delegate from Oriente, articulated the first position. He argued that, if approved, the Communists' proposed article would in fact "create" the problem that they sought to oppose—"such discrimination of race which, to my knowledge, does not exist in Cuba." This, however, was an isolated claim. All other delegates who intervened in the debate recognized that discrimination was indeed a problem requiring a solution. Another delegate of the Partido Liberal, José Manuel Cortina from Havana, asserted that he agreed with the substance of García Agüero's proposal and claimed that the debate was limited to finding the best procedure to guarantee the equality of all Cubans. This, he argued, should be done "in a way that stimulates the progressive evolution of the concept [of equality] within a spirit of harmony and fraternity. . . . Here we are not discussing, nor can we discuss as a possibility, that a part of the Cuban people be in a situation of inferiority. . . . The convention by unanimity wishes to do justice to all the components of Cuban society, regardless of their color, their race."

Defining equal access to work (Article 74) was even more controversial. At stake was whether, in the pursuit of equality—a goal on which all delegates nominally agreed—the Cuban state should take an interventionist role in the distribution of employment and redress previous inequities through the introduction of racially defined policies. The Communists advocated guaranteeing the participation of black workers in all economic sectors in a proportion similar to their percentage in the total population of each province. This, party delegates noted, reproduced in fact one of the demands made by the National Federation of Societies of the Colored Race.[38] The Communists later softened their position, proposing that blacks should have a "fair" representation in all *new* employments rather than in all trades and industries. By limiting quotas only to new jobs, they argued, the main objection of those opposed to the principle of proportionality was taken into account—namely, that this policy would create racial divisions and conflicts among workers.

In order to neutralize the Communists' radical formula, conservatives were forced to advance an alternative proposal that, while eliminating the proportional allocation of employment according to race, unequivocally stated that racial discrimination in hiring and promotion practices was unconstitutional. Thus it was the ABC, one of the most conservative parties, that submitted a competing proposal to the convention for discussion. It read: "As an essential part of its permanent social policy, the Ministry of Labor will oversee that no discriminatory practices of any kind prevail in the distribution of employment opportunities in industry and commerce. In the removal of personnel and in the creation of new positions . . . it is mandatory to distribute employment opportunities without distinctions of race or color. . . . The law will establish that any other practice will be punishable."[39]

The convention's debate around these two proposals—those sponsored by the Communists and by the ABC—brought to the forefront the different ways in which the issue of discrimination was approached and exposed the true ideological colors of the participants. Opposition to the proportional allocation of jobs—even those of new creation—echoed the usual arguments that such a policy would threaten the unity of the Cuban "moral race" and generate conflicts that would "deeply affect Cuba's fraternity, which must be protected by all means."[40] As the ABC's delegate Jorge Mañach stated, discrimination was a "moral" and "psychological" problem that had to be solved, but only through "indirect and delicate" means. The Communists countered that their proposal could not "create" divisions that existed already. In a long and well-reasoned exposition, delegate César Vilar from Oriente—described by U.S. authorities as someone with "an appreciable following among the negroes and workers"[41]—explained how blacks were kept in the worst-paid positions in all economic sectors and argued that the solution to this problem could not be left in the hands of those who had created it to begin with.[42]

Although both Communist proposals were defeated, the party, and the interests it represented, did accomplish several significant things in the convention. Some of the concerns voiced by the delegates of the Unión Revolucionaria were introduced into the constitutional text. For instance, their demand that a complementary law punishing racial discrimination be passed six months after the approval of the Constitution was incorporated, in a modified way, in one of the "transitory" provisions. It prescribed that the law should be approved in one of the three legislative sessions following the convention. Likewise, although the Communists' efforts to guarantee a proportional distribution of jobs and appointments failed, labor rights were defined in a way that was unequivocally antidiscriminatory and, even more important, a government body—the Ministry of Labor—was charged with oversight.[43]

Perhaps the most important achievement, however, was that the Communists had forced the convention to publicly discuss and acknowledge the existence of racial discrimination in Cuba. Never before had racism been debated so openly at the level of the national government. In the process, delegates of other parties, who in different circumstances might have chosen to ignore the issue, were forced to address it and to justify their positions. It is worth noting that, after the Communist proposal on equality was voted down, a large number of delegates felt compelled to "explain" their vote. Although one of them asserted that he was not using the opportunity "to make political propaganda through the microphone, or to gain voters for [his] party or [his] candidacy," that is precisely what he and other delegates were doing. One after another, those who voted against the proposal emphasized that they had done so out of technical considerations, for no disagreement existed about the need to promote the equality of all Cubans.[44]

Such explanations were even more necessary because the Communist delegates called for roll votes on these issues, eliminating the possibility for those voting against to remain anonymous. And the Communists did more: they publicized the names of the delegates opposed to their proposals. Thus, when Liberal delegate José Manuel Casanova came to the convention's next session, he was handed an "accusatory pamphlet . . . in which the delegates who had voted against the proposals submitted by the representatives of the Cuban Communist Party were angrily criticized." This, Casanova complained, was "not fair," for no delegate had refused cooperation in this "matter of justice." It was not proper, he added in a presentation to the convention, to characterize "some delegates as heroic and dedicated defenders of the rights of the Cuban race of color and other delegates as heartless enemies of those rights."[45]

The conservative press's charges of "racism" only reinforced the image that the Communists were the most resolute defenders of Afro-Cubans' rights.[46] Furthermore, the Unión Revolucionaria Comunista was the only party that had taken the recommendations of the National Federation of Societies of the Colored Race into the convention. Its prestige and influence before Afro-Cubans and their organizations were consequently enhanced, prompting other delegates to insist that the Communists were not the only ones fighting against discrimination. Auténtico labor leader and delegate Eusebio Mujal, for instance, explained that he had coauthored the Communist proposal on labor rights, implying that the Communists should not be construed as the only defenders of Afro-Cubans' rights.[47] His own party also deserved some credit.

Competition for labor and Afro-Cuban support had brought the Communists and Auténticos together on this occasion, but it would separate them in the future. Indeed, competition between these two groups for the control of organized labor turned ferocious in the 1940s. Since the constitutional question of discrimination was defined, at least in part, as a labor question, organized labor could play a leading role in the struggle against racial discrimination. The Constitution had established a system in which only organized groups could exact benefits and concessions from the state.[48] Those in control of the recently organized Confederación de Trabajadores de Cuba (CTC, Confederation of Cuban Workers) were thus in position to advance the cause of racial equality to no small degree. For instances of discrimination apart from labor, the Constitution had promised a complementary law that would establish concrete sanctions against those who violated the principle of equality. In both scenarios—either labor-related or not—state institutions such as the Ministry of Labor, the courts, and Congress had vital roles to play. In a sense, the struggle for a racially inclusive and egalitarian Cuba had been postponed again, for without specific laws the constitutional principles were nearly impossible to enforce. This time, however, the struggle had been fully transferred to the realm of the state.

POPULAR FRONT POLITICS:
THE RISE OF COMMUNIST INFLUENCE

While the convention was in session, the political parties prepared for the general elections to be held on July 14, 1940. Under the new system, it was imperative that different interest groups not only organize but also secure influence and access to the government. Both coalitions campaigned intensely to place their candidates in office. Batista and Grau again engaged in political battle.

Emboldened by their success in the elections to the constitutional convention but conscious of their minority status within the coalition, the Communists worked hard to consolidate their position in support of Batista's candidacy. Batista had given them, to the dismay of the propertied classes and the Auténticos, the opportunity to reorganize the CTC. In exchange, he expected the Communists to deliver votes and the crucial support of organized labor. And the party delivered: when Batista campaigned across the island in early 1940, he was favorably impressed by its capacity to mobilize workers. In town after town, reports agreed, the Communists' followers turned out in large numbers and were the best organized.[49]

Reports also agreed on another point: blacks and mulattoes made up the bulk of the Communist demonstrators and Batista's supporters more generally. In Matanzas, the U.S. consul asserted, the "number of colored people" attending a rally of the Socialist Democratic Coalition "was very noticeable, especially in the ranks of the Communist Party." The consul in Cienfuegos estimated, in turn, that two-thirds to three-fourths of participants in another coalition gathering were black. Elsewhere it was noted that Batista's appeal resided with the poorer elements, whereas Grau enjoyed the support of the wealthy and the middle class—a "much higher type of people." When Batista visited Holguín (Oriente province) in June, the two main white clubs in the city, El Liceo and Colonia Española, refused to host a banquet for him, which was instead organized by a local Afro-Cuban society.[50]

The propertied class strongly objected to Batista's alliance with the Communists, who were identified with social and racial chaos and whose influence had evidently increased through their control of the labor confederation. An equally ominous sign was the nature of Batista's political platform, a fairly progressive one that included agrarian reform, substantial benefits to workers, a campaign against illiteracy, and public health programs among its goals. Wholeheartedly supported by the Communists, the platform also advocated the need to pass "a practical and legislative policy that will make effective the equality of opportunities and rights for all Cubans without distinction of race or color."[51]

Some elements of the campaign further reinforced the worst fears of the propertied class concerning Batista and his Communist allies. Using the favorable conjuncture of the elections and the constitutional convention, labor mobilization was on the rise. In January and February 1940—coinciding with the beginning of the grinding season—more than twenty sugar mills in the provinces of Matanzas, Santa Clara, and Camagüey went on strike. Workers' demands were sweeping. In addition to a 20 percent wage increase for all industrial and field workers, they petitioned for adequate housing facilities, running water, paid vacations, free medical treatment, schools, and subsistence land for the off-season. Employers were put on the defensive, noting that the government hesitated to repress strikes "because of the probable effect on Colonel Batista's presidential aspirations." In Central Washington, located in Manacas, Santa Clara, the two CTC delegates—described by the mill administrator as "flashily dressed negroes"—assured the workers that "as they all belonged to Batista's party they could get anything they wanted, provided they held out long enough."[52]

Workers' assessment of the political conjuncture was correct. Indeed, employers acknowledged that CTC leaders had chosen "an opportune time" to launch these strikes.[53] Mill administrators were compelled to grant wage increases in order to maintain some sense of authority. Otherwise, workers could appeal to the secretary of labor, who, the manager of the Tuinucú Sugar Company asserted, invariably sided with labor. Even worse, employers were forced to also grant increases to nonstriking workers who were not affiliated with CTC unions in order to preserve the prestige of the "good elements" in labor organizations.[54]

Further working to the advantage of workers and the confederation was the fact that competing political groups tried to intervene in labor disputes as a way to gain the support of the unions, forcing Batista to adopt a decidedly pro-labor position. During a strike in the printing trades in Havana, for instance, candidate Grau "offered his services" to the workers, expecting that in return they would join his party. So did a leader of the ABC. Communist leaders Peña and Roca thus conferred with Batista, warning that if the strike was not settled to the satisfaction of the CTC, a large portion of the labor element that supported his candidacy would be "demoralized." Batista immediately instructed the chief of police to release all detained workers and demanded that the secretary of justice settle the strike in favor of the CTC.[55]

The Communists also used the elections to advance their radical agenda for racial equality, leading to the usual charge that the party's goals and tactics were "racist." The appeal of this accusation, voiced not only by property owners but also by members of the overwhelmingly white professional class and by conservative political leaders, should not be underestimated. This charge resonated with myths and fears deeply ingrained in Cuban imagery, such as those of the "black peril" and the indivisibility of the racially harmonious Cuban nation. These images were being freely used in order to stall the growing influence of the Communists. In a typical case, a social organization of businessmen named Agrupación Nacional Acera del Louvre, whose members identified themselves as "Friends of the Americans," published a leaflet warning "the race of color" that the association was ready to repel the "Communist offensive" in the island. In a letter sent to acting president Federico Laredo Brú in the midst of the electoral campaign, it asked him to adopt energetic measures against "the reds," pledging the support of all "social elements" against the Communists' attempts to promote "class hatred, racism, and anti-Americanism" in Cuba.[56] Similar arguments were also voiced by political leaders, who warned that the Communists' "demagogic campaign" might result in a violent racial conflict. As a group of politicians who asked Batista to disassociate himself from the Communists asserted, "[B]lacks must be helped, but not poisoned."[57]

The anti-Communist crusade adopted an even clearer racial character in Santiago de Cuba, where the party enthusiastically supported the candidacy of Justo Salas Arzuaga, an Afro-Cuban affiliated with the Partido Liberal, for mayor. Although Salas had accumulated a long and prominent record of public service as a House representative (1930–32), provincial councillor

(1922–26), alderman, and functionary in the local customs house, his candidacy was interpreted as a Communist attempt to give blacks control of the city.[58] According to the party's daily, *Noticias de Hoy*, the local "aristocracy" had launched the slogan "No black mayor for Santiago" and were touring the city in their luxury automobiles "buying votes and conducting a racist campaign." Reflecting his own prejudice and fears as well as those of the local white elite with whom he maintained close links, the U.S. consul in Santiago reported: "[T]he political campaign has largely resolved the contest into a racial issue of whites versus blacks. To the Negroes, it offers a new and unsurpassed opportunity to assert their power, gain control of the municipality from the whites, and . . . obtain graft and sinecures. The cry 'Down with the whites' is frequently heard now and comes close to being the slogan of their political meetings." Whites in Santiago, the same authority asserted, complained that blacks were getting "fresher" all the time, demanding entrance into beaches, hotels, restaurants, and bars that had been traditionally off-limits to them.[59]

Labor and other forms of popular mobilization enhanced the Communists' position as true representatives of the masses. Through their access to the executive—which was thoroughly controlled by Batista—the Communists ensured that most of the strikes that developed in early 1940 were settled in favor in workers. This proved conclusively that unions had much to gain from affiliating with the CTC and that the confederation had the ability to influence government decisions. In Santiago, Justo Salas was elected mayor, a result that Blas Roca celebrated as a Communist triumph: "[I]t was our party that helped him and made him succeed." Indeed, Salas's largest vote had come from the Communists, who ranked second in the city.[60] The party also elected five of the twenty-five members of the city council—of whom at least two were black or mulatto.[61] Furthermore, Batista won in a fairly clean election, and the party managed to elect 10 representatives to the House (out of 162), including well-known Afro-Cuban labor and party leaders such as Lázaro Peña, Salvador García Agüero, Blas Roca, and Jesús Menéndez Larrondo.[62]

The campaign demonstrated that the Communists had become an important political force, but it provided some other enduring lessons as well. First, the effectiveness of the party was based on its capacity to make alliances with other political groups. This capacity, in turn, was largely dependent on its ability to control the labor confederation and mobilize workers for electoral purposes. Even at the height of the party's power in the mid-1940s, the number of party militants was never large enough to make the Communists electoral contenders on their own. Without their labor base, contending political groups realized, the Communists' electoral strength was virtually negligible. And since it was the government that had given them the opportunity to organize the CTC to begin with, it followed logically that a different administration might favor one of the other groups that vied to control the organization. The Communists thus had to choose their political allies carefully, for an unsympathetic government could threaten their leadership in the confederation and even their viability as a political party. In short, the Communists had been trapped by the logic of the political system. While using it to their advantage, they helped reproduce a system that might ultimately undermine their existence as a party.

A less obvious but equally important lesson came out of these early Communist incursions into electoral politics. It would be considerably more difficult to wage the battle against racial discrimination than to advance labor demands. For one thing, labor-related demands met with resistance only among employers, whereas racially defined goals tended to generate opposition among larger sectors of the voting population. In this sense, both the constitutional convention and the mayoralty race in Santiago provided an unequivocal message. Any attempt to aggressively alter deeply embedded racist mores would meet with widespread resistance. The Communists' radical proposals to the convention had elicited substantial opposition. Salas had been elected, but not without widespread opposition from the white population of Santiago. Always astute, Batista correctly sensed the political environment and tended to compromise on the issue of race. For instance, when a new commanding officer for Oriente's military district was to be appointed in late 1939, Batista bypassed black major Gregorio Querejeta, his first choice for the post, "out of respect for the susceptibilities of the whites." Instead, he named Lieutenant Colonel Ramón N. Gutiérrez, a "pure white" known to have "a pronounced feeling against the Negroes," to lead the armed forces in the province.[63]

Structural obstacles further hindered the Communists' attempts to advance a radical antiracist agenda. With high rates of unionization and a national organization that could mobilize thousands of members across regions and economic sectors, labor was in a privileged position to assert effective pressure on the state. No comparable organization existed among Afro-Cubans. The National Federation of Societies of the Colored Race was supposed to play this role, but most Afro-Cubans did not belong to any of its member clubs and the leadership of the federation was composed almost entirely of black and mulatto professionals with limited influence on the masses of Afro-Cuban manual workers. The latter found in the unions an adequate vehicle for their most pressing demands. Furthermore, the workings of the political system facilitated the resolution of labor conflicts, but they made the adoption of radical antidiscrimination policies much more difficult. Whereas the former could be channeled through the executive and settled by presidential decrees, the latter implied legislative action. The complementary laws required by the Constitution to punish discrimination had to be approved by the national Congress—and its lack of activity was notorious in the 1940s.

The Communists understood that only under strong popular pressure would the legislature agree to tackle a problem that the constitutional convention had addressed only reluctantly. In order to create the political momentum to pass its antidiscrimination law, the party used its influence in the labor movement and worked closely with feminist, youth, and Afro-Cuban organizations. The Communists sought to influence these organizations and their political agendas by placing some of their militants in positions of leadership. They helped organize, for instance, the first National Women's Congress in 1939 and the Federación Democrática de Mujeres Cubanas in 1948, which was later characterized as "Communist-inspired, Communist-controlled and Communist-directed." The general secretary of the 1939 congress was Edith García Buchaca, later president of the Women's Federation. Two of the federation's vice presidents had been members of the 1939 congress's executive committee as well.[64]

The Communists also placed representatives in the most important youth associations and in the regional and national federations of Afro-Cuban societies. Severo Aguirre was in the executive committee of the Agrupación Jóvenes del Pueblo, a group created in Santiago de Cuba around 1937 and believed to be composed "almost entirely of young negroes."[65] In turn, Salvador García Agüero was one of the organizers of the first congress of the Hermandad de Jóvenes Cubanos, held in 1938 with the participation of more than three hundred groups from across the island. The U.S. Embassy reported that both organizations, the Hermandad and Jóvenes del Pueblo, united in early 1940 with the purpose of "supporting the Communist Party in the forthcoming elections."[66] Together with Serafín Portuondo Linares, García Agüero also belonged to the executive committee of the Federación Nacional de Sociedades. In the late 1940s, the federation's president, Quirino García Rojas, was at least a Communist sympathizer.[67] In Matanzas, the secretary of the provincial federation was Antolín Dickinson Abreu, a sugar labor leader and party member since the early 1930s; another leader of the party in the province, Cesáreo Sánchez, led the societies in the area of Pedro

Betancourt.[68] In Camagüey, the party was represented by Francisco Guillén and Felicita Ortiz, who was also prominent in the Women's Federation.[69] Another female leader, Esperanza Sánchez Mastrapa, represented Gibara in Oriente's Federación Provincial de Sociedades.[70]

Not only did the Communists get some of their militants elected to the leadership of these organizations, but the party was always careful to include some Afro-Cubans among them. Sánchez Mastrapa, Felicita Ortiz, and Consuelo Silveira, all of whom played prominent roles in the women's movement, were either black or mulatto; Severo Aguirre, the student leader, was also black. The same principle was applied to the party's leadership, its candidates for office, and the labor confederation. Out of seventeen national Communist leaders identified in a 1940 U.S. Embassy "Who's Who" report, six were Afro-Cuban. In a similar 1948 source, at least ten out of thirty-one "prominent Cuban communists" were identified as black or mulatto.[71] Afro-Cubans represented 32 percent of the delegates to the party's national assembly in 1944 and 30 percent in 1948, 40 percent of party-elected House representatives in 1940, and 33 percent of its elected senators and 50 percent of its House representatives in 1944. Out of sixty-five identified candidates for aldermen positions in 1944, seventeen were nonwhite; eight of the twenty-five members of the national executive committee of the party in 1948 were Afro-Cuban.[72] The Communists probably had the only party whose leadership so closely reflected the social composition of its members, among whom blacks and mulattoes represented about one-third of the total.[73] Unsympathetic outsiders could only interpret this as conclusive proof of the organization's "racist" goals: "[T]he Negroes, realizing their power, have been replacing the whites in the principal positions and have gained the control of the party, placing it at the service of the specific interests of their race. . . . The principal leaders, not only of the PSP [Partido Socialista Popular, Popular Socialist Party—communist] but likewise of the CTC and the labor unions, belong to the colored race."[74]

With the solid support of the labor confederation and counting on their close links with other organizations, the Communists attempted to pass a bill that would specifically regulate the constitutional statement against racial discrimination (see figure 6.1). Introduced by Representative Blas Roca in the House as early as January 1941, the "Law of Education and Sanctions against Racial Discrimination" contained two separate sections. The first part defined discrimination using language that was nearly identical to that of the amendment introduced by García Agüero in the constitutional convention. But the law contained concrete criminal sanctions as well. It prescribed

¡Hombre o Mujer Negro!

¿Quién lucha por tu igualdad?
¿Quiénes exigen respeto a tu
dignidad humana?
¿Quién propone la Ley contra
la discriminación racial?

¡Lucha junto a ellos!

¡AFILIATE AL PARTIDO SOCIALISTA POPULAR!

FIGURE 6.1. *Communist electoral propaganda. This poster calls voters to join the Communist Party and support its struggle for racial equality. "United, Equal. Black man or woman! Who fights for your equality? Who demands respect for your human dignity? Who is promoting the Law against racial discrimination? Join their fight! Join the Partido Socialista Popular!"* From Noticias de Hoy, *September 22, 1951. (Biblioteca Nacional "José Martí")*

imprisonment from six months to three years for those who violated the law, four-year suspensions for public functionaries, and fines and the eventual closure of institutions in which discrimination was practiced. The second section created a Cuban Institute of Inter-Racial Cooperation under the Ministry of Education. The institute would launch educational campaigns to demonstrate the "falsehood of racist theories," supervise public and private schools' curricula, and publicize the role played by Afro-Cubans in the struggles for independence and under the republic.[75]

The party deemed this and other complementary laws to be of the utmost importance and called on workers, peasants, and the general citizenry to join in the struggle to have them approved. "Without them [the complementary laws], the equality of blacks and women, the right to strike, the right to unionize, the suspension of peasant evictions, will all be a dead letter," proclaimed a Communist manifesto soon after the national elections. "We must give priority to drafting the laws that complement the new constitution, which is being attacked by reactionaries . . . to avoid its implementation," a party journal advocated. "We must explain continuously what these laws mean; that without them it is not possible to apply the Constitution."[76]

Since discrimination was largely a labor question, the Communists saw the CTC as a major player in their campaign to stir public opinion in favor of the law and in their struggle against racism more generally. No significant labor conference, congress, or demonstration occurred without the Communist-controlled unions demanding congressional action on the complementary legislation. This was the first item on the agenda of the CTC's Second National Congress in December 1940. It was still the first resolution on social legislation adopted by the organization's fifth congress in 1947.[77] The CTC also instructed its unions to actively propagandize the issue in the labor press and to take concrete steps to guarantee the hiring and promotion of black workers, particularly in those sectors and activities in which discrimination was more blatant.[78]

Under Communist leadership, some unions brought pressure on employers to promote blacks into positions that were customarily closed to them. The most noted of these cases took place at the Havana Electric Company. Due to the activism of the Union of Motorists and Conductors, which had created a "Tramway Committee against Discrimination," the first black tramway conductor was promoted to the position in 1947.[79] In the Ariguanabo textile mill, the Communist-controlled union launched a strike in 1944 based, among other reasons, on the fact that the U.S.-owned factory employed only fourteen blacks in a total labor force of four thousand employees. The Communists also denounced Woolworth and other stores where Afro-Cubans found no employment opportunities. And when a black worker was passed over for promotion in a dry-cleaning facility in Havana, the Communist-controlled union took the employer to court.[80]

The CTC also campaigned on a number of issues that were of great benefit to Afro-Cuban workers, even though they were not defined in racial terms. One example was Decree 3185, which established a forty-four-hour week with wages paid for forty-eight hours and regulated the constitutional principle of equal pay for equal work. The significant wage increases that the CTC managed to obtain in the 1940s through presidential decrees favored all unionized workers, regardless of race. Between 1940 and 1952 more than 450 decrees regulating salaries and wages were approved. Batista's administration alone granted general wage increases ranging from 10 to 25 percent in 1941 and 1944; real nonagricultural wages more than doubled between 1940 and

1952.[81] Furthermore, the Communists sought to extend these benefits to nonunionized sectors in which an Afro-Cuban presence was quite prominent, such as domestic work. They organized the Union of Domestic Workers—whose leader, Elvira Rodríguez, was black—and submitted a law extending all labor benefits to them.[82]

The campaign in favor of the complementary laws was supported also by the Communist-controlled Federación Democrática de Mujeres Cubanas. The 1939 Women's Congress had already passed several resolutions that reproduced the radical views of the party concerning the race question, including proportional distribution of employment and appointment of black women to the executive boards and electoral lists of all political parties. In turn, the first congress of the Women's Federation, held in 1950, agreed to lend the movement's "strong support" to the approval of the Communists' law against discrimination. In her report to the assembly, mulatto representative and party militant Esperanza Sánchez Mastrapa elaborated on the need for such a law from the perspective of Afro-Cuban women: "To the inequalities that women suffer in all social relations in our country . . . black and mulatto women must add those based on skin color. This is an even more cruel violation of Article 20 of the Constitution."[83]

The party's natural ally in the struggle against discrimination was, of course, the Federation of Societies of the Colored Race, in which most of the Afro-Cuban intelligentsia was grouped. Although party leaders were critical of these societies, which they believed helped to consolidate and reinforce racial segregation, the Communists actively enlisted their support to force congressional action on their proposal.[84] "To advance the struggle against discrimination," a party internal report asserted, "we will have to count on the most influential sector of the black population, namely the Black Societies—political, revolutionary, of racial defense, religious—which have a long tradition in our country." Party militants were instructed to join the Afro-Cuban clubs, to promote the "education" of their members concerning the true nature and origin of discrimination, and to incorporate the societies into the Communists' general struggle "for the establishment of the socialist and communist regime in the nation."[85]

To no small degree, the Communists' efforts bore fruit. Particularly in 1944, when their law was again introduced—this time by García Agüero in the Senate—an impressive movement involving dozens of Afro-Cuban clubs from across the island demanded the passage of the law. Again, the timing of the campaign had been carefully chosen: it coincided with the national elections. In the midst of the electoral campaign, candidate Ramón Grau San

Martín was invited by Unión Fraternal, together with other political figures, to speak at the club and to define his position concerning racial discrimination and the complementary law.[86] But the Afro-Cuban clubs also made sure that electoral promises were not easily forgotten. Before and immediately after president-elect Grau and members of Congress took office, they were flooded with requests to support the Communists' legal project. At a gathering of twenty-five Havana societies in early October, they unanimously agreed to send messages to the Senate and the House of Representatives demanding the passage of the law. The Havana federation also asserted publicly that it hoped Grau would follow through on his promises and that substantial numbers of Afro-Cubans would be promoted to positions of power within the administration.[87]

Pressure also came from the other provincial federations. The Pinar del Río federation sent letters to the provincial legislators, requesting their favorable vote for the law and demanding to know their position on the issue. The Matanzas federation replicated this strategy in its own province, also securing the endorsement of the governor and former presidential candidate Carlos Saladrigas.[88] In Las Villas, the town council of Santa Clara passed a resolution supporting the law, and in response to a request from the provincial federation, all the elected mayors sent a letter of endorsement to Congress. The campaign was seconded in Oriente by the Provincial Council of Veterans and the descendants of Maceo.[89] In addition to these concerted efforts, the Afro-Cuban clubs and societies also sent individual letters and telegrams to the president, requesting his support. Club Atenas, which did not belong to the Federation of Societies, released a manifesto denouncing the persistence of "racist discrimination" in the island and demanding the passage of the law.[90]

Nevertheless, the campaign failed. The proposed law was submitted to the Senate Commission on Constitutional and Political Rights, where it was defended by Communist senator Juan Marinello, receiving a favorable vote.[91] However, the Senate did not act on the proposal, sending it instead to yet another commission and indefinitely postponing its discussion. A national demonstration organized by the Afro-Cuban clubs in Havana's National Amphitheater in August 1945, attended by Grau and some cabinet members, failed to break the deadlock. So did the Second National Convention of the federation, which demanded again the approval of the project. By 1947 the National Federation of Societies of the Colored Race sourly admitted in a public declaration that, all its efforts notwithstanding, the law remained in a congressional drawer. The presidents of both houses had not included the proposal in the legislative agenda, and Grau had done nothing to get the support of his own party, which after 1946 had a congressional majority.[92]

Neither the Communists nor their allies in the Afro-Cuban clubs gave up, however. If Grau's administration had been a fiasco on almost every conceivable count, a new election provided another opportunity to pressure Congress and force the president to include the antidiscrimination law among his priorities. Using methods that by now had become customary in Cuban electoral politics, the leading candidate, Carlos Prío Socarrás of the ruling Partido Revolucionario Cubano, was invited to speak from the tribune of Club Atenas. Prío was not as vague as Grau was when dealing with this issue—Grau's statements usually were lost in a vast repertoire of empty slogans such as "Cubanness is love" and "Let there be candy for everyone"— but the candidate did not have much to offer in providing a solution to a problem whose existence he did not deny. "It is a national shame," Prío declared, "that the problem of racial discrimination must figure in a government program.... Discrimination creates divisions, the possibility of a social cataclysm, the affirmation of a principle of despicable fascism." He described discrimination as "mainly an economic problem" that persisted because the Fifty Percent Law had not been applied as intended. When it came to his government program, however, Prío's promises were almost as empty as Grau's: "We must fight against that [discrimination]: we must remedy this ill.... We must keep promoting deep and wide social justice in Cuba, so that divisions do not penetrate the consciousness of the nation."[93]

But Prío had at least recognized publicly the existence of discrimination and committed himself to doing something about it. Furthermore, during the electoral campaign he had also promised to promote blacks and mulattoes to positions of leadership within the administration, raising the expectations of Afro-Cuban office seekers. "Never before has the black Cuban been in as advantageous a position as he is now before a new government," Afro-Cuban journalist Manuel Cuéllar wrote in 1948. Again using the electoral momentum, in 1948 the Communists submitted for the third time their proposed law against discrimination—on this occasion through Congressman Aníbal Escalante. Although their past campaigns had failed to have the law approved, they had at least achieved a desirable result: the need to pass the complementary law against discrimination had been included in the legislative programs of all major parties.[94]

By 1948, however, the Communists' capacity to mobilize public opinion in support of their proposal had been seriously impaired. After eight years of fierce competition with the Auténticos, the Communists had lost control of

CARTELES   ¡YA ERA HORA!

FIGURE 6.2. *"It Was About Time!" This cartoon depicts the expulsion of Communist labor leader Lázaro Peña from the* CTC. *From* Carteles, *July 20, 1947. (Biblioteca Nacional "José Martí")*

the CTC in 1947, when they proceeded to form their own labor confederation, which did not enjoy legal recognition or government support (see figure 6.2). By 1951, it was estimated that out of some two thousand local unions nationally, the Communists remained in control of only forty.[95] All of the national federations had fallen under the umbrella of the government-sponsored, non-Communist CTC. Losing its labor base was a major blow to the party, which in 1948 for the first time won fewer votes than in the previous election. By 1950, the Communists could barely find a political party willing to accept them as electoral allies. A year later, the number of voters affiliated with the party had declined, compared to 1949, by almost 60 percent.[96]

Militants of the Partido Socialista Popular were also displaced from leadership positions in the different labor federations, which joined the government-sponsored CTC. Aracelio Iglesias, the Afro-Cuban leader of the Havana Stevedores Union, was replaced in his post and assassinated in October 1948. All Communists were taken off of the Executive Board of the National Federation of Maritime Workers, whose new general secretary, a black labor leader named Gilberto Goliath, was an Auténtico.[97] The Afro-Cuban Communist leader of sugar workers, Jesús Menéndez, was killed in February 1948. The same month, three inspectors from Prío's Ministry of Labor, accompanied by soldiers, took over the Federación Provincial de Trabajadores de Oriente, headed by yet another Afro-Cuban Communist, Juan Taquechel.[98] Shortly thereafter, the Communist radio station Mil Diez, which ranked sixth in the country in terms of audience, was closed down. By 1949 the CTC had made it a goal to outlaw the Communist Party altogether, and the conservative press announced that the Cuban labor movement had been "liberated."[99]

ANTICOMMUNISM

The Communists had been removed from the leadership of organized labor, but they remained a force to be reckoned with. The "tragedy," U.S. authorities noted, was that the Communist labor leaders were in fact more competent, honest, and better organized than the Auténticos.[100] Furthermore, they had left behind a legacy that the new leaders could not easily ignore. The Communist CTC had effectively represented the interests of labor and obtained significant benefits and wage increases for unionized workers during the 1939–47 period. The Communists also had championed the struggle for racial equality, demanding the approval of the complementary legislation, denouncing instances of racial discrimination, and occasionally forcing employers to hire and promote Afro-Cuban workers to better-paid positions. In order maintain some sense of legitimacy as CTC leaders, the Auténticos had little choice but to continue these traditions.

The new leadership of the confederation moved aggressively to consolidate its role. Labor mobilization did not recede. In fact, to the dismay of employers, the demands of organized labor increased. "The overthrow of the Red leaders that tyrannized labor organizations has accomplished nothing," admonished *Diario de la Marina*, "because the same antisocial principles . . . continue to dominate 'anti-Communist' labor organizations." The conservative press noted that the new leaders of the CTC had increased wage and other labor demands so that they could not be accused of ignoring workers, and that the government was eager to show a favorable record of "social conquests." "In the eyes of the government," the same newspaper asserted, "ownership of property is a kind of crime."[101]

The Auténtico labor leaders were much slower in appropriating the agenda for racial equality. Indeed, the issue of racial equality, which had been prominent in every major manifesto or public act of the Communist-controlled unions, virtually disappeared from the list of demands of organized labor. Among the 255 requests that the thirty-one national federations comprising the CTC submitted to President Prío in May 1951, not one referred to racial equality or the lack of a complementary law on the subject.[102] Auténtico labor leader Marcos Hirigoyen admitted that the unions had done little to eliminate discrimination. "If union leaders, with the support of their organizations, used direct action to demand the observation of the workers' registry as Cubans and workers, and not as men of this or that color, there would be no discrimination in Cuba."[103]

The Communists, in turn, kept fighting against discrimination. As mentioned above, the Partido Socialista Popular submitted its law to Congress for the third time in 1948. The party used its remaining labor base and its presence within the Federation of Societies to keep the issue alive and to maintain its claim over it. When the party tried to organize a "Democratic National Front" in 1950 and 1951, the struggle against racial discrimination figured prominently among its goals and demands.[104] Furthermore, the Communists also used race to disqualify their critics. For instance, referring to the anti-Communist Congress of Telephone Workers in October 1947, they pointed out the noticeable lack of "brown" faces among those attending the assembly. They also attacked the new leadership of the CTC for displacing Afro-Cubans from the executive board of the organization.[105]

Criticism of the CTC, the Auténticos in general, and the government also came from Afro-Cuban societies that were not linked to the Communist

Party, particularly the prestigious Club Atenas. By 1951, the Afro-Cuban clubs had become increasingly impatient with President Prío's total disregard for his electoral promises concerning the need to fight against discrimination. During the elections, Prío had pledged to appoint blacks and mulattoes to government posts, but the proportion of Afro-Cubans in the administration remained dismally low. During his term, Grau had named two Afro-Cubans as generals, two blacks or mulattoes as cabinet members, and several Afro-Cubans as section heads, including the chief of police.[106] Under Prío, even this limited Afro-Cuban presence in the government declined.[107] The "almost complete absence of black representatives" in the government, an editorial in *Nuevos Rumbos* remarked, had created widespread skepticism in the black population toward the administration.[108] Worse, perhaps, was the fact that as late as August 1951 Prío had not yet recommended that Congress approve the law against discrimination. In an open letter to the president, the directors of Club Aponte recalled his electoral offers and compelled him to support the law. "You promised that your government would end this degrading situation [of discrimination]. . . . Stick to your word on this historic issue." A similar petition was made by Club Atenas, whose president, Auténtico senator Prisciliano Piedra, had introduced his own antidiscrimination law in Congress.[109]

Piedra's proposal, which basically reproduced the Communist law except in its "educational" section, could only be interpreted by the party as an attempt to steal its hard-earned primacy in the antidiscrimination struggle. As a senator in the ruling party, Piedra expected his proposal to receive favorable action, for by 1950 it had become evident that one of the main obstacles preventing the approval of the Communist proposal was the affiliation of its proponents. Other political parties were reluctant to let them receive the credit for the antidiscrimination law. The Partido Socialista Popular condemned Piedra's initiative as an electoral "trap," which sought to create confusion and divisions, by someone who had never defended Afro-Cuban rights in his long political career, which had begun in the early 1920s.[110] The Federation of Societies, in which the Communists maintained some influence, acknowledged as well that submitting a new proposal weakened their campaign in favor of the law, for the Senate and the House could not legally consider two different proposals on the same issue. A few days later, Piedra offered to withdraw his proposal in a public letter to President Prío.[111]

If the interests involved in the approval of the law were contradictory, their assessment of political timing was not. As in the past, the campaign in favor of the law intensified during the period preceding the national elections of June 1952. An editorial published in the monthly of Club Atenas amounted to nothing less than electoral blackmail: "The government of President Prío still has a few months left in power. If he truly wants to win the forthcoming battle of June 1, it would be convenient for him to take note of what we have said. We will know how to use consciously the rights given to us by the Constitution."[112]

Prío and the Auténticos could not afford to ignore these threats, for the outcome of the 1952 elections was far from guaranteed. In fact, opinion polls suggested that the leading candidate was that of the oppositionist Partido del Pueblo Cubano Ortodoxo (Party of the Cuban People, Orthodox), created in 1947 as an alternative to the scandalous corruption and graft of the Auténtico administrations.[113] In his new address to Congress in October 1951, Prío briefly acknowledged the need to regulate discrimination.[114] Although he remained opposed to giving the Communists credit for the initiative, he could not evade the issue any longer. Pressure was coming not only from the Communist ranks but also from prominent Afro-Cuban figures within his own party and anti-Communist groups that advocated reformism as an alternative to Communist propaganda.[115] In short, Prío had to find a formula that, while regulating discrimination, did not work to the political advantage of his enemies.

The official CTC provided such a formula. Following the agreements of their seventh congress, the leaders of the confederation initiated a movement against discrimination in the fall of 1951. In September, the secretary of social relations of the CTC, Afro-Cuban Reinaldo Hastié, called for a meeting with representatives of student organizations, the Federación de Sociedades de la Raza de Color, and Afro-Cuban society page reporters to organize a "common front" against racial discrimination. Out of this and other preliminary meetings, the Frente Cívico Cubano Contra la Discriminación Racial (Cuban Civic Front against Racial Discrimination) was organized, which also had the support of Atenas and Unión Fraternal, the two most important Afro-Cuban clubs in the capital.[116]

Responding favorably to the front's campaign, and in order to placate the many critics of his administration, in early November, Prío issued a decree regulating Article 74 of the Constitution. The decree established that the constitutional provision would have to be "immediately fulfilled," that "racial discrimination in the filling of vacancies or newly created positions in industry and commerce" was punishable, and that the lists of unemployed workers from which candidates were selected would contain no reference to their race or color. The Ministry of Labor was charged with investigating any instance of discrimination and was authorized to pursue industrial or commercial establishments that did not comply with the law. The decree also noted that its effects were not retroactive, that it did not impair any "lawfully vested rights," and that it did not fix "percentages of a discriminatory nature" in the distribution of employment.[117]

The decree had been issued in response to the combined pressure of several groups. In turn, it set new forces in motion. Claiming victory, the Frente Cívico immediately began to make contacts with the National Federation of Retail Workers to promote the hiring of blacks in commercial establishments, where they were greatly underrepresented. They demanded that the director of sports end discriminatory practices in amateur sports and especially in baseball, in which the exclusion of blacks had become a "scandal." Representatives of the front also paid a visit to the minister of labor and the president to thank them for the decree and to request their personal intervention with employers in order to create opportunities for blacks.[118]

The front's activities were complemented by other groups that saw the decree as an unprecedented opportunity to break the traditional white monopoly over certain occupations. Unión Fraternal—whose president, Rogelio Piedrahita, was a member of the executive board of the Frente Cívico—reproduced the decree and gave a copy to each member of the club so that they were fully aware of its content. In Las Villas, the president of the Sociedad El Gran Maceo called for a meeting with all the Afro-Cuban clubs in the province to study the proposals of the Frente Cívico. Another organization, the Comité Conjunto Pro-Justicia Ciudadana, congratulated the front and the CTC for their success "in the crusade that led to the approval of the decree" against discrimination, but it asserted that in order to make those gains "real," blacks should be represented in all government offices and on the Auténtico's electoral ticket as well.[119]

Prío and Minister of Labor Edgardo Buttari further legitimized the Frente Cívico and the Auténtico-sponsored CTC by meeting privately with representatives of the retail sector to insist on their support in hiring Afro-Cubans. In late November, the president asked the managers of some of the most noted department stores in Havana—Fin de Siglo, El Encanto, Sears and Roebuck, and La Filosofía—to include black women on their staffs. Meanwhile, Minister Buttari met with the president of the Association of Commercial Streets and asked for his cooperation in this matter.[120] Prío also used the commemoration of Antonio Maceo's death to publicly criticize discrimination and, utilizing the dominant discourse of *mestizaje*, to appeal to the unity of all Cubans. "This country is not the making of a privileged race. . . . To introduce divisions between blacks and whites . . . is to betray Cuba." In a clear allusion to his own decree and to the Communists, Prío also asserted that Cubans had reached harmony by promoting "public freedoms and social justice."[121]

The mainstream press hailed the government's policy and Prío's speech as definite steps toward the solution of the so-called black problem in Cuba. It was particularly laudatory about the "discreet" and "gradual" approach the administration had taken to tackle this issue.[122] This was of course an unveiled reference to the Communists and their active campaign against race discrimination, which one journalist claimed did more harm to the nation than tuberculosis.[123] "When the Communists led the labor syndicate and with governments that were very close to them, black Cubans envisioned only remote promises of legislation," charged Reinaldo Hastié. From the pages of *Diario de la Marina*, conservative Afro-Cuban journalist Gastón Baquero also welcomed Prío's decree, noting that the "communist revolution" prospered only in places where social injustices prevailed.[124]

If the government approach was discreet and gradual, so were the results of its policies. A few highly educated, light-skinned mulatto women found employment in Havana's luxury stores during the 1951 Christmas season, but that was about all the decree accomplished in practice. From the Federación de Sociedades, the Communists dismissed the decree as "useless," while angrily criticizing the creation of the Frente Cívico as an electoral maneuver of the Auténticos against the complementary law. Furthermore, they noted in January 1952 that the few Afro-Cuban women hired in the department stores had been dismissed after the shopping season, exposing the "hypocrisy" of Prío.[125]

The Communists were not alone in their criticism. Pastor Albear, then a senatorial candidate with the Ortodoxos, ridiculed the decree as a "mockery" against Afro-Cubans. The regulation, Albear charged, took cases of discrimination away from the judicial system and placed them under the jurisdiction of the Ministry of Labor, where they were handled through a mere administrative procedure—clearly not what the Constitution intended. A writer in the black journal *Amanecer* also referred to the decree as a mockery and claimed that it did not provide effective protection "of any kind." Other less well known Afro-Cubans were also skeptical. A reader of *Atenas* questioned how meaningful it was to employ several young women in a few commercial establishments and wondered whether he should support the activities of the Frente Cívico. The editors of the journal agreed that this did not solve the problem and warned that the complementary law was needed to fight against instances of discrimination that were not related to employment opportunities and promotions.[126]

The decree as such did not provide a solution, but the whole campaign, which involved the president and received ample coverage in the mainstream press, again placed the issue of race at the center of Cuban national politics and drew public attention to the persistence of discrimination in the island. In a sense, the Communists had been successful. After more than ten years of systematic propaganda and mobilization, even their enemies recognized that some government action was required in this area, if only to deprive the Communists of one of their most effective political tools. Furthermore, regardless of whether the campaign was driven by electoral calculations, it produced another unexpected result: in December 1951, the House of Representatives approved the Communists' Law of Education and Sanctions against Racial Discrimination, which they had initially submitted to Congress eleven years before.[127]

These undeniable successes notwithstanding, the struggle to enact a law regulating discrimination was far from over. It still had to be approved by the Senate, in which the Partido Socialista Popular had no representation. More important, however, was the fact that the popular forces that might have been mobilized at such a crucial moment were deeply divided. The official CTC supported its own initiative, the Frente Cívico, and hoped to work within the framework of Prío's decree. The Federación de Sociedades remained committed to the approval of a complementary law, but in its Fourth National Convention of February 1952, the Communists were expelled from its executive board. The new president was none other than Prisciliano Piedra, for whom the post represented an important step toward his reelection as senator. Piedra and the Communists had clashed over the complementary law, the activities of the Frente Cívico—which he earnestly supported—and the efficacy of Prío's decree. Representatives of other Afro Cuban clubs realized that rather than being a powerful and efficient ally, the Communists had become an obstacle blocking their access to government resources, which were crucial for many societies to survive. Thus, by early 1952, the Federación de Sociedades, just like the CTC, had been captured by the Auténticos. Government control of the national leadership of both organizations was now complete.[128]

The successful incorporation of these organizations into the state machinery introduced opportunities, but it also placed limitations on their activities. Although the CTC continued pressing for labor demands, the confederation was rife with internal divisions, racketeering, and corruption. Furthermore, the political interests of many of its leaders frequently clashed with those of ordinary workers. When the stevedores union of Santiago de Cuba went on strike to protest the loading of bulk sugar in 1955, it was opposed by its own National Federation of Maritime Workers. The union, local sources reported, sought the advice of Afro-Cuban Communist leader Juan Taquechel, former president of the workers federation in the province. The national federation replied by asking the government to intervene in the local union and replace its leaders.[129]

Divisions were evident in other ways. In 1949, the powerful unions of electrical and telephone workers held a congress of independent unions and went on to form their own federation, which competed with the official CTC and the Communists for the support of labor. In 1951, the National Federation of Tobacco Workers threatened as well to withdraw from the CTC due to the interference of the national leadership in the federation's business. Its leader, mulatto union organizer Manuel Campanería, accused Mujal of power abuses and racism and was expelled from the board of the Auténtico's Comisión Nacional Obrera.[130] By late 1951, a group of Auténtico labor leaders recognized that "the balance" of the CTC's work since 1948 had been "negative," as demonstrated by the fact that it had not been able to achieve unity between the working masses and the new union leaders. "The high leadership of the CTC," they accused in a public document, "has introduced its tactics of shady deals, obedience to government dictates, and personal transactions into social conflicts." This had "broken syndical authority" and discredited the workers' movement. Not surprisingly, in the late Prío administration and beyond, organized labor began to lose some of its hard-earned benefits.[131]

A similar process took place in the Federation of Societies of the Colored Race, whose growing dependency on government subsidies seriously impaired its capacity to follow an independent political agenda. Precisely because of these subsidies and other benefits such as jobs in the public sector, good relations with the state were assiduously cultivated. Replicating their successful public "homage" to Machado, the Afro-Cuban clubs organized banquets honoring both Grau and Prío.[132] The election of Senator Piedra as president of the federation further solidified these links, but at the same time it exposed the federation to the politicking and corruption typical of the Auténtico administrations. Piedra's election was itself hotly contested—and not only by the Communists—as an electoral maneuver of Prío and the ruling party. Even his election as president of Club Atenas had been surrounded by scandal, prompting several members of his own club to initiate judicial action against him.[133] Further conflicts within the federation arose around the administration and use of $30,000 donated by Prío to construct a private beach for the societies. Piedra was accused by some of his former supporters of stealing the money and using it for personal purposes. Leading the charge was Reinaldo Hastié, friend and collaborator of the CTC's general secretary, Mujal, who asked for a vote of censure against the executive board, which he claimed—together with his archenemies the Communists—had been imposed from outside. Piedra counterattacked that "everybody" had participated in spending the money and in turn accused Hastié of stealing $10,000 that the CTC had allegedly allocated for the activities of the Frente Cívico.[134] Beyond these mutual accusations, what transpired from the meeting was that, just like the CTC, with the displacement of the Communists, the "anti-red" front had been broken and personal aspirations and rivalries threatened the integrity of both organizations.

BATISTA'S AUTHORITARIAN REGIME

The military coup led by Batista in March 1952 helped to consolidate these trends. After a timid initial attempt at resistance, the leadership of the CTC negotiated an arrangement with the de facto government that guaranteed the status of the confederation and its leaders. Mujal's main concern was that the new government would deliver the CTC to the Communists or to labor activists from Batista's own Partido Acción Unitaria.[135]

The Federation of Societies followed suit. In a public manifesto issued shortly after the coup, its president, Prisciliano Piedra, requested that all Afro-Cuban clubs "display their frank and strong support for the new leaders of the nation." At the same time, Piedra asked again for the approval of the complementary law against discrimination and the inclusion of qualified Afro-Cubans in the new administration.[136]

This was not just political opportunism. Many Afro-Cuban professionals whose livelihoods depended on appointments in the inflated government bureaucracy saw the coup as an opportunity for social advancement after four years of Prío's neglect. "We expect a lot from Batista," an Afro-Cuban local leader of the Partido Acción Unitaria in Matanzas asserted. "Batista is 'the man' of the sepia people," concurred journalist Felipe Elosegui.[137] Expectations consequently ran high. According to press reports, a large number of black and mulatto politicians, friends of "the general" or of some of his closest collaborators, had visited the presidential palace in the days following the coup, seeking appointments. As usual, only a few succeeded, although in numbers large enough to give the impression that this would be a government friendly to black people.[138] Two Afro-Cubans were appointed to Batista's first cabinet, Miguel Angel Céspedes as minister of justice and Justo Salas—the former mayor of Santiago—as minister without portfolio. Several more were appointed to the Consultive Council, an advisory board created by Batista to replace Congress. These included such well-known political figures as veteran Generoso Campos Marquetti, Aquilino Lombard, Gustavo Urrutia, journalist Gastón Baquero, and Luis Oliva Pérez, a prominent member of Club Atenas. The press secretary of the club, David Grillo, who was also affiliated with the Partido Acción Unitaria, was being considered to head a department. Journalist Manuel Cuéllar Vizcaíno was named director of social affairs in the Ministry of Information, an office charged with promoting social and cultural projects "leading to national integration." Two Afro-Cubans were in charge of the departments of street cleaning and radio. A personal friend of Batista and protégé of Prisciliano Piedra, Ulises Sánchez Querol, was appointed chief of inspectors in the treasury.[139]

Albeit limited, the presence of these Afro-Cubans in the administration gave them the opportunity to exercise some influence in government decisions, channel some patronage to their followers, and support the Afro-Cuban clubs, which represented their main institutional base. Thanks to the efforts of Councilman Oliva, the government granted $50,000 to seven Afro-Cuban clubs in Havana to build an "inter-social club" that all members could attend. A month after the coup, representatives of the MOPI, an organization that campaigned for racial equality and was led by one of the founding members of the Frente Cívico, handed a list of petitions to Batista. The requests ranged from a petition for a fellowship for Afro-Cuban soprano Olimpia Cabrera to a demand that the government take energetic measures against discrimination. "The general cannot disappoint us," the MOPI declared to the press.[140] Through the mediation of First Lady Marta Fernández de Batista—who attempted, with little success, to emulate Eva Perón's parallel welfare system—Afro-Cuban piano player Zenaida Manfugás received another fellowship to pursue studies in Europe. And in 1952, Batista granted $500,000 to the Nacional Federación de Sociedades to construct an exclusive private beach for members of the Afro-Cuban clubs.[141]

Government action was not limited to a few fellowships and donations. Badly needing popular support, the Batista administration also took some token action in the always difficult area of regulating race discrimination by law. The coup had interrupted the possibility—admittedly remote—that the

Communists' Law of Education and Sanctions would pass in the Senate after being approved by the House of Representatives. It had also interrupted the activities of the Frente Cívico, whose very existence was intimately linked to the Auténticos and the deposed administration.[142] In response to petitions from the Federation of Societies, MOPI, and other organizations, a decree issued in June 1952 regulating the labor exchange— where available unemployed workers were registered—established that jobs would be distributed "without discrimination of any class" and that positions would be filled "without distinctions of race or color."[143] The decree paraphrased some of the passages of Prío's regulation, but it was in fact less comprehensive. Among other things, it included no specific sanctions against violators of the law, although it referred them to the criminal code.

Some Afro-Cuban politicians continued to press for a comprehensive antidiscrimination law. The decrees of Prío and Batista referred to labor; other social areas remained untouched, and racist practices were particularly brutal in those areas, especially in recreational facilities and more or less exclusive establishments that customarily excluded Afro-Cuban customers under the pretext that they were "clubs" for members only. Furthermore, instances of discrimination in these places were frequently more blatant than those involving hiring of personnel. The rejection of an Afro-Cuban job seeker could be always framed as an issue of "ability"—an important loophole that both decrees included. The extent to which racial separation permeated the social life of the middle and upper sectors of society is demonstrated by the fact that the Federation of Societies sought funds to establish its own exclusive, private beach. During the 1950s, when Havana became a tourist and gambling mecca, virtual segregation was prevalent in ample sectors of the entertainment business, in private schools, and even in public squares and parks across the island.[144]

Thus Afro-Cuban activists persisted in their efforts to secure an explicit antidiscrimination law. Theoretically, it was possible to prosecute those who violated Article 20 of the Constitution—which proscribed discrimination because of race, color, or sex—by seeking application of the Código de Defensa Social (the criminal code). But the article was difficult to enforce because it did not clearly define what constituted discrimination. This was true even if the courts were sympathetic, which, some Afro-Cubans claimed, they were not.[145] Seeking to correct this vagueness, at least two attempts were made to have such a law approved in the 1950s. A proposal endorsed by Club Atenas and Unión Fraternal was submitted to the Consultive Council by

Afro-Cuban councilman Oliva in 1952. After the spurious electoral process of 1954, Senator Aquilino Lombard introduced yet another proposal in the Senate.[146] None was approved.

Oliva's proposal defined discrimination along lines that were very similar to those included in the Communists' project and in Piedra's law. The following people were guilty of discrimination: those who, based on race or color, violated citizens' rights to freely access all streets, parks, squares, promenades, and other public spaces; those who prevented individuals from establishing residence in any neighborhood or area; and the owners and managers of commercial, industrial, recreational, and educational establishments who denied employment or refused service in public spectacles, bars, beaches, and "analogous places" or blocked access to educational institutions of any kind. Finally, the law also penalized people who promoted ideas of inferiority or superiority of individuals "due to ethnic reasons."

As with previous proposals, this effort encountered opposition in the Consultive Council. The legal opinion given by another member of the council argued that it was counterproductive to expose prejudices that should be eliminated by "cultural means." These issues, the speaker argued, should be dealt with in an effective but "quiet" way, for the exposure of these "social blots" would only discredit a civilized country like Cuba. He thus proposed that discrimination be regulated within the criminal code as a crime of "injury."[147] This position prevailed. In January 1955, the Council of Ministers issued a succinct regulation, Law-Decree 1933, modifying the Código de Defensa Social and including among the "felonies against the right of equity" any "acts of discrimination against another person on grounds of sex, race, color, or class, and any other discrimination detrimental to human dignity."[148]

This law-decree elicited little interest and was poorly publicized. Instead of enacting a comprehensive antidiscrimination law, such as that proposed by Oliva, the Council of Ministers penalized discrimination without clearly defining it and, more to the point, without giving it the legal and political visibility that a separate law would have provided. After the fiasco of Prío's decree, whose limited practical impact had been the subject of public scorn, Afro-Cubans must have grown skeptical of these legal maneuvers. When asked about the decree, the president of Club Atenas asserted that, since it was available, Afro-Cubans should make use of it, but he was neither enthusiastic about nor supportive of the law.[149] Perhaps the best proof that the decree was not deemed to be sufficient by many Afro-Cubans is the fact that barely a few months had passed before Lombard submitted another proposal for a complementary law. Reflecting the growing frustration of Afro-

Cuban intellectuals with gradual and nonconfrontational approaches, the new bill reintroduced the notion of proportional representation in all public and private employments. But this notion continued to elicit considerable opposition. When the Frente Cívico advanced this possibility in a meeting with the minister of labor in 1951, it became the subject of intense and widespread criticism.[150] The chances that the Lombard bill would be passed were quite simply nil.

The failure of the Cuban state to implement the constitutional mandate of racial equality had several important consequences in the short run—which is where peoples' lives take place. It discredited the state, together with the Constitution from which it drew legitimacy, and all its representatives, regardless of political affiliation. It also cast serious doubts about—if not outright rejection of—the dominant integrationist ideology of *mestizaje* and its capacity to create a nation that was truly for all. Even more to the point, it further discredited the leading Afro-Cuban institutions, notably the Federation of Societies and Club Atenas. The inability of these institutions to represent effectively the concerns of most Afro-Cubans irrespective of class had become painfully obvious. Undisguised, too, was their subordination to the group in power. Politics, politicking, and corruption had permeated the institutional life of the federation and some of the most important Afro-Cuban clubs to such a degree that any illusion of autonomy had been effectively shattered. Thus, Piedra's leadership of the federation was challenged following the coup, for his main claim to power was his friendship with former president Prío, whom he referred to as "my brother."[151] In Club Atenas, several members organized a group to "rescue" the society from its leadership. The club continued to prosper through the 1950s, but only through its intimate connections with high government representatives, who constantly participated in its banquets, lectures, and public acts. In 1954, Batista gave Club Atenas the Order of Carlos Manuel de Céspedes, the highest decoration of the Cuban government.[152]

But the ultimate expression of government intervention in the affairs of the Afro-Cuban clubs was the creation, by government decree, of a national club of Cuban societies named after Juan Gualberto Gómez in 1954. Its most immediate purpose was to construct the private beach and recreational facilities for which Batista had allocated $500,000. The government had decided to create its own club for Afro-Cubans, explained Batista in a speech at Unión Fraternal, because "black representatives" had been unable to reach an agreement concerning the location of the private beach and how to spend the money. The Council of Ministers would appoint the directors of the institution. Among those being considered for the job were Miguel A. Céspedes; José Pérez González, a labor leader who at the time was minister without portfolio; Gastón Baquero; and Club Atenas's president, engineer Felix O'Farrill. They were all close to Batista and the administration. Another prominent black leader close to the regime, veteran Generoso Campos Marquetti, eventually became the president of the Federation of Societies.[153]

The unwillingness of Cuban politicians to approve the complementary law and use the power of the state to fight discrimination led a group of Afro-Cuban professionals and entrepreneurs to seek autonomous solutions to their traditional subordination in society. To them, even more than to Afro-Cuban manual workers, "integration" and "fraternity" had failed to provide concrete opportunities for social advancement. "Integration is a utopia in the Cuban environment," asserted an Afro-Cuban intellectual, because it implied a social will that did not exist.[154] To build what they defined as an independent economic base, these Afro-Cubans looked to the United States, where a sector of the African American population had succeeded financially. Like many in the island, Afro-Cuban professionals followed social events and maintained contacts with some of their peers to the north. The U.S. Embassy in Havana encouraged those contacts and, as part of its anti-Communist crusade after the war, propagandized the achievements of the population of color in that country.[155] Atenas and other clubs organized trips to the United States, which often resulted in plans to develop Afro-Cuban businesses in the island. Journalist Pedro Portuondo Calás attended some of the annual conferences that the U.S. Department of Commerce organized to study the economic situation of the "colored" population.[156] Another journalist, José Daniel García, tried several times to promote U.S.-style enterprises geared toward Afro-Cubans. He first promoted, without success, a "grocery" and in 1953 made contacts with the Fuller Brush Company to introduce its products in the island. García called on Afro-Cuban consumers to support his efforts, for Fuller would open employment opportunities for blacks and would also distribute cosmetic products that were especially designed for "the color of [their] skin." Other entrepreneurial attempts included a commercial cooperative funded by Alipio Zuasnábar in Havana and similar establishments elsewhere.[157]

Perhaps the most notorious effort to organize a black autonomous economic base was launched by lawyer Juan René Betancourt in the 1950s. Betancourt had been a leader of the Federation of Societies in Camagüey and had organized a committee against discrimination while attending the University of Havana. He had participated in cross-racial movements to promote

Afro-Cuban rights and had become disenchanted with their results. "Neither civic nor political institutions have ever attempted to conduct a serious, conscious effort... to solve a problem that is not of blacks, but of all Cubans," he wrote in 1954. According to Betancourt, in order to eliminate discrimination and prejudice it was imperative to address their "economic causes," which he claimed could be done only through "cooperation." His scheme called for 100,000 Afro-Cubans each to invest one peso (equal to one dollar) in a lucrative enterprise, creating jobs and wealth for Afro-Cubans. This was the purpose of his Organización Nacional de Rehabilitación Económica (ONRE, National Organization of Economic Rehabilitation), of which several branches were organized in Havana in the 1950s.[158]

Neither Betancourt's ONRE nor other racially defined entrepreneurial attempts succeeded. They were not supported by black and mulatto manual workers, leading to the complaint—which Afro-Cuban professionals had voiced since at least the 1910s—that the "black family" was hopelessly divided.[159] Indeed, these efforts were condemned to failure because they assumed that race identities were, as in the United States, powerful enough to mobilize consumers along racial lines—an assumption that was not realized in practice.

Although these efforts to follow a separate, racially defined route of improvement were made precisely because of the failure of Cuban governments to address Afro-Cubans' grievances, the Batista regime was, according to various sources, perceived as being favorable to blacks. As a Cuban staff member in the U.S. Embassy reported, "Batista is generally assumed to have considerable sympathy for the Negro and his problems (he is, of course, widely thought to have some small proportion of Negro blood himself) and is generally assumed also to find a large percentage of his political support among the Negro part of the Cuban population."[160] This assumption was based as much on Batista's token support of Afro-Cuban professionals and their clubs as it was on the nature and social composition of the organized opposition to his regime. Resistance to the coup sprang initially from the Partido Ortodoxo and from university students, two groups in which blacks were poorly represented. The Ortodoxos included the members of the dissolved ABC and had been frequently attacked for the low presence of blacks among their rank and file.[161] When they signed the so-called Pact of Montreal with Prío and the Auténticos, not a single Afro-Cuban was present. As in the Machado period, the visible face of the opposition was white.[162]

Opposition came from the Communists as well, but the party had been considerably weakened by repression and by its own electoral opportunism.

Batista's initial position toward the Communists was not openly confrontational, but given the cold war environment, he was soon forced to adopt stringent measures against them. First, nothing short of strident anticommunism would guarantee U.S. support. Second, the traditional opposition constantly sought to delegitimize Batista in the eyes of U.S. authorities by emphasizing his former contacts with the Communists, thus contributing to the anti-Communist hysteria. The regime reacted by moving swiftly against the party. In 1953, the Partido Socialista Popular and its daily, *Noticias de Hoy*, were banned. Party sympathizers were barred from holding office in the unions in 1954. The dreaded Bureau of Repression of Communist Activities was created a year later. And a 1957 decree gave the Ministry of Labor and the CTC the right to purge workers with communist "ideas" from the public utility companies.[163] A U.S. diplomat in the island reported with satisfaction that under Batista the Communists were going through their "most difficult period."[164]

Using the same arguments that had been employed against him, Batista sought in turn to discredit any opposition to his regime as Communist-inspired. A demonstration of university students in January 1953 was described by the president as "of a frankly Communist type," even though he recognized that it was led by Auténtico and Ortodoxo groups. The attack on the Moncada barracks in Santiago in July 1953, led by former Ortodoxo activist Fidel Castro, was likewise depicted as "communistic," resulting in the detention and prosecution of Lázaro Peña and Joaquín Ordoqui. Other party leaders such as Marinello and Roca were also linked to the attack and forced to go underground.[165] "This is the government's version of Communism," explained a journalist in 1957. "[T]hose who do not support the regime are Communists. . . . To be truthful, if something has given communism new currency among us it has been [the coup of] March 10. If one believes the government, more than half the Cuban population is Communist."[166]

Batista's charges that acts of civic and armed resistance against his regime were inspired by the Communists were indeed preposterous. Rather, the assault on the Moncada barracks and the organization of the 26th of July Movement (M-26-7) were the works of a group of young idealists who had not prominently participated in national politics before and who were not formally linked to any political organization in the island. The Communists, in fact, did not initially support their struggle and characterized it as "petit bourgeois adventurism."[167]

The social composition, leadership, and goals of the M-26-7 contributed to reinforcing the notion that blacks were sympathetic to Batista or, at the very least, unsympathetic toward the revolutionaries. Although no concrete evidence could be displayed to corroborate such an assertion, various observers noted that blacks and mulattoes were poorly represented in the movement, whose main social base, they said, rested with the middle class. "The younger educated persons of Cuba appear to be definitely opposed to Batista and consider him an armed dictator," reported an attorney from Virginia who visited the island in 1957.[168] Felipe Pazos, who had been president of the Cuban National Bank and was actively opposed to Batista, asserted in 1958 that "support from the negro element in Oriente ha[d] been and continue[d] to be lukewarm" toward Castro and his rebels. "Many negroes from Santiago are nominally aligned with the Batista regime," he claimed. Other observers agreed that blacks were "less revolutionary-minded" than other groups.[169]

This, however, does not mean that blacks did not participate in the struggle against Batista, much less that they supported the regime. Although support for the M-26-7 was initially drawn from urban professionals and university students—groups in which Afro-Cubans were poorly represented—the participation of blacks and mulattoes in the movement was far from negligible. Between one-fifth and one-fourth of those who attacked the Moncada barracks in 1953 were nonwhite. There were also several Afro-Cubans among those who came with Fidel Castro from Mexico in the boat *Granma* in 1956.[170] Once the movement expanded its contacts with local labor unions after 1957, the participation of blacks in organized acts of resistance probably increased even further. In an M-26-7 cell captured by the Batista police in Artemisa in July 1957, Afro-Cubans represented 30 percent of the membership. In four groups of "subversives" captured in Havana in April 1958, Afro-Cubans represented 25 percent.[171] An African American journalist reported later that many top officers in the Rebel Army were "colored" and that as many as 50 percent of the troops could be classified as such. Although these figures were based on North American perceptions of race, there is little doubt that blacks were well represented among the rebels. Their proportion was high enough for Afro-Cuban scholar Carlos Moore to claim later that discrimination against black soldiers might have led to a racially motivated civil war.[172]

Some Afro-Cubans also achieved positions of prominence and command within the revolutionary forces. In addition to the well-known case of Commandant Juan Almeida, blacks and mulattoes in leadership positions included Major Calixto García Morales, appointed head of the army in Santa Clara in early 1959; Captain Marcos Girón, second in command of the Havana police; and Captain Enrique Benavides, who was in control of the Hotel

Havana Riviera and said to be "destined" for a high position in the government. Furthermore, some of Fidel Castro's personal bodyguards were also black.[173]

The perception that blacks had limited or no participation in the struggle against Batista or that they were in fact allied to the Batista regime has lasted to this day. Contributing to these perceptions was the fact that the social organizations in which blacks were best represented—the Afro-Cuban clubs and the unions—were effectively controlled by the government, lending credibility to the idea that they did not oppose the regime. One can explain the lack of visibility of Afro-Cubans in the struggle using the same argument with which Farber analyzes the situation of workers—who are also said to have played no role in the anti-Batista struggle: they "had no readily available institutions through which they could express or organize their discontent." Among the forty-two civic and professional institutions that demanded Batista's resignation in March 1958, not a single Afro-Cuban society was listed.[174] Likewise, although blacks and mulattoes were fairly well represented in Batista's army, their participation in positions of leadership was minimal. It is noteworthy that when in January 1959 *Bohemia* published a "Gallery of Assassins" that included twenty-three top army and police commanders, not one of them was Afro-Cuban.[175]

Contributing to these perceptions was the almost complete silence of the anti-Batista forces concerning race and racial discrimination. In his notable defense after the Moncada attack, known as "History Will Absolve Me," Castro analyzed the numerous ills of the Cuban republic: discrimination was not listed. It is obvious that Afro-Cubans were not excluded from his concept of "people"—which referred to the unemployed, agricultural and industrial workers, peasants, and the lower classes in general—but they were not singled out as a group with special grievances to be redressed in the future. This silence is very surprising given Castro's allegiance to the ideals of Martí, in which the issue of racial equality figured prominently. "Our purpose is to continue his [Martí's] work, because we are loyal to his ideas . . . because we are ready to turn into a reality the Cuba that he dreamed about," the leader of the M-26-7 declared in a 1955 interview.[176]

Not that the movement completely ignored the issue of race, as is often claimed.[177] The "Manifesto No. 1 to the People of Cuba," dated August 1955, called for the "establishment of adequate measures in education and legislation to put an end to every vestige of discrimination for reasons of race." But this document had limited circulation, and more important, subsequent programmatic documents referred to the race question in very vague terms or made no allusion to the problem. For instance, the "Program-Manifesto of the Movement," released in Mexico in 1957, asserted that the M-26-7's ideal was the "organic unity of the nation" and that "no group, class, race, or religion should sacrifice the common good to benefit its particular interest." The program stated as well that the revolution's social order would "incorporate all, without privilege or exception," but not a single word was said about the persistence of racial discrimination in the island.[178] And at least some Afro-Cubans were listening, for Betancourt recalled later his frustration with the revolutionary program for not giving proper attention to racial injustices. In Oriente, where questions of race were of course too salient to be ignored, the leadership of the M-26-7 commissioned a study of the race issue in order to incorporate it into the movement's program.[179]

As in the crisis that led to the fall of the first republic, the importance of race in the 1950s conflict was enhanced by the participants on both sides of the struggle, who manipulated the issue for their own political ends. Some of Batista's spokesmen appealed to blacks in support of the regime, claiming that they should expect nothing from the revolutionaries. Senator Rolando Masferrer, better known for his private army of thugs, "The Tigers," used his reputation as a promoter and defender of Afro-Cuban rights to discredit the rebels.[180] Masferrer printed and distributed fliers in Santiago claiming that Fidel Castro and his followers were antiblack. A similar position was taken by Afro-Cuban journalist Vasconcelos, who in 1957 was Batista's minister of communications: "If the 26th of July triumphed, the black masses of Cuba would return to slavery and workers to complete helplessness. . . . It [the M-26-7] finds support in the professional middle class, so favorable to prejudices. . . . I bet you don't see a majority of workers, peasants, and blacks in the 26th of July."[181]

If the regime used race to rally support, some sectors of the opposition did exactly the same by agreeing with the government's propaganda. Rather than challenging the assumption that blacks supported Batista, groups such as the Organización Auténtica—an armed branch of Prío's followers—used racially charged icons to depict Batista and his army as a bloodthirsty gang of primitive savages with pronounced beastly features (see figure 6.3). They referred to Batista as "el mulato malo" and the "black beast," reinforcing the image that this was a struggle between the white, educated middle class and an ignorant, bloody, and predominantly black army—a struggle between civilization and barbarism, progress and regression.[182] As a group of "Cuban mothers" who wrote to the U.S. Embassy in Havana stated, Batista was a "beast" who belonged in "the African jungle."[183] Only the Communists

FIGURE 6.3. *"They Are All the Same! Punishment Will Be the Same for All." In this cartoon, Batista and his supporters are depicted by the opposition as black beasts. From* Panfleto, *December 1, 1954. (United States National Archives)*

contested the notion that Batista's government had been beneficial to blacks in any way.[184]

So if, on the one hand, the impending triumph of the revolutionary forces represented a new opportunity to create the nation for all that Martí had envisioned and that the leadership of the M-26-7 claimed to incarnate, on the other hand, there were groups, even within the anti-Batista coalition, that perceived Afro-Cubans as supporters of the regime. As during the struggle against Machado, for these groups it followed only naturally that blacks and mulattoes would have little claim to a new, post-Batista Cuba. Betancourt envisioned this reality in 1958: "Blacks as such have never had any reason, nor do they have it now, to support any government. Nevertheless, there it is the propaganda saying the opposite, so when the president of the republic leaves power, the antiblacks will have enough material to assert that this was the government of blacks, even though they have been as subordinated as usual in the public administration."[185]

In a sense, the situation was even more ambiguous than during the fall of the first republic. Some Afro-Cuban clubs and societies had been linked to the Machado regime, but under Batista the Afro-Cubans' main social organization, the Federation of Societies, had become fully discredited because of its open collaboration with the regime. If under Machado a radical sector of organized labor had remained hostile toward the regime, under Batista the CTC had become indistinguishable from the government itself. Neither the unions nor the Afro-Cuban societies were in a position to effectively advance the cause of Afro-Cuban rights in a postrevolutionary Cuba. There was still the clandestine Partido Socialista Popular, but it was not until 1958 that the Communists joined the armed struggle against Batista.[186] Their participation granted them political survival, but it was unlikely that the Communists would play a leading role in the new government. In short, whether the "real" revolution promised by the M-26-7 meant building the inclusive and egalitarian nation envisioned by Martí and sanctioned in the 1940 constitution remained to be seen.

The black problem cannot be liquidated automatically just because a
revolution has triumphed.
—Juan René Betancourt, "Fidel Castro y la integración nacional" (1959)

Without true equality among all Cubans, Republic and Revolution would be
ill-fated lies.
—Salvador García Agüero, "Va bien Fidel" (1959)

Our Revolution . . . has eliminated from Cuban life the humiliating spectacle
of discrimination because of skin color.
—José Felipe Carneado,
    "La discriminación racial en Cuba no volverá jamás" (1962)

In fact, that which one calls "revolution" in Cuba is nothing but the
domination of one *class*, of one *race* over another class, another race.
—Carlos Moore,
    "Le peuple noir a-t-il sa place dans la révolution cubaine?" (1964)

In the early morning of January 1, 1959, Batista fled the country. Rebel
Army forces moved into the main cities, took control of garrisons and other
strategic points, and began filling the vacuum left by the collapse of the
previous regime. Although opposition to the dictatorship included a wide
spectrum of groups and organizations, the Rebel Army led by Fidel Castro
was unquestionably the center of political and military power after the revolution. Fidel Castro moved into Havana among cheering crowds, promising
to redress Cubans' historic claims for social justice, economic independence,
and national sovereignty. "This time," he asserted in a January 2 speech in
Santiago de Cuba, "the revolution is for real."[1]

The shortcomings of the republican past, distant as well as recent, became
the revolution's first claim to political legitimacy. The mostly unfulfilled
program of the 1940 constitution gave those shortcomings a sense of urgency and visibility. They ranged from the inability of republican governments to promote economic diversification; eliminate corruption, the dread-
ful *latifundia*; or remedy chronic unemployment.

Prominent among these shortcomings was the republic's failure to build the *patria* with all and for all envisioned by Martí. Although by the end of the second republic Afro-Cubans had succeeded in entering many areas of employment that had been previously closed to them, they remained systematically barred from some occupations and economic sectors. White-collar jobs in banks, upscale stores, and company offices were for the most part reserved for whites. In some industries, the unions gave priority to employee relatives when filling job openings. In the process, they helped reproduce traditional racial patterns in the distribution of employment. Blacks were also disproportionally represented among the unemployed, and they were the bulk of the inhabitants of the shanty towns in Havana and other cities. They were also overrepresented in the prison population.

Racial barriers were particularly visible in areas of social life, in which open racial segregation was not uncommon. Blacks and mulattoes were discriminated against in luxury hotels, restaurants, cabarets, bars, beaches, and social clubs. Their children could not attend the best private schools even if they had the financial means to afford them. Segregation was also evident in some public spaces, such as the central parks of several towns across the island. Blackness remained a formidable barrier against social ascent and mobility, particularly in the higher strata of society. Meanwhile, whereas the governments of the second republic had done little to tackle racism in any systematic way, mobilization and political demagoguery had given the issue national visibility and helped expose the inefficacy of the constitutional program of 1940.

Yet some scholars imply that it was only after 1959 that race became an issue in Cuban politics. David Booth asks, "Why did then color become an issue with the advent of the revolution?" One could easily turn this question around: How could race not have been an issue under the revolution? Race remained a major social identity with significant influence on individual chances for mobility in the late 1950s. Those who pose Booth's question somehow imply—and sometimes assert explicitly—that prerevolutionary Cuba was a racially harmonious society, that revolutionary authorities exaggerated the sufferings of Afro-Cubans for political purposes, or even that it was they who created a racial division that did not exist before.[2]

THE REVOLUTION'S "MOST DIFFICULT PROBLEM"

The question posed by Booth and others has some merit, however, given that race and discrimination did not figure prominently in the political program or the propaganda of the M-26-7. Although it is unthinkable that race would have simply disappeared from public debates or lost social significance because of the revolutionary triumph, it does not necessarily follow that Castro and other revolutionary leaders had to publicly admit, much less condemn, racially discriminatory practices in Cuban society.[3] Yet in a March 22, 1959, speech given at the presidential palace, Castro spoke at length about racism, called on Cubans to eliminate discrimination, and asked them to forge a "new *patria*." According to Carlos Moore, Castro was forced to tackle the issue in order to avert a racially motivated "civil war." Moore asserts that the black members of the Rebel Army were being discriminated against and denied accommodation and service in the same hotels that housed their white comrades, which led to "a series of violent incidents across the island."[4] Other authors simply imply that, in the alleged absence of a real social problem, Castro's speech merely sought to rally the support of the Afro-Cuban population.[5]

What these authors neglect to mention is that discussions about race and the meanings of the revolution for Afro-Cubans began as early as January 1959. Race and racism did not become issues only when Castro spoke about them. Rather, these issues were brought to public attention by various social and political actors who perceived the revolution as an unprecedented opportunity to redress previous inequities. In the process, they exercised pressure on the government to adopt concrete antidiscrimination measures.

The Communists were again active in this movement. The party had been outlawed under Batista, but it reemerged in early January. Its daily, *Noticias de Hoy*, resumed publishing on January 6 with a front-page declaration that highlighted the "most immediate tasks" that the provisional government should undertake, including the formulation of a "real and effective policy against race discrimination."[6] Following the first meeting of the party's national committee—attended by such well-known Afro-Cuban leaders as Blas Roca, Nicolás Guillén, and Salvador García Agüero—a public letter was sent to then president Manuel Urrutia enumerating sixteen measures that should be implemented by the revolutionary government. The first two measures requested national application of the agrarian reform launched by the Rebel Army in the territory under its command during the insurrection. The third asked for an official antidiscrimination policy and for concrete steps to guarantee blacks' access to all jobs, the armed forces, and state institutions, including the diplomatic service.[7]

The need to eliminate discrimination and promote "real equality" among all Cubans was emphasized by the revolutionary labor movement as well. Under the leadership of the M-26-7, a labor congress had been convened in November 1958 with the participation of several groups, including the Communists. The program of the revolutionary labor federation contained demands such as better pay and union rights. It also included a strong statement against "odious racial discrimination." Originally broadcasted by Radio Rebelde, this agenda was widely publicized in January 1959 by the M-26-7 and the Communist press.[8] When the CTC called on workers to attend the rally at the presidential palace on March 22—at which Fidel Castro spoke at length about racism—one of its slogans was "Against racial discrimination!"[9]

Afro-Cuban intellectuals also voiced their hope that racism would finally be eliminated under the revolution. In articles published in *Revolución*—the official daily of the M-26-7—and *Bohemia*, lawyer Juan René Betancourt, then provisional president of the Federation of Societies, countered Batista's propaganda that had presented Fidel Castro as antiblack and compared the Rebel Army with the Liberation Army of 1895. Betancourt's pieces were not just a panegyric on the new authorities, however. He also called on revolutionary leaders not to replicate the "mistakes" of 1895, warning that a socioeconomic problem such as race would not be solved automatically just because a revolution had triumphed. In order to achieve the long-sought national integration, claimed Betancourt, it was necessary to organize blacks into a unified social movement. Using language similar to that of the Afro-Cuban intellectuals of the 1930s, Betancourt asserted that there would not be a "real revolution" in Cuba if the question of racial equality was either ignored or silenced. He complained about the lack of blacks in positions of leadership in the new government and demanded justice for those who had been "always forgotten." While Fidel Castro used history to legitimize the revolution and the emerging order, Betancourt did so to demand effective equality for Afro-Cubans.[10]

The question of race emerged not just in political programs or press articles. The new authorities had no choice but to confront this issue in a myriad of social situations, from racially defined spaces within parks to patriotic celebrations held in racially defined social clubs. Thus, according to witnesses, segregation practices in several parks in the province of Las Villas were challenged when officers of the Rebel Army, accompanied by groups of black and mulatto citizens, walked through the sections that were traditionally reserved for whites.[11] When Afro-Cuban major Calixto Morales, military governor of Las Villas, was invited to attend meetings honoring the birthday of José Martí on January 28 by both the Afro-Cuban society El Gran Maceo and the white club El Liceo de Santa Clara, he asked the directors of the latter to invite the members of El Gran Maceo to their celebration. For many blacks and mulattoes, an Afro-Cuban journalist noted, it was the first time they set foot in the exclusive Liceo. In another unprecedented act, the conservative club Colonia Española opened its doors several weeks later so Afro-Cubans could attend a poetry reading performed by the great mulatto poet Nicolás Guillén. Race, segregation, and inequality were issues that revolutionary authorities could not ignore.[12]

Attentive to the demands and needs of the popular sectors, whose support was deemed crucial for the survival of the revolutionary government, Fidel Castro listened. It is inaccurate to state that it was not until March 22 that Castro mentioned or criticized racial discrimination in Cuba. He referred to the issue on at least three previous occasions, first in an interview with U.S. journalists in January, then in speeches to workers the following month.[13] "Everybody knows," Castro told the workers of the Shell Oil refinery on February 6, "the tragedy confronted by women and by blacks. We know that these two sectors are discriminated against. They talk for instance about racial discrimination, which is true." Castro not only recognized that there was discrimination but also noted that the issue was being publicly raised and discussed. Then, on March 22, he asserted that the revolution had four main battles to fight: the battle to reduce unemployment, to raise the living standards of the poor, to bring down the cost of living, "and one of the most just battles that must be fought, a battle that must be emphasized more and more . . . the battle to end racial discrimination at work centers."[14]

Castro identified two forms of discrimination in Cuba: one that barred blacks from access to cultural centers and another, "the worst," that denied them access to jobs. Opposing the notion that an antidiscrimination law was necessary, Castro went on to state that the "hateful, repugnant" discrimination could be changed through a campaign condemning public manifestations of racism. He also promised to improve public schools, in which children of all colors studied and played together, and to build recreation centers open to all citizens. Together, he asserted, all Cubans would gradually build a "new fatherland" free of discrimination.

If popular pressures brought the issue of race to the attention of the revolution's main leader, Castro's declaration set the stage for an unprecedented assault on racism. Before March 22, public discussions about race had been dominated by requests to the government to act in this area. Afro-Cuban intellectuals such as Betancourt had complained about the lack of attention given to blacks and were clearly anxious to see the revolutionary government define its position on the question of race. Castro's speech had not only legitimized those claims, turning them into a central principle of the revolution's program, but also called for social mobilization against those responsible for racist behavior. The speech of the then first minister created unprecedented opportunities to challenge traditional patterns of race relations in Cuba.

But the potential subversion of traditional racial hierarchies also met with opposition. As in the early years of the republic—when planters like Edwin Atkins complained that blacks were venturing into spaces that had been previously closed to them—or the 1930s—when the "best" citizens of Santiago complained that blacks were getting "fresher" all the time—Fidel Castro's appeal to end discrimination in employment and recreational places was interpreted by the wealthy, some sectors of the middle class, and even some workers as an assault on their dearest values: family, decency, and religion. According to a witness of these events, a number of "very respectable white ladies" left the country because, since Castro's speech, "blacks had become impossible." "In the well-to-do neighborhoods of Havana, Santa Clara, and Camagüey," this witness recounts, "there was general uproar. The counter-revolution . . . disseminated the rumor that Fidel Castro had invited black men to invade the country's aristocratic sanctuaries to dance and revel with the vestal virgins who, up to that moment, had managed to avoid the terrible contact with the black skin."[15]

Other sources confirm these impressions. Afro-Cuban journalist Sixto Gastón Agüero agreed that the speech had caused "alarm" and that a significant number of white Cubans were troubled by the possibility of eliminating racial barriers in entertainment activities that were deemed to fall within the private sphere. According to Agüero, the notion that blacks and whites would attend public dances together had created the strongest opposition. A U.S. report reproduced the perceptions of those who resented the elimination of traditional racial barriers in private spaces, asserting that many blacks in Havana had mistaken "liberty for licence and whether or not the entertainment appealed to them invaded not only expensive resorts but gatherings in private homes. Protests indicated to the authorities only that the unwilling hosts were counter-revolutionaries guilty of American-style prejudice."[16]

Like other authorities before him, Castro soon realized that eliminating racial divisions would be considerably more difficult to achieve than he had initially envisioned. Opposition to total and unqualified integration crossed political, class, and even color lines. It was not just the wealthy or the "aristocrats"—who opposed the revolutionary program on several grounds—who resented sharing leisure and other social activities with blacks. The "petit bourgeoisie" and some workers displayed similar indignation when it came to integrating their most personal circles. As a white self-employed salesman stated, a black man should be given opportunities "of the economic type, so he could enjoy a job and have his home," but not "social ones." He elaborated: "For example, 50 blacks can be working in a factory and 50 whites, and get along well, and be friends, and all that, but comes the time to share your house, no, no, you are black, and I'm white. . . . I'm not in agreement with integration in its totality."[17]

Nor was this attitude shared exclusively by counterrevolutionaries. People who wholeheartedly supported the revolution and were, in Sixto Gastón Agüero's words, ready to die for its leader were nonetheless scandalized by the notion of blacks and whites dancing together. Well-to-do mulattoes who had earned a pass into whiteness in Cuba's socioracial hierarchy through education, "decency," and income perceived the crumbling of racial barriers as a threat to their precarious social position.[18] Even some blacks, unused to such public exposure of their inferior status, found it hard to accept the challenge entailed by the potential overhaul of traditional racial roles.[19] Though Fidel Castro was not the first national political figure to condemn discrimination publicly, his speech mounted an unprecedented attack on one of the central tenets of Cuba's complex system of race relations: the separation of public and private spaces. In 1959, as on previous occasions during the republic, an attempt to integrate spaces that were socially defined as private met with resistance across a variety of social groups. This resistance demonstrated that a radical program of integration might endanger national unity.

And unity was the priority. The revolutionary program was already eliciting powerful opposition from within and without and could only be implemented with massive popular support. As Castro himself recognized in the same speech, the revolution needed "the most determined and absolute support of all the people." In a televised press conference held just three days after the speech, the prime minister again condemned racial discrimination, but he partially restored the traditional public/private divide concerning integration.[20] Although Castro angrily criticized those who called themselves Christian, educated, or revolutionary while being racist, he also asserted that the revolution would not "impose" limitations on individuals and their personal habits. "I did not say," he clarified, "that we were going to open the exclusive clubs for blacks to go there to dance or to entertain themselves. I did not say that. People dance with whomever they want and . . . socialize with whomever they want."

Castro also challenged the notion that after his speech blacks had become, as a white woman told him, "impossible." "What do [whites] want?" he asked of those who complained about blacks' alleged misbehavior. "[Whites] had [blacks] cleaning automobiles all their lives, they had them cleaning shoes and begging, they could not go to school to get a good education, and now they want blacks to be more refined than those who went to study in Paris. Now they want blacks to even speak French, please!"

Yet the prime minister called on Afro-Cubans to be more "respectful" than ever before, asked them not to give any excuses to those who opposed the revolution's integrationist goals, and argued that racist attitudes would be changed through education and persuasion. Indeed, he remained opposed to passing antidiscrimination legislation and fighting racism through legal means.

Thus Castro's March 25 words were open to various interpretations. The speech unequivocally asserted that racial discrimination was socially and morally wrong. However, emphasis was placed on employment, described by Castro as the "truly cruel and inhuman" variant of discrimination. By contrast, private and personal spaces would be respected. Change in these areas would be gradual, achieved through the color-blind education of new generations of Cubans—a point that the most conservative press did not fail to emphasize.[21] Those who resented Castro's antiracist pronouncement were chastised, but, as on previous occasions during the republic, blacks were asked again to be patient and respectful—not to seek aggressively a redefinition of their traditional social places. These expectations could be easily used to delay integration, for any misbehavior could be interpreted as an indication that Afro-Cubans were not "prepared" to benefit from the revolution's program of racial integration.

But the speech was not ambivalent in some of its key statements. Not only was discrimination wrong, but also it was anti-Cuban and counterrevolutionary. Revolution and racism, Castro stressed beyond any doubt, were incompatible concepts. Most important, the prime minister called on writers, intellectuals, and journalists to debate race issues, to educate the public, and to demonstrate scientifically that prejudice and discrimination were absurd. In sum, Fidel Castro called for a public debate about racism and characterized discrimination as a national shame that ought to be eliminated in the new Cuba. This, by itself, created unprecedented opportunities to launch an assault—perhaps even the final assault—against discrimination and racist ideologies in the island.

Several groups seized this opportunity and, with the support of the state, led an antiracist campaign unparalleled in Cuban history. In April and May 1959 an outburst of conferences, lectures, and symposia analyzing the roots and effects of racial discrimination took place. The University of Havana held a "Forum against Racist Discrimination." The Cuban Association of the United Nations held a "Forum about Ethnic Prejudice in Cuba," presided over by white intellectual and professor Elías Entralgo. A roundtable about discrimination, with the participation of the minister of social welfare, the dean of the National Association of Journalists, and others, was televised in early April.[22] Around the same time, a group of prominent intellectuals, including Entralgo, Salvador García Agüero, and Nicolás Guillén, organized the Provisional Committee of Orientation and National Integration to launch a national movement in support of "the revolutionary attitude defined by the prime minister." On April 5, the committee held its first meeting, which was attended by Comandante Ernesto "Che" Guevara. Out of this assembly was created the Movement of National Integration with branches in several provinces, municipalities, and workplaces. In August, the Provincial Committee of Havana organized a series of public lectures across the province, including rural areas, to disseminate the revolution's antiracist doctrines.[23] Another series of conferences on racial integration, organized by the state-sponsored Department of Culture, were also staged in August. Invited by the Provincial Federation of Societies (the Afro-Cuban clubs), the minister of labor attended a meeting at the Club Marbella and gave a talk about "racial discrimination and unemployment." Still another movement, the National Campaign for Racial Integration, was organized by the Federation of University Students and some Afro-Cuban clubs, such as Unión Fraternal and Atenas.[24]

Several political, civic, and religious organizations supported the campaign and made public pronouncements in support of Castro's speeches, including the Partido Socialista Popular (communist), the Socialist Youth, numerous unions (see below), the Masons, professional organizations such as schoolteachers' groups, the Catholic Workers Youth, and even the Cuban Council of Protestant Churches.[25] In Santa Clara, university students organized cross-racial dances; fraternity banquets were organized in Santiago.[26] Journalists and writers published dozens of articles debating the origins of and solutions for racial discrimination. Fidel Castro had called on intellectuals to address the issue; the revolutionary press responded. *Noticias de Hoy* published long interviews with well-known intellectuals such as Fernando Ortiz and Entralgo. Communist Party leaders Carlos Rafael Rodríguez and García Agüero published articles supporting Castro's speeches and highlighting the Communists' historic role in the struggle against racism. A series of articles analyzed the psychological dimensions of prejudice and urged psychiatrists to scientifically study the problem.[27] The theme was also covered, though less prominently, by *Revolución*, *El Avance Revolucionario*, and other newspapers.[28]

The campaign against discrimination was also fueled by frequent references to the issue in some of the speeches of the revolutionary leaders. In addition to Fidel Castro himself, who kept talking about discrimination at public events, guerrilla commanders Raúl Castro and Guevara raised the issue frequently. On May 1, 1959, for instance, Raúl Castro and Guevara addressed workers' rallies in Havana and Santiago. They both spoke about the need to advance the revolution's antidiscrimination program. "Our revolution," Raúl Castro stated, "will wage the final battle against the ill-fated prejudice of racial discrimination. The unity of all people is as important to the revolution as the integration of all Cubans is to the nation." "Slavery," Guevara was saying at the same time in Santiago, "did not end in Cuba until January 1, 1959." When Guevara accepted a Doctor Honoris Causa from the Universidad Central in Santa Clara in December, he asserted that the "essential" function of the university in the "new Cuba" was to "paint itself with black, paint itself with mulatto, not only among students, but also among teachers." In a press conference in July, Fidel Castro, in turn, anticipated that through persuasion and "intelligent measures" Cuba was "approaching a process of abolition of racial prejudices."[29]

These "intelligent measures" were being implemented in two main areas: the gradual desegregation of public and recreational facilities and the design of policies that, although couched in color-blind language, created opportunities for the poorest in society, among whom blacks were of course overrepresented.

The process of desegregating recreational facilities and lifting racial barriers in occupations that had been traditionally closed to blacks was slower and more painful than is usually realized. Some authors question the importance of this process, implying that racial segregation had little bearing on the lives of many, if not most, Afro-Cubans.[30] Although some facilities were out of reach of all the poor, regardless of race, racial desegregation was critical because it turned the abstract goals of racial equality and national integration into concrete, tangible political acts with immediate results. Indeed, the issue was deemed potentially explosive enough for the government to follow a gradual approach.

The beaches became the first target of the revolutionary authorities. Most of the best beaches in the country had been privatized, linked to social clubs or expensive hotels, and open only to members and guests. Since most of these clubs were openly discriminatory, Afro-Cubans were in fact barred from access to these beaches. Previous governments had offered as a solution the creation of separate recreational facilities on "popular beaches" or exclusive beaches for black clubs. In his March 22 speech, Fidel Castro announced that all beaches would be open to the public and that "the people" would be able to attend the country's best beaches, including exclusive resort areas such as Varadero, Santa María del Mar, or Tarará. Two weeks later, the private beaches in Santiago, Havana, and elsewhere were declared public. The official announcement, however, carefully noted that the people would have access to "the sand and the sea" only. Private buildings, swimming pools, restaurants, bars, and other club facilities remained off-limits and were to be used only by members. Furthermore, the authorities warned that, in addition to respect for private property, "order and decency required by the behavior of a civilized people" were expected. The beaches had been declared social property; club facilities remained private and beyond the reach of the black and the poor. Confrontation over these spaces had been, for the time being, postponed. Fidel Castro had hinted that this would be the official policy when he toured some of Havana's beaches and clubs in mid-February. Speaking at the club of bank employees on the Santa María beach east of Havana, Castro asked for cooperation concerning public access to beaches, but he reassured club members that their "privacy" would be respected.[31]

An equally gradual, nonconfrontational approach was followed in the desegregation of parks. Although some officers of the Rebel Army entered, accompanied by black civilians, the white sections of parks and challenged their traditional racial boundaries, the full desegregation of parks was frequently achieved through remodeling. Rather than confront embedded racist habits, the authorities chose to rebuild the parks and destroy their traditional, racially significant layouts. The new parks, they hoped, would not be associated with a historic geography of race and power. "The humanist revolution," the official in charge of the remodeling in Santa Clara declared, "has its origin precisely in all social injustices. One of these injustices is racial discrimination. . . . That is why the Revolutionary Government is building a new [Leoncio] Vidal park in Santa Clara, where white and black children can look at each other in the happiness of being equal members of a fatherland that is with all and for the good of all." The old flowerpots that had divided the white and black areas were removed and replaced with an undivided walkway, together with a recreational area for children. "This is how the revolution works," asserted *Revolución* concerning the opening of the new park; "this is a step forward in the unity of all Cubans."[32]

The gradual approach through which the revolutionary leadership hoped

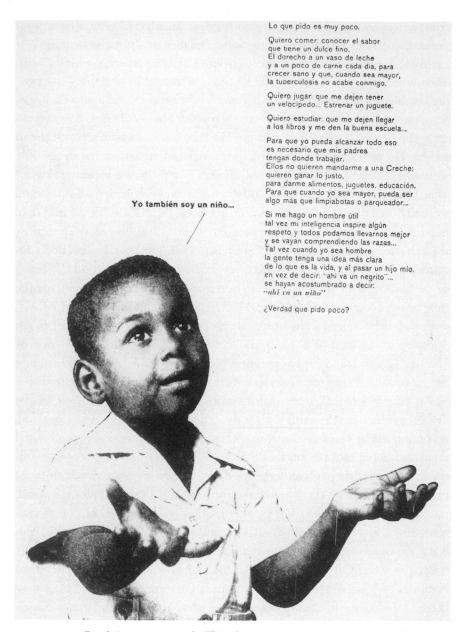

Lo que pido es muy poco.

Quiero comer: conocer el sabor
que tiene un dulce fino.
El derecho a un vaso de leche
y a un poco de carne cada día, para
crecer sano y que, cuando sea mayor,
la tuberculosis no acabe conmigo.

Quiero jugar: que me dejen tener
un velocípedo... Estrenar un juguete.

Quiero estudiar: que me dejen llegar
a los libros y me den la buena escuela...

Para que yo pueda alcanzar todo eso
es necesario que mis padres
tengan donde trabajar.
Ellos no quieren mandarme a una Creche:
quieren ganar lo justo,
para darme alimentos, juguetes, educación.
Para que cuando yo sea mayor, pueda ser
algo más que limpiabotas o parqueador...

Si me hago un hombre útil
tal vez mi inteligencia inspire algún
respeto y todos podamos llevarnos mejor
y se vayan comprendiendo las razas...
Tal vez cuando yo sea hombre
la gente tenga una idea más clara
de lo que es la vida, y al pasar un hijo mío,
en vez de decir: "ahi va un negrito"...
se hayan acostumbrado a decir:
"ahi va un niño"

¿Verdad que pido poco?

Yo también soy un niño...

FIGURE 7.1. *Revolutionary propaganda. This advertisement was published in the* M-26-7 *daily in early 1959 and calls for racial harmony and equality. From* Revolución, *April 2, 1959. (Biblioteca Nacional "José Martí")*

to eliminate discrimination and eventually achieve racial integration also became explicit in some of the propaganda of the period. An advertisement published repeatedly in *Revolución* during April and May 1959 exemplifies this point. It portrayed a black boy pleading for a better future (see figure 7.1). The text read:

> I don't ask for much. I want to eat, get to know the taste of a pastry. The right to a glass of milk and a little bit of meat every day, to be healthy so, when I grow up, tuberculosis does not consume me. I want to play, to have a tricycle . . . to have a new toy. I want to study, to access books and a good school. In order for me to reach all that, it is necessary that my parents have a place to work. They don't want to send me to an institution. They want to earn what is fair in order to give me food, toys, education, so when I grow up, I can be something besides a shoeshine boy, or a valet. If I become a good man, perhaps my intelligence will generate some respect, and we all can get along and the races will understand each other. Perhaps when I become a man, people will have a clearer idea about life so that when one of my children goes by, instead of saying "there goes a 'negrito' [little black]," they will come to say, "*there goes a child.*" Isn't it true that I don't ask for much?

The central message of this advertisement was unmistakable: socioracial hierarchies and traditions would not be transformed overnight. Instead of aggressively asserting their right to an equal place in society, Afro-Cubans were *asking* for such basic things as food, education, and work. In turn, racial ideas would "perhaps" begin to change when a new generation of Cubans, educated in a climate of racial harmony, acquired the knowledge needed to understand that skin color did not define humanity. Change would be achieved without confrontation. The needs represented by the boy in the advertisement were immediate, but Afro-Cubans were expected to wait for these benefits to be given to them.

When confrontation did occur—and, given the radicalization of the revolutionary process, it was virtually unavoidable—it was couched in the language of class rather than race. The process of desegregation of the social clubs, for instance, was done in the name of "los sin nada" (the have-nots): workers, peasants, and humble employees and professionals. Beginning in late April 1960, one full year after opening the beaches to the public, the government moved against the private clubs and nationalized them. The first club to be claimed as social property was the ultra-exclusive Havana Biltmore Yacht and Country Club, which was renamed Cubanacán. It was an ideal first target: the club symbolized both the exclusivity of the elite and its intimate links with foreign, mainly American, investors. As one journalist wrote, it was a club "of foreign name and composition, therefore counterrevolutionary." Amid growing confrontation with the U.S. government, the expropriation of the Havana Biltmore came to represent an act of national affirmation by the Cuban "people," a concept that was identified with workers, peasants, and the humblest sectors of the population.[33]

Accused of accepting a million-dollar gift from Batista, the club was reopened as a *círculo social obrero* (workers social circle). Membership quotas varied according to the income of members. By late 1960, 55 percent of members earned less than $100 per month; another 23 percent had a monthly income of between $100 and $150. "The families that are using the workers social circle are low-income families," Fidel Castro noted with satisfaction. The leader of the revolution called for the creation of similar institutions across the country, "one circle in each town . . . one in each sugar mill." By October 1961, thirteen clubs had been transformed into *círculos sociales obreros* in Havana alone.[34]

Although these expropriations were done in the name of the people, they included not only such upper-class bulwarks as the Havana Yacht Club, the Miramar Yacht Club, and the Vedado Tennis Club but also clubs that belonged to professional associations and employees, such as the electrical workers' Cubanaleco. The revolution was claiming as workers' property facilities that already belonged to workers. But some of these clubs, their social composition notwithstanding, had been as discriminatory as those of the elite. The clubs of railway and electrical workers, for instance, did not allow blacks on their premises, even though their bylaws were silent on the issue of race. By January 1960, the railway workers' club had been desegregated due to an integrationist movement led by the union. Cubanaleco remained open only to whites. Seizing the momentum created by Fidel Castro's antiracist declarations and the ensuing national campaign against discrimination, a cross-racial "Integration Committee" was organized within the union and began to fight against the color line in the club. "It is not fair," it argued, "that those who face death together at the top of the electric posts cannot have leisure together in a club that belongs to all." Quoting an article of the club bylaws that stated that anyone on Havana Electric's payroll could become a member of the club, the committee asserted that it was only demanding that the club follow its own regulations. "We do not ask for any privilege. We demand a right."[35]

Yet the process of desegregating the club encountered resistance among club members. Caught between competing demands, the general secretary of the union proposed a solution that was not too different from the one applied in the case of the parks: to build a new club for electrical workers at Guanabo Beach. This, Afro-Cuban journalist Roger Fumero noted, was only a maneuver to dissipate tensions while maintaining the "infamous color line" in Cubanaleco. The union leaders would have to open the club to blacks, warned the journalist. Otherwise, Fidel Castro would do it for them. "Union leaders never dared face this problem [before]. But it is evident that things are different now. Now . . . [there is] a government that has fought against all injustices, and its main leaders have recognized that the problem of discrimination exists in Cuba." Whereas union leaders hesitated over how to tackle the issue of discrimination at the club, revolutionary authorities did not: several months later, Cubanaleco was taken over by the state, turned into a workers social circle, and opened to all.[36]

State intervention was also crucial in lifting racial barriers in employment. This process was considerably slower and more difficult than the desegregation of beaches, parks, or social clubs. Numerous unions publicly supported Fidel Castro's antidiscrimination pronouncements and passed resolutions demanding that employers hire black workers.[37] Especially in those sectors in which Afro-Cubans had seldom found job opportunities, such as banks, retail stores, and cigarette factories, the unions' stand, combined with the explicit condemnation of discrimination from above, created opportunities that had not existed before. Correctly sensing the weakness of their position in the new environment, employers tended to compromise. Otherwise, workers would appeal to the authorities, something that, a lawyer representing sugar companies in the island noted, should be avoided by all possible means. "The hand of Cuba's destiny at present is held by the organized labor movement," a manager at a U.S. firm in Oriente asserted.[38]

Thus, when the Federation of Bank Workers stipulated in its collective bargaining agreement that the union would control 50 percent of new hires in order to appoint black workers, employers agreed. Some managers of bank and other companies even took the initiative and began hiring Afro-Cuban workers themselves.[39]

But as the example of electrical workers and their club shows, in some cases the unions themselves were the problem. Given the large number of unemployed and underemployed workers in the island, competition for jobs was fierce. Many unions favored the employment of sons and close relatives of existing employees, a policy that employers supported in order to maintain a better grip over the labor force. In companies that traditionally did not employ blacks, the "lists of job seekers" were composed almost exclusively of whites: Afro-Cubans knew in advance that their chances of getting hired were nonexistent and did not bother to apply.[40] In sum, to alter significantly the racial composition of the occupational structure, it was necessary to confront embedded interests, habits, and hiring practices that had contributed to maintaining color lines in jobs. State action was required.

Yet the revolutionary leadership remained opposed to passing a law that would force employers to hire a predetermined quota of black workers—a position that the Communists still defended in 1960. The revolutionary government did take legal steps, but in a way that would lead to the gradual integration of workplaces and minimize racially defined confrontation. The new Organic Law of the Ministry of Labor, approved in January 1960, established that all new employees would be hired through the Ministry of Labor. In order to distribute jobs with "justice and equality," the ministry would conduct a labor census to determine the number, skills, place of residence, family income, and needs of the unemployed. With this information at hand, the ministry would then create a national registry of job seekers in which the unemployed would be randomly assigned a number. Only the ministry could fill vacancies. Neither unions nor employers could hire workers who had not been selected by the ministry out of the national registry. "This way," the official organ of the ministry proclaimed, "the Revolutionary Government will eliminate completely all sorts of discrimination in certain labor sectors." According to the secretary of labor, the census—which was actually conducted in April 1960—would guarantee that all Cubans would have equal opportunities for employment and eliminate race discrimination in employment.[41]

African American writer Julian Mayfield, who visited the island in the summer of 1960, commented on the impact of these measures: "Take an example. . . . The proprietor of a barbershop in a lush hotel like the Havana Libre . . . would never have considered hiring a colored barber before the revolution. But the decision is no longer his."[42]

The notion of forcing a color-blind distribution of employment through state intervention was of course not new. The principle was included in the Constitution of 1940 and was later upheld, but with little practical impact, in Prío's and Batista's decrees of 1951 and 1955. The situation, however, was "different" in 1960, according to Afro-Cuban journalist Fumero. Since family income and needs were weighed when filling vacancies, the new system was not, in fact, color-blind. It tended to benefit the poorest, among whom blacks were overrepresented.[43] More to the point, the capacity of the government to influence hiring practices increased significantly when, in the fall of

1960, foreign and domestic industries and companies began to be nationalized. By 1963, 70 percent of agriculture, 95 percent of industry and transportation, 75 percent of retail trade, and 100 percent of banking activities had
come under the direct control of the state. Thus the state had become Cuba's
main employer.[44]

Other government policies helped diminish social inequalities, including
those associated with race, and contributed to the long-term goal of national
integration. The nationalization of private schools in July 1961 destroyed one
of the most enduring pillars of racism in Cuban society. Most of these
schools were segregated. The 1961 massive literacy campaign, in turn, provided not only basic reading and writing skills to the poorest in society but
also brought Cubans of different social backgrounds together. Urban residents came to know the harshness of rural life firsthand. Middle-class citizens became personally involved in confronting poverty and ignorance.
Blacks and whites joined in this effort, both as teachers and as students.
Among the voluntary teachers participating in the campaign, 30 percent were
black or mulatto. Adult education was also expanded and special schools
created to address the needs of underprivileged groups such as domestic
workers, a large number of whom were Afro-Cuban females.[45]

Likewise, the lowering of rents and the 1959 creation of the National Institute of Housing benefited low-income families. The institute was charged
with the construction of cheap housing for workers and took on the task of
building houses for residents of the largely black shantytowns and slums. By
1961, for instance, the residents of the infamous Havana shantytown of Las
Yaguas had been transferred to a new housing complex that had been built in
what was traditionally a middle-class neighborhood. In Santiago, the shantytown "Manzana de Gómez" was in the process of being destroyed by early
1960, and similar neighborhoods, such as "Honduras" and "Debajo del
Puente" (literally, "under the bridge"), were being studied to provide their
residents with material support so they could build their own houses.[46] Scholarship students from poor families were lodged in the mansions of the
wealthy, who by 1961 had fled the country en masse. More than a thousand
ex–domestic workers enrolled in training courses for administrative and
commercial jobs in 1962 were housed at the Hotel Nacional, previously one
of Havana's most exclusive hotels.[47] Havana's traditional geography of race
and wealth was being drastically altered.

Individuals of different social and racial backgrounds were further indoc-
trinated in the values of a new, integrated society through mass organizations
such as the Revolutionary Militias, the Committees for the Defense of the

Revolution, and the Federation of Cuban Women. All these organizations were color-blind concerning membership. They served to channel revolutionary enthusiasm, mobilize and control the population, and give symbolic power to groups whose participation in Cuba's political life had been minimal before. Observers noted, for instance, that among those in the militia in 1960, "there were many who had been unable to fill prestigious roles in the old order, including a noticeably high proportion of negroes and middle-aged women."[48]

The effects of this process of radical change cannot be easily summarized. The lives of all Cubans were affected, and people responded to the revolutionary changes in different ways, which depended largely on their social origin. The predominantly white upper class and the most affluent sectors of the middle class left the country and found refuge in Miami, Florida, where they attempted to re-create a Cuba that no longer existed. The lower classes rallied in support of the revolution and its leader. According to a survey conducted in 1962, 70 percent of workers had a favorable attitude toward the revolution. The percentage was even higher among black workers: 80 percent approved of Castro's government. As early as September 1959, a U.S. State Department report considered blacks to be one of the sources of support for the revolutionary government.[49]

Most blacks and mulattoes benefited materially from the national redistribution of income and resources implemented by the revolution. Perhaps equally important, for the first time they were, together with other disadvantaged groups, at the center of government attention and given the opportunity to participate substantially in areas that had been closed to them. In this sense, the desegregation of parks, beaches, schools, and recreational facilities was critically important. It allowed Afro-Cubans to assert their recently acquired status in very concrete ways. A black industrial worker interviewed by Maurice Zeitlin in 1962 elaborated on the importance of this process: "I am most proud of what the revolution has done for the workers and the *campesinos* [peasants]—and not only at work. For example, Negroes couldn't go to a beach or to a good hotel, or be *jefes* [managers, supervisors] in industry, or work in the railroads or in public transportation in Santiago. This was because of their color! . . . But now, no—all of us—we're equal: the white, the Negro, the mulatto." Other Afro-Cuban workers concurred: "Here, there's not a place that my child can't enter, or anyone else's—whether he's poor, or Negro, or whoever." "We can frequent any place we want, beaches, hotels, movies," said another. Even some black emigrants otherwise hostile toward the revolution admitted that blacks were "like everybody else.

The same as the white."[50] No one captured better what these transformations meant for many Afro-Cubans than Nicolás Guillén in his noted poem "Tengo" (I Have), written in 1964:

> I have, let's see:
> that being Black
> I can be stopped by no one at
> the door of a dancing hall or bar.
> Or even at the desk of a hotel
> have someone yell at me there are no rooms,
> a small room and not one that's immense,
> a tiny room where I might rest.
>
> .   .   .   .
>
> I have that having the land I have the sea,
> no country clubs,
> no high life,
> no tennis and no yachts,
> but, from beach to beach and wave on wave,
> gigantic blue open democratic:
> in short, the sea.
> I have, let's see:
> that I have learned to read,
> to count,
> I have that I have learned to write,
> and to think,
> and to laugh.
> I have that now I have
> a place to work
> and earn
> what I have to eat.
> I have, let's see:
> I have what was coming to me.[51]

Some white workers found it hard to adjust to these changes and resented what they perceived as an official bias toward Afro-Cubans. Particularly difficult was the social and physical closeness that integrated schools, recreational facilities, and mass organizations imposed on blacks and whites. "My sons were militiamen," explained a white sugar worker in 1962, "but they resigned because of communism, and, too, they weren't happy because there were many Negroes in the battalion who thought they were better than others." This perception that blacks felt as if they were "better" than whites or were "better off" than whites in the island was shared by several white workers interviewed by Fox in 1970, who resented the dismantling of traditional racial hierarchies. "[T]he black has more rights than the whites. . . . [T]he black is worth more than the white," declared a farmworker from Oriente. A former soldier concurred: "[T]he black gets more consideration. . . . The white man there [in Cuba] isn't worth a thing. A Negro is worth more than a white." According to a bread salesman, whites in Cuba were living "under the boot of the black." Blacks "abused" whites because they had gained membership and leading positions in the Committees for the Defense of the Revolution, the militias, and similar organizations.[52]

Not only had the revolutionary government taken decisive, although careful, steps toward the desegregation of most social spaces and the racial integration of the population, particularly the youth; it had also created an "ideal" that had become dominant in the discourse and imagery of the new society. Revolutionaries and, after 1961, Communists could not be racist. Racism was identified with social groups subservient to imperialist interests: the white, pro-Yankee, antinational bourgeoisie that had fled the country. Thus, not only was racism anticommunist or counterrevolutionary; it was also antinational and a perilous sign of ideological "backwardness."

Given the enormous influence that the state and its mass organizations exerted in most areas of national life, most members of society felt compelled to comply with this ideal and adapt to the new environment. As a black actor interviewed by Elizabeth Sutherland in 1968 explained, whites could not "very well be openly racist anymore." Blacks and whites acted "as though" they had achieved "the ideal of brotherhood," the actor noted, when in fact it was still just an ideal. But the facts that racial brotherhood had become the ideal and that people felt required to act accordingly were themselves significant achievements in a country in which racial barriers, and even segregation, had been rampant only a decade before.[53] The testimony of a white professional, interviewed by historians Duharte and Santos in 1994, exemplifies how ordinary whites were forced to cope with the issue of race:

I was born in Camagüey in 1951. . . . This province has always been considered to be one of the most racist in Cuba and I believe that to be the case. In my family you would breathe racism constantly. . . . My grandmother never sat by a black in a bus or a taxi. . . . [S]he would not admit blacks to her table either. . . . Like many youth at the time, when I was twelve I went to junior high school in Havana. There, I had to face the problem from a different angle. For the first time I had direct contact with blacks; they were in my classroom . . . even in my dormitory. This was a tremendous experience for me. I don't recall having a marked aversion to them, due perhaps to revolutionary propaganda, which had been claiming for several years that we were all equal. Whoever did not share that feeling was considered counterrevolutionary.[54]

Revolutionary authorities, in turn, took the ideal at face value. As early as 1962, they began claiming that Cuba had eliminated racial discrimination. Among other successes, the Second Declaration of Havana, issued in February 1962, asserted that the revolution had "eradicated discrimination because of race or sex" in Cuba. Writing the same year, a Communist Party official concurred: "Our patriotic, democratic, and socialist revolution has eliminated from Cuban life the odious and humiliating spectacle of discrimination because of skin color." The dominant discourse was summarized by Fidel Castro himself when he argued that discrimination in Cuba had disappeared along with class privileges. He also noted that it had "not cost the revolution much effort to resolve that problem."[55]

This became the dominant theme in public discourse, echoed in official documents, journalistic pieces, and even scholarship. The revolution had solved Cuba's historic race problem: racism and discrimination were things of the past. The initial campaign against discrimination waned after 1962, leading to a growing public silence on the issue—except to note Cuba's success in this area. What had been the subject of a fruitful and unprecedented public debate in the early postrevolutionary years eventually became a taboo. As one of Sutherland's informants stated, "The problem in Cuba is that there is a taboo on talking about racism, because officially it does not exist anymore. And nobody, black or white, wants to talk about it." If openly racist acts were deemed to be counterrevolutionary, attempts to debate publicly the limitations of Cuba's integration were likewise considered to be the enemy's work. As in the past, the ideal of racial brotherhood worked in complex, often contradictory ways.[56]

Several factors contributed to making race and discrimination nonissues in public debates. First, silence was congruent with the gradual, nonconfrontational approach followed by the revolutionary leadership on the issue of race. The authorities admitted that racism and prejudices would not wither away overnight, but these attitudes were conceptualized as "remnants" of a past that would disappear in due time. Silence was institutionalized also because some of the political actors that might have objected to the revolution's policies in this (or any other) area were not in the position to do so. The Communists had always contended that the struggle against racism involved at least two fronts: a legal one, in which discrimination would be penalized, and a cultural one, which entailed an education campaign to eradicate socially accepted ideas about race. The leaders of the party defended the need to approve an antidiscrimination law—despite Castro's opposition to this idea—through 1960. But by 1961, the Partido Socialista Popular had become a partner in the ruling coalition. Although the party's position strengthened along with the establishment of closer ties to the Soviet Union, its role within the leadership remained subordinate.[57] The Communists' revolutionary credentials were frequently challenged immediately after the revolution's triumph because of their belated support for armed struggle and their previous ties to Batista. Thus the party could not afford the political luxury of having an independent voice. Furthermore, it is doubtful that party leaders felt the need to keep pressing for additional measures concerning the race question. After Fidel Castro declared the revolution to be of "socialist" character in 1961, the Communists had no reason to promote further an explicit antidiscrimination agenda. They had always believed that race differences would automatically disappear under socialism, as they had allegedly done in the Soviet Union and other socialist countries.[58]

Afro-Cuban intellectuals, who had tenaciously complained during the whole republican period about the shortcomings of Cuba's racial democracy, could have continued to address racism. But by the mid-1960s, this group had lost its main bases of institutional support: the Afro-Cuban clubs and the black press. Opportunities to publish a regular column devoted to "black issues" in the mainstream press—not an uncommon practice in prerevolutionary Cuba—had also disappeared. The press had been placed under strict government control.

The revolution's integration program left little room for racially defined voices or institutions to persist, much less to thrive. However, the Afro-Cuban societies were not dismantled overnight. Many survived much longer than the exclusive clubs of the bourgeoisie. When the government closed them, it was usually for alleged procedural reasons, such as lack of proper registration or failure to pay fees and taxes. Furthermore, the black societies were not singled out as preferred targets of government action. Rather, they were eradicated together with numerous other associations—civic, fraternal, professional, and mutual aid—that supposedly obstructed the process of redefining Cuba's civil society along lines deemed to be appropriate by the revolutionary government. In September 1961, more than 170 of these associations were closed by provincial authorities in Havana alone.[59]

The Afro-Cuban societies were in a weak position to resist. The leadership of the national and provincial federations had been dangerously close to Batista; many clubs received government subsidies. In January 1959, a process of "revolutionary seizures" of the societies began, similar to that which took place after the fall of Machado. Atenas was the first club whose board of directors was replaced by a group of disenchanted members who described themselves as "revolutionary youth." They replaced the old board—which they publicly accused of cooperation with Batista and CTC leader Eusebio Mujal—and informed the new chief of police about their action.[60]

The National Federation of Societies was also "revolutionarily seized" in January 1959. Leading the movement for its seizure was lawyer Juan René Betancourt, who claimed to be qualified for the task because his own organization, ONRE, was, aside from the federation, the largest in the country. Betancourt also argued that ONRE's leading figures had either been members of revolutionary organizations or at least remained aloof from the corruption of Batista's regime. "We were perfectly qualified to assume at that moment the defense of the race and the leadership of the federation," Betancourt asserted later. He became the self-appointed provisional president of the organization, sent telegrams to all affiliated societies notifying them about the changes, and began a public campaign demanding that the government clarify its position concerning the so-called black problem.[61]

In other cases, it was through government intervention that previous leaders were replaced. In early March, the directors of the National Club of Societies Juan Gualberto Gómez—the exclusive Afro-Cuban beach resort built with Batista's money in Marbella—were suspended from their duties by a decree issued by the minister of education. A government *interventor* (intervener) was appointed to run the club until a new board was elected. Instead, the government representative ordered the club in February 1960 to open its doors to Cubans of all colors.[62]

It was not only club directors that were being challenged from within and without. After Fidel Castro's speech in late March, the very existence and purposes of the black clubs were debated. Some Afro-Cuban intellectuals angrily criticized them as obstacles in the revolution's road to national integration. In his report to the Forum about Racist Discrimination held at the University of Havana in April 1959, for instance, journalist Manuel Cuéllar Vizcaíno warned that "racist associations, either of whites or blacks," should receive no financial support from the revolutionary government, for they were all "anti-Cuban." By early 1960, Cuéllar claimed that Afro-Cuban societies had lost their purpose and would become a hindrance in the process of integration. He criticized Atenas for offering only recreational activities and complained that young club members had not taken exams for diplomatic careers. In his view, Atenas and other clubs not only were doing little to advance the program of the revolution but also had failed to take advantage of whatever opportunities were being created by the revolutionary government.[63]

Another Afro-Cuban journalist, Roger Fumero, supported Cuéllar's criticism. Fumero charged that, in light of the revolution's integrationist goals, there was no reason for the Federation of Societies to exist any longer. He also criticized Unión Fraternal, the second most important Afro-Cuban club, for clinging to its traditional social functions while failing to support the "democratic projections" of the revolutionary government. An Afro-Cuban reader of his column agreed: the leaders of the black societies acted as if a revolution had not taken place and were only concerned with parties and personal gain.[64]

These criticisms showed that Afro-Cubans did not share a common view about the roles their traditional institutions should play in the new environment or about the process of national integration more generally. Some, such as Betancourt, saw the societies as a bastion from which to articulate a racially defined autonomous movement that would promote the advancement of blacks as a corporate group. Thus Betancourt stressed that the societies "must never allow any government to tell them who should be their national leader; they must never again subordinate the happiness of the race to government charity." Concretely, he hoped to use the National Federation of Societies as a way to implement his plan for a black cooperative movement across the island.[65] But other Afro-Cuban intellectuals, including Cuéllar and Fumero, adamantly opposed any effort that would consolidate the separation of blacks and whites, especially at a time in which the government seemed determined to create unprecedented opportunities for effective racial equality. Journalist Sixto Gastón Agüero criticized even the dominant notion of integration, claiming that Cubans were already ethnically, biologically, and culturally integrated. What remained was to create awareness about this process and eliminate the very notion of "race" from social consciousness. Given that it was not likely that the Afro-Cuban societies would advance this process, they should be eliminated.[66]

Using similar arguments, the Communists also criticized Betancourt's efforts. The creation of a racially integrated and egalitarian nation, they argued, could not be achieved without the joint effort of blacks and whites. Those who opposed unity, Salvador García Agüero charged in an angry critique of Betancourt, were enemies of the revolution, the fatherland, and blacks themselves. He referred to Betancourt's "black doctrine" as a racist ideology that would only perpetuate segregation, resentment, and isolation among Cubans of different colors.[67]

The Afro-Cuban clubs tried desperately to adapt to the new environment. They participated in the antidiscrimination campaign launched in 1959 and 1960 and in revolutionary programs that did not have a specific racial content. Several societies, for instance, collected money to support agrarian reform, industrialization, or the literacy campaign. Some clubs, such as Atenas, elected leaders who had been active in the struggle against Batista. Others sought legitimacy by changing their names: in 1961 the Jóvenes del Vals society became Jóvenes del Vals Revolucionario. Many invited members of the Rebel Army or the M-26-7 to attend their public functions or lent their facilities to revolutionary organizations for free.[68]

But to no avail. The existence of racially defined associations was perceived by revolutionary leaders to be in blatant contradiction to the revolution's goals concerning racial integration. Many of the societies' traditional roles were being taken over by other institutions or had otherwise lost relevance in postrevolutionary society. The Afro-Cuban clubs had performed mutual-aid functions and provided services such as schooling, health care, and recreation that were being opened to all, regardless of race. They had provided Afro-Cuban professionals and politicians with a constituency that was critical to their aspirations for social recognition and ascent. But in the emergent institutional order, those roles were being played by mass and revolutionary organizations.

In many cases, the societies that were liquidated from above were virtually dead already. Although limited, the available evidence is nonetheless conclusive: the number of Afro-Cubans affiliated with the clubs declined considerably under the revolution. The membership of Jóvenes del Vals dropped from 127 in 1956 to 38 in 1962; that of Unión Fraternal, from 3,212 in 1951 to only 211 in 1965. In Atenas, the number of voting members declined by two-thirds: from 292 in 1957 to 91 in 1959.[69]

Because of its social composition, its ties to Batista, and conflicts among its members, the government "intervened" in the operation of Atenas. In July 1961, the *interventor* decreed the dissolution of the society, arguing that it was not fulfilling the ends for which it had been created and that it had been "abandoned" by its members. However, there is evidence that at least until late 1960 the members of Atenas tried to maintain some institutional life, holding elections and calling for meetings. Outside intervention most likely prevented further engagement and accelerated the process of abandonment invoked as one of the reasons for dissolution.

Other societies survived longer into the revolution, and some, especially religious societies (see below), were never formally eliminated. Unión Fraternal and Jóvenes del Vals Revolucionario were not dissolved until August and September 1966, respectively. In both cases, authorities argued that the associations had not released information concerning elections, meeting minutes, and similar documentation.

Allegedly, these associations were being eliminated on purely technical grounds due to the lack of diligence of their directors, who had repeatedly failed to file the timely documentation required by law. But there is little doubt that, at best, by the mid-1960s the Afro-Cuban societies were being perceived by the revolutionary government as hindrances to its agenda. A new law of associations approved in 1965 placed their supervision and control under the Ministry of the Interior, the organ charged with preventing crime and counterrevolutionary activities.

Furthermore, some of the societies were closed despite resistance. When Unión Fraternal was dissolved and its properties assigned to government institutions, for instance, its president sent a long letter to the chief of public order protesting the decision. He invoked the society's glorious past, its involvement in the War of Independence, its antidiscrimination efforts during the republic, and its staunch support for all the revolutionary programs as evidence that it should remain open. That Unión Fraternal was nonetheless closed strongly suggests that the government was not proceeding on legalistic considerations alone. In the eyes of the new authorities, the societies had become not only useless but also counterproductive. They had fought against discrimination, but this problem had been avowedly eradicated by the revolution. They gave voice to a social group that allegedly did not need it any longer because its members had been fully integrated into all social activities. The 1961 resolution dissolving Atenas spelled it out clearly: among other reasons, the club was being closed because "discrimination due to race, sex, age, or social condition had disappeared" in Cuba's socialist society.

The Afro-Cuban clubs represented an affront to the government's vision of a color-blind society and a potential challenge to the official discourse of a discrimination-free Cuba. Indeed, in the early years of the revolution, the clubs and Afro-Cuban intellectuals had occasionally challenged local authorities for not promoting the revolutionary ideals of equality and even the central government for the absence of blacks in positions of command.[70] The clubs gave blacks and mulattoes the opportunity to articulate a common discourse according to which justice and equality were their own achievements rather than benefits handed down by the revolutionary government.[71] "There is a tendency," an Afro-Cuban actress stated in 1968, "to assume that the Revolution 'gave' blacks their freedom—gave us the right to enter white society, to have the same things they have. It is an essentially paternalistic attitude. And it creates resentment."[72] The clubs and the black press were potential channels to articulate such resentment and break the official silence of race. They had to be eliminated.

This, however, does not mean that race disappeared as a socially relevant identity from Cuban life or even that it was erased from all forms of public discourse. Debates about racism in Cuban socialism moved into the private sphere, in which notions of race continued to affect social relations in a myriad of ways. But the issue of race retained a prominent place in two areas of public discourse: culture and international politics.

TO MAKE A TRUE CUBAN CULTURE

The revolution was conceived by its leaders and many Cubans as a process not only of political or economic transformations but also of cultural change. As in the 1930s, the new Cuba required a new culture, one that would exalt autochthonous values and traditions and rescue forms of popular expression that had been forgotten, ignored, or simply rejected under the republic. In this process, a plethora of cultural institutions were created or reorganized in the first two years of the revolution. These included the Instituto Cubano de Arte e Industria Cinematográficos (ICAIC, Cuban Institute for the Art and Industry of the Cinema); the National Council of Culture, subordinated to the Ministry of Education; the National Theater of Cuba; and the National Publishing House.

It was nearly impossible to exalt popular traditions without acknowledging the African roots of national culture. Already by the 1950s, the notion that Cubanness could not be understood without reference to its black ingredients was widely accepted. This acceptance was neither unproblematic nor universal, but it was nonetheless widespread. The works of anthropologists Fernando Ortiz, Rómulo Lachatañeré, and Lidya Cabrera, all of whom emphasized the dominant role of "lo negro" in Cuban folklore, were highly respected and frequently invoked as proof that Cuba was a mestizo nation. Blackness was also central to the work of some of the best painters of the period, such as Wilfredo Lam. Although commodified and aesthetically "filtered" to please North American tourists and white middle-class Cubans, rhythms and dances of perceived African origin had become established forms of national expression. The 1930s "black craze" had subsided, but blackness remained central to the way the Cuban nation was imagined and its culture represented.

In turn, the growing identification of the revolutionary leadership with the poor led to a renewed interest in the cultural expressions of the "people"—a concept that was increasingly identified with the dark lower classes. Moreover, the public condemnation of racial discrimination and Fidel Castro's invitation to debate questions of race in the mass media created unprecedented opportunities to attempt a full reassessment of Cuba's national culture and of the "place" and importance of its Afro-Cuban components. For many intellectuals, black and white, this was indeed a unique opportunity to create an authentic Cuban culture.

Thus cultural themes figured prominently in the debates that followed Castro's speeches in March 1959. Public lectures and roundtables discussed the importance of African influences in Cuban music, visual arts, and other forms of expression. As early as May 1959, a law to "stimulate folkloric traditions" was submitted to the Council of Ministers for consideration.[73] Cultural events that traditionally had been all-white domains were symbolically integrated. For instance, for the first time ever, the 1959 Miss Cuba pageant was presided over by a black man, Comandante Juan Almeida, who personally delivered the trophy to the white winner of the beauty contest. The incident, the U.S. Embassy reported, had caused "strong resentment" in the population, but it was nonetheless repeated. In 1960, Almeida presided over the choosing of Carnival's "queen" in Havana.[74] In a contest to select the best "Cuban dolls" for the "Cuban Christmas" of 1959 sponsored by the Department of Culture of the Ministry of Education, two of the three main awards—including the first prize—went to dolls representing Afro-Cuban figures. Also for the first time, in 1961 black models and hairstylists competed in the annual beauty contest sponsored by the Club of Hairstylists and the National Federation of Barbers in Havana. "Beauty," a newspaper noted, "has no specific color."[75]

This environment was propitious enough for some Afro-Cuban intellectuals to bring into the public sphere issues and cultural expressions that had been traditionally hidden or demeaned as "black things." Foremost among them was Santería, which had never been fully accepted as a genuine expression of Cubanness. Afro-Cuban activists and writers called for a reassessment of Santería as a legitimate and dignified form of popular religion rather than as witchcraft practiced by ignorant blacks.[76] Likewise, the social and cultural meanings of groups such as the Abakuá—a secret all-male fraternal society of African origin that used to appear only in the police chronicle of the daily press—began to be reexamined. Some *potencias* (Abakuá groups) donated money to agrarian reform and declared support for the revolution. When the harbor at Havana was sabotaged, Fidel Castro asserted that he did not doubt the loyalty of dockworkers, many of whom were affiliated with the Abakuá. By early 1960, the noted Afro-Cuban ethnomusicologist Odilio Urfé was engaged in the organization, for the first time ever in Cuba, of a national congress of the Abakuá.[77]

Other Afro-Cuban intellectuals challenged dominant ideas about race, nationality, and national culture. Journalist Gastón Agüero published a tract arguing that the Cuban nation was already culturally integrated and that only racism and prejudice prevented the acknowledgment of this historical reality. Cubans had to be educated in a new spirit, one in which the very concept of "race" had no place. Another Afro-Cuban writer, Walterio Carbonell, agreed that Cubans had to be exposed to a different education, but he argued that it was first necessary to destroy dominant interpretations of national history and culture, which had been fabricated by the white bourgeoisie. "To demolish the ideological conceptions of the bourgeoisie is to make Revolution," claimed Carbonell. In his seminal *Crítica: Cómo surgió la cultura nacional*, the author criticized those who spoke about the rescue of national culture while maintaining and reproducing an "aristocratic interpretation" of the formation of *cubanidad*. The culture of the slave owners, claimed Carbonell, could not be that of revolutionary Cuba. Rather, it was necessary to create a new "historical consciousness" that gave Africa and its descendants the place they deserved in the formation of the Cuban nation.[78]

Carbonell despaired over the inability of some revolutionaries to free themselves from the influence of what he termed the "bourgeois conceptions" of culture. He also criticized the fact that former slave owners were still regarded as founding fathers of the Cuban nation and Cuban culture. His critique indicated that although there was consensus about the need to create an authentic national culture, the "authenticity" and importance of its various components remained contested. As mentioned above, not even Afro-Cuban intellectuals shared a common vision about this process. Some institutions interpreted the "recovery" of Cuban values as a mandate to issue popular editions of Cuban "classic" authors such as José Antonio Saco or José de la Luz y Caballero, prime exponents of the bourgeois culture that Carbonell so angrily criticized.[79]

But other institutions did contribute to creating the "historical conscious-ness" that Carbonell and others advocated. By 1960 the recently created ICAIC was planning several documentaries and animated films that referred to Afro-Cubans, their history, and the fallacies of racism. A movie about the struggles staged by the peasants of Realengo 18, many of whom were black, was released in 1961. The cast included several black actors, and some of the characters were interpreted by residents of the Realengo, located in the mountains of eastern Cuba.[80]

One of the institutions that initially contributed the most to the task of creating a new national culture was the Teatro Nacional de Cuba (TNC, Cuban National Theater), whose Department of Folklore staged its first public performance in February 1960. Under the leadership of noted white ethnomusicologist Argeliers León, the Department of Folklore was con-ceived as a tool for Cubans to become "owners of [their] own culture," a process that mirrored and contributed to the economic and political inde-pendence created by the revolution. Unlike the tourist-oriented spectacles through which Afro-Cuban culture had been represented, León's produc-tions were designed to maintain the "authenticity" of popular forms of cultural expression and to promote them in mainstream society.[81] The early work of Danza Nacional de Cuba (Cuban National Dance), another depart-ment of the TNC, was conducted with the utmost respect and admiration for Santería and its practitioners.[82]

As part of its mandate, the Department of Folklore organized the Seminar of Folklore Studies in 1960, at which some of the best young researchers of Afro-Cuban culture were trained.[83] León also published *Actas del Folklore*, a journal that included research papers on Santería, the Abakuás, and other forms of popular culture—including those of non-African origin. One of the participants in the seminar recalled later: "The intention was . . . to give new vitality, more weight, and greater value to the African influences expressed through the music and dance used in popular culture, and to return this . . . to the people."[84]

The experiment of the TNC was unique in several ways. To guarantee the authenticity of the presentations, they were staged by real practitioners of Santería and other Afro-Cuban religions. These performers had been trained in their households and communities, not in dance or music academies. Most of them were lower-class blacks and mulattoes whose practices had been traditionally hidden from the society at large. Furthermore, this was an un-precedented institutional effort, backed and supported by the state, with the purpose of researching the African roots of Cuban culture and educating the public in the aesthetic values of a new national culture.

Yet this does not mean that the revolution's cultural institutions were going to promote Santería or other Afro-Cuban religions. Since its creation, the Department of Folklore made clear that its mission was to present "the pure value of the songs, dances, and poetry" associated with the religions. The beliefs themselves were left to be practiced in private. Although the mere public presentation of Afro-Cuban ritual dances and songs helped significantly to legitimize these religions and emphasize the centrality of African elements in the formation of the Cuban culture, a systematic reassessment of Santería as a true religion—and not just a popular rite or superstition—did not take place. By 1961, Carbonell argued that the silence surrounding the progressive political and cultural roles played by the Afro-Cuban religions in the formation of the Cuban nationality was "suspicious."[85]

Paradoxically, this silence coexisted with the promotion of so-called Afro-Cuban folklore. In 1962, two new institutions took over the functions that had been initially concentrated in the Department of Folklore of the TNC. To promote research about the "cultural expressions of the Cuban people" and to create a "museum of Cuban ethnology," the National Institute of Ethnology and Folklore was organized. The decree creating the institute explained that although the Cuban people had created their own forms of language, dance, music, poetry, and myths, Cubans still lacked a true "cultural unity." The main purpose of the institute was to "integrate" these forms into a national culture that would represent and contribute to consolidation of the revolution. León became the director of the new institution and launched the publication of the important serial *Etnología y Folklore*.[86]

To continue public performances of popular songs and dances, the Conjunto Folklórico Nacional (CFN, National Folkloric Ensemble) was created. One of its founding members was young ethnomusicologist, composer, and writer Rogelio Martínez Furé, who had attended the seminar of folklore sponsored by the TNC in 1960. Martínez Furé described the purposes of the ensemble: "The Conjunto Folklórico Nacional [was] created to satisfy a need of our country, which did not have an institution that would collect dancing and musical expressions of national character and integrate them into the new socialist culture. . . . The *conjunto* . . . must select those forms of true artistic value and organize them according to the demands of modern theater, but without betraying its folkloric essence." The CFN followed in the footsteps of the Department of Folklore of the TNC in that the troupe was originally formed with dancers, musicians, and informants who were active practitioners of Santería and other popular forms of cultural expression. In mid-1963 the CFN staged its first public performance in Havana, with a program that was mostly devoted to Afro-Cuban themes. A year later it represented Cuba in the Festival of Nations in Paris, also touring Spain, Belgium, and Algeria. The image that revolutionary Cuba began to export as its own was largely defined by its African ancestry.[87]

Both the institute and the CFN were seen by their founding members and by authorities as catalysts in the process of creating an authentic national culture. And to no small degree, they were. Especially in the early stages, the work of these institutions was permeated with enthusiasm and respect for the cultural expressions they were supposed to investigate and represent. But institutionalizing "scientific research" and "spectacles" as two separate areas reflected some of the ambiguities that characterized the revolution's approach to integration. The institute intended to research Cuban popular traditions, catalog them, monitor their evolution under socialism, and ultimately store them in the newly created Museum of Ethnology. The CFN would organize theatrical spectacles, selecting cultural forms of "artistic value" and depriving them of their sacred, ritual foundation. Although Martínez Furé was—as León before him—clearly committed to maintaining the authenticity of these presentations, they resulted in the secularization of Afro-Cuban sacred culture, a process that some black intellectuals criticized as "folklorization."[88] In a sense, the institute and the CFN were charged with keeping alive the historic memory of these cultural expressions precisely because revolutionary authorities believed they were about to die in the new Cuba. And just as the revolution had "solved" the problem of discrimination by eliminating the most visible forms of segregation, it was creating a national culture by integrating the equally visible expressions of Afro-Cuban traditions. The rest—remaining forms of discrimination and prejudice and the religious content of the Afro-Cuban songs and dances—were "remnants" of the past that, it was assumed, would disappear in due time.[89]

Thus the artistic value of these expressions was not necessarily linked to the complexity, vitality, and, in Carbonell's words, progressive social function of the Afro-Cuban religions, which were frequently referred to as "rites." By the mid-1960s it was clear that the religions of African origin were not perceived as progressive cultural forms but were in fact deemed to be obstacles to the construction of socialism and the formation of the "new man." But Santería and other Afro-Cuban religions had not been singled out for discouragement.[90] Their treatment was part of an assault on religions in general, and the Catholic Church in particular, that had reached its climax in late 1961.[91] The assumption of Marxism-Leninism as the official ideology of the government, the organization of the Partido Comunista de Cuba in 1965, and the confrontation with the Catholic hierarchy all contributed to a climate of religious intolerance. Moreover, the emphasis on education and the formation of a highly politicized (that is, Marxist) "new man" clashed with the "opium of the masses" with which orthodox Communists identified religions. At best, religions were seen as relics of a past of ignorance and exploitation that the revolution had set out to destroy. Even after the gradual rapprochement between the revolutionary leaders and the Catholic Church began in 1969, the party still portrayed religions as "a helpful ideological element for the dominant classes in societies where exploitation is common."[92]

These dogmatic perceptions of religion were perhaps accentuated in the case of Santería, which party ideologues conceived of as little more than a grotesque collection of primitive rites. The state-church conflict of 1961–62 had been characterized by criticism of the Catholic Church as a reactionary institution and of priests as counterrevolutionary agents. Attacks on Christian dogma had not been a dominant theme. Judging by official publications, however, the perceptions of party officials about Afro-Cuban religions were seriously prejudiced and reproduced, in fact, many of the stereotypes that had identified these religions with witchcraft in the past.[93] As *El Militante Comunista* put it in 1968, "Santería is a coarse mix of mythological elements from various African regions. . . . Its practitioners pride themselves on their knowledge of the virtues of plants, which is more primitive, for instance, than that of medieval alchemists. . . . A religion is primitive when it has not even created abstractions. . . . To us [their practices] turn our stomachs, but for a primitive mentality they have a logic." Quoting the racist tract of Rafael Roche Monteagudo, originally published in 1908, the unnamed author of this article asserted that Santería was "ridiculous," that its *orishas* (deities) had a "monstrous and repulsive appearance," and that practitioners spent their lives dancing and looking at shells. These beliefs, the author continued, had to be "fought against" in school textbooks as harmful and antiscientific "nonsense." "It is undeniable," the article concluded, "that these remnants of the past make people unhappy and do not contribute at all to the construction of socialism."[94]

This was not an isolated piece. Santería was depicted in similar terms in other publications geared toward the political education of the population. A documentary devoted to Santería and released by the ICAIC in 1964 was entitled *Superstition*. An anonymous article published in the section "Ideological Work" of *Trabajo Político* referred to Santería as "obscurantism," a "primitive" belief from which practitioners had to be "liberated." Although it had "folkloric value," Santería was said to clash with "the age in which we live and with the type of society and of man that is being created in our *patria*." Thus Afro-Cuban religions were represented not only as a remnant of the past from which ignorant practitioners had to be freed but also as a cultural form antagonistic to the new society and the new citizen under construction. Believers were viewed as potential social deviants, if not downright antisocial, whose behavior was characterized by drunkenness, vagrancy, and a concern for their religious community rather than for socialist society as a whole.[95]

No group exemplifies these perceptions better than the Abakuá societies. Members of these societies were considered to be dangerous to society just by belonging to the group. "It is a fact," a police journal reported on the Abakuás, "that many of the members display a high level of social dangerousness and a predisposition to commit crimes." Another study characterized members of the group as selfish and antisocial because of their "relentless individualism." The "sect" attracted the "worst elements" of society and had become a refuge for "bandits, counterrevolutionaries, and thieves." The Abakuás were also criticized for not accepting women in the societies, a restriction said to be common among "all primitive peoples."[96]

Critics blamed prerevolutionary society for the ignorance of practitioners of Afro-Cuban religions. As a result, they were to a degree exonerated from their faults. But ignorance, low cultural level," and religious obscurantism were deemed factors contributing to antisocial conduct, thus the subject of special attention from state organs charged with the prevention and repression of criminal activities. Although the revolutionary government did not repress the observance of Afro-Cuban religions in a systematic way, it tried to limit their growth, imposed limitations on their practice, and associated them with crimes and counterrevolutionary forms of behavior. Whether they were considered ignorant or antisocial, religious practitioners were depicted by party officials as inferior members of society in need of uplifting and enlightenment. The environment was repressive enough for practitioners to hide the colors of their saints in ways that were not obvious to authorities, work colleagues, and society at large.[97]

Practitioners were not prosecuted because of their beliefs. Yet Afro-Cuban religions were invoked in criminal cases as predictors of social dangerousness and linked directly to a culture of criminality.[98] In a 1966 murder case, for instance, the twenty-one-year-old accused, a member of an Abakuá society, was described as someone who lived in a circle of "gangsters, criminals, and killers." The cause of the killing was not known, but the court inferred that it was due to conflicts between rival Abakuá *potencias*. In another 1966 murder case, the accused was characterized as "a youth who, due to his low cultural level and his links to antisocial elements, has become a true psychopath, that is, an individual who tends to break all the norms of civilized society, the law, and morality. . . . He is a member of the sect of '*ñáñigos* or *abakuás*,' which in its current form . . . constitutes nothing else but an association of criminals."

Likewise, when a member of the Sociedad Hijos de Sarabanda Corta Lima—a society of *palo* followers, an Afro-Cuban religion of Bantu origin—was tried for murder, the crime was linked to his membership in the group of *paleros*. According to the court, "[G]iven his religious affiliation, characterized by machismo and a false concept of manliness, he [the accused] killed his enemy." In turn, the same court was puzzled when hearing the case of a young man who had fired a shot at someone, because the accused had decided to be initiated as a *ñáñigo* despite having a "high cultural level" and coming from a "decent and morally adjusted household."

Given the state's pejorative perceptions of Afro-Cuban religions, it is not surprising that some policies were aimed directly at discouraging, and occasionally even preventing, the conducting of religious ceremonies.[99] In the mid-1960s, a measure was passed prohibiting initiation ceremonies of Santería, although it was revoked later. Also, during this period several religious associations requested official cancellation from the registry of the Ministry of the Interior. They usually alleged loss of membership and incapacity to fulfill legal requirements as reasons for dissolution.[100] Authorities saw this as a natural process—a function of generational change and a consequence of the construction of socialism. But it seems reasonable to assume that the negative social environment, born out of official condemnation, also played a role. Whereas religious associations could be an easy target for monitoring and repression, individual practitioners were not. Loss of membership and requests for cancellation might well have been strategies to further hide Santería from the watchful eyes of authorities and society.

Indeed, this seems to have been the strategy followed by the members of the Casino Africano San Antonio from Santa Isabel de las Lajas association in Las Villas.[101] In September 1966, the president of the society wrote to the official in charge of the registry of associations in the region requesting cancellation. No explanation was offered. Casino Africano, which had been founded in 1913, had only twenty-six active members by December 1965: sixteen men who paid 20 cents per month and ten women who paid 10 cents per month. Its annual budget amounted to less than $52. In February 1967 it was officially dissolved, its goods—including a small house—given to the Institute of Housing and other state institutions.

Three years later, however, the former president of the association wrote a letter to Celia Sánchez, personal aide to Fidel Castro, requesting the reopening of the Casino Africano. His letter portrayed a quite different story, claiming that the society had been closed against his will and that something similar had happened to other associations. He addressed Celia, as she was popularly known, as a "comrade of struggle and ideals," for she had allegedly received the *santo* Ochún (Virgen de la Caridad del Cobre) from a notorious Santera (Santería practitioner) from Cruces who was an acquaintance of his. It is unknown whether Celia responded to this letter, but in January 1971, the former president of Casino Africano sought to formally register the association again. In his letter to the authorities, he noted that the purpose of the society was to "perpetuate the memory and respect for [their] ancestors." The new directive vowed to support the "triumphant revolution," asserted that "decency" and "irreproachable behavior" would be observed, and offered to maintain the institution at the "highest possible cultural level."

The local chief of the registry was not moved by all these offerings couched in the rhetoric of revolution. In fact, he was outraged. In his secret report to provincial authorities, he noted that the Casino Africano had been closed at the request of its own members and that no association had been arbitrarily dissolved in the region, as the former president of the society had told Celia Sánchez. But the official himself provided the clues needed to reconcile what appear to be radically different recollections of the same events. When the directives of the Casino Africano requested cancellation in 1966, this official reported, initiation ceremonies "were not being authorized. They also had to pay for stamps and other fees. None of this exists today, quite the contrary. It is since the time that initiations have been authorized that the directives of the society bothered to request registration." He asserted that if the purpose of the society was truly to "maintain the tradition of their ancestors," the members would not have canceled it before. That they could not perform some of their basic functions seems to have played no role in his assessment. The official opposed registration, claiming that this would only encourage "backwardness and ignorance." Whereas authorities perceived the 1966 cancellation as a spontaneous decision, association members deemed it an imposition.

By 1971 these ceremonies had been authorized again, but they required special permission from the local police district. Santeros were interviewed in advance and asked to identify the participants, the types of rituals to be performed, and the origin of the materials required for ceremonies—many of which could be obtained only on the black market. Authorization was not automatically granted, and attendance of minors was strictly prohibited. "I had to insist for many weeks to get permission for the ceremony," explained a Santera from Pogolotti (Marianao, Havana) who was initiated in 1974. "Finally, the chief of police in the area said that I could do it, but he warned me not to have any minors there—'If I hear that there is a child there I will cancel the whole thing,' he said." Another Santero reported that his family tried to initiate him in 1972, but they could not because "it was prohibited for minors."[102] Even after the accommodation that characterized the government's approach toward religion in the 1970s, there is little doubt that Afro-Cuban religions were being merely tolerated. A mid-1970s movie portrayed Abakuás as groups that generated marginality and "a code of parallel social relations that is the antithesis of social integration." In the early 1980s, epidemiological studies conducted by the Ministry of Health still identified participation in Afro-Cuban religions as "pathological behavior."[103]

The official silence on race ultimately prevented a public discussion about the social functions of Santería along the lines suggested by Cuéllar Vizcaíno, Carbonell, and other Afro-Cuban intellectuals in the early years of the revolution. Along with other religious beliefs, the Afro-Cuban religions were characterized by the ruling Communist Party as opiates for the people. The party's orthodox and conservative language made no explicit reference to race, but terms such as "primitive" and "cultural level" had clear racial implications and were rightly interpreted by the population as veiled references to blackness. Folkloric spectacles were no substitute for a serious reassessment of Santería in which practitioners themselves had the opportunity to vindicate their beliefs as true religions and cultural forms of which all Cubans could be proud. Moreover, even some of these spectacles lost visibility during the late 1960s—the Conjunto Folklórico Nacional, for instance, did not stage any international tours between 1964 and 1970. In sum, the lack of a public debate about race and racism facilitated the survival and reproduction of the very racist stereotypes that the revolutionary leadership claimed to oppose. Historically, a unique opportunity had been lost.

However, efforts to promote the African roots of national culture were not meaningless. They contributed to reinforcing the notion that African elements were central to Cubanness and exposed ordinary Cubans of all colors to a different vision of themselves and their nation. The creation of the "Sábados de la Rumba" by the CFN, for instance, brought African cultural elements to the heart of what had traditionally been a white middle-class neighborhood: Vedado.[104] At the same time, the work of painters such as Manuel Mendive celebrated the African origins of the nation.[105] A few young writers explored the complexities of race, exposed embedded racist myths, and found pride in blackness.[106]

The image of a mixed nation with African roots also became an identity for export and allowed the government to identify itself with the struggle of peoples of color worldwide. Through this identification, race became a major issue in Cuba's foreign policy.

INTERNATIONALIZING BLACKNESS

The importance of this identification with other nonwhite peoples increased as tensions between the governments of Cuba and the United States escalated. In its search for allies within and outside the United States, the issue of race became a central pillar of Cuba's international policy. Cuban authorities soon realized that African Americans could be a valuable ally and that racism was a formidable political weapon to counteract the negative campaign waged by the U.S. mainstream press against the revolutionary government. As early as February 1959, Fidel Castro responded to negative reports in the U.S. media concerning the killing of Batista's war criminals by reminding the U.S. government about its own race problems. Likewise, when the U.S. government voiced concern and opposition to agrarian reform, the Cuban press and leaders responded that the United States should first address its own domestic social problems, such as racial discrimination.[107]

Seeking the support of black Americans, in 1959 and 1960 the Cuban government organized, and in some cases even financed, the visits of African American intellectuals and public figures so they could see the revolution's accomplishments firsthand. Representatives of the black press were included among the 150 journalists that Havana invited in January 1959 as part of "Operation Truth," which sought to counteract negative publicity in the United States and elsewhere. The government also invited a group of congressmen, but only two—one of whom was Adam Clayton Powell, a representative from Harlem—accepted.[108]

More government-sponsored tours followed. In late 1959, the Cuban Tourist Commission invited a group of African Americans to visit the island during Christmas and paid all expenses. Among other activities, they were to attend a banquet with Fidel Castro and President Osvaldo Dorticós. Participants included heavyweight boxing champion Joe Louis and the editors and publishers of several major black newspapers. The message that the Tourist

Commission wished to send was quite explicit: revolutionary Cuba welcomed African American tourism.[109] Another delegation, also financed by the Cuban government, was invited for the July 26 festivities in 1960. This group included authors Julian Mayfield, John Henrik Clarke, and LeRoi Jones and activist Robert F. Williams, who was on his second trip to see the Cuban "social miracle."[110]

To no small degree, the Cuban government's campaign was successful. Sympathetic accounts of the revolution and its leader flooded the African American press in the early months of 1959 and beyond.[111] Black journalists cheered the revolution's efforts to eliminate racism and reported Fidel Castro's public statements against racial discrimination. In the process, they could not avoid making comparisons with the situation in the United States, where white-supremacist groups were officially tolerated.

The initial campaign was fairly successful because the interests of Cuban authorities coincided with those of many African Americans in several ways. The revolution triumphed at a time when the civil rights movement in the United States had achieved some successes, but its most difficult battles still laid ahead. The Cuban ability to dismantle segregation and the most visible manifestations of racism in such a short period of time gave both revolutionary authorities and African Americans the opportunity to question the degree of determination of the U.S. government to eliminate racism at home and the alleged superiority of American democracy. Just as Castro challenged the moral authority of the United States to judge the actions of his government, African American activists questioned the U.S. concern for Cuban war criminals when blacks' rights were being violated daily at home. "The important lesson in the Cuban experience," Mayfield wrote in 1960, "is that great social change need not wait on the patient education of white supremacists. . . . Surely a powerful and secure government like that of the United States could, if it chose, achieve remarkable results. If the democratic press, of which we boast, needs several generations to achieve what the Cubans have done in 18 months, then there is something wrong with it."[112]

Castro's most conspicuous overture toward black America took place during his visit to the United Nations in October 1960. Offended by the way the Cuban delegation had been treated in a midtown-Manhattan hotel, Castro decided to stay in the Theresa Hotel in Harlem—a move that he himself characterized as "a big lesson to people who practice discrimination." Interviewed by the *Afro-American*, Castro asserted that in Harlem he felt like he was in his own country, adding that the Cuban delegation had been discriminated against in midtown Manhattan. Not invited to a luncheon organized by President Dwight Eisenhower in the lavish Park Avenue Waldorf Astoria Hotel, Castro declared that he was "honored to lunch with the poor and humble people of Harlem."[113] Even those African Americans who did not sympathize with revolutionary Cuba appreciated the gesture, for, as Mayfield stated, "anybody so completely rejected by white America must have some good points."[114]

Cuba's initial gestures toward African Americans were driven by the need to counteract the negative publicity that revolutionary policies were getting from the mainstream media and politicians in the United States. This need was less evident after January 1961, when the United States broke off diplomatic relations with the Cuban government. Rather than appealing to all African Americans, after 1961 Cuban authorities shifted their emphasis toward the most radical sectors and activists within the black liberation movement—people who in many cases were at the fringes of the civil rights movement. The Cuban government identified these groups as allies who were fighting imperialism from within. These groups and activists, in turn, supported revolutionary Cuba because they shared a common enemy. As a 1961 "Declaration of Conscience by Afro-Americans" signed by a large number of intellectuals and political activists involved with the Fair Play for Cuba Committee stated, the enemies of the Cuban revolution were African Americans' own enemies: "[T]he Jim Crow bosses of this land where we are still denied our rights. The Cubans are our friends, the enemies of our enemies."[115]

One of the signers of this declaration was Robert F. Williams, who, as Van Gosse rightly asserts, "made the most telling connection between the rising anger of African-Americans and the island revolution."[116] Williams had become notorious for advocating blacks' "self-defense" in Monroe, North Carolina. The head of the local branch of the National Association for the Advancement of Colored People, he had been criticized by his own organization for his support of the Cuban revolution and his involvement in the Fair Play for Cuba Committee. Indeed, Williams traveled several times to Cuba during 1959 and 1960, where he claimed to have "experienced [his] first freedom as a human being." When Castro went to Harlem during his visit to the United Nations, Williams sent him a public invitation to visit North Carolina, calling him "the greatest humanitarian leader of our time."[117]

Amid growing racial violence in Monroe and facing charges of kidnapping, Williams left the United States and sought political asylum in Cuba. He lived there until 1966, continued to publish his newsletter, *The Crusader*, and began broadcasting Radio Free Dixie from Havana. Both the newsletter and the radio broadcast underscored the differences between "racism-free" Cuba and racist America. In the words of U.S. authorities, Radio Free Dixie called "upon American Negroes to engage in force and violence against the American Government." A 1965 police journal charged that, through Williams, the Cuban government was preparing a black revolt in the United States. "Castro arming Southern Negroes," reported the *Police Gazette*.[118]

Williams was only the first radical African American activist to be given sanctuary in revolutionary Cuba. Others would soon follow. In 1968, one of the founding members of the Black Panther Party, Eldridge Cleaver, arrived on the island, remaining in hiding for several months. A few months later another high-ranking member of the party and a former bodyguard of Cleaver, William Lee Brent, hijacked a plane from Oakland, California, to Havana. The Panthers' leader, Huey Newton, also went to Cuba in 1973. A leading member of the Black Liberation Army, Assata Shakur, staged a spectacular escape from jail in 1979 and went to Cuba, where she still lived in the mid-1990s.[119]

Radical African American activists found not only refuge in the island but also diplomatic, political, and military support. According to Cleaver, there was even talk of opening a permanent training unit for black militants in Cuba.[120] As with the initial campaign to gain African Americans' support, this cooperation was based on common interests and judgments concerning the nature of racism and the struggle for its elimination. The Cuban authorities wanted to embarrass the U.S. government internationally and promote social conflicts at home. So did these African American militants. Castro believed that capitalism engendered racism; they agreed. Castro had demonstrated that social change was possible through revolutionary violence. Groups such as the Black Panther Party had appropriated the rhetoric and substance of this lesson. "We must destroy both racism and capitalism," Newton advocated in 1968. "It is useless to talk about becoming free unless you talk about engaging in armed struggle against racism and capitalism and imperialism in North America," the minister of education of the Panthers asserted. The Cubans considered the pacifist civil rights movement a maneuver to "confuse and deter the legitimate struggle of the black North American people." The Panthers agreed, describing pacifist activists as "begging-oriented" and modern exponents of the traditionally servile "house negro."[121]

There was agreement on yet another important point. African Americans' liberation struggle was part of a larger, international confrontation between colonial or neocolonial peoples and white imperialism. As Williams asserted in a 1962 broadcast of Radio Free Dixie, "[W]e are not going to be free until we join the rising tide of humanity in South America, Asia, and Africa in the final assault against the racist, imperialist, and fascist forces of the U.S.A." African American militants argued that blacks constituted "an oppressed nation" that had "essentially the same relationship to American capitalism as other colonials and semi-colonials have to Western capitalism."[122] Stokely Carmichael endorsed this thesis in his speech to the first conference of the Organization of Latin American Solidarity (OLAS) in Havana in 1967: "We greet you as comrades because it becomes increasingly clear to us each day that we share with you a common struggle; we have a common enemy. Our enemy is white Western imperialist society. . . . Our people are a colony within the United States; you are colonies outside the United States." Carmichael declared that African Americans were training urban guerrilla groups inspired by the Cuban revolution and Che Guevara. He was treated as an honored guest by the Cuban government.[123]

It is hardly surprising that African American radicals would be inspired by Cuba's example. Besides the fact that Cuba had undertaken a campaign against racism at home, the revolution had made Africa a central concern of its foreign policy. From the visit of Guinea's president Sékou Touré to Cuba in 1960, to Che Guevara's fighting in the Congo in 1965, to Castro's own visit to Guinea, Sierra Leone, and Algeria in 1972, Cuba had supported the anticolonial struggle in Africa since the 1960s. Thus, for the African American militants, revolutionary Cuba was not only a safe haven but also a source of ideological legitimacy and one of their most important international platforms.[124]

Yet agreements between the Cuban government and the African American militants were neither universal nor unproblematic. This is because Cuba's international campaign of solidarity with oppressed black peoples around the world was staged for a domestic audience, as figure 7.2 shows. Cuba could take a leading role in the worldwide struggle against racism because it had allegedly eliminated racial discrimination at home. The social subordination of African Americans and the violence that characterized the process of desegregation in 1960s America were systematically announced to the Cuban population through the government-controlled media. Cubans were reminded, on almost at a daily basis, that they lived in a superior society.[125]

Although radical African American militants did not dispute the superiority of Cuba's revolutionary society, their insertion into the national political scene was fraught with difficulties. As representatives of "black power," these militants were in many cases adamant about the need for blacks to mobilize separately—a notion that contradicted the integrationism of the

FIGURE 7.2. *"We Want Castro!" This cartoon was published during Fidel Castro's visit to Harlem in 1960. From* Noticias de Hoy, *September 21, 1960. (Biblioteca Nacional "José Martí")*

Cuban revolution. Moreover, African American militants used the example of the revolution in Cuba to claim that gradualist approaches were a white maneuver to perpetuate racism, but in several areas the Cuban government itself had endorsed a gradual, nonconfrontational approach when dealing with the race question.

Thus many of these African American militants grew increasingly impatient with and critical of the Cuban government and its antidiscrimination agenda. Williams left the island in 1966 and went to China, where he sent a public letter to Castro denouncing the lack of cooperation of Cuban officials concerning his revolutionary activities in Havana. Cleaver stayed in Cuba for just a few months, becoming an outspoken critic of the revolution thereafter. Carmichael had been given red-carpet treatment by Havana, but he claimed subsequently that the Cuban example was irrelevant to the cause of black liberation because of its emphasis on cross-racial class struggle. Less famous African Americans who came to experience life in Cuba shared these misgivings and criticisms.[126]

Contradictions also emerged because some of the internal consequences of Cuban solidarity with black America were neither anticipated nor desirable to the authorities. Some of the African American leaders who visited or lived in Cuba—Williams is a prime example—spoke frequently at workers' rallies and other public meetings across the island. Others, such as Carmichael, were publicized and treated as heroes. Either way they reached ordinary Cubans with messages that were not always acceptable to the authorities because their purpose, struggles, and doctrines were defined in racial terms. Carmichael, for instance, spoke about racial oppression not only as a form of economic exploitation—the position advanced by the Cuban government—but also as a form of cultural exploitation. In his speech to the OLAS conference in Havana, he asserted: "Black Power not only addresses itself to exploitation, but to the problem of cultural integrity."[127]

At a time when the Communist Party and Cuban authorities were discouraging, if not overtly repressing, Afro-Cuban cultural expressions such as Santería, these statements had clear implications for Cuban society. Visiting Cuba in 1967, Sutherland reported that Carmichael's visit had a significant impact among Afro-Cubans, who "seemed to be watching and listening with particular intensity." Some Afro-Cubans adopted at least some of the external symbols that these militants displayed—such as the Afro hairstyle—and perhaps part of the substance of their message.[128] In 1967, a group of young Afro-Cuban intellectuals attempted to draft a paper on race and culture in Cuba to be submitted to the World Cultural Congress to be held in Havana in January 1968. Other unconfirmed reports assert that Cuban blacks attempted to articulate some sort of autonomous discourse in various ways, but they always met with official resistance.[129]

In the long term, however, Cuba's support for the African American struggle and the anticolonial struggle in Africa contributed significantly to the government's project of national integration. At a minimum, Cuban solidarity paved the way for the island's unprecedented participation in African politics in the 1970s and 1980s. Foreign policy may have been used to distract attention from domestic race problems, as Carlos Moore asserts.[130]

But the heavy presence of Africa (and the West Indies in the 1970s and early 1980s) in Cuban life facilitated the ascent of blacks within the state bureaucracy and the armed forces and helped to modify embedded social perceptions about African culture, population, and politics.[131] The massive participation of black and white Cubans in the African wars and civilian missions after 1975 would not have been possible without such changes. Nor is it likely that in the absence of such changes Castro would have been able to proclaim that Cuba was a Latin-African nation, as he did in 1975.[132]

Identification with Africa and its descendants in the diaspora also gave the Cuban government the opportunity to construct a notion of Cubanness that was in stark contrast with that of its archenemy: the exile community in Miami. Whereas the revolution's "true" Cubanness was identified with the poor and blacks, the identity of the so-called worms was portrayed as the quintessence of all the ills the revolution had avowedly eliminated: class exploitation, foreign dependency, and racism. Nowhere were the racial implications of foreign policy clearer than in the conflict with Cuban exiles.

The Cuba that exiles attempted to reconstruct in Miami and other communities in the United States was in many ways the antithesis of the new Cuba that the revolution was attempting to build in the island. It was, to begin with, socially and demographically different. The 1953 Cuban census had reported that blacks and mulattoes made up 27 percent of the total population. Their proportion among U.S. exiles was about 13 percent in the 1960s and 16 percent in the 1970s. The educational and occupation profile of the exile community was also, initially, very different from that of the island population, with an overrepresentation of professionals, entrepreneurs, and white-collar employees. In addition to strident anticommunism, its racial and social composition made Cuban Miami the perfect antithesis to Cuba's revolutionary society.[133]

These contrasts were further magnified by factors over which the Cuban exiles had little control. Whereas revolutionary Cuba prided itself on being a racially harmonious, discrimination-free society, the exiles arrived in a city that in the early 1960s was, for the most part, still segregated.[134] To the racial tensions of the host community, they added a new layer, for many African American residents firmly believed that the Cuban refugees were getting the lion's share of public dollars and being given preferential treatment in employment and other opportunities. As the black weekly *Miami Times* editorialized in 1961, "Negroes are complaining that the Cubans are given preference and in some instances are being replaced by the refugees. While we sympathize with the unfortunate Cubans we feel that charity should begin at home." Testifying before a Senate committee later that year, the executive director of the Greater Miami Urban League confirmed that there was considerable "resentment and hostility in the Negro community" toward the Cubans, who were pushing blacks out of jobs and accepting employment at "reduced pay rates."[135]

The perception that Cubans have been favored to the detriment of African Americans in Miami has lasted to this day.[136] Together with other factors, this idea fueled the anger that led to racial violence in the city in 1968, 1980, and 1989. Prior to the 1968 riot, for instance, there was discussion in the local black press of whether episodes of violence similar to those happening in other American cities would ever happen in Miami. Resentment toward Cubans was already high due to a strike that they had launched in 1967— "they are not grateful for the opportunity given them by American business," a journalist charged. When a black teacher in Miami warned that those who "planted seeds of hate" between African Americans and Cubans were inciting violence, her remarks provoked a strong reaction. A letter to the editor of the *Miami Times* reflected the anger of the community: "Who is this . . . writer who seems to be so concerned about riots, but not the conditions . . . that cause riots? . . . Who is this Negro . . . who is so much concerned about the economic advancement of Cubans, but fails to comprehend that Negroes as an ethnic group make up the lowest ring of the economic scale in Miami!" What the teacher had dubbed "rumors" concerning allegations that Cubans took blacks' jobs this writer called "facts." He said he did not approve of rioting, but he concluded that blacks in ghettos elsewhere were trying to send a message and that it was time to "start listening." Several months later, a violent riot erupted in the black section of Liberty City in Miami, to which the Cubans responded by arming themselves. In a report issued by a local task force for the National Commission on the Causes and Prevention of Violence, the "steady loss of jobs by Negroes to Cubans" was singled out as one of the factors leading to the riot.[137]

The Cuban presence was considered an underlying factor in the riot of 1968, but it was seen as one of the main causes of the May 1980 riot, which erupted again in Liberty City. Although it was the acquittal of several white policemen charged with killing an African American insurance agent that triggered street violence, observers were unanimous in their assessment that resentment over the public help given to the Cuban refugees who were coming by the thousands through the Mariel boatlift had led to the fury of Miami's blacks.[138] While the federal government pledged to welcome the Cuban *marielitos* with open arms, rumors about a slash in funding of food stamps and other social programs circulated in the black sections of Miami. To add insult to injury, although Cuban refugees were welcome, those from Haiti were systematically denied asylum and the benefits associated with such status.[139]

The 1980 riot could not have come at a better time for Cuban authorities, who were deeply embarrassed by the spectacle of tens of thousands of Cubans leaving the island. In contrast to previous migration waves, that of Mariel reflected the social and demographic composition of the general population. Many came from poorer sectors of the population; blacks and mulattoes were still grossly underrepresented, but their proportion was significantly higher than among previous exiles. Indeed, the *marielitos'* socio-demographic composition threatened to undermine the representation of Miami as the social, racial, and political antithesis of revolutionary Cuba. Havana responded by depicting them as *escoria*, the scum of Cuba's socialism. Revolutionary Cuba could not afford to have a nonwhite, nonelitist Miami.[140]

The 1980 riot, in turn, allowed Cuban authorities the opportunity to remind the population about the racist nature of U.S. society. The official press referred to Miami as a "racial hell in capitalist paradise" and grimly depicted the fate of the *marielitos*. It was emphasized, for instance, that the Ku Klux Klan had sent an airplane to fly over the refugee camps with a banner that read: "The KKK is here." According to the Cuban press, the *marielitos* were competing with native blacks for low-paying, menial jobs and had joined the city's underworld of unemployment, drug addiction, and homelessness. The popular weekly *Bohemia* published a photograph of a black handcuffed *marielito* who looked as scared "as if he were looking at the white robes of a Klansman." The Cuban press also emphasized that many *marielitos* had ended up in U.S. jails, where they had no legal guarantees, reinforcing the image of the United States as a society dominated by racism and the rejection of the poor.[141]

In fact, the new immigrants were rejected even by the Cuban-American community.[142] Their social composition represented a threat not just to the revolution's representation of Miami. It also threatened the community's image as "the cream of the crop" of Cuban society. For once, Cuban authorities and their enemies agreed: these low-class, dark immigrants were indeed scum and lumpen. Thus, the resettlement and assimilation of Afro-Cuban *marielitos* were particularly difficult. Not only did they lack relatives in the community, but also they were black. At the Fort Indiana Gap camp in Pennsylvania, for instance, the proportion of blacks among residents increased from 14 percent in May 1980 to 50 percent three months later. An official of a resettlement agency said that churches were willing to sponsor Cuban refugees but that they preferred nuclear families and "want them white."[143]

The 1980 riot helped to restore the Cuban representation of Miami as a "racist hell," and Cuban-American politics through the 1980s reinforced the notion that the community was passionately racist. Nothing helped to consolidate this image more than Cuba's Africa policy. While Cuban troops were fighting the invasion of the South African army and its Union for the Total Independence of Angola (UNITA) allies in Angola, leaders of the right-wing Cuban American National Foundation (CANF) were lobbying in support of Jonas Savimbi, the UNITA leader. The fact that the congressional black caucus, the TransAfrica organizations, and other influential African American voices were critical of Savimbi did not seem to affect the CANF's decision. In 1988, the chairman of the organization announced that he would travel to Angola to meet Savimbi and to encourage Cuban soldiers to defect. While Cuba offered massive medical assistance to Angola and other African countries, a team of Cuban-American physicians offered their services to Savimbi's UNITA. Some Cuban-Americans even criticized the negotiations to withdraw Cuban troops from Angola, claiming that this would work to the benefit of its Marxist regime, for South African troops would be "precluded from re-entering Angolan territory."[144]

The association between the exiles and apartheid was further reinforced when they opposed Nelson Mandela's visit to Miami in June 1990. Mandela had praised Cuba for its support in the struggle against apartheid and for its human rights record. Disregarding the feelings of other sectors of the community, the city council of Miami yielded to Cuban-American pressure and refused to welcome Mandela. African Americans deemed this an insult and retaliated with a boycott against holding conventions in the city until officials apologized. When Mandela visited Havana in July 1991, the ideological split between the African American and Cuban communities of Miami grew even wider. Whereas the former welcomed Mandela's warm reception in Havana as something "wonderful," Cuban-Americans called Mandela a "communist" who had turned a deaf ear to the denunciations of human rights abuses in the island while praising Cuba for its "unparalleled" fight against racism. The exiles' support for racism and apartheid was denounced by Mandela himself: "Who are they [Cuban-Americans] to call for the observance of human rights in Cuba? They kept quiet for 42 years when human rights were being attacked in South Africa. . . . [They] have supported the apartheid regime for the last 40 years."[145]

Thus, it has not been particularly difficult for the Cuban authorities and media to propagate the image of a racially troubled Miami and of Cuban-Americans as bastions of racism. As *Granma*, the official newspaper of the Cuban Communist Party, asserted in 1994 in reference to the exiles, "[T]hey work as the empire's lackeys, declaring a Noble Peace Prize winner like Nelson Mandela persona non grata, burning Latin American flags or acting as a containing wall against Miami Haitians or Afro-Americans."[146]

The Cuban media has connected racism, Miami, and counterrevolution even when this connection was not obvious. The 1992 riot in Los Angeles is a good example. An editorial published by *Granma* asked whether this was the same government that was trying to incriminate Cuba in the international community because of its human rights record, whether this was the American "paradise" to which some wanted to emigrate. While President George Bush was visiting Miami and declaring that the Cuban revolution would fall, the editorial continued, the social explosion was about to start in the United States. The connection between racial violence, U.S. hostility toward Cuba, and Miami was therefore explicitly made. A *Christian Science Monitor* journalist who was visiting Havana reported that Afro-Cubans reacted in "horror" as the government "played the images of the Los Angeles riots over and over again on Cuban television."[147]

Cuba's identification with Africa and African Americans helped the revolutionary government advance its domestic agenda of national integration even if questions of race were not publicly debated after the early 1960s. Its cultural and foreign policies helped to emphasize the centrality of Africa in the formation of *cubanidad* without risking racial divisions internally. Meanwhile, authorities believed that remaining racial differences would automatically disappear through implementation of the revolution's egalitarian policies. This, in turn, would lead to the creation of a new social consciousness, one in which the very notion of race would be absent. By 1981, more than twenty years after the triumph of the revolution, it became possible to measure the impact of Cuban socialism on racial inequality and to ascertain how successful the revolution's class-based approach had been in eliminating racial differences.

RACIAL INEQUALITY: TWENTY YEARS LATER

For the first time since 1959, the Cuban census in 1981 released information according to race. The 1970 census had included this variable, but no racial figures were compiled in the published version. Race was also absent in serial demographic publications.

According to the census, in which respondents had the opportunity to identify their own race among four discrete categories—"white," "black," "mestizo," and "Asian"—by 1981 the Cuban population was 66 percent white, 12 percent black, and 22 percent mestizo (Asians represented only 0.1 percent of the total). The white proportion had declined significantly compared to 1953 (73 percent) and was the lowest in twentieth-century Cuba—not a surprising result, given that the vast majority of emigrants since the 1960s had been white. Contrary to what might be expected, however, the proportion of blacks was similar to that reported in the census of 1953. It was the percentage of mestizos that had increased significantly, from 14.5 percent in 1953 to 22 percent in 1981.

Scholars and journalists have questioned the accuracy of these figures, arguing that the proportion of nonwhites in the total population "must" have been much higher than 34 percent. Some even suggest that the census was a deliberate attempt to whiten the country.[148] Their criticism, however, implies that there is a true, immutable blackness, not just a social representation of it. This is a valid argument only if one assumes that by 1981 racial categories were defined along lines similar to those prevalent in 1953—that is, that no change had occurred in the social definitions of black, white, or mestizo. This is not likely to be the case.

The mulattoization of the Cuban population might be the result of various factors not necessarily related to the "real" degree of "race miscegenation" in the country. It could be the result of intermarriage, which anecdotal references indicate increased significantly after 1959.[149] It could also reflect a broader acceptance of the notion that Cuba is a mixed, mestizo nation or a process of upward mobility. Individuals who, due to their low status, would have been considered "negros" in the past saw themselves as mestizos or mulattoes in 1981. If this is the case—and there is compelling evidence in this direction—the racial composition of the population as reported by the census could reflect both the changes that took place since 1959 (mobility) and the resilience of the past, as indicated by the fact that such mobility was still identified with whitening. Indeed, as will be discussed to some extent in the next chapter, racial ideologies that associate whiteness with education, beauty, and other socially positive traits are quite prevalent in contemporary Cuba. The aphorism "to be white is a profession" summarizes these perceptions, which lead to popular concerns with "improving the race" (adelantar la raza).[150] Since "race" is defined by a number of social and cultural factors, in addition to phenotypical features, the growing proportion of mulattoes in the population is probably a reflection of the educational and occupational mobility experienced by younger generations of Afro-Cubans.

Other census results point to this coexistence of postrevolutionary change and prerevolutionary social realities. However, the transformations are so vast that they can only be described as impressive. By the early 1980s, Cuban society had made remarkable progress in the reduction of racial inequality in a number of crucial areas, including education, health care, and employment. Racial inequality persisted in some areas, but the trend was unequivocally toward equality.

The revolution's impact on racial equality and the singularity of the Cuban case can be understood better in comparative perspective. For instance, by 1981, life expectancy in Cuba was not only close to that of developed countries in absolute numbers but was almost equivalent for blacks and whites. Although a white/nonwhite gap of one year still existed, it was significantly lower than the gap in Brazil (6.7 years) or the United States (6.3 years). Life expectancy reflects broad social conditions, including access to nutrition, health care, maternal care, and education, and thus these differences are significant.[151]

This pattern held for educational achievement as well. Illiteracy was basically eliminated in the island in the early 1960s, but by 1981 inequality in education had disappeared even at the university level. The proportion of blacks and mulattoes who had graduated from high school was in fact higher than the proportion of whites, an indication that blacks had made good use of the educational opportunities created by the revolutionary government. Conversely, in the United States and Brazil, large differences according to race remained in education (see table 7.1).

The expansion and socialization of education eventually influenced the racial composition of the occupational structure. As table 7.2 shows, the index of dissimilarity (a summary measure of inequality) in the Cuban labor market in the early 1980s was three to four times lower than in the United States or Brazil. The proportion of blacks and mulattoes employed in the professions (one-fifth of the labor force) was virtually identical to that of whites in the island, whereas in Brazil it was three times lower. Of workers employed in the Cuban medical sector, 31 percent were black or mulatto, a proportion only slightly lower than blacks and mulattoes' share of the population (34 percent, according to the 1981 census).

But the distribution of the racial groups in the different occupations was still unequal. Although Afro-Cubans were not greatly overrepresented in

TABLE 7.1. Percentage of Population Aged 25 or Over Having Completed High School or College, by Race, Brazil, Cuba, and United States, 1980s

Country	Whites	Blacks	Mulattoes	Differences W/B	W/M
Brazil (1987)					
High school	13.9	5.3	8.0	8.6	5.9
College	9.2	1.0	2.0	8.2	7.2
Cuba (1981)					
High school	9.9	11.2	9.6	−1.3	0.3
College	4.4	3.5	3.2	0.9	1.2
United States (1987)					
High school	56.4	52.8	—	3.6	—
College	20.5	10.7	—	9.8	—

Sources: Cuba, *Censo 1981. República de Cuba*, 16:2, 67–70; Andrews, "Racial Inequality in Brazil and the United States."
Note: W: whites; B: blacks; M: mulattoes.

blue-collar jobs (35 percent), their proportion in some sectors, such as construction (41 percent), was larger than their population share. Likewise, whereas 13 percent of whites worked in managerial positions, the proportion of blacks (7 percent) and mulattoes (9 percent) was significantly lower. Even taking these qualifications into account, however, it is safe to state that the incidence of racism in the Cuban labor market was limited, particularly against mulattoes. Furthermore, since these figures are not age-specific, at least part of the remaining differences could be attributed to historical factors and past discrimination.

Progress was also obvious in the area of black and mulatto representation in leadership positions—an area in which the Cuban government has been frequently criticized. Since the early years of the revolution, Afro-Cuban intellectuals of different ideological persuasions insisted on the need to open, once and for all, leadership positions to blacks and mulattoes. As Moore asserted in 1964, "The right to govern, not the right to be governed, this is the problem. . . . After six years of 'Revolution,' including four of 'socialism,' the government . . . does not have a single black member in its cabinet!"[152] Moore's complaint was not without foundation. In fact, at least in the upper

Category	Brazil			Cuba			United States	
	W	B	M	W	B	M	W	B
Professions	9.0	2.5	3.8	22.2	22.1	22.9	15.5	11.2
Administration	16.7	4.2	6.7	12.8	7.1	8.7	27.9	22.3
Sales	9.0	4.0	6.5	6.4	6.9	6.5	10.5	5.0
Nonagricultural manual labor	26.0	27.9	25.6	23.1	29.2	24.2	31.7	37.1
Service	10.7	22.6	13.0	7.3	9.4	8.6	11.4	22.3
Agriculture	22.7	31.5	38.6	18.2	12.9	18.3	2.8	2.0
Other/unknown	6.0	7.2	5.8	10.0	12.4	10.8	0.0	0.1
Index of dissimilarity	—	23.9	18.3	—	11.1	4.1	—	16.3

Sources: Cuba, *Censo 1981. La población de Cuba*, 117–18; Andrews, "Racial Inequality in Brazil and the United States," 249–50.
Note: W: whites; B: blacks; M: mulattoes.

---

echelons of the government and the PCC, changes in the racial composition of the leadership were extremely slow. Blacks and mulattoes represented only 9 percent of the Central Committee of the PCC elected in 1965, an estimated 7 percent in 1975, and about 12 percent in 1980. Their proportion was not higher in the provincial executive bureaus: 8 percent in 1974.[153]

Nonwhites were much better represented in other positions of command. Following prerevolutionary trends, more than one-third of the members of the National Executive Committee of the CTC were black or mulatto in 1974. Among delegates to the Municipal Assemblies of Popular Power Organs in 1976, their proportion amounted to 28 percent. According to the 1981 census, 24 percent of those classified as "dirigentes" (people in leadership positions of various kinds) were either black or mulatto. Six years later the percentage of nonwhites in management positions had increased slightly. According to a census conducted in 1986 to determine the social composition of the leadership at the national, provincial, and municipal levels, blacks and mulattoes represented 27 percent of the total (table 7.3).[154]

TABLE 7.3. Percentage Distribution, Managers in Government Establishments (*Dirigentes de Establecimientos*), by Race, 1987

Category	Whites	Blacks	Mulattoes
Municipal	71.9	12.1	16.0
Provincial	73.8	10.9	15.3
National	72.7	12.7	14.6
Total	72.5	12.1	15.4
Percent in adult population	66.1	12.0	21.9
Index of representation	110	101	70

Source: Cuba, *Censo nacional de cuadros del estado*, 5:126–29.

That a census of the social composition of the leadership was conducted is itself an expression of the Cuban government's attention to questions of representation. Indeed, in the third congress of the PCC in 1986, Castro elaborated at length about the need to increase the number of women, youth, and blacks and mestizos in the highest echelons of the PCC. In his closing speech to the congress, Castro broke the long-standing official silence on race: "The hypocritical societies that practice racial discrimination are afraid to talk about this, but revolutionary societies are not. . . . If you do not feel embarrassed to say white or blond, why do you feel embarrassed to say black, or mulatto, or mestizo? Why? Especially in this country, where we are children of mixed blood. This is our greatest source of pride, because it is not a bad mixture, it is an excellent mixture. Ask imperialism whether or not this is true."

Castro's public admission that racism and discrimination had "an effect" that was "still" part of Cuban society was congruent with the dominant discourse that these were remnants of the past, but the official recognition of their existence was certainly new. In his speech, Castro himself gave some clues as to why these realities were being acknowledged. He spoke of the "hundreds of thousands" of blacks and mulattoes who had graduated from technological schools and universities, "outstanding" people who had to be represented in the leadership of society. The revolution's own success had created groups and tensions that ultimately undermined the official silence on race. "The correction of historic injustice cannot be left to spontaneity," Castro asserted. "It is not enough to establish laws on equality and expect total equality. It has to be promoted in mass organizations, in party youth. . . . We cannot expect women, blacks, mixed-race people to be promoted spontaneously. . . . We need to straighten out what history has twisted." In response, the third congress of the party elected a Central Committee in which blacks and mulattoes represented 28 percent of the total, a twofold increase since 1980.[155]

History's "twists" were evident in other ways. Racial inequality had been greatly reduced in areas in which government performance had been successful, such as health care, education, and employment. But in areas of limited government success, racial inequality remained much wider. For instance, despite efforts to the contrary, a strong correlation between race, the regional distribution of the population, and the quality of the housing stock persisted through the 1980s. A traditional geography of race and poverty had not been dismantled, largely because of the government's failure to provide adequate housing to all the population.[156] No neighborhood was racially exclusive—this was true, for the most part, in prerevolutionary Cuba also—but in the most dilapidated areas of the big cities, the proportion of blacks and mulattoes was greater than that of whites.

In Havana, the municipalities of Habana Vieja and Centro Habana exemplify well the persistence of these residential patterns. Blacks and mulattoes represented 36 percent of the city's population in 1981, but they amounted to 44 and 47 percent, respectively, of the residents of the aforementioned municipalities. Whereas 13 percent of city residents lived in tenement houses, in Habana Vieja and Centro Habana the proportion of tenement dwellers was three to four times higher. Only 14 percent of the city's population lived in these municipalities, yet they contained 47 percent of the houses in the city with structural damages. The proportion of houses in which sanitary services were collectively used was also three to four times higher in Habana Vieja (36 percent) and Centro Habana (24 percent) than in Havana as a whole (9 percent). Households in these municipalities also ranked consistently lower than the provincial average in the availability of appliances.[157]

These residential areas, characterized by high densities of nonwhites and a physically deteriorated environment, were also perceived as sites of criminal activities. According to police authorities, the geography of crime remained tied to race and poverty.[158] Of the areas officially classified by the Policía Nacional Revolucionaria (National Revolutionary Police) to be *focos delictivos* (criminal centers) in Havana in 1987, 31 percent were located in the three municipalities with the highest proportions of blacks and mulattoes in the city: Habana Vieja, Centro Habana, and Marianao (which comprised only 20 percent of the city's total population). These *focos* included some shanty-towns, such as El Palo, Isla de Simba, Las Yaguas, and Isla del Polvo in Marianao, or tenement houses, such as Mercaderes 111 in Habana Vieja and Romeo y Julieta in Centro Habana. In many cases they were communities that had been rebuilt in the early years of the revolution to replace previous shantytowns.[159] Yet a study commissioned by the attorney general of Cuba in 1987 found that, in more than 70 percent of cases, the designation of an area as a *foco* did not reflect rates of crime higher than the city's average. It was police perceptions that turned these heavily black, low-income areas into *focos delictivos*. Crime rates were actually higher in neighborhoods considered "better" by police authorities.[160]

The persistence of racial inequality in the criminal system and the association between race and crime remained obvious in other ways. According to a Ministry of the Interior report, the yearly average number of criminal acts between 1976–80 and 1981–85 increased nationally by 11 percent. The growth in some of the provinces with a large black and mulatto population was significantly higher: 57 percent in Granma, 29 percent in Santiago de Cuba, and 50 percent in Guantánamo. In the same period, the yearly national average number of murders increased by 46 percent, from 216 in 1976–80 to 315 in 1981–85. The increase in the three provinces mentioned above amounted to 70 percent.[161]

Impressionistic reports also assert that blacks and mulattoes were over-represented in the prison population. According to an organization of political prisoners in the Combinado del Este prison, in the late 1980s, eight out of every ten prisoners were black. This, they concluded, destroyed "the myth proclaimed by the Cuban revolution that it has established racial equality." A U.N. commission that visited two Cuban prisons in 1988 reported that "a large number of prisoners were black," a reality that was acknowledged by the vice president of the Council of State who accompanied the visitors. The functionary explained that the number of blacks in prison was disproportionate to their population share because despite "the substantial achievements of the Revolution," the majority of blacks were still in the poorest strata of society. This, he claimed, "is by no means the expression of a policy of racial discrimination, but a left-over from the past."[162]

Whether these racial differences can be explained as "left-overs" is of course open to question, but it seems safe to state that, just as in prerevolutionary Cuba, blacks' delinquency rates remained higher than those of whites through the 1980s. A provision in the penal code that can be particularly telling about racialized perceptions of crime is that of *peligrosidad social* (social dangerousness). The history of this criminal provision is itself revealing. It appeared in the Cuban criminal code of 1936—under the influence of contemporaneous Italian criminal law—to provide for the repression of individuals with "a certain unhealthy, congenital or acquired predisposition" to commit crimes. The penal code of 1979 changed the legal definition of dangerousness, but it still allowed for the repression (including reeducation through internment) of individuals with "a special proclivity" to commit crimes. In other words, a person whose conduct was deemed to be "manifestly against the norms of socialist morality" could be deprived of freedom even without committing acts defined as crimes in the law. Included among these precriminal behaviors were habitual drunkenness, vagrancy, drug addiction, and other forms of "antisocial conduct."[163]

Such a broad definition of antisocial behavior created room for racialized notions of proper conduct to be enforced more freely than under the specific provisions of the penal code. Data to assess the racially differentiated impact of the "social dangerousness" provision are scant, but the results of a study commissioned by the attorney general of Cuba in 1987 are revealing. Out of a total of 643 cases of *peligrosidad* submitted to the courts in Havana City between May and December 1986, 345 subjects were black and 120 were mulatto. Nonwhites represented a staggering 78 percent of all the individuals considered to be socially dangerous. This proportion was more than double their share in the total population. Whereas there were 5,430 white adults living in the city for each white person facing charges of social dangerousness, the ratio among blacks (excluding mulattoes) was 1 in 713. Blacks (again, excluding mulattoes) were declared to be socially dangerous 7.6 times more often than whites and 3.4 times more often than mulattoes. Social dangerousness was essentially used to typify the conduct of blacks, particularly of young blacks. Fully 84 percent of the socially dangerous subjects were between the ages of sixteen and thirty.[164]

Despite its inadequacies, the information reviewed here provides a picture of the role of race in 1980s Cuban society that is complex and contradictory. The structural changes implemented by the revolutionary government did benefit large sectors of the black population, but such gains were concentrated in areas in which the revolution had been particularly successful. Prominent among these were education, health care, and employment. Progress was also evident in the area of leadership representation. Moreover, the acknowledgment in 1986 that the "heritage" of racism had not been totally eliminated under Cuba's socialism demonstrated that the state remained committed to the ideal of a racism-free society and pointed to the possibility of further advances.

Conversely, the government's failure to meet housing demands allowed for the survival and reproduction of traditional residential patterns that combined race with poverty and marginality. This also limited the impact of the revolution's educational program, high rates of schooling notwithstanding.[165] The chance that young blacks would grow up in these poorer areas remained significantly greater than that of whites. More important, perhaps, is that social perceptions about marginality and crime continued to be racially bounded, a clear indication that the ideal of a color-blind society had not been fulfilled by the 1980s. The revolution's gradual approach to the race question had been fairly successful in eliminating inequality, but mainly in those areas in which generous government spending had created unprecedented opportunities for mobility and minimized competition.

In summary, the achievement of racial equality in socialist Cuba was largely dependent on government performance. However, the capacity to perform is precisely what the government most lacked in the 1990s, when the collapse of the Soviet Union led to what the Cuban government called "the special period."

People don't change inside. A strong wind has to blow. . . . Even so, there are deep roots that remain and struggle to resurface.
—Manuel Granados, *Adire y el tiempo roto* (1967)

Tourist firms look like South African companies in times of Peter Botha. You go there and they are all white. And I wonder: Where am I, in Holland?
—Gustavo, Afro-Cuban singer (1994)

The Cuban economy stagnated in the late 1980s under the "rectification period" launched after the third congress of the Communist Party in 1986. This program called for a reversal of the market-oriented pragmatism that characterized the 1971–85 years, a recentralization in decision making, and the reintroduction of mass mobilizations and voluntary work as forms of labor organization. Then, following the collapse of the Soviet Union and Cuba's trading partners in Eastern Europe, the economy entered a depression. Between 1989 and 1993 the gross domestic product declined by as much as 40 percent. In 1986, Fidel Castro and the Communist Party had agreed that it was necessary to promote further racial equality in areas in which change had been too slow, but by the early 1990s, it was evident that such advances would have to be made with shrinking resources.[1]

The problem was not only that resources were not available to eliminate inequality in areas in which previous advances had been modest, however. Resources were lacking even to maintain previous levels of social welfare. Moreover, after 1993 the Cuban government was forced to introduce a number of market-oriented measures to foster productivity and stimulate Cuba's stagnant economy. These included the legalization of U.S. dollars, different forms of self-employment, foreign investment, and "free" agricultural markets. Although this program led to a modest recovery after 1995, Cuban authorities themselves recognized that it was not without a price. The new economic policies unavoidably provoked increasing inequality and resentment in a population that was used to living in a highly egalitarian social setting. As a high-ranking government official remarked in 1993, "This will create differences among people, greater than what we have now and greater than we are used to having since the revolution. . . . [T]he inequality or privilege that can be created are realities we must allow." "We are aware," the same official declared in 1995, "that some of the measures that we are applying are not in agreement with the aspirations of equality . . . which have guided our revolutionary conceptions."[2]

Although privileges and inequalities had to be allowed, Cuban authorities probably expected that the crisis would not have a racially specific impact. The relatively high levels of equality and effective racial integration that Cuban society had achieved by the 1980s should have guaranteed a color-blind impact of market forces. Individuals should have been affected according to their position in society and employment, regardless of race. Yet substantial evidence indicates that under the so-called special period, racial inequality and racially defined social tensions have increased substantially.

RE-CREATING INEQUALITIES

These economic changes have affected large sectors of the population, regardless of race, education, and other socially relevant variables. As Cubans in the island themselves recognize, the origins and nature of the crisis are not racially defined. "The issue isn't race," a black scientist asserted in 1993, referring to the crisis. A black female physician agreed: "Here there are not black and white differences. We are all living through the special period."[3] A similar perception was prevalent among two hundred respondents to a survey conducted in Havana and Santiago de Cuba in 1994. Although a higher percentage of blacks (22 percent) than whites (7 percent) considered the crisis to have racially differentiated effects, the dominant view was that it affected blacks and whites equally.[4]

Yet some of the reforms introduced by the government affect different social groups dissimilarly and have racially differentiated consequences. The most obvious example is that of the legalization of dollars, which has tended to fragment Cuban society along the lines of those who have access to dollars and those who do not. For the most part, Cubans receive hard currency from two main sources: family remittances and links to the Cuban dollar economy, represented mainly by tourism and the joint ventures and foreign companies that have opened businesses in the island. Workers in some productive sectors have also received dollar payments in the last few years, but these amounts are small compared to what can be obtained in tourism jobs or through family remittances (for instance, workers in the biomedical research sector have received $70 once or twice a year). Some artists, artisans, writers, and scholars also obtain dollars through their work.

Family remittances are probably the most important source of hard currency for ordinary Cubans. Economic officials in the island estimated that in 1997 annual remittances amounted to about $800 million. Given the racial composition of the Cuban diaspora, it is reasonable to assume that blacks' access to these funds is rather limited. According to the 1990 U.S. census, 83.5 percent of Cuban immigrants living in the United States identify themselves as white.[5] Assuming that dollar remittances are evenly distributed among white and nonwhite exiles and that they stay, roughly, within the same racial group of the sender, then about $680 million out of the $800 million that enter the island every year would end up in white hands. What this means is that per capita remittances to the island would amount to about $85 per year among whites. The comparable figure for nonwhites would be less than half this amount.

Given their limited participation in the remittances, blacks' opportunities to participate in the dollar economy are basically reduced to the competitive tourist sector, the most dynamic and lucrative in the Cuban economy. The desirability and attractiveness of tourist jobs are such that a large number of professionals have abandoned their occupations to seek employment in this sector. Consequently, competition for these jobs has escalated.

Tourism is an area in which blacks should have privileged access, for in the early 1980s they had comprised a significant proportion of the labor force employed in hotels, restaurants, and similar services. Of those employed in "services," 38 percent, according to the 1981 census, were black or mulatto—a percentage slightly above blacks and mulattoes' population share.[6] Yet there is widespread consensus that nonwhites are currently underrepresented in the tourist sector and face significant obstacles to both finding jobs and getting promotions. Of respondents to a 1994 survey conducted in Havana and Santiago, 40 percent agreed that blacks do not have the same employment opportunities as whites in this sector.[7] The testimony of the manager of a tourism corporation—a white female, forty-five years old—which was recorded by historians Rafael Duharte and Elsa Santos in a study about prejudice in Santiago de Cuba in 1994, is revealing:

Yes, it is true, there is a lot of racial prejudice in the tourist sector. I have worked there for about a year and I know that there is a lot of racism. In my corporation, for instance, out of five hundred workers there are only five blacks. . . . There is no explicit policy stating that one has to be white to work in tourism, but it is regulated that people must have a pleasant aspect, and blacks do not have it. . . . In the fanciest store in the city—La Maisson—all workers are white and out of fourteen models only one is mulatto. It is so rare to find black women in tourism that when there is one, people comment that she must be going to bed with an important boss. The few black men who work in tourism always perform manual labor, such as driving trucks or lifting merchandise in the warehouses. They never work directly with the tourists, or even in cleaning jobs; all of these workers are white. I know a black woman who told me her experience when she tried to find work in tourism. She has a degree in economics, is a specialist in computing, and speaks English, French, and German. She went to the interview very well dressed, even though she herself confessed that everything was borrowed. Well, it was very unpleasant because in the end she was not accepted, but they did not give her a specific reason. . . . The person who interviewed her did not know how to handle the situation because he could not tell her, "We do not accept you because you're black." . . . I think that her knowledge should have counted; after all, some white women working in tourism are also ugly, even if they are white. A few days ago a representative of a tourism corporation said publicly that he does not want blacks in his corporation because "*el negro* never finishes what he starts."[8]

Although getting a job in such a competitive sector is certainly hard for everyone, some "aesthetic" and cultural factors are frequently noted to justify the exclusion of blacks on the ground that they lack the physical and educational attributes needed to interact with tourists. These factors are usually incorporated in the concept of "good presence," a racialized construct that is based on the belief that blackness is ugly and that blacks—their formal schooling notwithstanding—lack proper manners, "cultural level," and education in their social relationships. A black female librarian from Santiago told the story of a friend who had been discriminated against while working in a tourist store: "I have a friend who finished, with very high grades, a course to work as a cashier in a tourist store. She is the darkest [*la más prieta*] of her group, has a good presence, is a young educated person, and . . . was denied the cashier position. All the cashiers are blond. After having a job designated for her in Havana, she has been transferred three times to different positions, so she is very upset and says that . . . if she denounces what has happened she might get fired."[9] "I do agree," a white tourist guide stated, "that there is an aesthetic criteria in the selection of tourism personnel that favors whites. In my company, out of sixty workers there are three blacks."[10]

Blacks are not only facing obstacles in attaining these jobs, however.

Given their representation in the sector through the 1980s, it must be inferred that at least some of these workers were displaced from their previous jobs and moved to less desirable occupations. Persistent rumors suggest that hotel managers have been giving preference to white workers and that "rationalization" programs (a term used to denote the downsizing of the labor force) have targeted blacks. In early 1994, for instance, the administration of the Habana Libre hotel fired dozens of workers to improve efficiency and quality of service. It was rumored that blacks had been singled out in the layoffs.[11] Thus, blacks have to cope not only with the racial prejudices of Cuban managers but also with those imported by foreign investors and their managerial personnel. But they are in a weak position to combat such prejudices, given that these investors are a key element in Cuban developmental strategy. The government is interested in providing them with as friendly an environment as possible, including the strict control of labor unions and their bargaining capacity. Although investors' access to labor is supposed to take place through the mediation of the government, they have, in Climent Guitar's words, "complete autonomy to select, hire, and, when necessary, fire the hotel's employees." In fact, a significant proportion of those who enter these jobs are hired directly by the managers and foreign investors, further limiting the state's capacity to guarantee a color-blind labor policy.[12]

Two additional factors tend to further increase the racially differentiated effects of the crisis and to fuel growing racial inequality under the special period. Because of blacks' relative concentration in areas that are overcrowded and that have a dilapidated housing stock, the opening of *paladares* (family-operated restaurants) is not an economic option for many black families. The other lucrative sector in which blacks are underrepresented is the private agricultural sector. Since the early decades of the century, the black peasantry was displaced from landownership, so Afro-Cuban rates of urbanization have been consistently higher than those of whites. According to an agricultural household survey conducted by a University of Havana research team in 1992, in a sample of rural communities across the island, whites represented 98 percent of private farmers and 95 percent of agricultural cooperative members.[13]

Most of these racially differentiated effects are clearly unintended and escape government control. Government policies to cope with the crisis have provoked social polarization— including a fast-growing income gap— but they are racial only in their consequences, not in their design.[14] The dollarization of the economy, for instance, has multiplied income differences according to race, but the government has no control over the distribution of the dollar remittances that members of the overwhelmingly white Cuban-American community send to their relatives in the island every year. Yet this does not explain blacks' underrepresentation in the tourist sector or in foreign corporations. As mentioned above, by the 1980s blacks had obtained levels of education comparable to those of whites and shared with them the benefits of expanded opportunities in white-collar employment. In fact, Afro-Cubans' slight overrepresentation in service jobs should have given them a competitive advantage in the expanding tourist economy. It must have been precisely because of these structural "advantages" that a racialized notion of suitability was constructed to define access to the most desirable sector of the Cuban economy. In other words, the underrepresentation of blacks in tourism cannot be explained as a function of structural conditions. It is, rather, a function of the pervasiveness of a racial ideology that portrays blacks as lazy, inefficient, dirty, ugly, and prone to criminal activities. In times of scarcity and growing competition for resources, this racist ideology has been used to justify the exclusion of Afro-Cubans from the benefits of the most attractive sector of Cuba's economy.

FROM PREJUDICE TO DISCRIMINATION

Despite its antidiscriminatory position and egalitarian social policies, the revolutionary government failed to create the color-blind society it envisioned in the early 1960s. The official silence on race contributed to the survival, reproduction, and even creation of racist ideologies and stereotypes in a society that, particularly in the 1960s, was still far from racially equal. What disappeared from public discourse found fertile breeding ground in private spaces, where race continued to influence social relations among friends, neighbors, coworkers, and family members. Supposedly harmless racist jokes reproduced traditional negative images of blacks. Racial ideologies were reproduced within the family and enforced in multigenerational households. The research of anthropologist Nadine Fernandez about the difficulties faced by interracial couples in Cuba convincingly demonstrates how traditional stereotypes have limited the choices of young couples.[15]

Still, the extent to which these racial ideologies permeate Cuban society and the intensity of racial prejudice in popular consciousness are somehow surprising. A survey conducted in Havana and Santiago in 1994 found that 85 percent of respondents agreed that prejudice is rampant in the island. A study conducted in three neighborhoods in Havana by the Centro de Antropología in 1995 found that 58 percent of whites considered blacks to be less intelligent, 69 percent believed that blacks did not have the same "values" and "decency" as whites, and 68 percent opposed interracial marriage.[16] To put these figures in perspective, in the United States in the early 1980s, the proportion of whites who declared that they were opposed to interracial marriage was actually lower (40 percent). Likewise, the proportion of whites who claimed to have no preferences concerning the racial composition of their neighborhood was lower in Havana (38 percent) than in the United States (42 percent).[17] Data compiled by Daniela Hernández in Santa Clara provide a less racist picture (for instance, 96 percent of white subjects declared that blacks and whites were equally intelligent and 65 percent opposed interracial marriage), but these results corroborate what we have known all along: that racial prejudice has not been obliterated in Cuba's postrevolutionary society.[18]

This ideology is frequently presented as a "left-over" or "remnant" from the past that is supposed to disappear in due time and whose impact is allegedly circumscribed to individuals and their most immediate family. Such representations are common in official discourse, journalistic pieces, and popular language. In 1986, for instance, the program of the PCC acknowledged that the "process of elimination" of "racial prejudices" had not been as "accelerated" as initially envisioned and that such beliefs affected "the psyche" of "a certain number of people." An article published in the popular magazine *Somos Jóvenes* in 1990 wondered if Cubans were "completely free" from the "ideological heritage" of racism. Another journal article asserted in 1991 that it would be a mistake to assume that the "vestiges" of centuries of racism and discrimination had totally disappeared under the revolution. After affirming that all Cubans had equal opportunities, the author admitted that "sometimes" such opportunities collided with "an inadequate family environment and other subjective factors."[19] To the limited extent to which they have researched these issues, most Cuban scholars share these notions.[20]

The characterization of racist ideologies as a "heritage" that affects only individuals serves several purposes. It obviously exonerates the revolutionary government and contemporary Cuban society from any responsibility in the production of racial stereotypes and prejudices. These ideas, the dominant discourse states, were created in the past—perhaps as long ago as the times of slavery. If they still affect some social relations (cross-racial marriages, for instance), it is because not enough time has lapsed. The implication, of course, is that they will eventually disappear even in the absence of systematic social and political action. Furthermore, although it is recognized that some action might be needed, the urgency of this problem is somehow diffused by its very nature: racist ideologies have a limited social incidence for they only affect private and family relations—areas over which the government has little control. As in Brazil, whites in Cuba blame anything (history, slavery) or anyone (foreign influence) but themselves for racism and discrimination.[21]

In fact, traditional ideas about race have found propitious conditions under the revolution to reproduce and perhaps even expand. For instance, the belief that Afro-Cubans continue to be primitive, lazy, and uncivilized regardless of educational achievement is frequently explained in terms of their low "cultural level"—the very notion used by the revolutionary government in the 1960s and 1970s to disparage Afro-Cuban religions and other forms of popular culture. The identification of social blackness with marginality, crime, and social dangerousness helped nurture the idea—very widespread in the Cuban population—that blacks are naturally predisposed to commit crimes. The very success of the revolution in creating equal opportunities in education, employment, and other social areas is now used to demonstrate blacks' inescapable inferiority. A forty-year-old white male physician interviewed by Duharte and Santos explained: "I have a theory that could be considered fascist, but to me blacks are inferior to whites in regard to their intelligence coefficient. In support of this theory I contend that in Cuba, where for thirty-five years blacks have had the same opportunities to study, there is no evidence that they can equal whites. How can one not think that genetic heredity affects them neurologically and makes them different, that is, inferior?" Another white male professional, fifty years old, concurred: "We took the chains off blacks and released them. . . . Now, thirty-five years later, they are worse off, less educated; instead of using the opportunity to improve themselves they continue to be *marginales* and criminals."[22]

By ignoring the advances made by Afro-Cubans on almost all fronts and avoiding a critical approach to the question of race, the state-sponsored media has also contributed to the persistence of some of these racist images. To begin with, black actors are conspicuously absent from television and are frequently relegated to stereotypical roles. "When I worked in television," a black female scriptwriter asserts, "I told the national director once that blacks' situation in TV was hopeless, because television does not reflect the reality of blacks. If the programs referred to the past, blacks appeared as maids or Santeros, but it was not like that, there was a class of black professionals. . . . The same today, with the black professionals created by the revolution. Blacks are always portrayed as *marginales*. . . . I would write a script with a black character and they would change it to a white." Her experience is by no means unique. When playwright and television writer Maité Vera attempted to place blacks in leading roles in some of her programs, she was criticized for promoting "reverse racism." "For many years," Vera explained in an interview with *Cuba Update* in 1991, "our creators . . . have acted as if they were blind to . . . this multicolor population which was not so mixed before."[23]

The same is true of movies. Afro-Cuban actors have assumed leading roles mainly in movies dealing with slavery, such as Sergio Giral's *El otro Francisco* (1974) and *Rancheador* (1977) or Tomás Gutiérrez Alea's critically acclaimed *La última cena* (1976). Gutiérrez Alea used an all-black cast in an earlier movie—*Cumbite* (1964)—but the story takes place in Haiti, not Cuba. Blacks and mulattoes figure prominently in Sara Gómez's *De cierta manera* (1974), but the movie deals with questions of marginality, *ñañiguismo*, and lack of social discipline. Conversely, questions of discrimination and prejudice have been dealt with only occasionally, such as in the conflicts surrounding the young interracial couple that heads the cast in Juan Carlos Tabío's *Plaff!* (1988).

Just as racial prejudices and stereotypes are conceptualized as a historic heritage, the absence of Afro-Cubans in the media has been explained in terms that avoid direct responsibility for the persistence of racist practices. The arguments range from the claim that these are "unconscious" choices, to technical problems, to issues of aesthetics. In the first scenario, it is claimed that directors and producers do not include blacks because they tend to interpret reality through their own eyes—although this begs the question of why there are so few Afro-Cuban directors to begin with. Others assert that technical problems such as "light absorption" prevent dark-skinned persons from fully participating in movies or television. Finally, some whites in television claim that scriptwriters do not include blacks because they subordinate their preferences to those of the public, who would not accept blacks in roles other than stereotypical ones. When asked about these explanations, however, a black television writer responded: "I do not think that there are technical problems with the illumination of blacks, or a shortage of black actors. I think that there are racial prejudices in the minds of the directors, who are those who make decisions."[24]

These strategies of silence and avoidance find an ideal complement in popular humor. Visitors to the island are often puzzled by the fact that, while most Cubans feel adamant about denying that they are racist, they tell racist jokes and use derogatory aphorisms quite freely. Supposedly harmless, these jokes constantly reproduce the image of blacks as foul-smelling, dirty, lazy, and criminally oriented. As with the case of government politics more generally—which for the most part are banned from public discussions—these jokes express social feelings and ambiguities that do not find outlets in more formal social settings. What is otherwise banned or taboo, popular humor expresses in socially acceptable ways.[25]

The ideology of racism was not created under the special period, but it acquired visibility and growing social acceptability during the 1990s. Indeed, despite the failure of government propaganda, which has claimed since the 1960s that all Cubans are equal and deserve full access to all sectors of national life, to eliminate racial prejudice, its impact should not be underestimated. This campaign created an ideal of egalitarianism that was shared by vast sectors of the population. Its complexities and contradictions notwithstanding, the postrevolutionary social environment was decidedly antidiscriminatory. Public discourse equated racism with a past of capitalism and class exploitation—a trait of the antinational, pro-American, white elite that had been displaced from power. To be racist was to be counterrevolutionary. Real revolutionaries were not supposed to be racist—at least not in public.

The association between revolution and racial fraternity/equality is a double-edged sword, however. It links the unacceptability of racism to the legitimacy, popularity, and support of the revolution—as represented by the government. But in the 1990s, the government lost legitimacy, support, and popularity, as well as economic resources. The erosion and deepening crisis of legitimacy of the current political system thus create new spaces for racist ideas and practices to operate and flourish. What used to be social and political anathema restricted, for the most part, to private spaces has become increasingly acceptable and public. These ideas, to use the expression of one of my collaborators in the island, are no longer confined to "people's heads." They result in concrete practices that are discriminatory in nature, as the example of the tourist sector shows. Diminishing government control over the hiring and promotion of personnel in the expanding private sector has created additional opportunities for these racially discriminatory practices to operate unhindered. Moreover, government enterprises are themselves reproducing these practices, at least in the most desirable sectors of the economy.

Not surprisingly, blacks have actively resisted displacement from the most lucrative economic activities through participation in the informal—and frequently illegal—economy, from prostitution to the black market, in order to access the indispensable hard currency. There is a widespread consensus that a large proportion of the so-called *jineteras* (prostitutes) are black or mulatto. This is not surprising. Blacks' participation in prostitution is explained not only by their disadvantageous position in the current situation but also by the tourists' own racialized notions of sexuality and pleasure. According to these notions, black sexuality is more appealing precisely because of the racial inferiority of black women and the unrestrained "primitiveness" of their sexual instincts, which makes them perfect sexual objects. Yet these very images, which associate blackness with unrestricted commercial sex, might construct as "black" women who would not be considered Afro-Cuban in other social relations. As Nadine Fernandez points out, the depiction of certain activities as "sex tourism" is mediated by notions of race, class, and gender. In fact, a 1996 study of the Cuban section of the Facultad Latino-americana de Ciencias Sociales claims that the majority of the *jineteras* are "mestizas" who would be considered white in other scenarios. Prostitution has become an element in the current definition of social blackness.[26]

In any case, Cuban tourist agencies are profiting from these images of tropical, unrestricted sexuality. They frequently advertise the island as a para-dise of sexual indulgence and promiscuity. "Cuba: the fire and passion of deepest Caribbean flavor," reads an advertisement for the Sol Palmeras Hotel in Varadero. "To be isolated is not to be lonely. This island deserves love," proclaims Cubatur. As Julia O'Connell Davidson, a sociologist at the University of Leicester who has conducted field research in the subject of sex tourism in the island, argues, for racially conscious white male tourists Cuba is paradise "in the sense that there, rather than being challenged, their racism is both implicitly and explicitly affirmed. They meet large numbers of Black women who really *are* sexually available, and, even more delightful for the white racist, people tell him that these Black women are sexually available because they are so 'caliente.'" The very existence of these dark-skinned *jineteras* is used to confirm the alleged moral deficiencies of black and mulatto women, further racializing the crisis that affects Cuban society.[27] As a visitor to the island noted in 1996, when elite women become involved with foreign-ers or artists and intellectuals aggressively seek to socialize with visitors in the hopes of getting grants or job offers, such activities do not convey social disapproval. "It's poor women of color who take the heat. And the fact that *jineteras* of color are now marrying Europeans at an unusually high rate makes them objects of envy in a country where many people are desperately looking for any means possible to emigrate."[28]

Other strategies of adaptation and resistance have become equally ra-cialized. For instance, the migration of people from the eastern provinces to Havana has been frequently interpreted as a black assault on the city. "These *negros orientales* [blacks from Oriente] are taking over," a white male profes-sional explained, referring to the "palestinos" (Palestinians), as these dark-skinned immigrants are known in Havana.[29] In fact, internal migrations are a function of the uneven development of the dollar economy in different regions of the country. The regional distribution of dollar stores can be used as a rough indicator of this phenomenon. Up to 1993, dollar stores were concentrated in tourist areas: it was illegal for Cuban nationals to access them. With the legalization of dollars, stores and services that operate in hard currency have been created in nontourism areas also, following the availability of dollars in the general population. In early 1996, 40 percent of these stores were located in Havana. Conversely, the eastern provinces of Granma, Santiago de Cuba, and Guantánamo had only 10 percent of the total.[30] Not surprisingly, the bulk of immigrants came from these disadvantaged areas—a process that mirrors migration flows in prerevolutionary Cuba. It is estimated that 50,000 people moved to Havana in 1996 alone and that in the first semester of 1997, 92,000 people tried to legalize their status in the city. The government reacted by banning all immigration to Havana in the spring of 1997, imposing fines on both the immigrants and their landlords, and requiring the immediate return of immigrants to their place of origin. An official in the Foreign Ministry's U.S. Department explained: "We had people living in subhuman conditions in Havana, without work. We went to these people and said, for example, 'Señor, you're from Guantánamo. You have left a house and job in Guantánamo. You need to continue your life in Guantánamo. You can't live in subhuman conditions here in a house built of trash.'" Whether massive deportations have taken place as a result of the law remains open to further verification. Officials claim that "no one has been put on a bus and sent back," but other sources assert that hundreds, even thousands, of people have been forced to leave the city and that the deportation order has been violently enforced.[31]

The presence of these Afro-Cuban immigrants in Havana was linked to an increase in violence and petty crimes—an increase recognized even by official sources—which also has been explained in racial terms. "Look, we all have problems," a white male professional states while talking about the immigrants, "but whereas I try to solve them through work or other legitimate ways, what blacks do is resort to robbery." According to a white female professional, this vision of blacks was shared even by government authorities: "A lot of stealing was going on and they were accused. Fidel offended them by saying something to the effect of 'Old Havana is full of Eastern delinquents.'"[32]

Thus the crisis of the 1990s resulted in growing social and racial tensions.

Based on racially charged notions such as "good presence" and "cultural level," Afro-Cubans have been denied opportunities in some of the most lucrative sectors of the economy, particularly in tourism. As is usually the case, the intensity of racist prejudices is related directly to the desirability of the sector in which the discrimination is taking place. Afro-Cubans' strategies of adaptation, which frequently involve participation in illegal activities such as prostitution, black-market activities, or plain robbery, are in turn used to demonstrate their alleged natural inferiority. Such inferiority is further evidenced, so the argument goes, by the fact that after four decades of socialism and antidiscrimination efforts, Afro-Cubans make up the bulk of the so-called criminals and *marginales*. Given these perceptions, it is not surprising that blacks are singled out as potential suspects by the police, as a journalist claims.[33] Indeed, racism is a self-fulfilling prophecy: it denies opportunities to a certain group due to their alleged insufficiencies and vices, and in turn, lack of opportunities creates the very insufficiencies and vices initially used to justify exclusion.

FIDEL'S "SECRET WEAPON"?

The revival of racism and racially discriminatory practices under the special period has led to growing resentment and resistance in the black population, which suddenly finds itself in a hostile environment without the political and organizational resources needed to fight against it. In this context, events such as the Malecón "riot" of August 5, 1994, begin to make sense. Spontaneous outbursts of rage and anger are typical of politically disorganized groups who perceive their situation as hopeless. Symptomatically, participants in this street protest stoned tourist stores while calling for "freedom" and political changes. As I have argued elsewhere, the surprise of the Cuban government concerning the racial composition of the rioters—according to an official report leaked to the press, blacks and mulattoes were in the majority—is more a function of its own prejudice and expectations than of any concrete sociological reality. The government expects young blacks to behave as passive "beneficiaries" of revolutionary gains, not as active protagonists for their own well-being and future.[34]

Perhaps because of these expectations, the reaction of the Cuban government to this process of racial polarization has been slow and inadequate. Given the lack of government action, it is even questionable whether in official circles there is awareness of the problem at all. The program of the fifth congress of the Communist Party contained an element of hope: while claiming that the revolution had "eliminated the institutional bases of racism" and worked to incorporate all Cubans, regardless of race, into the country's life, it called for maintaining "the just policy" of increasing black representation in positions of command.[35] Even if this policy had been fully implemented, its impact would have been limited: positions within the government bureaucracy are not, for the most part, as desirable as they were in the past, and they certainly do not provide material benefits comparable to those in the dollarized sector. Yet a visible increase of blacks in the power structure would have sent an unequivocal message to managers in the private sector (Cuban and foreign) that the government opposes racial exclusion and that racially discriminatory practices would not be tolerated. Instead, the 1997 congress of the party elected a Central Committee that was actually whiter (13 percent) than those elected in 1991 (16 percent) and 1986 (28 percent).[36] The proportion of blacks and mulattoes among the candidates to the National Assembly of Poder Popular in the 1997 elections (about 21 percent) was higher than their proportion in the PCC but still low considering their share in the total population. Furthermore, this figure does not indicate significant improvement over the racial composition of the candidates in the elections of 1993 (19 percent).[37] It was not until early 1999—when a delegation from the U.S.-based Trans-Africa Forum visited the island after the question of race was debated in a congress of the Union of Writers and Artists and raised the issue of discrimination with authorities and several conferences were devoted to discussing this theme—that government leaders took note and began to emphasize again the need to promote blacks and mulattoes to positions of leadership.[38]

Yet the belief that Afro-Cubans represent a source of support for the government—Castro's "secret weapon"—is quite widespread. It is argued, for instance, that blacks are terrified at the prospect of the return of the white Cuban-American exiles, but the limited available evidence does not support this assertion.[39] Even if we accept the notion that the Cuban-American community is racist, it does not follow that blacks in the island fully endorse this vision or, more to the point, that they are politically paralyzed as a result. Perceptions in Cuba about the Cuban-American community are in fact less negative than the government might wish. The government itself has contributed to this process by softening its rhetoric about the exiles, by presenting them as economic emigrants, and by welcoming their dollars. A survey conducted by CID-Gallup in Cuba in 1994 found that 75 percent of respondents referred to Cuban-Americans in affectionate terms. In a survey on racial attitudes conducted in Havana and Santiago the same year, only 27 percent of whites and 33 percent of blacks agreed with the proposition that the Miami exiles were racist. Only 39 percent of black respondents believed that, upon their return, the white exiles would bring racism back into the island, and this proposition was supported mainly by older (forty years old and over) blacks (51 percent). Only 18 percent of younger respondents agreed with the statement.[40]

It is also argued that Afro-Cubans benefited from the revolution to such a degree that they would perceive its end as a major social reversal. This argument is based on much more solid evidence. According to various surveys and studies conducted in the island between 1994 and 1995, most Cubans agree that the 1959 revolution represented a major step toward the improvement of race relations and the elimination of racism and inequality. The 1994 Havana/Santiago survey found that 76 percent of the population believed that blacks' situation improved along with that of the rest of the population; 62 percent of whites and 73 percent of blacks and mulattoes agreed that Afro-Cubans' situation would be worse without the revolution. The Gallup survey reported even more optimistic returns: 90 percent of the respondents affirmed that skin color did not significantly affect opportunities or the way people were treated; 94 percent believed that "persons of color have the same access as whites to a good education," and a similar proportion agreed that they have equal opportunities to get "a good job" (90 percent) or "a position in society" (91 percent). In the study conducted in Havana in 1995, 81 percent of whites, 75 percent of blacks, and 71 percent of mestizos agreed that substantial progress had been made toward the elimination of race discrimination. In Santa Clara, according to Hernández, 94 percent of whites and 83 percent of blacks and mulattoes agreed with a similar proposition.[41]

Whether this perception translates into an unconditional support for the government is, however, an altogether different question. In fact, one of the conclusions from the 1994 survey conducted in Havana and Santiago was that generational differences were more important in determining perceptions about the revolution, its achievements, its shortcomings, and the impact of the special period than racial ones. This result was coincident with the findings of the CID-Gallup survey, which found younger Cubans to be less satisfied with their personal life on the island. This is true for both blacks and whites. The current crisis has eroded some of the emblematic achievements of the Cuban revolution to such a degree that young blacks no longer perceive the restoration of capitalism as a major reversal. The incapacity of the Cuban government to maintain its previous levels of social assistance, the deterioration of social programs that persist, and the introduction of limited market reforms with their legacy of increasing inequality and social polarization are all factors that have contributed to undermining the legitimacy of the political order. It should be noted, also, that the participation of Afro-Cubans in the cross-racial dissident movement is far from negligible. Some of the best-known leaders of the opposition, such as Vladimiro Roca and Félix Bonne Carcassés, are black or mulatto.

The very racialization of the crisis might lead to racially defined forms of organization and resistance, further fueling racial tensions in the island. It is perhaps worth mentioning that although the vast majority of respondents to the 1994 survey on racial attitudes opposed the formation of an all-black organization, 16 percent of the younger black respondents considered this type of organization to be a necessity. Racial exclusion breeds racially defined social responses. Unless some of the existing institutions (such as the courts) or organizations (such as the unions or the PCC) effectively represent Afro-Cuban concerns and take on the struggle for racial equality, the creation of a racially defined organization might be increasingly perceived as the only way to counteract discrimination in the labor market and other areas of social life.

Initial steps toward the eventual emergence of racially defined forms of social and political mobilization have been taken already. Although most of the groups that emerged in the 1990s limited their activities to emphasizing the importance of black culture in any representation of *lo cubano*, others sought to effect social changes more generally.

This is the case of the Cofradía de la Negritud (Fraternity of Blackness), created in early 1999.[42] The Cofradía was created to make the Cuban state and society fully aware of the "growing racial inequality" that has taken place in the country and to demand the adoption of adequate measures to reverse this process. Its members have argued that the growing income gap experienced during the special period has a strong "racial content" and that the "historical disadvantage" of the black population "increased substantially . . . compared to the previous decade." The members of the Cofradía have also complained about the lack of official action and predicted that racial inequality might reach a "critical level" in the future.

The program of the Cofradía has clear precedents in previous organization efforts among Afro-Cubans. Following dominant interpretations of Cuban nationalism, its members claim to pursue the "noble aspirations" of those who fought to create a *patria* for all, without racial differences. Indeed, the opening statement of their program is a quote by José Martí. Moreover, the Cofradía claims to follow the teachings of Juan Gualberto Gómez, the great Afro-Cuban advocate of integration, and vows to promote the "fraternity" of all Cubans regardless of skin color. Like most Afro-Cuban associations since the creation of the republic, the Cofradía seeks to work within the parameters of a racially integrated nation and calls for the understanding, solidarity, and support of all Cubans.

Yet, as on previous occasions, the very creation of the Cofradía denotes the frustration of a sector of the black population with state institutions and their skepticism and ambivalence concerning cross-racial forms of mobilization. Building upon Afro-Cubans' longtime traditions of self-help, their program calls for blacks to promote their own initiatives, increase their self-esteem, "rescue and promote the values of the black family," and establish contacts with black organizations in the island and abroad. Their slogan is self-explanatory: "Let us help ourselves and we will be helped." These pronouncements bear a strong resemblance to the purposes of past organizations, such as Juan René Betancourt's ONRE, created at times when Afro-Cuban intellectuals were equally frustrated with the inability of government authorities to eliminate discrimination.

The Cofradía also follows long-established patterns when it declares to be a social organization that does not pursue political purposes. But just as the Afro-Cuban clubs became sites of political mobilization during the republic, the founding members of the Cofradía acknowledge that their project and actions might be easily interpreted as being of a political nature.

Whether this or any other racially defined organization will be allowed to operate peacefully is, at best, doubtful. The existence of black organizations defined in terms other than cultural or religious would openly call into the question the government's record in the sensitive area of race relations and would likely result in charges of "reverse racism." In addition, as the spectacular surge of Santería in the 1990s shows, there are actors in Cuban society who persist in ignoring, silencing, or demeaning the African roots of *cubanidad*. In a document issued in 1993, the annual conference of the Methodist Church complained that Afro-Cuban "cults" were proliferating under the disguise of "national culture" and that they were promoted in the state-owned media, whereas the Christian faith received no support. "Satanism has acquired the status of folklore," the document asserted. Likewise, the refusal of the Catholic hierarchy to allow a meeting between Pope John Paul II and Santeros exemplifies the Church's long-standing denial of the importance of the Afro-Cuban religions and their practitioners, which Cardinal Jaime Ortega reportedly called "pseudo-religions."[43]

The terms "cults" and "pseudo-religions," one could argue, are just restatements of "brujería," the demeaning term used to describe Afro-Cuban religions at the turn of the century. Although most Cubans surely agree that the nation ought to be for all, the concrete meanings of *cubanidad* remain open to contending interpretations.

Speaking before the grave of Antonio Maceo in 1951, President Carlos Prío elaborated on his vision of *cubanidad*. "Cuba," he declared, "has its own voice, which is neither white nor black. Just as Martí is white and Maceo is black, our culture is white with Spain and black with Africa." Almost fifty years later, in his welcoming remarks to Pope John Paul II, Fidel Castro characterized the nation in similar terms. "They [the Africans] made a remarkable contribution to the ethnic composition and the origins of our country's present population in which the cultures, the beliefs, and the blood of all participants . . . have been mixed."[1] It would be difficult to find two figures who are less alike in Cuban modern politics, yet these two presidents agreed on at least one thing: Cuba is a mixed nation in which there is little room for racial differences, much less discrimination.

This national discourse of *mestizaje* and racial fraternity has led to often contradictory social effects. It has contributed to minimizing or even ignoring, as some scholars contend, the specific claims for justice of the population of African descent. Yet it has also opened avenues for their participation in the nation—and not merely in a representational sense. Dominant interpretations of this ideology have delegitimized racially defined forms of political mobilization as racist and antinational, but they have also facilitated and encouraged other forms of social action. And whereas persistent racism and inequality have reinforced social identities associated with race, the reluctance of political regimes to acknowledge the social implications of race has contributed to the formation of competing identities from above. Particularly after 1959, the politics of distribution and social ascent contributed to the creation of new identities, such as "revolutionary" and "people."

This rhetoric of integration and equality notwithstanding, the fact is that perceptions of race continue to affect social relations in Cuba. But this is a reality that most political leaders in the island have chosen to ignore. Indeed, the very governments that have pledged allegiance to the ideal of a racially integrated nation, as they all have done since the early republic, also have implemented policies that resulted in the survival and reproduction of socially constructed perceptions of race. This was the case even during the postrevolutionary period, when the Cuban state used its considerable power and prestige to eliminate racism from the island. In some cases, such as the denigration and repression of African-based religions practiced by diverse political regimes throughout the twentieth century, the state has reinforced and legitimized the traditional association between blackness and backward-ness. This was certainly true in the early republic, when different administrations actively sought to de-Africanize Cuba. It remained true during the second republic, the "nationalization" of Afro-Cuban cultural practices not-withstanding, and persisted under the revolution. Particularly during the 1960s, the revolutionary authorities regarded Afro-Cuban religion as a cul-tural atavism incongruent with the construction of a modern, technically oriented socialist society—an obstacle of the past that had to be removed. For ordinary citizens, this has meant that whereas it is un-Cuban to be unequivocally racist, it might be patriotic to disparage Afro-Cubans and their culture.

More often than not, however, it is the failure of the government to act that has contributed the most to the continuing significance of race in Cuban society. The state's limited intervention in "private" social spaces has meant that racism has been allowed to operate virtually unhindered in this sphere. Thus, in the first republic, when government regulation of social and eco-nomic affairs was minimal, racial discrimination permeated vast sectors of the labor market and a large number of social activities. Racially exclusionary practices expanded even into spaces deemed to be public, such as parks, promenades, and upscale hotels.

Even after government intervention in the economy and society increased after the 1930s, private spaces remained bulwarks of discrimination and segregation. At least in this sense, the new Cuba that the so-called revolution of 1933 was supposed to create was not new at all. Indeed, during the second republic, many public establishments presented themselves as private clubs precisely to legally exclude black customers from their premises. Further-more, it was in those areas in which the state succeeded the most in opening opportunities for all, such as public education, that a growing private sector expanded to accommodate the demand for racial exclusivity by the white middle and upper classes. The Communists understood this reality well and mounted an assault on private schooling in 1941; their main goal was to regu-late the curriculum and admission policies of these institutions. They failed. The great Afro-Cuban intellectual and politician Juan Gualberto Gómez also attacked the public-private dichotomy when black spectators and athletes were barred from the Havana Yacht Club in 1930, but his voice went largely unheard.

It was not until the revolution of 1959 that systematic efforts were made to bridge the perceived gap between public and private. The revolutionary government not only destroyed the institutional bulwarks of racial segregation in the island, such as private schools, social clubs, and recreational facilities, but also sought to socialize younger generations in a new egalitarian and color-blind social ethic. With the expansion of the boarding-school system in the early 1970s, thousands of youths were removed from their families and sent to live in multiracial settings in which they learned the new socialist culture. Meanwhile, the nearly universal socialization of the means of production eliminated most private economic activities and facilitated the entry of Afro-Cubans into occupations and jobs that had been previously closed to them. The emigration of vast sectors of the middle and upper classes facilitated this process.

The impact of this radical program of social engineering should not be underestimated. By the late 1970s and early 1980s even unsympathetic observers acknowledged that significant progress had been made toward building a nation that was truly for all. Measurable inequality had decreased or almost disappeared in a number of areas; some behavioral patterns had begun to change. For instance, fragmentary but solid evidence suggests that cross-racial dating and marriage were on the rise. As sociologist Orlando Patterson puts it, in the final analysis "integration must mean intermarriage."[2] Perhaps the best indicator that race had lost social and political relevance in the island is the fact that by 1986 the leadership of the Communist Party felt comfortable enough to raise publicly the issue of black representation in the government.

The revolution's impact on traditional patterns of race is full of paradoxes, however. The youth were socialized in a new ethic through public education, yet the housing shortage meant that in practice they had to conform to the behavioral patterns sanctioned by their parents in multigenerational households. The government wiped out the pillars of institutional racism but in other ways remained prisoner of the very past it sought to erase. It advocated, as previous administrations had before 1959, dealing with race through a gradual and nonconfrontational approach. Furthermore, the authorities' adherence to a conservative interpretation of the national ideology of racial equality, according to which there was no racial problem in Cuba, foreclosed any public discussion of the issue. While some organizations were working in every community across the island to change ingrained cultural practices at the household level, there was no organized voice to prioritize issues of race. For instance, the Federation of Cuban Women worked with communities to eliminate the traditional subordination of women and denounced instances of gender discrimination, but no organization performed a comparable role concerning race discrimination. The Communist Party had become part of the government. The Afro-Cuban societies had disappeared. There was no competition among political parties for the black vote. And while previous governments had been equally uncomfortable acknowledging the continuing significance of race in Cuban society, no administration before 1959 had been able to silence the issue. Only the revolutionary government, controlling the media, was in the position to impose an effective ban on public discussions of race. Thus the ultimate irony is that the same government that did the most to eliminate racism also did the most to silence discussion about its persistence.

It is also a paradox that three decades after the revolutionary triumph of 1959, when the new generation born and raised in socialist Cuba came of age, the whole experiment began to unravel. As George M. Fredrickson states, the "salience of ethnic status and consciousness" depends on the power relationships between social groups perceived as racially or ethnically different. The access of a subordinate group to physical resources, political power, and cultural recognition can improve its social status and even "gradually erode" the ideological pillars of racism. But the process, as Fredrickson himself notes and the Cuban experience confirms, is, unfortunately, reversible.[3] The generation born around 1959 grew up in a relatively egalitarian environment and was socialized in what was for the most part a color-blind social ethic, but this generation was also raised under the belief that socialism, *patria*, and social justice were all the same thing. In other words, the social unacceptability of racism had been linked to the fortunes and legitimacy of a political regime that by the mid-1990s was lacking both. If instances of discrimination previously had been condemned due to their "counterrevolutionary" character, in the 1990s they became increasingly acceptable precisely because of the progressive discrediting of the regime. In the new social and economic environment, the cumulative social and cultural changes that had taken place since 1959 could not be realized fully. Instead, a new logic of market relations, private economic activities, and exclusive social and recreational spaces began to reappear in Cuban society. One of the most noted symbols of the old bourgeoisie, the elitist Havana Biltmore Yacht and Country Club, reopened in 1997. The first club nationalized by the revolutionary government and turned into a "workers circle" in 1960, it was also the first to reopen, catering as it had in the past to foreign investors and their partners in the island.

The gradual reintroduction of market relations in the 1990s did not have to result in growing social polarization along racial lines, however. That it did is indicative not just of how ingrained perceptions of race are in Cuba's social landscape or of the difficulties involved in uprooting racism from the social consciousness. It is also indicative of how politics and racially neutral government policies (such as the "dollarization" of the 1990s) can lead to growing racial inequality. The creation of a nation that is truly for all requires systematic and consistent state action over a long period of time. Since the early years of the republic they helped create, Afro-Cubans have known this, and they have struggled to be included in the polity. It is unlikely that they will forget this lesson any time soon. In fact, after four decades of massive social mobility, education, and radical integration, Afro-Cubans are better prepared than ever to assert their equal place in society. This might sound overtly optimistic. But it is not just optimism. Rather, it reflects the assertiveness of young Afro-Cubans who are confident about the future. As a black doctor stated in 1992, "We are too educated and politically aware to let go what we have gained. We are not going back."[4]

NOTES

ABBREVIATIONS

AHPC   Archivo Histórico Provincial, Cienfuegos
ANC   Archivo Nacional de Cuba, Havana
BBC   Braga Brothers Collection, Latin American Library, University of
        Florida, Gainesville, Florida
LC   Manuscript Division, Library of Congress, Washington, D.C.
USNA   United States National Archives, Washington, D.C.

INTRODUCTION

1. Sally Dinkel, "Exile's End," *Town & Country* (July 1993): 114.
2. Throughout this book, the terms "black" and "Afro-Cuban" are used interchangeably to denote people deemed to be nonwhite in Cuba. The label "Afro-Cuban" is frequently rejected by Cuban scholars on the ground that it does not reflect accurately the process of racial and cultural integration of the Cuban "people." In conversations with scholars in the island, some agree that the term could be used in the area of "culture" but remain opposed to a general use of the label. These objections are basically the same voiced in 1939 by intellectual Alberto Arredondo (*El negro en Cuba*, 107–15), who argued that the term was a tautology because "Cuban" was already "Afro." Despite these valid objections, I have chosen to use the label to emphasize the singular historical experience of those Cubans who are defined in terms of their African ancestry in a society that has never been color-blind. As long as the dream of a raceless nation remains a project, the term "Afro-Cuban" serves to emphasize the centrality of blackness in the formation of *cubanidad*.
3. Carneado, "La discriminación racial," 67. On this position, see Serviat, *El problema negro*; Cannon and Cole, *Free and Equal*; MINREX, *Cuba, Country Free of Segregation*; Juan Sánchez, "Un mal del pasado. Aspectos de la discriminación racial," *Bohemia* 65, no. 21 (May 1973): 100–106; Green, *Cuba*; and King, *How Cuba Uprooted Race Discrimination*. Please note that throughout all translations are mine unless otherwise noted.
4. Omar López Montenegro, "Castro Is a Calculating Racist—Here's Why," *Miami Herald*, July 30, 1993; Montaner, *Informe secreto*, 101. For additional examples of this critical position, see Moore, "Le peuple noir" and *Castro, the Blacks, and Africa*; Clytus, *Black Man in Red Cuba*; and Cleaver, *Soul on Ice*, 107–9.
5. Casal, "Race Relations in Contemporary Cuba" and *Revolution and Race*; Booth, "Cuba, Color and the Revolution"; Thomas, *Cuba*; Domínguez, *Cuba: Order and Revolution* and "Racial and Ethnic Relations"; Masferrer and Mesa-Lago, "The Gradual Integration of the Black in Cuba"; McGarrity, "Race, Culture, and Social Change in Contemporary Cuba"; and Fernandez, "The Color of Love."
6. Casal, "Race Relations in Contemporary Cuba," 11.
7. The idea, however, has some currency in (white) political discourse and popular imagery, at least among exiles. For examples, see José Miguel Gómez Barbera,

"¿Dónde está la discriminación?," *El Nuevo Herald*, August 22, 1993; Liz Balmaseda, "Cuban Miami Should Be Candid on Issue of Race," *Miami Herald*, August 11, 1993.

8. Thomas, *Cuba*, 1117–26; Masferrer and Mesa-Lago, "The Gradual Integration"; Castellanos and Castellanos, *Cultura Afrocubana*, 2:401–29.

9. Casal, *Revolution and Race*, 1–4; Casal, "Race Relations in Contemporary Cuba," 12–18.

10. Pérez-Stable, *The Cuban Revolution*, 5–6.

11. M. Martínez, "Carta topográfica," *Diario de la Marina*, May 19, 1929.

12. Good examples of this literature are the biographical works of Horrego Estuch: *Juan Gualberto Gómez, Martín Morúa Delgado*, and *Maceo, héroe y carácter*. See also Griñán Peralta, *Maceo, análisis caracterológico*; Pérez Landa and Rosell Pérez, *Vida pública de Martín Morúa Delgado*; Franco, *Antonio Maceo*; Savignón, *Tres ensayos*; and Córdova, *Flor Crombet*.

13. For examples, see Serra, *Para blancos y negros*; Arredondo, *El negro en Cuba*; Cuéllar Vizcaíno, *Unas cuantas verdades*; Pinto, *Un artículo* and *El Dr. Mañach y el problema negro*; and Grillo, *El problema del negro*. Of similar character are the works of Betancourt: *El negro, Prejuicio, ensayo polémico*, and *Doctrina negra*.

14. Excellent analyses of this process are Moore's *Nationalizing Blackness* and Kutzinski's *Sugar's Secrets*. For additional useful references, see Arce, *La raza cubana*, and Ramos, "Cubanidad y mestizaje."

15. Pérez-Stable, *The Cuban Revolution*, 5.

16. Lockwood, *Castro's Cuba*, 128. As early as 1962 the Second Declaration of Havana asserted that Cuba had eliminated racial discrimination ("II Declaración de la Habana," in *Documentos de la Revolución*, 68).

17. As a young black person interviewed by Sutherland in 1967 said, "[T]he problem is that there is a taboo on talking about racism, because officially it does not exist anymore." See Sutherland, *The Youngest Revolution*, 149. See also Landau, "A New Twist," 55.

18. Betancourt went into exile, where he was highly critical of government policies; see, for instance, his "Castro and the Cuban Negro." Carbonell remained in Cuba but was ostracized; see Moore, *Castro, the Blacks, and Africa*, 99.

19. For overviews of Cuban postrevolutionary historiography, see Zanetti Lecuona, "Realidades y urgencias de la historiografía," 119–28; Ibarra, "Historiografía y revolución," 5–16; Pérez, "In the Service of Revolution," 144–52.

20. For an example, see López Segrera, *Raíces históricas de la revolución cubana.*

21. Fernández Robaina, *El negro en Cuba*.

22. Scott, *Slave Emancipation*, "Relaciones de clase e ideologías raciales," and "The Lower Class of Whites"; Ferrer, "Social Aspects," "Esclavitud, ciudadanía," and "To Make a Free Nation."

23. Fermoselle, *Política y color en Cuba*; Orum, "The Politics of Color"; Helg, *Our Rightful Share*; Pérez, *Cuba between Empires, Cuba under the Platt Amendment*, and "Politics, Peasants, and People of Color"; see also Benjamin, *The United States and Cuba*.

24. Moore, *Nationalizing Blackness*; Kutzinski, *Sugars' Secrets*; Helg, "Race in Argentina

and Cuba"; Pruna and García González, *Darwinismo y sociedad en Cuba*; García González, "En torno a la antropología y el racismo"; Daniel, *Rumba*; Martínez, *Cuban Art*.

25. Fernández Robaina, *Hablen paleros y santeros*; Alvarado, "Relaciones raciales en Cuba"; Guanche, "Etnicidad y racialidad"; Menéndez Vázquez, "Un cake para Obatalá"; Duharte and Santos, *El fantasma de la esclavitud*.

26. Holt, "Marking," 7.

27. Helg, *Our Rightful Share*, 3; Castellanos and Castellanos, *Cultura Afrocubana*, 2:327.

28. Helg, *Our Rightful Share*; Fernández Robaina, *El negro en Cuba*. See also Rout, *The African Experience*, 301–8.

29. Castellanos and Castellanos, *Cultura Afrocubana*; Masferrer and Mesa-Lago, "The Gradual Integration of the Black in Cuba." For a discussion of the changes of racial inequality in different moments of the republic, see de la Fuente, "Race and Inequality in Cuba."

30. Carnoy, *Faded Dreams*, 41. Carnoy calls similar explanations in the United States "pervasive racism."

31. Helg, *Our Rightful Share*, 6–7, 16. For a brief discussion of the UNESCO studies and their influence, see Skidmore, "Race and Class in Brazil," 11–24, and "Bi-Racial U.S.A. vs. Multi-Racial Brazil," 373–86.

32. Hanchard, *Orpheus and Power*, 74; Burdick, "The Myth," 40. For additional examples, see Whitten, *Black Frontiersmen*, 199; Rout, *The African Experience*, 318; Hasenbalg, "Race and Socioeconomic Inequalities in Brazil," 25–41; and Valle Silva, "Updating the Cost of Not Being White in Brazil," 42–55.

33. Fernandes, *The Negro in Brazilian Society*; Van den Berghe, *Race and Racism*; Hasenbalg, *Discriminaçao e desigualdades raciais no Brasil*; Wood and Carvalho, *The Demography of Inequality in Brazil*; Lovell, "Race, Gender and Development in Brazil"; Andrews, "Racial Inequality in Brazil and the United States."

34. Wright, for instance, contends that Venezuelan elites "demonstrated an *amazing* propensity to assimilate miscegenated individuals" (my emphasis), given that, since independence, blacks and *pardos* (mixed-race people) "held powerful positions in regional and national elites" (*Café con Leche*, 7–9). In other instances, mobility of blacks is explained as a function of their cultural "whitening," that is, their distancing from "blackness"; see Wade, *Blackness and Race Mixture*, 5–6, and, for Cuba, Helg, *Our Rightful Share*, 121–22.

35. Andrews, *Blacks and Whites in São Paulo*, 4.

36. In particular, they have facilitated cross-racial mobilization in the organized labor movement throughout the region, although labor historiography has paid scant attention to these issues. For a recent summary, see Andrews, "Black Workers in the Export Years." For Cuba, see Scott, "Relaciones de clase e ideologías raciales," and de la Fuente, "Two Dangers."

37. Wilson, *The Declining Significance of Race*, 4–7.

38. For a critique of this position, see Reich, *Racial Inequality*, 76–108. Reich argues that racism benefits capitalists but that the reproduction of racial inequality does not depend on employers' conscious intentions.

39. Greenberg, *Race and State in Capitalist Development*, 26–28.

40. For an excellent discussion, see Pérez, *Cuba under the Platt Amendment*.

41. Pérez-Stable, *The Cuban Revolution*, 37 (emphasis in original).

42. Greenberg, *Race and State in Capitalist Development*, 26.

43. Love, "Political Participation in Brazil," 8–9; Andrews, *Blacks and Whites in São Paulo*, 43; Foner, *Reconstruction*, 604–9; Kousser, *The Shaping of Southern Politics*; Fredrickson, *Black Liberation*, 14; Arellano Moreno, *Breve historia de Venezuela*, 390–431; Lombardi, *Venezuela*, 217–20.

44. "El programa conservador," *La Lucha*, August 29, 1907.

45. Helg, *Our Rightful Share*, 6–7, correctly stresses that this emphasis on merits conveniently overlooked the historic subordination of Afro-Cubans.

46. My analysis of the middle class has benefited greatly from the recent literature on race, class, and gender in the Jim Crow South, particularly Brown and Kimball, "Mapping the Terrain of Black Richmond"; Gilmore, *Gender and Jim Crow*; and Shaw, *What a Woman Ought to Be*. For a study that deals with similar questions in Brazil, see Andrews, *Blacks and Whites*, 125–46.

47. Seidman, "Workers in Racially-Stratified Societies," 1–6; Andrews, "Black Workers in the Export Years," 7–29, and *Blacks and Whites*, 54–60; Chomski, *West Indian Workers*, 33–59.

48. Wright, *Café con Leche*, 97–111; Andrews, *Blacks and Whites*, 184–85. Concerning the Mitchell incident, see Chapter 4.

49. Domínguez, *Cuba: Order and Revolution*, 4.

50. Quoted by Pérez-Stable, *The Cuban Revolution*, 3.

51. Laurence Glasco, "A Cuban Surprise: Racism Is Almost Nonexistent in Cuba," *Pittsburgh Post-Gazette*, July 1, 1991.

52. Holt, "Marking," 7.

53. Fernandez, "The Color of Love"; Safa, *The Myth of the Male Breadwinner*, 132–36.

54. Ricardo E. González, "Race at Heart of Cuban Crisis," *Miami Times*, September 1, 1994.

CHAPTER ONE

1. The interaction between race, the abolition of slavery, and the formation of a nationalist coalition is studied in Scott, *Slave Emancipation*; Cepero Bonilla, *Azúcar y abolición*; and Ferrer, "Social Aspects of Cuban Nationalism," "To Make a Free Nation," and "Esclavitud, ciudadanía y los límites de la nacionalidad cubana." The role of race in the 1895 war is also studied in Helg, *Our Rightful Share*. For a discussion of the general goals of the war, see Pérez, *Cuba*, 156–78.

2. The U.S. intervention has been studied in great detail by Pérez, *Cuba between Empires* and *Cuba under the Platt Amendment*, 3–87.

3. Wood to Platt, Havana, January 12, 1901, LC, Leonard Wood Papers, 30 (emphasis in original).

4. Scott, *Slave Emancipation*, 45–62; Ferrer, "Social Aspects of Cuban Nationalism," 37–56.

5. For discussions of Martí's ideas on race, see Ortiz, "Martí and the Race Problem," 253–76; Stabb, "Martí and the Racists," 434–39; Armas, "Jose Martí: La verdadera y única abolición," 333–51; Castellanos and Castellanos, *Cultura Afrocubana*,

2:274–86; and Helg, *Our Rightful Share*, 45. A useful compilation of Martí's writings about race is Martí, *La cuestión racial*.

6. Martí, "My Race," in *Our America*, 313.
7. Ibid. (my emphasis).
8. Martí, "Our America," in *Our America*, 84–94.
9. Martí, "The Dish of Lentils," in *Our America*, 315–16; Ferrer, "To Make a Free Nation," 225–41.
10. Martí, "My Race" and "Basta," in *Our America*, 308, 312.
11. My discussion here follows Ferrer's careful analysis of the formation of a nationalist ideology during the period of insurgency, from the 1860s to the 1890s. See her "To Make a Free Nation."
12. Partido Moderado, *Programa oficial*, reprinted as "La candidatura presidencial del Partido Moderado," in *La Discusión*, September 10, 1905.
13. "El General Menocal y 'Labor Nueva,'" *Labor Nueva* 1, no. 1 (February 20, 1916): 1.
14. "La nota del día," *La Discusión*, September 23, 1908.
15. Ibid.
16. "Lo que era la esclavitud en Cuba," *La Discusión*, November 13, 1908; "Unidad de razas," *La Lucha*, September 3, 1907; "Palabras del doctor Varona," *Labor Nueva* 1, no. 3 (March 5, 1916): 3. For a statement that is virtually identical to that of Varona, see Mañach, "El problema negro," in *Pasado Vigente*, 123–24. Mañach's essay was written in 1931.
17. Quoted in Chargé d'Affaires to the Secretary of State, Havana, February 23, 1910, USNA, RG 59/837.00/1284; "Lo que era la esclavitud."
18. See the discussion of this interpretation in Helg, *Our Rightful Share*, 105–6.
19. Orestes Ferrara, "Deberes y derechos de la raza de color," *Labor Nueva* 1, no. 1 (February 20, 1916): 5–6.
20. Mañach, "El problema negro," 129–32; A. Indalecio Cosío, "La opinión de un imparcial," *La Prensa*, August 26, 1915; René Lufríu, "Personalidad," *Aurora*, April 30, 1914. Mañach maintained these views during his prolific intellectual life. See his "Avispas por la ventana," *Bohemia*, March 17, 1949, 55, 96, and the critique of black author Angel C. Pinto, *El Dr. Mañach y el problema negro*.
21. M. Martínez, "Carta topográfica," *Diario de la Marina*, May 19, 1929; Mañach, "Glosas. El problema negro y la palabra oscura," *Diario de la Marina*, May 12, 1929.
22. José Manuel Poveda, "Voces nuevas," *La Prensa*, September 5, 1915.
23. Cosío, "La opinión de un imparcial."
24. See the letter of M. F. Sánchez to Tristán [Ramón Vasconcelos] and his comments in "Un nuevo lío," *La Prensa*, December 12, 1915.
25. Tristán, "Opinión de un cenfoguense," *La Prensa*, August 21, 1915; Julio M. González Torres, "Sociedades que nos honran. Luz de Oriente," *Adelante* 1, no. 2 (July 1935): 19–20; Juan Jiménez Pastrana, "Indagaciones. Las Sociedades Cubanas y el problema negro," *Nuevos Rumbos* 2, no. 5 (November 1947): 33; David Grillo, *El problema del negro cubano*, 144; Betancourt, *El negro*, 85–86.
26. For an example, see the discussion by Cuban anthropologists about ocular diseases in the island, studied by Naranjo Orovio and García González, *Racismo e inmigración en Cuba*, 186–93.

27. Castellanos, "Los menores delincuentes," 81–111, and *La delincuencia femenina en Cuba*, 12–13.

28. Mariblanca Sabas Alomá, "Sobre problemas raciales: Lección a un lector que no sabe leer," in Pinto, *Un artículo y tres cartas*, 19–23.

29. Gustavo Urrutia, "Armonías. Abolido el racismo en el registro civil" and "Armonías. Dígase hombre," *Diario de la Marina*, June 4 and 21, 1950; Aracelio Azcuy, "Reparación de una injusticia," *Atenas* 2, no. 7 (November 1951): 10.

30. Lino D'Ou, "Restituir no es ceder," *Labor Nueva* 1, no. 4 (March 12, 1916): 6. For a later example of the same discourse, see Carlos Fernández Cabrera, "Elogio del negro cubano," *Nuevos Rumbos* 1, no. 8 (August 1946): 6.

31. For the use of Martí in the struggle for racial equality, particularly by the Partido Independiente de Color, see Fernández Robaina, *El negro en Cuba*, 104–9.

32. Serra, *Carta abierta*, 3–4. See also "Charla semanal," *Labor Nueva* 1, no. 10 (April 23, 1916): 3.

33. Juan de Dios Cepeda, "Manifiesto impreso Partido Independiente de Color dirigido a todos los hombres de color," Placetas, October 20, 1909, ANC, Fondo Especial, leg. fuera, no. 9-22; Juan de Dios Duany, "Manifiesto impreso 'Mal presagio. El microbio moral en nuestra sociedad,'" ca. 1910, ANC, Fondo Especial, leg. 4, no. 128.

34. Inocencia Alvarez, "Lo que somos," *Diario de la Marina*, February 10, 1929. For additional examples, see Catalina Pozo y Gato, "Al margen de ciertas campañitas," *Alma Mater*, October 24, 1933. This discourse was voiced also by the black societies after the 1930s; see Gustavo Urrutia, "Opresores y oprimidos," *Adelante* 4 (September 1935): 6; "Reiteran su firme posición democrática las Sociedades Negras," *Noticias de Hoy*, October 39, 1943; and "Editorial," *Atenas* 3, no. 10 (October 1954): 5.

35. The question of the participation of Afro-Cubans in the Liberation Army remains elusive, especially since reports of their proportion varied according to the racial ideology of the observer. Different authors have advanced estimates that coincide roughly. Pérez sets black participation at 40 percent among officers in his *Cuba between Empires*, 106; Ibarra, *Cuba, 1898–1921*, 187, mentions 60 percent, including soldiers and officers; Fermoselle, *Política y color en Cuba*, 26, asserts that 40 percent of generals and colonels in the army were black. Using new methodologies and sources, Michael Zeuske is currently attempting to determine the participation of ex-slaves and blacks in the Liberation Army in the region of Cienfuegos. The social composition of the Cienfuegos brigade is studied also by Orlando García Martínez, who has found that 18 percent of its senior officers were black or mulatto. See Zeuske, "La participación de los ex-esclavos en el Ejército Libertador: El ejemplo de la región de Cruces y Lajas," and García Martínez, "La Brigada de Cienfuegos: Un análisis social de su formación," papers presented at "Taller de Historia," Cienfuegos, March 5–7, 1998.

36. Barnet, *Biography of a Runaway Slave*, 194.

37. A Commission of the PIC to William Taft, Havana, November 22, 1912, USNA, RG 59/837/960. See also Helg, *Our Rightful Share*, 153.

38. Ricardo Batrell Oviedo and Alejandro Neninger, "Manifiesto al pueblo de Cuba y

a la raza de color," *La Discusión*, August 11, 1907; Jorge Castellanos, "La llaga racial al desnudo," *Noticias de Hoy*, September 24, 1952. Examples of this discourse are countless; for a sample, see Víctor Muñoz, "¡Si fuésemos francos!," *Labor Nueva* 1, no. 5 (March 19, 1916): 4–5; Julián González, "Blancos y negros," *Labor Nueva* 1, no. 11 (April 30, 1916): 6–7; and Nicolás Guillén, "El camino de Harlem," *Diario de la Marina*, April 21, 1929.

39. For an introduction to black journalism, see Trelles, "Bibliografía de autores de la raza de color"; Deschamps Chapeaux, *El negro en el periodismo cubano*; and Fernández Robaina, *Bibliografía de temas afrocubanos*. Black issues received attention also in the mainstream press, and some of the most important papers in the country devoted regular columns to the "colored people." In 1915–16 *La Prensa* published "Palpitaciones de la raza de color," a column produced by Ramón Vasconcelos under the pseudonym of Tristán; *Diario de la Marina* published Gustavo E. Urrutia's column "Armonías" (1928–36) and his very influential Sunday page, "Ideales de una raza" (1928–30). Black "social" life—that is, the activities of black clubs and the black middle class—was covered in social columns, such as the "Notas Sociales" that Raúl Suárez Mendoza wrote for *Ahora* (1933) and Pedro Portuondo Calás's "Motivos Sociales" published by *El País* during the late 1930s and 1940s. In the 1950s, when the chronicles of black societies were disappearing from the press, *El Tiempo* published Felipe Elosegui's "1000 noticias en sepia" and Manuel Cuéllar Vizcaíno's "Aire libre."

40. See Chapter 3.

41. Nicolás Guillén, "La conquista del blanco" and "El blanco: He ahí el problema," *Diario de la Marina*, May 5, June 9, 1929. See also the comments to the first article by Mañach, "Glosas: El problema negro," and Pinto, "Ladrándole a la luna," *Nuevos Rumbos* 1, no. 4 (March 1946): 9.

42. Masdeu, *La raza triste*, 28–29. Masdeu was a white author. The novel is dated 1920, but in the introduction Masdeu claims it was written "when he was young," while working in the sugarcane fields. In the second edition of the novel in 1942, he states that it had been written "about thirty years" before.

43. They were Mayor Generals Jesús Rabí, chief of the Second Army (Oriente), and Pedro Díaz, chief of the Sixth Army (Pinar del Río). For biographical sketches on these and other Afro-Cuban officers, see "Número-album consagrado a la revolución cubana," *El Fígaro* 15 (February 1899).

44. Atkins, *Sixty Years in Cuba*, 297, 306; Barnet, *Biography of a Runaway Slave*, 190.

45. Barnet, *Biography of a Runaway Slave*, 197.

46. Barnada, Pedro Varela, and others to Leonard Wood, Santiago de Cuba, January 11, 1900, LC, Leonard Wood Papers, 28.

47. "La prensa," *Diario de la Marina*, September 1, 1899, morning ed.; "El general Banderas," *La Lucha*, September 6, 1899.

48. "Los soldados de Maceo," *La Lucha*, May 22, 1902; "La República conmemora el 10 de Octubre," *La Discusión*, October 11, 1905.

49. For a few examples, see "Asuntos varios. Pensión," *Diario de la Marina*, May 15, 1900, evening ed.; "Prominent People," *Diario de la Marina*, January 31, 1900, evening ed.; Cuba, Cámara de Representantes, *Diario de Sesiones* 42, no. 10 (May 28,

1924). In this session, the House of Representatives provided a pension to the family of Pedro Díaz and a donation to the sister of Guillermo Moncada.

50. "El General Jesús Rabí," *La Lucha*, September 5, 1915; "Se teme que la enfermedad del General Rabí tenga un fatal desenlace," *La Lucha*, September 21, 1915; "¡Ha muerto el General Jesús Rabí!," *La Prensa*, December 5, 1915; "Rafael Serra Montalvo" and "Entierro de un representante," *La Lucha*, October 25 and 26, 1909; "Crespón de luto," "Los funerales del señor Morúa," and "El sepelio del señor Morúa," *La Lucha*, April 29 and 30, May 1, 1910.

51. Hevia Lanier, *El Directorio Central*, 24. About the Directorio, see also Horrego Estuch, *Juan Gualberto Gómez*, 11; Helg, *Our Rightful Share*, 35–43; and Montejo Arrechea, *Sociedades de Instrucción*, 80–110.

52. Lino D'Ou, "Rasgos i perfiles. Manuel Delgado," *Diario de la Marina*, January 6, 1929; "Ese negro no: Ese General," *El Político*, September 7, 1930.

53. Juan Jérez Villarreal, "Lino Dóu, el hijo de Bárbara," *Diario de la Marina*, February 24, 1929; Lino D'Ou, "Sobre dos puntos" and "El dilema," *La Prensa*, August 19 and 25, 1915; Longan to the Chief of Military Information Division, Guantánamo, July 1907, USNA, RG 395/1008/53, item 71; Gerardo Castellanos, "Murió Lino D'Ou," *Estudios Afrocubanos* 4, nos. 1–4 (1940): 39–46.

54. Lino D'Ou, "Rasgos i Perfiles. Pancho Antúnez, Laudelino García y Lino D'Ou" and "Rasgos i Perfiles. Juan Travieso," *Diario de la Marina*, February 3, April 7, 1929; Nicolás Guillén, "Ramón Canals," *Diario de la Marina*, November 3, 1929.

55. "Maceo," *La Lucha*, December 7, 1906; "El pueblo de Cuba," *La Prensa*, May 20, 1916, about the inauguration, by the president, of a bronze statue of Maceo; "La conmemoración del 7 de diciembre," *La Lucha*, December 8, 1925. For examples of official acts in Congress, see "Oración fúnebre," *Diario de la Marina*, December 8, 1928; "Sesión solemne en honor del Mayor General Antonio Maceo," in Cuba, Cámara de Representantes, *Diario de Sesiones* 53, no. 12 (December 9, 1929). The law declaring December 7 a national holiday is reproduced in "Héroes y maestros," *Boletín Oficial del "Club Atenas"* 1, no. 11 (November 20, 1930): 5.

56. "Los restos de Maceo y Panchito Gómez," *La Lucha*, September 19, 1899; Helg, *Our Rightful Share*, 105.

57. Nilo Zuasnábar, "Lo que queremos," *Fragua de la Libertad* 1, no. 7 (July 4, 1942): 1, 11.

58. But even a writer as racist as Mustelier had to recognize Maceo's virtues as a patriot, although he claimed that the general was not a brilliant military chief in his *La extinción del negro*, 26–29. Concerning the minimization of racism in Maceo's life, see Antonio Iraizoz, "Reparos a un libro sobre Maceo," *Cúspide* 2, no. 12 (December 15, 1938): 2–3.

59. Lorenzo Díaz Valencia, "La sonrisa del extinto," *Aurora* 1, no. 9 (December 1, 1914): 3; Lino D'Ou, "Maceo," *Labor Nueva* 1, no. 15 (May 21–28, 1916): 8–9. For an example of the elites' interpretation of Maceo's legacy, see Enrique José Varona, "Maceo," *Labor Nueva* 1, no. 15 (May 21–28, 1916): 6.

60. George Duroy, "Lo que me dijo la estatua," *Labor Nueva* 1, no. 15 (May 21–28, 1916): 16–17.

61. José Enrique Morúa, "Antonio Maceo y la revolución cubana," *Labor Nueva* 1, no. 15 (May 21–28, 1916): 13–14.

62. "Memorandum re: Racial Problem of Cuba," enclosed in Sumner Welles to the Secretary of State, Havana, September 29, 1933, USNA, RG 84/800/143.

63. Barnet, *Biography of a Runaway Slave*, 194; Pepper, *To-Morrow in Cuba*, 141.

64. For a good critical study of the dominant ideas of race in the North Atlantic world, see Tucker, *Racial Research*.

65. About the impact of the U.S. intervention on race relations in the island, see Duke, "The Idea of Race," 87–109; Helg, *Our Rightful Share*, 91–98; Orum, "The Politics of Color," 47–64; and Epstein, "Social Structure," 192–203. See also Pérez, *Cuba between Empires*.

66. Duke, "The Idea of Race," 87; "The Questions of the Day," *La Lucha*, September 7, 1899; Pepper, *To-Morrow in Cuba*, 315; Orum, "The Politics of Color," 48–49.

67. Wood to McKinley, Havana, April 12, 1900, LC, Leonard Wood Papers, 28.

68. John A. Gardner to the Secretary of State, Havana, October 18, 1910, USNA, RG 59/837.4061; Bryce, "The Relations of the Advanced and the Backward Races," 18–19; Paul Beck, "Office Memoranda," Havana, April 15, 1920, USNA, RG 165/2056-196.

69. Smith, "The Color Line," 49, 122–23.

70. Quoted by Tucker, *Racial Research*, 65.

71. John A. Gardner, "Havana Is World's Wickedest City," *Cleveland Press*, January 27, 1911.

72. "La nota del día," *Diario de la Marina*, January 18, 1901, evening ed. For similar perceptions, see Paul Beck to the Director of Military Intelligence, Havana, April 14, 1919, USNA, RG 59/837.504/147; Rabbi Jacob Goldstein, "Our 'Little Sister' Cuba," 1921, USNA, RG 59/837.00 P81/13; and Lindsay and Winter, *Cuba and Her People*, 85.

73. Henry Norweb to the Secretary of State, Havana, January 14, 1946, USNA, RG 59/837.00/1-1446. Statements like this were not exceptional, despite the decline of scientific racism after the 1930s. For additional examples, see Thompson to Freeman Matthews, Matanzas, August 7, 1935, USNA, RG 84/800, in which he elaborates on the features of the "Latin mind," and "The Ambassador's Memo," Havana, August 15, 1939, USNA, RG 84/800, on Cubans' "lack of honor and integrity."

74. Quoted by Dolz y Arango, "Discurso inaugural," 163.

75. "Our 'Failures' with the Inferior Races," *La Lucha*, September 7, 1899, English ed.

76. Barringer, "The American Negro," 446; "Los miguelistas contra el tío Sam," *La Discusión*, August 27, 1907, quoting the *Havana Daily Telegraph*.

77. Pepper, *To-Morrow in Cuba*, 150–53; Lindsay and Winter, *Cuba and Her People*, 104–5, 135; Bullard, "The Cuban Negro," 623–30; Major Albert Gallatin to the Director of Military Intelligence, Havana, February 3, 1919, USNA, RG 165/2056-133.

78. About the French influence in Latin American and Cuban medicine and eugenics, see Stepan, *"The Hour of Eugenics,"* 72–79.

79. Mestre, "Las leyes de la herencia," 163–93.

80. Beers had founded the National Committee for Mental Hygiene, which advocated the eugenic segregation and sterilization of the mentally defective. See Larson, *Sex, Race, and Science*, 59–62. About the Cuban league, see Mestre, "La higiene mental," 203–18.

81. Francisco M. Fernández, "La esterilización de los criminales reincidentes para evitar el aumento de la criminalidad," Cuba, Sanidad y Beneficiencia, *Boletín Oficial* 3 (January–June 1910): 412–16; "Revista de revistas: La esterilización de los imbéciles," *Revista Bimestre Cubana* 22 (1927): 625–27; Simeón Poveda Ferrer, "Mi criterio," *La Prensa*, September 28, 1915.

82. Stepan, *"The Hour of Eugenics,"* 174–82.

83. *Transactions of the First Pan American Conference*, 208, 219–21.

84. Montalvo, "El problema de la inmigración en Cuba," 524–38. See also Naranjo and García González, *Racismo e inmigración*, 152–64; and Pruna and García González, *Darwinismo y sociedad*, 131–38.

85. Figueras, *Cuba y su evolución colonial*, 236–38; S. Giraudy y Betancourt, "Lo que debe ser nuestra república," *La Discusión*, September 22, 1903; Orestes Ferrara, "La lucha presidencial en Cuba," *La Reforma Social* 17, no. 4 (August 1920): 346–50. Figueras's book has been analyzed by Helg, "Race in Argentina and Cuba," 48–52.

86. "La nota del día," *Diario de la Marina*, January 18, 1901, evening ed.

87. Brief summary of letter from Cesar Madrid to Mr. Caffery, Havana, 1934, USNA, RG 84/800/535; "La prensa," *Diario de la Marina*, October 17, 1901, morning ed.

88. Wisan, *The Cuban Crisis*, 452–53; "La raza de color," *Diario de la Marina*, April 12, 1901, morning ed.

89. "El censo," *Diario de la Marina*, April 22, 1900, morning ed.

90. About this obsession, see Tucker, *Racial Research*, 33–36.

91. A representative of President McKinley estimated in 1899, for instance, that half of the black population had been "destroyed" during the struggle. See Porter, *Industrial Cuba*, 104–5.

92. U.S. War Department, *Report on the Census*, 97; for similar opinions, see Pepper, *To-Morrow in Cuba*, 147–49, and Figueras, *Cuba y su evolución colonial*, 238. For a counterview, see Lindsay and Winter, *Cuba and Her People*, 106–7.

93. For an example of scientific explanations of blacks' higher mortality as a consequence of racial inferiority, see Smith, "The Color Line," 223–27.

94. "La raza de color, lenta, pero segura, va desapareciendo del territorio nacional," *La Lucha*, September 8, 1915; Heape, "The Proportion of the Sexes," 305–11. Another analysis dealing with differential growth rates according to race is the remarkable study by Juan Guiteras, "Estudios demográficos."

95. Mustelier, *La extinción del negro*, 35–39.

96. The effects of immigration on the labor market are explored below in Chapter 3.

97. *El Popular*, quoted in "La prensa," *Diario de la Marina*, October 3, 1900, morning ed.

98. For examples of how the discourse of tropical decadence was echoed in the Cuban press, see "The Questions of the Day," *La Lucha*, September 29 and 30, 1899, English ed. For an example of the Cuban scientists' work to the contrary, see Guiteras, "Estudios demográficos." For similar works in Latin America, see Stepan, *"The Hour of Eugenics,"* 89–90.

99. Ley de Inmigración y Colonización, July 11, 1906, in Pichardo, *Documentos*, 4:273–76.

100. Jackson to the Secretary of State, Havana, August 14 and 26, 1910, USNA, RG 59/837.55/21155/9 and 10.

101. Unknown to William W. Craib, n.p., September 26, 1913, and Luis V. Abad, Secretary of Fomento de la Inmigración to the Cuba Company, Havana, August 27, 1913, Cuba Company Papers, ser. 1, box 9, 142, University of Maryland, McKeldin Library, College Park, Maryland.

102. Zanetti and García, *United Fruit Company*, 208–10; unknown to Craib, n.p., September 26, 1913, Cuba Company Papers, ser. 1, box 9, 142; Hugh Gibson to the Secretary of State, Havana, September 18, 1912, USNA, RG 59/837.55/19.

103. Merrill Griffith to the Secretary of State, Santiago de Cuba, May 31, 1916, USNA, RG 59/837.55/33; "El problema de la inmigración haitiana y jamaiquina," *La Lucha*, February 6, 1917; "El problema de inmigración clandestina," Cuba, Sanidad y Beneficiencia, *Boletín Oficial* 17 (January–June 1917): 140–41; H. D. Clum, "Sanitary Conditions," Santiago de Cuba, June 7, 1923, USNA, RG 59/837.124/59.

104. H. J. Dickinson to Enoch Crowder, Antilla, June 23, 1923, USNA, RG 59/837.124/58; Alfredo Zayas, "Mensaje al Congreso," Cuba, *Gaceta Oficial*, November 8, 1921, 8847–48; Juan Guiteras to the Secretary of Sanitation and Welfare, Havana, November 7, 1919, USNA, RG 59/837.124/19; "3,000 Cases of Malaria Reported in Santiago," *Havana Evening News*, December 2, 1926.

105. Zayas, "Mensaje," 8849–50; *Transactions of the First Pan American Conference*, 205–9, 323; Fernando Méndez Capote, "Discurso de apertura del IV Congreso Médico Nacional," Cuba, Sanidad y Beneficiencia, *Boletín Oficial* 19 (January–June 1918): 254–58; "VI Congreso Médico y de la Prensa Médica," *Crónica Médico-Quirúrgica de la Habana* 51, nos. 1–6 (January–June 1925): 19.

106. V. Harvard, "Report on the Malarial Situation in the Provinces of Camagüey and Oriente," Havana, May 23, 1918, USNA, RG 59/837.124/6; Bailey K. Ashford to the American Minister, Havana, January 1, 1920, USNA, RG 59/837.124/29.

107. This figure was calculated using the reports of Instituto Finlay, *Boletín Semanal*, 1940–44. A sample of two weekly reports was used each year, one corresponding to the end of June, and the other to the end of December (about 4 percent of total registry). I purposely excluded the reports from January to June, the *zafra* period, when a seasonal working population was larger in Camagüey and Oriente.

108. Merrill Griffith to the Secretary of State, Santiago de Cuba, June 1, 1916, USNA, RG 59/837.55/34.

109. Billiken, "El peligro negro"; Tristán, "El artículo del Gráfico," *La Prensa*, March 23, 1916; "Cuba. Caso antillano," *Revista de Avance* 3, no. 39 (October 15, 1929): 287–88; Edward I. Nathan, "Cuba's Population Problems," Santiago de Cuba, April 24, 1928, USNA, RG 59/837.55/83; Carlos Manuel Cruz, "Inmigración útil y necesaria," *Diario de Cuba*, April 21, 1928; "Tierra y población en las Antillas," *Revista de Avance* 1, no. 16 (November 30, 1927): 87–88.

110. Castellanos, "El homicidio en Cuba." I have calculated the figures of female delinquency from the data contained in the photographic album reproduced by

Castellanos, *La delincuencia femenina en Cuba*. The data of the prison population correspond to 1927, as reproduced in Cuba, Comisión Nacional de Estadísticas y Reformas Económicas, *Cuadros estadísticos de los penados*.

111. Castellanos, *La brujería y el ñañiguismo en Cuba*, 107; "Gente no deseable," *Diario de la Marina*, November 23, 1922; "Abajo con las autoridades corruptas," *La Noche*, March 21, 1924. About cases of *brujería* involving Antilleans, see "Un lynchamiento en Regla," *La Lucha*, June 29, 1919; "Savage Instincts of Negro Must Be Extirpated," *Havana Post*, June 29, 1919; and "Haitiano come-niños," *La Política Cómica*, November 6, 1921.

112. Bullard, "The Cuban Negro," 625–27; Pepper, *To-Morrow in Cuba*, 155; Lindsay and Winter, *Cuba and Her People*, 107–8.

113. My analysis of *brujería* follows Helg's work on the subject. For a detailed discussion of some of the most notable cases in the early republic, see her *Our Rightful Share*, 107–16, 238–39. See also Reinaldo Román, "An Indignant Public Opinion: The Cuban Press and the Negros Brujos Scares (1904–1943)," paper presented at the Second CRI Conference on Cuba and Cuban-American Studies, Miami, March 18–20, 1999.

114. "¿Crimen por brujería?," "La brujería en la Habana," and "Los crímenes de la brujería," *La Lucha*, July 26, 1906, June 14, 1907, March 20, 1910.

115. For numerous examples during the 1910s–1930s, see Castellanos, "La lucha policíaca contra el fetichismo," *Revista de Técnica Policial y Penitenciaria* 4, nos. 2–3 (August–September 1936): 231–72; see also Roche y Monteagudo, *La policía y sus misterios*, 186–208.

116. "La Cámara botará una ley contra los brujos" and "En sesión extraordinaria la Cámara," *La Lucha*, June 28, July 4, 1919; Cuba, Cámara de Representantes, *Diario de Sesiones* 31, no. 30 (July 4, 1919): 18–20; 31, no. 36 (July 13, 1919): 11–13; "Prohibidos por gobernación los ritos de brujería," *Diario de la Marina*, November 22, 1922.

117. See the discussion of Castellanos in "Un diagnóstico criminológico," 200–204.

118. Serra, *Carta abierta*, 9; El Negro Falucho, "Carta abierta al Sr. Director del Nuevo Criollo," *El Nuevo Criollo*, October 8, 1904; "Continúa el Sr. Antonio Poveda," *El Nuevo Criollo*, November 11, 1905; Batrell Oviedo and Nenínger, "Manifiesto."

119. Marcel Levargie, "Haiti y la emigración cubana," *La Prensa*, February 7, 1916; Ramiro Neyra y Lanza, "La prensa y la inmigración antillana," *Labor Nueva* 1, no. 9 (April 16, 1916): 6–7; Juan de Bravo, "El negro y la política," *La Prensa*, January 22, 1916; Lino D'Ou, "Suaviter in modo," *Labor Nueva* 1, no. 5 (March 19, 1916): 5–6.

120. At times, however, Antilleans were presented as honest, hardworking people. Also, Haiti was not presented as the savage and primitive country depicted in the mainstream press but as the first free land in the Americas. See Levargie, "Haiti y la emigración cubana," and D'Ou, "Suaviter in modo." For an early attempt, see Risquet, *Rectificaciones*, 187.

121. "Charla semanal," *Labor Nueva* 1, no. 5 (March 19, 1916): 3; 1, no. 7 (April 2, 1916): 3–4; "Vitam impendere vero," *La Prensa*, April 5, 1916; Lino D'Ou, "Un

postulado," *Labor Nueva* 1, no. 13 (May 14, 1916): 3; Gustavo Urrutia, "Haitianos y jamaiquinos," *Diario de la Marina*, June 30, 1928.

122. For the reactions of organized labor, see Chapter 3.

123. John Russell to the Secretary of State, Havana, November 2, 1928, USNA, RG 59/837.5538/17; Noble Judah to the Secretary of State, Havana, May 31, 1929, USNA, RG 59/8375552.

124. Gustavo Urrutia, "Ideales de una raza. Cuba será blanca . . . o no será," *Diario de la Marina*, June 28, 1928.

125. Frederick Todd, "Special Report: 'Trend in Immigration into Cuba,'" Havana, March 2, 1929, USNA, RG 59/837.55/85; Harry F. Guggenheim, "General Conditions Report," Havana, February 7, 1931, USNA, RG 84/800/556; C. R. Cameron, "Proposed Cuban Migration Law," Havana, June 12, 1936, USNA, RG 84/855.

126. "La ley del 50 por 100 no quita trabajo," *Alma Mater*, December 9, 1933.

CHAPTER TWO

1. Carnoy, *Faded Dreams*, 11 (emphasis in original).

2. Love, "Political Participation in Brazil," 9; Kousser, *The Shaping of Southern Politics*, 224–51. The Cuban figures are based on Cuba, *Censo 1907*, 357, and "Official Vote," *La Lucha*, November 16, 1908. The estimated turnout in the 1908 elections coincides with that of Domínguez, *Cuba: Order and Revolution*, 26.

3. The literature about this period and the so-called race war of 1912 is profuse. Some scholars have emphasized white racism in their analyses. The most recent and best-documented study along these lines is Helg, *Our Rightful Share*; see also Fernández Robaina, *El negro en Cuba*, and Portuondo Linares, *Los independientes de color*. Other interpretations stress the revolt; the limited popular appeal of the party; and, in the case of Pérez, "Politics, Peasants, and People of Color," the underlying structural conditions that made the revolt possible. See also Orum, "The Politics of Color," and Fermoselle, *Política y color en Cuba*.

4. Some studies, such as Helg, *Our Rightful Share*, 228, and Aguilar, "Cuba," 44, characterize the post-1912 period as one of widespread racism. Others consider that 1912 did not have a lasting effect on Cuban society and politics. For examples, see Portell-Vilá, *Nueva historia*, 144–52, and Castellanos and Castellanos, *Cultura afrocubana*, 2:327.

5. Helg, *Our Rightful Share*, 228; Casal, "Race Relations," 14; Booth, "Cuba, Color, and the Revolution," 148; Evenson, *Revolution in the Balance*, 109.

6. This characterization is based on Domínguez, *Cuba: Order and Revolution*, 11–12.

7. Grillo, *El problema del negro*, 67.

8. "La población de Cuba," *La Lucha*, September 21, 1899. The assessment of *La Lucha* was correct. See Elihu Root to Wood, Washington, D.C., February 28, 1900, LC, Leonard Wood Papers, 28; "Datos," *Diario de la Marina*, February 19, 1901, morning ed.; "The Questions of the Day," *La Lucha*, October 31, 1899.

9. "En palacio," *La Unión Española*, January 3, 1900, evening ed.; Martínez Ortiz, *Cuba*, 1:113–14; Wood to Root, Havana, February 23, 1900, LC, Leonard Wood

Papers, 28. For a general discussion of this process, see Pérez, *Cuba between Empires*, 303–14, and Orum, "The Politics of Color," 67–69.

10. Wood to Elihu Root, Havana, February 8, 1900, LC, Leonard Wood Papers, 28; Martínez Ortiz, *Cuba*, 1:130. The electoral law was published as *Ley electoral*.

11. Wood to Root, Havana, February 23, 1900, February 8, 1901, LC, Leonard Wood Papers, 28, 29.

12. "Asuntos varios. El sufragio universal" and "Asuntos varios. Manifestación," *Diario de la Marina*, March 21, 23, and 26, 1900.

13. "La prensa" and "Asuntos varios. La comisión electoral," *Diario de la Marina*, February 17 and 20, 1900, morning ed.

14. Only two Afro-Cubans were elected to the convention, Juan Gualberto Gómez and Morúa Delgado. Among the elected "substitutes" there was at least another person deemed to be black, General Agustín Cebreco from Oriente. See "Asuntos varios. La convención," *Diario de la Marina*, August 15, 1900, and Martínez Ortiz, *Cuba*, 1:179.

15. Cuba, Convención Constituyente, *Diario de Sesiones* 18 (January 27, 1901): 206. The suffrage discussion is reproduced in *Diario de Sesiones* 20 (January 30, 1901): 272–86. For the view of a contemporary opposed to universal suffrage, see Martínez Ortiz, *Cuba*, 1:204–6.

16. These figures are calculated using the occupation government's own estimates and the returns of the 1899 census. See Orum, "The Politics of Color," 70–71, and U.S. War Department, *Report on the Census*, 206. The 1907 figures come from Cuba, *Censo 1907*, 357.

17. Mustelier, *La extinción del negro*, 30. For an example of the press' concerns about the proportion of Afro-Cubans in the voting population, see "Datos," *Diario de la Marina*, February 19, 1901, morning ed.

18. Lino D'Ou, "A iguales esfuerzos iguales consecuencias," *Labor Nueva* 1, no. 26 (August 20, 1916): 4; Caamaño de Cárdenas, "Con sello rápido," *La Prensa*, August 2, 1915. A devastating critique of the kind of populist rhetoric developed by candidates in electoral periods is made by Gerardo del Valle, "Para Concejal," in *1/4 Fambá y 19 cuentos*, 94–99.

19. Pedro Portuondo Calás, "Palabras," *Renovación*, March 20, 1932.

20. Pérez-Medina, "The Situation of the Negro," 296; Betancourt, *Doctrina negra*, 15–16; Cuéllar Vizcaíno, "Aire libre," *Tiempo*, September 4, 1952. The issue also surfaces in literature; for examples, see Hernández Catá, "La piel," in *Los frutos ácidos*, and Masdeu, *La raza triste*, 173–75.

21. Paul Beck, memoranda, Havana, April 20, 1920, USNA, RG 165/2056-196. A similar testimony about blacks increasing their demands "before every election" is provided by Henry Watterson, "The Illogical Cuban," *The Cuba News* 4, no. 4 (February 27, 1915): 1, 4–5.

22. "¡No hubo quórum!," *La Discusión*, July 8, 1901; "Los enemigos de la independencia," *El Mundo*, April 27, 1901. A similar attack on universal suffrage and the "barbarism of number" was being staged in the United States by a number of scientists in the eugenics movement; for an excellent discussion, see Tucker, *Racial Research*, 70, 91, 102–6.

23. "La prensa," *Diario de la Marina*, March 17, 1900, morning ed.; "Los debates del 'Ateneo,'" *La Discusión*, November 19, 1905. The debate in the Consultive Commission can be followed in Cuba, Comisión Consultiva, *Diario de Sesiones* 1, nos. 14–16 (March 5–8, 1907).

24. "Los debates del Ateneo. Discurso pronunciado por el doctor Alfredo Zayas," *La Discusión*, November 20, 1905.

25. These quotations are taken from the following articles, all published in *El Nuevo Criollo*, November 11 and 25, 1905: Enrique Ponce Herrera, "El señor Varona"; "Será derrotada"; "Aunque se vista de seda"; and Serra, "Sobra de información" and "La Sociedad Jurídica y 'La Doctrina de Martí.'" See also Serra, "La brasa a su sardina," *La Discusión*, May 13, 1904.

26. "Politics in Cuba," *Havana Post*, November 14, 1901. In this aspect my work follows Orum's pioneering study of race in electoral politics during the early republic; see his "The Politics of Color."

27. "Asuntos varios. Por Masó," *Diario de la Marina*, October 29, 1901, morning ed.; "La llegada del General Masó," *La Discusión*, October 28, 1901; Bartolomé Masó, "Al país," *Diario de la Marina*, October 31, 1901, evening ed.; "El programa de Masó," *La Discusión*, July 30, 1901. According to the *Havana Post*, Masó's manifesto had actually been written by Afro-Cuban patriot Juan Gualberto Gómez; see "Maso Throws Down the Gauntlet," November 2, 1901.

28. "Asuntos varios. El General Bandera," "Llegada del General Masó," "Asuntos varios. Por Masó," and "Asuntos varios. Los partidarios de Masó en Cárdenas," *Diario de la Marina*, October 24 and 28, 1901, evening ed., October 29, December 12, 1901, morning ed.

29. "Mítin en Guanabacoa," *Diario de la Marina*, November 28, 1901, morning ed.; "Americans Are Attacked at Maso Meeting," *Havana Post*, November 19, 1901; "La prensa," *Diario de la Marina*, November 24, 1901, morning ed.

30. "Game of Politics Becoming Mixed," *Havana Post*, November 2, 1901; "La prensa," *Diario de la Marina*, November 7, 1901, morning ed.

31. "La presidencia de la república. El programa de Estrada Palma," *La Discusión*, September 23, 1901; "Las elecciones," *La Unión Española*, June 18, 1900, evening ed.; "Los partidarios de Estrada Palma" and "La nota del día," *Diario de la Marina*, November 25 and 27, 1901, evening ed.; "Algo más sobre razas," *La Discusión*, November 23, 1901.

32. "El mítin de Remedios" and "En tierra camagüeyana," *La Lucha*, July 31, August 7, 1905; "Lo de Guantánamo" and "La propaganda del insulto, en Baracoa," *El Cubano Libre*, September 4 and 15, 1905; Castillo, Roja, Failde, Vázquez, and Sánchez to Jorge Valera, n.p., May 18, 1906, ANC, Fondo Especial, leg. 7, no. 114.

33. "La Concha me dio licencia," "Las claves," and "Apunta pueblo," *El Nuevo Criollo*, March 11, May 27, 1905.

34. "El porque [*sic*] de la necesidad," *La Lucha*, October 16, 1908; "'War or Free Nation' Intervention Must End," *Havana Post*, November 19, 1906; Julián Betancourt, "Réplica a mis adversarios" and "Los veteranos y Montoro," *El Mundo*, September 11 and 25, 1908; "¡Alerta raza de color!," *El Triunfo*, September 20, 1908; "De Colón," *La Lucha*, September 9, 1908.

35. Eligio Hernández, "A la raza de color," "Ecos de Banes," and "Movimiento político en la isla," *La Discusión*, September 12, 15, and 16, 1905; "La obra del engaño," *El Nuevo Criollo*, September 30, 1905.

36. "Movimiento conservador" and "Digamos la verdad," *El Cubano Libre*, July 20, 1907, September 9, 1908; Mario Garcia Menocal, "Manifiesto al país," *La Lucha*, October 23, 1908.

37. For an idea of the press campaign around the Montoro-Rabí hug, see the following, all published on September 11, 1908: "Los reconquistadores de la república," *La Discusión*; "La campaña presidencial conservadora," *El Cubano Libre*; and "Los conservadores en el Nacional," *El Mundo*. See also "La semana," *Avisador Comercial*, September 12, 1908. About the presence of Afro-Cuban generals in the PC, see also "Los veteranos de la independencia con el Partido Conservador," *El Cubano Libre*, September 9, 1908.

38. "Dos cartas decorosas," *El Nuevo Criollo*, January 21, 1905. On this incident, see Fernández Robaina, *El negro en Cuba*, 51, and Portuondo Linares, *Los independientes de color*, 15.

39. [Serra], "Aclaraciones" and "Invitación," *El Nuevo Criollo*, February 11, May 27, 1905.

40. "A través de la Isla. Del Perico" and "A través de la Isla. De Colón," *La Lucha*, September 13 and 20, 1905.

41. Ulises de Croacia, "A los electores de la raza de color," "Es natural y lógico," and "El Sr. Risquet," *El Nuevo Criollo*, October 7 and 28, 1905; "La reelección de Risquet," *La Discusión*, October 6, 1905.

42. "Desde Santiago" and "Todo con los Nacionales," *El Nuevo Criollo*, September 2, October 22, 1905; "La fusión de los liberales," *El Mundo*, September 3, 1908; "Juan Gualberto Gómez," *La Discusión*, September 5, 1908; "Después de la coalición," *El Cubano Libre*, September 12, 1908; "Juan Gualberto siempre liberal," *La Lucha*, October 30, 1908.

43. Riera, *Cuba política*, 57–66, 78–81; Simeón Poveda, "Sobre la raza de color," *El Nuevo Criollo*, November 18, 1905.

44. "Palpitaciones de la raza de color. Duro y a la cabeza," *La Prensa*, November 12, 1915; "Iniciativa plausible," *La Lucha*, April 19, 1910; D'Ou, "La evolución de la raza de color," 333–37. The list of elected officials is based on Riera, *Cuba política*, 142–49, and "Los representantes elegidos," *La Lucha*, November 24, 1908. Many of the pictures of the black Liberal candidates were published in *La Lucha* in September and October.

45. D'Ou, "La evolución de la raza de color," 333–37.

46. Lino D'Ou, "Sobre dos puntos" and "No más denominaciones," *La Prensa*, August 15, 1915, January 11, 1916. For an excellent description of this practice, see also Masdeu, *La raza triste*, 173–75.

47. Bullard, "The Cuban Negro," 623–30. Black participation in the Liberal revolt has been studied in Orum, "The Politics of Color," 113–24, and Helg, *Our Rightful Share*, 137–38.

48. "En defensa de la paz. El ejemplo de Rabí," "Adhesiones patrióticas," and "La convulsión radical," *El Cubano Libre*, August 17, 20, 22, and 25, 1906; "La pertur-

bación del orden público," *La Discusión*, August 18, 1906; "El general Pedro Díaz," *La Lucha*, August 23, 1906.

49. "Movimientos armados" and "Ataque y toma de Guanajay," *La Lucha*, September 1 and 17, 1906.

50. "¿Partido negro?," *La Discusión*, December 17, 1906; Longan to the Chief of the Military Information Division, Santiago de Cuba, November 30, 1908, USNA, RG 395/1008/53/283.

51. Bullard, "The Cuban Negro," 630.

52. For overviews of the committee's activities, see Serra, "A los liberales de color," in *Para blancos y negros*, 82–83; Fernández Robaina, *El negro en Cuba*, 37–45; Horrego Estuch, *Juan Gualberto Gómez*, 176–78; and Helg, *Our Rightful Share*, 125–27.

53. "Justicia para todos" and "Los veteranos de color. El Comité de acción," *La Lucha*, May 28 and 30, 1902.

54. "Current Topics. Committee of Colored Men Call on President," "Por la raza de color. Su ingreso en la policía," and "La asamblea de la raza de color," *La Lucha*, June 9 and 23, 1902.

55. "La verdad ante todo" and "Los veteranos de color. El Comité de acción," *La Lucha*, May 30, 1902.

56. "El alcalde y la raza de color" and "A la raza de color," *La Lucha*, June 21, November 1, 1902.

57. "La nota del día," "Lógica pura," and "La agitación de los elementos de color," *La Discusión*, August 6, 7, and 11, 1907.

58. "Manifiesto al pueblo cubano y a los ciudadanos de color," Camagüey, August 1907, ANC, Fondo Especial, leg. fuera de caja, no. 6-4; versions of this manifesto were published in "La nota del día," *La Discusión*, August 31, 1907, and "La raza de color," *Diario de la Marina*, September 3, 1907, morning ed.; see also Fermoselle, *Política y color*, 109–11, and Helg, *Our Rightful Share*, 145.

59. "El movimiento de la raza de color" and Lino D'Ou, "Obstrucción," *La Discusión*, September 17, October 1, 1907.

60. This notion was endorsed also by Batrell and Nenínger in their famous "Manifiesto al pueblo de Cuba." The original manifesto is located in ANC, Fondo Especial, leg. fuera, no. 8-21.

61. "Manifiesto a los ciudadanos de color del pueblo cubano," Camagüey, September 6, 1907, ANC, Fondo Especial, leg. fuera, no. 8-35.

62. Fermoselle, *Política y color*, 111.

63. The program of the PIC is analyzed in Portuondo Linares, *Los independientes de color*, 19–21; Fernández Robaina, *El negro en Cuba*, 64–66; and Helg, *Our Rightful Share*, 147–49.

64. *Havana Daily Telegraph*, quoted in "Los miguelistas contra el tío Sam," *La Discusión*, August 27, 1907; "El mítin miguelista," *La Discusión*, August 26, 1907. For additional examples of the relationship between Gómez and Estenoz, see "Carta canta" and "Más humanidad," *La Lucha*, August 27 and 28, 1907.

65. "La nota del día," "Estenoz contra José Miguel," and "La actitud de Estenoz," *La Discusión*, September 23, November 9 and 10, 1908.

66. "Provincia de la Habana. Votación total," *La Lucha*, November 19, 1908.

67. "Asuntos varios. Círculo de la Unión Democrática," *Diario de la Marina*, June 20, 1900, evening ed.

68. "La huelga general" and "Sobre la huelga," *La Unión Española*, September 26 and 27, 1899, morning ed.

69. "Nuestros industriales," *El Nuevo Criollo*, December 31, 1904; Cuéllar Vizcaíno, *Doce muertes famosas*, 78.

70. Evaristo Estenoz, "A mis amigos," *El Nuevo Criollo*, September 30, 1905.

71. "Borrando los últimos vestigios," *La Discusión*, December 5, 1905; "La incorporación de Estenoz," *La Lucha*, August 20, 1906; Cuéllar Vizcaíno, *Doce muertes famosas*, 74–78.

72. "La prensa," *Diario de la Marina*, September 25, 1908, morning ed.; Helg, *Our Rightful Share*, 157.

73. "La partida del Caney," "La visita presidencial a Oriente," and "El general Ivonnet," *El Cubano Libre*, September 16 and 23, October 3, 1903; "Los sublevados del Caney," *La Lucha*, September 16, 1903.

74. Jackson to the Secretary of State, Havana, April 26, 1910, USNA, RG 59/837.00/1943/377; Jackson to the Secretary of State, Havana, August 31, 1910, USNA, RG 59/837.00/426.

75. Jackson to the Secretary of State, Havana, October 20, 1910, USNA, RG 59/837.00/431. The relationship between the PC and the PIC is studied by Portuondo Linares, *Los independientes de color*, 187–93, and Helg, *Our Rightful Share*, 178–79.

76. "Aquellos vientos . . ." and "Las cosas en su punto," *La Lucha*, February 14, April 25, 1910.

77. "El congreso," *La Lucha*, February 12 and 15, 1910; "El Señor Morúa Delgado y el Partido Independiente de Color," *La Lucha*, February 13, 1910; Morúa Delgado, *Integración cubana*, 239–45. The final version of the amendment can be seen in *Gaceta Oficial*, May 14, 1910.

78. "Viaje del Presidente," *La Lucha*, March 11 and 15, 1910; "El Presidente en Vuelta Abajo" and "El doctor Zayas en Artemisa," *La Lucha*, March 30, April 24, 1910; Jackson to the Secretary of State, Havana, March 31, 1910, USNA, RG 59/837.00/21; "Los nuevos secretarios," *La Lucha*, April 16, 1910.

79. "La raza de color y los racistas," *La Lucha*, June 7, 1912.

80. Fermoselle, *Política y color en Cuba*, 182–87. Portuondo Linares, *Los independientes de color*, 173–76, emphasizes the "anti-imperialism" of the PIC, but since 1910, the party had tried to obtain official U.S. recognition and support based on the Platt Amendment. Helg, *Our Rightful Share*, 190, stresses that seeking U.S. recognition was not inconsistent with the Platt Amendment.

81. "Proclama impresa del Partido Independiente de Color," Cárdenas, April 24, 1910, ANC, Fondo Especial, leg. 4, no. 132; Manuel Pardo Galindo Azuaga to Licenciado Alberto Ponce, April 24, 1910, ANC, Audiencia de Santiago de Cuba, leg. 28, no. 16.

82. Beaupré to the Secretary of State, Havana, February 19, 1912, USNA, RG 59/837.00/571.

83. Telegrams, Beaupré to the Secretary of State, Havana, May 27, 1912, USNA,

RG 59/837.00/622 and 626; Manuel Rionda to W. E. Ogilvie, May 29, 1912, BBC, RG 2, ser. 2, vol. 31.

84. The press campaign is carefully studied in Helg, *Our Rightful Share*, 173–77, 194–97.

85. Beaupré to the Secretary of State, Havana, June 14, 1912, USNA, RG 59/837.00/793; Portuondo Linares, *Los independientes de color*, 252–53.

86. D. A. Galdós to Van Horne, Camagüey, June 2, 1912, Cuba Company Papers, ser. 1, box 15, 180, University of Maryland, McKeldin Library, College Park, Maryland; A. H. Scales, Commanding Officer of the USS *Prairie*, to the Secretary of Navy, Manzanillo, June 8, 1912, USNA, RG 59/837.00/767; George Bayliss to Beaupré, Antilla, June 1, 1912, USNA, RG 59/837.00/763; "Relations Strained. Black Rebellion Unabated," *The Cuba News*, June 1, 1912; "Los Estados Unidos y la rebelión," *La Ultima Hora*, June 11, 1912.

87. William Taft to José Miguel Gómez, May 27, 1912, USNA, RG 59/837.00/614; "Relations Strained. The Week's Developments," *The Cuba News*, June 1, 1912.

88. Beaupré to the Secretary of State, Havana, June 1, 1912, USNA, RG 59/837.00/655; Galdós to Van Horne, Camagüey, June 7, 1912, Cuba Company Papers, ser. 1, box 15, 180.

89. George Bayliss to Beaupré, Antilla, June 15, 1912, USNA, RG 59/837.00/827; Chas Ham to Holaday, Palma Soriano, June 25, 1912, USNA, RG 59/837.00/877; G. C. Peterson to M. H. Lewis, Guantánamo, July 20, 1912, USNA, RG 59/837.00/912. For a detailed account of the repression, see Helg, *Our Rightful Share*, 221–25.

90. Gómez to Taft, Havana, May 26, 1912, USNA, RG 84/801/388.

91. Beaupré to the Secretary of State, Havana, May 28, 1912, USNA, RG 59/837.00/633; B. Anderson to Beaupré, Caibarién, June 8 and 11, 1912, USNA, RG 59/837.00/794 and 813; Max Baehr to Beaupré, Cienfuegos, June 8, 1912, USNA, RG 59/837.00/794.

92. "Monteagudo," *La Lucha*, July 17, 1912. Ortiz's military career is discussed in Chapter 3.

93. "El movimiento racista. Consejos oportunos" and "Alocución al elemento tranquilo de color del barrio del Pilar," *Diario de la Marina*, June 11, 1912, morning ed.; "El movimiento racista. Alocución del alcalde de Matanzas," *Diario de la Marina*, June 12, 1912, evening ed.; Vidaurreta a Menocal, Santa Clara, June 11, 1912, and "Fiscal de la Audiencia de Oriente al Secretario de Justicia," Santiago de Cuba, May 30, 1912, ANC, Secretaría de la Presidencia, leg. 110, no. 2.

94. "Las ligerezas . . . o lo que sea," *La Ultima Hora*, June 11, 1912; Beaupré to the Secretary of State, June 12, 1912, USNA, RG 59/837.00/745; Bayliss to Beaupré, Antilla, June 15, 1912, USNA, RG 59/837.00/827.

95. Orum, "The Politics of Color," 212–13. For an explanation of Afro-Cubans' response that emphasizes their fears of victimization, see Helg, *Our Rightful Share*, 170–71, 207.

96. Lewis, Lewis, and Rigdon, *Cuatro hombres*, 20.

97. Comandante Tomás Aguilar, "Al Gral. Evaristo Estenoz," and Tirso Calderón Barrera, "A la raza de color," *El Triunfo*, September 27 and 30, 1908; "De Man-

zanillo," *La Lucha*, September 26, 1908; "Tribuna libre," *Diario de la Marina*, September 20, 1908, morning ed.

98. "La agitación en Güines. Manifiesto al país," *La Lucha*, April 26, 1910; Julio Franco, "Réplica a la raza de color de Cárdenas," January 1910, ANC, Fondo Especial, leg. 4, no. 135. This manifesto was contested in Francisco Real, "Manifiesto impreso del Partido Independiente de Color," Cárdenas, January 20, 1910, ANC, Fondo Especial, leg. fuera, no. 10-15.

99. "Un almuerzo a Rabí," "Contra el racismo. Manifiesto patriótico," and "El Consejo Nacional de Veteranos," *La Lucha*, September 13, 1908, May 15, 1910, May 22, 1912; "El General Pedro Díaz," *La Ultima Hora*, June 11, 1912.

100. "La cuestión racista. Manifiesto de las sociedades de color" and "Contra el racismo. Dos manifiestos," *La Lucha*, May 3 and 5, 1910; "Telegramas oficiales. Protesta," "Manifiesto," and "Protesta," *Diario de la Marina*, June 2, 1912; "Recortes de prensa," 1910, ANC, Fondo Especial, leg. fuera, no. 9-29; "A la raza de color de Cárdenas," 1912, ANC, Fondo Especial, leg. fuera, no. 4-22; "Los actuales sucesos. Importante asamblea de la raza de color," *La Lucha*, June 10, 1912.

101. "Iniciativa plausible," *La Lucha*, April 19, 1910; "El movimiento racista. Un manifiesto," *Diario de la Marina*, June 4, 1912, morning ed.

102. Basilio Valle, "El problema actual," *Labor Nueva* 1, no. 22 (July 23, 1916): 5–6; Felix Fernández, "Gracias," *La Prensa*, November 13, 1915; Ruiz Suárez, *The Color Question*, 47.

103. Beaupré to the Secretary of State, Havana, June 11, 1912, USNA, RG 59/837.00/765; Beaupré to the Secretary of State, Havana, June 10, 1912, USNA, RG 59/837.00/735.

104. Masdeu, *La raza triste*, 228.

105. "Expansion Introduces Race Prejudice," *Illinois Record*, February 18, 1899, quoted in Marks, *The Black Press*, 98; Pepper, *To-Morrow in Cuba*, 143; "Out of Cuban Racial Troubles May Grow Political Party," *Tampa Tribune*, January 31, 1910. I thank Gary Mormino for sharing the latter with me.

106. "Tómense medidas," *La Prensa*, November 30, 1915; "Grave incidente en el parque de Cienfuegos," *El Mundo*, March 26, 1916; "Incidentes enojosos" and "Problema cubano," *La Prensa*, March 29, June 20, 1916.

107. "Report Fighting in City of Santa Clara," *Havana Post*, January 19, 1925; "El problema racial en Santa Clara" and "El conflicto racial se ha agravado en la capital de las Villas," *La Lucha*, January 12 and 19, 1925; "Más cordura," *La Discusión*, January 19, 1925.

108. On the complex nature of city spaces as sites of civic contestation, see Brown and Kimball, "Mapping the Terrain," 296–346.

109. "La sociedad villaclareña en un gesto hidalgo," *La Discusión*, January 22, 1925; "El cisma racial de Santa Clara va a tener patriótica solución," *La Lucha*, January 22, 1925.

110. "Protestan diversos elementos," "Patrióticas declaraciones del Comandante Sandó," and "Repercuten en Pinar del Río los sucesos de Santa Clara," *La Lucha*, January 24, February 2 and 3, 1925; "La agitación racial en la República" and "El

representante Garriga," *La Discusión*, January 24, February 8, 1925; "Regret Race Clash," *Havana Post*, January 22, 1925.

111. "Los sucesos en el parque de Santa Clara" and "Carta del Coronel Carvison," *La Lucha*, January 28, February 3, 1925; Mella, "Los cazadores de negros resucitan en Santa Clara," *Juventud* 2, no. 11 (March 1925): 5–6, reprinted in Mella, *Documentos y artículos*, 165–67.

112. "Se teme un nuevo choque racista," *La Discusión*, February 7, 1925; "No pueden negarse a unos elementos derechos que se reconocen a otros," *La Lucha*, January 23, 1925.

113. Beaupré to the Secretary of State, Havana, January 15 and 17, 1913, USNA, RG 59/837.00/969, 971.

114. "Se aproxima una nueva revolución racista" and "El racismo en Oriente," *La Lucha*, September 11 and 14, 1915; "¿Se conspira o no se conspira?," *La Prensa*, September 28, 1915.

115. "Manejos misteriosos de los racistas" and "Los racistas siguen despertando sospechas," *La Prensa*, September 29, October 2, 1915; "¿El centro de la conspiración racista está en la capital de la República?" and "Frases hirientes del negro 'Totó,'" *La Lucha*, September 12 and 14, 1915; "Regla Mayor Fears Negroes," *Havana Post*, September 16, 1915.

116. "La opinión del gobierno sobre el racismo," *La Prensa*, September 30, 1915; "El paralítico Lacoste," *La Lucha*, September 16, 1915; "Negroes Loyal to Government," *Havana Post*, September 17, 1915; "De Guantánamo," *La Prensa*, November 12, 1915.

117. Tristán, "Lo de Oriente," *La Prensa*, September 14, 1915; "Nuestro criterio. Juegos peligrosos," *La Prensa*, November 10, 1915. See also Helg, *Our Rightful Share*, 240.

118. Andrew de Graux, "Report on Trip through the Island," Havana, August 30, 1919, USNA, RG 59/837.00/1573; "Llamamiento a los hombres de color," *La Lucha*, July 5, 1919.

119. "Monteagudo" and "Hablando con Monteagudo," *La Lucha*, July 17 and 21, 1912.

120. "Habla el General Rego," "Entrevista con Nuñez," and Antonio Escobar, "Los culpables liberales," *La Lucha*, June 26 and 30, July 20, 1912; Gómez, "A nuestro pueblo," *Diario de la Marina*, December 2, 1928; Cuba, Cámara, *Diario de Sesiones* 19 (April 30, 1913): 21–22.

121. Gibson to the Secretary of State, Havana, September 21, 1912, USNA, RG 59/837.00/924.

122. "Campaña presidencial," "El Club Morúa Delgado," and "El recorrido triunfal de Menocal y Asbert," *La Lucha*, May 10, July 24, September 23, 1912.

123. "¡Pobre Cuba!," "Descomposición," and "¡Ah, José Miguel!," *La Lucha*, September 23 and 24, October 19, 1912.

124. See the following articles, all published in *La Opinión*: "Por qué José Miguel no puede ser presidente," February 3, 1920; "José Miguel por el campo de sus hazañas racistas," August 7, 1920; and "La bárbara carnicería de mayo y la raza de color," October 27, 1920. The issue also figured in *La Lucha*: "Editorial. Frente al desorden," November 26, 1919; "La cordialidad de José Miguel," February 1,

1920; and "El general José Miguel Gómez encarna, a pesar de negarlo, una política de exclusivismos y rencores," September 6, 1920.

125. "La mancha negra," "Chucho, barre con todos los negros," and "Los negros de Cuba son unos salvajes," *La Opinión*, February 13, October 25, 1920, February 5, 1921; Harold D. Clum to Boaz Long, Santiago de Cuba, October 1, 1920, and Long to the Secretary of State, Havana, October 8, 1920, USNA, RG 59/837.00/1808, 1802; "Una hoja suelta," *La Opinión*, February 17, 1920.

126. See the following, all published in *La Opinión*: José A. Beltrán, "Viene Tiburón," August 13, 1920; "Manifiesto cívico a los hombres de color de Matanzas," October 26, 1920; "La raza de color de las Villas," February 17, 1921; and "El gesto hermoso, digno y patriótico del Club Moncada," August 9, 1920.

127. "Los elementos de color" and "Ha quedado constituído el Directorio," *La Opinión*, February 27, March 3, 1920; "Una organización" and "Extiende su organización política en la República la agrupación anti-Miguelista," *La Lucha*, March 3 and 15, 1920.

128. "Sí, Tiburón es un racista!," *La Opinión*, February 15, 1921; "La raza de color," Francisco Duany Méndez, "A un Miguelista que escribe insolencia de 'Macua,'" and "El asombro de Tiburón," *La Opinión*, February 17, March 4, August 7, 1920.

129. "Innoble campaña conservadora," *El Reconcentrado*, August 28, 1912; "Los liberales en Matanzas," *La Lucha*, September 21, 1912; "La voz de los racistas," *El Heraldo de Cuba*, September 15, 1916; "General Gómez," *Havana Post*, September 11, 1920.

130. "Memorandum re: Racial Problem of Cuba." For opinions of Gómez's popularity with blacks, see Major N. W. Campanole to the Director of Military Intelligence, Havana, September 28, 1920, USNA, RG 165/2657-Q; Beck, Office Memo, Havana, April 15, 1920, USNA, RG 165/2056/196.

131. Holaday to Hugh Gibson, Santiago de Cuba, August 17, 1912, USNA, RG 59/837.00/920; "Las elecciones," *La Lucha*, November 6, 1912.

132. Williamson to Sumner Welles, Washington, D.C., November 15, 1920, USNA, RG 59/837.00/1979. Calculations about the electoral results in Oriente are based on N. W. Campanole, "Report on Observations in 1920 Cuban Elections in Oriente Province," Havana, November 22, 1920, USNA, RG 165/2657-Q-54, and Cuba, *Censo 1919*, 410–11.

133. White to the Secretary of State, Havana, August 27, 1920, USNA, RG 59/837.00/1747; "El día 23 postularán los Conservadores," *El Mundo*, May 12, 1920.

134. "El general Menocal y Labor Nueva," *Labor Nueva* 1, no. 1 (February 20, 1916): 3; "La boleta liberal," *La Prensa*, September 16, 1916.

135. "Charla semanal," *Labor Nueva* 1, nos. 33 and 34 (October 15 and 22, 1916): 3; Alejandro E. Sorís, "En broma," and Tristán, "El sacrificio de Cataneo y Cuesta," *La Prensa*, April 3, July 29, 1916; Riera, *Cuba política*, 233–45.

136. Junta Provincial Electoral de Santa Clara, "Resultado del escrutinio provincial," in Long to the Secretary of State, November 12, 1920, USNA, RG 59/837.00/1888; "El gobierno del General Gómez," *La Opinión*, February 18, 1920.

137. "Gracias," *Labor Nueva* 1, no. 33 (October 15, 1916): 4; Sorís, "En broma"; "Funcionario competente," *La Opinión*, September 24, 1920.

138. Chapman, *A History of the Cuban Republic*, 313; Orum, "The Politics of Color," 259–60.

139. Ortiz, *La decadencia*, 16. About the Zayas period, see Pérez, *Cuba*, 229–48, and Aguilar, "Cuba," 48–50.

140. Abelardo Pacheco and Vicente Ferrer Ortega, "La situación del elemento de color," *Unión Nacionalista*, September 11, 1928; Benjamin, *The United States and Cuba*, 51.

141. Brief biographical sketches of most of these figures appear in *Renovación*, March 20, 1932. See also "El Dr. Miguel Angel Céspedes," *Diario de la Marina*, September 6, 1928; Harry F. Guggenheim, "General Conditions Report," Havana, January 3, 1931, USNA, RG 84/800/494; and Muñoz Ginarte, "Comentos sin comentarios," *Diario de la Marina*, December 15, 1929.

142. Gerardo Machado, "Cuba os recibe con los brazos abiertos," *El País*, March 13, 1930; "Héroes y maestros. El siete de diciembre," *Boletín Oficial del Club Atenas* 1, no. 11 (November 20, 1930): 5; Lino D'Ou, "Juan Gualberto Gómez," *Diario de la Marina*, May 5, 1929.

143. "Investigating Ku Klux Klan," "Ku Klux Klan Will Be Dissolved," and "Camagüey Klan Warning," *Havana Post*, September 2, 9, and 30, 1928; "La Ku Klux Klan de Camagüey," *Unión Nacionalista*, September 10, 1928.

144. H. Clark, "Membership of the Twelve Cuban Congress," Havana, April 17, 1925, USNA, RG 165/2657-Q-255; Riera, *Cuba política*, 323–28, 333–47; "Boleta muestra provincial, elecciones parciales 1926," Havana, Camagüey, and Oriente, USNA, RG 59/837.00/2616. See also *Renovación*, March 20, 1932, and the list of candidates published in *El Político*, July 13, 1930. Since it is not possible to identify accurately all members of Congress, the number of blacks in the legislature may have been higher than I have indicated.

145. "Memorandum re: Racial Problem of Cuba." See also Jesús Masdeu, "Cómo nos ven," *Diario de la Marina*, April 14, 1929.

146. "Política al día" and "Homenaje al Presidente G. Machado," *La Lucha*, August 19, 23, and 31, 1928; "Hablaba la raza de color," *Diario de la Marina*, September 6, 1928.

147. "El homenaje de las sociedades de color," *Diario de la Marina*, September 6, 1928; "Machado y las sociedades de color" and "Brillante homenaje," *La Lucha*, September 5 and 6, 1928; Antonio Pardo Suárez, "Palpitaciones del momento," *La Lucha*, September 7, 1928.

148. Pérez-Stable, *The Cuban Revolution*, 39. The literature about the Machadato is very extensive. For useful overviews, see Soto, *La revolución del 33*; Aguilar, *Cuba 1933*; and Tabares del Real, *La revolución del 33*.

149. Abelardo Pacheco, "La situación del elemento de color," *Unión Nacionalista*, September 7 and 10, 1928; "Miguel Mariano Gómez," *El Político*, December 5, 1930.

CHAPTER THREE

1. For overviews of immigration to Cuba, see Maluquer de Motes, *Nación e inmigración*; Naranjo Orovio, "Trabajo libre e inmigración española en Cuba: 1880–1930," 749–94; Iglesias, "Características de la inmigración española en Cuba,"

270–95; Alvarez Estévez, *Azúcar e inmigración*; and Pérez de la Riva, "Cuba y la migración antillana, 1900–1931," 3–75.

2. For a discussion in Latin America, see Andrews, "Black Workers in the Export Years," 7–29, and Godio, *Historia del movimiento obrero latinoamericano*, 47–50.

3. Cuban historiography has acknowledged these divisions but has paid little attention to their concrete operation. For some examples, see Cabrera, *El movimiento obrero*, 37; Instituto de Historia, *Historia del movimiento obrero*, 1:179–80; and Córdova, *Clase trabajadora*, 91–100.

4. Atkins, *Sixty Years in Cuba*, 306; "Escasez de trabajadores," *Diario de la Marina*, June 19, 1900, evening ed.; "Invitación," *La Unión Española*, February 8, 1900, evening ed.

5. "Escasez de braceros," *Diario de la Marina*, January 1, 1901, morning ed.; Cuba, Military Governor, *Civil Report . . . 1901*, 5:75.

6. These and other immigration figures are calculated from Cuba, Secretaría de Hacienda, *Inmigración y movimiento de pasajeros*, 1902–31.

7. Jackson to the Secretary of State, Havana, January 16, June 27, 1911, USNA, RG 59/837.55/15 and 18.

8. For sugar production data and the proportion of eastern provinces in the national output, see Guerra, *Azúcar y población*, 227–30; Ayala, "Social and Economic Aspects of Sugar Production," 95–124; and Pérez de la Riva, "Cuba y la migración antillana," 3–75, especially 23–27.

9. Gonzalez to the Secretary of State, Havana, November 15 and 27, 1918, USNA, RG 59/838.5637/1; Morgan to the Secretary of State, Havana, November 29, 1918, USNA, RG 59/838.5637/2; Department of State to American Legation, Washington, D.C., December 14, 1918, USNA, RG 59/838.5637/2a; Blanchard to the Secretary of State, Port-au-Prince, December 31, 1918, USNA, RG 59/838.5637/3.

10. Russell to the Secretary of State, Port-au-Prince, October 28, 1927, USNA, RG 59/837.504/312; C. B. Curtis to the Secretary of State, Havana, July 26, 1928, USNA, RG 59/837.5538/11; Gross to the Secretary of State, Port-au-Prince, July 19, 1928, USNA, RG 59/838.5637/7.

11. "Haitian Decree Reaches Cuban Dept. of State," *Havana Post*, August 18, 1928; Curtis to the Secretary of State, Havana, October 11, November 2, 1928, USNA, RG 59/837.5538/15 and 17.

12. "Zafra libre sin braceros antillanos," *Heraldo de Cuba*, August 18, 1928; Judah to the Secretary of State, Havana, April 14, 1928, May 31, 1929, USNA, RG 59/837.50/42 and 52.

13. "Haitian Decree"; Horace J. Dickinson, "Importation of Haitian Labor into the Antilla District," Antilla, September 24, 1928, USNA, RG 59/837.5538/14.

14. Foreign Policy Association, *Problems of the New Cuba*, 285.

15. Decreto no. 2232, October 18, 1933, in Pichardo, *Documentos*, 4:1, 78–82.

16. In 1924 these complaints led to an international scandal. See Cuba, Secretaría de Estado, *Documentos diplomáticos*. See also "Memorandum para el Sr. Secretario de Estado and M. to Manuel Rionda," Havana, January 25, 1924, BBC, RG 2, ser. 10c,

box 58; "El gobierno está preocupado con la reclamación inglesa," *La Discusión*, January 15, 1925.

17. "Ley Provisional de Nacionalización del Trabajo" (November 8, 1933), in Pichardo, *Documentos*, 4:1, 98–100; "La Ley del 50 por 100 no quita trabajo," *Alma Mater*, December 9, 1933. For a more detailed discussion of the social conflicts related to these laws, see Chapter 5.

18. Naval Attaché, "Memorandum for the Ambassador," Havana, February 25, 1941, USNA, RG 84/832; Pérez de la Riva, "La migración antillana," 53; Fernando Ortiz, "En el solar de la prieta," *Bohemia*, May 15, 1949, 20–22, 88; Bervin, *Mission a la Havane*, 22.

19. Juan de Zengotita, "Cuba's Manpower Resources," Havana, June 15, 1955, USNA, RG 59/837.06/6-1555.

20. Pérez, *Cuba under the Platt Amendment*, 71–72; Trelles, "La hacienda," 323–42.

21. Pérez, "Politics, Peasants, and the People of Color," 523, and *Cuba*, 195–99.

22. U.S. War Department, *Report on the Census of Cuba, 1899*, 555–59; Pepper, *To-Morrow in Cuba*, 151; Hinton, "Cuban Reconstruction," 92–102. About the sugar expansion in the northern part of Oriente, see also Zanetti and García, *United Fruit Company*, 53–79.

23. Ramiro Guerra, "Como nos ven," *Diario de la Marina*, January 13, 1929; Nelson, *Rural Cuba*, 171; Cuba, Ministerio de Agricultura, *Memoria del Censo Agrícola*, 466–71.

24. Kindsay and Winter, *Cuba and Her People*, 135; Pepper, *To-Morrow in Cuba*, 150.

25. Foreign Policy Association, *Problems of the New Cuba*, 41.

26. Atkins, *Sixty Years in Cuba*, 295; Luis Felipe Rodríguez, "La Guardarraya," in *Ciénaga y otros relatos*, 289–94.

27. Hartwell Johnson, "General Survey of Political and Economic Conditions," Matanzas, December 22, 1933, USNA, RG 84/800/145; Edward S. Benet to Butler J. Wright, Matanzas, June 1, 1938, USNA, RG 84/800.

28. Cuba, Comisión Nacional de Estadística y Reformas Económicas, *Cuadros estadísticos en relación con los ingenios*; Ferrocarriles del Norte de Cuba, *Boletín Quincenal, edición extraordinaria*, Ciego de Avila, 1923, 42–49; CNOC, *IV Congreso*, 71.

29. Clark, "Labor Conditions in Cuba," 778.

30. Scott, "Race, Labor, and Citizenship," 12.

31. Edwin Schoenrich to Samuel Dickinson, Santiago de Cuba, January 2, 1934, USNA, RG 84/800.

32. Conrado Becquer, interviewed by the author, Havana, March 18, 1998; Zanetti and García, *United Fruit Company*, 244–45; Morales y Patiño, "La higiene," 367–78; Pérez Pérez, *Huelga del 55*, 8–9.

33. Percival Farquhar to Sir William C. Van Horne, n.p., November 1, 1900, Cuba Company Papers, ser. 1, box A, 263–65, University of Maryland, McKeldin Library, College Park, Maryland; Iglesias, "La explotación del hierro," 100–101; Clark, "Labor Conditions in Cuba," 685; "Economic Conditions in the Interior Portion of the Havana Consular District," Havana, May 26, 1927, USNA, RG 59/837.00/2663.

34. Pérez-Medina, "The Situation of the Negro in Cuba," 294–98; Le Riverend, *Historia económica de Cuba*, 234.

35. Zanetti and García, *United Fruit Company*, 435–36; Hartwell Johnson, "General Survey of Political and Economic Conditions"; Vogenitz to Wright, Cienfuegos, May 28, 1938, USNA, RG 84/800/5; Arthur J. Dukes to Wright, Nuevitas, June 2, 1938, USNA, RG 84/800.

36. Clark, "Labor Conditions in Cuba," 779.

37. The 1899–1919 censuses define as urban any city with a population of 1,000 or more. Because this definition is significantly altered later, I have used centers of 5,000 or more to study differential rates of urbanization by race. For a general discussion of urbanization in Cuba, see Dyer, "Urbanism in Cuba," 224–33, and CEDEM, *La población de Cuba*.

38. Barnet, *Biography of a Runaway Slave*, 190.

39. L. L. and Bernard, "The Negro in Relation to Other Races," 310.

40. Wilson, *The Declining Significance of Race*, 62–87; Jaynes and Williams, *A Common Destiny*, 271–74. For an overview of the literature, see Trotter, "African Americans in the City," 438–57.

41. Crowder to the Secretary of State, Havana, August 25, 1925, USNA, RG 59/837.00/2597; "Economic Crisis," *Havana Post*, March 29, 1927; Guggenheim, "General Conditions Report," Havana, April 11, 1930, USNA, RG 84/170-G; Trelles, "La hacienda," 323–42. All the figures about sectoral growth have been calculated from the censuses.

42. Edward L. Reed, "Confidential Dispatch," Havana, August 5, 1930, USNA, RG 84/326; Guggenheim, "General Conditions Report," Havana, June 9, 1931, USNA, RG 84/800/729.

43. National income figures are based on Alienes y Urosa, *Características fundamentales*, 52.

44. Benet to Wright, Matanzas, June 1, 1938, USNA, RG 84/800; Zanetti and García, *United Fruit Company*, 227; Guggenheim, "General Conditions Report," Havana, April 10, 1931, USNA, RG 84/800/644.

45. For an overview of unemployment, see Mesa-Lago, *The Labor Force*. The growth of industrial output is studied in Pérez-López, "An Index of Cuban Industrial Output."

46. Pérez-López, "An Index of Cuban Industrial Output"; Alienes, *Características fundamentales*, 47–48; Dyer, "Urbanism in Cuba," 228.

47. Tamayo, "La vivienda en procomún," 23–31.

48. Chailloux Cardona, *Síntesis histórica*, 111, 135; "Los barrios de indigentes," *El Mundo*, November 28, 1951; Herminio Portell Vilá, "De cómo viven los habaneros pobres," *Bohemia*, December 9, 1951, 66–67, 83.

49. Novás Calvo, "La luna de los ñáñigos," 83–105; Ames, "Negro Family Types," 159–63. Ames's figure probably included what according to Cuban racial constructions would be "mulattoes," for he considered "Negro" "those having predominantly Negroid characteristics."

50. Chailloux Cardona, *Síntesis histórica*, 149; Convención Nacional, *Programa*, 4.

51. Serra, *Para blancos y negros*, 46; George Duroy, "Machacando en hierro frío," *Labor Nueva* 1, no. 13 (May 14, 1916): 6; Gustavo Urrutia, "La vivienda del pobre," *Diario de la Marina*, November 21, 1929.

52. Benjamín Muñoz Ginarte, "Comentos sin comentarios. ¡Tierras! ¡Tierras propias!," *Diario de la Marina*, June 16, 1929.

53. Muñoz Ginarte, "Comentos sin comentarios. Al doctor Ramiro Guerra," *Diario de la Marina*, February 10, 1929.

54. Vogenitz to Wright, Cienfuegos, October 18, 1939, USNA, RG 84/800/34; Milton Patterson Thompson, "Cuban Immigration Problems," Matanzas, October 9, 1936, USNA, RG 84/855. The Spanish control of the commercial sector has been studied in García Alvarez, *La gran burguesía comercial*, 91–104, and Naranjo Orovio, "Análisis histórico de la emigración," 503–26.

55. Gustavo Urrutia, "La defensa," *Diario de la Marina*, April 22, 1928. Urrutia went back to this issue in "La cuestión económica del negro," *Diario de la Marina*, July 17, 1929.

56. The sudden increase in the foreign whites' index of participation among merchants in the 1931–43 period suggests that most Spanish merchants did not become naturalized Cubans during the 1930s. The nationalization of labor law targeted foreign "workers" and had little impact among the merchants. Since the proportion of Spaniards in the working population decreased, the index of representation of the foreign merchants increased artificially.

57. Gustavo Urrutia, "Dicen de París . . . ," *Diario de la Marina*, May 7, 1928; Betancourt, *Doctrina negra*, 62–63; García Buchaca et al., *El II Congreso*, 20; FDMC, *Informes y resoluciones*, 29.

58. "Promete Prío combatir la discriminación racial" and "Destacadas figuras del comercio," *Prensa Libre*, November 15 and 28, 1951.

59. Felipe Elosegui, "1000 noticias en sepia," *Tiempo*, December 1 and 2, 1951; Sergio Carbó, "Bellas y dulces muchachas de color," *Prensa Libre*, December 12, 1951; "Afirma Buttari que no existe la discriminación," *Prensa Libre*, December 15, 1951; José Luis Massó, "Reportaje de actualidad. Ha caído una gran barrera racial," *Bohemia*, December 9, 1951, 48–49, 111; "Lanzadas a la calle," *Noticias de Hoy*, January 11, 1952.

60. Arredondo, *El negro en Cuba*, 57; Foreign Policy Association, *Problems of the New Cuba*, 475–76; Clark, "Labor Conditions in Cuba," 771.

61. Lazcano, *Constitución de Cuba*, 2:516; Nicolás Guillén, "El camino de Harlem," *Diario de la Marina*, April 21, 1929. In the Ferrocarriles del Norte de Cuba, an American-owned company, not only were the twelve upper employees of the general administration white, but among the 101 employees in the departments of accounting, fares, and shops and others, there was not a single Afro-Cuban employed. See Ferrocarriles del Norte de Cuba, *Boletín Quincenal, edición extraordinaria*, Ciego de Avila, 1923.

62. "Datos cubanos. Movimiento de las empresas de tranvías eléctricos durante 1924–25," *Revista Bimestre Cubana* 22 (1927): 274.

63. "La lucha contra los discriminadores," *El Organizador* (March 1947): 2; Carlos

Rafael Rodríguez, "Un paso importante en la lucha contra la discriminación racial," *Fundamentos* 7, no. 65 (March 1947): 2325–29; unknown to the American Embassy, Havana, January 7, 1947, USNA, RG 59/837.00B/1-747.

64. "Saludan ingreso de un negro," *Noticias de Hoy*, January 7, 1947; "La discriminación nacional y racial en la industria cubana," *Nuevos Rumbos* 2 (January–February 1947): 25.

65. Foreign workers represented only 23 percent of the labor force employed by the phone companies in 1924. See "Datos cubanos. Los teléfonos de servicio público en 1924," *Revista Bimestre Cubana* 21 (1926): 759. For specific graphic examples that show the racial composition of the phone unions, see the following articles, all published in *Unidad*: "IV Consejo Provincial del Sindicato de las Villas" (March 1947): 22, 31; "De nuestro baluarte oriental" (May 1947): 9; and "Delegaciones provinciales asistentes al IV Congreso" (November 1952): 33–35. For Afro-Cubans' denunciations, see "Editorial," *Atenas* 2, no. 7 (November 1951): 5, 22.

66. Pepper, *To-Morrow in Cuba*, 152.

67. The proletarianization of urban artisans is analyzed in two articles published in the "Ideales de una raza" column in *Diario de la Marina*: Ramiro Guerra, "Nuevas y fecundas orientaciones," January 13, 1929, and Muñoz Ginarte, "Comentos sin comentarios," January 27, 1929.

68. "Datos cubanos. Movimiento de las fábricas de tabaco en el año de 1924," *Revista Bimestre Cubana* 22 (1927): 108; Cuba, Comisión Nacional de Estadística y Reformas Económicas, *Estadística . . . de cigarros y tabacos en el año 1926*; Arredondo, *El negro en Cuba*, 63; Lazcano, *Constitución de Cuba*, 2:516; CNOC, *IV Congreso*, 71.

69. "Datos cubanos. Resumen de la estadística de destilerías y su producción," *Revista Bimestre Cubana* 22 (1927): 757–59.

70. "Cuartillas traspapeladas," *La Prensa*, January 11, 1916; Neyra y Lanza, "La prensa y la inmigración antillana," *Labor Nueva* 1, no. 9 (April 16, 1916): 6–7.

71. Neyra y Lanza, "La prensa y la inmigración antillana"; Daniel Braddock, "Living Conditions in Cuba," Havana, August 26, 1958, USNA, RG 59/837.01/8-2658; "Classified Advertisements," *Havana Post*, July 28, 1922; "Editorial. La ley y los hábitos mentales," *Carga* 1, no. 13 (February 1944): 2–3.

72. For a brief description of Afro-Cuban female activities in the early 1900s, see Clark, "Labor Conditions in Cuba," 718. For a denunciation of black women's displacement from the labor market due to immigration, see "Un poco de etnología," *La Prensa*, October 13, 1915.

73. Female activity rates are explored in de la Fuente, "Race and Inequality in Cuba," 158; Masdeu, *La raza triste*; and Arredondo, *El negro en Cuba*, 63.

74. For a "favorable" assessment of this immigration and a summary of the debate, see Maluquer de Motes, "La inmigración española en Cuba," 137–47.

75. The index of dissimilarity measures differences between two population groups. In table 3.4 it measures differences in the occupational distribution of immigrants, native whites, and blacks.

76. Atkins, *Sixty Years in Cuba*, 315.

77. Clark, "Labor Conditions," 768–69 (my emphasis).

78. Frank Garrett to Whigham, Jatibonico, October 22, 1913, Cuba Company Papers,

ser. 1, box 9, 135; F. Gerard Smith to Leandro Rionda, Francisco, February 15, 1917, BBC, RG 10, ser. 10a, box 8.

79. "La huelga de bahía," *La Lucha*, July 9 and 19, 1904; "Movimiento obrero. Los estibadores," *La Lucha*, July 16 and 17, 1906; Beaupré to the Secretary of State, Havana, May 8, 1912, USNA, RG 59/837.5401/23; "Noticias del puerto. Jamaiquinos," *Diario de la Marina*, March 11, 1921; "Estibadores cesanteados injustamente," *La Lucha*, August 15, 1928.

80. Unknown to Galham, Camagüey, November 30, 1916, and M. K. to Whigham, Richmond, November 29, 1916, Cuba Company Papers, ser. 1, box 23, 913 and 204.

81. Craib to George Whigham, Jatibonico, December 20, 1916, Cuba Company Papers, ser. 1, box 20, 264; Horace Dickinson to C. B. Hurst, Antilla, June 13, 1922, USNA, RG 59/837.00/2232; "El antagonismo," *La Lucha*, July 4, 1924; "Strike Conspiracy," *Havana Post*, October 13, 1917; Jos Wells to the Secretary of State, Antilla, June 17, 1921, USNA, RG 59/837.504/211.

82. "Huelga general," *La Lucha*, November 2, 1902; "La huelga de los aprendices," in Instituto de Historia, *El movimiento obrero*, 1:193–95; "La huelga general. La Liga General de Trabajadores Cubanos," *La Lucha*, November 14, 1902. About the Liga's purposes, see "Los obreros," *La Lucha*, September 29, 1899, and "Otra huelga," *La Unión Española*, January 22, 1900, evening ed.

83. Instituto de Historia, *Historia del movimiento obrero*, 1:150 (emphasis in original).

84. "La huelga del alcantarillado de la Habana," in Instituto de Historia, *El movimiento obrero*, 1:289–92; [Partido Socialista], "Manifesto to All Workers," enclosed in Victor Berger to the Secretary of State, Washington, D.C., February 19, 1912, USNA, RG 59/837.0132/1.

85. Flaxer, "Memorandum on Labor Unions," in Guggenheim to the Secretary of State, Havana, June 18, 1931, USNA, RG 84/850.4/747.

86. "La prensa," *Diario de la Marina*, October 25, 1901, morning ed.; "A la Cámara," *El Nuevo Criollo*, February 18, 1905; "Información obrera," *El Mundo*, September 11, 1908; "Obreros de la Patria," *La Lucha*, October 7 and 9, 1909; Congreso Nacional Obrero, *Memoria*, 277, 299, 321.

87. Among those petitioning for these laws were Afro-Cubans Juan Bravo and Gustavo Vargas Soler from the Camagüey railway workers. See Juan Bravo, "Sensaciones," *Juvenil*, January 19, 1913; about Soler, see Congreso Nacional Obrero, *Memoria*, 172.

88. The proportion was later increased to 75 percent. At least two attempts had been made in the early 1920s to have a similar bill considered in Congress, one by the Regla Town Council in 1922, the other by the Movement of Veterans and Patriots in 1923. See Crowder to the Secretary of State, Havana, March 7, 1922, and "Memorial to Congress Presented by the National Assembly of Veterans and Patriots," Havana, August 30, 1923, USNA, RG 59/837.032/53 and 837.00/2345.

89. "Pintoresca sesión en la Cámara" and "Continúan los debates," *La Lucha*, November 5 and 10, 1925; "House Adopts Native Labor Legislation" and "Remainder of Native Labor Law Approved," *Havana Post*, November 5 and 11, 1925; "Project of Law Introduced in the House of Representatives by Representative Lombard," USNA, RG 59/837.504/278.

90. "La Cámara de Comercio de Santiago de Cuba" and "Las Cámaras de Comercio de Rodas y de San Antonio de los Baños protestan," *La Lucha*, November 27 and 29, 1925; "Nuevitas Chamber of Commerce Protests" and "Guantánamo Chamber of Commerce Opposed," *Havana Post*, November 20, December 19, 1925; "Economic Corporations Oppose Passage of Lombard Labor Bill," *Evening News*, November 21, 1925.

91. "American Chamber of Commerce Calls Special Session" and "American Chamber of Commerce Protests," *Havana Post*, November 13 and 24, 1925; Crowder to the Secretary of State, Havana, November 30, 1925, and Department of State to Embassy in Havana, Washington, D.C., November 14, 1925, USNA, RG 59/ 837.00/2602 and 837.504/275; Pérez, "Aspects of Hegemony," 62–63.

92. Crowder to the Secretary of State, Havana, November 13, 1925, January 29, 1926, USNA, RG 59/837.504/275 and 292.

93. Excerpts from *Heraldo* and *El Día*, from "Cuban Press on the Events of the Day" and "Lombard Measure May Affect Cuban Politics," *Havana Post*, November 8, 1925, January 26, 1926; "La ley del setenta y cinco por ciento," *La Lucha*, November 14, 1925.

94. The study of cross-racial mobilization in the labor movement in Cuba is undertaken in Scott, "Relaciones de clase e ideologías raciales," 127–50, and Dumoulin, "El primer desarrollo," 3–66.

95. Lino Castelló, "Francisco Lamuño," *El Hombre Nuevo*, October 13, 1919; "Argentina, Cuba, España" and "El mítin de Martí," *¡Tierra!*, November 20 and 27, 1909. See also Dumoulin, "El primer desarrollo," 34–35.

96. "Nueva protesta de la Federación Obrera de la Habana," "La viril protesta obrera," and "Manifiesto protesta de la Liga Antimperialista," in Rosell, *Luchas obreras*, 83–84, 95–98, 108–10 (emphasis in original).

97. J. M. Cruz Tolosa, "Como nos ven. A Domingo Mesa," *Diario de la Marina*, February 17, 1929; Lindsay and Winter, *Cuba and Her People*, 155. The opportunities for graft in public office are re-created by Jesús Masdeu in his 1931 novel, *Ambición*.

98. Carrión, "El desenvolvimiento social," 6–27; Gabriel Sánchez, "La protección del estado," *Labor Nueva* 1, no. 27 (August 27, 1916): 8–9.

99. "Arbitrariedad," *La Lucha*, September 6, 1899; "Patriotismo con jaba," *La Lucha*, May 27, 1902; El Negro Falucho, "Quia nominor leo," *El Nuevo Criollo*, December 24, 1904; "Víctima de libertad," *La Lucha*, September 5, 1905; "El cacique Antonio Bravo," *El Nuevo Criollo*, October 7, 1905.

100. Sierra, *Para blancos y negros*, 205–6.

101. "Cuartillas traspapeladas," *La Prensa*, January 11, 1916; "Tribuna libre," *El Globo*, May 12, 1927; Elosegui, "1000 noticias en sepia," *Tiempo*, November 16, 1951.

102. "Los Auténticos revolucionarios," *Ahora*, December 12, 1933; Owen W. Games, "Fortnightly Political Report," Santiago de Cuba, December 2, 1936, USNA, RG 84/800; "Del ambiente político," *Acción Socialista* 24, no. 657 (March 1945): 9.

103. Lindsay and Winter, *Cuba and Her People*, 155–56; Juan Jiménez Pastrana, "El estilo maceico de la república," *Atenas* 2, no. 8 (December 1951): 14–17, 23.

104. "Datos cubanos. Empleados del estado cubano," *Revista Bimestre Cubana* 22 (1927): 763; "El incremento de la burocracia," *Diario de la Marina*, February 8, 1931.

105. Trelles, "La hacienda," 325. An excellent literary re-creation of this problem can be found in Masdeu's *Ambición*, in which the protagonist obtains two imaginary government jobs, each one worth $250 per month. The monthly salary for his "real" job was, however, only $75.

106. Serra, "De actualidad," *El Nuevo Criollo*, February 11, 1905; Helg, *Our Rightful Share*, 87.

107. "Asuntos varios. Mítin en Guanabacoa," *Diario de la Marina*, November 28, 1901, morning ed.; "A la Antorcha de Trinidad," *El Nuevo Criollo*, November 5, 1904; Simeón Poveda Ferrer, "Sobre la raza de color II," *El Nuevo Criollo*, November 25, 1905. See also Orum, "The Politics of Color," 113–29; Helg, *Our Rightful Share*, 100–103; Fernández Robaina, *El negro en Cuba*, 46–67; and Castellanos and Castellanos, *Cultura Afrocubana*, 2:288–308.

108. Ricardo Batrell Oviedo and Alejandro Nenínger, "Manifiesto al pueblo de Cuba," ANC, Fondo Especial, leg. fuera, no. 8-21; "¿Partido negro?," *La Discusión*, December 17, 1906; Evaristo Estenoz, "A mis amigos," *El Nuevo Criollo*, September 30, 1905; Magoon, *Report of Provisional Administration*, 326.

109. Hugh Gibson to the Secretary of State, Havana, November 10, 1911, USNA, RG 59/837.00/502; "Como se cubaniza," *Cuba*, January 17, 1912; "Aviso del gobierno de Washington," *La Opinión*, January 17, 1912; Arredondo, *El negro en Cuba*, 65.

110. "Comunicación mecanografiada del Secretario de la Presidencia al Secretario de Justicia," Havana, October 23, 1933, ANC, Secretaría de la Presidencia, leg. 87, no. 91.

111. Alfredo Martín Morales, "Claroscuro," *Labor Nueva* 1, no. 4 (March 12, 1916); Fernández Robaina, *El negro en Cuba*, 193; Masdeu, *La raza triste*, 177.

112. Pérez, *Cuba between Empires*, 338–44; Helg, *Our Rightful Share*, 96–97.

113. "Asuntos varios. La guardia rural," *Diario de la Marina*, January 12, 1901, evening ed.; "La prensa," *Diario de la Marina*, October 11, 1901, morning ed.; "Report of Captain H. J. Slocum," in Cuba, Military Governor, *Civil Report . . . 1902*, 3:68; Batrell Oviedo and Nenínger, "Manifiesto."

114. "La Prensa," *Diario de la Marina*, October 11 and 17, 1901, morning ed.; "El Centro de Veteranos y Wood," *El Mundo*, October 16, 1901; "Asuntos varios. La artillería cubana," *Diario de la Marina*, January 19, 1902, morning ed.; Cuba, Military Governor, *Civil Report . . . 1902*, 1:191.

115. "Armed Forces of Cuba, 1906–1934," USNA, RG 165/2012-153; Trelles, "El progreso y el retroceso," 348–49.

116. Decrees 539 and 541, Havana, May 8, 1924, USNA, RG 165/2657-Q143; de Graux, "Memo to the War Department," Havana, January 21, 1919, USNA, RG 165/2012-55.

117. Serra, "A los liberales de color," October 1906, in *Para blancos y negros*, 80–84; "A la Antorcha de Trinidad," *El Nuevo Criollo*, November 5, 1904; Batrell Oviedo and

Nenínger, "Manifiesto"; Máximo Gómez to Leonard Wood, Havana, January 6, 1900, LC, Leonard Wood Papers, 28; "Notas sueltas. El general Díaz," *La Lucha*, September 9, 1899.

118. "G-2 Report: Prominent Officers in the Cuban Army," Havana, January 6, 1922, USNA, RG 165/2012-90; "Una injusta preterición," *La Discusión*, January 24, 1925; Van Natta to the Chief of Military Intelligence, Havana, July 30, 1918, USNA, RG 165/2012-16; Romilio Portuondo Calá, "El primer piloto negro con licencia," *Magazine de Hoy*, October 1, 1944.

119. Lino D'Ou, "El Brigadier González," *Cúspide* 2, no. 10 (October 15, 1938); "El alcalde y policía de Camajuaní," *La Lucha*, August 21, 1907.

120. "Comandante Arsenio Ortiz," n.d., USNA, RG 165/2657-Q-126; Long to the Secretary of State, Havana, September 27, 1920, USNA, RG 59/837.00/1778; "El Cmte. Arsénico Ortiz," *La Política Cómica*, May 3, 1931; "La agresión al chacal Ortiz," *Bohemia*, November 26, 1933, 14, 59; J. Hobson to the Director of Military Intelligence, Havana, October 24, 1920, USNA, RG 165/2657-Q-46; Schoenrich to Guggenheim, Santiago, April 27, 1931, USNA, RG 84/800.

121. H. Freeman Matthews to the Secretary of State, Havana, September 16, 1933, USNA, RG 84/820/259. I estimated this percentage using the figures included in "Resume of Cuban Army Strength," February 28, 1933, USNA, RG 165/2012-100.

122. Hartwell Johnson, "General Survey of Political and Economic Conditions," Matanzas, December 22, 1933, USNA, RG 84/800/145; "The Crusher of Revolutions," *Havana Post*, November 12, 1933; T. N. Gimperling, "G-2 Report: Alleged Dissension and Communism in the Cuban Army," Havana, October 30, 1933, USNA, RG 165/2012-133; Gimperling, "Commissioned Officers," Havana, January 4, 1934, USNA, RG 165/2012-119; Richard S. Hooker Jr., "Squadron Intelligence Report," Havana, January 5, 1934, USNA, RG 84/820/322.

123. William Blocker, "Fortnightly Political Report," Santiago, December 13, 1935, USNA, RG 84/800; Military Attaché, "Memo," Havana, March 12, 1935, USNA, RG 84/800/2880; Milton Thompson to Elis O. Briggs, Matanzas, September 4, 1935, USNA, RG 84/800.

124. William Blocker, "Fortnightly Political Report," Santiago de Cuba, December 13, 1935, USNA, RG 84/800; Willard L. Beaulac, "General Conditions Report," Havana, September 22, 1938, USNA, RG 84/800/1130; Ellis O. Briggs to the Secretary of State, Havana, December 4, 1943, USNA, RG 84/800/5329.

125. Edwin Schoenrich to Samuel S. Dickson, Nuevitas, December 26, 1933, USNA, RG 84/800; Johnson to Dickson, Matanzas, January 4, 1934, USNA, RG 84/800/309; Caffery to the Department of State, Havana, February 21, 1934, USNA, RG 84/800/173; "Al pueblo de Cuba," *Adelante* 6 (November 1935): 20; Al País, "¡El Partido Comunista ante los últimos atentados a los negros!," Havana, April 6, 1936, ANC, Fondo Especial, leg. 5, no. 193; Thompson to H. Freeman Matthews, Matanzas, May 18, 1936, USNA, RG 84/800; Thompson to Briggs, Nuevitas, September 16, 1941, USNA, RG 84/800.

126. Cuéllar Vizcaíno, *Unas cuantas verdades*, 7–12; Thompson to Briggs, Nuevitas, September 16, 1941, USNA, RG 84/800.

127. "Almuerzo del presidente con los jefes policíacos," *Revista de la Policía* 1, no. 8 (August 1945): 13; John Speakes to James Wright, Havana, August 1, 1945, USNA, RG 84/843; E. W. Timberlake, "Distribution of Troops," Havana, May 19, 1938, USNA, RG 84/822/5576. For Afro-Cubans' views on their participation in the police force after the 1933 revolution, see "De Calimete," *Adelante* 1, no. 2 (July 1935): 20; Cuéllar Vizcaíno, *Unas cuantas verdades*, 5, 10; and Elosegui, "1000 noticias en sepia," *Tiempo*, December 7, 1951.

128. Barber, "Military Intelligence Division: Who's Who on Lt. Col. Gregoria [*sic*] Querejeta," Havana, May 7, 1941, USNA, RG 165/2012/168; "Ascendido el capitán Querejeta," *Diario de la Marina*, November 14, 1933; Norweb to the Secretary of State, Havana, December 3, 1946, USNA, RG 59/837.00/2526; "Decretados ascensos," *El Crisol*, February 4, 1942; Mallory to the Secretary of State, Havana, December 15, 1948, USNA, RG 59/837.20/12-1448.

CHAPTER FOUR

1. Quoted in Epstein, "Social Structure," 200.
2. This quote is taken from Masdeu's novel *Ambición*, 12.
3. For a concrete example in which the right to education is linked to Martí's republic "with all and for all," see the short story of Afro-Cuban author Tomás Savignón, "Mi amigo blanco," *Diario de la Marina*, August 10, 1930.
4. For a few examples, see "Apunta pueblo," *El Nuevo Criollo*, May 27, 1905; Francis White to the Secretary of State, Havana, August 13, 1920, USNA, RG 59/837/1734; "Machado Announces Platform," *Evening News*, September 11, 1924.
5. Nicolás Guillén, "Proyecto de entrevista con el Sr. Gómez Estévez," *Diario de la Marina*, October 6, 1929.
6. Hinton, "Cuban Reconstruction," 96.
7. El Negro Falucho [Serra], "Se triunfará esta vez?" and "A un 'negro oriental,'" *El Nuevo Criollo*, September 2, 1905, November 12, 1904; Batrell Oviedo, *Para la historia*, 172.
8. "La política," *El Nuevo Criollo*, April 22, 1905. For examples of Afro-Cubans' perceptions of black education in the United States, see Juan Antiga, "El negro en los Estados Unidos," *Labor Nueva*, April 2, 1916, 4–5, and "La instrucción de los negros en los Estados Unidos," *Diario de la Marina*, December 2, 1928.
9. "Directorio Central," 1887, ANC, Registro de Asociaciones, leg. 428, no. 13454. For a general discussion of the Directorio's work on education, see Helg, *Our Rightful Share*, 36–37.
10. Tristán [Ramón Vasconcelos], "Una cuantas verdades," *La Prensa*, August 14, 1915; "Unión Fraternal," ANC, Registro de Asociaciones, leg. 427, no. 13447; "Club Unión Fraternal," 1910, ANC, Registro de Asociaciones, leg. 1200, no. 25047; "Asociación Centro de Cocheros," 1900, ANC, Registro de Asociaciones, leg. 1331, no. 27279; "El primer paso," *El Nuevo Criollo*, August 5, 1905.
11. On North American views and practices concerning education, see Pérez, "The Imperial Design," 35–52, and "North American Protestant Missionaries," 53–72; Crahan, "Religious Penetration."
12. For school registration and attendance during 1900–1920, see "Sección de es-

tadística," *La Instrucción Primaria* 10, nos. 1–2 (September–October 1911): 67; "El gobierno del Dr. Zayas," *La Lucha*, October 17, 1924; and Cuba, Secretaría de Educación, *Estadística general, 1931–1936*, 36.

13. Ortiz, *La decadencia cubana*, 6. See also Ortiz, "El Doctor de la Torre," 8–14; Trelles, "El progreso y el retroceso," 347; "Cifras pavorosas," *La Prensa*, May 14, 1916; and "El analfabetismo," *La Discusión*, January 11, 1925.

14. Carlton Bailey, "Report: Education in Cuba," Havana, December 10, 1926, USNA, RG 59/837.42/21; CEPAL, *Cuba*, 87.

15. "Asuntos varios. Apertura de un colegio" and "Asuntos varios. Comité del barrio del Príncipe," *Diario de la Marina*, March 7, October 5, 1900, morning ed. See also Magoon, *Report of the Provisional Administration*, 325–28.

16. I have used the ten-to-nineteen-year-old group to measure literacy for two reasons. The first is a methodological one: the use of a limited age group permits me to measure the evolution of literacy and education during the years immediately preceding the census, when most of the members of this group would have acquired their literacy. Second, this age group is consistently listed in all censuses.

17. Convención Nacional, *Programa*, 4. For a report on the problems faced by the public school system, see C. R. Cameron, "Regulation of Private Schools in Cuba," Havana, February 28, 1936, USNA, RG 84/842.

18. Lowry Nelson, "Literacy of the Cuban Population," [1946], USNA, RG 59/837.42/3-146; John E. Hoover to Frederick B. Lyon, Washington, D.C., June 5, 1946, USNA, RG 59/837.002/60546; Rodolfo Rodríguez, "Presupuestos fastuosos y escuelas miserables," *Bohemia*, December 2, 1951, 40–42, 103; Truslow, *Report on Cuba*, 404.

19. Summary of Presidential Message, Havana, November 7, 1932, USNA, RG 84/800/1430; *Inter-American Statistical Yearbook 1942*, 911; Cuban Economic Research Project, *A Study on Cuba*, 427; "Statistics on the Cuban Educational System," Havana, September 10, 1959, USNA, RG 59/837.43/9-1059; Truslow, *Report on Cuba*, 404.

20. Massip, "La crisis de los institutos," 183–215; *Inter-American Statistical Yearbook 1942*, 914; "Anuncia el Ministro de Educación," *El Mundo*, July 18, 1942; Edward Bash to the Department of State, Havana, September 10, 1959, USNA, RG 59/837.43/9-1059.

21. J. Butler Wright, "Cultural and Propaganda Activities," Havana, April 19, 1938, USNA, RG 84/842/702; "Memorandum," Havana, March 21, 1933, USNA, RG 84/800/1550; Pérez, "North American Protestant Missionaries," 67.

22. Colegio de Belén, *Album*; Colegio Champagnat, *Memoria*; Riolai, "Obras benéficas: 'La Domiciliaria,'" and Esperanza de Zubizarreta, "Obras benéficas: 'Sagrado Corazón,'" *Labora* 1, no. 4 (October 15, 1920): 15–20; 2, no. 1 (January 15, 1921): 15–20.

23. Crahan, "Religious Penetration," 220; Havana Military Academy, *Memoria*. Testimonies about La Progresiva were obtained through interviews with Dr. María D. Maicas, Mexico City, December 21, 1994; Engineer Victor Ezpeleta, Mexico City, January 4, 1995; Dr. Yolanda Maicas, Havana, July 30, 1996; and Dr. Noel González, Havana, August 4, 1996. For a panegyric of the school, see Tony Delahoza,

"La Progresiva," *Bohemia*, November 12, 1950, 52–54. About Edison, see Instituto Edison, *Anuario*.

24. The full campaign is reproduced in *Por la escuela cubana*. For a defense of private education, see "Un triunfo de la cultura y la cubanidad bien entendida," *Diario de la Marina*, July 24, 1941.

25. The Communist Party introduced the law again in 1945. See Juan Marinello, "La Constitución cubana y la enseñanza privada," *CTC* 6, no. 65 (July 1945): 26–29; 6, no. 67 (August 1945): 30–31, 44–45, and "Proyecto patriótico," *Voz Gráfica* (May 1945): 12–13.

26. "Cuban Press on the Events of the Day. Urges Limited Classes," *Havana Post*, October 13, 1925; Daniel Braddock, "Report: Living Conditions in Cuba," Havana, August 26, 1958, USNA, RG 59/837.01/8 2658.

27. *Por la escuela cubana*, 86.

28. Marinello, *La cuestión racial*, 18.

29. Gustavo Urrutia, "Armonías," *Diario de la Marina*, February 24, 1929; Instituto de Segunda Enseñanza, *Memoria anual*, 1901–8; Cuba, Escuela Normal para Maestras, *Memoria anual*, 1915–16, 1924–25; González y Venegas, "Origen y desarrollo," 300–353; Cuba, Escuela Normal para Maestros, *Memoria*.

30. Dolz y Arango, "Discurso inaugural," 161–89; Wright, "Institutions of Higher Learning in Cuba," Havana, November 13, 1939, USNA, RG 84/842/2552; Herminio Portell Vilá, "Memorandum about Education in Cuba," Havana, June 20, 1945, USNA, RG 59/837.42/6-2245; Universidad de la Habana, *Datos estadísticos*.

31. Cuba, Comisión Nacional de Estadística, *Estadística de los matriculados*, 1927, 1930; "Datos cubanos. Alumnos de la Universidad Nacional, 1925–1926," *Revista Bimestre Cubana* 22 (1927): 924; Betancourt, *El negro*, 87; Universidad Católica, *Yearbook*.

32. Andrew de Graux to the Military Attaché, Havana, August 30, 1919, USNA, RG 59/837.00/1573; Marinello, *La cuestión racial*, 18; Pinto, "Una soberana idiotez," *Nuevos Rumbos* 1, no. 3 (January–February 1946): 5; J. Milla Chapelli, "Perfiles," *Diario de la Marina*, June 16, 1929.

33. Serra, *Para blancos y negros*, 83; "Dr. Tranquilino Maza Cobián," *Labor Nueva* 1, no. 21 (July 16, 1916): 7; Raúl C. Urrutia, "Vanity-Case. Dr. T. Maza Cobián," *Diario de la Marina*, January 13, 1929; Felipe Elosegui, "1000 noticias en sepia," *Tiempo*, November 27, 1951.

34. Gustavo Urrutia, "Ideales de una raza. ¡Cállense . . . y esperen!," *Diario de la Marina*, July 8, 1928.

35. Nelson, "Literacy of the Cuban Population"; Cuba, Secretaría de Educación, *Estadística general 1931–1936*, 38; Cuban Economic Research Project, *A Study on Cuba*, 427.

36. "Charla semanal," *Labor Nueva* 1, no. 8 (April 9, 1916): 3–4.

37. José Jucayo and Frank Guáimaro to the President of the United States, Havana, February 14, 1922, USNA, RG 59/837.00/2205.

38. Paul Beck, office memoranda, Havana, April 15, 1920, USNA, RG 165/2056-196; de Graux to the Military Attaché, Havana, August 30, 1919, USNA, RG 59/837.00/1573.

39. For a listing of prominent Afro-Cubans in the late nineteenth century, see Risquet, *Rectificaciones*, 147–84.

40. Gustavo Urrutia, "El único arquitecto," *Diario de la Marina*, July 1, 1928; E. R. Agüero, "Tocando la realidad," *La Prensa*, May 23, 1916. A similar argument concerning Afro-Cuban women was made in Catalina Pozo y Gato, "Con su permiso, amigo," *La Mujer*, November 15, 1930, 4, 20.

41. L. L. and Bernard, "The Negro in Relation to Other Races," 311.

42. Ruiz Suárez, *The Color Question*, 23.

43. Arredondo, *El negro en Cuba*, 61; Hernández Catá, "La piel," in *Los frutos ácidos*, 115–84; Masdeu, *La raza triste*, 76.

44. Nicolás Guillén, "Baró: Un autosuperado," *Diario de la Marina*, October 20, 1929; Tristán, "La escala de Joe," *La Prensa*, August 24, 1916; "Dr. Tranquilino Maza Cobián," *Labor Nueva* 1, no. 21 (July 16, 1916): 7; Raúl C. Urrutia, "Vanity-Case."

45. Nicolás Guillén, "La Dra. Matehu," *Diario de la Marina*, January 5, 1930; "¡Salve . . . oh salve!," *Diario de la Marina*, September 1, 1929; Consuelo Serra, "Intimidades," *Diario de la Marina*, June 1, 1930. These cases resemble those studied by Shaw in the United States in *What a Woman Ought to Be*.

46. Betancourt, *Doctrina negra*, 13, 78.

47. For a similar argument concerning Brazil, see Andrews, *Blacks and Whites*, 163–65.

48. Gilmore, *Gender and Jim Crow*, xix; Urrutia, "Ideales de una raza. ¡Cállense . . . y esperen!"

49. Lino D'Ou, "Otro rasero," *Labor Nueva* 1, no. 27 (August 27, 1916): 3–4; Tristán, "Variaciones sobre un mismo tema," *La Prensa*, October 8, 1915; and Gustavo Urrutia's comments to Aldereguía, "La tuberculosis en la raza negra," *Diario de la Marina*, September 15, 1929.

50. Gustavo Urrutia, "El negro que tenía que cambiar de domicilio," *Diario de la Marina*, May 2, 1928; Tristán, "No es la sufrida" and "De una jovencita," *La Prensa*, November 16, December 13, 1915; José Manuel Poveda, "Voces nuevas," *La Prensa*, September 5, 1915.

51. Tristán, "Comparsas," *La Prensa*, March 2, 1916; Francisco Mendoza Marrero, "El carnaval pasa," *La Prensa*, March 12, 1916; D'Ou, "Otro rasero."

52. Bullard, "The Cuban Negro," 624–25.

53. Cuba, *Censo 1907*, 458; Cuba, *Censo 1931*, table 17; Gustavo Urrutia, "Armonías. Deberes sociales," *Diario de la Marina*, August 18, 1929. For a summary of marriage rates among whites and blacks, see de la Fuente, "Race and Inequality," 147–48.

54. Lino D'Ou, "Surge et ambula," *Labor Nueva* 1, no. 23 (July 30, 1916): 4; Gustavo Urrutia, "Armonía. Deberes"; Tristán, "Tres puntos" and "Opinión de un cenfoguense," *La Prensa*, August 16 and 21, 1915; Neyra Lanza, "Ya era tiempo," *La Prensa*, October 4, 1915.

55. Caridad Chacón de Guillén, "Mi opinión," *La Prensa*, September 29, 1915; "Reflecciones femeninas," *La Prensa*, August 31, 1915.

56. Gerónimo Guerra, "A cuharetear," *La Prensa*, September 1, 1915; "Cuartillas traspapeladas," *La Prensa*, January 11, 1915. After the 1930s, Afro-Cuban intellectuals frequently explained blacks' lower marriage rates as an economic problem.

For examples, see Betancourt, *Doctrina negra*, 8–9, and Pinto, *El Dr. Mañach y el problema negro*, 31–45.

57. Brown and Kimball, "Mapping the Terrain," 329.

58. Gustavo Urrutia, "Incidencia y reflexión," *Diario de la Marina*, April 20, 1930.

59. Castellanos, "La briba hampona," 95; Ann Nevins, "As Others See Us," *Cuban Topics*, April 6, 1929, 4. For similar remarks, see Pepper, *To-Morrow in Cuba*, 153, and Hinton, "Cuban Reconstruction," 98–99.

60. Elosegui, "1000 noticias en sepia," *Tiempo*, February 23, 1952; "Denúnciase ante el Tribunal Supremo" and "Llamamiento al Presidente," *Noticias de Hoy*, March 22 and 23, 1947; "Editorial" and Elosegui, "Benito Martí," *Nuevos Rumbos* 2, no. 3 (March–April 1947): 3–4, 6–7.

61. Cuéllar Vizcaíno, "Aire libre," *Tiempo*, September 19, 1952.

62. Gustavo Urrutia, "Armonías. Rayos ultra-violetas," *Diario de la Marina*, March 16, 1930; Elosegui, "1000 noticias en sepia," *Tiempo*, April 10, 1952.

63. Gerardo Machado, "Cuba os recibe," *El País*, March 13, 1930; "Informaciones: (Incidentes del Habana Yacht Club)" and "Adhesiones valiosas," *Boletín Oficial del Club Atenas* 1, no. 4 (April 20, 1930): 5, 7; Gustavo Urrutia, "Un bochorno para Cuba," *Diario de la Marina*, March 30, 1930.

64. "Directrices," *Revista de Avance* 4, no. 45 (April 15, 1930): 98, 126. The reaction of the mainstream press is reproduced in *Boletín Oficial del Club Atenas* 1, no. 4 (April 20, 1930): 6–10. For a defense of the Havana Yacht Club, see "Impresiones," *Diario de la Marina*, March 31, 1930.

65. "Manifestaciones del ilustre patricio Juan Gualberto Gómez," *Boletín Oficial del Club Atenas* 1, no. 4 (April 20, 1930): 6. His statement is reproduced in *Diario de la Marina*, March 30, 1930.

66. Elosegui, "1000 noticias en sepia," *Tiempo*, November 22, 1951; "Niegan servicio" and "Fobia discriminadora," *Noticias de Hoy*, December 21 and 22, 1939.

67. Elosegui, "1000 noticias en sepia," *Tiempo*, December 5, 1951; "Clausurados cuatro bares" and Jorge Castellanos, "La llaga racial," *Noticias de Hoy*, September 13 and 24, 1952; Salvador García Agüero, "Desagravio a Maceo," *Noticias de Hoy*, May 23, 1953.

68. Felipe Elosegui, "El caso del hotel Andino," *Noticias de Hoy*, September 22, 1940; Francisco Ichaso, "Deporte. Kid Chocolate o el negrito," *Revista de Avance* 3, no. 35 (June 15, 1929): 182; Gustavo Urrutia, "La primera derrota de 'Chocolate,'" *Diario de la Marina*, October 6, 1929.

69. For the Mitchell case, see "Expediente compuesto por escritos dirigidos al Presidente," 1937, ANC, Secretaría de la Presidencia, leg. 39, no. 14. About the Sevilla hotel, see Cuéllar Vizcaíno, "Aire libre," *Tiempo*, September 11, 1951.

70. Urrutia, "El negro que tenía que cambiar"; "Vivienda y discriminación," *Nuevos Rumbos* 1, no. 9 (September–October 1946): 3; "Interesan del Congreso," *Noticias de Hoy*, October 6, 1944; Nicolás Guillén, "El camino de Harlem," *Diario de la Marina*, April 21, 1929; Aracelio Azcuy, "Negros en el cinódromo," *Atenas* 2, no. 4 (August 1951): 10.

71. Nicolás Guillén, "La conquista del blanco," *Diario de la Marina*, May 5, 1929; Urrutia, "Armonías. Rayos."

72. Urrutia, "La primera derrota."

73. For good introductions to the study of the *cabildos* and *sociedades* before independence, see Montejo Arrechea, *Sociedades de Instrucción*, and Hevia, *El Directorio*.

74. Among these were the Centro de Cocheros and the Redención society (1912), which grouped workers from the building trades. See ANC, Registro de Asociaciones, leg. 1134, nos. 23761–62, leg. 446, no. 14799. See also Montejo Arrechea, *Sociedades de Instrucción*, 54.

75. "Manifiesto de los hijos de Papá Silvestre" (1915), in Castellanos, *La brujería y el ñañiguismo*, 56–60; "Sociedad Nación Congo-Portugués, 1922," AHPC, Registro de Asociaciones, leg. 22, no. 418; Roche y Moteagudo, *La policía y sus misterios*, 181. See also the testimony of Ortiz about a Congo *cabildo* in "Preludios étnicos," 158–59.

76. ANC, Registro de Asociaciones, leg. 713, nos. 18314–18.

77. Long to the Secretary of State, Havana, October 8, 1920, USNA, RG 59/837.00/1802; del Valle, "Para concejal," in *1/4 Fambá*, 94–99.

78. "Sociedad de Instrucción y Recreo Club Moncada," AHPC, Registro de Asociaciones, leg. 33, no. 706.

79. The society from Regla was later called the Centro Juan Gualberto Gómez and in 1929 became, after a fusion with another local group, the Sociedad Progresista Juan Gualberto Gómez. See "Nueva directiva," *Diario de la Marina*, January 12, 1901, evening ed., and Gustavo Urrutia, "Armonías," *Diario de la Marina*, January 26, 1930. The Quiebra Hacha society is mentioned in D'Ou, "La evolución de la raza de color," 335.

80. "Los brujos ante la corte," *La Lucha*, June 28, 1912; "Cartas dirigidas a Juan G. Gómez por el Centro Juan Gualberto Gómez de Regla, 1898–1928," ANC, Adquisiciones, leg. 53, no. 4076, leg. 54, no. 4089; Elosegui, "1000 noticias en sepia," *Tiempo*, October 17, 1951; "Pide a Batista una beca," *Tiempo*, April 29, 1952.

81. Tristán, "Tempestad en un vaso de agua," *La Prensa*, October 14, 1915. The case of Atenas is discussed below. For examples of lottery funds being used to subsidize Afro-Cuban societies, see "Expediente referente a las solicitudes de las Sociedades e Instituciones de color, 1943–1944," ANC, Secretaría de la Presidencia, leg. 4, no. 93; "Notes about 'La renta de la lotería,'" in J. N. C., "Memorandum," Havana, June 22, 1944, USNA, RG 84/891; Cuéllar Vizcaíno, "Aire Libre," *Tiempo*, September 9, 1952, and *Unas cuantas verdades*, 10; and Gustavo Urrutia, "Armonías: Las 'sociedades de color' y discriminación en el trabajo," *Diario de la Marina*, August 12, 1952.

82. For a concrete example involving Senator Joaquín Pedraza and the Luz de Occidente society (San Cristobal, Pinar del Río), see "Una cuestión," *Cuatro Páginas*, November 29, 1941.

83. *Reglamento*, art. 1.

84. "Club 'Unión Fraternal,' Vegas, Nueva Paz," ANC, Registro de Asociaciones, leg. 1200, nos. 25047–49; "Asuntos varios. Divina Caridad," *Diario de la Marina*, February 12, 1902, morning ed.; Raúl C. Urrutia, "Vanity-Case," *Diario de la Marina*, August 11, 1929; Alberto Coffigny Ortiz, "Crónica social," *Diario de la Marina*, April 6, 1933.

85. "Unión Sagüera, breve reseña histórica" and "¡Adelante Trinidad!," *Renovación*,

March 20, 1932; "Desde Lajas" and "De Peña Blanca. Atenas Occidental," *La Discusión*, January 17 and 27, 1925; Julio M. González Torres, "Societarias," *Adelante* 1, no. 2 (July 1935): 18; Bonifacio Romero Pérez, "Nuestro discurso," *Atenas* 2, no. 7 (November 1951): 18–20.

86. Juan Domingo Roche, "Acuarelas. Los deportes en Cuba" and "El Senador Alberto Barreras," and Roche, "Píldora deportiva," *Diario de la Marina*, February 3, March 24, May 5, 1929; "La ODAC," *Fragua de la Libertad* 1, no. 6 (June 18, 1942): 12.

87. Apolo, "Epístola," *Juvenil* 1, no. 19 (March 1, 1913); Enrique Andreu, "Postulados y corolarios," and Tristán, "Un ejemplo edificante," *La Prensa*, October 21, November 8, 1915; Tristán, "La Asociación de Jóvenes Cristianos," *La Prensa*, September 16, 1916.

88. "Sociedad de Socorros Mutuos del Gremio de Cocheros de Color 'Nuestra Señora de la Caridad,'" 1881, ANC, Gobierno General, leg. 97, no. 4441; "Asociación 'Centro de Cocheros,'" ANC, Registro de Asociaciones, leg. 446, no. 14799; Tristán, "Tempestad en un vaso de agua," *La Prensa*, October 14, 1915.

89. See the following, all published in the column "Palpitaciones" of *La Prensa* in 1915: Andreu, "Un grito de alarma," December 19; Tristán, "Unas cuantas verdades," August 14; "Suicidio social," September 22; and "Paso inicial," November 10.

90. Tristán, "Paquete postal," *La Prensa*, August 6, 1915.

91. "Jóvenes de L'Printemps" and "Crónica," *Labor Nueva* 1, no. 2 (February 27, 1916): 11; 1, no. 7 (April 2, 1916): 10; "Club Jóvenes del Vals," ANC, Registro de Asociaciones, leg. 1158, nos. 24248–59.

92. Brown and Kimball, "Mapping the Terrain," 329–31; Gilmore, *Gender and Jim Crow*, 75–77; Andrews, *Blacks and Whites*, 140–41.

93. César Bascaro, "Booker T. Washington," and Abelardo Vasconcelos, "Clarinada," *Labor Nueva* 1, no. 6 (March 16, 1916): 10; 1, no. 34 (October 22, 1916): 7; Fabián Gotario, "Los arreboles de una idea," Manuel González Jiménez, "Hierros y bronces," and González Jiménez, "Un año . . . ," *Aurora* 1, no. 1 (April 15, 1914): 5–6; 1, no. 4 (June 1, 1914): 1–3; 2, no. 14 (April 15, 1915): 4.

94. See the section "Personalidad" of *Aurora*, where white intellectuals such as Julio César Gandarilla, René Lufríu, and Francisco González published their opinions about the new society.

95. Francisco González, "Hierros y bronces," "Nuevas rutas," and "Verbo de juventud," *Aurora* 1, no. 4 (July 1, 1914): 1; 1, no. 10 (December 15, 1914): 1; "Menos palabras," *Juvenil* 1, no. 17 (January 19, 1913): 1.

96. Juan de Bravo, "Sensaciones," and Apolo, "Epístola," *Juvenil* 1, no. 17 (January 19, 1913): 8–9; 1, no. 19 (March 1, 1913); José del C. Velasco, "Nuestro elemento representativo," *Aurora* 1, no. 7 (August 10, 1914): 9–10; S. Beyris, "Lo que debemos hacer," *Labor Nueva* 1, no. 24 (August 6, 1916): 9 (reproduced in *La Prensa*, August 10, 1916). An excellent analysis of the Afro-Cubans' organizational options is done in Lino D'Ou, "El dilema," *La Prensa*, August 25, 1915.

97. "Y dice el Dr. Céspedes," *La Prensa*, August 18, 1915.

98. "Habla Juan Gualberto" and "La Asociación," *Diario de la Marina*, December 2, 1928.

99. Tristán, "A un señor de Melena," *La Prensa*, October 5, 1915.

100. See the following, all in *La Prensa* in 1915: Poveda, "Voces nuevas," September 5; José Enrique Morúa, "Plato fuerte," September 7; and Varona, "Mi carta," November 7.

101. Tristán, "Paquete"; Caamaño de Cárdenas, "Con sello rápido," *La Prensa*, August 2, 1915.

102. This point was emphasized later in Cuéllar Vizcaíno, *Unas cuantas verdades*, 18–19.

103. "Club Atenas," ANC, Registro de Asociaciones, leg. 1112, nos. 23267–70; Belisario Heureaux, "Del tiempo pasado," *Boletín Oficial del Club Atenas* 1, no. 10 (October 20, 1930): 2; "Nuestros socios fundadores," *Atenas* 2, no. 5 (September 1951): 8; Marino Barreto, "Rápidas," *La Lucha*, November 23, 1919. See also Ruiz Suárez, *The Color Question*, 86–89; Helg, *Our Rightful Share*, 244; and Fernández Robaina, *El negro en Cuba*, 120.

104. See "Movimiento de socios" and "Solicitudes de ingreso," *Boletín Oficial del Club Atenas* 1, no. 4 (April 20, 1930): 4; 1, no. 10 (October 20, 1930): 6–7.

105. Tristán, "Paquete"; N. Lesnar, "Palabras de mujer," *La Prensa*, August 10, 1915; Calixta M. Hernández, "La influencia" and "El hogar," *Diario de la Marina*, May 5, July 7, 1929.

106. Hernández, "Divagaciones," *Diario de la Marina*, June 16, 1929; Pozo y Gato, "Con su permiso." The best study of Cuban feminism is Stoner's *From the House to the Streets*, which devotes little attention to the racial question.

107. "Obelisco al General Quintín Bandera," *Boletín Oficial del Club Atenas* 1, no. 4 (April 20, 1930): 2. For examples of contact with white politicians, see "Junta Directiva. Acuerdos."

108. For the discussion in the House, see Cuba, Cámara de Representantes, *Diario de Sesiones* 44, no. 9 (May 1, 1925): 97–108. For an earlier attempt to pass a similar law, see *Diario de Sesiones* 40, no. 34 (July 5, 1923): 16, and "Escritura #243 de cesión," July 3, 1926, ANC, Registro de Asociaciones, leg. 1112, no. 23268. The new headquarters were inaugurated on May 11, 1929. See Muñoz Ginarte, "Comentos," and Ramírez Ross, "Atenas," *Diario de la Marina*, May 19, June 2, 1929.

CHAPTER FIVE

1. Historiography about the so-called 1933 revolution is profuse. For useful introductions to the subject, see Pérez, *Cuba*, 251–66; Domínguez, *Cuba: Order and Revolution*, 54–109; and Tabares del Real, *La revolución del 33*.

2. For an analysis of these organizations, their composition, and their agendas, see Pérez, *Cuba*, 231–48.

3. Ortiz, "Informe," in Municipio de la Habana, *Las comparsas populares*, 15.

4. This vision was sustained by North American historian Charles Chapman. See Fernando Ortiz to Charles E. Chapman, Havana, June 3, 1926, USNA, RG 59/837.41/1.

5. R. D. Coulter to the Secretary of State, Miami, January 29, 1911, USNA, RG 59/837.00/458; E. L. Hallman to the President, Norristown, Pennsylvania, September 9, 1910, USNA, RG 59/837.00/428.

6. Billiken, "Arreglando el mundo: No se admiten cubanos," *La Prensa*, August 30, 1915; Un Guajiro Cubano to Enoch Crowder, Havana, February 1921, USNA, RG 59/837.00/81.

7. The concept of "Latin race" was used frequently by the press in the early republic to oppose Anglo-Saxon influences over the island. For examples, see "La prensa," *Diario de la Marina*, December 22, 1901, January 8, 1902, March 18, 1902, all morning eds. The Latin race was also celebrated in the "Festival of the Race" or "Day of the Race" (October 12), which became a national holiday in 1922. See Ortiz, "La sinrazón de los racismos," 161–83.

8. Some Afro-Cuban intellectuals challenged prevalent scientific notions about race. See, for instance, J. M. Asanza, "Sinopsis," and Juan Finot, "Concepciones," *La Prensa*, May 29, July 9, 1916. For a discussion of the validity of anthropometric studies to measure intelligence, see Rafael Gómez, "Las razas humanas," *Labor Nueva* 1, no. 21 (July 16, 1916): 4–5.

9. Ortiz, "Ni racismos ni xenofobias," 6–19, *El engaño de las razas*, and "La sinrazón de los racismos," 161–83. See also "Aprobada una moción cubana," *Diario de la Marina*, May 1, 1956.

10. For different uses of this concept, see Gustavo Urrutia, "La raza cubana," *Diario de la Marina*, June 26, 1928; Arce, *La raza cubana*; and Beci, *El igualitarismo*, 65–67.

11. About this process, see Barkan, *The Retreat of Scientific Racism*.

12. Stepan, *"The Hour of Eugenics."*

13. Cuba, MINSAP, *Dr. Enrique Lluria Despau*, 39–43.

14. Mario Luque, "Un gran libro cubano," *Cuba y América*, August 22, 1905, quoted in ibid., 95–97.

15. For examples, see Cepeda, *Eusebio Hernández*, and Rodríguez Expósito, *Dr. Enrique Núñez y Palomino*.

16. Guiteras, "Estudios demográficos," 405–21.

17. Percentages calculated from Cuba, Junta Superior de Sanidad, *Informe mensual* (1904–7), and Cuba, Sanidad y Beneficiencia, *Boletín Oficial* (1910–34). For the 1930s, see Cuba, Consejo Nacional de Tuberculosis, *Resumen*. For an excellent overview of the disease in Cuba, see Díaz-Briquets, *The Health Revolution*, 67–72.

18. Barnet, "Concepto actual," 19–36; Cuba, Military Governor, *Civil Report, 1902*, 1:164.

19. Ramírez Ros, "Cultura utilitaria," *Labor Nueva* 1, no. 1 (February 20, 1916): 9–10. See the following, all published in *Diario de la Marina* in 1929: "Ideas del Dr. J. A. Taboadela sobre la tuberculosis," September 29; Taboadela, "Nuevas consideraciones sobre la tuberculosis," October 6; Armando Leyva, "Como nos ven," September 1; and Gustavo Aldereguía, "La tuberculosis en la raza negra," September 15.

20. Kutzinski, *Sugar's Secrets*, 13.

21. N. M. Choleatt to the Secretary of State, Havana, September 15, 1915, USNA, RG 59/837.42/7; Ramón Vasconcelos, "Desde la celda número ocho," *Heraldo de Cuba*, April 7, 1921.

22. Moore, *Nationalizing Blackness*, 23–26.

23. Marinello, "25 años de poesía cubana," 366–88. For an introduction to the vast

literature on this poetic movement, see "Literatura afrocubana" in Instituto de Literatura, *Diccionario*, 24–26.

24. Ortiz, "Más acerca de la poesía mulata," 26–28; Marinello, "25 años de poesía cubana," 386.

25. Nicolás Guillén, "Sóngoro cosongo," in *Obra poética*, 1:114. On the contemporary impact of Guillén's poems, see Boti, "La poesía cubana," 343–53.

26. Moore, *Nationalizing Blackness*, 134–35.

27. See Martínez, *Cuban Art*, 74–81, 105–9, for a specific discussion of Abela. For contemporary comments on Abela's paintings of black cultural practices, see Adolfo Zamora, "Eduardo Abela, pintor cubano," *Revista de Avance* 3, no. 30 (January 15, 1929): 18–19.

28. Ramos, "Cubanidad y mestizaje," 107; Ortiz, "Por la integración cubana," 258.

29. Moore, *Nationalizing Blackness*, 189.

30. It was Havana's Municipal Advisory Commission of Tourism that requested authorization for the *comparsas* to resume. See "Comunicación del Alcalde de la Habana," in Municipio de la Habana, *Las comparsas populares*, 7–8, 29–32.

31. "The Carnival of Havana" and "Cuba's Coming Carnival," *Havana Chronicle* 2, no. 20 (February 1940): 1–2; 3, no. 1 (January 1941): 1. For a description of the *comparsas* as a primitive spectacle, see Norweb to the Secretary of State, Havana, March 17, 1944, USNA, RG 59/837.00/3-2746.

32. "Carnival," *Havana Telegram*, February 8, 1937; "Second Paseo of Carnival" and "Third Carnival Parade," *Havana Post*, February 9 and 10, 1937. For a detailed discussion of the controversies surrounding the *comparsas*, see Moore, *Nationalizing Blackness*, 62–86.

33. Winant, *Racial Conditions*, 29.

34. Kutzinski, *Sugar's Secrets*, 145, 12–13, 9. For a nuanced analysis of this process in the realm of music, see Moore, *Nationalizing Blackness*, 132–46, 219–21.

35. Ortiz, "Más acerca de la poesía mulata," 25–33, 439–41.

36. Andreu, "El pintor Alberto Peña," 114–25; García Agüero, "Un comentario final," 129–32; Andreu, "La muerte de Peñita," 115–17; Martínez, *Cuban Art*, 82–85, 160–61.

37. García Agüero, "Un comentario final," 126–28; Domingo Argudín Lombillo, "Pro-arte: El escultor Teodoro Ramos," *Diario de la Marina*, September 8, 1929; Walter H. Pearl, "History of the Plastic Arts in Cuba," *Havana Post*, June 9, 1940; Ramos Blanco, "Por un arte nacional," *Grafos* 35 (February 1936); Ramos Blanco, "Contribución de la forma negra en las artes plásticas," *Atenas* 2, no. 8 (December 1951): 8–9, 18–19.

38. García Agüero, "Presencia africana," 114–27; Moore, *Nationalizing Blackness*, 134.

39. Clotilde Pujol, "What Is Cuban Music," *Havana Post*, June 9, 1940.

40. García Agüero, "Presencia africana," 114–27.

41. Guirao, *Orbita de la poesía afrocubana*, xv.

42. Efraín Hidalgo, "Cubanidad hipotética," *Nuevos Rumbos* 2, no. 2 (January–February 1947): 22.

43. For some examples of repression against Santería practitioners in the 1930s, see Castellanos, "La lucha policíaca," 231–78. In the late 1940s Santería was still

frequently portrayed as a bloody African ritual; the following articles, published in *Bohemia* (a weekly with a wide national circulation), are examples of this trend: José Quilez Vicente, "¡La sombra repulsiva del feroz santero!" and "¡Entre danzas diabólicas!," April 8, July 8, 1945, and José A. Maestri, "Los ritos africanos: El bembé," November 12, 1950. For a protest of the black societies against this campaign, see G. A., "Comentarios de actualidad," *Nuevos Rumbos* 1, no. 2 (December 1945): 4.

44. Quoted in Kutzinski, *Sugar's Secrets*, 141.

45. Serra, *Carta abierta*, 11; Lino D'Ou, "El autóctono subrogado," *Boletín Oficial del Club Atenas*, November 20, 1930, 2–3.

46. Gustavo Urrutia, "Opresores y oprimidos," *Adelante* 4 (September 1935): 6–7.

47. This is the interpretation voiced by Afro-Cuban radical activist Manuel Machado in "Coronel Jaumá," *Alma Mater*, December 17, 1933.

48. Pérez-Medina, "The Situation of the Negro in Cuba," 298; Matilde S. Menéndez, "¿Racismo o política?," *La Correspondencia*, February 28, 1936; Gastón Mora y Varona, "La cuestión social," *Diario de la Marina*, February 24, 1929; Vasconcelos, "Al margen de los días. Complejos," in Municipio de la Habana, *Las comparsas populares*, 33–37.

49. Quoted in Ibarra, *Cuba: 1898–1921*, 354.

50. "Incorporation" is used here in the sense discussed in Collier and Collier, *Shaping the Political Arena*, 3–23.

51. H. Freeman Matthews, "Affiliation Tendencies of Cuban Labor Unions," Havana, April 18, 1934, USNA, RG 84/850.4/323; Beals, *The Crime of Cuba*, 248–49.

52. On the Communists' efforts to organize workers across racial and ethnic lines, see Carr, "Mill Occupations and Soviets," and de la Fuente, "Two Dangers, One Solution."

53. "Manifiesto," in Rosell, *Luchas obreras*, 108–10 (emphasis in original).

54. Instituto de Historia, *Historia del movimiento obrero*, 1:256–57; "Plataforma electoral del Partido Comunista de Cuba," in Rosell, *Luchas obreras*, 188–211. About the CNOC's program, see Policía Judicial, "Memorandum," Havana, July 17, 1930, USNA, RG 84/800B.

55. Edwin Schoenrich to Guggenheim, Santiago de Cuba, July 13, 1931, and Guggenheim, "General Conditions Report," Havana, August 8, 1931, USNA, RG 84/800/4 and 809.

56. Wakefield, "Political Situation in the Nuevitas Consular District," March 17, 1931, USNA, RG 84/800; González Echevarría, *Orígen y desarrollo*, 87; Lewis, *Marcus Garvey*, 106–7.

57. "Memo: Racial Problem of Cuba," enclosed in Benjamin Sumner Welles to the Secretary of State, Havana, September 29, 1933, USNA, RG 84/800/143; Welles to the Secretary of State, Havana, September 30, 1933, USNA, RG 84/800/324; Rubén Martínez Villena, "Las contradicciones internas del imperialismo yanqui," in Cuba, MINED, *Documentos*, 176–93.

58. CNOC, *IV Congreso*, 73–74; "Proyecto de Resolución del II Pleno del Comité Central de Ala Izquierda Estudiantil," Havana, February 1934, ANC, Fondo Especial, leg. 3, no. 117.

59. For early documents of the PCC, see "Convocatoria y actas del congreso de fundación," in Instituto de Historia, *El movimiento obrero*, 1:443–57; "Acta número dos del Comité Central del Partido Comunista de Cuba," in Rosell, *Luchas obreras*, 73–74; "Juvenil Communist League of Cuba, Morón Sectional Committee," September 14, 1933, USNA, RG 84/800B/141.

60. Torres Molina, *Apuntes*, 19–24, 63–68; Carr, "Identity, Class and Nation," 24.

61. The Comintern theses and discussions are reproduced in Foner and Allen, *American Communism and Black Americans*, 163–200.

62. For examples of this campaign, see Unión de Torcedores de Santiago de Cuba to U.S. Consul, Santiago de Cuba, July 6, 1931, and H. Freeman Matthews, "Communism in Cuba," Havana, March 23, 1934, USNA, RG 84/800/4 and 800B/127; "Memo: Racial Problem of Cuba," "Plataforma electoral del Partido Comunista," and "CNOC: Manifiesto de agosto de 1933," in Rosell, *Luchas obreras*, 188–211, 277–80.

63. CNOC, *IV Congreso*, 69–75; "Manifiesto del Primer Congreso Regional de Unidad Sindical," Santiago de Cuba, August 22, 1934, in Instituto de Historia, *El movimiento obrero*, 2:786; Committee of the Oriente District of the PCC, "To the Workers," September 1933, USNA, RG 84/800/132. About the "faja negra," see also Grobart, "Preguntas y respuestas sobre los años treinta," in *Trabajos escogidos*, 94–98, and Serviat, *El problema negro*, 116–22.

64. Several African American activists visited the island during this period and supported the campaign for black self-determination. A noted example is that of William Patterson, the national secretary of International Labor Defense in the United States who went to Cuba in May 1934. A California-educated lawyer, Patterson joined the Communist Party in the 1920s and distinguished himself in the defense of the Scottsboro case. On Patterson's activities in Cuba, see "Un distinguido abogado," *Ahora*, May 25, 1934. On his career, see Naison, *Communists in Harlem*, 14–16, and Johnpoll and Klehr, *Biographical Dictionary*, 311–12.

65. Schoenrich to Guggenheim, Santiago de Cuba, July 13, 1931, USNA, RG 84/800/4; "Communist Party of Cuba, Dist. of Sta. Clara, Regional Com. of Cienfuegos," September 1933, USNA, RG 84/800.

66. A similar process took place in the United States. See Naison, *Communists in Harlem*, 18–19.

67. See Chapter 6 for numerous examples of these alliances.

68. "Cuba será pronto un república comunista," *Diario de la Marina*, November 13, 1934; "Report concerning the Development of the Communist Party in Cuba," 1946, USNA, RG 59/837.00B/8-746.

69. "Communist Activities in Cuba," Havana, February 10, 1940, USNA, RG 84/820.02/2824. For charges against the PCC for inciting racial troubles, see Alfonso Fors, Jefe de la Policía Judicial, to Secretario de la Presidencia, Havana, January 31, 1931, USNA, RG 84/800.1/562; "Memo: Racial Problem of Cuba"; and "Report concerning the Development of the Communist Party," 12–14.

70. Arredondo, *El negro en Cuba*, 80–98; Agustín Alarcón, "¿Nación negra? ¡No!," *Adelante* 18 (November 1936): 12.

71. "¡Revolucionarios, alerta!," September 7, 1933, ANC, Fondo Especial, leg. 1, no. 160; Pérez, *Cuba under the Platt Amendment*, 321.

72. Pérez, *Cuba under the Platt Amendment*, 323–24.

73. Ramón de la Cruz to Leandro Rionda, Havana, December 1, 1933, BBC, RG 2, ser. 10c, box 97.

74. Hartwell Johnson, "General Survey of Political and Economic Conditions," Matanzas, December 22, 1933, USNA, RG 84/800/145; José Rionda to Manuel Rionda, Havana, September 30, 1933, BBC, RG 2, ser. 10c, box 129.

75. For a summary of this legislation, see Dumoulin, "La regulación estatal," 12–22; Domínguez, *Cuba: Order and Revolution*, 87–88.

76. The PCC recognized later that its opposition to the provisional administration had been a mistake; see "Summary of Speech of Marin (Cuba)," July 30, 1935, USNA, RG 84/800B/120A.

77. Alvarez Estévez, *Azúcar e inmigración*, 205.

78. "Constituído un comité," *Alma Mater*, October 11, 1933; "La ARN contra la aprobación," *Ahora*, November 8, 1933.

79. Edward Reed, "Summary of Legislative Decrees," Havana, November 21, 1933, USNA, RG 84/804.4/234; "El pueblo en masa," *Alma Mater*, December 16, 1933; Samuel Dickson to the Secretary of State, Havana, December 28, 1933, USNA, RG 84/800/278.

80. Dickson to the Secretary of State, Havana, December 23, 1933, and Welles to the Secretary of State, Havana, December 6, 1933, USNA, RG 84/800/276 and 478.

81. "La A.R.N.," *Alma Mater*, November 28, 1933; Convención Nacional, *Programa*, 11; Arredondo, *El negro en Cuba*, 145–59; Arce, *La raza cubana*, 27.

82. Enrique Bringuier, "Es necesario que se cumpla la ley," *Alma Mater*, December 2, 1933.

83. See, for example, the declarations of Afro-Cuban leader Sandalio Junco in "Expone Sandalio Junco su criterio," *Alma Mater*, December 5, 1933; see also CNOC, *IV Congreso*, 69.

84. Dickson, "Summary of Legislative Decrees," Havana, January 15, 1934, USNA, RG 84/804.4/360; "La Federación Obrera de la Habana" and "Obreros," *Alma Mater*, December 1 and 7, 1933; "Conferencia de emergencia de la CNOC," *Ahora*, December 11, 1933.

85. "Los sindicatos hacen firme . . . oposición," *Alma Mater*, December 10, 1933; H. Freeman Matthews, "General Conditions Report," Havana, November 21, 1934, USNA, RG 84/800/1948.

86. Albert Nufer to the Ambassador, Havana, December 19, 1933, USNA, RG 84/850.4.

87. Nufer to the Ambassador, Havana, December 5, 1933, USNA, RG 84/850.4/506.

88. "La cubanización," *Ahora*, December 3, 1933; Arredondo, *El negro en Cuba*, 146.

89. "Report: Communism in Cuba," Havana, August 4, 1933, USNA, RG 84/800B.

90. "¡Revolucionarios, Alerta!," Havana, September 1933, ANC, Fondo Especial, leg. 1, no. 160.

91. Sheridan Talbot to Jefferson Caffery, Santiago de Cuba, July 19, 1935, USNA, RG 84/822; Hernan Vogenitz to Caffery, Cienfuegos, July 2, 1935, USNA, RG 84/800.

92. Milton Patterson Thompson to H. Freeman Matthews, Matanzas, March 12, 1936, USNA, RG 84/800; Edward S. Benet, "Military Affairs," Matanzas, June 14, 1938, USNA, RG 84/800.

93. The cartoon was rightly criticized by Afro-Cuban intellectuals. See "Insidia?," *Adelante* 12 (May 1936): 10; Gustavo Urrutia, "Armonías: Serenidad," *Diario de la Marina*, April 19, 1936.

94. "¡Revolucionarios, Alerta!"; "Cubanos, alerta!," *Adelante* 4 (September 1935): 4; "Impresiones," *Diario de la Marina*, August 27, 1935.

95. Urrutia, "Opresores," 6–7; "¡Revolucionarios, Alerta!"; José a. Plá to Urrutia, in "Armonías," *Diario de la Marina*, February 12, 1934; see also Directorio Social Revolucionario "Renacimiento," "Manifiesto," Havana, 1934, ANC, Fondo Especial, leg. 10, no. 26.

96. Lumen, *La revolución cubana*, 238–39; Ricardo Riana Jaumá, "Sargento Vasconcelos," and Manuel Machado, "Coronel Jaumá," *Alma Mater*, December 10 and 17, 1933.

97. Ernesto Pinto Interián, "En torno a la convención de sociedades," *Adelante* 12 (May 1936): 11.

98. "Memo: Racial Problem of Cuba."

99. Comité Revolucionario Pro-Reorganización de Sociedades Negras, "A las autoridades y pueblo en general," Santa Clara, 1933, ANC, Fondo Especial, leg. 4, no. 129; Directorio, "Manifiesto." On the role of the Afro-Cuban youth in the "revolution," see Serapio Páez Zamora, "La misión revolucionaria de la juventud negra," *Adelante* 16 (September 1936): 8.

100. Directorio, "Manifiesto"; Arredondo, "Un ¡hurra! por Adelante," *Adelante* 24 (May 1937): 7–8.

101. Directorio, "Manifiesto"; "La Asociación Adelante," *Adelante* 1 (June 1935): 3.

102. Calixta Hernández de Cervantes, "Feminismo" *Adelante* 2 (July 1935): 14; Raúl Suárez Mendoza, "A la mujer cubana" and "La mujer pinareña," *Ahora*, October 20 and 21, 1933.

103. "Ocho sociedades . . . representadas," *Diario de la Marina*, May 7, 1928.

104. Raúl Suárez Mendoza, "La convención de sociedades," *Ahora*, October 20, 1933; "La convención," *Adelante* 10 (March 1936): 3; Pinto Interián, "En torno a la convención," 11.

105. "Iniciativas plausibles," *Adelante* 17 (October 1936): 3; Dictinio Polanco Bidart, "Réplica al Dr. Pinto," *Adelante* (May 1937): 20.

106. Convención Nacional, *Programa*, 3–15. On the discussions surrounding this program, see Pastor de Albear, "La convención," and Gustavo Urrutia's responses "Orientación," "Aclaraciones," and "Complemento jurídico," *Diario de la Marina*, February 14, 16, 18, and 19, 1936.

107. "Asteria Nacional Revolucionaria," Havana, 1933, ANC, Registro de Asociaciones, leg. 289, no. 8239; "Asteria pide una cooperación" and "Los dirigentes de Asteria," *Alma Mater*, December 5 and 10, 1933; Gustavo Urrutia, "Armonías," *Diario de la Marina*, May 13, 1933.

108. H. Freeman Matthews to the Secretary of State, Havana, July 24, 1935, USNA, RG 84/800/3689; "Los concejales electos," *Diario de la Marina*, February 25, 1936.

109. "Una bomba en Asteria," *Alma Mater*, December 28, 1933.
110. "Una bomba . . . en el Club Atenas," "Al pueblo de Cuba," and "Cuatro bombas," *Ahora*, November 14 and 16, December 5, 1933; Comité Central del PCC, "Al país," Havana, April 6, 1936, ANC, Fondo Especial, leg. 5, no. 193.
111. "El Ku Klux Klan Kubano," *Diario de la Marina*, October 30, 1933, quoted in Fernández Robaina, *El negro en Cuba*, 135; KKKK, "Boletín No. Uno: Cubanos blancos a defendernos," September 30, 1933, USNA, RG 84/800/176. See also Lumen, *La revolución cubana*, 238–39.
112. Gustavo Urrutia, "Armonías," *Diario de la Marina*, February 1, 1934.
113. "Cómo se desarrollaron los lamentables sucesos" and "Trinidad," *Heraldo de las Villas*, February 6 and 13, 1934; "Los sucesos de Trinidad" and "En Trinidad no hay problemas de raza," *La Correspondencia*, February 13 and 21, 1934; Hernández Llórens, "Notas," 364–65.
114. Hernan Vogenitz, "Cienfuegos Political Report," July 2, 1935, USNA, RG 84/800.
115. Jesús Plasencia, "¿Hitler en Trinidad?," *Aurora* 13, no. 3 (March 1934): 5; Comité por los Derechos del Negro, "Manifiesto," Havana, February 16, 1934, ANC, Fondo Especial, leg. fuera, no. 7-37; Knox Alexander to Samuel S. Dickson, Cienfuegos, January 2, 1934, USNA, RG 84/800.
116. At least two of the fifteen members of the Council of State, a body with legislative functions, were black: Dr. Oscar Edreira, then president of Atenas, and Dr. Nicasio Silverio. See H. Freeman Matthews to the Secretary of State, Havana, January 24, 1935, USNA, RG 84/803/2498.
117. Comité por los Derechos del Negro, "Manifiesto"; "Detenida el hacha," *Bandera Roja*, November 26, 1934; Matthews to the Secretary of State, Havana, October 31, 1934, USNA, RG 84/800/1757; "En Trinidad," *Diario de la Marina*, November 8, 1934; "Mayor Protested by Negroes Quits," *Havana Post*, November 8, 1934.
118. Caffery to the Secretary of State, Havana, March 7, 1934, USNA, RG 84/800/210. Gustavo Urrutia, however, noted that the decree could be used to fight "negro phobia" as well; see his "Armonías," *Diario de la Marina*, March 14, 1934.
119. In Havana alone eighteen unions that seconded the strike were banished. The first general secretary of the CNOC, César Vilar, went into exile; the new leader, Lázaro Peña, was imprisoned in 1936. See "Sindicatos" and "14 gremios," *Diario de la Marina*, March 19 and 21, 1935, and "Ocupan documentación roja," *El Avance*, May 13, 1936.
120. "Varias detenciones," "Oportunas declaraciones . . . de Minerva," "Albores Club," and "Los elementos de color," *La Correspondencia*, February 13–17, 1936.
121. Partido Comunista de Cuba, "Al país," Havana, April 6, 1936, ANC, Fondo Especial, leg. 5, no. 193; "La nota del día," *La Discusión*, February 20, 1936.
122. Vogenitz, "Fortnightly Political Report," Cienfuegos, August 9, 1935, USNA, RG 84/800; Arthur Dukes to J. Butler Wright, Nuevitas, October 3, 1937, USNA, RG 84/800; Matthews to the Secretary of State, Havana, June 18, 1934, USNA, RG 84/800/678.
123. "El A.B.C. y los cubanos de color" and "El ABC," *Diario de la Marina*, August 2,

1933, July 6, 1934. See also the ABC manifesto enclosed in Matthews to the Secretary of State, Havana, June 30, 1934, USNA, RG 84/800/776.

124. ABC, *El ABC*, 35. For a discussion of the ABC that is clearly sympathetic to the party, see Aguilar, *Cuba 1933*, 118–21.

125. Matthews to the Secretary State, Havana, November 22, 1934, USNA, RG 84/800/1964; "La CNOC," *Ahora*, June 18, 1934; "The Anaesthesia of Imperialism" (translation of an article from *Mella*, September 1933), in USNA, RG 84/800B/132; Lumen, *La revolución cubana*, 239.

126. Caffery to the Secretary of State, Havana, June 25, 1934, USNA, RG 84/800/732.

127. Felipe Elosegui, "1000 noticias en sepia," *Tiempo*, November 22, 1951.

128. T. N. Gimperling, "Batista's Control of Troops" and "Who's Who on Commissioned Personnel," Havana, October 24, November 15, 1933, USNA, RG 165/2012/132-33.

129. Pérez-Stable, *The Cuban Revolution*, 42.

130. Cuba, *Plan Trienal*. For a sympathetic view of Batista's work, see Cabús, *Batista*. For a critical overview of the period, see Pérez, *Cuba*, 277–79.

131. A good indicator of the importance of organized labor is the proportion of labor-related laws and decrees among the total number of regulations, which, after 1933, was always consistently higher than before. For an excellent analysis, see Domínguez, *Cuba: Order and Revolution*, 87–89.

CHAPTER SIX

1. Pérez, *Cuba*, 281.

2. Willard Beaulac, "Weekly Summary," Havana, October 15, 1938, USNA, RG 84/800/1219. Other fascist organizations included Afirmación Nacional, created in 1934 by some Spanish businessmen led by José Rivero, editor of *Diario de la Marina*; Falange Española, organized in 1938 also by upper-class Spaniards; and the Legión Nacional Revolucionaria Sindicalista, which sought to spread fascist propaganda in labor circles. See Department of State, "Anti-American Domestic Groups in the Other American Republics," Washington, D.C., February 26, 1943, USNA, RG 84/820.02. On the question of fascism in Cuba, see also Naranjo Orovio, *Cuba: Otro escenario*.

3. A concrete example of early alliances with other groups is provided by the Comité por los Derechos del Negro, which the Communists created after the lynching of Proveyer in Trinidad (see Chapter 5). For the United States, see Ottanelli, *The Communist Party*, 49–80.

4. Hobsbawm, *The Age of Extremes*, 142–56.

5. "El discurso de Urrutia en la Unión Fraternal," *Cuatro Páginas*, November 22, 1941.

6. "Las sociedades de color," *El Crisol*, January 7, 1942; Gustavo Urrutia, "Armonías," *Cuatro Páginas*, January 24, 1942, and "Armonías," *Diario de la Marina*, February 14, 1934.

7. Nilo Zuasnábar Suárez, "El negro en la Constituyente," *Rumbos*, June 14, 1939. See also Ernesto Pinto Interián, "En torno a la convención de sociedades negras," *Adelante* 12 (May 1936): 11.

8. Plá to Urrutia, Camagüey, February 1, 1934, in "Armonías," *Diario de la Marina*, February 12, 1934.

9. Domínguez, *Cuba: Order and Revolution*, 57.

10. Ramón Vasconcelos, "Punto largo," *El País*, October 24, 1939; Marinello, *La cuestión racial*, 13–14.

11. Labor laws figured prominently in the legislative program of all parties represented in Congress prior to the constitutional convention. Roughly 20 percent of all legislative proposals dealt with labor issues. For examples, see "Treinta y tres leyes seleccionó el Comité Liberal," *El País*, August 2, 1936; "Treinta y cuatro leyes acordó el Partido Acción Republicana," *Diario de la Marina*, August 4, 1936; and "Programa mínimo aprobado por el Comité Nacionalista," *Diario de la Marina*, August 12, 1936. See also Domínguez, *Cuba: Order and Revolution*, 87–89.

12. Carlos Mendieta, leader of Unión Nacionalista, quoted in Agustín Acosta, "Conferencia," in Atenas, *Los partidos políticos*, 60.

13. Beaulac to the Secretary of State, Havana, October 13, 1938, USNA, RG 84/800/1205.

14. Carlos Saladrigas, "Conjunto Nacional Democrático: Exposición del programa," in Atenas, *Los partidos políticos*, 273.

15. ABC, *El ABC*; Francisco Ichaso, "Algunos aspectos del ideario del ABC," in Atenas, *Los partidos políticos*, 104–5; Acosta, "Conferencia," 62–63.

16. Marinello, "La cuestión racial en el trabajo, la inmigración y la cultura," Claudio E. Miranda del Pozo, "Conferencia," and Rafael Iturralde, "Partido Popular Cubano: Su intervención en los destinos públicos," in Atenas, *Los partidos políticos*, 124, 136, 330–31.

17. Acosta, "Conferencia," 62–64; Saladrigas, "Conjunto," 273; Ichaso, "Algunos aspectos," 105–6. This position was endorsed also by the Partido Demócrata Republicano, led by former Conservative president Mario García Menocal, and by the Partido Nacional Revolucionario. See Alberto Boada Miquel, "Problemas constitucionales," and Pablo Lavín, "Ensayo de valorización política," in Atenas, *Los partidos políticos*, 231, 401–2.

18. Marinello, *La cuestión racial*, 137; Miranda del Pozo, "Conferencia," 123–25; Iturralde, "Partido Popular," 331.

19. Roca, "Por la igualdad de todos los cubanos," in Atenas, *Los partidos políticos*, 265.

20. On the PRC(A), see Partido Revolucionario Cubano, "Al pueblo de Cuba," Havana, May 1, 1935, USNA, RG 84/800/3414; "Es preciso llegar al gobierno," *Luz*, August 5, 1937; and Guillermo Martínez Márquez, "El Autenticismo revolucionario," in Atenas, *Los partidos políticos*, 312–13. On the Liberals, see Gustavo Gutiérrez, "La discriminación racial ante la Convención Constituyente," in Atenas, *Los partidos políticos*, 189–201.

21. Milton Thompson to J. Butler Wright, Santiago de Cuba, March 17, 1939, Edward Benet to the Wright, Matanzas, May 2, 1939, and Hernan C. Vogenitz to Wright, Cienfuegos, October 5, 1939, USNA, RG 84/800.

22. "Resumen del escrutinio," *Diario de la Marina*, November 21, 1939; Thompson to Wright, Santiago, November 21, 1939, USNA, RG 84/800. The Communists

received 22 percent of the vote in Santiago and 12 percent in the province of Oriente as a whole.

23. The other two were Antonio Bravo Acosta, a mulatto lawyer from Santiago elected on the ticket of the Partido Demócrata Republicano headed by Menocal, and José Maceo González, a physician from Palma Soriano (Oriente) elected by the Partido Nacional Revolucionario. Maceo González, either the son or nephew of Antonio Maceo, allegedly had "a reputation for agitating on the racial issue." See Thompson to Wright, Santiago de Cuba, February 7, 1940, USNA, RG 84/800.

24. In Havana, of nineteen Communist candidates, five were black or mulatto. They were, in addition to Roca and García Agüero, Lázaro Peña, Severo Aguirre, and Consuelo Silveira. In Matanzas, at least two out of six candidates were black. See "¡Cubanos: Todos a las urnas!," *Noticias de Hoy*, November 15, 1939, and Benet to Wright, Matanzas, October 27, 1939, USNA, RG 84/800.

25. Thompson to Wright, Santiago de Cuba, February 17, 1949, USNA, RG 84/800. It is noteworthy that the Communists did not mention Cordero when referring to their black delegates. See Arnaldo Escalona, "Genuinos representantes," *Noticias de Hoy*, November 19, 1939.

26. "No interferirá al Congreso la Asamblea Constituyente," *El Crisol*, November 23, 1939. For the Communist response, see Arnaldo Escalona, "Refutan . . . a los doctores Bravo Acosta y Manuel Capestany," *Noticias de Hoy*, November 26, 1939.

27. In an effort to maintain their grip over black voters, the leaders of the Liberal Party increased the proportion of nonwhites in prominent positions during the 1930s. By 1939 the provincial party leaders of Havana, Matanzas, and Santa Clara were black or mulatto: Vasconcelos, Prisciliano Piedra, and Capestany. Both Vasconcelos and Capestany were in the Senate. The Liberals also made Representative Marcelino Garriga, who was black, president of the House.

28. Thompson to Wright, November 21, 1939, and Thompson to Beaulac, February 10, 1940, USNA, RG 84/800.

29. Enclosed in Thompson to Wright, November 28, 1939, USNA, RG 84/800 (emphasis in original).

30. Marcelino Hernández Ferrer, "Labor de Unión Revolucionaria Comunista," *Diario de Cuba*, November 25, 1939.

31. "Government to Face Test" and "Majority of Opposition," *Havana Post*, November 14 and 21, 1939. For a good overview of the parties participating in the election, see "Cuban Political Parties," Havana, May 1939, USNA, RG 84/800.

32. This discussion follows Domínguez, *Cuba: Order and Revolution*, 100–101.

33. In Sancti Spíritus, for instance, the Afro-Cuban clubs organized a banquet for the military chief of the province, who supervised the elections. See Vogenitz to Wright, Cienfuegos, October 3, 1939, USNA, RG 84/800/29. See also Zuasnábar Suárez, "El negro en la constituyente"; Convención Nacional, *Programa*, 6–7; and Grillo, *El problema del negro*, 59–62.

34. Benjamín Muñoz Ginarte, "Discurso de apertura," in Atenas, *Los partidos políticos*, 11.

35. Wright to the Secretary of State, Havana, May 3, 1940, USNA, RG 84/801.1/235.

36. This discussion is based on Cuba, Convención Constituyente, *Diario de Sesiones*, April 27, 1940, 20–27.

37. In the Cuban legal system, based on Roman law, the abstract constitutional principles had to be codified in laws "complementary" to the Constitution.

38. Blas Roca, "Proyecto de bases constitucionales sobre trabajo y regimen de la propiedad," Havana, March 12, 1940, USNA, RG 84/801.1/17; Marinello, *La cuestión racial*, 12–13.

39. The discussion of both amendments, submitted by the Communists and the ABC, is reproduced in Cuba, Convención Constituyente, *Diario de Sesiones*, June 7, 1940, 4–12, and Lazcano, *Constitución de Cuba*, 2:512–28.

40. See the speech of Cortina against the amendment, in Lazcano, *Constitución de Cuba*, 2:514.

41. Thompson to Beaulac, Santiago de Cuba, February 10, 1940, USNA, RG 84/800.

42. Lazcano, *Constitución de Cuba*, 2:515–22.

43. Cuba, *Constitución de la República*, arts. 20, 74, and unique art., "transitory" to third title, 7, 21, 81.

44. Cuba, Convención Constituyente, *Diario de Sesiones*, April 27, 1940, 23–27.

45. "El dictamen sobre trabajo y propiedad" and "Democracia y politiquería," *Noticias de Hoy*, April 5, May 11, 1940; Cuba, Convención Constituyente, *Diario de Sesiones*, May 2, 1940, 14–15.

46. For examples, see "Un parto de la demagogia," *¡Alerta!*, April 5, 1940; "Apuntes del director," *Cuba Nueva en Acción*, May 11, 1940.

47. Cuba, Convención Constituyente, *Diario de Sesiones*, May 2, 1940, 15–16; Lazcano, *Constitución de Cuba*, 2:524.

48. On this political system, see Domínguez, *Cuba: Order and Revolution*, 56–57.

49. Arthur Jukes to George Messersmith, Nuevitas, July 3, 1940, Joaquín García, "Political Memorandum," Santa Clara, July 1, 1940, Francisco Cause, "Political Memorandum," Caibarién, July 2, 1940, and Horace Dickinson to Messersmith, Antilla, June 29, 1940, USNA, RG 84/800.

50. Benet to Messersmith, Matanzas, June 30, 1940, Vogenitz to Messersmith, Cienfuegos, June 30, 1940, and Dickinson to Messersmith, Antilla, June 29, 1940, USNA, RG 84/800.

51. "Platform of the Coalition (Government) Parties," Havana, January 6, 1940, USNA, RG 84/800/2681; Blas Roca, "La plataforma nacional," *El Comunista* 2, no. 4 (February 1940): 235–41.

52. Beaulac to the Secretary of State, Havana, January 20, 1940, USNA, RG 84/800.4/2737; Jukes to Beaulac, Nuevitas, February 1, 1940, and A. F. N., "Memorandum: Trip to Central Washington," Havana, February 5, 1940, USNA, RG 84/800.4.

53. Coert du Bois to Beaulac, Havana, January 18, 1940, USNA, RG 84/800.4/2732.

54. José Rionda to Manuel Rionda, Havana, January 29, 1940, BBC, RG 2, ser. 10c, box 129.

55. Du Bois, "Memorandum: Printing Trades Strike," Havana, March 11, 1940, USNA, RG 84/850.4/18.

56. Agrupación Nacional Acera del Louvre, [Proclama], Havana, May 9, 1940, enclosed in Beaulac to the Secretary of State, Havana, May 18, 1940, USNA, RG 84/800B/302; Evelio and Rafel Reyna to Federico Laredo Brú, Havana, May 6, 1940, USNA, RG 84/800B/253.

57. Ramón Hermida, Alfredo Botet, Maximiliano Smith, Fernando Sirgo, and Juan J. Remos to Batista, Havana, February 1, 1940, USNA, RG 84/800/2834; Beaulac, "Conversation with Dr. Emilio Núñez Portuondo," Havana, April 21, 1941, USNA, RG 84/800B/1924.

58. On Salas's background, see "Los alcaldes municipales," *Acción Ciudadana*, January 31, 1945, 9; Riera, *Cuba política*, 309, 345.

59. Zenin Carnet, "A pesar de la reacción," *Noticias de Hoy*, July 16, 1940; Thompson to Messersmith, Santiago de Cuba, July 6, 1940, USNA, RG 84/800.

60. "Con la ayuda de las fuerzas que apoyan a Batista," *Noticias de Hoy*, September 17, 1940. For the electoral results in Santiago, see "Con plena conciencia ciudadana" and "El nuevo alcalde de Santiago," *Libertad*, July 16 and 17, 1940.

61. "Cómo quedó formada la cámara municipal de Santiago," *Noticias de Hoy*, July 17, 1940.

62. Riera, *Cuba política*, 491–512.

63. Thompson to Wright, Santiago de Cuba, July 14, 1938, and Thompson to Beaulac, Santiago de Cuba, December 19, 1939, USNA, RG 84/800.

64. "Conclusiones del Congreso Nacional Femenino," Havana, April 18–22, 1939. I thank Barbara Ray for sharing this evidence with me. About the FDMC, see A. John Cope to the Secretary of State, Havana, January 31, 1949, USNA, RG 59/837.00B/1-3149; "Acuerdos del Consejo," *Mujeres Cubanas* 1, no. 6 (January 1951): 12.

65. Owen Games, "Fortnightly Political Report," Santiago de Cuba, May 3, 1937, and Jukes to Wright, Nuevitas, October 13, 1937, USNA, RG 84/800; Vogenitz to Wright, Cienfuegos, November 8, 1939, USNA, RG 84/800/40.

66. "Contestan los miembros de la Hermandad de Jóvenes Cubanos," *El País*, January 30, 1938; Beaulac to the Secretary of State, Havana, February 6, 1940, USNA, RG 84/800B/2803.

67. García Rojas was one of the sponsors of the Communist-inspired Association for the Defense of Democratic Rights, created in 1948. See Earl T. Crain to the Secretary of State, Havana, October 21, 1949, USNA, RG 59/837.00B/10-2149.

68. "Movimiento favorable a la ley de sanciones," *Noticias de Hoy*, October 11, 1944; "List of Leaders . . . in the Communist Party," Matanzas, June 9, 1941, USNA, RG 84/800B.

69. "La reunión de federaciones y sociedades negras," *Noticias de Hoy*, October 26, 1943.

70. Romilio Portuondo Calá, "Una mujer negra," *Magazine de Hoy*, October 8, 1944.

71. "Communist Activities in Cuba," Havana, June 15, 1940, USNA, RG 84/820.02/421; "A List of Prominent Cuban Communists," Havana, January 9, 1948, USNA, RG 59/837.00B/1-948.

72. "Al pueblo de Cuba," *Noticias de Hoy*, January 25, 1944; Riera, *Cuba política*, 491–546; Sergio Aguirre, "El PSP y la igualdad racial," *Noticias de Hoy*, May 7, 1948. See

also the column "Candidatos socialistas en diversos municipios" published by *Noticias de Hoy* in April and May 1944 for data on the candidates for local office.

73. Among new party recruits in 1942, for instance, Afro-Cubans represented 35 percent. According to Blas Roca, in 1946 blacks and mulattoes made up 36 percent of total affiliates. See Fabio Grobart, "Una emulación de tipo especial," *Fundamentos* 2, no. 16 (November 1942): 575–77, quoted in Domínguez, *Cuba: Order and Revolution*, 102, 555, and Henry Norweb, "Estimate of Significance of Communist Party," Havana, March 29, 1946, USNA, RG 59/837.00B/3-2946.

74. "Report concerning the Development of the Communist Party of Cuba," enclosed in Norweb to the Secretary of State, Havana, August 7, 1946, USNA, RG 59/837.00B/8-746. The party changed its name from Unión Revolucionaria Comunista to Partido Socialista Popular in 1944.

75. Roca, "Penas y educación contra la discriminación racial," *Fundamentos* 4, no. 33 (May 1944): 14–30; "Interesan del Congreso," *Noticias de Hoy*, October 6, 1944.

76. "A todo el pueblo de Cuba," *Información*, September 7, 1940; Manuel Luzardo, "El resultado de las elecciones y las tareas del Partido," *El Comunista* 2, nos. 10–11 (August–September 1940): 672–84.

77. Messersmith to the Secretary of State, Havana, December 10, 1940, USNA, RG 84/850.4/1269; "Resolución del V Congreso," *El Organizador* (June–July 1947): 6–7.

78. For examples of coverage of this campaign in the labor press, see "Los nueve puntos," *Voz Gráfica* (December 1940): 15; Francisco Goiry, "El proyecto de ley contra la discriminación," *CTC* 6, no. 66 (August 1945): 20–21, 46; "La prensa obrera y las leyes complementarias," *El Organizador* (September 1946): 1; Roger Fumero, "Discriminación racial," *Voz Gráfica* (May 1946): 4; and "Contra la discriminación," *Boletín de Organización* (August 1946). About the CTC directives to promote blacks in the workplace, see Peña, *¡La unidad es victoria!*, 30–31, and "Informe de los camaradas Lázaro Peña, Oscar Amable, Martín Gonzalez y Nicolás Hernandez," Havana, January 8, 1949, USNA, RG 59/837.00B/3-1049.

79. "Saludan el ingreso de un negro," *Noticias de Hoy*, January 7, 1947; "La discriminación nacional y racial en la industria cubana," *Nuevos Rumbos* 2 (January–February 1947): 25; Rogelio Gutiérrez, "La lucha contra los discriminadores," *El Organizador* (March 1947): 2.

80. S. B., "Memorandum," Havana, November 14, 1944, USNA, RG 84/840.1; J. J. M., "Strike at Ariguanabo," Havana, October 26, 1944, USNA, RG 84/850.4; Harry W. Story to Gordon L. Burke, Santiago de Cuba, March 13, 1944, USNA, RG 84/800B; "Se inició el juicio por discriminación," *Noticias de Hoy*, November 27, 1943.

81. For an excellent analysis of this process, see Domínguez, *Cuba: Order and Revolution*, 74–75, 87–89.

82. Elvira Rodríguez, "Domésticos, no esclavos," *Boletín de Organización* (August 1946): 6; "La ley y los hábitos mentales," *Carga* 1, no. 13 (February 1944): 2–3; Sarah Pascual, "Las trabajadoras domésticas hablan," *Boletín de Organización* (February 1947): 21, 23.

83. "Conclusiones del Congreso Nacional Femenino," 17–18; FDMC, *Informes*, 26–38.

84. For a Communist critique of the Afro-Cuban societies, see Blas Roca, "La discriminación de los negros," *Fundamentos* 3, nos. 22–23 (June–July 1943): 311–22.

85. "Informe de los camaradas Peña, Amable, Gonzalez y Hernandez," 147–48.

86. Humberto Hernández, "Ciclo de conferencias en Unión Fraternal," and "Protestan de la actitud del Dr. Grau," *Noticias de Hoy*, April 7 and 19, 1944.

87. "Resueltamente se manifiestan" and "Campaña contra la discriminación," *Noticias de Hoy*, October 3, November 10, 1944.

88. "Están contra la discriminación los pinareños," "Apoya el proyecto . . . el gobernador matancero," and "Se pronuncian . . . diversos congresistas," *Noticias de Hoy*, November 18, December 5 and 17, 1944.

89. "Intenso movimiento," "Cobra impulso en todo el país," "Los veteranos contra la discriminación," and "Piden la Ley contra la discriminación los Maceo," *Noticias de Hoy*, November 14 and 22, December 7 and 9, 1944.

90. "Telegramas mecanografiados dirigidos al Presidente de la República," ANC, Secretaría de la Presidencia, leg. 63, no. 2; Angel Bertematy García, "La ley contra la discriminación racial," *Fragua de la Libertad* 4, no. 18 (May 10, 1945): 4.

91. "Discutirán en breve la ponencia contra la discriminación" and "Aprobada la ponencia de Marinello," *Noticias de Hoy*, November 21 and 23, 1944.

92. "Weekly Summary," Havana, August 17, 1945, USNA, RG 59/837.00/8-1745; "Refuta la Federación de Sociedades Negras," *Noticias de Hoy*, November 26, 1947; Juan Jiménez Pastrana, "La Constitución cubana del 40 y el problema negro," *Nuevos Rumbos* 2, no. 3 (March–April 1947): 11–12, 22, 24–25.

93. "Fijó Prío su línea de gobierno," *El Mundo*, May 6, 1948; Gabriel Arango Valdés, "El discurso de Prío y la discriminación racial," *Nuevos Rumbos* 3 (June–July 1948): 18–19, 33; Grillo, *El problema del negro*, 75–79.

94. V. Lansing Collins to the Secretary of State, Havana, October 6, 1948, USNA, RG 59/837.00/10-648.

95. Irving Lippe, "Summary of Labor Developments," Havana, October 3, 1951, USNA, RG 59/837.06/10-351.

96. For a summary of party votes and affiliations in the 1940s, see "Estado comparativo" and "Alcanzará el PRC(A)," *El Mundo*, December 11, 1949, October 24, 1951.

97. Mallory to the Secretary of State, Havana, October 19, 1948, USNA, RG 59/837.5043/10-1948; "El asesinato de Aracelio Iglesias," *Fundamentos* 8, no. 81 (November 1948): 683–86. On the Maritime Federation, see Norweb to the Secretary of State, Havana, February 11, 1948, USNA, RG 59/837.00/2-1148.

98. Andrés Solís, "Un líder que no olvidaremos," *Voz Gráfica* (February–March 1950): 4–5. Victims of this labor-related violence included Auténticos as well. The most noted, but hardly unique, case was that of ex-Communist Afro-Cuban labor leader Sandalio Junco, who was shot in Sancti Spíritus in 1942. Junco was a member of the Auténtico Comisión Obrera Nacional when he died. See "Tres muertos," *El Mundo*, May 9, 1942, and "Hay que reaccionar como cubano y como negro," *Fragua de la Libertad* 1, no. 5 (June 5, 1942): 7.

99. Alfredo T. Quílez, "¿Se libera el obrerismo cubano?," *Carteles*, July 20, 1949, 25.

100. John T. Fishburn, "Notes on Cuban Labor," Havana, July 28, 1953, USNA, RG 59/837.06/7-2853.
101. This and similar press releases are enclosed in Butler to the Secretary of State, Havana, September 30, 1948, USNA, RG 59/837.00/9-3048. For a similar complaint, see "Por una política laboral rectamente ajustada," *Diario de la Marina*, May 13, 1951.
102. "Demands Made by the Different Labor Federations," Havana, May 1, 1951, USNA, RG 59/837.06/5-1551.
103. Mario Barrera, "Rincón obrero," *Prensa Libre*, December 1, 1951.
104. For this campaign in the Communist-controlled labor press, see "Frente Democrático," *Unitario* 4, no. 7 (July 1951); "Tarea inaplazable," *La Chaveta* 2 (August 1951); "Editoriales," *La Dalila* 15, no. 7 (July–August 1951); "Derrotemos a los criminales," *Adelante!* 5, no. 3 (July 1951).
105. "Un congreso anti-comunista," *Boletín de Organización* (October 1947): 5; Blas Roca, "El decreto sobre la discriminación racial y las masas," *Noticias de Hoy*, November 17, 1951.
106. The Afro-Cuban generals had been Gregorio Querejeta and Hernández Nardo; the ministers had been José Manuel Casado (Interior) and Francisco Benítez (Labor). See Cuéllar Vizcaíno, *Unas cuantas verdades*, 10–11; Severo Aguirre, "El PRC no defiende a los negros," *Noticias de Hoy*, May 5, 1948; and Felipe Elosegui, "1000 noticias en sepia," *Tiempo*, September 18, 1951.
107. Afro-Cubans who had been included in Prío's cabinet included Ramón Vasconcelos and Casado, who had been minister of the interior under Grau. See Butler to the Secretary of State, Havana, February 4, 1950, USNA, RG 59/737.00/2-450; Sergio Aguirre, "Cordialidades. La raza de los buenos," *Noticias de Hoy*, November 23, 1951; and "Clausurado anoche el Congreso Auténtico," *El Mundo*, November 21, 1951.
108. "El nuevo presidente y las leyes complementarias," *Nuevos Rumbos* 4, no. 1 (November 1948): 3–4. On Afro-Cubans' disappointment with the administration, see also Grillo, *El problema del negro*, 80–81.
109. "Carta abierta del Club Aponte" and "Editorial," *Atenas* 2, no. 4 (August 1951): 6, 8. On the impact of these statements, see Felipe Elosegui, "1000 noticias en sepia," *Tiempo*, August 29, 1951.
110. García Agüero, "La discriminación, la ley y la trampa," *Fundamentos* 10, no. 95 (February 1950): 128–34. Piedra's proposal is reproduced in his "Empleos dignos para personas decentes," *Atenas* 2, no. 6 (October 1951): 7, 32.
111. "Llama la Federación de Sociedades Negras a la lucha," *Noticias de Hoy*, January 26, 1950; "Así trabajamos contra la discriminación racial," *Atenas* 2, no. 4 (August 1951): 7.
112. "Editorial," *Atenas* 2, no. 4 (August 1951): 8.
113. Raúl Gutiérrez Serrano, "El pueblo opina sobre el gobierno," *Bohemia*, December 16, 1951, 124–27, 146–49; Carlos Lechuga, "El último survey," *El Mundo*, December 13, 1951. On the Ortodoxos, see Farber, *Revolution and Reaction*, 122–30.
114. Prío, "Mensaje al Congreso," *Gaceta Oficial*, October 26, 1951, 93.

115. For instance, the National Anti-Communist Federation of Cuba requested Congress to "pass legislation complementary to the Constitution on racial discrimination, because this constitutes one of the points of our democracy and has been used by the native Communists as a propaganda item." See Henry Hoyt to the Secretary of State, Havana, March 13, 1951, USNA, RG 59/737.001/5-351.

116. Felipe Elosegui, "1242 noticias en sepia," *Tiempo*, September 15 and 18, 1951; Grillo, *El problema del negro*, 87–88.

117. "Decreto 4832," *Amanecer* 1, no. 1 (February 1952): 18; "Por medio de una decreto declaran punible la discriminación," *Diario de la Marina*, November 7, 1951.

118. "Entra en vigor el decreto," *Prensa Libre*, November 7, 1951; Felipe Elosegui, "1000 noticias en sepia," *Tiempo*, November 29, 1951.

119. Felipe Elosegui, "1000 noticias en sepia," *Tiempo*, November 28, 1951; "Reunión contra la discriminación," *El Mundo*, November 15, 1951; "Contra la discriminación racial," *Prensa Libre*, December 13, 1951.

120. "Destacadas figuras del comercio" and "Emplearán más jóvenes," *Prensa Libre*, November 28, December 13, 1951; "Apoya el Conjunto de Calles," *El Mundo*, December 20, 1951.

121. "Fustigó el Presidente Prío a la práctica de la discriminación," *El Mundo*, December 9, 1951. The speech was widely publicized and was also reproduced by *Tiempo* and *Prensa Libre*.

122. For a good summary, see Aracelio Azcuy, "La nota discordante," *Prensa Libre*, December 12, 1951. Azcuy reproduces comments from all major Havana newspapers.

123. Sergio Carbó, "Bellas y dulces muchachas de color," *Prensa Libre*, December 12, 1951.

124. "El Diario pregunta" and Gastón Baquero, "Nota sobre el prejuicio racial," *Diario de la Marina*, November 11 and 30, 1951.

125. On the Frente, see Honorio Muñoz, "Contra la discriminación," "El llamado Frente Cívico trata de confundir," and "Es antidemocrático el Frente Cívico," *Noticias de Hoy*, January 17, 20, and 22, 1952. On the Afro-Cuban women employed in the department stores, see "Lanzadas a la calle las jóvenes negras," *Noticias de Hoy*, January 11, 1952.

126. Pastor Albear, "Es una burla a la raza de color el decreto sobre la discriminación," *Prensa Libre*, November 29, 1951; Angel Jubiel Varona, "¿Hacia dónde debemos ir?," *Amanecer* 1, no. 3 (April–May 1952): 16; "Nuestros lectores opinan," *Atenas* 2, no. 8 (December 1951): 4.

127. Henry Hoyt, "Summary of Action Taken in House of Representatives," Havana, December 28, 1951, USNA, RG 59/737.21/12-2851.

128. "No podrá detener la lucha," *Noticias de Hoy*, February 26, 1952; Felipe Elosegui, "1000 noticias en sepia," *Tiempo*, November 21 and 22, 1951, February 24 and 27, 1952.

129. Juan de Zengotita, "Labor Developments," Havana, March 31, 1955, USNA, RG 59/837.06/3-3155.

130. John Cope to the Secretary of State, Havana, May 25, 1949, USNA, RG 59/837.504/5-2549; "Piden garantías" and "Se inaugurará hoy el Congreso de los Tabacaleros," *El Mundo*, November 13, December 2, 1951. The accusation of racism was based on the expulsion of four Afro-Cuban labor leaders from the executive committee of the Auténticos' Comisión Obrera. See "Trata la CTC de la crisis en la Federación Tabacalera," *Prensa Libre*, October 19, 1951.

131. "Obreros: Repertorio de acusaciones," *Bohemia*, November 4, 1951, 71; "Declaraciones de Orizondo," *Prensa Libre*, October 26, 1951. On the effects of the Prío administration on labor, see Domínguez, *Cuba: Order and Revolution*, 89–90.

132. "Las sociedades de color," *Revista de Policía* 1, no. 9 (September 1945): 32; Norweb to the Secretary of State, Havana, August 9, 1946, USNA, RG 59/837.00/8-946; Felipe Elosegui, "1000 noticias en sepia," *Tiempo*, January 22, 1952.

133. Armando Rabilero, "La Federación Nacional de Sociedades" and "Impediremos la formación de una CTK negra," *Noticias de Hoy*, February 27 and 29, 1952.

134. Felipe Elosegui, "Una turbulenta reunión," *Amanecer* 2, no. 7 (January 1953): 22–24; García Agüero, "Una plaga sobre las sociedades," *Noticias de Hoy*, October 22, 1952.

135. "La CTC en Columbia," *Tiempo*, March 14, 1952; Barrera, "Rincón obrero," *Prensa Libre*, December 5, 1951.

136. "Texto del manifiesto dirigido por la Federación de Sociedades Cubans al Jefe del Gobierno," *Amanecer* 1, no. 3 (April–May 1952): 5; García Agüero, "Otra vez Prisciliano," *Noticias de Hoy*, October 15, 1952.

137. "Habla el PAU," *Prensa Libre*, December 18, 1951; Felipe Elosegui, "1000 noticias en sepia," *Tiempo*, April 20, 1952.

138. The Afro-Cuban journal *Amanecer* reported, for instance, that Batista had surrounded himself with a group of collaborators that included blacks, some of whom had been appointed to "positions of importance" within the government. See "Editorial. No por . . . , por cubanos," *Amanecer* 1, no. 3 (April–May 1952): 2.

139. This information is based on a variety of sources. See "Proclama sobre los propósitos y estatutos del nuevo gobierno," Havana, March 10, 1952, USNA, RG 59/737.00/3-1052; Felipe Elosegui, "1000 noticias en sepia," *Tiempo*, March 14 and 19, April 13, 1952; Cuéllar Vizcaíno, "Aire libre," *Tiempo*, September 27, 1952; and "Ojos y oídos: Nicolás Esquivel" and "El novato del año," *Amanecer* 1, no. 6 (August–December 1952): 8–10.

140. "El camino expedito," *Amanecer* 2, no. 3 (April 1953): 10; "Pide a Batista," *Tiempo*, April 29, 1952. On MOPI, see also Mario Carrión, "Integración nacional," *Amanecer* 2, no. 3 (April 1953): 3.

141. Agustín Tamargo, "Zenaida Manfugás," *Amanecer* 1, no. 6 (August–December 1952): 8–9; Cuéllar Vizcaíno, "Aire libre," *Tiempo*, September 9, 1952.

142. Concerning the lack of activity of the Frente after the coup, see Felipe Elosegui, "1000 noticias en sepia," *Tiempo*, March 19 and 26, 1952.

143. "Proyecto de Decreto-Ley presentado al Consejo de Ministros por Jesús Porto carrero," Havana, June 8, 1952, ANC, Fondo Especial, leg. 13, no. 141.

144. To mention but one notorious case, in 1953, African American singer Josephine

Baker was denied accommodations at the Hotel Nacional. See Earl T. Crain, "Joint Weeka no. 7," Havana, February 19, 1953, USNA, RG 59/737.00(W)/2-1353. For additional examples, see Chapter 4.

145. For a strong condemnation of the judicial system for promoting discrimination, see "Los tribunales de justicia," *Fragua de la Libertad* 1, no. 6 (June 18, 1942): 1.

146. Oliva's project is reproduced almost in its entirety in Grillo, *El problema del negro*, 126–30. For Lombard's proposal, see "Moción al Senado de la República," Havana, September 16, 1955, ANC, Fondo Especial, leg. 4, no. 136.

147. Grillo, *El problema del negro*, 130–37.

148. "Ley-Decreto No. 1993," *Gaceta Oficial*, January 24, 1955, enclosed in Carlos Hall, "New Law-Decree against Discrimination," Havana, February 14, 1955, USNA, RG 59/837.411/2-1455; "Acuerdos del Consejo," *Prensa Libre*, January 25, 1955.

149. Fernando Villaverde, "Habla el Presidente del Club Atenas," *Prensa Libre*, February 2, 1955.

150. Barrera, "Rincón obrero," *Prensa Libre*, December 13, 1951; "Afirma Buttari que no existe discriminación racial," *Prensa Libre*, December 15, 1951; Raoul A. Gonsé, "Verdades: El problema de la discriminación racial," *El Mundo*, December 19, 1951.

151. "La presidencia de Atenas," *Amanecer* 1, no. 6 (August–December 1952): 10. See also the accusations made by the president of the Havana Federation against the leaders of the National Federation for their "politicking," in Astenógenes Batista, "Una carta," *Tiempo*, July 14, 1957.

152. "Contra la entrega del Club Atenas," *Carta Semanal*, March 12, 1958; Juan R. Gómez Gómez, "Síntesis de una obra de gobierno," *Atenas* 3, no. 10 (October 1954): 7–10.

153. Cuéllar Vizcaíno, "¿Medio millón desairado?," *Tiempo*, January 25, 1955; "Designará el General Batista directiva de Sociedades Cubanas," *Tiempo*, March 6, 1955; Lisandro Otero, "¡La confraternidad humana no permite discriminación!," *Bohemia*, April 21, 1957, 86–87, 94.

154. Vegueri, *El negro en Cuba*, 30.

155. Grillo, *El problema del negro*, 47–53. In 1943 the American ambassador paid a courtesy visit to the Afro-Cuban club Luz de Oriente in Santiago de Cuba. See "En la Sociedad Luz de Oriente," *Libertad*, February 27, 1943. The Soviet Embassy had also made overtures to the black population, and in 1944 the Soviet press attaché was invited to speak at Club Atenas. See Humberto Hernández, "Conferencias educativas," *Noticias de Hoy*, April 8, 1944, and Jack West, "Memorandum for the Ambassador," Havana, May 2, 1944, USNA, RG 84/800B/6780.

156. Gómez Gómez, "Síntesis de una obra," 9; "Notas sociales," *La Verdad*, August 25, 1951; "La raza de color en los Estados Unidos," *Amanecer* 1, no. 4 (May–June 1952): 8; Serviat, *El problema negro*, 138–40.

157. Grillo, *El problema del negro*, 149–54; "Habla José Daniel García," *Amanecer* 2, no. 3 (March 1953): 10–11; "Nuestra obra," *Amanecer* 2, no. 4 (April 1953): 15. On Zuasnábar's cooperative, see Cuéllar Vizcaíno, *Unas cuantas verdades*, 9, and "¿Qué pasa, Justo Luis?," *Amanecer* 2, no. 4 (April 1953): 10. See also Astenógenes

Batista, "¿Tiene el negro cubano interés de levantarse creando comercios?," *Amanecer* 2, no. 3 (March 1953): 6–7.

158. Betancourt, *Doctrina negra*, 24–25, 59, 63–64; "Ejecutivo de la ONRE en Pogolotti," *Tiempo*, July 14, 1957. For a characterization of Betancourt's ideas as "petit bourgeois nationalism," see Serviat, *El problema negro*, 135–38.

159. Astenógenes Batista, "¿Nuestra gentes es remisa?," *Tiempo*, September 6, 1957.

160. Hall, "New-Law Decree against Discrimination."

161. The Ortodoxos of course defended themselves against these charges. See "Hablan los Ortodoxos," *Prensa Libre*, October 13, 23, and 27, 1951.

162. Photographs of participants appeared in the press. See "Ortodoxos y Auténticos," *El Crisol*, June 1, 1953, and "El Compromiso de Montreal," *Carteles*, June 14, 1953.

163. "Ley-Decreto 1170," October 30, 1953, USNA, RG 59/737.00/11-1653; "La defensa de la democracia," *Información*, May 5, 1955; Andrés Valdespino, "El Decreto 538: ¿Contra el comunismo o contra la libertad?," *Bohemia*, April 7, 1957, 51, 99–100. For a discussion of party activities under Batista, see Farber, *Revolution and Reaction*, 161–65.

164. Earl T. Crain, "Joint Weeka no. 28," Havana, September 18, 1953, USNA, RG 59/737.00(W)/9-1853.

165. "Batista Dubs Student Riots 'Communistic,'" *Havana Post*, January 17, 1953; Rojas, *La generación del centenario*, 91–93; "Blas Roca y Marinello," *¡Alerta!*, July 27, 1953.

166. Valdespino, "El Decreto 538," 99–100.

167. Bonachea and San Martín, *The Cuban Insurrection*, 25.

168. William Fears to the Department of State, Accomac, Virginia, March 29, 1957, USNA, RG 59/737.00/3-2957.

169. "Memorandum of Conversation, Dr. Felipe Pazos," Washington, D.C., October 14, 1958, USNA, RG 59/737.00/10-1458; "Developments in Cuba," Havana, September 5, 1959, USNA, RG 59/737.00/9-559.

170. Thomas, *Cuba*, 1560–61, 894; Domínguez, "Racial and Ethnic Relations," 279.

171. "Peligrosa red de saboteadores," *Tiempo*, July 4, 1957; "Ocho nuevos detenidos," *El Crisol*, April 7, 1958; "Acusados de Atentado," *Información*, April 8, 1958. The best empirical study of links between the M-26-7 and organized labor is García Pérez, *Insurrection and Revolution*.

172. C. W. Mackay, "First Hand Report on Cuba," *Afro-American*, January 31, 1959. For a similar claim by another African American journalist, see Charles Howard, "The Afro-Cubans," *Freedomways* (Summer 1964): 375–82. See also Moore, "Le peuple noir," 199.

173. Ricardo Bernal, "La Universidad Central, la reforma agraria y la integración nacional," *Noticias de Hoy*, May 8, 1959; Mackay, "So This Is Havana" and "Inside Castro's Cuba," *Afro-American*, February 7 and 14, 1959.

174. Farber, *Revolution and Reaction*, 157; Daniel Braddock to the Department of State, Havana, March 26, 1958, USNA, RG 59/737.00/3-2658.

175. "Galería de asesinos," *Bohemia*, January 11, 1959, 152–58.

176. Ramón Coto, "Responde Fidel Castro," *Bohemia*, November 10, 1955, 15, 81–83.
177. Thomas, *Cuba*, 1121; Masferrer and Mesa-Lago, "The Gradual Integration," 373.
178. "Manifesto No. 1 [26th of July Movement] to the People of Cuba" (August 8, 1955), in Bonachea and Valdés, *Revolutionary Struggle*, 270; "Program Manifesto of the 26th of July Movement," in Bonachea and Valdés, *Cuba in Revolution*, 132–33. See also Bonachea and San Martín, *The Cuban Insurrection*, 154–59.
179. Betancourt, *El negro*, 167; Carlos Nicot and Vicente Cubillas, "Relatos inéditos sobre la acción revolucionaria del líder Frank País," *Revolución*, July 30, 1963. For examples of Afro-Cubans participating in the M-26-7 in Santiago, see Nils Castro, "Universidad: 21 aniversario," *Mambí* (October 1968): 94–97.
180. Masferrer had developed this reputation for allowing the publication in his newspaper *Tiempo* of regular columns devoted to black questions. In 1951 an Afro-Cuban club from Havana proposed to organize a function to honor the senator. See Felipe Elosegui, "1000 noticias en sepia," *Tiempo*, December 6, 1951.
181. On Masferrer, see Earl Smith, "Joint Weeka no. 29," Havana, July 17, 1957, USNA, RG 59/737.00(W)/7-1757, and Betancourt, *El negro*, 167. On Vasconcelos, see Luis Manuel Martínez, "Habla Ramón Vasconcelos," *Tiempo*, July 9, 1957.
182. Salvador (Saviur) Cancio Peña, "Temblad, granujas!," *Panfleto*, November 15, 1954; Cancio Peña, "El día del gran Arrastre!," *Panfleto*, December 1, 1954. Note that the expression "mulato malo" was probably used here to denote that Batista was in fact a "dark" mulatto, as opposed to a light "mulato avanzado" or "bueno" in Cuban racial terminology.
183. Daniel Braddock to the Department of State, Havana, August 14, 1959, USNA, RG 59/737.00/8-1459.
184. García Agüero, "Desagravio a Maceo," *Noticias de Hoy*, May 23, 1953; Roca, *Los fundamentos*, 97.
185. Betancourt, *El negro*, 193.
186. Smith to the Secretary of State, Havana, March 25, 1958, USNA, RG 59/737.00/3-2558; Farber, *Revolution and Reaction*, 164–65.

CHAPTER SEVEN
1. *Revolución*, January 3, 1959, quoted in Pérez-Stable, *The Cuban Revolution*, 3.
2. Booth, "Cuba, Color and the Revolution," 155; Thomas, *Cuba*, 1120–21; Masferrer and Mesa-Lago, "The Gradual Integration," 373–74; Fagen, "Revolution," 10–15.
3. This sense of the inevitable is conveyed in Carneado, "La discriminación racial," 60–61.
4. Moore, "Le peuple noir," 199. I have been unable to corroborate these assertions by Moore.
5. See the works mentioned above, note 2.
6. "Unión: Tarea de la hora," *Noticias de Hoy*, January 6, 1959.
7. Daniel Braddock to the Department of State, Havana, February 2, 1959, USNA, RG 59/737.001/2-259; "Carta al ciudadano presidente," *Revolución*, January 31, 1959.

8. Park F. Wollam, "Events in Oriente," Santiago de Cuba, October 11, 1958, USNA, RG 59/737.00/10-1158; "El programa del FONU," *Noticias de Hoy*, January 11, 1959.

9. "Exhorta la CTC," *Revolución*, March 18, 1959.

10. Betancourt, "La cuestión racial," *Revolución*, January 17, 1959, and "Fidel Castro y la integración nacional," *Bohemia*, February 15, 1959, 66, 122–23. See also Gastón Agüero, *Racismo y mestizaje*, and Alcibíades Poveda, "Un problema social en Santiago de Cuba," *Revolución*, February 9, 1959.

11. This information was provided by Cuban historian Carlos Venegas during a conversation with the author in Cienfuegos, March 5, 1998. Venegas is a native of Trinidad. Another historian from Santa Clara, Hernán Venegas, also asserted that this had happened in Santa Clara.

12. These incidents are described in Ricardo Bernal, "La Universidad Central, la reforma agraria y la integración nacional," *Noticias de Hoy*, May 8, 1959. See also the perceptions of an African American journalist about these changes in Ring, *How Cuba Uprooted Race Discrimination*, 12.

13. "Necesitamos paz," *Revolución*, January 23, 1959; "Discurso pronunciado . . . en la Refinería Shell el 6 de febrero de 1959" and "Discurso pronunciado en la Plenaria Nacional convocada por la FNTA el 9 de febrero de 1959," in Castro, *Discursos para la historia*, 1:62, 84.

14. The speech was published entirely in *Noticias de Hoy*, March 24, 1959, and *Revolución*, March 23, 1959.

15. Depestre, "Lettre de Cuba," 121.

16. Gastón Agüero, *Racismo y mestizaje*, 11–13; Foreign Areas Studies Division, *Handbook for Cuba*, 89. César García Pons also mentions the "discomfort" provoked by Castro's speech in "El Dr. Castro y la discriminación," *Diario de la Marina*, March 29, 1959.

17. Fox, "Race and Class," 429.

18. Depestre, "Lettre de Cuba," 121; Gastón Agüero, *Racismo y mestizaje*, 13.

19. The uneasiness of some blacks concerning these drastic social changes is evident in the testimonies gathered by Fox in "Race and Class," 432–34. It is also evident in the anecdote mentioned above concerning the celebration of Martí's birthday in Santa Clara in January 1959. Although most members of El Gran Maceo accepted the invitation of the white social club, some chose not to participate. See Bernal, "La Universidad Central."

20. "¡A ganar la batalla de la discriminación!," *Revolución*, March 26, 1959.

21. The front-page headline in *Diario de la Marina*, March 26, 1959, for instance, read: "Dr. Castro Explained That Racial Discrimination Is an Issue That Requires a Process of Education. To End Discrimination Does Not Mean Forcing Anyone to Dance, If They Don't Want to Dance." The headline published in the *Times of Havana* on the same day read: "Social Changes Take Time."

22. Cuéllar Vizcaíno, "Discriminación," *Nuevos Rumbos* 8 (April 25, 1959): 5–9; Elías Entralgo, "Forum sobre prejuicios étnicos en Cuba," *Nuevos Rumbos* 10 (August 9, 1959); "Campaña contra la discriminación racial," *Revolución*, April 8, 1959.

23. "Integrarán Comité Nacional de Integración," "Habló Ernesto Guevara," and

"Reunión del Comité," *Noticias de Hoy*, March 31, April 7, August 25, 1959; "Anuncian en Marianao," *Revolución*, November 28, 1959; "Ciclo de mesas," *Noticias de Hoy*, September 9, 1960.

24. "Conferencias sobre integración," *Noticias de Hoy*, August 23, 1959; "Hablará el Ministro del Trabajo," *Revolución*, August 29, 1959; "Conferencia," *Revolución*, May 30, 1959.

25. "La unidad de blancos y negros" and "Unidad juvenil," *Noticias de Hoy*, March 25, April 30, 1959; "Reforma de la enseñanza," *Revolución*, April 18, 1959; "Statement of the Cuban Council of Protestant Churches," Havana, July 15, 1959, USNA, RG 59/837.413/7-1759.

26. Bernal, "La universidad central"; "Banquete," *Noticias de Hoy*, May 7, 1959.

27. The following list is only a sample of the coverage provided by *Noticias de Hoy* in 1959: "Cubano es más que blanco," March 28; "Don Fernando," April 4; José Felipe, "Racismo" and "Peligro negro," May 10 and 13; Diego González, "Los reflejos [I, II, III]," March 31, April 5, April 7; García Agüero, "Va bien Fidel," March 24; and Carlos Rafael Rodríguez, "A las filas," March 27.

28. "Zona rebelde: La discriminación racial" and "El humanismo," *Revolución*, March 25, May 23, 1959. *Avance Revolucionario* devoted two regular columns to issues of race in 1959: Roger Fumero's "Glosas del tiempo" and Tello Téllez's "Reflejos sociales." See also Alejandro Acosta, "La discriminación racial," *Sierra Maestra*, November 8, 1959.

29. "Discurso de Raúl Castro," *Noticias de Hoy*, May 3, 1959; "Speech of Ernesto 'Che' Guevara at Santiago de Cuba," Havana, May 4, 1959, USNA, RG 59/737.00–May Day/5-459; Guevara, *Escritos y discursos* 4:45–50; Castro, *Conferencia*, 37–39.

30. Thomas, *Cuba*, 1120–21; Betancourt, "Castro and the Cuban Negro," 272–73. See also Moore's discussion about the meanings of these measures in "Le peuple noir," 208–9.

31. "Se abren las playas," *Revolución*, April 11, 1959; "Mantendrán balnearios privacidad," *Revolución*, February 17, 1959; "Moncada: Siete años después," *Trabajo* 3 (July 1960): 66–71.

32. O. Fernández, "Hermano negro," *Revolución*, August 21, 1959; "Tendrá Santa Clara" and "Nuevo parque," *Revolución*, August 26, November 23, 1959; "Contra la discriminación racial en Cruces," *Noticias de Hoy*, April 1, 1959.

33. "Trascendencia social y humana de los círculos obreros," *Trabajo* 7 (November 1960): 90–93.

34. Ricardo Cardet, "Alegría fraternal," *Combate 13 de Marzo*, October 27, 1961.

35. Roger Fumero, "Glosas del tiempo" and "¿Dos 'Cubanalecos' para qué?," *El Avance Revolucionario*, January 22 and 25, 1960; Tello Téllez, "Reflejos sociales: ¿Dos 'Cubanalecos' para qué?," *El Avance Revolucionario*, February 22, 1960.

36. Tello Téllez, "Reflejos sociales: El extraño silencio de Fraginals" and "Reflejos sociales: ¿Dos 'Cubanalecos' para qué?," *El Avance Revolucionario*, February 17 and 22, 1960; Cardet, "Alegría fraternal."

37. "El humanismo," *Revolución*, May 23, 1959; "Proletarias: La discriminación," *Nuevos Rumbos* 10 (August 9, 1959): 7–9; "Un Comité de Integración en la Beck," *Noticias de Hoy*, May 12, 1959; "Demands . . . Workers in the Distribution of

Motion Pictures," Havana, April 22, 1959, USNA, RG 59/837.062/5-459; "Crean Comité de Integración los tabaqueros," *Noticias de Hoy*, April 8, 1959.

38. Ramón de la Cruz to the Manatí Sugar Company, Havana, July 13, 1960, BBC, RG 4, ser. 45, box 2, folder "Labor-Cuba"; Richard Milk to the Secretary of State, Preston, December 24, 1959, USNA, RG 59/737.00/12-2459.

39. "Contra la discriminación los bancarios," *Noticias de Hoy*, April 9, 1959; "Empleará un banco a trabajadores negros," *Revolución*, May 22, 1959; Fumero, "Glosas del tiempo," *El Avance Revolucionario*, March 18, 1960; Roca, *Los fundamentos*, 98.

40. About these practices, see the perceptive article by Lázaro Peña, "Debemos combatir practicamente la discriminación racial desde los sindicatos," *Noticias de Hoy*, March 29, 1959.

41. "Recuento de la labor revolucionaria del Ministerio del Trabajo," *Trabajo* 1 (May 1960): 84–94; Augusto Martínez Sánchez, "Conferencia," *Trabajo* 1 (May 1960): 66–67.

42. Mayfield, "Cuba Has Solution to Race Problem," *Afro-American*, October 1, 1960.

43. "Los nuevos empleos son para los que más los necesitan," *Trabajo* 6 (October 1960): 4–5.

44. Mesa-Lago, "Economic Policies and Growth," in *Revolutionary Change*, 283.

45. Jolly, "The Literacy Campaign," 190–219; "La revolución reivindica a las clases explotadas," *Combate 13 de Marzo*, August 8, 1961. Black participation in the literacy campaign is quite apparent in Manuel Octavio Gómez's documentary *Historia de una batalla* (1962). This visibility was further enhanced by the fact that one of the campaign martyrs—Conrado Benítez, a volunteer teacher who was assassinated by counterrevolutionary bands in the Escambray mountains in 1961—was black.

46. Lewis et al., *Cuatro hombres*, 126–39; "La revolución transforma 'Las Yaguas,'" *Revolución*, February 18, 1959. For Santiago, see Cuba, *Statistics from the Ministry of Social Welfare*, 19.

47. Jolly, "The Literacy Campaign," 210.

48. MacGaffey, "Social Structure and Mobility in Cuba," 106.

49. Zeitlin, *Revolutionary Politics*, 77; "Developments in Cuba since Castro Assumed Power," September 5, 1959, USNA, RG 59/737.00/9-559.

50. Zeitlin, *Revolutionary Politics*, 85, 75; Fox, "Race and Class," 436.

51. Guillén, *¡Patria o muerte!*, 190–95.

52. Zeitlin, *Revolutionary Politics*, 77; Fox, "Race and Class," 427–30.

53. Sutherland, *The Youngest Revolution*, 150.

54. Duharte and Santos, *El fantasma de la esclavitud*, 100–103.

55. "II Declaración de la Habana" (February 4, 1962), in *Documentos de la revolución cubana*, 68; Carneado, "La discriminación racial," 54; Lockwood, *Castro's Cuba*, 128.

56. Sutherland, *The Youngest Revolution*, 149. Both Sutherland (ibid., 146) and Moore ("Le peuple noir," 205) note that the campaign against racism waned after 1962 or 1963. My research confirms these assertions.

57. This was particularly the case after the restructuring of the Integrated Revolutionary Organizations in 1962. See Domínguez, *Cuba: Order and Revolution*, 210–18.

58. Roca, *Los fundamentos*, 98–99.

59. The list of societies was published in *Combate 13 de Marzo*, August 27, September 1, 2, and 8, 1961.

60. "Destituyeron a la Junta Directiva del 'Atenas,'" *Revolución*, January 26, 1959.

61. Betancourt, *El negro*, 156–60. Betancourt recounted this story differently later, asserting that he had been appointed by the government to occupy the federation. See his "Castro and the Cuban Negro," 270–71.

62. "Destituyen a directivos," *Revolución*, March 24, 1959; Roger Fumero, "Deja de ser el Club Marbella un centro separatista," *El Avance Revolucionario*, February 19, 1960.

63. Cuéllar Vizcaíno, "Discriminación"; Roger Fumero, "Glosas del tiempo," *El Avance Revolucionario*, March 24, 1960.

64. Roger Fumero, "Glosas del tiempo" and "Mensaje," *El Avance Revolucionario*, January 20, April 23, 1960. The letter written by Jesús Muñiz was printed in Fumero, "Carta con breve preámbulo," *El Avance Revolucionario*, April 22, 1960.

65. Betancourt, *El negro*, 158–60.

66. Agüero, *Racismo y mestizaje en Cuba*, 226–42; Roger Fumero, "Glosas del tiempo: Más sobre 'Racismo y Mestizaje en Cuba,'" *El Avance Revolucionario*, April 21, 1960.

67. García Agüero, "Negrismo no: Integración," *Noticias de Hoy*, August 26, 1959. See also Betancourt's critique of the Communists in his "Castro and the Cuban Negro," 270–74.

68. "Conferencia sobre integración," "Festival en Aponte," and "Excepcional aporte a la R.A. en Matanzas," *Revolución*, May 30, April 29, June 12, 1959; Tello Téllez, "Reflejos sociales: El homenaje de ayer," *El Avance Revolucionario*, March 1, 1960; "Club Jóvenes del Vals," ANC, Registro de Asociaciones, leg. 1159, no. 24261; "Unión Fraternal de Jaruco," *Noticias de Hoy*, September 30, 1960; Cabrera Torres, *La rehabilitación*.

69. "Club Jóvenes del Vals"; "Unión Fraternal," ANC, Registro de Asociaciones, leg. 1225, nos. 25614–16; "Club Atenas," ANC, Registro de Asociaciones, leg. 1112, nos. 23267–70. The discussion below is based on these sources.

70. "A Guanajay no ha llegado la política justa de la integración nacional," *Noticias de Hoy*, May 10, 1959; Cuéllar Vizcaíno, "Discriminación," *Nuevos Rumbos* 8 (April 25, 1959): 5–9.

71. For an example of this sort of discourse in the clubs, see Tello Téllez, "Palabras para jóvenes," *El Avance Revolucionario*, February 12, 1960.

72. Sutherland, *The Youngest Revolution*, 150. Examples of this "paternalistic attitude" can be found in the leaders' dealings with black counterrevolutionaries, whom they considered double traitors. For examples, see Lavretsky, *Ernesto Che Guevara*, 163, and Montaner, *Informe secreto*, 98–100.

73. Antonieta Henríquez, "Ciclo de conferencias sobre integración racial," and R. Seoane, "En Cuba," *Noticias de Hoy*, August 23 and 30, 1959; "En poder de Urrutia un proyecto para estimular las tradiciones folklóricas," *Noticias de Hoy*, May 24, 1959.

74. "Eligen a Miss Cuba," *Revolución*, July 6, 1959; Daniel M. Braddock to the Depart-

ment of State, Havana, September 9, 1959, USNA, RG 59/937.61/9-959; "Corona esta noche el Comandante Almeida a la Reina del Carnaval," *El Avance Revolucionario*, February 6, 1960; "Coronará Almeida a reina," *El Crisol*, February 3, 1960.

75. "Muñecas de trapo," *Revolución*, December 10, 1959; H. Núñez Lemus, "La belleza sigue siendo arma femenina," *Combate 13 de Marzo*, October 19, 1961.

76. Betancourt, *El negro*, 86; Cuéllar Vizcaíno, "Discriminación."

77. "Excepcional aporte a la R.A. en Matanzas"; Tello Téllez, "Apuntes sobre un Congreso Abacua," *El Avance Revolucionario*, April 1, 1960.

78. Agüero, *Racismo y mestizaje*, 226–33; Carbonell, *Crítica*, 20, 32–36.

79. For instance, the Dirección General de Cultura of the Ministry of Education published in 1960 the work of racist author Saco, *Colección de papeles científicos, históricos, políticos*. Another printing house, Lex, also published several works by Saco, Luz y Caballero, and Domingo del Monte. For Carbonell's assessment of these authors, see his *Crítica*, 34–40.

80. "Cine cubano: Otra obra de la revolución," *Trabajo* 8 (December 1960): 172–73; Mario Rodríguez Alemán, "Realengo 18," *Combate 13 de Marzo*, August 16, 1961. For an introduction to Cuba's movie industry in the early years of the revolution, see Pat Aufderheide, "Cuba Vision: Three Decades of Cuban Film," in Brenner et al., *The Cuba Reader*, 498–506.

81. Argeliers León, "La expresión del pueblo en el TNC," *Actas del Folklore* 1, no. 1 (January 1961): 5–7. About the Teatro Nacional de Cuba, see Hagerdon, "Anatomía," 219–38.

82. Ramiro Guerra, "Hacia un movimiento de danza nacional," *Lunes de Revolución*, July 13, 1959. See also Salvador Massip's excellent documentary *Historia de un Ballet* (1962), which documents the earliest efforts of Danza Nacional to study and stage Afro-Cuban dances.

83. These included Rogelio Martínez Furé, Miguel Barnet, Rafael López-Valdés, and Alberto Pedro. They all contributed some of their work in the seminar to *Actas del Folklore*.

84. Interview with Cuban anthropologist Rafael López-Valdés by Hagerdon, Havana, December 30, 1991, in Hagerdon, "Anatomía," 222.

85. León, "La expresión del pueblo en el TNC," 5; Carbonell, *Crítica*, 108–12.

86. "Creación del Instituto de Etnología y Folklore," *Actas del Folklore* 1, nos. 10–12 (October–December 1961): 33–35; Enrique González Manet, "Transforma la revolución las costumbres del cubano," *Bohemia*, May 11, 1962, 16–18, 97.

87. Martínez Furé, *Conjunto Folklórico Nacional*, and "Obra de fundación," in *Diálogos imaginarios*, 248–56.

88. Moore, "Le peuple noir," 218–19. The critique of "folklorization" was shared by some of the Afro-Cuban intellectuals interviewed in Sutherland, *The Youngest Revolution*, 151.

89. The same assumption was behind the foundation of the Santería Museum in Guanabacoa in 1964. About this institution, see José Luis Hernández, "El Museo de Guanabacoa," *Areíto* 1, no. 3 (July 1988): 8–12.

90. This assertion is made in Moore, "Le peuple noir," 219.

91. About the relations between church and state in post-1959 Cuba, see Kirk, *Between God and Party* (for the 1961 conflict, see 102–9), and Crahan, "Freedom of Worship," 211–19.

92. Kirk, *Between God and Party*, 127–43. The rapprochement was facilitated by a number of public documents released by the Catholic Church, reprinted in Hageman and Wheaton, *Religion in Cuba*, 279–308.

93. Domínguez, "Racial and Ethnic Relations," 280.

94. "Ciencia y religión: La santería," *El Militante Comunista* (October 1968): 82–90.

95. Bernabe Hernández, *Superstición* (1964), film; "Santería," *Trabajo Político* 4 (December 1968): 48–57.

96. "Los ñáñigos o abakuá," *P.N.R.* (January–March 1972): 2–16; "La Sociedad Secreta Abakuá (Ñáñigos)," *Revista Jurídica* 1 (1969): 13–24.

97. The author of "Ciencia y religión: La santería," for instance, asserted that practitioners disguised their ritual colors in watch bracelets (87).

98. Excerpts of the cases discussed below are taken from "La Sociedad Secreta Abakuá," 18–24.

99. Some authors have denied, however, that Santería was ever repressed, claiming that state opposition was due to counterrevolutionary activities. See Miguel Barnet, "Algunas palabras necesarias," *Areíto* 1, no. 3 (July 1988): 5–7.

100. "Sociedad Santa Bárbara, Cienfuegos," AHPC, Registro de Asociaciones, leg. 9, no. 201; "Sociedad Espiritista Casino Africano San Antonio, Santa Isabel de las Lajas," AHPC, Registro de Asociaciones, leg. 54, no. 6. Of course, some societies were never canceled, such as Hijos de San Antonio and Hijos de San Lázaro, both from Guanabacoa. See Ramón Valdés Guanche, "La Asociación Hijos de San Antonio," *Areíto* 1, no. 3 (July 1988): 20–22, and "En el munanso simbilico con el Tata Enkise," *Areíto* 1, no. 3 (July 1988): 23–24.

101. This is based on the dossier of the Sociedad Espiritista Casino Africano San Antonio.

102. Santera Coralia Crespo, interviewed by the author, Havana, March 13, 1998; Babalao Carlos Terry Calderón, interviewed by the author, Cienfuegos, March 6, 1998. The opposition to minors' participation in the Afro-Cuban religions is also evident in "La Sociedad Secreta Abakuá," 17.

103. The movie quoted is *De cierta manera* (1974), directed by Sara Gómez. For a good analysis of this and other movies concerning questions of race, see Martínez-Echazábal, "The Politics of Afro-Cuban Religion," 16–22. For the Ministry of Health information, see McGarrity, "Race, Culture, and Social Change," 199.

104. The Sábados de la Rumba were organized in 1982, but Saturday performances of the CFN began in 1975. See Martínez Furé, "Obra de fundación," in *Diálogos imaginarios*, 255–56.

105. On Mendive's work, see Martínez Furé, "Manuel Mendive: Los pinceles de Elegba" (1968), in *Diálogos imaginarios*, 243–47, and the documentary *Motivations* (1988), dir. Marisol Trujillo.

106. For introductions to the question of race in literature, see García Barrio, "The Black in Post-Revolutionary Cuban Literature," 263–70, and Olliz-Boyd, "Race Relations in Cuba," 225–33. Some important texts of the period, such as a

section of Granados's *Adire y el tiempo roto* (1967) and a poem of Excilia Saldaña (1967), have been translated into English and reproduced in Pérez Sarduy and Stubbs, *Afrocuba*. Nancy Morejón is one of the authors whose work is well known, particularly her superb poem "Mujer Negra," which was published in English in "The Poems of Nancy Morejón," *Black Scholar* (Summer 1983): 50–53. On Morejón's work, see Efraín Barradas, "La negritud hoy: Nota sobre la poesía de Nancy Morejón," *Areíto* 6, no. 24 (1980): 33–39, and Howe, "Nancy Morejón's 'Mujer Negra,'" 95–107.

107. Mariano Faget to Dwight Eisenhower, Miami, November 27, 1959, USNA, RG 59/737.00/11-2759; "Discurso de Fidel Castro en el Congreso Nacional de la FNTA," *Revolución*, December 15, 1959; Park F. Wollam, "Events in Oriente Province," Santiago de Cuba, June 17, 1959, USNA, RG 59/737.00/6-1759.

108. "150 Newsmen Get Cuban Invitation" and "Adam C. Powell among Visitors," *Chicago Defender*, January 21 and 22, 1959.

109. "Castro, Joe Louis Confer in Havana," *Chicago Defender*, January 4, 1960; "Castro Opens Cuba's Doors for U.S. Negro Tourist Trade," *Pittsburgh Courier*, January 16, 1960. See also Gosse, "The African-American Press," 266–80.

110. Clarke, "Journey to the Sierra Maestra," *Freedomways* (Spring 1961): 32–35; Jones, "Cuba libre," in *Home*, 11–62; Ring, *How Cuba Uprooted Race Discrimination*, 6–9; Mayfield, "Cuba Has Solution to Race Problem," *Afro-American*, October 1, 1960.

111. The reactions of the black press to the Cuban revolution are studied in Gosse, "The African-American Press," 266–80, and Ring, *How Cuba Uprooted Race Discrimination*, 6–14.

112. Mayfield, "Cuba Has Solution." For additional examples, see Gosse, "The African-American Press," 271–72.

113. Steve Duncan, "Premier Talks to Afro," and Alvin White, "Fidel Calls Harlem 'An Oasis in Dessert,'" *Afro-American*, October 1, 1960. On Castro's visit to Harlem, see also Gosse, *Where the Boys Are*, 149–51; Rosemari, *Fidel and Malcolm X*; and Moore, *Castro, the Blacks, and Africa*, 78–82, which describes these events as "The Harlem Show."

114. Mayfield, "The Cuban Challenge," *Freedomways* (Summer 1961): 185. A similar point was made in the editorial "Castro Visit," *Afro-American*, October 1, 1960.

115. "Declaration," *Afro-American*, April 29, 1961, reprinted in Ring, *How Cuba Uprooted Race Discrimination*, 15. About the Fair Play for Cuba Committee, see Gosse, *Where the Boys Are*, 137–73.

116. Gosse, *Where the Boys Are*, 152–54.

117. "NAACP Hits Official's Support of Castro Rule," *Afro-American*, April 22, 1961; "Invites Castro to Visit South," *Chicago Defender*, September 27, 1960.

118. U.S. Congress, Committee on the Judiciary, *The Tricontinental Conference* (Washington, D.C.: U.S. Government Printing Office, 1966), 7, in Robert F. Williams Papers, box 11, CIA Documents, 1961–68, University of Michigan, Bentley Historical Library, Ann Arbor, Michigan; George Roberts, "Castro Arming Southern Negroes," *National Police Gazette* (July 1965): 5, 18, in Williams Papers, box 7, Clippings 1963–66.

119. Cleaver, *Soul on Ice*, 108; Brent, *Long Time Gone*, 131–46; Pearson, *The Shadow*, 268–75; Shakur, *Assata*, 266–74.

120. Cleaver, *Soul on Ice*, 107. U.S. authorities claimed that African Americans were being trained in terrorist tactics in Cuba. For a few examples, see U.S. Congress, Committee on the Judiciary, *The Tricontinental Conference*, 6–7.

121. Castro, *Discursos en los aniversarios de los CDR*, 102–3; Huey Newton, "Black Power and the Revolutionary Struggle," *Tricontinental* 3 (November 1968): 5–12; George Murray and Joudon M. Ford, "Black Panthers: The Afro-Americans' Challenge," *Tricontinental* 10 (January–February 1969): 96–111. For concrete examples of endorsement of armed violence versus pacifist approaches by the Cubans, see "Legítima lucha del negro Norteamericano," *OLAS* 5 (1966): 5–7, and "The Rebellion of North American Black People," *Tricontinental* 3 (September 1968): 57–58.

122. "Radio Free Dixie Broadcasts to U.S.A." (October 13, 1962), Williams Papers, box 11, CIA Documents, 1962–68, folder 2; Cruise, *Rebellion or Revolution?*, 94, 105–10. For a discussion of the colonial thesis of black America, see Haines, *Black Radicals*, 57–70.

123. James Forman, "Estados Unidos 1967: Marea Alta de Resistencia Negra," *Tricontinental* 6 (May–June 1968): 22–51. On Carmichael's visit to Cuba, see also Carson, *In Struggle*, 274–76.

124. The details of Cuban involvement in Africa are fairly well known and will not be reproduced here. By far the best-documented study of the Cuban Africa policy during this period is Moore's highly controversial *Castro, the Blacks, and Africa*. For Che's participation in the war in the Congo, see Taibo II et al., *El año que estuvimos en ninguna parte*. For the Cuban participation in the independence of Guinea-Bissau, see Gleijeses, "The First Ambassadors," 45–88. On Castro's visit to Africa, see *El futuro es el internacionalismo*, 11–102.

125. Examples of this media campaign are too numerous to cite here. Typical are the popular documentaries of Santiago Alvarez: *Now* (1965) and *LBJ* (1968).

126. Williams to Castro, Peking, August 23, 1966, Williams Papers, box 11, CIA Documents 1961–68; Cleaver, *Soul on Ice*, 107–9; Moore, *Castro, the Blacks, and Africa*, 260–62; Clytus, *Black Man in Red Cuba*.

127. Carson, *In Struggle*, 274–75.

128. On the rejection of Afro hairstyles, see Sutherland, *The Youngest Revolution*, 152–53, and Saul Landau, "A New Twist on Race in Cuba," 53.

129. Sutherland, *The Youngest Revolution*, 154–55, 162–63. The effort of these Afro-Cuban intellectuals is mentioned in Booth, "Cuba, Color and the Revolution," 172 n. 126, and Moore, *Castro, the Blacks, and Africa*, 307–12. Moore cites other cases of black organizing (see ibid., 304–16), but his information relies on individual oral sources that are difficult to confirm.

130. Moore, *Catro, the Blacks, and Africa*.

131. To mention but one indicator of this presence, between 1974 and 1980 eleven heads of state of African countries visited Cuba, and the island established diplomatic relations with twelve African states. In 1980 Cuba was also visited by Jamaica's Michael Manley (twice) and by Grenada's Maurice Bishop. In turn,

Fidel Castro returned to Africa in 1976, 1977, and 1978, visiting thirteen countries in all. He also visited Jamaica in 1977. See Franklin, *Cuba and the United States*, 107–65. The social and cultural effects of Cuba's involvement in Africa might be contradictory, however. For many Cubans, this experience might have reinforced stereotypes about the "primitiveness" and "inferiority" of Africans and of blacks more generally. Derogatory remarks about Angolans were quite common among Cubans who returned from civilian and military missions there. This is a theme that needs further research.

132. Taylor, "Revolution, Race," 19–41. Castro's quote is taken from "En el congreso del pueblo," *Bohemia*, January 2, 1976, 55. On the relations between Cuba, Africa, and the Caribbean during the 1970s and 1980s, see Domínguez, *To Make a World Safe*; Falk, *Cuban Foreign Policy*; and Erisman and Kirk, *Cuba's International Relations*.

133. These figures are taken from Pedraza's "Cuba's Refugees," 273–75. Also of interest concerning the initial migration waves are Aguirre, "Differential Migration," and Fagen and Brody, "Cubans in Exile."

134. Dunn, *Black Miami*, 171–241.

135. "Refugee Problem" and "Negroes Losing Jobs to Cuban Refugees," *Miami Times*, November 11, December 16, 1961.

136. This assertion is based on a careful reading of the section "Street Talk" published in the *Miami Times* in 1993–98. Even when dealing with nonrelated subjects, African American residents frequently refer to the Cubans and the advantages they have received.

137. Dave Bondu, "Around Miami," *Miami Times*, May 26, 1967; "Riots Are Efforts of Communist Infiltration" and R. Gibson, "Letter to the Editor," *Miami Times*, August 4 and 11, 1967; John Egerton, "Cubans in Miami: A Third Dimension in Racial and Cultural Relations" (1969), in Cortés, *The Cuban Experience*, 4, 13, 23.

138. Marable, "The Fire This Time," 2–18.

139. On the 1980 riot and its connection to the Mariel influx, see Porter and Dunn, *The Miami Riot*, and Portes and Stepick, *City on the Edge*, 18–60.

140. About the characterization of the Mariel exiles as scum, see "Imágenes de Mariel," *Bohemia*, May 2, 1980, 54–59; "Noticias de Mariel. El tiempo sigue mejorando y la escoria navegando" and "Fidel, el primero de mayo," *Bohemia*, May 9, 1980, 44–45, 51–59. For an academic attempt to depict these emigrants as *escoria*, see Hernández and Gomis, "Retrato del Mariel," 124–51.

141. "En el 'paraíso' capitalista," *Cuba Internacional* 127 (June 1980): 9; Mario Kuchilan Sol, "¡Helos allí en su 'paraíso'!," *Bohemia*, June 13, 1980, 78–80; Julio A. Martí, "Una celda para Santy," *Cuba Internacional* (January 1991): 51–54.

142. Strong evidence supports this claim. For a good summary, see Portes and Stepick, *City on the Edge*, 22–37.

143. Elice Higginbotham, "The New Immigrants" and "The Difficulties of Resettlement," *Cubatimes* 1, no. 2 (Summer 1980): 23–26; 1, no. 3 (Fall 1980): 7–10; Portes and Stepick, "Unwelcome Immigrants," 493–514; Alma Guillermo Prieto, "Cubans of 1980 'Freedom Flotilla' Encountering Hardships," *Washington Post*, July 18, 1984.

144. "Cuban Exile Leaders Going to Angola," *Washington Post*, March 26, 1988; Mirta

Ojito, "Miami Medics Aid Angola Rebels," *Miami Herald*, February 6, 1988; Leonardo Cano, "Propaganda anticubana," *Bohemia*, July 20, 1990, 62–64; Jaime Suchlicki, "Do We Really Want Angola Agreement?," *Miami Herald*, August 21, 1988.

145. Portes and Stepick, *City on the Edge*, 176–78; Alfonso Chardy, "Blacks, Cubans See Mandela Trip in Different Ways," *Miami Herald*, July 27, 1991; Mimi Whitefield, "Mandela Salutes Cuba," *Miami Herald*, July 27, 1991; Whitefield, "Mandela Defends Bond with Castro, Rejects Criticism by S. Florida Exiles," *Miami Herald*, July 28, 1991; Lee Hockstader, "Castro Heaps Praise on Visiting Mandela," *Washington Post*, July 28, 1991.

146. Félix Pita Astudillo, "Emigration, 'Exile' and Political Manipulation," *Granma International*, April 27, 1994. On the image of Miami in the Cuban media, see also Cano, "Propaganda anticubana"; Nicanor León Cotayo, "Los agoreros de Miami," *Granma*, March 16, 1990; and Andrés Gomez, "Miami," *Granma*, January 5, 1994.

147. "A ese 'horno de iras,' ¡jamás!," *Granma*, May 6, 1992; Vincent James, "Black Cubans Call for Change," *Christian Science Monitor*, June 16, 1992.

148. For a summary of various estimates and the implications of this debate, see Moore, *Castro, the Blacks, and Africa*, 359–62.

149. Robert del Quiaro, "Five Faces of Cuba," *Washington Post*, February 11, 1973; Mayra Beatriz, "Amor: En blanco y negro," *Somos Jóvenes* (February 1990): 2–9. The best study of interracial couples in Cuba is Nadine Fernandez, "Race, Romance, and Revolution."

150. For numerous examples of how these ideas permeate popular consciousness, see Duharte and Santos, *El fantasma de la esclavitud*, 82–83, 95, 105–7.

151. For a discussion of how these figures were estimated, see de la Fuente, "Race and Inequality," 131–68. For sources, see table 7.1.

152. Moore, "Le peuple noir," 209. On the perception of other Afro-Cuban intellectuals, see Cuéllar Vizcaíno, "Discriminación," and Betancourt, *El negro*, 167–68.

153. Given that they are based on picture identification and sources that are far from adequate, these figures should be regarded as only tentative estimates. See Domínguez, "Racial and Ethnic Relations," 283; Montaner, *Informe secreto*, 107–8; and Domínguez, "Revolutionary Politics," 33. Figures for the provincial bureaus were obtained through picture identification from "Asambleas de balance," *El Militante Comunista* (June 1974): 24–191.

154. "El nuevo secretariado ejecutivo nacional de la CTC," *Bohemia*, November 23, 1973, 54–55; Casal, *Revolution and Race*, 16–20; Cuba, CEE, *Censo . . . La población de Cuba*, 117–18.

155. "Speech by President Fidel Castro Ruz at the Closing Ceremony of the Third PCC Congress" (February 7, 1986), in Foreign Broadcast Information Service, *Daily Report, Latin America* 6:027, February 10, 1986, 10–22; Castro, *Informe Central*, 503; Nelson Valdés, "The Changing Face of Cuba's Communist Party," *Cuba Update* 7, nos. 1–2 (Spring 1986): 1, 4, 16.

156. On the housing shortage, see Mesa-Lago, *The Economy of Socialist Cuba*, 162–64.

157. These figures are taken from Cuba, CEE, *Censo 1981*, 3:cxxi–cxliv.

158. Since the early 1960s these areas were considered sites for marginality and anti-social behavior. Youths from these areas, many of whom were black, were singled out for participation in various reeducation efforts. For a graphic example of this policy, see ICAIC's 1968 documentary, *Una isla para Miguel*.

159. For a view of these barrios, see José Luis Sanchez's documentary, *El Fanguito* (1990).

160. As coordinator of a research team of the attorney general of Cuba, I had the opportunity to visit these areas in 1987 and talk to the residents. Our results were included in an (unpublished) report entitled "Focos delictivos en la Habana."

161. Cuba, MININT, Sección de Estadística, *Informe*.

162. U.N., Economic and Social Council, Commission on Human Rights, *Consideration of the Report of the Mission Which Took Place in Cuba in Accordance with Commission Decision 1988/106* (E/CN.4/1989/46), 29, 319.

163. Evenson, *Revolution in the Balance*, 156–58.

164. Alejandro de la Fuente and Alejandro Vázquez, "La peligrosidad en ciudad de la Habana (1986)," unpublished report to the Office of the Attorney General, 1987.

165. This reality was acknowledged by the minister of interior in 1987. See "Palabras del Diputado a la Asamblea Nacional y Ministro del Interior José Abrahantes," in Cuba, MININT, *Una política consecuente*, 11–27.

CHAPTER EIGHT

1. For an introduction to the economic situation under the "rectification" and "special" periods, see Mesa-Lago, *Breve historia económica*, 127–74.

2. The first speech is quoted in Douglas Farah, "Cuba Opts to Legalize the Dollar," *Washington Post*, July 25, 1993, the second in "Con los que aman y fundan," *Correo de Cuba* (1995): 46. Concerning the reforms introduced by the Cuban government, see Mesa-Lago, *Are Economic Reforms Propelling Cuba to the Market?*

3. Mimi Whitefield, "Blacks' Support for Castro Erodes," *Miami Herald*, August 9, 1993.

4. For a discussion of the methods, coverage, and results of this survey, see de la Fuente and Glasco, "Are Blacks Getting 'Out of Control'?," 53–71.

5. Concerning the racial composition of the Cuban community in the United States, see Pedraza, "Cuba's Refugees," 273–75.

6. Cuba, CEE, *Censo . . . La población de Cuba*, 119.

7. De la Fuente and Glasco, "Are Blacks Getting 'Out of Control'?," 62–64. This perception is shared by some of the informants in Serrano, "Mujer, instrucción, ocupación y color de la piel," 119–31.

8. Duharte and Santos, *El fantasma de la esclavitud*, 126–27.

9. De la Fuente and Glasco, "Are Blacks Getting 'Out of Control'?," 65.

10. Duharte and Santos, *El fantasma de la esclavitud*, 126.

11. A Cuban official who requested to remain anonymous confirmed this rumor in a personal conversation with the author in 1996. One of the informants in Duharte and Santos, *El fantasma de la esclavitud*, 124, asserts that this had been a "big scandal" and that the hotel's manager had to apologize on television. On labor conflicts in the Habana Libre, see Clissold, "Balancing Economic Efficiency." In

"Cuba's Employment Conundrum," Clissold also reports the rumor that whites were being preferred over blacks in hotel positions.

12. "Climent Guitart: A Hotelier Moves into Cuba," *Cubanews* 2, no. 1 (January 1994): 11; Gunn, "Cuba's Employment Conundrum."

13. I thank Carmen Diana Deere for sharing this information with me.

14. One Cuban economist estimated that the income gap grew from 4:1 in 1989 to 25:1 in 1995 (quoted by Gunn, "Cuba's Employment Conundrum").

15. Fernandez, "The Color of Love," 99–117; Fernandez, "Race, Romance, and Revolution."

16. De la Fuente and Glasco, "Are Blacks Getting 'Out of Control'?," 62–64; Alvarado, "Estereotipos y prejuicios raciales," 89–115.

17. U.S. data are taken from Schuman, Steeh, and Bobo, *Racial Attitudes in America*.

18. Hernández, "Raza y prejuicio racial en Santa Clara," 75–86.

19. Alina Martínez Triay, "En el centenario de la abolición de la esclavitud," *El Militante Comunista* (October 1986): 14–23; Mayra Beatriz, "Amor: En blanco y negro," *Somos Jóvenes* (February 1990): 2–9; Esther Mosak, "Al tiempo hay que ayudarlo," *Cuba Internacional* 258 (June 1991): 34–36.

20. Alvarado, "Relaciones raciales en Cuba," 37–43; Guanche, "Etnicidad y racialidad," 51–57; Caño, "Relaciones raciales," 58–65. See also the testimonies of Cuban scholars quoted in Pedro Juan Gutiérrez, "Razas: Diferentes pero iguales," *Bohemia* 89, no. 2 (1997): 8–13.

21. Andrews, *Blacks and Whites*, 168.

22. Duharte and Santos, *El fantasma de la esclavitud*, 118–19, 99.

23. Ibid., 132–33; Esther Mosak, "White Mirrors: Film and Television Workers Talk about Racial Representation," *Cuba Update* (November 1991): 28–30.

24. This discussion relies on the testimonies of some television workers compiled by Duharte and Santos in *El fantasma de la esclavitud*, 132–35, and on Mosak, "White Mirrors," 28–30.

25. For a discussion of racial jokes in the island, see Fernandez, "Race, Romance, and Revolution," 152–59.

26. Fernandez, "Back to the Future? Women and Tourism in Cuba," paper presented at the meeting of the American Anthropological Association, Washington, D.C., November 19–23, 1997; Elena Díaz, Esperanza Fernández, and Tania Caram, "Turismo y prostitución en Cuba," unpublished paper, Havana, FLACSO, 1996.

27. Davidson, "Sex Tourism in Cuba," 39–48; Davidson and Sanchez Taylor, *Child Prostitution and Sex Tourism*, 24–25.

28. Coco Fusco, "Hustling for Dollars," *Ms.* (September–October 1996): 62–70.

29. Testimony of a white male professional, thirty-nine years old, interviewed by the author, Havana, August 1998.

30. Pablo Alfonso, "Torrente de dólares del exilio a Cuba," *El Nuevo Herald*, January 9, 1996.

31. Genevieve Howe, "Cuba: Regulating Revolution," *Z Magazine* (April 1998): 32–38.

32. For the first testimony, see note 29 above; the second is quoted in Howe, "Cuba: Regulating Revolution," 37.

33. This assertion, which one hears often in Cuba, is made by independent journalist

Manuel Vázquez Portal in "In Cuba: It's a Crime to Be Black," *Miami Herald*, December 1, 1998.

34. For a discussion of the Malecón riot, see de la Fuente and Glasco, "Are Blacks Getting 'Out of Control'?," 53–54. For a reaction in the Cuban press that labeled participants "lumpen," see Marcos Alfonso, "Tranquilidad en la capital," *Juventud Rebelde*, August 7, 1994.

35. Cuba, Partido Comunista de Cuba, *Proyecto*, 6–8.

36. These are tentative figures, created using picture identification. See "Comité Central del PCC," *Granma*, October 11, 1997, and Cuba, Partido Comunista de Cuba, *IV Congreso*, 364–90.

37. "Los candidatos del pueblo," *Granma*, February 2–6, 1993; "Los candidatos del pueblo," *Granma*, December 19–23, 1997. *Granma* published a detailed profile of the candidates in 1997 but did not include race: Marcos Alfonso, "Radiografía electoral," December 9, 1997.

38. See de la Fuente, "Silence, Race, and the 'Special Period': An Update," *Cuban Affairs* 5, nos. 1–2 (Spring–Summer 1999): 3, 13. For Cuban officials' acknowledgment of the problem, see Susana Lee, "El primer requisito," *Granma*, April 23, 1999.

39. For examples of this assertion, see William Raspberry, "Black Cubans and Castro," *Washington Post*, May 24, 1995; "Black Cubans Fear U.S. Racism," *Miami Herald*, October 10, 1994; and Ricardo González, "¿Por qué no hay balseros negros?," *El Nuevo Herald*, September 12, 1994.

40. Mimi Whitefield and Mary B. Sheridan, "Encuesta intenta medir pulso," *El Nuevo Herald*, December 18, 1994; "Gallup Poll in Cuba," *Cuba Update* (February–March 1995): 9; de la Fuente and Glasco, "Are Blacks Getting 'Out of Control'?," 67–68.

41. See Whitefield and Sheridan, "Encuesta"; de la Fuente and Glasco, "Are Blacks Getting 'Out of Control'?," 60–62; Alvarado, "Estereotipos y prejuicios raciales," 107–9; and Hernández, "Raza y prejuicio racial en Santa Clara," 78–80.

42. I am deeply grateful to Engineer Norberto Mesa Carbonell, the founder of the Cofradía de la Negritud, for sharing with me the organization's program and additional information.

43. Pablo Alfonso, "Mensaje de la iglesia metodista," *El Nuevo Herald*, September 28, 1993; Orlando Márquez, "Entrevista al Eminentísimo Señor Cardenal Jaime Ortega Alamino," *Verdad y Esperanza* (January 1998): 4–8.

EPILOGUE

1. "Fustigó el Presidente Prío a la práctica de la discriminación," *El Mundo*, December 9, 1951; "La tierra que Usted acaba de pisar se honra," *Granma*, January 22, 1998.

2. Patterson, *The Ordeal of Integration*, 193.

3. Fredrickson, *The Comparative Imagination*, 87–88.

4. Quoted in Vincent James, "Black Cubans Call for Change," *Christian Science Monitor*, June 16, 1992.

BIBLIOGRAPHY

ARCHIVES

Archivo Histórico Provincial, Cienfuegos (AHPC)
  Registro de Asociaciones
Archivo Nacional de Cuba, Havana (ANC)
  Adquisiciones
  Audiencia de la Habana
  Audiencia de Santiago de Cuba
  Donativos y Remisiones
  Fondo Especial
  Gobierno General
  Registro de Asociaciones
  Secretaría de la Presidencia
Library of Congress, Manuscript Division, Washington, D.C. (LC)
  Leonard Wood Papers
United States National Archives, Washington, D.C. (USNA)
  Foreign Service Post Records, RG 84
  General Records of the Department of State, RG 59
  Records of the U.S. Army Overseas Operations, RG 395
  Records of the War Department, RG 165
University of Florida, Latin American Library, Gainesville, Florida
  Braga Brothers Collection (BBC)
University of Maryland, McKeldin Library, College Park, Maryland
  Cuba Company Papers
University of Michigan, Bentley Historical Library, Ann Arbor, Michigan
  Robert F. Williams Papers

AFRO-CUBAN PERIODICALS

(Published in Havana unless otherwise noted)

Adelante, 1935–38
Amanecer, 1952–53
Atenas. Mensuario Cultural de Afirmación Cubana, 1951–54
Aurora, 1914
Boletín Oficial del Club Atenas, 1930
Cuatro Páginas, 1941
Fragua de la Libertad, 1942–45
Juvenil, 1913
Labor Nueva, 1916
El Nuevo Criollo, 1904–6
Nuevos Rumbos, 1945–48, 1959
Renovación (Sagua la Grande), 1932
Rumbos, 1939

OTHER PERIODICALS

(Published in Havana unless otherwise noted)

Acción Ciudadana (Santiago de Cuba), 1945
Acción Socialista, 1944–45
Actas del Folklore, 1961
Adelante!, 1951
Afro-American (Baltimore), 1959–61
Ahora, 1933–35
¡Alerta!, 1943–53

Alma Mater, 1933
Archivos del Folklore Cubano, 1924–30
Aurora (Organo Oficial de la Unión de
    Empleados de Cafés . . . y Similares),
    1934
El Avance, 1936
El Avance Revolucionario, 1959–60
Avisador Comercial, 1908
Bandera Roja, 1934
Bohemia, 1917–98
Boletín de Organización (Federación de
    Trabajadores de la Habana), 1946–48
Bulletin of the Pan American Union
    (Washington, D.C.), 1917–20
Carga, 1944
Carta Semanal, 1958
Carteles, 1924–50
La Chaveta, 1951
Chicago Defender, 1959–60
Christian Science Monitor (Boston), 1992
Combate 13 de Marzo, 1961
El Comunista, 1940
La Correspondencia (Cienfuegos), 1924,
    1934–36, 1943
El Crisol, 1939–60
Crónica Médico-Quirúrgica de la Habana,
    1924–26
CTC, 1945
Cuba, 1912
Cuba, Capital and Country (Beverly,
    Mass.), 1908
Cuba, Escuela Normal para Maestras de
    la Habana, Memoria anual
    correspondiente al curso académico, 1915–
    16, 1924–25
Cuba Contemporánea, 1913–27
Cuba Internacional, 1980–91
The Cuba News, 1912–15
Cubanews, 1994
El Cubano Libre (Santiago de Cuba),
    1903–8
Cuban Topics, 1928–30
Cuba Nueva en Acción, 1939–42
Cuba Review (New York), 1905–10
Cubatimes, 1980

Cuba Update, 1991–95
Cuba y América, 1905–13
Cúspide, 1937–39
La Dalila, 1951
Diario de Cuba (Santiago de Cuba), 1928,
    1939–44
Diario de la Marina, 1899–1959
La Discusión, 1900–1909, 1917, 1925,
    1936
Estudios Afrocubanos, 1937–45
Etnología y Folklore, 1962–69
Ferrocarriles del Norte, Boletín Quincenal
    (Ciego de Avila), 1923
El Fígaro, 1899–1909
Freedomways, 1961
Fundamentos, 1941–53
El Globo, 1927–29
Grafos, 1936
Granma, 1965–98
Havana, the Magazine of Cuba, 1929
Havana Chronicle, 1940–41
Havana Daily Telegraph, 1906–8
Havana Evening News, 1923–27
Havana Evening Telegram, 1925–26, 1937
Havana Post, 1900–1908, 1910–53
Heraldo de Cuba, 1916, 1920–21, 1928
Heraldo de las Villas (Santa Clara), 1934
El Hombre Nuevo, 1919
Información, 1940–58
Instituto de Segunda Enseñanza de la
    Habana, Memoria anual correspondiente
    al curso académico, 1901–8
Instituto Finlay, Boletín Semanal
    Epidemiológico Sanitario, 1940–44
La Instrucción Primaria, 1902–12
Juventud, 1925
Labora, 1920–21
El Liberal (New York), 1935
Libertad (Santiago de Cuba), 1940–43
La Lucha, 1899–1931
Luz, 1937–41
Mambí (Santiago de Cuba), 1968
Miami Herald, 1988–91
Miami Times, 1961–67, 1993–98
El Militante Comunista, 1968–86

La Mujer, 1930
Mujeres Cubanas, 1951
El Mundo, 1901, 1905–8, 1916, 1920–21, 1928–29, 1942–51
Negro World (New York), 1925–31
La Noche, 1913, 1924
Noticias de Hoy, 1939–63
El Nuevo Herald (Miami), 1994–98
OLAS, 1966
La Opinión, 1912, 1916, 1919–21
El Organizador, 1943–47
El País, 1930–36
Panfleto, 1954
Patria y Libertad, 1918
Pittsburgh Courier, 1960
P.N.R., 1972
La Política Cómica, 1916–31
El Político, 1930
La Prensa, 1913–16
Prensa Libre, 1951–55
El Reconcentrado, 1912
La Reforma Social, 1920
Revista Bimestre Cubana, 1910–58
Revista de Avance, 1927–30
Revista de Instrucción Pública, 1918–20, 1925–28
Revista de la Facultad de Letras y Ciencias, 1905–30

Revista de Policía, 1945
Revista de Técnica Policial y Penitenciaria, 1935–36
Revista Jurídica, 1969
Revista Parlamentaria de Cuba, 1922–27
Revista Popular Cubana, 1907
Revolución, 1959–63
Siempre, 1944
Sierra Maestra (Santiago de Cuba), 1959
La Tarde, 1924
Tiempo, 1946–57
¡Tierra!, 1909
Times of Havana, 1959
Trabajadores, 1992–94
Trabajo, 1960
Trabajo Político, 1968
Tricontinental, 1968–69
El Triunfo, 1908, 1920–21
La Ultima Hora, 1912
Unidad, 1947–52
La Unión Española, 1899–1900
Unión Nacionalista, 1928
Unitario, 1951
La Verdad, 1951
Verdad y Esperanza, 1998
Voz Gráfica, 1941–45
La Voz Obrera, 1933
Washington Post, 1973–93

GOVERNMENT DOCUMENTS

Cuba. *Censo de la República de Cuba bajo la administración provisional de los Estados Unidos, 1907.* Washington, D.C.: Oficina del censo de los Estados Unidos, 1908.

——. *Censo de la República de Cuba, año de 1919.* Havana: Maza, Arroyo y Caso, 1920.

——. *Constitución de la República de Cuba.* Havana: Compañía Editora de Libros, 1940.

——. *Gaceta Oficial.* 1910–55.

——. *Informe general del censo de 1943.* Havana: P. Fernández y Cía, 1945.

——. *Plan Trienal de Cuba.* Havana: Cultural S.A., 1938.

——. *Statistics from the Ministry of Social Welfare.* Havana: mimeo, 1960.

Cuba. Cámara de Representantes. *Diario de Sesiones.* 1905–6, 1911–13, 1919, 1923–29.

——. *Memoria de los trabajos realizados.* 1920–21.

Cuba. Comisión Consultiva. *Diario de Sesiones.* 1907.

Cuba. Comisión Nacional de Estadísticas y Reformas Económicas. *Cuadros estadísticos de los penados de ambos sexos que se encontraban cumpliendo condena en los establecimientos penales de la República en 30 de junio de 1927.* Havana: mimeo, 1927.

———. *Cuadros estadísticos en relación con los ingenios y su zafra en 1925 a 1926*. Havana: [Secretaría de Hacienda], 1927.

———. *Estadística de los matriculados y graduados en la Universidad de la Habana*. Havana: mimeo, 1927, 1930.

———. *Estadística en relación con la elaboración de cigarros y tabacos en el año 1926*. Havana: n.p., 1928.

———. *Estado demográfico correspondiente al quinquenio de 1925 a 1929*. Havana: mimeo, [1930?].

Cuba. Comité Estatal de Estadísticas (CEE). *Censo de población y viviendas 1981. La población de Cuba según el color de la piel*. Havana: INSIE, 1985.

———. *Censo de población y viviendas 1981. República de Cuba*. 16 vols. Havana: CEE, 1983.

———. *Censo nacional de cuadros del estado. Dirigentes de establecimientos, resumen nacional 1987*. 5 vols. Havana: CEE, 1989.

Cuba. Consejo Nacional de Tuberculosis. *Resumen general de los trabajos efectuados por el "Tuberculosis Survey de Cuba."* Havana: Ciudad Militar, 1938.

Cuba. Convención Constituyente. *Diario de Sesiones*. 1901, 1940.

Cuba. Escuela Normal para Maestros de la Habana. *Memoria correspondiente al curso académico de 1928 a 1929*. Havana: La Propagandista, 1929.

Cuba. Junta Superior de Sanidad. *Informe mensual sanitario y demográfico*. 1904–7.

Cuba. Military Governor. *Civil Report of the Military Governor, 1901*. 15 vols. Havana: n.p., 1902.

———. *Civil Report of the Military Governor, 1902*. 6 vols. [Havana]: n.p., 1903.

Cuba. Ministerio de Agricultura. *Memoria del Censo Agrícola Nacional, 1946*. Havana: P. Fernández y Cía, 1951.

Cuba. Ministerio de Educación (MINED). *Documentos de Cuba republicana*. Havana: MINED, 1972.

Cuba. Ministerio del Interior (MININT). *Una política consecuente en la prevención del delito y la justicia penal*. Havana: Poligráfico MININT, 1987.

———. Sección de Estadística. *Informe del quinquenio 1981/85*. Havana: mimeo, 1986.

Cuba. Ministerio de Relaciones Exteriores (MINREX). *Cuba, Country Free of Segregation*. Havana: MINREX, Dirección de Información, [1965].

Cuba. Ministerio de Salud Pública (MINSAP). *Dr. Enrique Lluria Despau*. Havana: Cuadernos de Historia de la Salud Pública, 1963.

Cuba. Oficina Nacional de los Censos Demográficos y Electoral. *Censo de población, viviendas y electoral, 1953*. Havana: P. Fernández y Cía, 1955.

Cuba. Partido Comunista de Cuba. *IV Congreso del Partido Comunista de Cuba: Discursos y documentos*. Havana: Editora Política, 1992.

———. *Proyecto: El partido de la unidad, la democracia y los derechos humanos que defendemos*. Havana: Editora Política, 1997.

Cuba. Presidencia. *Memoria de la administración del Presidente de la República*. Havana: Rambla y Bouza, 1910–28.

Cuba. Sanidad y Beneficiencia. *Boletín Oficial*. 1910–34.

Cuba. Secretaría de Educación, Negociado de Estadística. *Estadística general, 1931–1936*. Havana: La Propagandista, 1936.

Cuba. Secretaría de Estado. *Documentos diplomáticos. Copia de la correspondencia . . . relativa al trato de los inmigrantes jamaiquinos*. Havana: Secretaría de Estado, 1924.

Cuba. Secretaría de Hacienda. *Inmigración y movimiento de pasajeros*. 1902–6, 1910–31.

———. *Movimiento de Población*. 1935, 1938.

Cuba. Secretaría de Sanidad y Beneficiencia. *Ordenanzas sanitarias*. Havana: Imprenta de Rambla, Bouza y Ca., 1914.

Cuerpo de Policía Nacional de la Habana. *Informe de los servicios prestados durante el año fiscal 1923–1924*. Havana: Talleres de "La Lucha," 1924.

Ley electoral municipal adicionada con el censo de población y la ley de perjurio. Havana: Imprenta de la Gaceta Oficial, 1900.

Magoon, Charles E. *Report of the Provisional Administration from October 13th, 1906, to December 1st, 1907*. Havana: Rambla and Bouza, 1908.

Transactions of the First Pan American Conference on Eugenics and Homiculture of the American Republics. Havana: Published by the Cuban Government, 1928.

U.S. Foreign Areas Studies Division. *Special Warfare Area Handbook for Cuba*. Washington, D.C.: American University, 1961.

U.S. War Department. Office Director, Census of Cuba. *Report on the Census of Cuba, 1899*. Washington, D.C.: Government Printing Office, 1900.

FILMS

Alvarez, Santiago. *Now*. 1965.

———. *LBJ*. 1968.

Giral, Sergio. *El otro Francisco*. 1974.

———. *Rancheador*. 1977.

Gómez, Manuel Octavio. *Historia de una batalla*. 1962.

Gómez, Sara. *De cierta manera*. 1974.

Gutiérrez Alea, Tomás. *Cumbite*. 1964.

———. *La última cena*. 1976.

ICAIC. *Una isla para Miguel*. 1968.

Massip, Salvador. *Historia de un ballet*. 1962.

Sánchez, José Luis. *El Fanguito*. 1990.

Tabío, Juan Carlos. *Plaff!* 1988.

Trujillo, Marisol. *Motivaciones*. 1988.

BOOKS, ARTICLES, AND PAPERS

ABC. *El ABC al pueblo de Cuba: Manifiesto-programa*. Havana: n.p., 1932.

Aguilar, Luis E. "Cuba, c. 1860–c. 1930." In *Cuba: A Short History*, edited by Leslie Bethell, 21–55. New York: Cambridge University Press, 1995.

———. *Cuba 1933: Prologue to Revolution*. Ithaca, N.Y.: Cornell University Press, 1972.

Aguirre, Benigno. "Differential Migration of Cuban Social Races: A Review and Interpretation of the Problem." *Latin American Research Review* 11, no. 1 (1976): 103–24.

Alienes y Urosa, Julián. *Características fundamentales de la economía cubana*. Havana: Banco Nacional de Cuba, 1950.

Alvarado, Juan A. "Estereotipos y prejuicios raciales en tres barrios habaneros." *América Negra* 15 (December 1998): 89–115.

———. "Relaciones raciales en Cuba. Notas de investigación." *Temas* 7 (July–September 1996): 37–43.

Alvarez Estévez, Rolando. *Azúcar e inmigración, 1900–1940*. Havana: Editorial de Ciencias Sociales, 1988.

Ames, David W. "Negro Family Types in a Cuban Solar." *Phylon* 11, no. 2 (1950): 159–63.

Andreu, Enrique. "La muerte de Peñita." *Estudios Afrocubanos* 2, no. 1 (1938): 115–17.

———. "El pintor Alberto Peña y su obra." *Revista Bimestre Cubana* 38 (1936): 114–25.

Andrews, George Reid. "Black Political Protest in São Paulo, 1888–1988." *Journal of Latin American Studies* 24 (1992): 147–71.

———. *Blacks and Whites in São Paulo, Brazil, 1888–1988*. Madison: University of Wisconsin Press, 1991.

———. "Black Workers in the Export Years: Latin America, 1880–1930." *International Labor and Working-Class History* 51 (Spring 1997): 7–29.

———. "Racial Inequality in Brazil and the United States: A Statistical Comparison." *Journal of Social History* 26, no. 2 (Winter 1992): 229–63.

Arce, Angel C. *La raza cubana*. Havana: n.p., 1935.

Arellano Moreno, Antonio. *Breve historia de Venezuela, 1492–1958*. Caracas: Italgráfica, 1974.

Armas, Ramón de. "Jose Martí: La verdadera y única abolición de la esclavitud." *Anuario de Estudios Americanos* 43 (1986): 333–51.

Arredondo, Alberto. *El negro en Cuba*. Havana: Editorial Alfa, 1939.

Atenas, Club. *Los partidos políticos y la Asamblea Constituyente*. Havana: Club Atenas, 1939.

Atkins, Edwin F. *Sixty Years in Cuba*. Cambridge, Mass.: Riverside Press, 1926.

Ayala, César. "Social and Economic Aspects of Sugar Production in Cuba, 1880–1930." *Latin American Research Review* 30, no. 1 (1995): 95–124.

Barkan, Elazar. *The Retreat of Scientific Racism: Changing Concepts of Race in Britain and the United States between the World Wars*. New York: Cambridge University Press, 1992.

Barnet, Enrique A. "Concepto actual de la medicina." *Anales de la Academia de Ciencias Médicas, Físicas y Naturales de la Habana* 29 (1902–3): 19–36.

Barnet, Miguel, ed. *Biography of a Runaway Slave*. Willimantic, Conn.: Curbstone Press, 1994.

Barringer, Paul B. "The American Negro: His Past and Future." In *Anti-Black Thought, 1863–1925*, 11 vols., edited by John David Smith, 7:435–57. New York: Garland, 1993.

Batrell Oviedo, Ricardo. *Para la historia. Apuntes autobiográficos*. Havana: Seoane y Alvarez, 1912.

Beals, Carleton. *The Crime of Cuba*. Philadelphia: Lippincott, 1933.

Beci, José Manuel de la Cruz. *El igualitarismo*. Havana: Imprenta Martí, 1939.

Benjamin, Jules R. *The United States and the Origins of the Cuban Revolution: An Empire of Liberty in an Age of National Liberation*. Princeton, N.J.: Princeton University Press, 1990.

Bergquist, Charles. *Labor in Latin America: Comparative Essays on Chile, Argentina, Venezuela and Colombia*. Stanford, Calif.: Stanford University Press, 1986.

Bervin, Antoine. *Mission a la Havane. Notes et souvenirs, 1942–1945*. Port-au-Prince: n.p., [1952].

Betancourt, Juan René. "Castro and the Cuban Negro." *The Crisis* (May 1961): 270–74.

——. *Doctrina negra. La única teoría certera contra la discriminación racial en Cuba*. Havana: P. Fernández y Cía, [1954].

——. *El negro: Ciudadano del futuro*. Havana: Cárdenas y Cía, [1959].

——. *Prejuicio, ensayo polémico*. Camagüey: n.p., 1945.

Bonachea, Ramón L., and Marta San Martín. *The Cuban Insurrection, 1952–1959*. New Brunswick, N.J.: Transaction Publishers, 1995.

Bonachea, Rolando E., and Nelson P. Valdés, comp. *Cuba in Revolution*. Garden City, N.Y.: Anchor Books, 1972.

——, eds. *Revolutionary Struggle, 1947–1958*. Cambridge, Mass.: MIT Press, 1972.

Booth, David. "Cuba, Color and the Revolution." *Science and Society* 11, no. 2 (Summer 1976): 129–72.

Boti, Regino. "La poesía cubana de Nicolás Guillén." *Revista Bimestre Cubana* 29 (1932): 343–53.

Brenner, Philip, et al. *The Cuba Reader: The Making of a Revolutionary Society*. New York: Grove Press, 1989.

Brent, William Lee. *Long Time Gone*. New York: Random House, 1996.

Brown, Elsa Barkley, and Gregg D. Kimball. "Mapping the Terrain of Black Richmond." *Journal of Urban History* 21, no. 3 (March 1995): 296–346.

Bryce, James. "The Relations of the Advanced and the Backward Races of Mankind." In *Anti-Black Thought 1863–1925*, 11 vols., edited by John David Smith, 8:1–44. New York: Garland, 1993.

Bullard, R. L. "The Cuban Negro." *North American Review*, March 15, 1907, 623–30.

Burdick, John. "The Myth of Racial Democracy." *NACLA* 25 (February 1992): 40–44.

Cabrera, Olga. *El movimiento obrero cubano en 1920*. Havana: Instituto del Libro, 1969.

Cabrera Torres, Ramón. *Hacia la rehabilitación económica del cubano negro*. Havana: n.p., 1959.

Cabús, José D. *Batista: Pensamiento y acción*. Havana: Prensa Indoamericana, 1944.

Cannon, Terry, and Johnetta Cole. *Free and Equal: The End of Racial Discrimination in Cuba*. New York: The Venceremos Brigade, 1978.

Carbonell, Walterio. *Crítica, cómo surgió la cultura nacional*. Havana: Editorial Yaka, 1961.

Carneado, José Felipe. "La discriminación racial en Cuba no volverá jamás." *Cuba Socialista* 2, no. 5 (January 1962): 54–67.

Carnoy, Martin. *Faded Dreams: The Politics and Economics of Race in America*. New York: Cambridge University Press, 1994.

Carr, Barry. "Identity, Class and Nation: West Indian Sugar Workers and Cuban Society, 1925–1934." Paper presented at American Historical Association convention, San Francisco, Calif., 1994.

——. "Mill Occupations and Soviets: The Mobilisation of Sugar Workers in Cuba, 1917–1933." *Journal of Latin American Studies* 28 (1996): 129–58.

Carrión, Miguel de. "El desenvolvimiento social de Cuba en los últimos años." *Cuba Contemporánea* 27 (September 1921): 6–27.

Carson, Clayborne. *In Struggle: SNCC and the Black Awakening of the 1960s*. Cambridge, Mass.: Harvard University Press, 1981.

Casal, Lourdes. "Race Relations in Contemporary Cuba." In *The Position of Blacks in Brazil and Cuban Society*, edited by Anani Dzidzienyo and Lourdes Casal, 11–27. London: Minority Rights Group, Report no. 7, 1979.

———. *Revolution and Race: Blacks in Contemporary Cuba*. Washington, D.C.: Woodrow Wilson International Center for Scholars, 1979.

Castellanos, Israel. "La briba hampona." *Revista Bimestre Cubana* 9 (1914): 94–104, 183–98, 253–59.

———. *La brujería y el ñañiguismo en Cuba desde el punto de vista médico-legal*. Havana: Imprenta de Lloredo y Ca., 1916.

———. *La delincuencia femenina en Cuba. Indices filiativos y album identoscópico*. Havana: Dorrbecker, 1929.

———. "Un diagnóstico criminológico." *Revista de Técnica Policial y Penitenciaria* 4, nos. 2–3 (August–September 1936): 200–204.

———. "Los estigmas somáticos de la degeneración. Su apreciación en las razas de color." *Vida Nueva*, October 15, 1927, 207–19.

———. "El homicidio en Cuba." *Revista de Técnica Policial y Penitenciaria* 3, nos. 1–3 (January–March 1936): 141–56; 3, no. 4 (April 1936): 263–80.

———. "La lucha policíaca contra el fetichismo." *Revista de Técnica Policial y Penitenciaria* 4, nos. 2–3 (August–September 1936): 231–78.

———. "Los menores delincuentes." *Revista Bimestre Cubana* 10 (1915): 81–111.

———. "El tipo brujo." *Revista Bimestre Cubana* 9 (1914): 328–44.

Castellanos, Jorge, and Isabel Castellanos. *Cultura Afrocubana*. 4 vols. Miami: Ediciones Universal, 1990–94.

Castro Ruz, Fidel. *Conferencia de prensa*. Havana: Capitolio Nacional, 1959.

———. *Discursos de Fidel en los aniversarios de los CDR, 1960–1967*. Havana: Instituto del Libro, 1968.

———. *Discursos para la historia*. Havana: n.p., 1959.

———. *Informe Central I, II y III Congreso del Partido Comunista de Cuba*. Havana: Editora Política, 1990.

Centro de Estudios Demográficos (CEDEM). *La población de Cuba*. Havana: Editorial de Ciencias Sociales, 1976.

CEPAL. *Cuba: Estilo de desarrollo y políticas sociales*. Mexico City: Siglo XXI Editores, 1980.

Cepeda, Rafael, ed. *Eusebio Hernández: Ciencia y patria*. Havana: Editorial de Ciencias Sociales, 1991.

Cepero Bonilla, Raúl. *Azúcar y abolición*. Barcelona: Editorial Crítica, 1976.

Chailloux Cardona, Juan M. *Síntesis histórica de la vivienda popular. Los horrores del solar habanero*. Havana: Jesús Montero, 1945.

Chapman, Charles E. *A History of the Cuban Republic: A Study in Hispanic American Politics*. New York: Macmillan, 1927.

Chomski, Aviva. *West Indian Workers and the United Fruit Company in Costa Rica, 1870–1940*. Baton Rouge: Louisiana State University Press, 1996.

Clark, Victor S. "Labor Conditions in Cuba." *Bulletin of the Department of Labor* 41 (July 1902): 663–793.

Cleaver, Eldridge. *Soul on Ice*. Waco: Word Books, 1978.

Clissold, Gillian Gunn. "Balancing Economic Efficiency, Social Concerns and Political Control." *La Sociedad Económica*, June 30, 1993.

——. "Cuba's Employment Conundrum." *Cuba Briefing Paper Series* 14 (May 1997).

Clytus, John. *Black Man in Red Cuba*. Coral Gables, Fla.: University of Miami Press, 1970.

Colegio de Belén. *Album conmemorativo 1914*. Havana: n.p., 1914.

Colegio Champagnat. *Memoria y premios, 1927–1928*. Havana: Seoane y Fernández, 1928.

Collier, Ruth Berin, and David Collier. *Shaping the Political Arena: Critical Junctures, the Labor Movement, and Regime Dynamics in Latin America*. Princeton, N.J.: Princeton University Press, 1991.

Commission on Cuban Affairs. *Problems of the New Cuba*. New York: Foreign Policy Association, 1935.

Confederación Nacional Obrera de Cuba (CNOC). *IV Congreso Obrero de Unidad Sindical*. Havana: n.p., 1934.

Congreso Nacional Obrero. *Memoria de los trabajos presentados al Congreso Nacional Obrero*. Havana: La Universal, 1915.

Conte, Rafael, and José M. Capmany. *Guerra de razas (negros contra blancos en Cuba)*. Havana: Imprenta Militar, 1912.

Convención Nacional de Sociedades de la Raza de Color. *Programa*. Havana: Imprenta Molina y Cía, 1936.

Córdova, Efrén. *Clase trabajadora y movimiento sindical en Cuba 1 (1819–1959)*. Miami: Ediciones Universal, 1995.

Córdova, Federico. *Flor Crombet (el sucre cubano)*. Havana: Cultural S.A., 1939.

Cortés, Carlos E. *The Cuban Experience in the United States*. New York: Arno Press, 1980.

Crahan, Margaret. "Religious Penetration and Nationalism in Cuba: U.S. Methodist Activities, 1898–1958." *Revista / Review Interamericana* 8, no. 2 (Summer 1978): 204–24.

Cruise, Harold. *Rebellion or Revolution?* New York: Morrow, 1968.

Cuban Economic Research Project. *A Study on Cuba*. Coral Gables, Fla.: University of Miami Press, 1965.

Cuéllar Vizcaíno, Manuel. *Doce muertes famosas*. [Havana]: n.p., n.d.

——. *Unas cuantas verdades*. Havana: n.p., 1948.

Daniel, Yvonne. *Rumba: Dance and Social Change in Contemporary Cuba*. Bloomington: Indiana University Press, 1995.

Davidson, Julia O'Connell. "Sex Tourism in Cuba." *Race & Class* 38, no. 1 (1996): 38–48.

Davidson, Julia O'Connell, and Jacqueline Sanchez Taylor. *Child Prostitution and Sex Tourism: Cuba*. Bangkok: ECPAT, 1996.

de la Fuente, Alejandro. "Race and Inequality in Cuba, 1899–1981." *Journal of Contemporary History* 30 (1995): 131–68.

———. "Two Dangers, One Solution: Immigration, Race, and Labor in Cuba, 1900–1930." *International Labor and Working-Class History* 51 (Spring 1997): 30–49.

de la Fuente, Alejandro, and Laurence Glasco. "Are Blacks 'Getting Out of Control'? Racial Attitudes, Revolution, and Political Transition in Cuba." In *Toward a New Cuba? Legacies of a Revolution*, edited by Miguel A. Centeno and Mauricio Font, 53–71. Boulder, Colo.: Lynn Rienner, 1997.

del Toro, Carlos. *El movimiento obrero cubano en 1914.* Havana: Instituto del Libro, 1969.

del Valle, Gerardo. *1/4 Fambá y 19 cuentos más.* Havana: Ediciones Unión, 1967.

Depestre, René. "Lettre de Cuba." *Presence Africaine* 56 (1965): 105–42.

Deschamps Chapeaux, Pedro. *El negro en el periodismo cubano del siglo XIX.* Havana: Ediciones R, 1963.

Díaz Briquets, Sergio. *The Health Revolution in Cuba.* Austin: University of Texas Press, 1983.

Documentos de la revolución cubana. Montevideo, Uruguay: Nativa Libros, 1967.

Dolz y Arango, Ricardo. "Discurso inaugural del curso académico de 1913 a 1914." *Revista de la Facultad de Letras y Ciencias* 17, no. 3 (November 1913): 161–89.

Domínguez, Jorge. *Cuba: Order and Revolution.* Cambridge, Mass.: Belknap Press of Harvard University Press, 1978.

———. "Racial and Ethnic Relations in the Cuban Armed Forces: A Non-Topic." *Armed Forces and Society* 2, no. 2 (February 1976): 273–90.

———. "Revolutionary Politics: The New Demands for Orderliness." In *Cuba: Internal and International Affairs*, edited by Jorge Domínguez, 19–70. Beverly Hills, Calif.: Sage, 1982.

———. *To Make a World Safe for Revolution: Cuba's Foreign Policy.* Cambridge, Mass.: Harvard University Press, 1989.

D'Ou, Lino. "La evolución de la raza de color en Cuba." In *Libro de Cuba*, 333–37. Havana: n.p., 1930.

Duharte, Rafael, and Elsa Santos. *El fantasma de la esclavitud: Prejuicios raciales en Cuba y América Latina.* Bonn, Germany: Pahl-Rugenstein, 1997.

Duke, Cathy. "The Idea of Race: The Cultural Impact of American Intervention in Cuba, 1898–1912." In *Politics, Society and Culture in the Caribbean*, edited by Blanca G. Sivestrini, 87–109. San Juan: Universidad de Puerto Rico, 1983.

Dumoulin, John. "El primer desarrollo del movimiento obrero y la formación del proletariado en el sector azucarero. Cruces, 1886–1902." *Islas* 48 (May–August 1974): 3–66.

———. "La regulación estatal de las relaciones obrero-patronales en Cuba, 1933–1958." Manuscript, 1987.

Dunn, Marvin. *Black Miami in the Twentieth Century.* Gainesville: University Press of Florida, 1997.

Dyer, Donald R. "Urbanism in Cuba." *Geographical Review* 47 (1957): 224–33.

Epstein, Erwin H. "Social Structure, Race Relations and Political Stability in Cuba under U.S. Administration." *Revista/Review Interamericana* 8, no. 2 (Summer 1978): 192–203.

Erisman, H. Michael, and John M. Kirk. *Cuba's International Relations: The Anatomy of a Nationalistic Foreign Policy*. Boulder, Colo.: Westview Press, 1985.

Evenson, Debra. *Revolution in the Balance: Law and Society in Contemporary Cuba*. Boulder, Colo.: Westview Press, 1994.

Fagen, Richard R. "Revolution—For Internal Consumption Only." *Trans-Action* (April 1969): 10–15.

Fagen, Richard R., and Richard A. Brody. "Cubans in Exile: A Demographic Analysis." *Social Problems* 11, no. 4 (Spring 1964): 389–401.

Farber, Samuel. *Revolution and Reaction in Cuba, 1933–1960: A Political Sociology from Machado to Castro*. Middletown, Conn.: Wesleyan University Press, 1976.

Federación Democrática de Mujeres Cubanas (FDMC). *Informes y resoluciones, I Congreso*. Havana: Editorial Cenit, 1950.

Federación Sindical de Trabajadores del Teléfono. *V Congreso Obrero Nacional de la Industria Telefónica. Memoria*. Havana: n.p., 1955.

Fermoselle, Rafael. *Política y color en Cuba. La guerrita de 1912*. Montevideo, Uruguay: Ediciones Géminis, 1974.

Fernandes, Florestan. *The Negro in Brazilian Society*. New York: Columbia University Press, 1969.

Fernandez, Nadine T. "The Color of Love: Young Interracial Couples in Cuba." *Latin American Perspectives* 23, no. 1 (Winter 1996): 99–117.

———. "Race, Romance, and Revolution: The Cultural Politics of Interracial Encounters in Cuba." Ph.D. diss., University of California at Berkeley, 1996.

Fernández Robaina, Tomás. "La Bibliografía de autores de la raza de color, de Carlos M. Trelles." *Revista de la Biblioteca Nacional José Martí* (September–December 1988): 141–51.

———. *Bibliografía de temas afrocubanos*. Havana: Biblioteca Nacional José Martí, 1985.

———. *El negro en Cuba, 1902–1958. Apuntes para la historia de la lucha contra la discriminación racial*. Havana: Editorial de Ciencias Sociales, 1990.

Ferrara, Orestes. *Elections or Mutiny: A Brief Survey of the Cuban Elections*. Havana: La Reforma Social, 1920.

Ferrer, Ada. "Esclavitud, ciudadanía y los límites de la nacionalidad cubana: La guerra de los diez años, 1868–1878." *Historia Social* 22 (1995): 101–25.

———. "Social Aspects of Cuban Nationalism: Race, Slavery, and the Guerra Chiquita, 1879–1880." *Cuban Studies* 21 (1991): 37–56.

———. "To Make a Free Nation: Race and the Struggle for Independence in Cuba, 1868–1898." Ph.D. diss., University of Michigan, 1995.

Figueras, Francisco. *Cuba y su evolución colonial*. Havana: Imprenta Avisador Comercial, 1907.

Folk, Pamela S. *Cuban Foreign Policy: Caribbean Tempest*. Lexington, Mass.: Lexington Books, 1986.

Foner, Eric. *Reconstruction: America's Unfinished Revolution, 1863–1877*. New York: Harper & Row, 1988.

Foner, Philip S., and James S. Allen, eds. *American Communism and Black Americans: A Documentary History, 1919–1929*. Philadelphia: Temple University Press, 1987.

Foreign Policy Association. Commission on Cuban Affairs. *Problems of the New Cuba*. New York: Foreign Policy Association, 1935.

Fox, Geoffrey E. "Race and Class in Contemporary Cuba." In *Cuban Communism*, 3rd ed., edited by Irving Louis Horowitz, 421–44. New Brunswick, N.J.: Transaction Books, 1977.

Franco, José Luciano. *Antonio Maceo, apuntes para una historia de su vida*. 3 vols. Havana: Sociedad de Estudios Históricos e Internacionales, 1951–57.

Franklin, Jane. *Cuba and the United States: A Chronological History*. Melbourne, Australia: Ocean Press, 1997.

Fredrickson, George M. *Black Liberation: A Comparative History of Black Ideologies in the United States and South Africa*. New York: Oxford University Press, 1995.

———. *The Comparative Imagination: On the History of Racism, Nationalism, and Social Movements*. Berkeley: University of California Press, 1997.

El futuro es el internacionalismo: Recorrido del Comandante en Jefe Fidel Castro por países de Africa y Europa Socialista. Havana: Instituto Cubano del Libro, 1972.

García Agüero, Salvador. "Un comentario final." *Revista Bimestre Cubana* 38 (1936): 126–32.

———. "Presencia africana en la música nacional." *Estudios Afrocubanos* 1, no. 1 (1937): 114–27.

García Alvarez, Alejandro. *La gran burguesía comercial en Cuba, 1899–1920*. Havana: Editorial de Ciencias Sociales, 1990.

García Barrio, Constance S. "The Black in Post-Revolutionary Cuban Literature." *Revista/Review Interamericana* 8, no. 2 (Summer 1978): 263–70.

García Buchaca, Edith, Esperanza Sánchez Mastrapa, and María I. Argüelles. *El II Congreso Internacional de Mujeres*. Havana: n.p., 1949.

García González, Armando. "En torno a la antropología y el racismo en Cuba en el siglo XIX." In *Cuba, la Perla de las Antillas*, edited by Consuelo Naranjo Orovio and Tomás Mallo Gutiérrez, 45–64. Aranjuez: Ediciones Doce Calles, 1994.

García Pérez, Gladys M. *Insurrection and Revolution: Armed Struggle in Cuba, 1952–1959*. Boulder, Colo.: Lynn Rienner, 1998.

Gastón Agüero, Sixto. *Racismo y mestizaje en Cuba*. Havana: Editorial Lid, 1959.

Gilmore, Glenda Elizabeth. *Gender and Jim Crow: Women and the Politics of White Supremacy in North Carolina, 1896–1920*. Chapel Hill: University of North Carolina Press, 1996.

Gleijeses, Piero. "The First Ambassadors: Cuba's Contribution to Guinea-Bissau's War of Independence." *Journal of Latin American Studies* 29 (1997): 45–88.

Godio, Julio. *Historia del movimiento obrero latinoamericano*. Buenos Aires: Cid, 1979.

González Echevarría, Carlos. *Origen y desarrollo del movimiento obrero camagüeyano*. Havana: Editorial de Ciencias Sociales, 1984.

González y Venegas, Caridad. "Origen y desarrollo de las Escuelas Normales de Cuba." *Revista de la Facultad de Letras y Ciencias* (July–December 1922): 300–353.

Gosse, Van. "The African-American Press Greets the Cuban Revolution." In *Between Race and Empire: African-Americans and Cubans before the Cuban Revolution*, edited by

Lisa Brock and Digna Castañeda, 266–80. Philadelphia: Temple University Press, 1998.

———. *Where the Boys Are: Cuba, Cold War America and the Making of a New Left*. London: Verso, 1993.

Granados, Manuel. *Adire y el tiempo roto*. Havana: Casa de las Américas, 1967.

Green, Gil. *Cuba . . . the Continuing Revolution*. 2nd ed. New York: International Publishers, 1985.

Greenberg, Stanley. *Race and State in Capitalist Development: Comparative Perspectives*. New Haven, Conn.: Yale University Press, 1980.

Grillo, David. *El problema del negro cubano*. 2nd ed. Havana: n.p., 1953.

Griñán Peralta, Leonardo. *Maceo, análisis caracterológico*. Havana: Cooperativa de Cultura Popular, 1962.

Grobart, Favio. *Trabajos escogidos*. Havana: Editorial de Ciencias Sociales, 1985.

Guanche, Jesús. "Etnicidad y racialidad en la Cuba actual." *América Negra* 15 (December 1998): 43–63.

Guerra, Ramiro. *Azúcar y población en las Antillas*. Havana: Editorial de Ciencias Sociales, 1970.

Guevara, Ernesto. *Escritos y discursos*. 9 vols. Havana: Editorial de Ciencias Sociales, 1972–77.

Guillén, Nicolás. *Obra poética, 1920–1972*. Havana: Editorial de Arte y Literatura, 1974.

———. *Prosa de prisa*. 3 vols. Havana: Editorial Arte y Literatura, 1976.

Guirao, Ramón. *Orbita de la poesía Afro-Cubana, 1928–37 (Antología)*. Havana: Ucar, García y Cía, 1938.

Guiteras, Juan. "Estudios demográficos." *Revista Bimestre Cubana* 8, no. 6 (November–December 1913): 405–21.

Hagerdon, Katherine Johanna. "Anatomía del Proceso Folklórico: The 'Folkloricization' of Afro-Cuban Religious Performance in Cuba." Ph.D. diss., Brown University, 1995.

Hageman, Alice L., and Philip E. Wheaton. *Religion in Cuba Today: A New Church in a New Society*. New York: Association Press, 1971.

Haines, Herbert H. *Black Radicals and the Civil Rights Mainstream, 1954–1970*. Knoxville: University of Tennessee Press, 1988.

Hanchard, Michael George. *Orpheus and Power: The "Movimento Negro" of Rio de Janeiro and São Paulo, Brazil, 1945–1988*. Princeton, N.J.: Princeton University Press, 1994.

Hasenbalg, Carlos A. *Discriminação e desigualdades raciais no Brasil*. Rio de Janeiro: Graal, 1979.

———. "Race and Socioeconomic Inequalities in Brazil." In *Race, Class and Power in Brazil*, edited by Pierre-Michel Fontaine, 25–41. Los Angeles: Center for Afro-American Studies, University of California, 1985.

Havana Military Academy. *Memoria, 1956–1957*. Havana: n.p., 1957.

Heape, Walter. "The Proportion of the Sexes Produced by Whites and Coloured Peoples in Cuba." *Philosophical Transactions of the Royal Society of London*, ser. B, 200 (1909): 271–330.

Helg, Aline. *Our Rightful Share: The Afro-Cuban Struggle for Equality, 1886–1912*. Chapel Hill: University of North Carolina Press, 1995.

———. "Race in Argentina and Cuba, 1880–1930: Theory, Policies, and Popular Reaction." In *The Idea of Race in Latin America, 1870–1940*, edited by Richard Graham, 37–69. Austin: University of Texas Press, 1992.

Hernández, Daniela. "Raza y prejuicio racial en Santa Clara: Un reporte de investigación." *América Negra* 15 (December 1998): 75–86.

Hernández, Rafael, and Redi Gomis. "Retrato del Mariel: El ángulo socioeconómico." *Cuadernos de Nuestra América* 3, no. 5 (January–June 1986): 124–51.

Hernández Catá, Alfonso. *Los frutos ácidos y otros cuentos*. Madrid: Aguilar, 1953.

Hernández Lloréns, Alberto. "Notas sobre la acción del Partido Comunista en el movimiento obrero de Trinidad." In *Los obreros hacen y escriben su historia*, 351–84. Havana: Editorial de Ciencias Sociales, 1975.

Hevia Lanier, Oilda. *El Directorio Central de las Sociedades Negras de Cuba, 1886–1894*. Havana: Editorial de Ciencias Sociales, 1996.

Hinton, Richard J. "Cuban Reconstruction." *North American Review* 168, no. 1 (January 1899): 92–102.

Hobsbawm, Eric J. *The Age of Extremes: A History of the World, 1914–1991*. New York: Pantheon Books, 1994.

Holt, Thomas C. "Marking: Race, Race-Making, and the Writing of History." *American Historical Review* 100, no. 1 (February 1995): 1–20.

Horrego Estuch, Leopoldo. *Juan Gualberto Gómez. Un gran inconforme*. Havana: Editorial Mecenas, 1949.

———. *Maceo, héroe y carácter*. Havana: La Milagrosa, 1952.

———. *Martín Morúa Delgado. Vida y mensaje*. Havana: Editorial Sánchez, S.A., 1957.

Howe, Linda S. "Nancy Morejón's 'Mujer Negra': Rereading Afrocentric Hermeneutics, Rewriting Gender." *Journal of Afro-Latin American Studies & Literatures* 1, no. 1 (Fall 1993–94): 95–107.

Ibarra, Ibarra. *Cuba: 1898–1921. Partidos políticos y clases sociales*. Havana: Editorial de Ciencias Sociales, 1992.

———. "Historiografía y revolución." *Temas* 1 (January–March 1995): 5–17.

———. *Ideología mambisa*. Havana: Editorial de Ciencias Sociales, 1967.

Iglesias, Fe. "Características de la inmigración española en Cuba, 1904–1930." In *Españoles hacia América. La emigración en masa, 1880–1930*, edited by Nicolás Sánchez-Albornoz, 270–95. Madrid: Alianza Editorial, 1988.

———. "La explotación del hierro en el sur de Oriente y la Spanish American Iron Company." *Santiago* 17 (March 1975): 59–106.

Instituto de Historia. *Historia del movimiento obrero cubano, 1865–1958*. 2 vols. Havana: Editora Política, 1985.

———. *El movimiento obrero cubano. Documentos y artículos*. 2 vols. Havana: Editorial de Ciencias Sociales, 1975.

Instituto de Literatura y Lingüística. *Diccionario de la literatura cubana*. 2 vols. Havana: Editorial Letras Cubanas, 1980–84.

Instituto Edison. *Anuario 1955*. Havana: Ucar García S.A., 1955.

Inter-American Statistical Yearbook, 1942. New York: McMillan, 1943.

Jaynes, Gerald D., and Robin M. Williams Jr. *A Common Destiny: Blacks and American Society*. Washington, D.C.: National Academy Press, 1989.

Johnpoll, Bernard K., and Harvey Klehr. *Biographical Dictionary of the American Left*. Westport, Conn.: Greenwood Press, 1986.

Jolly, Richard. "The Literacy Campaign and Adult Education." In *Cuba: The Economic and Social Situation*, edited by Dudley Seers, 190–219. Chapel Hill: University of North Carolina Press, 1964.

Jones, LeRoi. *Home: Social Essays*. New York: William Morrow, 1966.

Kirk, John M. *Between God and Party: Religion and Politics in Revolutionary Cuba*. Tampa: University of South Florida Press, 1989.

Kousser, J. Morgan. *The Shaping of Southern Politics: Suffrage Restriction and the Establishment of the One-Party South, 1880–1910*. New Haven, Conn.: Yale University Press, 1974.

Kutzinski, Vera M. *Sugar's Secrets: Race and the Erotics of Cuban Nationalism*. Charlottesville: University Press of Virginia, 1993.

L. L., and J. S. Bernard. "The Negroes in Relation to Other Races in Latin America." *Annals* 140 (November 1928): 306–18.

Landau, Saul. "A New Twist on Race in Cuba." *Monthly Review* 42, no. 9 (February 1991): 53–58.

Larson, Edward J. *Sex, Race, and Science: Eugenics in the Deep South*. Baltimore: Johns Hopkins University Press, 1995.

Lavretsky, I. *Ernesto Che Guevara*. Moscow: Progress Publishers, 1976.

Lazcano y Mazón, Andrés M. *Constitución de Cuba*. 3 vols. Havana: Cultural S.A., 1941.

Le Riverend, Julio. *Historia económica de Cuba*. Havana: Instituto del Libro, 1967.

Lewis, Oscar, Ruth M. Lewis, and Susan M. Rigdon. *Cuatro hombres. Viviendo la revolución: Una historia oral de Cuba contemporánea*. Mexico City: Joaquín Mortiz, 1977.

Lewis, Rupert. *Marcus Garvey: Anti-Colonial Champion*. Trenton, N.J.: Africa World Press, 1988.

Lindsay, Forbes, and Nevin O. Winter. *Cuba and Her People of To-Day*. Boston: L. C. Page, 1928.

Lineamientos económicos y sociales para el quinquenio (1986–1990). Havana: Editora Política, 1986.

Lockwood, Lee. *Castro's Cuba, Cuba's Fidel: An American Journalist's Inside Look at Today's Cuba*. New York: Macmillan, 1967.

Lombardi, John V. *Venezuela. La búsqueda del orden. El sueño del progreso*. Barcelona: Editorial Crítica, 1985.

López Segrera, Francisco. *Raíces históricas de la revolución cubana (1868–1959). Introducción al estudio de las clases sociales en Cuba en sus relaciones con la política y la economía*. Havana: UNEAC, 1978.

Love, Joseph L. "Political Participation in Brazil, 1881–1969." *Luso-Brazilian Review* 7, no. 2 (1970): 3–24.

Lovell, Peggy A. "Race, Gender and Development in Brazil." *Latin American Research Review* 29, no. 3 (1994): 7–35.

Lumen, Enrique. *La revolución cubana, 1902–1934*. Mexico City: Ediciones Botas, 1934.

MacGaffey, Wyatt. "Social Structure and Mobility in Cuba." *Anthropological Quarterly* 34 (1961): 94–109.

McGarrity, Gayle L. "Race, Culture, and Social Change in Contemporary Cuba." In

Cuba in Transition: Crisis and Transformation, edited by Sandor Halebsky and John M. Kirk, 193–205. Boulder, Colo.: Westview Press, 1992.

Maluquer de Motes, Jordi. "La inmigración española en Cuba: Elementos de un debate histórico." In *Cuba, la perla de las Antillas*, edited by Consuelo Naranjo Orovio and Tomás Mallo Gutiérrez, 137–47. Aranjuez: Ediciones Doce Calles, 1994.

———. *Nación e inmigración: Los españoles en Cuba (ss. XIX y XX)*. Barcelona: Ediciones Jucar, 1992.

Mañach, Jorge. "La crisis de la alta cultura en Cuba." *Revista Bimestre Cubana* 20 (1925): 129–63.

———. *Pasado vigente*. Havana: Editorial Trópico, 1939.

Marable, Manning. "The Fire This Time: The Miami Rebellion, May, 1980." *Black Scholar* (July–August 1980): 2–18.

Marinello, Juan. *La cuestión racial en la Constitución*. Havana: n.p., 1940.

———. "25 años de poesía cubana. Derrotero provisional." *Revista Bimestre Cubana* 39 (1937): 236–39, 366–88.

Marks, George P. *The Black Press Views American Imperialism, 1898–1900*. New York: Arno Press, 1971.

Martí, José. *La cuestión racial*. Havana: Editorial Lex, 1959.

———. *Obras escogidas*. 3 vols. Havana: Editorial de Ciencias Sociales, 1992.

———. *Our America*. New York: Monthly Review Press, 1977.

Martínez, Juan A. *Cuban Art and National Identity: The Vanguardia Painters, 1927–1950*. Gainesville: University Press of Florida, 1994.

Martínez-Echazábal, Lourdes. "The Politics of Afro-Cuban Religion in Contemporary Cuban Cinema." *Afro-Hispanic Review* (Spring 1994): 16–22.

Martínez Furé, Rogelio. *Conjunto Folklórico Nacional*. Havana: Consejo de Cultura, 1963.

———. *Diálogos imaginarios*. Havana: Editorial Arte y Literatura, 1979.

Martínez Ortiz, Rafael. *Cuba. Los primeros años de independencia*. 2 vols. Paris: Editorial Le Livre Libre, 1929.

Masdeu, Jesús. *Ambición*. Havana: Tipografía Artística, 1931.

———. *La raza triste*. 2nd ed. Havana: Imprenta Obrapía, 1943.

Masferrer, Marianne, and Carmelo Mesa-Lago. "The Gradual Integration of the Black in Cuba: Under the Colony, the Republic, and the Revolution." In *Slavery and Race Relations in Latin America*, edited by Robert Brent Toplin, 348–84. Westport, Conn.: Greenwood Press, 1974.

Massip, Salvador. "La crisis de los institutos de 2a. enseñanza." *Revista Bimestre Cubana* 19 (1924): 183–215.

Mealy, Rosemari. *Fidel and Malcolm X: Memories of a Meeting*. Melbourne, Australia: Ocean Press, 1993.

Mella, Julio Antonio. *Documentos y artículos*. Havana: Editorial de Ciencias Sociales, 1975.

Memorias inéditas del censo de 1931. Havana: Editorial de Ciencias Sociales, 1978.

Menéndez Vázquez, Lázara. "¿Un cake para Obatalá?" *Temas* 4 (October–December 1995): 38–51.

Mesa Rodríguez, Manuel I. *Martín Morúa Delgado*. Havana: El Siglo XX, 1946.

Mesa-Lago, Carmelo. *Are Economic Reforms Propelling Cuba to the Market?* Coral Gables, Fla.: North-South Center, 1994.

——. *Breve historia económica de la Cuba socialista*. Madrid: Alianza, 1994.

——. *The Economy of Socialist Cuba: A Two-Decade Appraisal*. Albuquerque: University of New Mexico Press, 1981.

——. *The Labor Force, Employment, Unemployment and Underemployment in Cuba: 1899–1970*. Beverly Hills, Calif.: Sage Publications, 1972.

——, ed. *Revolutionary Change in Cuba*. Pittsburgh: University of Pittsburgh Press, 1971.

Mestre Arístides. "La higiene mental en los Estados Unidos y en Francia. Nuestra liga y su programa." *Revista de la Facultad de Letras y Ciencias* (July–December 1929): 203–18.

——. "Las leyes de la herencia y la biología aplicada." *Revista de la Facultad de Letras y Ciencias* (July–October 1918): 163–93.

Mitchel, Michael. "Blacks and the Abertura Democrática." In *Race, Class and Power in Brazil*, edited by Pierre-Michel Fontaine, 95–119. Los Angeles: Center for Afro-American Studies, University of California, 1985.

Montalvo, José R. "El problema de la inmigración en Cuba." *Revista Cubana* 8 (1888): 524–38.

Montaner, Carlos A. *Informe secreto sobre la revolución cubana*. Madrid: Ediciones Sedmay, 1976.

Montejo Arrechea, Carmen Victoria. *Sociedades de Instrucción y Recreo de pardo y morenos que existieron en Cuba colonial*. Veracruz, Mexico: Instituto Veracruzano de Cultura, 1993.

Moore, Carlos. *Castro, the Blacks, and Africa*. Los Angeles: UCLA Center for Afro-American Studies, 1988.

——. "Le peuple noir a-t-il sa place dans la Révolution Cubaine?" *Presence Africaine* 52 (1964): 177–230.

Moore, Robin. *Nationalizing Blackness: Afrocubanismo and Artistic Revolution in Havana, 1920–1940*. Pittsburgh: University of Pittsburgh Press, 1997.

Morales y Patiño, Oswaldo. "La higiene en los centrales azucareros." *Crónica Médico-Quirúrgica de la Habana* 51, no. 9 (September 1925): 367–78.

Morro, Juan del. "La Sociedad del Folklore Cubano." *Revista Bimestre Cubana* 18 (1923): 47–52.

Morúa Delgado, Martín. *Integración cubana y otros ensayos*. Havana: Impresora Nosotros S.A., 1957.

Municipio de la Habana. *Las comparsas populares del carnval habanero, cuestión resuelta*. Havana: Molina y Cía, 1937.

Mustelier, Gustavo E. *La extinción del negro. Apuntes político sociales*. Havana: Imprenta de Rambla, Bouza y Ca., 1912.

Naison, Mark. *Communists in Harlem during the Depression*. Urbana: University of Illinois Press, 1983.

Naranjo Orovio, Consuelo. "Análisis histórico de la emigración española a Cuba, 1900–1959." *Revista de Indias* 174 (1984): 503–26.

——. *Cuba, otro escenario de lucha: La guerra civil y el exilio republicano español*. Madrid: CSIC, 1988.

——. *Cuba vista por el emigrante español, 1900–1959*. Madrid: CSIC, 1987.

——. "La población española en Cuba, 1880–1953." In *Cuba, la Perla de las Antillas*, edited by Consuelo Naranjo Orovio and Tomás Mallo Gutiérrez, 121–36. Aranjuez, Spain: Doce Calles, 1994.

——. "Trabajo libre e inmigración española en Cuba, 1880–1930." *Revista de Indias* 52, nos. 195–96 (1992): 749–94.

Naranjo Orovio, Consuelo, and Armando García González. *Racismo e inmigración en Cuba en el siglo XIX*. Aranjuez, Spain: Ediciones Doce Calles, 1996.

Nelson, Lowry. *Rural Cuba*. Minneapolis: University of Minnesota Press, 1950.

North, Joseph. "Negro and White in Cuba." *Political Affairs* 42, no. 7 (July 1963): 34–45.

Novás Calvo, Lino. "En el cayo." *Revista de Occidente* 36 (April–June 1932): 235–69.

——. "La luna de los ñáñigos." *Revista de Occidente* 35 (January–March 1932): 83–105.

Olliz-Boyd, Antonio. "Race Relations in Cuba: A Literary Perspective." *Revista / Review Interamericana* 8, no. 2 (Summer 1978): 225–33.

Ortiz, Fernando. "La crisis política cubana. Sus causas y remedios." *Revista Bimestre Cubana* 14 (1919): 5–22.

——. *La decadencia cubana*. Havana: Imprenta y Papelería "La Universal," 1924.

——. "El Doctor de la Torre y la crisis cultural." *Revista Bimestre Cubana* 18 (1923): 8–14.

——. *El engaño de las razas*. Havana: Editorial Páginas, 1945.

——. "Martí and the Race Problem." *Phylon* 3 (1942): 253–76.

——. "Más acerca de la poesía mulata. Escorzos para su estudio." *Revista Bimestre Cubana* 37 (1936): 23–39, 218–27, 439–43.

——. "Ni racismos ni xenofobias." *Revista Bimestre Cubana* 24 (1929): 6–19.

——. "Por la integración cubana de blancos y negros." *Revista Bimestre Cubana* 51 (1943): 256–72.

——. "Preludios étnicos de la música afrocubana." *Revista Bimestre Cubana* 64 (1949): 87–194.

——. "La sinrazón de los racismos." *Revista Bimestre Cubana* 70 (1955): 161–83.

Orum, Thomas T. "The Politics of Color: The Racial Dimension of Cuban Politics during the Early Republican Years, 1900–1912." Ph.D. diss., New York University, 1975.

Ottanelli, Fraser M. *The Communist Party of the United States: From the Depression to World War II*. New Brunswick, N.J.: Rutgers University Press, 1991.

Patterson, Orlando. *The Ordeal of Integration: Progress and Resentment in America's "Racial" Crisis*. Washington, D.C.: Civitas, 1997.

Pearson, Hugh. *The Shadow of the Panther: Huey Newton and the Price of Black Power in America*. Reading, Mass.: Addison-Wesley, 1994.

Pedraza, Silvia. "Cuba's Refugees: Manifold Migrations." In *Origins and Destinies: Immigration, Race, and Ethnicity in America*, by Silvia Pedraza and Rubén G. Rumbaut. Belmont, Calif.: Wadsworth, 1996.

Peña, Lázaro. *¡La unidad es victoria!* Havana: n.p., 1942.

Pepper, Charles M. *To-Morrow in Cuba*. New York: Harper & Brothers, 1899.

Pérez, Louis A., Jr. "Aspects of Hegemony: Labor, State, and Capital in Plattist Cuba." *Cuban Studies* 16 (1986): 49–69.

——. *Cuba: Between Reform and Revolution.* New York: Oxford University Press, 1988.

——. *Cuba between Empires, 1878–1902.* Pittsburgh: University of Pittsburgh Press, 1983.

——. *Cuba under the Platt Amendment, 1902–1934.* Pittsburgh: University of Pittsburgh Press, 1986.

——. "The Imperial Design: Politics and Pedagogy in Occupied Cuba, 1899–1902." In *Essays on Cuban History: Historiography and Research*, 35–52. Gainesville: University Press of Florida, 1995.

——. "In the Service of Revolution: Two Decades of Cuban Historiography, 1959–79." In *Essays on Cuban History: Historiography and Research*, 144–52. Gainesville: University Press of Florida, 1995.

——. *Lords of the Mountain: Social Banditry and Peasant Protest in Cuba, 1878–1918.* Pittsburgh: University of Pittsburgh Press, 1989.

——. "North American Protestant Missionaries in Cuba and the Culture of Hegemony, 1898–1920." In *Essays on Cuban History: Historiography and Research*, 53–72. Gainesville: University Press of Florida, 1995.

——. "Politics, Peasants, and People of Color: The 1912 'Race War' in Cuba Reconsidered." *Hispanic American Historical Review* 66 (August 1986): 509–39.

Pérez de la Riva, Juan. "Cuba y la migración antillana, 1900–1931." In *Anuario de Estudios Cubanos 2*, 3–75. Havana: Editorial de Ciencias Sociales, 1979.

——. "Los recursos humanos de Cuba al comenzar el siglo: Inmigración, economía y nacionalidad (1899–1906)." In *Anuario de Estudios Cubanos 1*, 7–44. Havana: Editorial de Ciencias Sociales, 1975.

Pérez Landa, Rufino, and María Rosell Pérez. *Vida pública de Martín Morúa Delgado.* Havana: n.p., 1957.

Pérez-López, Jorge. "An Index of Cuban Industrial Output, 1930–1958." Ph.D. diss., University of New York at Albany, 1974.

Pérez-Medina, M. A. "The Situation of the Negro in Cuba." In *Negro: An Anthology*, edited by Nancy Cunard, 294–98. New York: Frederick Ungar, 1970.

Pérez Pérez, Ángel. *Huelga del 55 en el central Estrella.* Havana: Departamento de Orientación Revolucionaria, 1974.

Pérez Sarduy, Pedro, and Jean Stubbs. *Afrocuba: An Anthology of Cuban Writing on Race, Politics and Culture.* Melbourne, Australia: Ocean Press, 1993.

Pérez-Stable, Marifeli. *The Cuban Revolution: Origins, Course, and Legacy.* New York: Oxford University Press, 1993.

Pichardo, Hortensia, ed. *Documentos para la historia de Cuba.* 4 vols. Havana: Editorial de Ciencias Sociales, 1969.

Pinto, Angel C. *Un artículo y tres cartas.* Havana: n.p., 1939.

——. *El Dr. Mañach y el problema negro.* Havana: Nuevos Rumbos, 1949.

Por la escuela cubana en Cuba libre. Havana: n.p., 1941.

Portell-Vilá, Herminio. *Nueva historia de la República de Cuba.* Miami: La Moderna Poesía, 1986.

Porter, Bruce, and Marvin Dunn. *The Miami Riot of 1980: Crossing the Bounds.* Lexington, Mass.: Lexington Books, 1984.

Porter, Robert P. *Industrial Cuba*. New York: G. P. Putnam's Sons, 1899.

Portes, Alejandro, and Alex Stepick. *City on the Edge: The Transformation of Miami*. Berkeley: University of California Press, 1993.

——. "Unwelcome Immigrants: The Labor Market Experiences of 1980 (Mariel) Cuban and Haitian Refugees in South Florida." *American Sociological Review* 50, no. 4 (August 1985): 493–514.

Portuondo Linares, Serafín. *Los independientes de color. Historia del Partido Independiente de Color*. Havana: Ministerio de Educación, 1950.

Pruna, Pedro M., and Armando García González. *Darwinismo y sociedad en Cuba, siglo XIX*. Madrid: CSIC, 1989.

Ramos, José Antonio. "Cubanidad y mestizaje." *Estudios Afrocubanos* 1, no. 1 (1937): 92–113.

Reglamento de la sociedad de la raza de color en Morón "La Unión." Morón, Cuba: A. del Cueto, 1899.

Reich, Michael. *Racial Inequality: A Political2DEconomic Analysis*. Princeton, N.J.: Princeton University Press, 1981.

Riera, Mario. *Cuba política, 1899–1955*. Havana: Modelo S.A., 1955.

Ring, Harry. *How Cuba Uprooted Race Discrimination*. 2nd ed. New York: Merit Publishers, 1969.

Risquet, Juan Felipe. *Rectificaciones. La cuestión político-social en la isla de Cuba*. Havana: Tipografía América, 1900.

Roca Calderío, Blas. *Los fundamentos del socialismo en Cuba*. Havana: Ediciones Populares, 1961.

Roche y Monteagudo, Rafael. *La policía y sus misterios en Cuba*. Havana: La Moderna Poesía, 1925.

Rodríguez, Luis Felipe. *Ciénaga y otros relatos*. Havana: Editorial Letras Cubanas, 1984.

Rodríguez Expósito, César. *Dr. Enrique Núñez y Palomino*. Havana: Cuadernos de Historia de la Salud Pública, 1968.

Rojas, Marta. *La generación del centenario en el juicio del Moncada*. Havana: Editorial de Ciencias Sociales, 1973.

Rosell, Mirta, ed. *Luchas obreras contra Machado*. Havana: Editorial de Ciencias Sociales, 1973.

Rout, Leslie B., Jr. *The African Experience in Spanish America*. Cambridge: Cambridge University Press, 1976.

Ruiz Suárez, Bernardo. *The Color Question in the Two Americas*. New York: Hunt, 1922.

Safa, Helen I. *The Myth of the Male Breadwinner: Women and Industrialization in the Caribbean*. Boulder, Colo.: Westview Press, 1995.

Savignón, Tomás. *Tres ensayos*. Havana: P. Fernández y Cía, 1951.

Schuman, Howard, Charlotte Steeh, and Lawrence Bobo. *Racial Attitudes in America: Trends and Interpretations*. Cambridge, Mass.: Harvard University Press, 1985.

Scott, Rebecca J. "Cuba: Questions sociales, raciales et politiques d'une transition à l'autre." *Problèmes d'Amérique Latine* 17 (April–June 1995): 3–16.

——. "Defining the Boundaries of Freedom in the World of Cane: Cuba, Brazil, and Louisiana after Emancipation." *American Historical Review* 99, no. 1 (February 1994): 70–102.

———. "Labor and the Exercise of Political Voice: Santa Clara, 1899–1906." Paper presented at the conference "Race at the Turn of the Century," New York University, April 1996.

———. "Relaciones de clase e ideologías raciales: Acción rural colectiva en Louisiana y Cuba, 1865–1912." *Historia Social* 22 (1995): 127–50.

———. *Slave Emancipation in Cuba: The Transition to Free Labor, 1860–1899*. Princeton, N.J.: Princeton University Press, 1985.

Seidman, Gay. "Workers in Racially-Stratified Societies: Introduction." *International Labor and Working-Class History* 51 (Spring 1997): 1–6.

Serra, Rafael. *Carta abierta al director de "Pueblo Libre."* New York: n.p., 1901.

———. *Para blancos y negros. Ensayos políticos, sociales y económicos*. Havana: El Score, 1907.

Serrano Peralta, Lourdes. "Mujer, instrucción, ocupación y color de la piel: Estructura y relaciones raciales en un barrio popular de la Habana." *América Negra* 15 (December 1988): 119–33.

Serviat, Pedro. *El problema negro en Cuba y su solución definitiva*. Havana: Editora Política, 1986.

Shakur, Assata. *Assata: An Autobiography*. Westport, Conn.: L. Hill, 1987.

Shaw, Stephanie J. *What a Woman Ought to Be and to Do: Black Professional Women Workers during the Jim Crow Era*. Chicago: University of Chicago Press, 1996.

Skidmore, Thomas. "Bi-Racial U.S.A. vs. Multi-Racial Brazil: Is the Contrast Still Valid?" *Journal of Latin American Studies* 25 (May 1993): 373–86.

———. "Race and Class in Brazil: Historical Perspectives." In *Race, Class and Power in Brazil*, edited by Pierre-Michel Fontaine, 11–24. Los Angeles: Center for Afro-American Studies, University of California, 1985.

Smith, William Benjamin. "The Color Line: A Brief in Behalf of the Unborn." In *Anti-Black Thought, 1863–1925*, 11 vols., edited by John David Smith, 8:45–315. New York: Garland, 1993.

Soto, Lionel. *La revolución del 33*. 3 vols. Havana: Editorial de Ciencias Sociales, 1977.

Stabb, Martin S. "Martí and the Racists." *Hispania* 40 (December 1957): 434–39.

Stepan, Nancy L. *"The Hour of Eugenics": Race, Gender, and Nation in Latin America*. Ithaca, N.Y.: Cornell University Press, 1991.

Stoner, K. Lynn. *From the House to the Streets: The Cuban Woman's Movement for Legal Reform, 1898–1940*. Durham, N.C.: Duke University Press, 1991.

Sutherland, Elizabeth. *The Youngest Revolution: A Personal Report on Cuba*. New York: Dial Press, 1969.

Tabares del Real, José A. *La revolución del 33: Sus dos últimos años*. Havana: Editorial de Ciencias Sociales, 1975.

Taibo, Paco I., II, Froilán Escobar, and Félix Guerra. *El año que estuvimos en ninguna parte. La guerrilla africana de Ernesto Che Guevara*. Mexico City: Planeta, 1994.

Tamayo, Diego. "La vivienda en procomún (casa de vecindad)." In *Tercera Conferencia Nacional de Beneficiencia y Corrección*, 23–31. Havana: Librería e Imprenta "La Moderna Poesía," 1904.

Taylor, Frank. "Revolution, Race, and Some Aspects of Foreign Relations in Cuba since 1959." *Cuban Studies* 18 (1988): 19–41.

Thomas, Hugh. *Cuba: The Pursuit of Freedom*. London: Harper & Row, 1971.

Torres Molina, Osvaldo. *Apuntes para la historia del movimiento comunista, obrero y campesino en Matanzas, 1869–1958.* Havana: Editora Política, 1984.

Trelles, Carlos M. "Bibliografía de autores de la raza de color." *Cuba Contemporánea* 43, no. 169 (January–April 1927): 30–78.

———. "La hacienda y el desarrollo económico de la República de Cuba." *Revista Bimestre Cubana* 22 (1927): 323–42.

Trotter, Joe W. "African Americans in the City: The Industrial Era, 1900–1950." *Journal of Urban History* 21, no. 4 (May 1995): 438–57.

Truslow, Francis Adams. *Report on Cuba.* Baltimore: Johns Hopkins University Press, 1951.

Tucker, William H. *The Science and Politics of Racial Research.* Urbana: University of Illinois Press, 1994.

Universidad Católica. *Yearbook, 1949–1950.* Havana: Ucar García S.A., 1950.

Universidad de la Habana. Secretaría General. *Datos estadísticos, curso académico de 1951–1952.* Havana: Universidad de la Habana, [1952].

Valle Silva, Nelson do. "Updating the Cost of Not Being White in Brazil." In *Race, Class and Power in Brazil*, edited by Pierre-Michel Fontaine, 42–55. Los Angeles: Center for Afro-American Studies, University of California, 1985.

Van den Berghe, Pierre L. *Race and Racism: A Comparative Perspective.* New York: Wiley, 1967.

Vegueri, Pascual Marcos. *El negro en Cuba.* Havana: n.p., 1955.

Wade, Peter. *Blackness and Race Mixture: The Dynamics of Race Identity in Colombia.* Baltimore: Johns Hopkins University Press, 1993.

Whitten, Norman, Jr. *Black Frontiersmen: A South American Case.* New York: Schenkman, 1974.

Wilson, William Julius. *The Declining Significance of Race: Blacks and Changing American Institutions.* Chicago: University of Chicago Press, 1980.

Winant, Howard. *Racial Conditions: Politics, Theory, Comparisons.* Minneapolis: University of Minnesota Press, 1994.

Wisan, Joseph E. *The Cuban Crisis as Reflected in the New York Press, 1895–1898.* New York: Octagon Books, 1965.

Wood, Charles H., and José Alberto Magno de Carvalho. *The Demography of Inequality in Brazil.* New York: Cambridge University Press, 1988.

Wood, Charles H., and Peggy A. Lovell. "Racial Inequality and Child Mortality in Brazil." *Social Forces* 70, no. 3 (March 1992): 703–24.

Wright, Winthrop. *Café con Leche: Race, Class and National Image of Venezuela.* Austin: University of Texas Press, 1990.

Zanetti, Oscar. "Realidades y urgencias de la historiografía social en Cuba." *Temas* 1 (January–March 1995): 119–28.

Zanetti, Oscar, and Alejandro García. *United Fruit Company: Un caso del dominio imperialista en Cuba.* Havana: Editorial de Ciencias Sociales, 1976.

Zeitlin, Maurice. *Revolutionary Politics and the Cuban Working Class.* Princeton, N.J.: Princeton University Press, 1967.

INDEX

Díaz, Pedro, 36, 37, 134
Dickinson Abreu, Antolín, 191, 227
Directorate of University Students, 94
Directorio Central de Sociedades de la Raza de Color, 37–38, 67, 140, 162, 167
Directorio de la Raza de Color (Camagüey), 68–69
Directorio de la Raza de Color (Havana), 67–68
Directorio Social Revolucionario "Renacimiento" (Afro-Cuban society), 201–3
Divina Caridad (Afro-Cuban society), 164
Domiciliaria, La, 145
Domínguez, Jorge, 17
Dorticós, Osvaldo, 296
D'Ou, Lino: on race and racism, 32, 52, 58, 154–55, 188; political activities, 38, 65, 67–68, 167, 169
Ducasse, Juan E., 36, 79
Duharte, Rafael, 278, 319, 324
Duke, Kathy, 40
Duncan, Robert T., 16

Edreira, Oscar, 85
Education: Afro-Cubans' access to, 6, 14, 18, 112, 140–49, 275, 309, 331; Afro-Cubans' perceptions of, 138–40, 151
Eisenhower, Dwight, 298
El Buen Camino (Afro-Cuban political group), 82
Elosegui, Felipe, 32, 158, 243
Employment: Afro-Cubans' access to, 6, 18, 95, 131, 273, 309–10, 331; government bureaucracy, 7, 66–67, 90–92, 128–32, 138, 169–70, 202–3, 310–11; liberal professions, 14, 128, 137–39, 143–45, 149–53, 309; rural guard, 59, 67, 71, 132–34; army, 59, 82, 132–37, 198, 226; mail service, 67, 131; police, 67, 131, 133–34, 136; agriculture, 107–8; mining, 109; retail

and commerce, 117–18, 319; transportation, 118–20; manufacturing, 120–21
Enríquez, Carlos, 183
Entralgo, Elías, 267
Escalante, Aníbal, 233
Escoto Carrión, Saturnino, 89, 92, 162, 167
Estenoz, Evaristo, 69–71, 73, 76
Estrada Palma, Tomás, 47, 61–63, 65, 67, 70–71, 83, 129–31, 134, 148
Estrampes, Miguel de, 132

Faílde, Miguel, 181
Fair Play for Cuba Committee, 298
Farber, Samuel, 252
Federación Cubana del Trabajo, 125, 189
Federación Democrática de Mujeres Cubanas (FDMC), 117, 227, 231
Federación Gastronómica, 197
Federación Obrera de la Habana, 197
Federación Provincial de Trabajadores de Oriente, 235
Federation of Bank Workers, 273
Federation of Cuban Women, 275, 337
Federation of Telephone Workers of Cuba, 120
Fénix, El (Afro-Cuban society), 164
Fermoselle, Rafael, 4
Fernández, Antonio, 125
Fernández, Francisco, 43
Fernández, Nadine, 322, 327
Fernández de Batista, Marta, 244
Ferrara, Orestes, 149
Ferrer, Ada, 4
Figueras, Francisco, 43
Fomento de la Inmigración, 101
Fox, Geoffrey E., 278
Francisco: sugar mill, 124
Fredrickson, George M., 338
Frente Cívico Cubano Contra la Discriminación Racial (Afro-Cuban organization), 118, 238–41, 245, 247
Frías, Pío Arturo, 92, 170